International Praise for *Bohemian Paris:*

"A thorough and vivid evocation of the City of Light in its heyday as capital of the avant-garde . . . Franck presents these players in the settings of their daily lives, pungently evoking crushing poverty, extravagant partying, fierce loving, and contentious wrangling that epitomize the bohemian lifestyle. . . . An impressive synthesis of historical detail and novelistic atmosphere."

—*Kirkus Reviews*

"Tender was the night in Montparnasse and Montmartre of the avant-garde. . . . This book shows us that, without art and its bohemians, the human spirit would disappear like a rabbit into a hat." —*Le Nouvel Observateur* (Paris)

"Franck spins lavish historical, biographical, artistic, and even scandalous detail into a narrative that will captivate both serious and casual readers. He illuminates Picasso's complexities . . . introduces us to the mannerly poet Max Jacob, and revisits Apollinaire, Jarry, Modigliani, Cocteau, Matisse, Hemingway, and Fitzgerald, among countless others—all set against the marvelously depicted backdrop of bohemian Paris. Though this era has been often treated, Franck's treatment is especially good; he is able to show how all these artists interacted while allowing them to remain individuals. This marvelous and informative work will inspire readers to become better acquainted with the works produced by these individuals."

—Carol J. Binkowski, *Library Journal* (starred review)

"This is group biography writ large, and Franck places Matisse and Picasso at the center, rival geniuses who by their vision, energy, and force of personality became the weighty stones that set up the best-defined ripples. . . . Franck is fascinated by the context in which the art was produced, and this he brings to life with passion and verve." —Belinda Jack, *The Literary Review* (London)

"It's not often that art books provide a good read, but Dan Franck's *Bohemian Paris* is an exception. . . . The text is as much about the weird and wonderful lifestyles of the fauvists, dadaists, cubists, and surrealists who flocked to *la ville lumière* in those heady days at the turn of the century." —*Midweek* (London)

"Alluring, and rich with stories." —*Marianne* (Paris)

For Simon Michaël Ouazana

BOHEMIAN PARIS

PICASSO, MODIGLIANI, MATISSE, AND
THE BIRTH OF MODERN ART

DAN FRANCK

Translated by Cynthia Hope Liebow

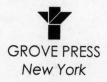

GROVE PRESS
New York

First published in Great Britain in 2001 by
Weidenfeld & Nicolson, London

First published in France in 1998 by Calmann-Lévy, Paris

This edition is printed by special arrangement with
Weidenfeld & Nicolson, London.

Published simultaneously in Canada
Printed in the United States of America

Library of Congress Cataloging-in-Publication Data

Franck, Dan.
   [Bohèmes. English]
   Bohemian Paris : Picasso, Modigliani, Matisse, and the birth of
modern art / Dan Franck ; translated by Cynthia Hope Liebow.
     p. cm.
   Translation of: Bohèmes.
   Includes bibliographical references and index.
    ISBN-13: 978-0-8021-3997-9
    1. Artists—Homes and haunts—France—Paris—Anecdotes.
2. Bohemianism—France—Paris—History—20th century.
3. Paris (France)—Intellectual life—20th century. 4. World War,
1914–1918—France—Art and the war. I. Title.

DC715 .F7513 2001
944'.361081'0887—dc21   2001050152

Grove Press
an imprint of Grove/Atlantic, Inc.
841 Broadway
New York, NY 10003

Distributed by Publishers Group West

www.groveatlantic.com

10 11 12 13 14   10 9 8 7 6 5

CONTENTS

List of Illustrations   ix
Preface   xi
Prologue   xvii

I THE ANARTISTS OF MONTMARTRE

THE MAZE OF MONTMARTRE   3
LITRILLO   9
LIFE IN BLUE   15
TWO AMERICANS IN PARIS   24
CYPRIAN   30
GUILLAUME THE BELOVED   44
THE LOVELY FERNANDE   56
THE BATEAU LAVOIR   60
THE WILD BEASTS' CAGE   65
WITH THE ACROBATS   74
THE TIME OF DUELS   79
GOSOL   85
AN AFTERNOON ON THE RUE DE FLEURUS   90
THE BORDELLO OF AVIGNON   95
THE GOOD DOUANIER   104
THE THEFT OF THE *MONA LISA*   112
SEPARATIONS   121
CUBISM   128
LEADERS OF THE PACK   134
THE CUBISTERS   140
GUILLAUME APOLLINAIRE GIVES A LITTLE HELP TO HIS FRIENDS   146
THE POET AND THE ART DEALER   153
CUBISM ON THE AUCTION BLOCK   157

II MONTPARNASSE GOES TO WAR

THE RUCHE   163
UBU ROI   167
2 AUGUST 1914   176
UNDER THE DIMMED STREET LAMPS   181
CHAÏM AND AMEDEO   184
THE VILLA ROSE   191
THE ARTILLERYMAN'S WOMEN   197
THE WRITER WITH THE SEVERED HAND   207
THE FRIVOLOUS PRINCE   214
THE COCK AND THE HARLEQUIN   221
THE POET'S WOUND   226
CAMOUFLAGE ART   231
MEANWHILE, IN AMERICA …   234
DADA & COMPANY   242
THE FRIENDS OF VAL-DE-GRÂCE   248
ADRIENNE MONNIER'S BOOKSHOP   253
PARTY DAYS IN PARIS   258
LOVE AT FIRST SIGHT   264
A PAINTER AND HIS DEALER   268
3, RUE JOSEPH BARA   273
LES MAMELLES DE TIRÉSIAS   276
PARIS–NICE   280
THE END OF THE GAME   284

III MONTPARNASSE, OPEN CITY

KIKI   289
DEATH COMES TO MONTPARNASSE   295
COMING TO BLOWS AT DROUOT   299
SURREALIST SCENES   304
THE WAKEFUL SLEEPER   310
DRESS DESIGNER TO THE ARTS   317
THE DRESS DESIGNER AND THE PHOTOGRAPHER   324
AN AMERICAN IN PARIS   328
A RADIATOR KNOB SIGNED BY RODIN   332
ONE COCKTAIL, TWO COCTEAUS   337
A GENERATION LOST AND FOUND   342
A WANDERING JEW   348
AT THE JOCKEY CLUB   355
PHOTOS, PHOTOS …   359
DR ARGYROL AND MR BARNES   364
SOUTINE'S CROSS   370
SCANDAL AT THE CLOSERIE DES LILAS   376

A LITTLE GEOGRAPHY OF SURREALISM   380
THE BAD BOYS OF THE RUE DU CHATEAU   385
SETTLING SCORES   390
THE SOFT DRINK KING   397
TAKEN IN PASSING   402
THE LAST OF THE BOHEMIANS   408

Notes   411
Selective Bibliography   418
Index   423

With thanks to Philippe Dagen,
for his helping hand

ILLUSTRATIONS

BETWEEN PAGES 142 AND 143

Picasso in the studio of the Bateau Lavoir in 1908 (*Photo: Gelett Burgess. Rights Reserved. RMN – Picasso Archives*)

Max Jacob in 1915 (*RMN – Picasso Archives*)

Utrillo, Suzanne Valadon and André Utter (*Le Masle-Documentation MNAM – CCI Collection*)

The Bateau Lavoir (© *ND-Viollet*)

The Lapin Agile cabaret c.1905 (© *Harlingue-Viollet*)

Picasso and Fernande Olivier in Montmartre in 1906 (*RMN – Picasso Archives*)
Guillaume Apollinaire and Annie Playden (*R.R., O. Beer Coll.*)

Lou (*R.R., O. Beer Coll.*)

Guillaume Apollinaire and Marie Laurencin (*R.R., O. Beer Coll.*)

The Douanier Rousseau in his studio in 1904 (© *Edimedia/Snark/ J. Warnod Coll.*)

Guillaume Apollinaire with the examining magistrate in September 1911 (*O. Beer Coll.*)

Derain, Madame Derain, Vlaminck, Kisling, Florents Fels, Juan Gris (*Jean Kisling Coll.*)

Guillaume Apollinaire (© *Edimedia/Snark*)

André Breton and Théodore Fraenkel in 1916–17 (© *Edimédia/Snark*)

Braque in military uniform, photographed by Picasso (*Picasso Estate, 1998. RMN – Picasso Archives*)

Alice Toklas and Gertrude Stein on the rue de Fleurus in 1923 (*Photo: Man Ray.* © *Man Ray Trust/ADAGP, Paris, 1998. The Erik Satie Foundation Archives*)

Commissioner Zamaron in his office at the Prefecture of Police (*Photo: Henri Manuel. R.R. Hachette Photothèque*)

Matisse in his studio in Issy-les-Moulineaux in May 1913 (*Photo: Alvin Langdon Coburn. R.R. MNAM-CCI Documentation*)

Picasso and Olga in London in 1919 (*Erik Satie Foundation Archives*)

Modigliani, Picasso and André Salmon at the Rotonde (*Photo: Jean Cocteau.* © *ADAGP, Paris, 1998.* © *Photothèque of the Museums of the City of Paris: Coroyer*)

Modigliani (*Marc Vaux Collection – MNAM-CCI Documentation*)

Jeanne Hébuterne at the age of twenty (*Hachette Photothèque*)

BETWEEN PAGES 238 AND 239

Alfred Jarry leaving his house in Corbeil in 1898 (© *Harlingue-Viollet*)

Paul Fort at the Closerie des Lilas, Boulevard du Montparnasse, in 1920 (© *Branger-Viollet*)

Foujita in 1928 (*Photo: A. Kertész.* © *Ministry of Culture - France*)

Arthur Cravan c.1902 (*Jacques Doucet Literary Library*)

Arthur Cravan in 1916 (*Hachette Photothèque*)

Session with a model at the painter Kees Van Dongen's studio in 1927 (© *Bonney/BHVP*)

Opening of the Jockey Club (*Photo: Man Ray.* © *Man Ray Trust/ADAGP, Paris, 1998.* © *Edimédia/Snark*)

Kiki of Montparnasse (*Photo: Man Ray.* © *Man Ray Trust/ADAGP, Paris, 1998. Hachette Photothèque*)

Zborowski and Soutine (*Photo: Paulette Jourdain. O. Beer Coll.*)

Soutine (*Photo: Paulette Jourdain. O. Beer Coll.*)

Jacques Prévert, Simone Prévert, André Breton, Pierre Prévert, in 1925 (*Photo: R.R., Fatras collection, Jacques Prévert estate*)

Blaise Cendrars (© *Martinie-Viollet*)

André Breton at the Théâtre de l'Œuvre (© *ADAGP, Paris, 1998.* © *Edimédia/Snark/Bibi Doucée*)

Jean Cocteau on the liner Ile-de-France in 1925 (© *Harlingue-Viollet*)

Raymond Radiguet in 1922 (*Photo: Man Ray.* © *Man Ray Trust/ADAGP, Paris, 1998. Erik Satie Foundation Archives*)

A ball in Montparnasse in 1925 (*Guy Selz Coll., Hachette Photothèque*)

Nancy Cunard (© *Bonney/BHVP*)

Louis Aragon (*Photo:* © *Jean Ristat/Diff. Gallimard. Elsa Triolet-Aragon Collection, CNRS*)

Elsa Triolet on the terrace of the Coupole in 1928 (detail) (*Elsa Triolet-Aragon Collection, CNRS. Published with the kind permission of M. Jean Ristat*)

A session of hypnosis (*Photo: Man Ray.* © *Man Ray Trust/ADAGP, Paris, 1998*)

Russian ball at the Bullier in 1929 (© *Museum of Judaic Art and History*)

Pascin at the Coupole in the spring of 1930 (*Henri and Jeanine Warnod Collection. Museum of Judaic Art and History*)

PREFACE

A world without art would be blind to itself. It would be confined within the boundaries imposed by simplistic rules. This is why totalitarian regimes, when they rise to power, set out to censor, prohibit and burn. This is how they destroy ideas, dreams, memory, and the expression of differences, which are the fertile soil from which artists spring.

The term 'artist', which describes rather than defines, never fails to provoke smiles and scepticism. While art is noble, significant, pure, and beautiful, the artist is negligible, trivial, often treated with disdain if not outright rejection. For substance has frequently been ignored in favour of form. Since Picasso's overalls, Vlaminck's wooden neckties, Braque's hats, and the surrealist battles, some naïve art lovers and other less well-meaning observers have taken the part for the whole, the disguise for the work of art, and forgotten (if they ever knew) that appearances can be extremely deceptive.

The painters of the Lapin Agile, like the poets of the Closerie des Lilas, did sometimes wear extravagant outfits, organize outrageous parties, whip out their revolvers at the drop of a hat and enjoy provoking the average bourgeois citizen in a thousand different ways, all for one basic reason: at the time, the average bourgeois citizen didn't have any use for them. He was entrenched within the boundaries of an old order while the pens and brushes of the time were experimenting with anarchism, as they would later do with communism and Trotskyism. The two worlds were irreconcilable.

But beyond matters of morals and dress, there is, more centrally, the question of art. An artist is, above all else, a producer of works of art. Picasso could wear whatever clothes he wanted, Alfred Jarry cock his pistol as often as he wished (which was frequently), Breton and Aragon get into fistfights with anyone they disliked; their behaviour mattered little next to the importance of the creative seeds they were sowing. Modern art was born and shaped in the hands of these sublime troublemakers. From 1900 to 1930, they didn't just lead the crazy artists' lives which earned them the hate of some and the envy of others: far more crucially, they were inventing the century's language.

But they were hated for this too. The scandals sparked off by *Ubu Roi* or the *Sacre du printemps*, the affairs of the 'wild beasts' cage' and the 'cubisters', and the uproar surrounding Matisse's *Bonheur de vivre* exhibited at the Salon des Indépendants in 1906, are good illustrations of the violence sometimes provoked by the avant-garde. Stravinsky, though subjected to endless criticism and ridicule, did not rebel against these virulent attacks; he felt that it was not up to the public to show indulgence for artists, but rather the artists' task to understand the public's occasional criticism. He himself would have shrugged his shoulders if he had heard his own works a year before he composed them.

The avant-garde always stirs up trouble. But society accepts it in the end. The most recent trends soon make the boldness of preceding generations look tame. In its time, impressionism had given rise to the same public outrage and critical anathema. Then neo-impressionism made its predecessor seem pale, before itself appearing dull and washed out next to the Fauves' horrors, which were in turn swept away by cubist monstrosities. In poetry, the Romantics were dethroned by the Parnassians, who were replaced by the symbolists, whom Blaise Cendrars was soon to see as 'already catalogued poets'. In music, Bach was the king of baroque tradition, Haydn, Mozart and Beethoven freed up the orchestra, paving the way for the great symphonic complexity of Berlioz, which soon seemed almost harmonious in the face of dodecaphony. As for Erik Satie, the critics of the time were barely willing to consider him a musician ...

At the dawn of the century, France was the capital of the avant-garde. But not only the avant-garde. In fact, two schools were present simultaneously in Montmartre alone. One continued in the tradition of Toulouse-Lautrec and included such artists as Poulbot, Utrillo, Valadon, Utter and others, none of whom ever provoked the passions stirred up by the group of the Bateau Lavoir. This group of artists followed fairly conventional rules; the others broke with tradition, in search of the art of the future. Mixing languages and cultures, drawing on incredibly diverse sources of inspiration, the Spaniards Gris and Picasso, the Dutch Van Dongen, the Polish-Italian Apollinaire, the Swiss Cendrars, and also the French Braque, Vlaminck, Derain and Max Jacob broke with the past to free painting and poetry from the constraints that weighed them down.

On the other side of the Seine, in Montparnasse, Modigliani, an Italian, Diego Rivera, a Mexican, Krogh, a Scandinavian, Soutine, Chagall, Zadkine, and Diaghilev, all Russian, and Léger, Matisse, and Delaunay, all French – to name just a few – were also enriching the century's artistic legacy. In the twenties, the American writers would arrive, as would Tzara the Romanian, the Swedes, more Russians, and other newcomers from still more lands … Paris would become the capital of the world. On the pavements, there would no longer be a handful of artists, as in Montmartre, but hundreds, thousands of them. It was an artistic flowering of a richness and quality never to be rivalled, even later in Saint-Germain-des-Prés. Painters, poets, sculptors, and musicians, from all countries, all cultures, classical and modern, met and mingled. Rich patrons of the arts and art dealers of the moment, models and their painters, writers and publishers, poverty-stricken artists and millionaires lived together, side by side.

Before the First World War, although Picasso had already become rich, most of his companions lived in utter poverty. After 1918, by contrast, they could buy themselves Bugattis and private homes. The era of the inspired but starving artist was coming to an end. Guillaume Apollinaire's death, two days before the armistice, also signalled the close of the first period, that of the pioneers. When Modigliani died in 1920, it was the end of a vagabond way of life which had also been that of Villon and Murger. With the Bulgarian Jules Pascin, the door shut for ever on the first thirty years of the century: the age of the bohemians.

They had chosen to live in Paris, a fraternal, generous city, which knew how to offer freedom to these people from foreign lands. Today, Picasso, Apollinaire, Modigliani, Cendrars and Soutine would not be in Paris. They would be rejected from the city, forced to live far from the Seine: the Spaniard punished for use of illicit substances, the Polish-Italian for possession of stolen goods, the Italian for disorderly conduct, the Swiss for house theft, the Russian for chronic poverty and barely concealed public begging.

There would be other motives for arrest. All would only serve to show that artists, today like yesterday, more often walk down the side of the road than straight down the centre. They remain what they have always been, that which makes them so unique: displaced persons.

To speak of yesterday's artists is to love today's. Memory is a reflection, a shadow, a projection. Down the decades, artists remain the brothers of their elders.

Quality was their prime concern. Modigliani, Soutine and Picasso, who never gave themselves to anything but their art, criticized Van Dongen and others for spending too much of their time in high society. For them, these companions of their early years had gone back on their word and their values, compromised themselves. They had become mere technicians, craftsmen of painting. But a craftsman is not an artist. One day, Pierre Soulages revealed to me the key to the difference between the two: 'The artist is looking for something. He doesn't know what path will lead him to his goal. The artisan takes paths he knows, to reach a goal which he also knows.' An illuminating remark.

The artist works alone. He has no staff, his is not a profession. Painting or writing are not just trades or crafts to him, they are the very breath of life. The tool itself is uncertain. If an idea dies, or the imagination becomes stagnant, if one's mind stops moving, nothing and no one can save a man suffocated by emptiness. And no one will replace him: the work of art is unique, as is he who produces it. The caryatids of Modigliani can be compared to no others. If Robert Desnos did once happen to buy a charcoal drawing by Picasso billed as a composition by Braque, it was because the two painters worked together during the great period of synthetic cubism.

Each of them was looking for something. Doubt is the eternal language of the artist faced with himself. The new work is never a certainty. It rests on nothing, not even on the preceding one. Success, curiosity are ephemeral. Each time, one must start again from scratch – from the abyss of nothingness. The artist lives on the breath of inspiration. If this forsakes him, all the rest goes with it. Such is the fate of the man who wrestles with the birth of a work of art.

The Bohemians was conceived in the studios of the Bateau-Lavoir artists, and grew to maturity on the pavements of the Ruche and of Montparnasse. It intersects with one of my novels, Nu couché.[*] It fills in its spaces, gaps and unrevealed secrets.

I wrote the two books at the same time, over a period of a few years, taking a break from one to work on the other, incapable of dividing them in two, of separating them. They are the Siamese twins of the same literary adventure: one is a novel, the other is a chronicle of the times. I couldn't have written Nu couché without The Bohemians and The Bohemians would not exist without Nu couché. The story of these men who made modern art grow and thrive in the soil of their diversity is so rich that a single book would not have allowed me to include all the pieces of the kaleidoscope that I had been accumulating for so many years. The two books are unlikely but stubborn companions. Having spent so much time with them, I have slowly lost sight of why I began to write them.

I wrote the novel first. In its original version, the book was unmanageable. It sank under its own weight. Reality drowned out fiction. The characters conjured up by my imagination were overshadowed by the real-life heroes of the Bateau-Lavoir and the Vavin neighbourhood. My protagonists certainly deserved a novel, but these figures were worthy of one as well.

I started again. I removed from Nu couché the ladders which had enabled

---

* Nu couché, Dan Franck, Editions du Seuil, Paris, 1988.

me to climb up to attack my fortress. I put them elsewhere. And I wrote the two books on parallel tracks.

Nu *couché* visits the workshops, the cafés and the whorehouses of the time through imagination, not relying on eyewitness accounts as a guide. It is like a painting set in a frame.

The Bohemians explores this painting, with all its shading and hidden treasures. In the voice of the storyteller, it tells the true tale of the Montmartre and Montparnasse artists.

I am not an art historian. A writer has his own language. This is mine. It is, in a way, another novel: the novel of the characters, places, and works of art that our century, as it turns the page, would carry off with it to a desert island, if it wanted to look back and rediscover itself in the cool shade of its memory.

PROLOGUE

One must try, at least for a while, to look
less horrible than before: clothes, shoes,
hair, and oh, that sad, tired face ...

Verlaine to Rimbaud

Two men were walking up the rue Didot, in the fourteenth arrondissement of Paris. They were schoolfriends, barely twenty years old. They moved quickly along the pavement without exchanging a word.

The walls of the Broussais Hospital came into sight on their left. They went under the archway and followed paths leading from one building to another until they reached a long, narrow room where they were asked to wait. The man they were looking for, a man who had been in prison several times, wasn't there.

They asked for him. They were told again to wait. Finally, a nurse led them to a very large room containing six iron beds arranged on either side of a window looking out on the garden.

The man they had come to see was in one of the middle beds, just to the right of the window. His name was written on a little sign above the pillow. He had grey hair, faun-like eyes, a broad forehead, and a beard grown wild. He wore a patient's cap and a rough-spun shirt with the hospital's name marked on it.

The two visitors introduced themselves. The man in bed hoisted himself up on one elbow, looked at them, and cleared the bed of the newspapers and books that were strewn all over it. He rose. Putting on an old pair of trousers, a stained cardigan, and a hospital robe, he led his visitors into the hallway, knotting the belt of the robe as he went.

They walked quickly towards the courtyard. There, for over an hour, they exchanged confidences, paying no attention to the sickly old people passing by, who stared at this strange trio composed of two students, firmly ensconced in their world, and this patient who looked like a tramp.

The three men said goodbye to each other.

A year later, the man had left the Broussais Hospital. One day in a Montmartre street, as he was walking with some difficulty, leaning on a cane, he ran into one of his young visitors of the previous year. He didn't recognize him. The young man introduced himself. They spoke for a moment.

'Will you buy me a drink?' the former convict asked. He pulled out a slim wallet and opened it, explaining that all the money he had in the world was right there. There were only a few coins ... He also said that a waiter, who had found him too shabbily dressed, had just thrown him out of the bistro where he had been sitting.

They entered a café and ordered a drink.

'Where are you living?' asked the student.

The other man shrugged his shoulders sadly. 'I don't really live anywhere, I move around ...'[1]

Thus spoke the poet, not at the end of the twentieth century but at the end of the nineteenth. The homeless man was Paul Verlaine. The two young men who went to see him were Pierre Louÿs and André Gide. Today, Verlaine would be sleeping in the Métro.

Poverty has a long and stubborn life.

I
THE ANARTISTS
OF MONTMARTRE

THE MAZE OF MONTMARTRE

Right at the top of the hill of Montmartre rises the Basilica of Notre Dame de la Galette. This astonishing edifice, one of the scandals of our times, mocks Paris even as it dominates her – material evidence of the power of the priests.

Le Père Peinard, 1897

As the century began, Montmartre and Montparnasse faced each other from afar: two hills which would be the birthplaces of the worlds of yesterday and today. Two shores of Haussmann's river; by constructing his buildings and avenues for the solid bourgeois class, the illustrious city planner pushed the troublesome white proletarian population to the city's outskirts: an old method for conserving the centre.

On the right bank was the Bateau Lavoir, on the left, the smoke-filled evenings of the Closerie des Lilas. Between the two flowed the Seine. And the entire history of modern art.

Montmartre had its Sacré Coeur, a kind of Byzantium-on-the-Seine. A block of white that rose and rose above the windmills, the vines, and the gardens.

Monsieur Thiers had set the ball rolling. By provoking Montmartre, he brought about the Commune. The Parisians have conserved the city cannons which were used there. And it is clearly not by chance that the Sacré Coeur was constructed on the exact spot where the Commune was launched: the church would force the people to pay for their revolutionary sins.

The basilica is enthroned above obscure hotels, riotous cabarets, flimsy shacks made of wood or tarred-over cardboard which seem to be marching up the side of the hill amid garlands of lilac and hawthorn. In the midst of this unruly maze, Isadora Duncan and her young students danced Greek-style, in bare feet and tunics, with carefree hearts. Montmartre was a village. One could sing, dance, eat and sleep there, all very cheaply. The private homes of the Avenue Junot had not yet been built. The houses of prostitution on the rue d'Amboise offered free dinners. The swishing skirts of La Goulue and the swaying hips of Rayon d'Or still made men swoon, and the footwork of Valentin le Désossé entranced audiences.* A notary's assistant by day and a dancer by night, he was the only man in the troupe of the Quadrille Réaliste, and his amazing agility thrilled the public of the Elysée-Montmartre, soon to be succeeded by the up-and-coming Moulin Rouge.

Bruant provoked the middle classes. Satie 'gymnopédized' at the Chat Noir, on the Boulevard Rochechouart, where Alphonse Allais was making his début. Rodolphe Salis directed the orchestra. Fifteen years before the turn of the century, this establishment disappeared, to be replaced by the Mirliton, while the paper Le Chat Noir continued to strike in every direction with its satirical claws. Allais went so far as to dip his pen in the inkwell of a more famous name: he signed his articles using the pseudonym Francisque Sarcey, who was a very real theatre critic, alive and well and writing articles which were widely followed in the review Le Temps. Another practical joke ... As for Jane Avril, the poet's mistress, she posed for Toulouse-Lautrec. Lautrec was a Montmartre painter, but he was not the first. The famous artists whose ghosts already peopled the cobbled streets of the neighbourhood were legion: Géricault, Cézanne, Manet, Van Gogh, Moreau, Renoir, Degas ... Those to come had not yet made names for themselves. They were only shadow figures for the time being. Momentarily holding their breath, they were learning in the museums, setting up shop wherever they could find a place, and awaiting their hour of glory. First in Montmartre, then in Montparnasse, and later, if the museums relayed their fame, throughout the world...

Was it out of self-protection, to cultivate its individuality, that Montmartre decided to fashion itself into a free commune? This may seem to have been not much more than a joke, and there was an element of that in it. But there was much more. There was also a desire for singularity, for liberty which, at the dawn of the century, led some of the area's residents to decide that the Place du Tertre should become the capital of an autonomous territory.

A vote was held. The proposal was passed by an absolute majority. Next, a mayor was elected. Jules Depaquit, illustrator by trade, was chosen as the first administrator of the Free Commune of Montmartre. He had earned the respect of his fellow citizens a few years earlier by having been dragged to the Prefecture of Police, after rumours that he was the author of the attack on the Véry restaurant on the Boulevard Magenta.

Although cleared of the charge – the true authors of the crime were

---

* La Goulue, ('the greedy one'), Rayon d'Or ('goldbeam'), and Valentin le Désossé ('Valentin the boneless', a nickname deriving from his extraordinary suppleness) were among the notable cabaret performers of the day; the Quadrille Réaliste was one of the most popular dance companies.

anarchists out to take revenge for Ravachol,* who had been arrested at a table in the establishment – Depaquit had gained fame from it. This would be further enhanced by the election, and soon he was being toasted in song by Francis Carco, praised by Roland Dorgelès, and admired by Nino Frank and Tristan Tzara, who saw him as one of the precursors of the Dada movement. He would also charm Picasso, who often came to listen to him recite poetry at the Lapin Agile.

Jules Depaquit left behind a script which Satie set to music for the Comédie Parisienne, and which was adapted for the theatre by Darius Milhaud and danced by the Ballets Russes in 1926, with a set by André Derain. Entitled *Jack in the Box*, this pantomime showed a man carrying a big clock, criss-crossing the stage over and over, without anyone being able to fathom what his role was. This was only revealed at the end of the last act: the man was a clockmaker.

Depaquit made a living by selling satirical drawings to newspapers that specialized in this art. He squandered all his earnings in bistros, which he would enter standing upright, and leave falling over himself. He had a very precise schedule: he would work like a devil for a week, and party for the next three. History does not tell us which of these phases gave rise to the brilliant and eminently political idea of obtaining the independence of his people, and the separation of Montmartre from the French state.

He preached the merits of this new statute in a thousand other communes, located for the most part in the Seine-et-Oise region near Paris, to which he was invited as the Minister Plenipotentiary of a nation in the process of being born. On the programme: wine and brass bands.

Within the boundaries of his own territory, Jules Depaquit had perfected an infallible method for getting free drink. When he was out of cash, he would enter a café, sad and tired, his coat on his back, suitcase in hand. He would be asked:

'Where are you going, M. Depaquit?'

'I'm returning to my country.'

'And where is that, your country?'

'Sedan.'

'Sedan! That far?'

'That far . . . Now you see why I'm so sad . . .'

Together they would despair. A bottle would be produced for consolation, and would be emptied to help cheer them up. When all had almost been forgotten, Jules Depaquit climbed onto the tables and shouted:

'Prussia invaded Sedan, but Montmartre will resist!'

* Ravachol was an anarchist-provocateur who used theft and violence to demonstrate his political principles.

And the troops of the Tertre were toasted for their bravery.

Generally, they had abdicated by the time dawn came, after having abundantly watered their furrows. But Depaquit, cheered on by his partisans, could not bring himself to capitulate. He was not Napoleon III.

One exception, perhaps, was the day on which all of Montmartre took up arms and donned the uniforms of the soldiers of 1870 to defend Francisque Poulbot, the Butte's painter of street urchins. Poulbot loved parties and parades. Each year, in order to console his girlfriend for the fact that they had not yet tied the knot, he organized a fake marriage that was attended by all the residents of the neighbourhood. Everyone wore a disguise for the occasion, then for the rest of the night, they danced, drank, and applauded the bride.

Poulbot got involved in a dispute with his landlord, who wanted to evict him. The painter called on his friends for help. He suggested they all don the uniform of the armies which had defended a besieged Paris before the violent explosion of the Commune, and that they barricade themselves in his lodgings, ready to show the landlord that it would cost him dearly to get at Poulbot.

The villain threw in the towel before the fatal hour. But Poulbot maintained the fraternal summons. And so, on the planned day, the streets and alleys of Montmartre filled with a battalion of cavalrymen, zouaves, lancers, artillerymen and associates, all armed with rifles and dressed in martial attire. If Roland Dorgelès is to be believed, late in the night the Montmartre troops were joined by soldiers from the National Guard, who arrived from Montparnasse dressed in a similar way and carrying tapered bayonets, which astounded the real policemen posted along the path of these fake soldiers, marching solemnly in rhythm.

The patrons fanned out onto the boulevards, taking aim at passers-by streaming out of movie theatres. They played at war until dawn. The armistice was signed after the troops of General Poulbot, sabres drawn and bugles trumpeting, had attacked the Moulin de la Galette.

The games and provocations of this merry band attracted tourists and curious onlookers, who drifted in from the boulevards in their top hats and waistcoats. Fortunately, the horse-drawn omnibus didn't go all the way up the Butte Montmartre but stopped at the Place Blanche, and there remained a long climb, through steep and narrow alleyways, up to the centre of the festivities.

Montmartre remained a place apart, protecting its singularity. It had its admirers, members of the same family – a family that hadn't yet revealed its younger branch, who would be more interested in the cross-pollination of the arts. The eldest of these would be named Pablo Picasso, André Salmon, Max Jacob and Guillaume Apollinaire...

For the moment, Depaquit and his friends were the leaders. Perched on café tables, Carco sang the 'Marseillaise', and Mac Orlan roused his pals by playing the bugle under their windows. They were all anarchists at heart. They ate, but not well, drank more than the average, slept here and there, wherever they could find a place, though not yet in the Métro, whose north–south line now joined Montmartre to Montparnasse. Their identity papers were not always in order, their address was not always permanent, and they occasionally stretched out a hand to beg. Some of them painted canvases which hardly sold, some made music, many were highly skilled in the art of eating off their neighbour's plate. But the neighbours were generous, and let them run up a bill without asking too many questions. On the stoves of the bistros, pots were kept boiling and stews ladled out for customers fallen on hard times: a kind of precursor of the latter-day soup kitchen. There, painters and poets drank toasts with the many free spirits who, at the beginning of the century, roamed the streets of Montmartre.

Of course, chance alone cannot explain their all finding themselves together in this particular neighbourhood, on the outskirts of the city, not far from the main boulevards. The steep, winding streets, which had seen hand-to-hand combat, housed men, newspapers, and a collective memory. The anarchist Libertad conducted his popular public talks on the rue Muller. The paper L'Anarchie, which had neither director nor editor-in-chief and whose moral and typographical code prohibited the use of capital letters, set up shop on the rue du Chevalier-de-la-Barre. The Libertaire was on the rue d'Orcel. Its editors met their friends and readers in the back room of the Zut, a café on the rue Norvins that the police were soon to close, to protect the ears of the state from the subversive talk of the café's regular customers. Steinlen, a Swiss painter who designed the Chat Noir posters, went elsewhere to preach his doctrine of coming revolution. And M. Dufy would soon have a police record for sheltering a fellow painter whose palette was daubed with the incendiary colours red and black.

In the years before the First World War, Juan Gris was pursued by the police and temporarily jailed, having been confused with Garnier, as central a fixture in Bonnot's band* as he was a target in the sights of the police. Pierre Mac Orlan, pedestrian and chronicler of the Butte, in his classic film Quai des brumes gives an electrician a task which the libertarians of the maquis often carried out: that of forging false identity papers. He helps out a deserter from the Colonial Army who has come to get a new identity. His gesture is accompanied by words that epitomize that time

---

* The members of Bonnot's band were among those responsible for a wave of politically motivated terrorism which swept France at the time; this anarchist branch was a radical faction of the international workers' movement.

and place. 'I've been spotted by the cops because of something that happened with an anarchist paper ...'[1]

Signac, Vallotton and Bonnard participated in lotteries in which their works were auctioned off for the profit of the *Révolté*, a free-thinking paper founded by Elisée Reclus and Jean Grave. Van Dongen, a friend of the anarchist writer Félix Fénéon, also participated. In 1897, he illustrated the Dutch translation of a work by Kropotkin, *Anarchy, Its Philosophy and Ideals*. And Vlaminck, loud and clear, trumpeted some rather devastating personal opinions – with no restrictions, and with some rather disturbing variations, alas, during the Occupation.

But the anarchists and the artists, however much they may have shared the same ideals, did not join forces when it came to acts of violence. The painters and poets didn't play around with the infernal machines of those who planted bombs. But they would often defend them. And they were always the first to cheer at games, farces, practical jokes, provocations and mayhem of all kinds. They too turned their back on the cosy, honeyed and well-ordered comfort of bourgeois homes. In Montmartre, as later in Montparnasse, the artists remained resolutely opposed to the perfect geometry of well-ordered structures. They were, quite simply, rebels.

LITRILLO

TO DRINK A LOT: To hit the bottle, to tipple,
to drink like a fish.

Aristide Bruant

Thousands of miles from Paris, plunged in his trans-Siberian prose, Blaise Cendrars despaired: 'Tell me, Blaise, are we very far from Montmartre?'

Before the war, the Butte was still the centre of everything, surrounded by the rest of the universe. The person who most contributed to building up and also, alas, to undermining Montmartre's influence was Utrillo. He didn't mean to do so, in the same way as he didn't mean to paint. That was just the way it happened. When his paintings of the Place du Tertre and the Moulin de la Galette were taken off to be auctioned at Drouot, all the amateur artists of Montmartre, and everywhere else, set about copying and pastiching his style. To begin with, they were just trying to put food in their stomachs. In the end, it was Montmartre which would be consumed...

Utrillo was a strange fellow. A native son, born in 1883 on the rue du Poteau, into a free-thinking if not altogether free family: their views were nonetheless closer to the philosophy of the anarchist review Le Père Peinard than to the scenes of conjugal felicity romanticized in verse by the poet Géraldy.

His mother was Suzanne Valadon. Short and plump-cheeked, she had extraordinarily luminous blue eyes which attracted men like flies. She was one of the few women who was not a dancer to have left her stamp on Montmartre's history. She was free both in thought and act, which could shock the conventional spirits of the times.

A country girl, she was the daughter of a cleaning woman, whose father had disappeared shortly after she was born. She came to Paris young, already knowing how to lie: she claimed to be even younger than she was, from a rich family, and gave a false first name – Suzanne only came later. At the time, she was officially known as Marie-Clémentine, and to the artists who used her as a model, Maria.

She had hundreds of odd jobs before becoming an acrobat with the Fernando Circus. After a bad fall, she had to change professions, becoming an artists' model. She posed, freely and whenever it suited her, for Puvis de Chavannes, Toulouse-Lautrec, and two well-known anti-Dreyfusards who signed the Barresian manifesto of the League of the French Nation in October 1898. These were Renoir and Degas: the latter encouraged her to paint.

She was the mistress of nearly all her mentors, and of Erik Satie. The musician sent her three hundred letters within the space of six months. He called her 'my little Biqui', which didn't move the beautiful Suzanne in the slightest. Their romance was short-lived and dramatic: the lady did not lack temperament.

She had one son, Maurice, about whose father we know little – in fact, almost nothing. Whatever some have said, Maurice was almost certainly not the son of the Catalan painter and art critic Miguel Utrillo, a great friend of Picasso during his first years in Montmartre. Most of Utrillo's friends thought, probably rightly, that Miguel was simply a generous lover who was happy to take on the role of father. There is also nothing to confirm Francis Carco's affirmation that the artist's father was a certain Boissy, a poor and alcoholic painter.

For several years, Suzanne Valadon led the free life of a single mother. She then married a well-to-do friend of Satie, a legal representative for a business firm, who sent Maurice to Saint Anne's hospital for the mentally ill. This husband was eventually replaced by André Utter, one of her son's best friends. Utter worked from time to time as an electrician, and more often as a painter. When she took him away from his canvases (so he could devote himself to hers), Suzanne Valadon was nearly forty-five. Utter was twenty years younger than her, and three years younger than Maurice. The stepfather was indeed the youngest of the trio – which was in fact a quartet since Valadon's mother also lived with them.

It may have been a strange family, but a family it was. Mother painted under the watchful eye of the two young men, one of whom was her son and the other her husband. The two were as close as brothers: closer, in fact, since they shared a passion for painting. From this point of view, the picture could not have been more harmonious, whatever the gossips might whisper.

The problem lay elsewhere, and had for a long time. Maurice had a weakness. He had been fond of the bottle from an early age. Not in quite the same way as his Montmartre friends who, painting with the sun when the light was best, worked during the day and drank at night. Utrillo drank all the time. For his mother, it was a tragedy. For him, agony. And for the neighbours, it was horrifying to hear the painter's howls when Utter and Valadon locked him up to dry him out. He insulted his mother and stepfather. He ripped up his canvases. He threw every object in reach out of the window. While Suzanne Valadon, in despair, cried and shouted and almost tore out her hair, her son would pick up his flute and play a sonata, though he scarcely knew how to read a score and barely understood even why one needed to close up the holes of the flute with one's fingers.

Everyone around him dreamed of just one thing: quiet. So let him paint instead. This is how he began, on the advice of a psychiatrist whom Suzanne had consulted at Saint Anne's. 'Find something to occupy him that will keep him away from wine,' the doctor had said. She encouraged him to paint, as Degas had with her several years earlier. She locked him up in a room with his brushes and tubes of colours, brought him a pile of postcards, and told him, 'I'll let you out when you've done all these.'

When Utrillo painted, nothing mattered except the work in progress. He forgot to eat and drink. But as soon as he had finished, he headed straight for a welcoming port, where the bottle was the anchor.

He hated painting outdoors. Having other people around to watch seemed invasive – it bothered him. In order not to be spied on, he would lean against a wall. And if someone persisted, he would turn on the intruder and chase him away with an explosion of fury and a barrage of insults. After several years spent raging against the curiosity of his contemporaries, who loved to watch painters at work, Utrillo was finally reduced to using only postcards as models in his portrayals of the little world of Montmartre.

Francis Carco, who saw him at work, described the quiet seriousness with which he chose from all the views he had collected, and the care and precision with which he enlarged his subject, noting the measurements with the help of a compass and ruler on the cardboard that he used as an easel. Dorgelès, also a friend, noted the painter's almost pathological perfectionism in making sure that everything was minutely and exactly reproduced:

> His production never seemed faithful enough to him. He counted the rows of stones, carefully covered the roofs, tore down the façades. To render colour, he crushed his tubes of paint and went into a rage when he couldn't find the right one. 'They're not in silver-white, the façades, are they? Not in zinc white ... They're made of plaster ...' He absolutely needed to obtain the exact same chalky white. He also had the baroque idea of painting the houses with a mixture of glue and plaster that he applied with a knife ... Often, he would use a church as subject ... 'I like that,' he would tell us, 'I like doing churches.'[1]

Friday was always a quiet day, in fact, because of the churches. Utrillo loved them. Especially the cathedral of Reims, because of his fanatical devotion to Joan of Arc. Friday was the day he devoted to the Maiden. His shelves and drawers were filled with medals, busts, various objects relating to the saint; he prayed for her soul.

On Saturdays, he would rejoin the familiar delights of hell. A doctor who lodged him once for several weeks confided to Francis Carco that he drank between eight and ten litres of wine a day. And one evening, having finished off everything in the cellar, he went into the couple's bedroom, discovered their stock of eau de Cologne and drank all five bottles.

On the Butte, the children of Montmartre called him Litrillo. They followed him with measured steps when, after having drunk away his distress, the painter wandered about the alleyways, his elbows pressed to his sides, muttering 'choo-choo-choo' and letting out imaginary puffs of smoke, imitating as best he could the demonic locomotive which, he said, had just been overturned, leaving one lone survivor in the world, Litrillo himself, 'choo-choo-choo' . . . Afterwards, he went home to play with a mechanical train, a real one, with rails fixed to the floor.

The poet André Salmon recounts that one day, after escaping from the watchful eyes of both his mother and his stepfather, Utrillo took refuge in a Montmartre hotel, his pockets filled with the materials necessary to make fireworks. And so he did, alone in his room, eventually setting the establishment on fire. It was soon surrounded by firemen and policemen, and while some in the crowd shouted 'Fire! Mayhem!' others were crying 'Fool! Madman!'

But he wasn't a madman, poor Maurice. And he protested publicly a little later, when Francis Carco published a book about him.[2] In complete disagreement with the portrait the writer had drawn of him, Utrillo locked himself up in his atelier on the rue Cortot and sent dozens of drawings sailing out of the window, on the back of which he had written, 'Monsieur Carco says I'm crazy. I am not crazy. I'm an alcoholic.'

When the bistro owners of Montmartre closed their doors to him, warned by Suzanne Valadon, he went out in search of liquor in the drinking dens of La Chapelle or the Goutte D'Or. He would come home with his face all swollen and puffy. The next day, his mother would receive a card posted the evening before by her son, who adored and admired her, on which he had scrawled simply, 'Not drunk!'

When he didn't have a penny left, he would trade a sketch for a glass of wine, or even absinthe. Worse still, he would sometimes just sit down on the pavement and give his works away to passers-by. For a few francs, he would agree to dedicate a canvas and deliver it himself. For a little less, he would sell his views of Montmartre in the stalls of Pigalle, or at Jacobi's, a retired butcher, or at Soulié's, a boxer who now dealt in art.

He owed his artistic salvation to a former clown and former pastry chef, who set up shop in what had once been a pharmacy on the rue Laffitte.

Clovis Sagot had made friends with the artists of the neighbourhood by offering them the candles and medicinal syrups he had discovered in the cellars of his dispensary. He claimed to be an art dealer, but many (notably Picasso, who was also his client) said that he was not much more than a second-hand goods trader. He did, however, know a lot about art. Enough, in any case, to have understood very quickly the profits to be made from painting. Just before the war, the Clovis Sagot gallery advertised in no uncertain terms:

2500% GAIN!

~

SPECULATORS!
Buy Art!
What you pay 200 Francs for
today will be worth 10 000
Francs in ten years' time.

~

You'll find all the young artists
at the Clovis Sagot Gallery

46, rue Laffitte

Clovis Sagot started small. He proposed buying Utrillo's canvases at a price of five francs for the small ones, ten francs for the medium-sized ones, and twenty francs for the largest ones. Maurice seized upon this unexpected opportunity, which would give him the money to drink all he wanted without going broke. He multiplied his views of Montmartre, and the number of glasses he downed. Then, urged on by Suzanne Valadon, he left Sagot for another dealer: Libaude, a former horse auctioneer who now directed a musical variety show, and who agreed to look after the son's affairs if the mother promised to vouch for him. Once the contract was signed, he offered to pay for a treatment to dry the artist out. Once again, it was useless.

Several years later, after Montmartre had moved to Montparnasse, the favourite model of all the painters of the day came to sit for Utrillo. Her name was Alice Prin. Foujita, Kisling, Man Ray and many others had already portrayed this lively and jocular young woman, whose pranks, manners and silhouettes were known to the entire world by now. She came to Utrillo's door; naturally, he too wanted to do her portrait.

He placed her in front of his easel, asked her to pose and painted for three hours. At the end of the session, 'Kiki de Montparnasse' asked if she could look at the portrait.

'Of course,' said Utrillo.

He moved away from the canvas. The young woman approached. She stared at Utrillo's drawing, petrified. Suddenly she burst out laughing, in the familiar laugh that was known in every bistro on the left bank. She leaned closer to make sure she wasn't mistaken. No, she had seen right. It wasn't her face which filled the canvas, nor her body. There wasn't a trace of her in the portrait. For three whole hours, Utrillo had been painting a little house in the country.

LIFE IN BLUE

There are now in France, as in all countries in fact, so many foreigners that it is not without interest to study the sensibility of those among them who, though born elsewhere, nevertheless came here young enough to be fashioned by high French culture and civilization. They introduce into their adopted country the impressions of their childhood, the liveliest of all, and enrich the spiritual heritage of their new land, in the same way as chocolate and coffee, for-example, have enriched the sphere of taste.

Guillaume Apollinaire

The Montmartre of the Mirliton, of the Moulin de la Galette and of the Quadrille Réaliste constituted a kind of national Montmartre. Its very names were an incantation, evocative of the grace and magic of a spot – the place du Tertre; of a time – the crossroads of two centuries; and of so many colourful characters – Bruant, Toulouse-Lautrec, La Goulue, Valadon, Utrillo, Mac Orlan, Carco, Dorgelès...

Mingling with these native artists, who had been living there for several years, were the foreigners. Painters too, but not only painters.

The France of the Second Empire had encouraged immigration, so as to have workers on hand for important building projects. Since then, the industry of mines and metals had been hiring willing manual labour as fast as it could find it. There were also the field-hands, many of them Polish, the students, many of them Romanian, and the intellectuals and artists fleeing the Tsarist persecutions, many of them Jewish. In this respect, France had a fairly good reputation: in 1791, it was the first country to give citizenship and equal rights to Jews, which had enhanced its image worldwide. At the beginning of the twentieth century, it was the incarnation of tolerance, the champion of human rights. Hundreds of painters and writers came to live in France, a country where they could freely express a richness, a sensibility, and a language which were all unwelcome at home. Modern art, born on the banks of Montmartre and Montparnasse, was the fruit of these multiple mixtures.

In its time, Bordeaux had welcomed a well-known Spaniard who had died within its walls: Francisco Goya. At the dawn of the century, another Spanish painter arrived in France: Pablo Diego José Francisco de Paula Juan Nepomuceno Mariá de los Remedios Crispin Crispiniano Santísima Trinidad Ruiz y Picasso.

The young man was nineteen. He had a reputation for being an extraordinary artist. At the age of ten, he could already draw as well as his teacher. When he was fourteen, his father deposited his own paints and brushes at his son's feet, giving up an art in which the youngster had already surpassed him. At sixteen, he brilliantly passed the entrance exams to Madrid's royal academy. When he arrived in Paris, he was no longer just a child prodigy.

He wasn't very familiar with France as yet and didn't plan to stay there long. Though he did not want to leave his native land, it was because it seemed to him too poor, too narrow, and his family was sometimes a burden. But if he was to remain on the other side of the Pyrenees for good, it seemed more likely that it would be in England, home of the pre-Raphaelites.

Picasso was in Paris for the 1900 World Fair. One of his works, Les Derniers Moments (which he covered over in 1903 with La Vie) was chosen to represent his country. For the occasion, he joined his Spanish friends in Montmartre. And he decided to stay.

In a drawing dating from this period, Picasso sketched himself with his companions in front of the entrance to the Fair. The drawing says a lot about the position which he already gave himself in the group: he is in front. Though he is smaller than the others, he has scribbled the world 'Me' under his figure, in large letters, more readable than the names marked under the profiles of those who follow him.

The five Spaniards have linked arms: the other four are Pichot, Ramon Casas, Miguel Utrillo and Casagemas. There is also one woman, Louise Lenoir, known as Odette when posing as a model, who was Picasso's mistress. These Spaniards already knew France well, particularly Montmartre. In Barcelona, in homage to the Parisian Chat Noir, they had founded a café-cabaret that they called Els Quatre Gats. It was there that, thanks to posters, Picasso had discovered European culture: impressionism, Cézanne, Gauguin, Rodin...

His friends were in Montmartre, so he came to Montmartre. A Catalonian painter, Isidre Nonell, lent him his studio on the rue Gabrielle. Later he lived on the Boulevard de Clichy, in a room that another Spaniard, Manyac, lent him for a while. His chunky figure, with a lock of hair falling onto his forehead above dark, lively eyes and the smell of tobacco wafting out of his short briar pipe, would soon become familiar to the inhabitants of Montmartre.

He was often to be seen in the company of his oldest companion, Manuel Pallarès, and a Catalonian writer, Jaime Sabartès, who would remain a faithful friend until his death. At Nonell's apartment, on the rue Gabrielle, Picasso lived with his friend Casagemas, whom he had known since the period of Els Quatre Gats.

Casagemas was probably the most 'politicized' of the artists of the

Spanish colony; he was linked with the libertarian movement. His signature can be found right next to Picasso's on the bottom of a petition demanding the liberation of the Spanish anarchists imprisoned in Madrid in 1900. Perhaps because of their friendship, Picasso would be suspected for a time by the French police of belonging to the anarchist movement. This suspicion would turn out to be unfounded, despite Picasso's real sympathy for the anarchist cause and for some of its champions: in 1909, he was revolted by the execution of Francisco Ferrer.*

Casagemas, aside from being politically active, was also sensitive, easily wounded, and very much in love. The object of his affections was a young girl who posed as a model in Montmartre, Germaine, and who sometimes spent a few hours in Picasso's bed. But Casagemas's affections were not returned. He spoke of suicide. To distract him from his problems, Picasso took him off to Spain. The bordellos there could not make him forget his passion. Casagemas returned to Paris. The night he arrived, he invited some friends to dinner at a restaurant on the Boulevard de Clichy. Germaine was one of them. Casagemas announced to them all that he was going to leave France to return to his country for good. The announcement provoked no reaction from the young woman. The painter renewed his proposals of marriage several times. She only shrugged. He drew a pistol from his pocket, shot at Germaine, but missed, then aimed the weapon at his own forehead and put a bullet through his brain.

Picasso, shaken by the tragic disappearance of his friend, painted several canvases portraying him, notably La Mort de Casagemas (1901) and Casagemas dans son Cercueil (1901). La Femme au chignon (1901), with her hard look and tight lips, is almost certainly a portrait of Germaine.

The death of Casagemas marked a turning point in his work. Until then, he had painted in the style of Toulouse-Lautrec. He admired the painter, having discovered his work at Els Quatre Gats. He chose people and subjects that would not have been foreign to the sensibility of his illustrious predecessor, and painted them in lively colours which the public liked. A good example is Le Moulin de la Galette (1900). His work was selling now. But little by little he began to abandon this style for a more tragic, internalized painting, which reflected the poverty in which the Spanish community of Montmartre was living. This was his blue period.

This period takes its name in part from Picasso's use of a blue monochromatism which is often said to have been inspired by El Greco. It evokes the melancholy, suffering, and poverty, often moral as well as material, that the artist saw around him shortly after his arrival in Paris. He visited the women's prison of Saint Lazare several times to see prisoners there. They appear often in his work and reflect the interest that Picasso

* Francisco Ferrer was a Spanish liberal opposed to Spain's colonial war in Mexico.

took at this time in a certain image of grief. Blue is an appropriate colour for this vision of the world and the conditions in which he was working, locked up all night in his studio, lit by a gas lamp.

He had the same three problems as all his friends at the time: how to earn enough money to enable him to live, to paint, and to eat.

The least poor of them all was the sculptor and ceramic artist Paco Durrio. He was a student of Gauguin and had remained friendly with him. He owned drawings, watercolours and about fifteen paintings by the exile of the Marquesas Islands, and it was he who introduced Picasso to his master's work.

Paco often offered to lodge him, and always shared whatever was on his table. When his friend didn't come to seek help, he would go out of his way to be kind, leaving a bit of bread or a can of sardines in front of Picasso's door. He was devoted to his companions, making a kind of cult out of his friendship. On his deathbed, he would confess, 'It's hell, leaving your friends.'

The person who most often benefited from this generosity was not Picasso but a Catalonian, Manuel Martinez y Hugué, known as Manolo. He was swarthy – black eyes, black hair – poor, devoted, resourceful, and had an elf-like love of jokes. He was the only one to whom Picasso still spoke in Catalonian. In bistros, he used to introduce Manolo as his sister. Manolo wanted to sculpt, but couldn't, for lack of clay and proper materials. So he painted, quite heroically, for no one bought his paintings. He managed to eat about every other day, slept wherever someone would let him, and pinched whatever he could find in shops.

One summer, Paco lent him his house. When he came home a few weeks later, the sculptor welcomed him somewhat awkwardly. He handed over the keys and took off. His friend inspected the house to make sure everything was still there. And so it was – everything except the Gauguins. Manolo had sold them to Vollard.

'You', Picasso declared one day to his friend, 'will never be executed by a firing squad.'

'Why?' asked Manolo.

'Because you would make them laugh too much!'

He was a past master of the art of scrounging enough to eat through playing clever games. He had perfected the technique in houses of worship. When he came to Paris, one of the first places he visited was a church. He found himself in the presence of a well-dressed churchgoer, who couldn't find a place to sit. A woman emerged from a dark corner of the nave. She proffered a chair, the man gave her a coin, he sat down, she disappeared. Manolo imitated the operation, and repeated it numerous times, which meant he could soon afford more substantial nourishment than a simple host dipped in holy water.

When he didn't go to the church, he practised the lottery method. Knocking on the doors of houses in Montmartre, he presented the drawing of a marble bust that he claimed he was in the midst of sculpting.

'A hundred sous for a number.'

In exchange for a coin, he gave the person in front of him a piece of paper with a number on it, and took his leave. Of course no one ever won: the bust did not exist. When he was asked what the winning number was, he would answer, '[André] Salmon's number!' A few years later, having finally earned enough to buy the material he needed, he duped Kahnweiler. The latter bought his sculptures regularly. For one of them, Manolo demanded more money than usual.

'Why?' enquired the merchant.

'Because it will be better than the others.'

'You always say that.'

'This time it's true.'

'Well, we'll see about that later.'

'In that case, I'm sorry, but I can't work.'

Kahnweiler was not just a dealer. He was an aesthete and a friend to his painters. Manolo, who knew this very well, insisted, 'It will be bigger than the others. I need more material, but you'll sell it for more money.'

'It's really a lot bigger?'

'Infinitely.'

So Kahnweiler included a few extra notes. Under his black mop of hair, Manolo's dark eyes shone with pleasure.

The summer passed. As the first autumn leaves began to fall, Kahnweiler received the sculpture from the Spaniard. It was a crouching woman, neither bigger nor smaller than his usual work. The dealer summoned the sculptor.

'You promised me a large piece.'

'And so it is.'

'I don't see ...'

'You haven't looked properly.'

Manolo stepped up to the statue. 'It's a woman ...'

'Yes, that I can see.'

'The woman is crouching down.'

'That I also see.'

'But what if she were to get up?'

'If she were to get up?' queried Kahnweiler, puzzled.

'Yes, then she would be big! Very big!'

The Spaniard Picasso managed to make out better than the regular hangers-on in the bistros. He had found an answer to the question of how to make a living: quite simply, he painted and sold his paintings. Already.

He was like the others, but at the same time different. Of all the artists who had matured together in Montmartre, he would not only become the richest in the end, but also the one who remained poverty-stricken and hungry for the shortest amount of time.

Picasso was too proud to send humorous sketches to the *Assiette au beurre*, the *Cri de Paris* or the *Charivari*, as Marcoussis, Gris, Van Dongen, Warnod and many others did. He was wary of the 'second vocation': 'When one has something to say, to express, any form of submission becomes intolerable.'[1] Rather than accepting the offers of the papers, he preferred to wait for the dealers to come to him.

The first of these, his fellow countryman Manyac, let him use a room in his apartment on the Boulevard de Clichy, and gave him a monthly allowance of one hundred and fifty francs in exchange for his work. It wasn't much, but it was enough to keep him from starving.

As long as Picasso's work continued in the style of Toulouse-Lautrec, Manyac supported him. But when he entered his blue period, the dealer began to back off: his paintings were impossible to sell. Picasso had to deal, for a time, with shopkeepers who sold art like others sold fruit and vegetables.

Most of them were simply dealers in second-hand goods. They set out their goods on the sidewalk in front of their shop. Squashed between an old iron and a pram without wheels, works by Utrillo, the Douanier Rousseau or Picasso could be spotted by passers-by.

Like the others, the Spaniard had to do business with Libaude and, especially, Clovis Sagot, with whom Utrillo had already had dealings. To begin with, the contact with the former pastry chef was easy: he seemed soft and malleable, like clay for a sculpture. And he truly liked painting. Or at any rate, colours. Things got a little more complicated when it came to talking about money. And when the artist himself didn't bring up the subject, Sagot took care to lead the conversation in this direction, as money was a subject he favoured above all others. Each time he arrived at Picasso's studio, with a bunch of flowers in his hand, he handed them kindly to the painter and asked, 'Do you like them?'

Picasso would nod.

'Do you think you could paint them?'

The Spaniard groaned.

'Well?'

'I don't know . . .'

'Of course you could!' the dealer would say. 'They're such lovely flowers!' He grabbed the bouquet and waved it in front of Picasso. 'I offer you flowers, you paint them, and then . . .'

Picasso didn't answer.

'And then, to thank me, you give me a little present: the painting!'

Sagot smiled his million-dollar smile. 'And what's more, I'm generous.
I'll leave you the flowers!'

One day, he offered to buy a few of Picasso's canvases.

'For how much?'

'Seven hundred francs.'

'Forget it.'

The painter left the rue Laffitte and went back to the Butte. The same evening, finding the cupboard alarmingly bare, he regretted his stand, and the next day returned to Sagot.

'You've changed your mind?'

'I don't have any choice.'

'Wonderful!' the dealer exclaimed. He opened his arms wide to embrace the artist.

'I'll take everything. For five hundred francs ...'

'Seven hundred!'

'Why seven hundred?'

'Yesterday ...'

'Yesterday was yesterday.'

Picasso, furious, left the shop.

Twenty-four hours later, after a day with nothing to eat, he came back.

'Today', cried Sagot, beaming, 'I'm in a good mood.'

'Which is to say?'

'Which is to say I'll give you three hundred francs for the lot.'

The artist gave up.

He also dealt with Soulié, the former boxer who had already cheated Utrillo. His shop was located just across from the Médrano Circus. Old Soulié was first and foremost an alcoholic, then an antiques and second-hand goods dealer who specialized in the purchase and sale of beds and old mattresses. He had started to sell art through a game of bartering: he would sell canvases to artists and they would pay with their drawings or gouaches when they had no other currency to propose. These works – by painters like Renoir, Lautrec and Dufy – were then exhibited directly on the sidewalk.

Soulié treated the artists more or less like ordinary customers, bargaining over everything, refusing to give them credit. One day, he came to Picasso's studio to order some paintings. He absolutely needed to have a bouquet of flowers for the next day: he had promised it to a customer. Picasso didn't have anything ready.

'Well paint me one, then!' the dealer suggested. 'That's not so hard, for you.'

'I don't have any white.'

'Why do you need white?'

'If you could give me a little advance, I could go buy some ...'

'Oh, forget about the white! It's so ordinary!'

Picasso painted a bouquet that Soulié bought from him for twenty francs. He carried it off while the paint was still drying. And that was a larger sum than usual, due to the fact that he had ordered it specially. Usually he only paid three francs for a gouache. And Picasso was no worse off than the others: it was from old Soulié that he bought, for five francs, a work by the Douanier Rousseau, *Portrait of Madame M.* The painting had been sitting on the pavement for days. The dealer noticed Picasso looking at it.

'Take her home! That lady would look good at your place.'

As the painter didn't seem to be able to make up his mind, he added, 'It's yours for a hundred sous! You can paint over it, and since it's a big one, if you do a fine bunch of flowers for me, I'll buy it back from you at the same price!'

Picasso bought the painting, but he didn't paint over it...

The first true art dealer he met was a woman, Berthe Weill. Her painters called her 'la Merweil'.* She was a small, cross-eyed woman who wore magnifying glasses for spectacles. She lived on very little, not taking much profit for herself on the sale of her paintings. She slept and ate at her gallery in the rue Victor-Massé: a simple shop in which works by Matisse, Derain, Dufy, Utrillo and Van Dongen hung from threads by clothes pins. Soon she would add paintings by Marie Laurencin, Picabia, Metzinger, Gleizes and, of course, Picasso. A lover of the arts, Berthe Weill contributed almost as much to the development of modern art as did Vollard, Paul Guillaume, Rosenberg and Kahnweiler. She helped Picasso considerably, having bought from him, through the intermediary of Manyac, a portion of his works dating from the Lautrec period, then, after the mediator had disappeared, some gouaches from the blue period. But only some.

If one goes by her account books, which she showed to Francis Carco in 1908, Berthe Weill bought Utrillo paintings for ten francs, Dufys for thirty francs, the same sum for Rouault, a Matisse for seventy francs and a Lautrec for six hundred francs. Picassos were valued between approximately thirty and fifty francs.[2] She sold the works on to fairly wealthy art lovers, such as André Level, the collector, Marcel Sembat, who was already an admirer of Matisse, and Olivier Saincère, who was to become secretary-general of the Elysée palace when Raymond Poincaré was in office. Thus this energetic little woman, so devoted to her painters, succeeded in making a reputation for Picasso beyond the narrow limits of the Butte Montmartre.

* When pronounced in French, 'la merweil' sounds very much like 'la merveille' or 'the marvel'. 'La mère Weil' also means 'the motherly Weill', a reference to her reputation for looking after her clients.

Berthe Weill had a strong character. The divisional commissioner of the nineteenth arrondissement was to find this out one day in 1917. In a gallery on the rue Taitbout, Berthe Weill had organized Modigliani's first exhibition. She had asked Blaise Cendrars to write a poem to accompany a drawing by the Italian painter on the invitations which she sent out.

On the evening of the opening, there were as many people inside the gallery as outside: inside were the art lovers, and in the street passers-by taken aback by the nudes exhibited in the window. They called a policeman, who brought in the commissioner. The latter made his message heard: the paintings had to be removed. Berthe Weill refused to comply. She was immediately summoned to the policeman's office. She crossed the street accompanied by the jeers and insults of overdressed men in gaiters and women in fancy hats.

The commissioner thundered, 'I order you to take down all that filth!'

'Why?' asked the gallery owner.

'Those nudes . . .'

The official was almost spitting with rage. When he managed to regain his self-control, he answered, his voice hoarse with anger, 'Those nudes . . . they have . . . hair!'

The exhibition had to be closed. To help Modigliani, who was living in utter poverty, Berthe Weill bought five of his paintings. She defended him as tenaciously as she had defended Picasso during his first Parisian years, when she herself had not felt sure about his works from the blue period. But, where the Spanish painter would one day become rich and famous, the Italian was never to find fortune. Or even a little luck . . .

TWO AMERICANS IN PARIS

I had shown two studies by Cézanne to a client. And right away, he
said: 'Don't want any of those things with all the empty spaces...'

Ambroise Vollard

Ambroise Vollard didn't like the blue period much either. He discovered
Picasso through Manyac, and sold some works by the Spanish painter in
1901, then some more from 1906. At the time, he had exhibited Manet,
Renoir, Cézanne, Van Gogh, Gauguin. His activity was in no way like that
of the antiques and used-goods salesmen or paint merchants whom Berthe
Weill resembled, at least at the start of the century.

Vollard had his own establishment. He was one of the first to buy
works by Derain and Vlaminck and to show interest in the sculptor
Maillol. He was close to Pissarro, who had introduced him to the
impressionists.

Ambroise Vollard had begun to come into his own when, in 1895, he
organized an exhibition of works by Cézanne which had been refused by
Durand-Ruel and the Bernheim brothers. In his memoirs, he describes in
great detail how much energy he had had to put into finding out where
the painter was living, as Cézanne was very careful not to give out his
address.[1] After having located him, he had a discussion with the artist's
son, to whom he spoke of his project for an exhibition. A few days later,
he received an enormous rolled-up package containing a hundred and
fifty works by the painter. Since he did not have much money at the time,
Vollard exhibited them framed only by rough wooden sticks. His fame,
and that of Cézanne, date from this event. It would enable Vollard to
devote himself to the painters he liked and admired, all the while pursuing
his vocation as a publisher of art books, which he loved. He would select
the best paper and the best engravers to publish works of his choice, and
would commission paintings by an artist to accompany the text. Thus he
published an edition of La Fontaine's fables illustrated by Chagall, a
volume of Verlaine's poetry with drawings by Bonnard, a work by Mirbeau
with artwork by Rodin...

In time, Vollard's gallery was to become one of the landmarks of the modern art world. It was located on the rue Laffitte, in the heart of the art dealers' neighbourhood in Paris, where Bernheim and Durand-Ruel were established (the latter had also opened a gallery in New York in 1886). Matisse, Rouault, Picasso and many other young artists often spent time in these spots, observing the works of their predecessors.

The display window of Vollard's gallery resembled no other. When Chagall noticed this, after having seen the Renoirs, Picassos and Monets exhibited on the rue Laffitte, he couldn't believe his eyes: everywhere there was nothing but dust, dirt, and old newspapers. And in this case, one could tell a book by its cover, for the inside was even worse! The visitor who entered discovered a desk, a stove, a Maillol sculpture, paintings sitting on the floor facing the wall, a few Cézanne canvases with no frames ... and dust, dust everywhere. One can understand Vlaminck's comment: he quipped that when he had had his first exhibition at Vollard's, he had sent his cleaning lady to the gallery every day to dust the furniture and the paintings.

Behind the desk, half-asleep, sat a man, a Creole from Réunion, aged about forty, tall, stout, balding, with a short beard. Renoir would say of him that he looked like a chimpanzee. Customers often thought that painting didn't really interest him. For Vollard hardly paid attention when people entered the gallery. He would open one eye, ask what they wanted, listen, start to get up and then sink down into his seat again, saying, 'Come back tomorrow.'

The next day, he would show them works that he had fetched from his Ali Baba-like cave, where a thousand treasures were stored. Having regained his seat behind the desk, he would wait until the visitor pointed to a canvas.

'That one?'

'Fifty francs,' answered Vollard without a moment's hesitation.

'Forty.'

'I said fifty. You're offering me forty. In that case it will be seventy.'

'What?!'

Vollard would shake his head, an indication that there was no point in arguing.

'And what proof do I have that this work is authentic?'

'None.'

'What do you mean, none?'

'The painting dates from 1830. I wasn't born then. How should I know?'

The customer would look at the dealer sceptically, and ask, 'Can you show me a few Cézannes?'

Vollard would show him some. The fellow was thrilled.

'How much for that one?'

'Two hundred francs.'

'Do you think Cézanne's market value is on the rise?'

'I haven't the faintest idea!'

The customer hesitated. Vollard condescended to give an explanation. 'I bought this painting for twelve francs last year. I'm selling it to you for twenty times that...'

'Which proves that its value is rising!'

'Which proves that it's rising at the moment. But who knows, tomorrow maybe the painting won't even be worth twelve francs any more!'

Behind his rough, unpleasant manners, Vollard concealed a crafty soul. He was like a cat on the hunt. When he wanted to acquire a painter's works, he did. He bought not just one or two paintings, but the entire production. This is how he proceeded with Vlaminck and Derain: fascinated by the pictorial violence of the Fauves, he went to the workshop first of one, then the other, and gruffly examined the works he found there.

'I'll buy,' he would say.

'What will you buy?'

'Everything.'

Most of the time, he didn't sign a contract: his word was enough. When he sold, and if he wanted to make the effort, he was no longer a cat but a fox. Thanks to Alice Toklas, we know about the games he played with Gertrude and Leo Stein.

One must try to imagine the scene. Two Americans, who had recently arrived in France, enter Vollard's gallery. The woman has a massive frame, like a peasant's, and is wearing laced-up leather sandals; her hair, cropped very short, further accentuates the manly appearance of her short, sturdy person; she has the handshake of a bodyguard, a trace of a smile; she talks in an animated and long-winded fashion. The man, stiff, somewhat severe-looking with his hat, red beard and overcoat, appears almost delicate at his sister's side. And Vollard is half-dozing behind his desk, wearing his legendary coat and his big, heavy shoes that are so old that the ends point up, like Turkish slippers.

He doesn't rise. He doesn't know that the greatest patrons of the arts in Paris are standing before him. Since their arrival in 1903, the Steins have been scouring the city's galleries and artists' workshops. They have a fortune to spend, and they're planning to spend it on art.

Impassive, sleepy, Vollard bides his time. Leo asks if they can see some landscapes by Cézanne. Vollard rises slowly. He descends the staircase leading to his treasures. Five minutes later, the dealer returns with a small canvas. He shows it to them. It's an apple.

'Excuse us,' says Gertrude. 'A piece of fruit is not a landscape ... We want to see a landscape.'

'Oh. Sorry,' says Vollard.

He disappears again, down the staircase. The Americans laugh.

When he returns, he is carrying a larger painting than the first one. He shows it to his two visitors. They inspect it attentively. This time, Leo speaks. He says, 'Monsieur Vollard, we don't mean to be rude, but we really would like to see a landscape. You've brought us a nude.'

Vollard looks at the painting in turn. It's a woman, seen from the back. 'Oh, do excuse me. I'll be right back.'

For the third time, he disappears down the staircase. He returns, a few minutes later, carrying a very large frame. 'You want to see a landscape? Here's a landscape.'

The painting is unfinished. There is indeed a landscape in it, but it is tiny. The rest of the canvas is empty.

'That's better,' admits Gertrude Stein. 'But if we could see a smaller, completely finished painting, we would be delighted.'

'I'll see what I can find,' grumbles Vollard.

He leaves again. Brother and sister wait. They hear steps. But it isn't the dealer: it's an oldish woman who emerges from the staircase, greets them in a friendly fashion, and vanishes into the street.

Leo and Gertrude look at each other. They don't understand what's happening. They laugh. Again they hear steps. And another woman appears. 'Good evening, monsieur, madame.'

She follows the first one into the rue Laffitte. Gertrude bursts out laughing and tells her brother her theory: the dealer is a madman, the two women who have just passed are painters who work in the basement of the gallery. Each time he has left, Vollard has asked them quickly to sketch an apple, a bit of a nude, a fragment of a landscape, then he's shown it to them, swearing it is a Cézanne. In fact, he has no Cézannes at all!

They laugh. But Vollard returns. He shows them another canvas, this time a real landscape, a finished painting. It is magnificent. The two Americans buy the work and leave.

Vollard would later tell his friends that he had had a visit from two nutty Americans who didn't stop laughing. He had quickly intuited that the more they laughed, the more they would buy.

He wasn't wrong. He had so amused them that the Steins came back soon, and often. In the same year, they bought two nudes by Cézanne, one Monet, two Renoirs and two Gauguins.

Vollard's basement was an absolute marvel, filled with a million treasures. It contained masterpieces, but also a kitchen and a dining room! For the dealer liked to entertain. He wasn't only clever and sullen. He was also curious, talkative on occasion, a great reader of popular literature; he loved to exchange gossip, and could be very courteous, especially to women, although he never married. In answer to a question from Vlaminck about his bachelor state, he answered that a wife would have asked him too many questions about Cézanne. 'Can you imagine? Having to explain, what a bore!'

At his table, the most frequently served dish was curried chicken, the speciality of his native island. The dealer hosted lunches and dinners for the artists and art lovers whom he liked most. Notably Rouault, who lunched with him nearly every day; and the irascible Degas, an anti-Semite and a pain in the neck, who had never forgiven Berthe Weill for setting up her gallery near where he lived. On the subject, Vollard liked to tell a story about a day when he had gone to see the painter to show him a canvas, and had by accident dropped a tiny bit of paper, a quarter of an inch wide, that fell through a crack in the floor. Degas had hurried over, crying, 'Watch it! You're making a mess in my studio!' The offending bit of waste was promptly picked up.

One evening when the dealer had invited him to dinner, Degas had made his acceptance of the invitation conditional upon seven points: there could be no butter in the cooking, no flowers on the table, only a thin mist of light could be visible, the cat had to be locked up, there must be no dog, the women were not to wear perfume, and dinner had to be served at precisely half past seven. Not an easy guest...

Vollard's friends knew that as soon as they had swallowed the last mouthful of the meal, their host would cross his hands behind his head, lean back against the wall, and drift off to sleep.

In fact, he was capable of sleeping anywhere. He could drop off at the table, in a carriage, behind his desk, and yet he constantly complained about having slept badly. He criticized his bed, which he swore to change (but which he always kept, as he did his coat and shoes which he promised to throw away ten times a week). This state of semi-somnolence made his friends – and his enemies – say that he had become rich while asleep. The painters for whom he posed, notably Renoir, begged him not to drift off during their sessions. To keep him awake, Bonnard made him hold a cat on his lap. Cézanne went so far as to seat him on a stool which was itself set on a platform supported by four posts.

'If you fall, the stool will fall too, dragging the pickets and the platform with it...'

'And then?'

'Well, that should wake you up!'

It was torture. After one hundred and fifteen sessions of posing and several unfortunate falls, the model asked, 'Are we almost done?'

'Not quite,' answered Cézanne.

'Are you at least satisfied?'

The painter stepped back, examined the canvas, and answered, 'I'm not dissatisfied with the front of the shirt...'

Ambroise Vollard would die in 1939 in an automobile accident. The chauffeur was driving while the dealer snored in the back seat. Two versions have been given of the accident. Some claim that the limousine hit a chicken coop and Vollard, having seen nothing coming because he was dozing deeply, had hit his head against the dashboard. Thus he had died in his sleep. But the tale may be too good to be true. Georges Charensol's version is more likely:[2] after the car had veered off the road, a bronze statue of Maillol's, which was sitting on the shelf over the back seat, fell and broke the art dealer's skull. Such was the death, in all probability, of Ambroise Vollard, touched by the double grace of Maillol and sleep.

CYPRIAN

Someone's talking about Max Jacob ... I see a firefly outlined against
the wall: it's Max, listening.

Raymond Queneau

A man had just left Vollard's and was walking up the streets of Montmartre,
his path hazily lit by the blue flame of gas lamps. He wore a Breton
shepherd's cloak in grey cloth lined with red flannel. He was balding,
with a large head and narrow shoulders. His mouth had smile-lines around
it, his eyes were sometimes mobile, sometimes steady. Unforgettable eyes.
He wore a monocle. The poverty common to many of the Butte's painters
was perceptible beneath his dignity and elegance.

To anyone who asked about his childhood, he would say that a band
of gypsies had kidnapped him when he was three years old; that his bones
were removed and he was cut up into pieces before being discovered
several years later in the courtyard of the Ecole Normale Supérieure, one
of France's finest schools.

There was no need to believe a word he said; the man was a poet.

He also had several other artistic talents: he was a painter, and always had
been. At the Lycée of Quimper, his art teacher had thought he was just a
doodler (revealing a shameful lack of perspicacity on the instructor's part).

His parents had wanted him to attend the Ecole Normale, but he chose
the Colonial Army, where he began to train. Lacking sufficient muscles,
and found to be short of breath, he was spared military service. One fine
day, with no luggage, no coat, just a few francs pinched from his mother's
wallet, he came to Paris, where he quickly discovered that a paintbrush
didn't bring much more in the way of revenue than a pen. He became in
turn piano teacher, tutor, office employee, art critic, street sweeper,
apprentice carpenter, lawyer's clerk, secretary, sales representative and
childminder.

His poverty was mind-boggling. He managed to dress with style, thanks
to the generosity of his father, a tailor in Quimper. And if he was walking
now in the direction of the Boulevard de Clichy, it was to meet the artist

whose sixty-four paintings he had just seen exhibited at Ambroise Vollard's – Pablo Picasso.

This art fascinated him. It had nothing to do, he explained, with the painting of those whose chief preoccupation was to move harmoniously from light to shadow, or the other way around. Nor did it resemble impressionism, a movement which was still not welcomed by the general public, despite the enthusiasm that was beginning to be felt for Renoir and Degas. It was not comparable to the works of the artists whom Max Jacob called 'the great decorators', supposed disciples of Delacroix and Rubens, who could fill entire walls with their vast works. It was close neither to the divided brushstroke of Signac, nor to those who imitated the symbolists, Puvis de Chavannes or Maurice Denis. It was less vehement than the work of Toulouse-Lautrec. And yet:

> He [Picasso] did imitate all that, but his imitations were caught up in such a whirlwind of genius that one felt only, in this exhibition of a great number of canvases, the explosive force of an entirely new and original personality.[1]

Max Jacob met the painter in the apartment he shared with Manyac on the Boulevard de Clichy. He told him how much he admired his work, as a dozen Spanish friends of Picasso, who were cooking beans on an alcohol burner, looked on. Picasso thanked him. The two men congratulated each other, shook hands, and embraced, without really being able to understand what in the world they were saying: the Spaniard spoke in his language, and the Frenchman in his. All they knew was that there was clearly some kind of magnetic attraction between them.

Picasso showed Jacob his work: dozens of canvases piled up one on top of another. Then he invited the visitor to eat and drink with his companions. Afterwards, they sang. As they didn't know the same tunes, Beethoven served as a common chorus: until late into the night, the guitars played melodies from his symphonies.

The next day, Max Jacob invited his new friend to come and visit him. The Spaniard turned up with all his friends as usual. Max read his verses to the assembled guests, who couldn't understand a word – only the general tone and gestures. That was enough. Picasso cried with emotion: he declared that Max Jacob was the only true French poet of his time. In exchange for the compliment, the only true French poet of the time offered some of his most precious possessions to his admirer: a Dürer wood engraving, rare authentic images of Epinal that he was one of the few still to collect, and all his Daumier lithographs.

Picasso drew him in to his band of Spaniards. They would laugh, sing, and dance far into the night. The group had several favourite hangouts.

The first was the Zut, a tavern on the rue Ravignan where all the anarchists of the Butte came to drink. It had three connecting rooms, each more sinister than the one before. Gas lamps lit the murky place, which was run by a little man with a cap and long beard, wearing brown velvet pants, clogs on his feet, and a bright red flannel belt. His name was Frédéric Gérard, Frédé for short. His bar was open to all the poor and rejected citizens of the city. Though he didn't know a single note of music, the tavern keeper played the guitar, sometimes the cello. He sang Parisian melodies, often accompanied by other performers who came to join him. Outside, the street was full of prostitutes, petty thieves, deserters, rival gangs with their knives out, looking for a fight, fraudsters, stamp forgers: the usual flora and fauna of the neighbourhood. The Zut's sign announced the tone: 'Beer'. It was the only alcohol available on the premises; there were no wines or liqueurs. Frédé poured the foam directly from the pitcher into glasses placed on the barrels that served as tables. Sometimes he would cook ham and eggs. When shots were heard outside, punctuating the young hotheads' fun, he reassured his immigrant friends that if the police came, he would hide them. They were all afraid of being forced to leave the country. But Frédé the bigmouth, Frédé the anarchist, was there to watch out for them.

He was a few years older than most of the others in the band, and he understood these free spirits who lived like schoolboys. They weren't burdened with the social and familial responsibilities that weighed so heavily on the respectable shoulders of those who lived further down the hills of Montmartre, away from the Butte. Here, the only family was one's group of friends. And the social and professional life they led was that of an artist: crazy and unpredictable. The manners of the painters and poets were nothing more nor less than the expression, in gesture and action, of the enthusiasms expressed in words by the anarchist Libertad and the *Père Peinard*.

In 1902, the Spaniard returned to his country for several months. When he came back, he shared several hotel rooms with a sculptor friend. He was ground down by poverty and discouraged by the poor sales of his canvases. Max, who was only five years older than him, played big brother and looked after the younger man – he called him 'little one'. In a show of amazing generosity, he managed to get himself a job as a handler for the Paris-France chain of department stores that his cousin directed. The poet swept the floor and delivered purchases in a wheelbarrow, and until he was fired eight months later for 'general incompetence', he shared his earnings with Picasso.

The two friends lived together in a room that Max had rented on the Boulevard Voltaire. The artists' life was very hard. One night, as they were gazing out of the window, the same thought came to both of them.

Picasso was the first to turn away. He took the poet's arm and said, 'We can't let ourselves have ideas like that.'

They took turns sleeping: Max slept at night while Pablo painted, and Pablo painted during the day while Max was out working. When they were together, in the evening, the Paris-France employee tried hard to encourage his friend, as Manyac, Berthe Weill and Ambroise Vollard had all moved away from him during his blue period.

Some days, using the pseudonym of Maxime Febur, Max would visit galleries where he would pass himself off as a rich collector. He would ask, 'Do you have any works by Picasso?'

Most of the time, the answer was no. They hadn't heard of him. Max pretended to be stupefied. 'How can that be? He's a genius! What a mistake for a gallery like yours not to exhibit an artist of such stature!'

For Picasso, Max Jacob was the incarnation of providence: not only did he help him, but he also helped him discover a world of letters that up until then hadn't represented anything more than hieroglyphics to him. And Picasso did as was his wont: he learned, he delved into whatever was offered, and he used it. As he would himself recognize, he wasn't a giver, but a taker.

For Max Jacob, things were simpler: Picasso was the most important person in his entire existence. 'He's the door to my whole life,' he would say. He took him as he was, all of him, without fussing over details. Fascinated, for instance, by his friend's vanity, he would watch in amazement as he carefully chose a pair of socks to match the day's underwear . . .

The poet celebrated the painter. The painter drew the poet. After Baudelaire and Delacroix, Zola and Cézanne, they led the waltz of pen and paint in their own time. Soon, other poets and painters would join them, notably Léger and Cendrars. Picasso himself would attract the attention of Salmon and Apollinaire, and then Cocteau, Eluard, Breton, Reverdy, René Char . . . But it was Max Jacob who first introduced him to Ronsard, Verlaine, Vigny, Baudelaire, Rimbaud and Mallarmé, opening up the vast horizon of poetry, which would strike a sensitive chord in him all his life. Max Jacob was first among the group of friends and followers of Picasso that succeeded his band of Spaniards; it was also Max Jacob who helped introduce him into fashionable circles and who arranged for him to meet the dress designers and artistic patrons, Paul Poiret and Jacques Doucet.

Picasso was not the only one to benefit from the poet's generosity and the abundance of opportunities he helped to arrange. For Francis Carco, too, 'the Butte would definitely have lost what was finest in its spirit' without Max Jacob.[2] The fact is undeniable.

First Montmartre, then Montparnasse, adored him. Whenever he appeared, he was cheered, welcomed, acclaimed. He went out in his black frock coat, top hat and monocle, into the very different types of society which it amused him to frequent. He was appreciated by bourgeois circles, with their comfortable lifestyles, for his intelligence, his humour, his appearance (which was not that far from theirs) and for his sometimes bawdy jokes. He was treasured by his impoverished friends for his generosity; he was always ready to share everything, and more besides. This convert from Judaism was a Breton, and proud of it. In society, he dazzled: 'a gossip and a poet, helpful, eager, chatty, deep, vain, mocking.'[3] But inside, he was terribly sensitive, emotional, capable of weeping, of begging someone's forgiveness. Witty, he could wield pithy remarks like a spear, aimed straight at the heart. He was appreciated by women for his exquisite manners – he who only truly loved men.

He did have a few female loves, though: one at least, three at most. The first was called Cécile, and would become Mademoiselle Léoni, the mistress of Matorel in *Saint Matorel*. No one knew her. Fernande Olivier mentions her existence, but probably never met her. But if one believes a letter written by Max Jacob to Apollinaire in 1904, he was planning to become engaged to her:

> I forgot to tell you yesterday that I'm no longer free this evening. I've promised to go to an engagement dinner ... Yes, it's my engagement! I'll be getting married in two or three months. This letter will serve as an invitation.[4]

The young lady was only eighteen years old; she worked in the Paris-France department stores. The romance was short-lived. According to his account, Max broke the affair off because he was too poor to be able to help her. He wept as he said goodbye.

After the war, one day, while he was sitting on the terrace of a café in Pigalle with his friends Juan Gris and Pierre Reverdy, a woman walked by. Max turned crimson and stammered out, 'Cécile!' The others stared as a plain, graceless matron walked by and disappeared into the neighbouring streets.

Whatever his successes or disappointments as a lover, Max Jacob was first and foremost one of the great poets of his day, mastering the alexandrine as skilfully as free verse and the prose poem. But he always remained modestly hidden behind others, making little of his talent, claiming to be only a minor poet. And this was true not only in the first years of the century when he was an unknown, but even later, when he had become an important figure who had acquired a certain fame – though that, for a poet, does not imply wealth, alas.

When Apollinaire published *Alcools*, Georges Duhamel, who was the critic for the *Mercure de France*, wrote that certain poems in the collection were plagiarized from Verlaine, Rimbaud and Moréas, and others inspired by Max Jacob. Max responded that the assertion was false: he claimed

never to have written a poem before meeting Apollinaire. This was untrue.
Max Jacob's greatest virtue, Valery Larbaud would say, was his humility.

In the thirties, when he was living in utter poverty, he agreed to appear on the stage. Every evening, in front of a full house, he would begin his show with this sentence: 'Ladies and gentlemen, you don't know me. No one knows me, despite the fact that I'm in the Larousse encyclopedia!'

He was a poet – a poet and not a novelist. The difference? He would explain it one day to Pierre Béarn, in the presence of Charles Trenet, a young man who happened to be in Max's minuscule Parisian apartment: 'The novelist will write "A green dress" and the poet will write "A dress the colour of grass".'[5]

He had worked as an employee in a firm. The directors asked him to write a speech to be read at the funeral of the son of one of the company's important suppliers. Max Jacob found out as much as he could about the bereaved supplier and prepared a detailed eulogy which praised the civic and moral virtues and the economic and financial talents of the deceased. But he was wide of the mark: the deceased in question had scarcely had time to prove himself, being only a child...

An edition of his first tale, *Le Roi Kaboul et le marmiton Gauvin*, was given to deserving students in an awards ceremony. It was a secular school, and he had been asked to replace the churches in the story by town halls, and the priests by teachers. This was rather in contradiction with his character: Max Jacob was no more an exemplar of moral values than he was a practising atheist.

He distributed the volumes himself, publishing them with his own funds or, on occasion, soliciting orders through Kahnweiler: this was the case with *Saint Matorel* (1911) and *Le Siège de Jérusalem* (1914), illustrated with etchings by Picasso. He himself financed the edition of the *Phanérogame* and the *Cornet à dés*.

'Live like a poet,' Picasso had said to him when he was working at Paris-France. This was probably a way of suggesting that he give up not only the delivery boy's wheelbarrow, but also the paintbrush. Max painted figurative gouaches, using paints, rice powder, the ashes from his cigarettes, the soot from smoke, coffee grounds, dust. He never did give up painting. But he did abandon the various odd jobs he had been doing up until then to make room for other activities: writing, of course, but also, fortune-telling.

He could read the lines of people's hands, or the dregs of a coffee cup; he knew the Cabbala and the language of the stars. He gave all his friends assorted talismans, drawings, stones, pieces of copper or iron engraved with incomprehensible hieroglyphics, fetishes of all sorts, sometimes covered with cabbalistic signs. Those he didn't like would receive heavy objects that the amateur astrologist advised them to keep on their person at all times; if they forgot, fate would be sure to punish them. So Max Jacob's enemies found themselves obliged to drag around an iron plaque in their briefcase, or a massive piece of granite in their pocket...

He had made a name for himself as an astrologer by publishing the horoscope of Joseph Caillaux* in L'Intransigeant. After that, he was constantly asked to predict the future, by everyone from the common folk of Montmartre, who paid him with soup or a pair of socks, to the dress designer Poiret, who was incapable of choosing a suit without asking Monsieur Max's opinion, to ladies of fashion who adored this strange little witty man whose presence was such a marvellous addition to their elegant dinners in Auteuil and Passy.

For Max Jacob's humour was legendary. Besides his talents as writer and astrologer, he could do imitations like nobody else. He imitated his parents (his mother was an operetta singer), politicians, cabaret performers, kicking his legs high in the air, turning up his trousers, showing his body hair, croaking out the high notes like a screeching dancer. Or he would play outraged old ladies, wearing a red rag around his head like a scarf. He loved to make a spectacle of himself. 'The need to please people is a frenetic passion with me,' he confessed.[6]

One evening, a fight broke out at the Lapin Agile. This happened often. Someone was wounded in the stomach with a corkscrew. This was less frequent. Max Jacob had to appear as a witness in a criminal court. He came, elegantly dressed. His account of the incident was asked for. He gave it in a soft voice, lisping, making sure that the only audible word in the whole account was 'corkscrew', which he pronounced at least ten times, as loudly as he could. The president of the court was enraged. Max Jacob was sent back to his seat. He began to whimper, protesting vigorously that if he had known he was going to be so badly treated, he would never have come ... Everyone present split their sides laughing, fortunately with less damage to their stomachs than the unlucky victim of the corkscrew.

At parties, his humour and his talents as an imitator were immensely popular. Fashionable Parisians, who had invited him because it was chic to show off this quirky eccentric with such excellent manners, would then climb the hills of Montmartre the next day to have the gentleman tell their fortune.

For the stylish bourgeoisie liked on occasion to slum it on the Butte. Dorgelès has described the men in their tailcoats visiting the painters' studios, less to buy their works than to ogle the models, whom they supposed, of course, to be the artists' mistresses. Meanwhile, their wives gawped at the

---

* Joseph Caillaux, a colourful left-leaning figure of the Third Republic, was Minister of Finance in several different governments and had a long and chequered career. In 1914 his wife created a stir by shooting the director of the Figaro, Gaston Calmette, who was carrying out a vicious press campaign against her husband.

old-fashioned gas lamps, the primitive kitchen-bathrooms, the rites of this more or less native population ... When they got out of their shiny automobiles or horse-drawn carriages, driven by coachmen clad in black, these women were uncomfortable. It was all very charming, Montmartre, but a little out of the way. Well, there were always the trees ... They turned up the hems of their elaborate dresses and hastened on to no. 7, rue Ravignan, where this cabbalist officiated, a man whom they often hadn't heard of but whom Paul Poiret, their darling dressmaker with his ever-so-refined taste, had recommended to them. They opened the door, and after the initial charms of this mysterious and enchanting neighbourhood, they were brusquely confronted with the harsh realities of the poets of this world.

A catastrophe ...

In 1907, Max Jacob lived at the end of a courtyard, in a kind of shed tucked in between two buildings, which looked straight out on to dustbins. The place was tiny (like all of his lodgings) and very dark. It looked like a storage space that had been emptied of its rubbish and brooms and rented out at a hundred francs a year. It was an accurate reflection, in any case, of the poet's extreme poverty. He wrote with a pen that cost two sous, ate rice pudding, borrowed fifty centimes to take the tram, tightened his belt so he could repay his debts as soon as possible, and spent the greater part of his meagre earnings on fuel for the oil lamp, which burned night and day since the single room was so dark. 'The politics of oil come before the politics of rice!' he joked, whenever anyone expressed sympathy. He had known worse, having already spent two or three winters in a room with no fire, huddled permanently in a coat and eating a pound of bread a day.

He cleaned the place carefully. The room was furnished with a mattress placed on four bricks, a table, a chair, and a trunk in which the poet kept his manuscripts. After much insistence, he had managed to get the owner to make an opening in the zinc of the roof to put a skylight there. On the largest wall, in chalk, he had drawn the signs of the zodiac, an image of Christ, a self-portrait painted at a time when he had had a beard, and various inscriptions, one of which immediately struck the eye: 'Never go to Montparnasse.'

Max received clients on Mondays. He was very courteous to his visitors, welcoming them himself and asking them to have a seat in a corner of the room, where several inhabitants of the neighbourhood were already waiting. Then he would go back to telling the fortune of the person he had been with when interrupted.

A magnificent four-panelled screen divided up the room. During the day, Max lent it to a German art lover who, after buying some paintings by the artists of the Bateau Lavoir, also acquired Max Jacob's manuscripts (perhaps even including the first drafts of *Saint Matorel*). When he promised to publish them, accompanied by etchings and gravings, Max looked at him with tears in his eyes. When the fellow offered him a few notes, Max thought he was in heaven. This divinity on earth asked if he could also have the screen. Max agreed. This was a shame: the four panels had been painted by Picasso. But when one learns that the young art lover (he is presented thus in accounts of the time) was named Daniel-Henry Kahnweiler, one immediately understands his interest in the screen.

The women who came from so far away to have their fortunes told were instantly struck by the smell of the place. They held their noses, assailed by the mixture of odours – tobacco, incense, oil, and ether. Tobacco, since Max smoked. Oil, since he needed light. Ether, since the poet was so fond of it that his room 'was more scented than an apothecary's shop'.[7]

Pierre Brasseur tells a story recounted to him by Max Jacob, which perfectly illustrates the moral contradictions experienced by the chief of druidism – a poetic movement which had between two and five members, and whose principal activity consisted in the pagan rite of cutting holly on the rue Ravignan.

> Honesty is a little house which smells of incense, which is very unpleasant, and which has only one door, immediately visible; dishonesty is much vaster, and smells of honey and alcohol; at first one can't find any door, although there are many. Beware, for this house is very tempting, and difficult to leave.[8]

Max Jacob would have liked to be a saint. And he probably thought that this was what was happening on 22 September 1909, at four o'clock in the afternoon. That day, as he was coming home as usual, Christ appeared to him on the wall of his humble abode. It was a fundamental revelation, which transformed his life and which he himself recounted as follows:

> After taking off my hat, I was getting ready, like a good bourgeois, to put on my slippers, when suddenly I cried out. On my wall was a Host. I fell to my knees, my eyes filled with tears. An ineffable sense of serenity descended upon me, and I remained unmoving, unable to understand what was happening. It seemed as though everything was revealed to me ... Also, as soon as my eyes had met the ineffable Being, I instantaneously felt divested of my human flesh, and two sole thoughts filled me: to die, to be born.[9]

Or, in more lyrical terms:

> I came home from the Bibliothèque Nationale; I put down my briefcase and looked for my slippers. When I raised my head, there was someone

there! On the wall! There was someone on the curtains: my chair fell   39
to the floor. I was stripped bare by lightning! Oh, unforgettable moment!
Oh, truth! Oh! Forgive me! He is in a landscape, in a landscape that I
once drew, but Him! Such beauty! Such elegance and gentleness! His
shoulders! His walk! He wears a robe of yellow silk, with blue lining. He
turns around, and I see his peaceful, radiant face.[10]

Other revelations would come to Max Jacob in his lifetime. Fairly
amusing ones, in general.

On 17 December 1914, while he was comfortably seated in a cinema,
absorbed in the cloak and dagger tribulations of the heroes of Paul Féval,
someone came and sat down next to him. Max had to pull his coat closer
to himself. He grumbled a little, laid his arm on the armrest of his seat,
and plunged back into the adventures of *La Bande des habits noirs*. Then his
eye strayed to the right. And there – stupor, perfection, dazzlement: his
new neighbour was none other than the Lord himself. Sitting calmly in a
cinema. Arms and legs crossed, one imagines, and, why not, perhaps
licking away at an ice-cream cone. Max was in a trance. The show was
not on the screen, but in the auditorium.

Another time, while praying in church, he heard a voice. 'Max! You're
so ugly!'

The sinner turned around. Whom did he see at his side? A woman in
white: the Virgin Mary. He cried, 'That's not true, Madam Virgin! I think
you're going a bit too far.'

He himself recounted this impromptu meeting to André Billy. One can
believe as much of it as one wants. The important thing is that he decided
to speed up the proceedings necessary for the cause – the cause of his
conversion.

He had been preparing himself ever since the visitor in the yellow silk
with the blue lining had materialized on his wall. But it wasn't easy: the
curé of the church of Saint Jean Baptiste, on the Place des Abbesses, made
fun of him a little, as did the curé of the Sacré Coeur. Why this ostracism?
'They must have obtained some damaging information about me,'
hypothesized Max Jacob.[11]

As for his friends, they just burst into gales of laughter. Picasso, whom
Max wanted to have as a godfather, proposed 'Fiacre' as a christening
name. Max was furious: in addition to the fact that the name, that of the
patron saint of gardeners and coachmen, was ridiculous, it was also a
veiled allusion to his sexual preferences.

Braving the mockery, the sneers, and the obstacles that the Church
placed in his path, the poet, cheerful, tragic clown that he was, finally
got what he wanted: after reflection, and after having examined him for
a long time to judge the sincerity of his faith, the fathers of Zion,

specialists in transfers of this nature, adopted the new member of their flock. Max was converted. The godfather magnanimously agreed to exchange Fiacre for Cyprian, a variant of one of his own first names.

Revelation and conversion were to change nothing in the new Catholic's manners. On the one hand, he prayed. In fact, he never stopped praying. To such an extent that his friends began to wonder: why so much? Vlaminck thought it gave him a kind of sensual pleasure, mixed with a tinge of masochism. He was probably not far wrong. For Cyprian had also become a proselytizer, sometimes in the most surprising circumstances. One evening in a dark corner of a cheap dive in Pigalle, he tried to convert a prostitute. He was kneeling down in front of her, holding her hands in order to persuade her.

'Embrace the faith!'

'Where is that?'

'Kiss . . .'

'Never when I work!'

The young woman, dumbfounded, watched curiously as this bald, monocled eccentric, dressed in a proper, if somewhat threadbare, black coat, told her stories about angels and the baby Jesus. Just then, her protector entered and took a different view of the situation. He rushed at this corrupter of his woman, grabbed him by the collar, seized his hands and broke both his thumbs.

But Max was not to be discouraged. He continued his efforts elsewhere. He soon had so many sins for which to reproach himself that the churches of Montmartre were no longer enough. He went further afield, where the priests didn't know him. It made confession easier: what with his taste for men, his passion for certain drugs and his diverse and immensely varied pranks and practical jokes, his whispered confidences in the confessional booth sometimes shocked or stunned the men in black who listened to him. Especially when he was a repeat offender.

On his way home, Max would make a detour by the all-night pharmacy near the Saint Lazare station. He would buy a bottle of ether. Locked in his room, he could sniff at his leisure, while conversing with God and the Virgin Mary. They were on familiar terms. He told them about his day, as if he were chatting with chums. The pharmaceutical vapours transported him onto a little white cloud where he settled cosily and often – a little too often in the opinion of the neighbours and the concierge, who also had to inhale the bitter odours.

Any scandals were always hushed up, though, because the poet was well liked. On the rue des Abbesses, he was known to all. He listened to the village gossip, passed it on to others, people confided in him, he bowed to the woman who owned the grocery store as though she were a princess . . . Who is to be believed, him or Utrillo, when this latter recounts that Max had once tried to rape him after having made him sniff ether? What difference does it make? Both of them were great figures of Montmartre, each in his own way. And that is another paradox concerning Max Jacob: he didn't like Montmartre. He mistrusted its 'pale little pimplets to whom legend has given a romantic halo' and its 'petty fraudsters', its 'little thieves'. He preferred the humanity of the working-class and bourgeois areas of Paris. He only lived in the neighbourhood because that's where his friends were. When they left, so did he, thanks to a miracle which gave him the means to leave.

The miracle was an accident. One day in January 1920, as he was crossing a street, he was hit by a car. He was left with several cuts and scratches but, more important, an indemnity. He confided to Vlaminck that he had prayed so hard to the Virgin Mary that she had finally taken pity on him. Rather than seeing him reduced to begging or dying of hunger, she had caused the accident. Thanks to the money paid by the insurance company, Max Jacob was able to live a little more comfortably – or at least a little less badly.

On the eve of his death, he was still able to see the bright side of life. Surrounded by two gendarmes, he sent several letters to his friends. In one of them, he wrote that the two policemen were being 'very nice' to him.

Nice because they had agreed to mail the letter. But they were taking him to Drancy. A few weeks before his arrest, on the register of the church of Saint Benoît, where he had gone on a retreat, Max had written: 'Max Jacob, 1921 [the date of his arrival there] – 1944'. It was prophetic. He already knew. On the road which was leading him to his death, he sent a letter to the priest of Saint Benoît:

> Dear Monsieur le Curé,
>   Please forgive this letter from a shipwrecked soul, written with the permission of the gendarmes. I want to tell you that I will soon be at Drancy. I've got a few conversions underway. I have confidence in God and in my friends.
>   I thank God for the suffering I am about to endure.[12]

He was sent to Drancy not as a Catholic but as a Jew. He sent out several cries for help to his friends, asking them to come to his aid. Guitry, Cocteau, Salmon, and several others intervened with the Gestapo and the German authorities. On 15 May 1944, they finally managed to obtain an order for his liberation. But it was too late: Max Jacob had died ten days earlier, ravaged by bronchial pneumonia.

One of his letters was to André Salmon. He begged him to find Picasso, so he could come to his rescue. It is not clear exactly what Picasso did, or even if he did anything. Some accuse him of not having lifted a finger, others simply of not having done enough for his friend; yet others forgive him on the grounds that he was a foreigner and thus himself on extremely shaky ground.

The deep, often overwhelming passion that Max Jacob had for Picasso caused him great suffering. The poet was quite paranoid. André Salmon told a story which illustrates just how sensitive he could be. One day, he read his friend a poem he was writing, in which there was a snake. Max returned home, where Picasso found him in tears: he thought Salmon had compared him to a snake.

If the painter failed to answer a letter from the poet, this was enough to make the latter fall into the depths of depression. The correspondence between the two men is eloquent on this topic:

Picasso to Max, in 1902:

> My dear Max, it's been longtime that I dont write you. Its not that I not think about you but I working lot thats why I dont write you.

Picasso to Max, in 1903:

> My dear Max, even if I dont write you very often you shouldnt think I forget you … I work as I can dont have enough dough to do the other things I want some days I not able to work and thats very bad.

Max, in 1904:

> Perhaps you haven't received my last card? In case this has happened, I'm sending you this one, which took no small doing since I haven't a penny and was obliged to sell some books to get a little money. There's no need for me to tell you that you're always welcome at my place…

Max, from Quimper, in 1906:

> My dear friend, I'm leaving tomorrow, April 16, at eight in the evening, and will be home the day after tomorrow at nine in the morning. What a treat it will be to see you all again! To see you again, my dear friend.[13]

In the innumerable epistolary exchanges between the two, the theme is always the same: Picasso is busy working, and Max is waiting for him.

He had a tic which his friends recognized. In his correspondence, his signature even more than the contents revealed the depth of affection that the poet had for those he was writing to: if the 'J' of 'Jacob' extended to the bottom of the page, that meant that he truly loved his correspondent.

If the consonant was written in small letters, then whatever honeyed words the text contained, invoking the purest of friendships, he did not harbour any real affection for the other. In Picasso's case, the 'J' is so long it seems to be sticking out its tongue.

In 1927, during a long silence on the painter's part, Max exploded in a letter to Jean Cocteau:

> I am not pleased with him! No, not at all! Is he afraid that ... but what exactly is he afraid of? That I'll invite myself to lunch? That I'll ask him for three francs? He wants to put an end to our closeness of the rue Ravignan? Already, before the war, all that was dead, destroyed...[14]

A little later, Paul Léautaud confirms:

> Max Jacob, who at the moment does not have a penny to his name, went to see him [Picasso]. Max Jacob did many favors for Picasso when he was just getting a start in life. He was a salesman in a novelty shop, only paid a pittance. Still, he found a way to give Picasso enough money to eat and to work as best he could at his painting. Max Jacob is, it would seem, a man incapable of asking for anything for himself. Picasso said to him, 'So, Max, how are things?' Max Jacob answered, 'Oh, not so good, you know, not good at all, at all.' Picasso replied, 'Come on, Max, everyone knows you're rich.' Max Jacob, with his typical subtlety, answered, 'Yes, Picasso, I know that you need me to be rich.'[15]

One of the last images that Max Jacob would conserve of his oldest friend, his brother, his companion of the early days, was that of a meal at Saint Benoît, on 1 January 1937. It seems that this was the only time Picasso visited the poet at his retreat. He arrived at the end of the afternoon, driven by his chauffeur, and accompanied by his son Paulo and Dora Maar. They had dinner together. Max levitated. Picasso made fun of him. Throughout the entire meal, he laughed at his host. In any case, this is how Max recounted their meeting. At midnight, when he was about to leave, Picasso offered to drive Max Jacob back to Paris. The poet protested, 'Oh, no!'

The heavy car set out towards the capital without him.

Seven years later, as he was himself heading north, towards the camp of Drancy where the religion of his childhood had condemned him to go, perhaps Max Jacob remembered an exchange he had had with Picasso during this dinner at Saint Benoît. The poet had asked the painter, 'Why did you come on New Year's Day?'

The painter had answered, 'Because New Year's is a day for the family.'

'You're wrong,' the poet had replied. 'New Year's is the day of the dead.'

GUILLAUME THE BELOVED

Exquisite! delicious! admirable! Mony, you are a divine poet, come
kiss me in the sleeping-car, my soul is fuckatative.

Guillaume Apollinaire

Picasso, Max Jacob, Guillaume Apollinaire. Soon, on the crest of the hills
of Montmartre, an art would be born that would set the world of painting
aflame. These three were the pioneering figures of modernity on the
move.

Max Jacob met Apollinaire in 1904. It was Picasso who took him to a
bar near the Saint Lazare station, the Austin Fox, where he had been with
the poet the day before. The Austin Fox was a hangout for jockeys, and
a meeting place for people catching trains, which was why Apollinaire
was often there: he still lived with his mother in nearby Vésinet.

The first time they met, Max was impressed by the elegance of the man
who would soon be his rival for Picasso's affections. Guillaume Apollinaire
was at this time a well-built young fellow, dressed in an English jacket
and a waistcoat with a pocket-watch dangling from it. He resembled a
moonstruck Pierrot, with his pear-shaped head. This description, made
by Max himself, corresponded trait for trait and curve for curve to a
portrait made by Picasso in 1908 of his other poet friend.

Max Jacob mostly saw Apollinaire in the same way as all the others
who knew him would see him: painters, writers, poets, art dealers,
publishers, the many friends, the few enemies.

Guillaume Apollinaire is seated at a table, smoking a little pipe. He
holds out a slightly limp hand to Picasso and Max Jacob without breaking
off the conversation he's carrying on with his neighbours, the stockbrokers,
the travelling salesmen. He's talking to them about Petronius and Nero.
He takes a book from his pocket, then another, and another: all the folds
of his clothes seem to conceal books of all kinds, prose, verse, philosophy,
curiosities, which Guillaume exhibits, hands over, takes back, reads. He
glances around, waxes enthusiastic, laughs, composes a quatrain, speaks
of a city, hums, describes an image, the smell of a tempting dish, the

accents of a *poskotznika*, exclaims suddenly, asks for a glass of stout, leans back and begins to hold forth on the subject of erotic literature, moves on to Buffalo Bill, to the Roman emperor Pertinax, to Paul Fort and Jean Papadiamantopoulos, produces an issue of *La Revue blanche* from one of his voluminous pockets, and asks all those present to reflect on the crucial question, about which he himself has spoken at length: why should Saïaphernès' tiara be scorned simply because it is fake?

Suddenly he gets up and says, 'Let's go for a walk.'

He then heads out into the Parisian night, trailing a bevy of artists and writers behind him, all across the city, from one strange place to the next, sometimes singing, stopping to note something intriguing, abruptly suggesting finding an automobile to take them out to Rueil, so they can stroll in the forest of Saint Cucufa.

The man was possessed by an insatiable curiosity. Anything new, unexpected, and unusual interested him. He was capable of stopping to watch carpenters building a wall and of admiring their work for several minutes, after which he would murmur, in total sincerity, 'Building is a real trade. Not like poetry ...'

He was extremely cultured, and his culture was extremely diverse. He spoke five languages. He had read everything. He had a passion for Nick Carter, Fantomas and Buffalo Bill and never missed an episode of their adventures, which he would read avidly while walking down the street. 'It's a poetical activity of the greatest importance!' he would exclaim.

He gave these popular novels in serial form to his friends. Soon, all of them were clearing out the library of Montmartre on the Boulevard de Clichy. They spent entire days reading. In the evening, all they could talk about were the adventures of Juve and Fandor. Max Jacob even considered creating a Society of the Friends of Fantomas.* This fictional hero would later be adopted by the surrealists – after all, were not his authors already almost writing surrealist prose, without knowing it, composing as they did with a rapidity worthy of the surrealists' 'automatic writing'? As for Cendrars, he went so far as to use Fantomas' name as the title of a poem. Better still: he conceived *Moravagine* as a kind of sequel to *Fantomas*. Yet the two works are not similar, aside from the diabolical rhythm of the adventures. One sprang from a writer's imaginary universe. The other was a commissioned job, accepted by a man who was a talented scribbler, confirmed socialite, and lover of fancy cars (Pierre Souvestre) and his ghostwriter, a journalist for the paper *Poids lourd* and the author of a guide on a thousand and one ways to assure the maintenance of one's automobile (Marcel Allain).

---

* Written by Pierre Souvestre and Marcel Allain and first published to much fanfare in 1911, *Fantomas*, a vast novelistic cycle in thirty-two volumes, was a great popular success in the years before the First World War.

Apollinaire explained to his friends how *Fantomas* was produced. The two authors worked for the publishing house Fayard: each month, they had to deliver a volume of approximately four hundred pages. The publisher's goal was simple: to sell more copies than Gaston Leroux with his popular detective hero Arsène Lupin.

Souvestre and Allain had perfected a method of collaboration. They would meet for three days, the time necessary to concoct a story and to plot its structure, following a detailed outline. After this, they would choose chapters at random, although they were prepared to trade some if one of them was suffering from a lack of inspiration. Then each went home and spoke into a dictaphone, which was installed close to a typist who took away the wax rolls without the authors even reading over what they had done. The final product was a style that raced along at a hundred miles an hour, with very messy grammar.

Though he recognized that the books were written 'any which way', Apollinaire admired their extravagant imagination, which he also found in the advertising campaign, the first of its kind, with which they were launched.

His own literary work was similarly characterized by the greatest variety, that same range of tastes and interests that gave his personality such charm and richness. Apollinaire wrote in verse and in prose: poems, calligrams, tales, articles, erotic stories. Because of the manners and morals of the time, and the fear of scandal, he concealed his best work under a false cover in an obscure corner of his personal library, the one that Picasso called the finest book he had ever read: *Les Onze mille verges*.

A few months after meeting Max Jacob and Picasso, Apollinaire became the director of an enigmatic review about 'physical development', for which the painter drew three sketches of the poet, nude, with muscles like a body-builder's, and a little head looking rather lost topping off this athlete's body. He also soon began to work as an editor, producing two collections, one of which was called *Les Maîtres de l'amour* and the other *Le Coffret du bibliophile*. He published the works of Aretinus and the Marquis de Sade, whom he thus helped to liberate from the dungeons of censure.

He had such a need to charm that few people were able to resist him. The paradoxes of his personality made him at ease in all situations. At Parisian dinner parties, Guillaume Apollinaire, in evening dress, bowed to the ladies, delicately brushing their white hands with a kiss. Here as everywhere, he would first make speeches like a scholar, then burst out into loud, childish, almost vulgar laughter. He was capable of the most exquisite courtesy, and the most clumsy clownishness. To the astonishment of his comrades, he dressed one day as an orthodox Jew, entered a whorehouse on the rue des Rosiers in the Jewish quarter and asked an assistant to the brothel-keeper whether the establishment respected the religious rules.

He bought *Le Temps*, explaining to the newspaper vendor that he suffered from chronic colitis and that *Le Temps*, if judiciously applied to the intestines, was an admirable cure for this malady. Still in the scatological vein, for which he had a particular fondness, he liked to walk in front of a pastry shop in the Passage Guénégaud which had an outside display window, and deposit a delicately scented fart right in front of the delicious cakes. More constructively, he cooked, for Vlaminck, pears in mustard, accompanied by dandelions flavoured with eau de Cologne...

At first sight, all these eccentricities did not fit with the image he liked to give of himself, that of a well-dressed bourgeois, with tie, waistcoat, and pocket-watch, who enjoyed a privileged life and many creature comforts. He was a bank clerk in an establishment on the rue de la Chaussée-d'Antin. Superstitious, he liked to have his fortune told, and avoided walking under ladders. He lived at his mother's comfortable home in Vésinet. His childhood had supposedly unrolled, like a silken carpet, on the steps of the great hotels of the Riviera, Italy, Nice, and Monaco. His full name was Wilhelm Apollinaris (a drink which appears in *Les onze mille verges*) de Kostrowitzky, the descendant of a former officer in the royal army of the Two Sicilys (and not of a prelate of the Catholic Church, as was long believed) and of the daughter of a Polish officer who had a post in the Pope's private chambers.

In point of fact, a lot of grand words were used to describe a more banal reality: Guillaume Apollinaire was a cross-breed and a foreigner. He was the son of a man who had abandoned his mother a few years after he was born, leaving behind him a mysterious whiff of romance, and of a woman, La Kostrowitzka, who seems to have been a kind of adventuress of love, a free thinker who dragged her children from rented room to hotel, scouring towns and holiday spots in search of fortune, lovers, and luck. At the time, all this represented the epitome of libertinage. Even worse, Guillaume was a Dreyfusard for a while, a supporter of libertarian theses, and a contributor to *Le Tabarin*, a newspaper with a dark reputation.

For unlike Max Jacob, Guillaume had already begun at the time they met to publish his work: not any books yet, but articles in *La Revue d'art dramatique* and *La Revue blanche* (whose editorial secretary, the writer Félix Fénéon, had been condemned for his anarchistic sympathies and had been defended on the witness stand by Mallarmé). The editorial staff of *La Revue blanche* was a prestigious one, and Guillaume was to rub shoulders there with a number of writers who were famous or soon to become so: Zola, Gide, Proust, Verlaine, Jarry, Claudel, Léon Blum, Octave Mirbeau, Jules Renard, Julien Benda...

With some friends, including Alfred Jarry and Mécislas Goldberg, among others, Apollinaire also founded a review – Le Festin d'Esope – which had an office in his mother's house and an editorial secretary, André Salmon. It would publish nine issues; in 1904, Apollinaire would print his L'Enchanteur pourrissant in its pages.

Apollinaire had several other activities already to his credit. Several years earlier, when he was barely twenty years old, he had written a short erotic book which was distributed surreptitiously: Mirely, ou le petit trou pas cher. And, even earlier, when he, his mother, and his brother Albert had arrived in Paris deprived of the funds which had enabled La Kostrowitzka to indulge up until then in an extravagant lifestyle, the poet earned money by writing promotional articles, an occupation not yet known by the name of advertising. He was also the ghostwriter for a well-known novelist who published Apollinaire's stories in serial form in Le Matin under his own name; and for a student who paid him to write his doctoral thesis on the writers of the Revolution.

Such was the life of a poet. When they weren't working as journalists, reporting on community events (like Salmon), or reviewing plays (like Léautaud), they published stories in the papers (like Alain-Fournier), or wrote licentious books for Jean Fort's bookshop in the Faubourg Pois-sonnière (like Alfred Jarry or Pierre Mac Orlan who, breaking with habit, even signed them with his real name, Pierre Dumarchey).

At the Fox bar, where Picasso and Max Jacob used to wait for their new friend to arrive after work, Apollinaire was continually enlarging the range of his talents. He was also a French teacher and a secretary; he had a degree from the Union of Stenographers. When he announced this, people would stare at him, astonished. And he would say, 'I can write as fast as I talk.'

'And what is the point of that?'

'No point. No point at all . . .'

All the less as he didn't write like Salmon or Jacob did. He had little need for a table. His method was more like that of Erik Satie, about whom he liked to note that he composed his works as he walked from Arcueil to Montparnasse, stopping to scribble down the notes by the light of street lamps. Like the musician, the poet strolled around Paris humming a melody to himself, always the same one, to which his rhymes and his verses then attached themselves – 'like a bee on a flower', wrote Max Jacob, who went on, 'This poetry was terribly inspired. He lengthened the notes to add a syllable or to remove one.' Paul Léautaud, the guest of Apollinaire and his wife one evening, heard the latter humming the same tune, as she copied out her husband's verses in a neat hand.

*

He looked rich, but was in fact poor. His mother – 'mama', as he called her – looked after some of their daily needs. She was a heavy drinker of both rum and whisky.

In Le Vésinet, in her large house situated right in the middle of a park, Vlaminck and Derain met La Kostrowitzka. She was walking her dogs, two setters with tawny coats. She had a whip in her hand. The two painters wondered if she used the same methods on her longtime lover, a certain Monsieur Weill (whom Max Jacob mistakenly took for Guillaume's father), who worked at the Stock Exchange and who had managed to find work for the Kostrowitzky sons – the neighbours claimed she did.

Albert, the younger of the two children, who gravitated in the circles of Marc Sangnier's Sillon Catholique,* was a calm, sensible and well-behaved young man. His mother listened to him with interest and admiration. The other son, the poet, whom she loved with a protective maternal love, was an enigma to her. He was useless on the Stock Exchange, at manual work, at almost everything he tried. He never had a penny in his pocket or knew where his next revenues would come from. He preferred the life of a poet to a stable, safe and respectable job as a bank clerk. Just what was a poet, anyway, she wondered.

Guillaume regularly weathered her maternal criticism without even thinking of answering back. He loved his mother, he defended her; he cursed Max Jacob for having written a song about her, which all his friends would sing in chorus when they wanted to make fun of him:

> Marrying Apollinaire's mother
> Apollinaire's mother
> Who'd look like fools then?
> Brother, oh brother!

He acted like an obedient little boy. His mother had read almost none of her son's works (he didn't send them to her) and when she took a look at L'Hérésiarque & Cie, she quickly fell asleep over these shocking and incomprehensible stories. One day she ran into Paul Léautaud, to whom she said, 'But my other son writes too! The one who's in Mexico.'

'What kind of literature?'

'Oh, very complicated things ... Articles in a financial paper.'

For her, Guillaume was something of a nuisance as a son. When he was in the Rhine valley, a twenty-one-year-old baby lost in the vastness of Germany where he was travelling as a tutor, she still wrote to him as though he were a little boy. She wanted to know what he was doing,

---

* The Sillon Catholique was a predominantly working-class Catholic movement of the beginning of the century.

how he spent his money, if he thought about his family; she practically instructed him to read German newspapers in order to learn the language and warned him not to put his money in his wallet where pickpockets, cleverer than he, would soon find it ... She reprimanded him because he forgot to write on Christmas Day, and reminded him to lick the stamps well before sticking them on the envelope, to buy shoes only if they didn't cost more than eight marks, not to drink except at meals (wine, beer, or even milk) and not to do anything foolish ... She asked if he changed the sheets often enough and washed himself thoroughly enough, and if his clothes were well darned and by whom. In an incredibly authoritarian tone, she demanded that he answer her letters and not just with his usual missives − written, she implied, by an imbecile. Finally, she suggested he work on his spelling:

> Take care when you write: it's shameful for a boy who has gone to a good school to be making spelling mistake [sic] all the time. I understand perfectly that they are only carelless [sic] mistakes but if you write that way to other people they'l [sic] judge your letters more harshly and it is shameful.[1]

Up until the age of twenty-seven, Guillaume lived with his mother. When he was twenty-eight and twenty-nine, he visited her every Sunday and would ritualistically bring her a sack of dirty laundry to wash each time. In exchange, he would take jars of home-made jam away with him. And he always left completely stuffed, having feasted on fish or noodles.

She never liked his friends. Neither the Montmartre ones, nor Vlaminck and Derain, whom Apollinaire first took home with him to Le Vésinet one evening when, with his wallet empty and his stomach crying out for sustenance, he thought that both he and his pals would have their hunger satisfied in the family dining room. He hoped that his mother would invite the three of them to share dinner with her guests. Instead, they were ushered into an antechamber, between the pool table and the music room. Sitting on a sideboard was a cage containing a blind monkey; he too was starving and had gnawed through the golden bars to the point of losing his sight.

Seated on their hard chairs, the three friends listened without a word to the sound of forks and knives coming from the room next door, salivating all the time. Dinner had started without them. They listened, through the appetizer, the main dish, the cheese platter, and the dessert. Even the monkey was silent. They were finally allowed into the dining room after the guests had departed along with their hostess − all fleeing the artists' arrival.

The leftovers were for them.

Guillaume Apollinaire had inherited an immoderate love of good food from his mother. 'Wine resonated in his stomach, meat crackled between his teeth,' wrote Chagall.[2] He liked to eat, even to stuff himself, gulping down dishes one after another, beginning again even when he wasn't hungry, or thirsty, when he was filled to the brim. He always had room for more.

When sitting at the table, eating, he would beam. His round cheeks full, his paunch comfortably installed between him and the meal, his collar open, his belt loosened a notch, he waited for the starting signal and plunged into the menu of dishes and wines. He chose among a wide variety of foods for, excepting red meat, he liked everything. He did have a preference for tripe, fancy teacakes with icing, and risotto, which he himself helped prepare for friends who came to dinner.

Apollinaire in a restaurant was a true spectacle. His napkin knotted around his neck, his false collar opened, stuffing himself with chicken or turkey, the bones of which he broke partly with his fingers, partly with his teeth, his little mouth became enormous and smeared with sauce, and his smile grew wider as dish after dish appeared. Suddenly, rising after consuming two platters of *boeuf gros sel* and three chops, he would say, 'Wait for me here. I have to go take a shit at the Lutetia.' For he knew the best washrooms in Paris, and always recommended them to his friends. When he returned, especially if Carco was at his table, the poet would finish his meal, then order a coffee and another little bowl of thick bouillon as a finishing touch.

If he was with Derain and Vlaminck, at Chartier's on the rue Montmartre for example, they would compete with each other to see who could eat the most. The rule was simple and extremely convivial: they had to try and eat every dish on the menu. And when they had finished, they would start again. The first to be full, and unable to swallow another mouthful, was the loser. Then they paid the bill. The person who paid was rarely Apollinaire.

When the poet ate out, he would generally discover that his pockets were empty when it was time to settle the bill. He would suddenly turn pale, and exclaim, 'Oh, I've left my wallet at home!' And when he had tried this trick as often as Depaquit had left for Sedan, he would appear to be the loser in the stuff-your-face contest, until finally Vlaminck would say, 'Oh, forget it, it's my round tonight.'

And immediately Apollinaire would order three more copious dishes, his appetite returning with his morale.

Apollinaire was extremely parsimonious, to say the least, whether through fear of want, or the anguish of the artist faced with irregular revenues, like a bird teetering on the tightrope of a royalty cheque. He had learned all about this sort of situation from watching his mother's uneven financial fortunes. These had known ups, downs, more ups, even more downs, and he had had to adapt. Guillaume had learned about money the hard way.

Still, he was never like Harpagon, contemplating his stocking with its savings; this was for the simple reason that he had no savings. He was often very poor, and never rich. He was a little like a child hanging on to his sixpence.

Soupault recounts that during the war he often accompanied Apollinaire, who was working at that time in the censorship department, to the buildings of the Stock Exchange. They would walk along the rue de la Banque, where there was an antiques dealer. Guillaume would stop at the boutique. He looked at everything: old keys, inkwells, busts, porcelain, weights and measures. He was entranced by these objects. He called the dealer over.

'How much for this vase?'

'Ten sous.'

'Ten sous?'

He contemplated it a while longer, enthralled, then put it back down, frowning. 'Ten sous is too much.'

Then, picking up an old pipe – a meerschaum or a briar pipe – he would run his fingers along the wood, admire its curves, and ask, 'And for this pipe?'

'Two sous.'

'Two sous? It's not worth that!'

Disappointed, he continued along his path. The next day, he returned, but even if the vase was now priced at five sous and the pipe at only one, he still wouldn't buy either.

There was an easy way to upset him: opening his closets and pretending to spirit away something in them. Apollinaire would pursue the offender, ordering, begging, demanding that this item which belonged to him be returned. He always managed to get it back, and always with a conciliatory exchange of remarks. Nobody held it against him. This weakness of his was well known, and accepted. The way to deal with it was simple: one just never asked him for anything.

This man who carefully counted every penny of his expenditure did not count at all when it came to expending energy on his love affairs. When he met Picasso and Max Jacob, he had just returned from London. He had gone there to make one last effort to win over a young girl he was desperately in love with, Annie Playden. He had met her three years before, at the home of the Vicomtesse de Milhaud. At the time, he was giving French lessons to the daughter of the house, Gabrielle, who was also being taught English by a British governess, the charming Annie. He had fallen in love with her in Paris and followed her to the Rhine valley, where the family had planted its aristocratic tent. This migration helped him forget another love, Linda, gave him the chance to visit Germany, and to write about the country – the *Rhénanes* and some admirable pages that he would come back to in *Le Poète assassiné* and *L'Hérésiarque & Cie.*

But what preoccupied him most, much more than the French classes given to the young Gabrielle, was the English governess. He sent her verses that he had already sent to Linda and that others would receive later, each imagining they were written solely for her. They had difficulty communicating, but as far as the young lady was concerned, she understood that he was courting her. And he probably managed to seduce her, to a point. 'I loved him physically, but our ideas and ways of thinking were far from each other,' confided the young lady.[3] In any case, in her letters, she called him 'darling'.

For nearly a year, they had a clandestine lovers' relationship. Then one sad day, Annie put an end to it: 'Kostro', as she called him, had a wild and passionate nature, which was often in conflict with the chaste and reserved temperament of the young woman. On one occasion, as they were walking along a cliffside, he challenged her: 'Either you marry me or I'll throw you to the bottom of the cliff.'

She managed to convince him that this was an unfair proposition, and left the next day. Guillaume found himself alone and abandoned.

It wasn't the first time, and wouldn't be the last. He knew how to attract women, but he didn't know how to keep them. He had been rejected before. He knew what it was to feel unloved, and it made him suffer. He wrote verses to them all, first to gain their affections, then to continue the liaison, finally to beg them to come back. Fiery and passionate, impetuous and sensual, he was ruled as much by sentiment as he was by eroticism. Nothing could stop him. Annie Playden wasn't interested in him any more? He didn't believe it.

But she resisted, and Guillaume returned to Paris for a while, where he flirted with a neighbour. When he learned that Annie was back in England, he rushed over to see her. He proposed elopement to his beloved, talked to her of marriage, children, wealth and fame, and showered her with hats and boas which frightened the young girl's restrained, conventional family. One evening, he laid a trap for her. He invited her to dinner at the home of one of his friends, an Albanian writer. Annie had got permission to stay out until nine. A few minutes before the ninth stroke of the bell, when dinner was nothing more than a memory, she heard scuffling in the next room. She went to see what was happening: the Albanian writer's girlfriend was putting sheets on a bed.

'Who's the room for?' she asked.

'Us!' answered Kostro smoothly.

At ten past nine, Annie Playden was back at home. She had used her parents' anger as an alibi.

Guillaume returned to Paris, dejected. Would he finally give up? The following year, he went back to London. This time, he asked his beloved if she would like to become a countess. This made no impression. To flee to France? Nor did this. What would it take to convince her?

'Nothing could!' exclaimed the young governess.

And as the poet continued to insist, she took a further step, tired of the struggle. She had crossed the Channel to escape him; now she would place an ocean between them. The Atlantic would separate them for ever, and even Apollinaire did not go so far as to pursue her to America.

But Annie would have her *Chanson du Mal-Aimé*, just as Louise, fifteen years later, would have her *Calligrammes*.

> Farewell, false, confounded love
> For the woman who went away
> For the one I lost
> Last year in Germany
> And whom I'll never see again.

When he returned from London in 1904, Apollinaire left the bank where he was working and became the editor-in-chief of the *Guide des rentiers*, a publication for people of private means. He didn't know anything about the stock market, but he pretended he did. When he later began to use his pen to defend modern art, becoming the troubadour of the artists in his circle, many pointed out, and not necessarily just to be unkind, that once again, he was talking of matters he knew nothing about.

As yet, though, he had written little on art. He would speak eloquently for hours at the Fox, as he would later at the Café de Flore. Those who moved in his circle included not only Picasso and Max Jacob, but also Alfred Jarry, a writer he admired, and Vlaminck and Derain, two Fauve painters he had met in the train from Le Vésinet to Paris. The group of friends was formed. All they needed now was a place of their own.

Picasso found it in 1904, when he returned from his fourth trip back to Spain. His friend Paco Durrio, the ceramic sculptor, had left the studio he occupied in Montmartre. It was a bizarre room in an unlikely spot, a building dating from 1860 where pianos had once been manufactured, and which had become an artists' residence thanks to the wooden panels dividing up the space. The building was constructed on the flank of a hill, and one had to enter on the top floor, then go down, slipping through dark corridors, which were boiling hot in the summer and icy cold in the winter. The sun entered the workshops through large windows looking out onto Montmartre. On the first floor, there was running water, but nowhere else. And there was only one toilet. The ceilings of the lower rooms served as the floors of the upper rooms. From one room to another, one could hear everything: the creaking mattress, punctuated by various groans, songs, cries, the sound of steps . . . The space between the wooden boards left no one in ignorance of the comings and goings of the neighbours. The doors barely closed.

But Picasso was enchanted. He avidly investigated this strange building, all in wood, which resembled nothing else in the world. He christened it the Trapper's House. But Max Jacob had another idea. The building vaguely resembled the flat-bottomed boats in which washerwomen scrubbed their sheets on the banks of the Seine. As a result, he gave it a name which would soon become known the world over: the Bateau Lavoir or 'Washing Boat'.

THE LOVELY FERNANDE

My eyes are scales, weighing the
sensuality of women.

Blaise Cendrars

Picasso lived at the very top, which was in fact the ground floor. On the door of the studio, in chalk, he had written these words, inspired by the names of certain cafés: 'Au rendez-vous des poètes.' When the visitor (and there were many of them) pushed open the door, he discovered a narrow passage opening onto a tiny bedroom with a rotting wooden floor. Then he entered a room furnished with a mattress and a rusty iron stove. An odour of black tobacco, gas, and linseed oil permeated the place. In the shadows, one could make out a basin which served as a sink, with a sliver of soap and a towel hanging from it. There was also a straw chair, easels, canvases of all sizes, tubes of paint on the floor, brushes, containers full of gasoline. A table with drawers lodged a tame white mouse, whom Picasso took care of, and who wasn't scared by the dog Frika, a friendly mutt. A big oil lamp provided the only lighting. In a corner of the room was a zinc tub filled with dozens of books. Here, a black trunk served as a seat. There, a pail full of water was waiting to be emptied. Everywhere, chaos reigned.

Except on the bed.

On the bed, stretched out languidly, was a young girl of twenty-three, tall, blonde, beautiful, exquisitely graceful, whom the painter contemplated with all the powerful magnetism of his intense black eyes. Her name was Fernande Olivier. She was his great love. She had replaced the women from the bordellos and several others who had come and gone, after having initiated the young Pablo into adulthood. She hadn't dethroned them all yet, but she would.

The first time he had seen Fernande was near the fountain on the rue Ravignan. Then he ran into her at the water faucet on the first floor. They had exchanged a few words; she also lived at the Bateau Lavoir. They caught sight of each other again on the Place Ravignan, where Picasso used to hang

eyes, penetrating and pensive, burning with a contained fire.[1] He seemed
ageless. She liked the contour of his lips, but didn't much like his thick nose,
which gave him a touch of vulgarity. He had a woman's hands. He was badly
dressed, awkward. She suspected he was shy and proud.

He was attracted by her style, her hats, a refinement in her person and
dress to which he was not accustomed. One rainy night, he ran into her
in the dark halls of the Trapper's House. In his hands he was holding a
cat he had just found in a gutter. He offered it to her.

She talked to him about her life, which had so far contained more
thorns than flowers. She had had an unhappy childhood, parents who had
rejected her, a salesman husband whom she had married to escape from
the hell of her family, a child lost, a difficult divorce after many beatings,
an affair with a sculptor who had encouraged her to become a model. A
few lovers. Some dreams, some disappointments...

Picasso was mad about her. One morning, he asked Apollinaire to help
him clean up his 'rendez-vous des poètes'. All day, they scrubbed the
floors, the walls and even the ceiling with a broom. In the evening, the
painter presented the studio to Fernande, hoping that she would soon be
under its spell...

And so she was, completely: felled to the floor, unconscious, victim of
the combined fumes of the eau de Cologne, terebenthine, oil and clorox.
She soon regained her senses, but she didn't stay long, and didn't declare
eternal love. She had her lovers, and he had the enigmatic Madeleine, a
mysterious model recognizable in La Femme au casque de cheveux and La Femme
à la chemise (she is, most notably, the figure in the magnificent Nu assis,
bought by Gertrude Stein).

Still, Picasso was very much in love. It wasn't a mere pang of desire, it
was a thunderbolt. He, the young Spaniard, still a little rustic, not very
well dressed, speaking broken French, a habitué of brothels, on the arm
of this stunning woman, with her chic clothes and her divine perfumes,
a little bourgeois, as all his women would be.

When she came to his studio, he devoured her with pleading eyes. He
would hide objects that she left behind. When she awoke, he would be
standing at her bedside, entranced. He forgot about his friends, forgot
about painting, except for painting her. He begged her to come and live
with him. She hesitated. She was afraid of his jealousy and his violence.
He showered her with criticism and reproaches, which frightened her a
little. But when he brought her gifts, she melted. He didn't have a cent,
but still managed to give her books, tea, bottles of perfume, the perfumes
which she loved, so strong and heady that wherever she was, one only
had to sniff the air to know she was present. Then someone would say,
'Ah, Madame Picasso is here!'

He drew her ceaselessly. She posed and watched. The studio was in a constant state of disorder, which didn't bother her. What did bother her was her host's lack of physical cleanliness, however touched she might be by his kindness and generosity. Fernande promised herself she would make him understand that when a woman comes to call, a man must be washed. She was already giving herself a role in the young man's education.

There was plenty of work to be done on that score. For in addition to all the rest, Picasso was jealous, of everything and everyone, as he would remain for the rest of his life. He could not bear his women or his friends to escape his grasp, unless he had himself planned for this to happen. He conducted himself with Fernande in the same way that he would behave with Françoise Gilot fifty years later: he advised the latter, only half in jest, to wear a veil on her head and a dress which came down to her feet. 'That way, you would belong less to others; they couldn't possess you, even with their eyes.'[2]

He wanted to cloister the beautiful Fernande away in his studio. She mustn't go out. She must give up posing for anyone else; already Picasso could not bear that the woman in his life should not be painted exclusively by him. Fernande posed once for Van Dongen, half nude, with one breast fully exposed (La Belle Fernande, 1906). She immediately got a slap for it. And a Homeric battle occurred one day when he suspected her of having deliberately attracted the eye of a customer seated in a bar. From then on, she no longer went out. He preferred doing all the household chores and errands himself, rather than taking the risk that she might exchange glances with someone.

This possessive side of his character amused his friends. Apollinaire gently made fun of the painter when he had him say, in La Femme assise:

> To really have a woman, you have to kidnap her, lock her up and keep her occupied all the time.[3]

Picasso blew hot and cold; he was never lukewarm. In this universe of crushing poverty, he traced multicoloured conjugal arabesques: she wouldn't work any more, he would buy her books, he would do everything for her.

One morning, he promised her a surprise for the evening.

'You're going to give me my portrait?'

He dug his hands into the pockets of his overalls, smiled enigmatically and repeated, 'A surprise . . .'

When she arrived that evening, he was waiting for her impatiently. He showed her some objects he had just acquired: a little oil lamp, a pipe with a long bamboo stem tipped with ivory.

'Is that a new kind of tobacco?'

He had her lie down on the braided rug on the floor. He lay down next to her. He went through some strange motions which she watched suspiciously: he opened a box which contained a dark paste resembling amber, rolled a little ball of it between his fingers, pierced it with the end of a needle, lit the oil lamp, heated the ball in front of the flame, placed it on the end of the pipe and breathed in. Then he handed the instrument to his companion. Thus it was that she discovered that at Picasso's, one smoked, and not only the black tobacco that he kept stuffed in his pouch. He was also very fond of opium.

They fell asleep towards morning.

She stayed at Picasso's for three whole days. Picasso worked at night. When she finally left, she was in love.

THE BATEAU LAVOIR

There was once a poet so poor, so badly lodged and so lacking in any kind of comfort that when he was offered a chair by the Académie Française, he asked if he could take it home.

André Salmon

She met Guillaume Apollinaire, and found him large, jovial, pleasant. He was well dressed, had a pear-shaped head, eyes set closely together, comma-shaped eyebrows, a small mouth, and a childlike nature. He was quiet, serious, gentle, emphatic, and charming.

Her impressions of Max Jacob were the following: he didn't look people in the eye when he spoke to them, his mouth was sardonic and cruel, his shoulders narrow, and there was something provincial about him. She was struck by the anxiousness that seemed to emanate from him, and by his nervousness with women.

Soon they were seeing each other every night, most of the time at Picasso's. Apollinaire often invited himself over for dinner. Max Jacob never did; he waited to be invited.

They ate at the table, sharing a napkin, a different corner of which belonged to each of them and about which Apollinaire wrote a story.[1] They often had Portuguese oysters, since at eight sous a dozen, it was a dish they could afford. And when they couldn't, they would go downstairs to the basement of the Bateau Lavoir and knock at the wooden door bearing the inscription, 'Sorieul, farmer', and try to buy, on credit, some of the artichokes, asparagus and onions which the tenant, by some unexplained miracle, managed to grow in his apartment.

Apollinaire would recite his verses, clumsily, without grace. Max Jacob, witty, hilarious, made them all laugh until dawn. In *La Femme assise*, portrayed by Apollinaire as Moïse Deléchelle, he is 'an ash-coloured man whose body, every bit of it, is musical'. And what did he do, this multi-toned, multi-talented man?

He beats upon his stomach to imitate the deep notes of the cello; from his feet come the raucous sounds of a rattle; the taut skin of his cheeks is like cymbals, as resonant as those of gypsies playing in a restaurant, and his teeth, which he taps with a pen, emit crystalline notes like those of orchestras composed of bottles – used as instruments by certain cabaret performers – or those of the large mechanical organs of merry-go-rounds at a fair.[2]

They improvised plays that they performed in costume. The dog, Flika, attached by a metal chain that she dragged behind her, was responsible for the sound effects. On the lower floors, the painter Jacques Vaillant increased the sound level with his wild, noisy parties. When calm was restored, the talk was of art, poetry, and literature. When Guillaume Apollinaire missed the last train to his mother's house in Le Vésinet, he slept over at the Bateau Lavoir, on a lumpy mattress, or in a hotel room on the rue d'Amsterdam.

In the morning, if it was winter and if the winter was a harsh one, Picasso would stay in bed, using the covers to try to keep warm. In the summer, he got up and painted in the nude. When someone knocked while he was working, he didn't open the door. If the visitor insisted, he would get rid of him with a torrent of abuse. If it was the pastry chef from the rue des Abbesses, Fernande would answer. She would shout, 'I can't open the door, I'm naked! Just leave the packages in front of the door!'

This was a tactic for weaseling out of immediate payment. The night before, she had placed an order, asking that the goods be delivered. Now, she promised to pay when she could...

There was another tactic, which consisted of stealing the milk bottles delivered at dawn on the doorsteps of apartments in wealthier neighbourhoods. But for that, one had to get up early...

When the visitor was an art dealer, the concierge would warn them. She lived in a nearby house and kept an eye on everyone entering the building, rushing to give the news when the person looked acceptable – that is, didn't look like a creditor. Then she would beat at the painters' doors and shout, 'This time, it's serious!'

If it was for Picasso, he would hide Fernande under the sheets and open the door. Trying to be amiable, he would welcome Sagot or Libaude. Aside from the fact that he didn't like them, he liked even less having to part with works that he sometimes considered still unfinished. Afterwards, he would be incapable of picking up a brush for several days.

They would console themselves with a meal at Azon's on the rue Ravignan. Thanks to André Salmon, they could eat there on credit and be served generous portions for many months to come. Noting that the restaurant's manager was an assiduous reader of Le Matin, the journalist-cum-poet-cum-writer had led her to believe he was the author of the paper's serial novel, which she adored. Denounced by friends and betrayed by photos, he had to resign himself to having a little less to eat ...

They also ate at Vernin's on the rue Cavallotti, a bistro popular with workers and office clerks. If the bill was too high, they could leave an object at the pawnshop in the neighbourhood, and come back and retrieve it as soon as they were able. On lucky days, if they were clever, they would manage to get a third party to pick up the bill. And if Max Jacob was there, everything was fine: his father would pay for the dinner. He had come to an arrangement with the bistro owner: Max would pay for his meals as often as he could, and if he owed money at the end of the month, his father would take care of it This was on one condition, however: that the menus would always be composed of a starter, a main dish, cheese or dessert, with coffee at lunch and a half-portion of red wine in the evening.

Behind his father's back, though, Max had renegotiated the pact. He could exchange the starter, main dish, cheese, dessert, coffee and wine for stout, quinquina, marc and other types of alcohol to which he treated his friends, thanks to his father's generosity. Thus they often managed to party happily, to the extent of the liquid equivalent of a meal a day.

When he came home, Picasso might take out his alcohol lamp, his pipe and his little box of opium. He had been introduced to this drug by a couple of users in the Closerie des Lilas in Montparnasse. Other habitués of the café also had a taste for opium, including, perhaps, Alfred Jarry, whose Les Minutes de sable mémorial contain a dose of opium, complete with burning lips, astral body and the inevitable hookah.[3] Blaise Cendrars probably did, as well, at Easter and in New York: 'I gave him some opium so he would go to Paradise more quickly.'

From 1910 on, cocaine would dethrone opium, following which the general consumption of drugs dropped; during the war, the use of narcotics was more strictly repressed. At the height of the Bateau Lavoir's popularity, it was opium that was most popular: it could be bought from navy officers who brought it back from China and Indochina. All one had to do was go to a boutique on the rue Croix-des-Petits-Champs, ask for 'a little box', put twenty-five francs on the counter, and one left the shop with the drug and all the material and instruments needed to use it.

Thus equipped, the guests at the Trapper's House would stretch out on the braided rug that Fernande had already tried out, then, all the while drinking cold lemon tea, would let themselves be transported to artificial paradises.

They sometimes took hashish too. If Fernande Olivier's account is to be believed, it could produce strange effects. One night when they had smoked some at the home of Princet, a mathematician who was more or less an insurance agent in Montmartre (and in whom, surprisingly, some have seen the real theoretician of cubism), Apollinaire was overcome by a sensation of ubiquity: he suddenly thought he was in a brothel. As for Picasso, he entered into a sort of painful trance, weeping and shouting, lamenting that since he had discovered photography, he had understood that his art was worth nothing, and the best thing to do was to kill himself.

The artists in Montmartre smoked frequently until 1908. That year, a German painter from the Bateau Lavoir, Wiegels (the Krauss of *Quai des brumes*), hung himself after having absorbed ether, hashish and opium. Picasso swore he would never touch the stuff again; Max Jacob continued to use it. Before the war, Guillaume Apollinaire smoked opium with Picabia (almost daily, the latter affirmed); he was still taking it when he met Lou; in the early months of 1915 he took the muse of *Calligrammes* to an opium parlour in Nice.

Most often though, rather than smoking, the artists drank. Except for Vlaminck, who drank nothing but water, and Picasso, who had only a very moderate taste for alcohol, the artists of the Butte accumulated rows of glasses on the bars of the neighbourhood's cafés.

Zut had been closed by the police due to anarchist activity there. But the customers had followed the owner, Frédé, to his new establishment. He had taken over the Cabaret des Assassins, previously run by the mère Adèle, a friend of La Goulue, who had herself succeeded André Gill, an illustrator and poet of the Commune. Le Lapin à Gill, rebaptized Le Lapin Agile, located on the rue des Saules, was to become one of the central spots for Montmartrian fun and games, and a preferred hangout for Picasso's friends. Carco, Dorgelès, and Mac Orlan were also regular customers. The sign showed a rabbit jumping out of a pot, in homage to the fricassee of rabbit cooked in wine that was a speciality of the mère Adèle.

Le Lapin Agile was a building drowning in greenery, with a bar, a dining room, a terrace, and a profusion of animals. The interior was dark, cleaned and polished every day by Frédé's wife, Berthe la Bourguignonne. Oil lamps with red lampshades dangled from wires hanging from the ceiling, diffusing the meagre light of a dive. On the walls hung a large white Christ sculpted by Wasselet, works by Utrillo, Poulbot and Suzanne Valadon, and a self-portrait of Picasso dressed as a clown (*Au Lapin Agile*, 1905). A large plaster fireplace served as a shelter for an army of white mice. They disputed their territory with a monkey, a tame crow, and, especially, Frédé's donkey Aliboron, known as Lolo, who grazed everywhere, nibbling at everything, and even painted on occasion; one of his works would be exhibited at the Salon des Indépendants in 1910, as we will see.

Berthe officiated at the ovens, and what they produced was excellent.

Frédé ran the cash register and gave credit. The customers drank well, sometimes heavily. The favourite drink, recommended by the owner and enjoyed by his guests, was the 'combine', a mixture of cherries, white wine, grenadine and cherry liqueur. At weekends, the bar and the big dining room were packed, filled with the restaurant's regular customers as well as curious diners from elsewhere who had come for the charm of Montmartre, and the atmosphere of this lively eatery with its women and its artists.

All of Montmartre came to the Lapin. This is where Picasso and Fernande met the exuberant Harry Baur (the painter nicknamed him El Cabo), and the very discreet Charles Dullin. The latter only really came to life when he indulged his love for the theatre by declaiming verses by Baudelaire, Rimbaud, Verlaine and Laforgue. He didn't just recite them, he spat them out. With his hair on end and his eyes shining, living the poetry as though it were consuming him, he captivated his audience, who always cut short their conversations to listen to him. After his performance, Dullin passed around a hat and was treated to a sandwich by Berthe.

Frédé loved to have Picasso and his friends in his establishment. The painter not only knew the restaurant well, but also the owner's family. He painted a portrait of Berthe's daughter, who would marry Pierre Mac Orlan: La Femme à la corneille (1904) shows Margot and her tamed bird. He brought Fernande, Jacob, Apollinaire and all the friends, painters and poets in his intimate circle. Picasso was the pivot around which all the others moved. When she saw him arrive at her house for the first time, accompanied by the fat Apollinaire, the tall, thin Salmon and the massive figures of Braque, Derain and Vlaminck, Gertrude Stein thought he looked like Napoleon escorted by his grenadiers.

The others may not have been grenadiers exactly. But Picasso was undeniably a born leader.

THE WILD BEASTS' CAGE

What I couldn't do in life, except by throwing a bomb – which would
have led me to the scaffold – I tried to achieve in art, in painting, by
using pure colour to a maximum.

Maurice de Vlaminck

'You've heard of Racine, La Fontaine, and Boileau?' Max Jacob asked
André Salmon ironically, a little after their first meeting. 'Well, that's us!'

The first time he came to the Bateau Lavoir, Salmon discovered Picasso
painting barefoot in his studio. The place was lit with candles. Leaving
his work, he showed his paintings to the newcomer. Like a demiurge, he
moved from canvas to canvas, pushing the easels and the frames, displaying
his work without the slightest comment, going from one corner of the
studio to another to find what he was looking for in the middle of all his
paintings. Salmon, like Jacob, Apollinaire and so many others before him,
was overwhelmed by the wealth of invention he discovered there that
night.

Tall, thin, a pipe-smoker like Picasso, Salmon was already writing
poems and was also a journalist. With Paul Fort, one of the central figures
of a Montparnasse that was just coming into being, he had founded a
famous review, *Vers et Prose*. Behind a dry, forbidding façade, he hid a great
talent for invention which vastly amused the little world of the Trapper's
House.

There was also André Derain, who lived in a studio on the rue Tourlaque
(the one which Bonnard had occupied), towards the bottom of the rue
Lepic. Derain, who had been born into a fairly comfortable social milieu,
had turned away from the more conventional career he would have had
if he had gone to the Ecole Polytechnique, the prestigious engineering
school, as his parents had wished, and instead followed the rockier paths
of painting and Montmartre. Nonetheless, he had conserved a pronounced
taste for manual work from his early industrial training. He loved to buy
old appliances at the flea market, which he then repaired and used in his
home. One of his favourite pastimes consisted of fashioning little cardboard
aeroplanes that he tried to get to fly. He collected broken-down musical

instruments and restored their musical soul. He read widely, and knew everything there was to know about the literature of his time. His painting, deep, ordered, solid, had something earthy and powerful about it that was also a characteristic of the man himself, with his imposing physical presence. His models recounted how he would sometimes take them on his lap to work, encircling their waist with one hand and painting with the other. He had not only to see, but also to touch.

Before moving to the rue Tourlaque, Derain had lived in Chatou, the village where he was born. This is where he met his great friend Vlaminck, with whom he often painted on the banks of the Seine, and whom he introduced to Matisse. This meeting would bring forth an unforgettable and scandalous progeniture: Fauvism.

The two companions had decided one day that they would become famous, and that the first of the two of them to bask in glory – symbolized for them by the publication of his photo in the paper – would treat the other to a gigantic meal. Vlaminck won the contest: one morning he arrived at Derain's home waving *Le Petit Journal*. His face graced the third page. Derain, stupefied, read the caption: he had before him an advertisement for Pink Laxatives, praised by Maurice de Vlaminck, artist-painter.

But they were both to become properly famous soon. Vlaminck, Derain, Manguin, Marquet, Camoin and especially Matisse would set off a scandal at the Salon d'Automne in 1905. This Salon had been created two years earlier to give young artists an opportunity to exhibit their works. It had a similar function to the Salon des Indépendants, which had been created by Seurat and Signac and had developed in protest against the official salons, juries, and awards. In every period, the artists rejected by the academies had withdrawn from the important shows – that is, when they hadn't been forcibly ejected from them by the censors. Thus Courbet in his time and later Degas, Pissarro and Manet would choose to exhibit in a Salon authorized by Napoleon III for the occasion: the Salon des Refusés.

Matisse, Vlaminck and their friends were, in turn, to provoke some friction at the third Salon d'Automne. They arrived with canvases whose frames they had made themselves from wood bought on credit from a carpenter in Chatou. They had distanced themselves from the pictorial rules that had accompanied impressionism and pointillism; in the eyes of Vlaminck, these led painting into a dead end. For Matisse, 'painting, in particular because it is *divisionist*,* destroys drawing'.[1]

These troublemakers represented light in another fashion, through the sole force of colour. The summer before the Salon was to take place,

* The term *divisionisme*, often used synonymously with *pointillisme*, is a pictorial technique consisting of applying on the canvas little spots of pure, juxtaposed colours. The colours, rather than mixing on the painter's palette, mix instead in the eye of the observer.

Matisse had written to Derain from Collioure, urging him to join him in order to discover the exceptional light of this village in the Western Pyrenees. Derain had come, and the two painters had worked side by side. Derain had discovered a new concept of light which was the equivalent of denying shadow. 'I let myself go, revelling in colour for its own sake,' he would write to Vlaminck.

His *Vues de Collioure* (1905) shows this clearly. As for *La Femme au chapeau* (1905) by Matisse, with its blues, its reds, its greens, this astounding dance of colours which was a slap in the face for many conservative visitors was greeted with both laughter and anger, not to mention the scepticism of some, like André Gide, who spoke of a 'reasoning', theorizing kind of painting, devoid of all intuition.

These painters were more in the tradition of Gauguin and Van Gogh's expressionism than that of Cézanne. Their works, vigorous in colours and contrasts, were grouped together in one single room that the art critic Louis Vauxcelles, very popular with conventional thinkers and totally hostile to modern art, called the 'wild beasts' cage', the *cage aux fauves*. Thus fauvism was born and baptized. Three years later, with others, this same critic compared Braque's painting, exhibited at Kahnweiler's, to cubes. Thus cubism got its name. The man, in his way, was a visionary . . .

The scandal was so great that the President of the Republic refused to inaugurate the exhibition. The press had a field day. *Le Figaro* spoke of a pot of paint thrown on the public's head. Among the compliments showered upon the Fauves, Vlaminck liked to exhibit an article from the *Journal de Rouen* of 20 November 1905:

> We now come to the most stupefying room of this salon which is already rich in sources of astonishment. Here, any description, any account, like any comment, all become impossible, as what we are shown has – aside from the materials used – no relation to painting whatsoever. Here we find nothing more than formless coloured streaks and dabs: blue, red, yellow, green, stains of colour juxtaposed any which way, the crude and naïve games of a child who is experimenting with a box of coloured pencils or paints that he has been given as a present.[2]

The art critics hadn't yet grasped the idea that painting no longer aimed at representing nature and the world objectively. For that, there was photography. Since the end of the nineteenth century, scandal had always come from the ways in which the artists were distancing themselves more and more from an outside reality and recomposing the world in their own way. They were no longer only interested in *representation* – as if it were possible, anyway, to transfer nature to a canvas – now, they were interested in *expression*. Negro art, in this respect, gave them many ideas.

After having shocked the art world over questions of light, before becoming totally irresponsible on the subject of form, the painters jumped into the fray with the critics, brandishing works where red was far from the most aggressive of the colours. They were the target of a thousand barbed spears – Matisse and Derain especially, but also Vlaminck.

More independent still than his friend from Chatou, Vlaminck's method for painting light was to crush tubes of paint onto the canvas. He worked instinctively, brutally, and paid no attention to theories and precepts. For a long time, he cultivated a certain violence, a quality which Derain, by contrast, gradually disciplined in himself. When Derain started to paint in decidedly too traditional and acceptable a fashion, taking the path of the schools and academies, Vlaminck broke with him.

Vlaminck, a reddish-blond man with naïve eyes planted in the middle of a stubborn, sometimes guarded face, was a bigmouth. He ate boisterously, shouted readily, laughed uproariously. He hated not only schools and academies, but also museums, cemeteries, and churches. He claimed that anarchism had led him to fauvism.

> I thus satisfied my desire to destroy the old conventions, to 'disobey', so as to recreate a sensitive, vibrant and liberated world.[3]

And he concluded by saying that if Ravachol had been a painter, he would have been the ultimate example of fauvism.

This was his opinion. Vlaminck had quite a lot of these, and never hesitated to express them vociferously. Or even with his fists. And what was true for him was also true for those close to him. Georges Charensol recounts that one day when Vollard was having lunch with him, he lost his appetite when he saw the painter's daughter, aged seven, light up a cigarette at the table. He remarked to her kindly that smoking, at her age ... The child, who could hardly have been called a well-brought-up young girl, turned to him and answered, 'What's it to you, old fool?'

Her answer pleased her father, who was not a great deal more amiable with his peers.

Vlaminck didn't really like Montmartre. He went there from time to time to party with his friends and then, at dawn, would walk back to the outskirts of Paris. At the time he met Picasso, he was relying on odd jobs to feed his wife and three children (his first canvases, created with a primitive paint straight out of the tube, cracked, victims of the bad quality of the paint and the easels). He participated in bicycle races and rowing contests, and scratched away at the violin in gypsy orchestras. He would also occasionally enter contests of strength at country fairs where, for a few francs, he had to fight huge musclemen and let himself be knocked to the ground before the end of the second round. Finally, he wrote books. He claimed that the raw materials for writing were cheaper than those needed for painting. He produced a few novels with evocative titles: *D'un Lit dans l'autre* and *La Vie en culotte rouge*.* Later, he would draft a devastating book of memoirs, in which he did not spare his friends of the time.

He thought that fortune had finally smiled upon him when he sold his first canvas at the Salon des Indépendants. But when he enquired about the buyer, he learned that he was a provincial fellow from Le Havre who had bought the two paintings he considered the ugliest to give to his son-in-law. The first was by Vlaminck, and the second by Derain.

The third member of their band was Georges Braque, who was born in the Normandy town of Argenteuil. His grandfather and his father directed a company of building painters, and both of them painted pictures in their spare time. Braque took courses at the school of Beaux Arts in Le Havre, where he worked with a painter who was also a decorator. He arrived in Montmartre in 1900, then gave up the kind of work his father did to devote himself to a more artistic and less artisanal kind of painting. He lived on the rue des Trois Frères and, in 1904, took a studio on the rue d'Orsel, not far from the Bateau Lavoir. He met Picasso in 1907, later than the others.

Tall, muscular, with dark, curly hair, calm and solid, with the strength of a bear, Braque impressed the girls he danced with at the Moulin de la Galette. When he took the omnibus which ran from Batignolles to Clichy to Odéon, crossing the Seine to the left bank, he would climb on to the top deck and sing, accompanying himself on the accordion.

Braque could be recognized by his blue overalls, his canary-yellow shoes and the hat that he wore shoved down over his head. For several months, the entire band wore the same hat: in a public auction, the painter had bought a hundred of them for a song, and had offered them round to all his friends.

Kees Van Dongen, a Dutchman, as hefty as Braque, red-headed and bearded, moved into the Trapper's House in 1905. He had tried his hand at all kinds of work: hawking newspapers on the central boulevards, painting houses, wrestling at fairs. Like many others, he also sold his drawings to the satirical review *L'Assiette au beurre*, and other drawings, of an erotic nature, to *Frou-Frou* or similar clandestinely distributed publications. He was one of the rare artists of the group from the Bateau Lavoir to have painted life in Montmartre, seeking his models among the prostitutes who walked the streets, the shopkeepers of the place du Tertre, or the dancers of the Moulin de la Galette; the others, although they lived there, turned away from the sources of inspiration which had animated

* 'From Bed to Bed' and 'Life in Red Knickers'.

the work of Willette, Utrillo, Poulbot and Toulouse-Lautrec.

Van Dongen, though living with the foreigners of Montmartre, painted like a Frenchman. His path would thus lie far from the upheavals of modern art (detesting all artistic theories, he didn't participate in Picasso's evenings) but led him rather to the heart of the Parisian salons where the ladies of fashion nested. They all dreamed of seeing themselves painted in pearls and earrings, by this giant who would soon be organizing grandiose and extravagant parties in his studio at Denfert-Rochereau.

André Salmon, always somewhat severe, criticized Van Dongen's painting, which was too colourful for his taste; he joked that the painter had confused his palette with the make-up cases of his models. As for Picasso, he would soon start to avoid Van Dongen, feeling that the man was more at home on the promenade at Deauville than anywhere else, and had become a society painter. He may also never have forgiven him for having done several portraits of Fernande Olivier, which sparked off a number of domestic quarrels. (The lovely Fernande, who became jealous in turn, defended herself by saying that Picasso had painted so many other women . . .)

At the Bateau Lavoir, Van Dongen had lived in such poverty that he never wanted to find himself in similar conditions again. He had shared a studio with his wife, Guus, and his little daughter Dolly. Guus was a vegetarian; at the Van Dongens', the chief dish was spinach. The family was friendly: it managed to survive in a small space where easels vied for room with the beds, the cradle, and the table, and they had to put up with the neighbours' racket, stifling heat in the summer, and bone-chilling cold in the winter. The few sous they managed to accumulate were barely enough to feed the child. Picasso, Max Jacob and André Salmon often had to chip in to buy talcum powder at the nearest pharmacy. When, finally, Dolly had fallen asleep, changed and fed, the Van Dongens counted their coins to see if they could afford something to eat themselves. They couldn't always . . .

When Vollard bought a few of his paintings, Van Dongen moved his small family to an apartment on the rue Lamarck and rented a studio for himself near the Folies Bergère. He finally put an end to the spinach, and disappeared from the Butte Montmartre, preferring the neighbourhood of the Palais Royal. There he would eat dishes cooked in rich sauces, and very red meat in a restaurant which he visited often and which, in its advertisement, boasted of the painter's patronage.

Where can one see Van Dongen putting
food into his mouth, chewing it, digesting it,
and smoking?

At **Jourdan's restaurant
10, rue des Bons Enfants**

Juan Gris also had a family. He came to the Bateau Lavoir in 1906 and moved into the studio that Van Dongen had left free. He was a young man of nineteen, with a swarthy complexion, dark eyes and dark hair. He was described by Kahnweiler, probably his best friend in Paris, as 'like a young dog, full of life, affectionate, kind, a little clumsy'.[5]

Like the others, Gris managed to survive in deplorable conditions. He sold drawings to the illustrated papers until Sagot began to buy his paintings. On the walls of his studio he inscribed, in pencil, figures corresponding to the items he had bought on credit from the merchants of the Butte. When he managed to make a little money, he asked Reverdy to do the sum, and then paid his debt.

Gris lived at the Bateau Lavoir, but stayed away from the commotion of the Lapin Agile. He drank little, except for coffee. He could be seen around the halls of the Trapper's House, melancholy and reserved. He stroked the dog of his fellow countryman, Picasso, with his left hand, saying that if she bit him, he would still have his right hand left for painting.

Picasso was extremely jealous of Juan Gris. He was not happy about the friendship that Gertrude Stein showed him, and still less Kahnweiler. In the twenties, Diaghilev commissioned Gris to do the sets and costumes for his new ballet, *Cuadro Flamenco*, then changed his mind and asked Picasso to do them. This affair did nothing to improve the relations between the two men. But in truth, the older man had very little with which to reproach his junior, except his independence, and the fact that he was also Spanish. Once again, Picasso wanted to be unique.

Gris remained at the Bateau Lavoir for over fifteen years. Two women shared his life: one was Josette, whom he had met in 1913, and the other was the mother of his son. When the weather was sunny, they hung the child up by the strings of his nappies from the window-frame. Picasso was as fond of this child as he had been attached to Van Dongen's little girl.

Gris died at the age of forty from leukaemia, which the doctors had confused with tuberculosis. His suffering was unbearable. He was living in Boulogne then, near Kahnweiler's home. From his garden, the latter could hear his friend's cries of agony.

When he learned of his fellow Spaniard's death, Picasso was very moved. Gertrude Stein, surprised by this show of grief after all the acrimony so often expressed between them, scathingly suggested to him that his tears were out of place...

Of all the painters of the Bateau Lavoir, Gris was the one who most kept his distance from Picasso's group of friends. The others shared everything: lodgings, meals, parties, even clothing. The little troop chose its clothes on Sundays, at the Marché Saint Pierre, the textile market in Montmartre.

Derain, in keeping with his painting of the period, adopted a Fauve style: green suit, red waistcoat, yellow shoes, white coat with black and brown checks, all directly imported from England. Later, in a more sober vein, he would choose blue, and nothing but blue: blue overalls to work in, and blue suits to be worn when he went out, carefully hung up in the closet in order of cleanliness.

Vlaminck, also a follower of the school of Chatou, favoured checked tweed, a hat decorated with a blue jay feather, and a magnificent multicoloured wooden tie that Guillaume Apollinaire admired for its multiple uses: it could serve as a club if one were attacked, or as a violin when it was turned over and the catgut strings on the other side were plucked.

When he wasn't dressed formally for an elegant dinner to which he had been invited for his wit and brilliant conversation, Max Jacob dressed like a magician, with silk cape, opera hat and monocle; or like a Breton, with a traditional coat, kabik, and braided buttonholes. André Warnod donned a velvet cape, Francis Carco spotless white gloves (he had four dozen pairs); Mac Orlan, who walked the streets of Montmartre with his basset hound at his heels, wore multicoloured sweaters and cyclist's stockings.

Picasso chose the overalls favoured by workers from the zinc mines, espadrilles for his feet, a cap, and a red cotton shirt with white dots, also purchased at the Marché Saint Pierre. He tried growing a beard (which can be seen in the *Autoportrait en bleu* of 1901), but soon shaved it off again. He began to hate the artistic look and painters who dressed and acted the part. This was one of the reasons why, when he had given up his legendary pair of overalls, he would criticize Modigliani and his extravagant behaviour. And yet already, in the period of the Bateau Lavoir, the Italian painter, who had come to Paris in 1906, distinguished himself from the others by the elegance of his attire: he wore velvet and his shirts were always sparkling clean. He dressed as conventionally as did Guillaume

Apollinaire, who was never known to sport the picturesque clothing favoured by some of his friends.

By dressing in these varied and sometimes outrageous outfits, the painters of the rue Ravignan were practically engaging in surrealism before the movement itself began. They would run down the streets at night shouting, 'Long live Rimbaud! Down with Laforgue!' sometimes setting off incidents that ended in fistfights. So it was on the day when, having crossed the Seine, they found themselves on the Pont des Arts where Derain, in a show of strength, twisted the railing of the staircase leading to the riverbanks. He and his wife got involved in a noisy spat, punctuated by blows and insults, until the police finally appeared on the scene and carted them off to the police station.

Everything disorderly was grist to the artists' mill, especially art, when it was not official art. They admired daring, desperate poets. Rather than going to the theatre, they preferred the dance hall of the Moulin de la Galette where, for four sous, they could dance quadrilles and fiery polkas all afternoon, which left both feet and soul enflamed. Soon, they would discover the unfamiliar forms of Negro art. In the mean time, the Montmartre painters liked to stroll down the central boulevards of the city, applauding other kinds of artist as iconoclastic as themselves: the boxers and the acrobats.

WITH THE ACROBATS

The child took my hand and I kept him with me, to protect me from misfortune.

Max Jacob

Picasso envied Braque and Derain, who knew how to box. He once tried putting on gloves and fighting with the latter. A direct punch from Derain's right fist sent Picasso reeling to the mat, and he never ventured another try. He simply observed, fascinated, the exchanges of blows in the boxing rings of the rooms where the group met.

They also went to the circus. Their favourite was the Médrano, which had succeeded the Fernando circus that Toulouse-Lautrec, Degas and Seurat used to paint; they went there several times a week. They were friendly with the clowns: Alex, Rico, Ilès, Antonio and especially Grock, who was just starting out. This love for the circus was a passion Apollinaire would cultivate until the end of his life, when he would go to applaud Guignol at the Buttes-Chaumont during the war; he was already a member of an association called 'Our Marionnettes'. In 1905, in La Revue immoraliste, which only ever published one issue, and in which he wrote on painting, literature, and theatre, he spoke of the Harlequins and the Colombines to be seen in Rome, establishing a link between Picasso and himself:

These are creatures who would enchant Picasso. Under the brightly coloured garments of these svelte acrobats, one feels that this is the authentic youth of the people, clever, skilful, talented at many things, poor, and often liars.

When he left the heights of Montmartre to go down to the Boulevard Rochechouart, where the circus was, Picasso entered a world of joviality and open-mindedness. He had never laughed so much as at the bar of the Médrano. He liked the atmosphere backstage even more than he liked the stage, and this is in fact how he painted the circus troupe: not performing but travelling, rehearsing, with their families, or simply going about their

occupations and everyday lives. This happy period, illustrated by the
reappearance of the theme of the acrobats in 1905, put an end to the
blue period. Picasso had entered his rose period, which for a long time
was mistakenly attributed to the appearance of Fernande in his life. In
fact, the openness to the world which characterizes this period had already
begun while he was with Madeleine.

Madeleine represents a pivotal point in Picasso's development, both on
an emotional level and in terms of his art. She was one of the few women
who would count in his life before Fernande's arrival on the scene. For
somewhat mysterious reasons, the painter would not mention her existence
until after Fernande's death, not even refuting the latter's statements when,
in speaking of Picasso, she gave herself the role that Madeleine had actually
played. According to Pierre Daix, only Max Jacob ever met this woman;
Pierre Daix had the information from Picasso himself, who confided in
him.

> One day, in 1968, on my arrival in Mougins, Picasso came out of the
> studio with a remarkable portrait, in profile, which he hadn't been able
> to find until then because the wrapping had got caught in the frame of
> one of the paintings in his collection. 'It's Madeleine,' he said to me,
> then, seeing my surprise, he added: 'I almost had a child with her ...'
> This detail took us back to 1904. But if one reflects on the theme of
> maternity and how it resurfaced in his work, one finds the splendid
> gouache of the *Maternité rose*, in which the face is much closer to
> Madeleine's angular face than to Fernande's.[1]

Picasso always thought of Harlequin as his double. When he painted
Famille d'Arlequin, giving Harlequin a baby, or *Famille d'acrobates avec un singe*,
it is his own fatherhood he is representing. And thus, by association,
Madeleine rather than Fernande. And it is not by accident that the painting
Maternité rose inaugurated what has been called Picasso's rose period.

This question of motherhood represented a real problem for the Picasso
couple: Fernande Olivier couldn't have a child. It was probably a trauma
for her, and it was also one for her lover. The rose period of their life
included a sombre episode which would remain secret for a number of
years.

In 1907, Fernande Olivier decided to adopt a child. She went to the
orphanage on the rue Caulaincourt and brought home a little girl. They
called her Raymonde (although André Salmon named her Léontine); no
one was ever able to learn her exact age, but she was probably about ten.
For several weeks, everyone took an enormous interest in her, and in the
new universe unfolding in the Trapper's House. Picasso, the good artist-
father, did a portrait of her in Indian ink (*Portrait de Raymonde*, 1907). But

the child took up a lot of space. She was noisy. He could no longer sleep for part of the day and work at night. Nothing was the same.

A solution had to be found, so one was sought. The answer was not terribly complicated: when a weight becomes too heavy to bear, it must be removed. Put elsewhere, back where it came from. Returned, so to speak. So after enjoying life with her new parents for three months, Raymonde was returned – against her father's will, it would seem – to her original status, that of an orphan, in the orphanage of the rue Caulaincourt. Max Jacob, the kindly Max Jacob, was given the difficult task of taking her back.

In *La Négresse du Sacré-Coeur*,[2] André Salmon has embellished the incident. If he is to be believed, Max, the good Samaritan, devoted and generous, was sharply rebuked by an employee of the orphanage, who accused him of being an unworthy father. He was informed of the rules: if he didn't see the light now and relent, he would never again have a chance to adopt the girl. The child burst into tears. So did Max. He took her to lunch in a restaurant, spending the last of the little money he had. When night fell, he brought her back to the rue Caulaincout. Then he left, almost running.

Had he taken ether that day?

The story was confirmed in an exchange with Hubert Fabureau.[3] But neither Fabureau nor Salmon mention the names of Fernande or Picasso. The two authors speak of 'an artist couple'; in *La Négresse du Sacré-Coeur*, Max Jacob appears as Septime Febur (a pseudonym he used to promote Picasso in galleries).

Why was so much care taken to conceal the story? Why did Picasso's flatterers protect him so well and for so long, only breaking the silence much later? Why has the entire early period at the Bateau Lavoir (preceding the birth of cubism) been represented in terms of the amusing adventures of an extraordinary whiz-kid?

It was because, even after only five years in Paris, Picasso was already at the centre of a network in which everything and everybody revolved around him, irrespective of whether the other people concerned were victims or beneficiaries of his power and of the strange fascination he seemed to hold for everyone he met. At the Bateau Lavoir, his presence was felt everywhere: some admired him, others defined themselves in relation to him, he inspired or was inspired by still others ... People were drawn to him both for what he did and for what he was. He was treated with kid gloves. He was sought out more often than he sought others. Even Guillaume Apollinaire – a little apart from the group because he didn't live in Montmartre and earned a better living in a different way, and because he distinguished himself from his companions by his dress, manners, and attitude – often appeared to be moving in his friend's orbit.

This was true in all areas, including the illustrations that the painter agreed to do for his poet friends and their books: he often didn't pay any special attention to the subject, simply contributing the fruit of his labours of the moment, sometimes sketches, or even rough drawings whose principal value resided in the fact that they were signed by him.

As the pillar around which all the others gathered, Picasso liked bringing people of different types together. He also enjoyed helping couples to form; in this respect, he had a generous soul. It was he who introduced Marie Laurencin to Guillaume Apollinaire, Marcelle Dupré to Georges Braque, and probably Alice Princet to André Derain.

He was also often caught up in quarrels between two warring parties. Until *Les Demoiselles d'Avignon*, criticism of his work was rare. It was universally admired, as was he. The Bateau Lavoir was like a laboratory, where ideas, viewpoints and discoveries were exchanged, the whole process taking place in an atmosphere of extraordinary artistic fraternity from which jealousy, for the moment and only in this domain, was banished. Except for Juan Gris, less sure of himself than the others, they all knew that one day they would overcome poverty and find their place in the sun. All they had to do was to manage to scrape through until that time came. They sat it out together, showing each other their new works, paintings and poems. It was a communal school, enriched by a variety of languages.

Art itself was thus not yet an arena of significant rivalry between them. It was the artist himself who provoked friction.

Which artist?

Picasso.

He was insanely jealous: of women, of men, of men flirting with women, of women not paying enough attention to him, of men not playing the role of disciple or admirer. It was thus only natural that he should spark off comparable jealousies concerning his own person.

This jealousy was purely emotional. Apollinaire, Max Jacob and André Salmon did not judge each other by their work, but they envied the roles of best, or first, given by Picasso to one or the other of them. The unhappiest of all was undoubtedly Max Jacob, dethroned by Apollinaire in poetry, by Fernande Olivier in Picasso's affections, and soon by Braque in terms of artistic creation.

One might imagine that these carefully orchestrated complicities were indestructible. But time would show that this was far from the case. They only lasted as long as the artists' poverty did, or for the time taken by each new revolution in painting. Picasso was close to Max Jacob, then abandoned him. He liked, then lost interest in André Salmon. He gave his friendship to Apollinaire, first in his heart for a time, but replaced him, after the war and the death of the author of *Alcools*, with Jean Cocteau. Everyone had recognized the painter as the standard-bearer of modern art. Many suffered emotional humiliations at his hands which were short-lived but left a lasting mark. As for Picasso, he strolled about imperially among his fellows, without paying attention to the complaints, the whining, the gossip and the little everyday misfortunes all around him. He was perfectly in his place. And his place was to be first in everything.

THE TIME OF DUELS

If I write, it's to infuriate my fellows; to get talked about and make a
name for myself. When one has a name, one has success with women
and in business.

Arthur Cravan

Fistfights aren't for gentlemen. On the rue Ravignan, in homage to Alfred
Jarry who liked to wave his pistol around in the Closerie des Lilas, the
artists amused themselves by crossing swords and exchanging fire every
time they had the chance.

Picasso kept his Browning on him at all times. He shot into the air to
get rid of people who annoyed him. He shot when he came home to the
Bateau Lavoir, the leader of a merry alcohol-soaked band. He fired out of
the window to wake up the neighbours.

One evening, he invited three Germans to come and see his works at
the Bateau Lavoir. Then he decided to take them to the Lapin Agile. Along
the way, the Germans tried to engage him in a discussion about art and
aesthetic theory. Picasso couldn't stand it. He drew his pistol and fired
into the air. The Germans fled.

When someone made disparaging remarks to him about Cézanne, once
again he waved his pistol and threatened them. When Berthe Weill
expressed some doubts about the amount of money she owed him, he
didn't answer, just took out his pistol and placed it on the table. Once, in
a café where he was bored, he shot a few bullets at the ceiling. But he
never aimed to hit anyone, and he never did.

As for Dorgelès, he would lie in wait, at a street corner, for the Don
Juan who had stolen his mistress. And Apollinaire, seated at a table in a
café, waited for Max Jacob, who had been chosen as a witness, to settle
the details of a duel to which he had challenged a literary critic, after his
devastating review of Apollinaire's work. In fact, the duel never took
place. All they crossed swords over in the end was which of the two
combatants would pay the bill for the drinks they consumed while the
witnesses were haggling over the details of the duel.

At the time, one sent one's witnesses like one sent flowers. The newspapers all had journalists who specialized in ferreting out feuds, insults, calumny, and the gossip of the fencing rooms where potential duellists practised their swordsmanship. They would turn up at dawn on the island of the Grande Jatte or the bicycle track of the Parc des Princes, preferred spots for combats, often chosen by the offenders or offendees.

Fortunately for the two friends of the Bateau Lavoir, although Picasso was the champion of the revolver, it was always without consequence, and although Apollinaire was the king of the duel, they were always called off.

The first time was in 1907. The second was a little before the war. The third time found him in opposition to Fabian Avenarius Lloyd, alias Arthur Cravan, who claimed to be Oscar Wilde's nephew on his mother's side. He was an impressive enemy: almost six feet tall and weighing two hundred pounds.

Cravan had a wide spectrum of activity, and his activities were provocative, anarchic, violent and a bit crazy. He seemed to have a great talent for this sort of thing. He had made a start on the benches of his secondary school, where a professor who had had the misguided idea of wanting to reprimand him had quickly found himself laid over the knees of the bad boy, his trousers pulled down, subjected to a sound spanking.

And that was just the beginning.

Expelled from school, Cravan went to Berlin, where he got into the unfortunate habit of walking around the city with four prostitutes hoisted on his shoulders. The police chief soon had him thrown out of the city, reminding him indignantly that Berlin was not a circus.

Paris was more tolerant. Cravan returned there and did some arithmetic: a night spent with a prostitute being less costly than a night at a hotel, he combined practical considerations with temptation and chose this option. He then tried his luck at being an actor-poet: when he was on stage, he would call for silence with a trumpet and a bludgeon.

He got a job as a salesman at Brentano's bookstore, but only managed to keep it for as long as it took him to throw a book at a customer who had asked him to hurry up.

To become better equipped to defend himself against the authority of the bosses, he perfected his boxing skills, becoming an amateur champion and getting frequent practice at the Closerie des Lilas: he would enter, insult the customers and fight with them until he was thrown out.

The jobs he claimed to have had were even more varied than Apollinaire's. He listed them without a moment's hesitation: he had been in turn, or sometimes simultaneously, a knight of industry, a sailor in the Pacific, a mule driver, an orange-picker in California, a serpent charmer, a hotel porter, a woodcutter in Australia, an ex-boxing champion in

France, the grandson of the Queen's chancellor, an automobile driver in Berlin, and a thief.

He was, first and foremost, a poet and a journalist, the director of a review that only ever published five issues, and which he distributed himself with the help of a produce merchant's barrow. It was called *Maintenant*. His reviews praised his uncle Oscar Wilde, and criticized anyone else.

Among his preferred targets:

Gide: There is nothing remarkable about his bone structure; his hands are those of a lazy man ... In addition, the artist's face is sickly; towards his temples, little leaves of skin detach themselves, similar to dandruff or a little bigger; as one would say vulgarly, 'he's peeling'.[1]

Suzanne Valadon: She does know some useful little formulas, but simplifying and being simplistic are not the same thing, old cow![2]

Delaunay: He has a mouth like an inflamed pig or the coachman of an aristocratic family ... Before meeting his wife, Robert was a perfect ass, and shared perhaps most of this beast's virtues.[3]

Marie Laurencin: There's a woman who needs to have someone lift her skirt and give her a big — somewhere.

Apollinaire, in the same article, was described as 'Jewish and serious' (Cravan took care to emphasize that he had no prejudice against Jews and even preferred them to Protestants).

In short, he would attack anyone and anything.

Guillaume Apollinaire sent his witnesses to the director of *Maintenant*. He was less offended for himself than he was angry about the slur on Marie Laurencin, who had been his companion for several years.

After delicate negotiations, the intermediaries managed to get Cravan to issue a double corrective notice. The new texts nuanced the earlier ones, without repudiating them altogether.

For Apollinaire: Monsieur Guillaume Apollinaire is not Jewish, but Roman Catholic. In order to avoid in the future any misunderstandings, which are always possible, I must add that Monsieur Apollinaire, who has a big belly, resembles a rhinoceros more than a giraffe; as for his head, it looks more like a tapir's than a lion's, and there is something of the vulture about him more than of the long-necked stork.

For Marie Laurencin: There's a woman who needs to have someone lift her skirt and give her a big astronomy lesson in her Variety Show.[4]

The affair was not pursued. Arthur Cravan would continue to create a stir for a while yet. Notably, he sold a real Matisse and a fake Picasso, which brought him enough money to go off to Spain at the beginning of the war. As for Apollinaire, he put his pen back into the inkstand, and reread the poems and articles he had written in praise of Marie Laurencin.

It was Picasso who had introduced him to the young lady in 1907. He had noticed her at the art dealer Sagot's gallery. At the time, Marie Laurencin was twenty. She was studying painting at the Académie Humbert, on the Boulevard de Clichy, in the same class as a certain Georges Braque.

Fernande Olivier described her as having the face of a goat, short-sighted eyes, a pointy nose, skin the colour of dirty ivory, long, red hands, and something of the perverse little girl about her. Not to mention that she was affected, liked to listen to herself talk, and played the ingénue.

Fernande hated her, probably because, in this group in which there were not many women, Marie Laurencin was her greatest potential rival for first place. André Salmon, more poetically but no less cruelly, summed up the same theme in a short phrase: 'an attractive ugly duckling.'[5]

And Apollinaire, relating in Le Poète assassiné the role played by the Bird of Bénin (Picasso) in the meeting between Tristouse Ballerinette (Marie Laurencin) and Croniamantal (himself), wrote:

> He [the Bird of Bénin] turned to Croniamantal and said to him:
> 'I saw your wife last night.'
> 'Who is she?' asked Croniamantal.
> 'I don't know, I saw her but I don't know her. She's a true young lady, just as you like them. Her face is dark and childlike, the face of one who is destined to make others suffer. And her graceful hands, which she lifts to push something away, lack that nobility which poets cannot love because it would keep them from suffering. I saw your wife, I said. She is ugliness and beauty.'[6]

It should be noted that these lines were written three years after they had separated . . .

Marie Laurencin was as thin as her lover was plump. But aside from their physique, they had many points in common, beginning with their family history: she was from a Creole family and had never known her father. She still lived with her mother, in Auteuil; Guillaume had just left his. He lived on the rue Léonie (later to become the rue Henner) and only went to Le Vésinet now for his ritual Sunday visit.

When she came to his place, Marie Laurencin skipped up the two floors of stairs, and left the same way. He followed her. He took her to the Bateau Lavoir, where she was more tolerated than liked. The artists there found something falsely ingenuous about her, which barely concealed her all too obviously bourgeois tastes. But what the others disliked, Apollinaire liked, for there were similar tendencies in himself. The kind Douanier Rousseau understood this very well, in fact, when he drew both of them (*La Muse inspirant le poète*, 1909) in such a way as to make them almost unrecognizable while conveying a symbolic truth: he was dressed as a public notary, and she was wearing the attire of a receptionist.

Apollinaire and his muse often entertained in the poet's new home. When invited to Apollinaire's, one was forbidden to get in the way, make a mess, or eat without being asked to. Picasso and Max Jacob, who had dinner there quite often, provoked their host's wrath one evening for the simple reason that while his back had been turned for a moment, they had dared to wolf down two slices of salami sitting on a dish on the table.

Apollinaire watched over the meal's preparation, and over his muse, who was learning to cook. If something was overcooked, there would be a scene. If something was underdone, there would be another one. Guillaume was demanding, bossy, rather tyrannical and as jealous as Picasso. In short, not the most easygoing of men to live with. He was satisfied when he saw the table well set, graced with tasty food and decent wine. Then Marie would be treated like his little ray of sunshine. He was even better natured when the guests, having put their heads and funds together, brought an extra item or two, capable of improving on the somewhat routine and repetitive contents of an Apollinaire dinner: the inevitable *boeuf en daube*, accompanied by a risotto. Still, this was better than the meal of raw apples sprinkled with cognac which Jean Metzinger and Max Jacob were served, on one strange occasion.

When all the necessary ingredients for a harmonious evening had been assembled, it was a treat to see the poet devour the appetizer (cucumbers, then snails), attack the main course, sometimes help himself to an additional portion of one of his favourite dishes (tripe), gobble down the dessert (little cakes with icing), and savour a surprise brought by a guest (caramels). Afterwards, having taken off his removable collar, the host rolled up his sleeves and helped clear the table.

When he and his companion were on good terms, conjugally speaking, Apollinaire could show a noteworthy gallantry. He wouldn't let anyone make fun of his dear Marie. He protected her from Max Jacob's barbs with as much zeal as he would have found to defend his mother's honour, had she been mocked by the same Max. This latter, as a joke, had also composed a little song about the muse:

Ah! I have an urge
To make a little angel with you
To make a little angel
By tickling your curves

Marie Laurencin

Maire Laurencin was certainly the poet's muse, just as Fernande Olivier was Picasso's inspiration. One was honoured in colours, the other in words, in *Alcools* and a part of *Calligrammes*. But, generally speaking, in Montmartre, it was rare for women thus to enter the lives of the poets and painters, to be transformed into paintings and poems.

Francis Carco recognized this, and expressed it in choice terms:

> Women never played an important role in our band of friends. We took them as they were, for a month or two, then they left again, of their own volition, and we wrote verses, thinking that they would have done just as well never to have come at all.[7]

This is obviously something of an exaggeration, as is often the case with Carco. But it was basically the truth. There were women, of course, at the Bateau Lavoir. Kees van Dongen was married, and Juan Gris too. But while these fine gentlemen were painting, the women chiefly looked after the family finances and the upkeep of the household, and not much more.

Luckily, this closed-minded attitude would not last long. In a few years' time, the women of Montparnasse, more numerous, would join those of Montmartre. History would not be the same if Suzanne Valadon, Fernande Olivier, and Marie Laurencin hadn't paved the way for their friends from the left bank, the Kikis, the Beatrice Hastingses, Marie Vassilieffs, Youkis, Gertrude Steins, Sylvia Beaches, Jeanne Hébuternes, Adrienne Monniers, and so many others, who would play a considerable role in the development of art after the First World War. Thus no one would surpass or even come close to the insufferable misogyny of a critic from the review *Vers et Prose* who, in 1907, recounted with envy the delight of Alfred de Musset one evening when he was able to walk through the Louvre all alone. Delight not because he was alone, but because he had 'escaped from his female contemporaries'.[8] And the journalist went on to tell of his own joy one evening when, similar in this to Musset, he had found himself on a Friday in Avignon. Why a Friday? Because that is the day on which, in memory of the Crucifixion, women did not go out in the streets. It was true heaven: 'One finally felt that one could admire the marvels of the place for itself.'

And who was this great man with such a strong preference for masculine company?

Charles Maurras.

GOSOL

Bringing forth order from chaos, that's
what creation is all about.

Guillaume Apollinaire

One morning, in the spring of 1906, a horse-drawn cab, driven by a coachman, stopped at the foot of the steps on the rue Ravignan. The man seated in it slowly emerged from the vehicle, told the coachman to go and have a seat in a bistro, and headed with a firm step towards the entrance to the Bateau Lavoir. The concierge, who had witnessed his arrival, figured that anyone who had come with such pomp could only be bringing good news for her tenants. She ran down the halls to Picasso's studio, pounded on the door, and announced, 'There's some fine folk on their way here, and it may be for you.'

'What kind of folk?' queried a voice from the other side of the door.

'The rue Laffitte kind. A dealer, and not just any dealer, looks like.'

The dealer was indeed from the rue Laffitte: it was Vollard. Having learned from Apollinaire that Picasso had abandoned the blue period for somewhat more lively works, he was curious to see what the artist was doing.

He saw. An hour later, as they happened to arrive in turn on the rue Ravignan, André Salmon and Max Jacob witnessed an extraordinary spectacle: the dealer was leaving the Trapper's House with two canvases which the poets recognized immediately as Picasso's. He placed them in the carriage, on the back seat, then with the same heavy step, went back into the house. A few minutes later, Vollard reappeared, carrying three more canvases, which he placed in the carriage. Soon it was four, then five. When he had finished, there were at least twenty paintings piled up on the seat.

Vollard sat down next to the coachman. The carriage turned and set off in the direction of the boulevards.

Max Jacob couldn't contain himself any longer; he had tears in his eyes.

He hugged André Salmon, and thanked all the gods in the heavens for having come to the aid of his venerated friend.

The year 1906 seemed full of promise. At the Bateau Lavoir, there had already been a visit from André Level, a collector who seemed a little bizarre but who had nonetheless bought some of Picasso's works. He had discovered the painter through Berthe Weill. He had a crazy story to tell but it was so generous that it had earned him the respect of the artists of the Bateau Lavoir. Lacking the means to acquire contemporary art all by himself, Level had got together with a few friends to found an association, 'La Peau de l'Ours',* which bought art for the community. Its eleven members contributed an annual subscription, which Level, who had become the manager, was authorized to spend on the purchase of art works. So he visited galleries and studios to discover young artists, whose works he then proposed to his 'associates'. Each painting he bought was distributed to a member of the group, chosen by the lottery. It was agreed that all the paintings would be put back on sale ten years after the founding of La Peau de l'Ours. A part of the profits would then be paid to the painters.

How could one not be tempted by such an idea? All the more so as, at Level's suggestion, the friends of the association had decided that in 1906 they would choose nothing but works by Picasso. And then, not long after this happy event, Vollard turned up as well. He bought two thousand gold francs' worth of paintings. That evening, the champagne flowed at the Bateau Lavoir. The next day, Picasso bought himself a wallet that he slipped into the inner pocket of his jacket, which he closed with a safety pin.

A few days later, he and Fernande Olivier left on vacation: first Barcelona, then Gosol, a Catalonian village hidden away in the mountains. Max Jacob and Guillaume Apollinaire escorted the couple to the Gare d'Orsay. They walked down the rue Ravignan, each of them hanging on to one handle of a heavy basket, in which the painter had stashed his tubes of paint and his brushes. There they hailed a carriage, which drove the boisterous lot of them to the station. On the platform, still more friends were waiting to see them off. It was a merry free-for-all.

The stay in Gosol lasted until the summer. Picasso was able to complete a painting there which he had begun the previous winter and hadn't been able to finish. A painting that would be of the utmost importance in the development of his work.

---

* 'La Peau de l'Ours' – literally 'the bear skin'. In French, the expression 'ne pas vendre la peau de l'ours avant de l'avoir tué' ('don't sell the bear's skin until it has been killed') is the equivalent of the English 'don't count your chickens before they're hatched'. Here it is a reference to the association's philosophy of buying works meant to appreciate in value and be sold years later.

A few months earlier, he had had another visit resulting in a sale which temporarily filled his purse. Brought by Henri-Pierre Roché, an odd couple had appeared one day at the door of the studio: they were Gertrude and Leo Stein. After having bought Cézanne paintings from Vollard, they had acquired Matisse's *La Femme au chapeau* in the 'wild beasts' cage' at the Salon des Indépendants. Then Leo had suddenly stopped short in front of a painting by Picasso exhibited at Sagot's. He had returned with his sister to show it to her. But she didn't like it.

'What bothers you, the legs?' Sagot had asked.

'The feet.'

'Cut them off!'

Of course, they didn't. Leo Stein finally bought the *Fillette au panier de fleurs* (1905) for one hundred and fifty francs. Then he had convinced his sister to come with him to the home of this Spanish painter of whom neither of them had ever heard before. Roché, who was friendly with the group from the Bateau Lavoir, since he knew all the artists in Paris, had agreed to introduce them. In the course of this first visit, the Steins had bought several paintings. Thanks to this sale, for a few weeks Picasso had been able to buy himself some materials, which meant he didn't have to recover old canvases in order to paint new ones.

Picasso and Gertrude rapidly became good friends. Fascinated by her appearance, the Spaniard offered to paint the American's portrait. She agreed. He wanted to paint her as Ingres had painted *Le Portrait de Monsieur Bertin*: seated, massive, a definitive statement.

The first session began. The painter positioned his model in a decrepit armchair. He himself sat on a chair facing the easel. With his nose practically touching the canvas, he drew a sketch first: Gertrude hunched up, her hands on her lap, her back slightly stooped; a presence that was almost masculine, motionless, as if in suspension.

Everything went well on the first day. The Stein family came to fetch its heroine when the session was over. Everyone was delighted. So delighted that they thought the painting, as it was then, could be considered finished; they were ready to pay for it, cart it off, exhibit it.

'What next?' exclaimed Picasso.

'You'd rather I come back tomorrow?' Gertrude asked, in her low, deep voice which corresponded exactly to the image of her the artist had created on the canvas.

She not only returned the next day, but the next, and the next, for several months. Every afternoon, she left the rue de Fleurus to hike up to Montmartre, entered the Bateau Lavoir, and sat across from the painter in the same worn-out armchair.

Sometimes Leo came to visit; occasionally Fernande would be present. She found the Steins a little ridiculous, especially Gertrude, with her corduroy velvet suits and laced-up sandals. But she had a grudging admiration for her tenacity, and it was much needed, to remain immobile for several hours a day while Picasso painted her, not saying a word.

In an effort at cordiality, Fernande offered to read to the model from Jean de La Fontaine's *Fables*. The offer was accepted. So the days passed with books and painting and conversation. Suddenly, after ninety sessions, Picasso threw up his brushes and threw in the towel. He explained, to Gertrude's consternation, 'I don't see you any more when I look at you.'

He had just painted the face.

He wiped it out.

And left for Gosol.

A sculptor friend had told him about this Catalonian village, praising it for its extreme simplicity. It was located in the Pyrenees, not far from Andorra. One could get to it on a mule, and once there, the rest of the world vanished. There was nothing but nature all around, the browns and the yellows of the mountains, the purity of a life unspoiled by modernity. The inhabitants, amiable and hospitable, were mainly smugglers. This was exactly what Picasso needed.

It was in Gosol that he took his first steps in a new direction which was to lead him, a year later, to the accomplishment of the artistic revolution represented by *Les Demoiselles d'Avignon*. Surrounded by the bare landscapes and the simple population, he refined his style. He was seeking what Gauguin had discovered in Tahiti: a purity, a form of primitivism. And something else, as well: novelty. He needed to define his difference from traditional art, while still reaffirming the values of his early work, when he had painted the poor people of Montmartre and the women prisoners of Saint Lazare. He wanted to add an element of criticism to his art: criticism of painting, of society, of established culture. He sought to overturn convention, to find himself again, to become once more a free-thinking sympathizer with the anarchist cause.

First, he painted in the manner of Ingres, whose *Le Bain turc* had fascinated him at the Salon d'Automne in 1905. This resulted in *Fernande à sa toilette*, an extremely traditional work. Then came a multiplicity of inspirations, from Iberian statues from before the Roman conquest, seen at the Louvre, to the Virgin of Gosol, dating from the twelfth century, with exaggerated features and oversized, empty eyes. There were Matisse's paintings, too, and Derain's...

Then Picasso looked deep into himself, sought, and found. He painted the *Grand Nu rose* (1906). It was Fernande, nude, against a pink background, with her hair up and her hands joined. The face is more sombre than the body, expressionless, the eyes without sockets; they are elongated, almost

split in the middle, deprived of all psychological subjectivity. It was the
sketch of a mask.

When he returned to Paris, fleeing a typhoid epidemic which had broken out in Gosol, Picasso went and stood in front of the portrait of Gertrude Stein, and without even seeing his model again, he painted in the head he had erased before, as if in a single stroke.

It too was the sketch of a mask. It was the foundation of the *Demoiselles d'Avignon*. And the first stuttering word in the language of a new art: cubism.

AN AFTERNOON ON
THE RUE DE FLEURUS

Matisse: colour. Picasso: form. Two
great preoccupations, one great goal.

Wassily Kandinsky

No. 27, rue de Fleurus. The house had two storeys, and an adjoining
workshop. On the house side, there were a few rooms, a bathroom, a
kitchen big enough to eat dinner in. The studio side consisted of an
enormous room, which contained polished Italian Renaissance furniture,
a stove, two or three tables bearing flowers and porcelain, a fireplace, a
massive cross hung between two windows, and had whitewashed walls
without an inch of bare space left on them. They were completely covered
with the works of Gauguin, Delacroix, El Greco, Manet, Braque, Vallotton,
Cézanne, Renoir, Matisse, Picasso, and others.

It wasn't a museum. And since, at the time, most of these paintings
weren't worth much, the door to the studio opened easily with a single
key: a flat American-style key that could easily be slipped in one's pocket,
a far cry from the enormous, noisy contraptions that Parisians clanked
about with in their pockets.

This is where the Steins lived. Every Saturday, they received guests in a
kind of open house. To be allowed in, all one had to do was answer the
hostess's ritual question – 'Who sent you?' – with the name of an artist
whose works were in the room.

One entered a vast studio where an extremely varied crowd – painters,
writers, poets – was gathered. Once a week, at the Steins', guests could
eat and drink all they wanted which, when one was a starving artist, was
not a negligible attraction. And if one was also interested in modern art,
the company was exceedingly interesting.

The man speaking at the end of the room, his fingers slipped into the
pockets of his waistcoat, surrounded by a crowd of admirers eager to
converse with him, was Guillaume Apollinaire. It was hopeless to try to
get the better of him in a discussion: he knew everything about everything,
and always won. Even Miss Stein, who was so often pleased with herself,

admitted to having only ever carried the day in a debate with him once, and then only because the poet was drunk.

The tall, sturdy man with a forbidding expression, standing in front of the fireplace, was Braque. He was unhappy because one of his works, placed above the hearth, was blackening under the steady assault of smoke. The two Cézanne watercolours near it were suffering the same fate. Braque grumbled, thinking that the next time he was asked to help hang paintings (the tallest of all, he held the paintings in place while the concierge hammered in the nail), he would request that his be moved to a better place. He wished he had said something at the last dinner. But there was a reason: at the table, each painter was seated across from his own canvases, next to his fellow painters. In these circumstances, it was hard to criticize...

On this particular evening, Picasso was present. As usual, he hardly said a word. He hated fancy social functions and had trouble expressing himself in French. He was watching the professorial Matisse, with an ironic expression, as the Frenchman gave an elegant discourse on some subject or another.

Picasso, on this particular day, was in a similar mood to that of his friend from the rue d'Orsel: a black rage. He had just noticed two of his paintings on the walls, but they seemed to have changed since they had left his studio. They were shinier than they should be. Gertrude Stein had had them varnished! Decidedly a woman who liked everything to be brilliant and showy...

Max Jacob tried to reason with him. He only managed to calm him down: Picasso didn't stalk out of the room that day, but he refused to set foot inside the studio on the rue de Fleurus for many weeks to come.

As he searched the room for Fernande Olivier, a man he didn't know came up to him and, gesturing towards the painting that the artist had finally finished on his return from Gosol, asked, 'Is that Gertrude Stein?'

'Yes.'

'It doesn't look like her.'

Picasso shrugged his shoulders. 'It doesn't make any difference: she will end up looking like it.'

Fernande was speaking with a small woman dressed in grey and black. She was young, with glass earrings dangling from her ears, but her quiet voice and prim manners made her seem older. She was often thought to be the chambermaid, but she was not. But watching her talk with Fernande Olivier, one could almost believe it. She was there and elsewhere at the same time, listening without hearing. Very dependent on Miss Stein, she didn't pay much attention to the conversation of Madame Picasso, about whom the hostess generally did not have much good to say: 'All she can talk about are three things: hats, perfume, and furs.'

But not this time. Now they were talking about the French lessons that Fernande could give her. Even as she answered the questions her future teacher was asking. Alice Toklas kept an eye on everything in the room: who was drinking, who wasn't drinking, who was eating, where were the cakes, were there enough of them, why wasn't Miss Stein there yet, would she be listened to attentively, should Alice intervene to get rid of the unwanted hangers-on who might trouble the exchange that the writer and patron of the arts would necessarily want to have with the painter-professor, Monsieur Matisse? And was Brancusi, who was coming up to them, going to spoil the harmony of the conversation?

Alice Toklas venerated her friend and employer and wanted to show her and the multiple facets of her personality off to best advantage. Gertrude liked to see herself as a literary diamond. She felt she was the innovative genius of the international literary world. The Picasso of literature. Alice helped her to believe it. It was her most important role, along with typing her friend's work.

Miss Stein had just appeared in the doorway to the studio. Today she was wearing a brown velvet dress which hugged her waist in a vice-like grip and enclosed her shoulders in a yoke from which her flesh escaped in undisciplined folds. To protect herself from the cold, she had put on heavy woollen stockings that she had shoved into her laced-up sandals, which made squeaky noises on the waxed floor.

With a glance around the room to make sure that all her guests had noticed her arrival, Miss Stein, satisfied on this point, handed a bundle of handwritten pages to Miss Toklas and asked her to type them, double-spaced, on the Underwood in the bedroom. Then she sighed and complained that writing was such a depressing business. But fortune was smiling on her: she had just sent a magnificent text to a New York review which had had the honour of publishing three of her pieces since the beginning of the year.

She headed towards the large painting by Picasso and settled in under her own portrait. Soon Henri Matisse, Robert Delaunay, and Maurice de Vlaminck, three avid scroungers, were standing in a circle around her.

Gertrude Stein was the orchestrator of these artistic get-togethers and she enjoyed the role. Seated under her portrait like Saint Louis dispensing his judgements under a tree, she handed out comments with an authoritative air, glaring angrily at anyone who dared to interrupt her. She couldn't stand the writers who didn't like the stories she'd published in American magazines, nor the painters who weren't her faithful followers; after all, wasn't she their benefactress, both materially and morally? She provided an exhibition space for those who refused to present their work in the official salons, which helped them to become known and get their work recognized. This was the case with Picasso. And who was responsible for the fact that Matisse now no longer had to worry about where his next meal was coming from? Gertrude Stein.

She liked the Matisses enormously. When she went to their home on the *quais*, near Saint Michel, she was always pleasantly surprised by the orderliness of their household. Picasso's style was pure bohemian; Matisse's was elegant poverty. One was offered as little to eat at one home as at the other, but on the left bank, this fact was better hidden. Madame Matisse knew how to cook *boeuf mironton*, and she was totally devoted to her husband's cause. One day, Matisse made her pose disguised as a gypsy, with a guitar in her hand. She fell asleep and the instrument fell to the floor. The family barely had enough to eat, but they preferred to go hungry and have the guitar repaired. Thus Matisse was able to finish the painting.

Another time, Gertrude Stein saw a magnificent basket of fruit on the table. It was not to be touched: it was reserved for the artist, for his work. So that the fruit wouldn't spoil, the temperature had been lowered in the apartment. Matisse painted his still life wrapped up in a coat, his hands covered with woollen gloves.

Gertrude Stein loved to invite Matisse and Picasso together. They admired each other's work, but didn't like each other very much, and spent all their time comparing and judging. A highly amusing spectacle.

Matisse and Picasso could be compared – the image comes from one of them – to the North Pole and the South Pole. The Frenchman had retained a stiffness and formality which perfectly suited the scribe's hand with which he drafted the official acts of the lawyer whom he worked for. He was serious, he didn't laugh. His family was composed not of friends but of his wife and daughter. He didn't often invite people to his home. When he spoke, it was always gravely, to convince someone of his point of view. 'He didn't know how to laugh, our fine painter of *la joie de vivre*,' noted André Salmon regretfully.[1]

Dorgelès, in a somewhat xenophobic article, described his 'worried beard' and 'austere spectacles', similar to those of a German military attaché, but then Dorgelès was edging ever closer to the right-wing *L'Action française* and would end up writing in the *Gringoire*.

The wittier Apollinaire found a pithier phrase: 'This wild beast is actually a refined creature.'* He described him at work, solemnly painting several canvases at once, spending a quarter of an hour on each one, quoting Claudel and Nietzsche if any students were in the room.

The Spaniard, by contrast, was a silent man. He expressed much with his eyes, and his eyes were mocking. He had rough manners where the

* He used the word 'fauve': 'Ce fauve est un raffiné.'

Frenchman was polite. He shunned formal cliques and salons. He had a passionate nature and showed it.

Yet the two painters had several things in common: their interest in the primitive, the friendship of their hostess, Gertrude Stein, the uneasy attention they paid to each other.

On the walls at the rue de Fleurus hung works by both of them. They themselves already knew what the Steins grasped as soon as they discovered their work: Matisse and Picasso were the two giants of modern art.

Each would have his defenders: for Matisse, it would be Leo and his brother Michael; for Picasso, it would be Gertrude. For the moment, the complicity between the brothers and the sister was still intact. But Matisse was already jealous of the solicitude that the American showed this Spaniard twelve years her junior; jealous too of Braque and Derain, who were drifting away from his world to approach the myriad mysteries of the Bateau Lavoir.

One question preyed on the professor's mind: what was it all about?

THE BORDELLO OF AVIGNON

This is the true Tahiti: that is, faithfully
imagined.

Paul Gauguin and Charles Morice

In Montmartre, as on the *quais* of Saint Michel, a cauldron was bubbling, containing a substance which no one had properly tasted yet, but which promised to be boiling hot: primitivism, and Negro art.

Picasso had been to Gosol, and Matisse had just come back from Collioure. The Spanish border lay between the mountain village and the little fishing port. But art knows nothing of borders. On the heights, Picasso was discovering a new simplicity, while far below, Matisse explored similar universes.

Gertrude Stein knew where and how the two influences crossed paths. One day – not a Saturday – Matisse was due to come and see her. On the rue de Rennes, he stopped short in front of a window in the shop belonging to Heymann, a dealer in exotic curiosities nicknamed the 'wild father'; he had seen a black African statuette in wood. He entered and bought it for fifty francs. It was a Vili statue from the Congo, representing a seated figure, with raised head and empty eyes. It was extraordinary in that its forms and proportions sprang more from imagination than from reality and that, contrary to the practices of Western sculpture, muscle tissue had no importance in the composition.

Matisse went on to the rue de Fleurus; a little later Picasso happened to stop in, and saw the object. This was after his return from Gosol. He observed it attentively for a long time, then went home to Montmartre. It had left an indelible impression on him.

The next day, Max Jacob found him in his studio, busy drawing strange heads, whose eyes, nose and mouth were connected with one stroke. (Max actually contradicted Gertrude Stein's account of the meeting, affirming that the Vili statue had been shown to Picasso by Matisse at his own home, during a dinner at which Apollinaire and Salmon were also present. But Apollinaire never mentioned it, and Salmon too seems to have forgotten the event.)

Matisse was familiar with Negro art: he often went to the Ethnography Museum at the Trocadéro, which specialized in objects from Oceania, Africa, and America, brought back by the colonials. These objects were piled up in dusty chests, when they weren't being exhibited in cases that had served as luggage during the voyages. Apollinaire was to protest against such a haphazard presentation of these extraordinary treasures, proposing that they be welcomed at the Louvre, where Picasso often went to admire the Iberic statuettes. (At this time, the Spanish painter hadn't yet started to go to the Trocadéro.)

In this game between the two men, a third person entered the arena, whose role would be decisive: André Derain.

Derain had been fascinated by Negro art for much longer than the others. He had been going to the Trocadéro museum for years, as well as to the British Museum where, in 1906, he discovered primitive works from New Zealand. He mentioned this often to Matisse during their mutual experiments with fauvism, and also to Vlaminck:

> I'm rather moved by my visits to London, and to the British Museum and the Negro Museum. It's quite unbelievable, wild with expression.[1]

It was Derain who urged Picasso to visit the Ethnography Museum. It was also he who would first show his friend a Fang mask, which made an impression on the Spanish painter comparable to that made by Matisse's Vili statue. This mask had a history, which predated the famous evening when Matisse brought his statue to the rue de Fleurus. Even if Gertrude Stein was almost certainly involved in that encounter between Matisse and Picasso, that does not make her the godmother of Negro art in Paris. Carco, Dorgelès, Warnod and Cendrars could all testify to this.

The godmother was in reality a godfather, by the name of Maurice de Vlaminck. One afternoon, when he was on the banks of the Seine at Argenteuil, where he had been painting for several hours, he left the river and walked into a café. He ordered white wine with Seltzer water. He had just taken his first sip when he noticed three strange objects sitting on a shelf between two bottles of Pernod. He got up, went over to look at them, and discovered three Negro sculptures. Two of them were painted in ochre red, ochre yellow, and white: they came from Dahomey. The other one was black, from the Ivory Coast. The painter was deeply affected – in his own words, 'shaken to the depths of my soul'. These statuettes were, for him, a revelation of Negro art. He bought them, paying for them with a round of drinks on the house. Then he stored them in his home.

A few days later, he had a visit from a friend of his father. The man noticed the African objects, and offered him three others: two statues from the Ivory Coast and a Fang mask, which his wife found so ugly she didn't want them disfiguring her living room. Vlaminck was thrilled. He hung the mask over his bed. When Derain saw it there, he was overwhelmed with emotion. He wanted to buy it. Vlaminck refused.

'Even for twenty francs?'

'Even for twenty francs.'

A week later, Derain returned. He offered fifty francs. Vlaminck agreed. His friend took the mask off to his studio on the rue Tourlaque. This is where Picasso saw it. And this is where his interest in Negro art was born.

It does not ultimately matter whether Matisse was first and Picasso second, or Picasso first and Matisse second. Other influences played a part: Gosol, for example, Collioure, Derain ... and of course, Gauguin.

For Gauguin was also fascinated by the Oceanic and African pieces that he had discovered during his time at the World Fair. A retrospective of his work organized around the theme of the *Tahitiennes* at the Salon d'Automne in 1906 was a decisive experience for Matisse, Picasso and Derain. It was from then on that they began to collect these treasures from another time, another culture, which laid down a challenge to traditional art and heightened the subjectivity of the artist to a degree never before known. The primitives, recognized as 'pure artists' by a Kandinsky still chiefly under Russo-Germanic influence, were only interested, in their words, in 'the inner essence, all external considerations being thus eliminated'.[2]

Matisse and Picasso little by little integrated Negro art into their production: Matisse by adding it to his paintings, Picasso by making Negro statuary the centre of his compositions. From this point on, the duel between Matisse and Picasso would no longer be carried out with subtle barbed shafts, but in public view, on immense canvases, in great masterpieces.

Matisse was the first to draw his weapon. At the Salon des Indépendants in 1906, he exhibited only one painting, but that one was to become a legend: *Le Bonheur de vivre*. This painting was monumental, both in its size (175 x 241 cm) and its novelty. It reflected a mixture of the primitivism that the artist had discovered in Collioure, with a carefully controlled fauvism, a dreamlike poetry reminiscent of Mallarmé's *L'Après-midi d'un faune*, and finally, a Gauguinesque distortion of body shapes. *Le Bonheur de vivre* represented a break with neo-impressionism.

For the critics, of course, it was a bonanza. Joining in the laughter and derision of those who turned their backs on it, they spoke of 'transcendental meanderings', of an 'empty canvas', of musical and literary thought with no visual content. They attacked his juxtaposition of colours, and the contours were felt to be sometimes too delicate, sometimes too heavy. They disliked the liberties taken with anatomy, and the abandonment of pointillism for flat-surface coloured brushstrokes. Even Signac, who had bought another scandalous painting, Luxe, calme et volupté, felt that Matisse had taken a wrong turn here – Signac who, with his friend Seurat, had himself suffered from the ostracism of the romantic impressionists, and whose work Pissarro had had to struggle to justify, faced with the influence of Monet and Renoir.

Matisse, who would show himself to be terribly conservative when the need to defend cubism arose, was thus, in 1906, at the forefront of the avant-garde. The previous year, at the Salon des Indépendants, Charles Morice, despite being a friend of Gauguin, had reproached Matisse in Luxe, calme et volupté for having joined the clan of the 'pointillistes and the confettistes'. It was the same story again a few months later with La Femme au chapeau; Matisse, at the time, was considered the most scandalous of innovators.

Even his faithful admirers had a moment of doubt. Leo Stein was also a bit nonplussed by Le Bonheur de vivre. He went to see it, then went again. In the end, the canvas came to be recognized by him for what it was: the great event of the Salon, the decisive work of the young century, and the one that would elevate Matisse to the grand master of modern painting. He bought it.

The following year, the painter created a similar stir, this time with the Nu bleu: souvenir de Biskra (1907), inspired by a trip he had taken to Algeria in the spring of 1906. The critics, once again, could not comprehend these bizarre forms, still deformed in the manner of Gauguin, this mask-like face, this skin of an iridescent blue. Louis Vauxcelles recognized that he just didn't understand what he termed a 'vacillating schematization', the chief architects of which were Matisse and Derain, who exhibited Les Baigneuses. Others described the painter as a 'crafty fellow', and his art as a 'universe of ugliness'.

Once again, Leo Stein and his sister bought the painting.

Meanwhile, far from the convent of Des Oiseaux – where the 'refined wild beast' was going to set up his academy, before falling back on the convent of the Sacré-Coeur, at the Invalides – Picasso was at work. In the disorder of the Bateau Lavoir, he pursued his own experiments with primitivism. Under Max Jacob's watchful, worried eye, he drew forms and figures that were reminiscent of the engravings in the caves of prehistoric man. After the Portrait de Gertrude Stein, he painted the Autoportrait (1906) and the Autoportrait à la palette (1906). Then he began several busts of women, notably the *Buste de femme à la grande oreille* (1907).

He was preparing his answer to Matisse, sharpening his knives. He knew his rival's work, having seen it at the Steins'. Like many others, he had been shaken by it. But he thought that those who saw Matisse's painting as something revolutionary were mistaken. Yes, it was a high point in art, but in classical art. It employed the most modern language, perhaps, but to express tradition. This was also Kandinsky's view at the time: he saw Matisse as one of the great masters of contemporary painting, a genius of colour, but a visceral impressionist who, like Debussy, had not broken with 'conventional beauty'.

Some thought that the artist had gone too far – but Picasso, in his heart of hearts, thought that Matisse had not gone far enough, had stopped too soon. The break, the real break with the past, would come about through Picasso himself.

In the winter of 1906, after months of trials and preparatory sketches, Picasso placed the tip of his brush on the throat of the man he meant to outdo. He began *Les Demoiselles d'Avignon* – for him, this work was to be his answer to Matisse's *Le Bonheur de vivre*.

The sketches show that he initially meant to represent a sailor in a bordello, and have a medical student enter a room where the young man and five women were standing. Why Avignon? Because, as he executed his work, Picasso was thinking of the calle d'Avignon (Avynyo), near where he had lived in Barcelona and where he bought his paper and paints. As for the sailor, he was inspired by Max Jacob: Max had told Picasso that he was from Avignon, a town which, at the time, housed a number of houses of prostitution. In the course of his preparatory sketches, Picasso had painted his poet friend dressed in a sailor's undergarments. Initially, one of the women was supposed to be Fernande Olivier, another Marie Laurencin, and a third Max's grandmother from Avignon (Picasso confirmed this to Kahnweiler in 1933).[3]

But as the work progressed, the sailor disappeared, and the student turned into a woman. When the painting was finished, it showed five women, four of whom were standing, nude. Their faces bore the print of Iberic statuettes and Negro masks. Unlike Matisse's masterpiece, which was full of curves and colours, and appears, today at least, extremely harmonious, Picasso's work was sombre and astonishingly violent. The bodies of the women were dismembered, fashioned with sharp angles, big feet, fat hands, breasts that jut out or no breasts at all, flattened, twisted noses, a leg streaked with blue, a lack of grace in certain of their movements, jowls, masks, gaping eyes staring out at the observer, hollow, black sockets, Iberic asymmetry on the right, Negro statuary on the left, clear geometries which prefigure cubism. Pierre Daix notes very justly that the painting's violence is reminiscent of the intensity of *Une saison en nfer*, and that Picasso was reading Rimbaud avidly while he was working on the canvas.[4]

But with Picasso, poetry disappeared, indolence vanished, Mallarméan dreams departed. This was a bordello, the crudest of realities. Picasso opposed this work, still greater than *Le Bonheur de vivre*, to Matisse's. His painting represented not the end, however modern, of an earlier universe, but the beginning of a new world. *Les Demoiselles* are to the *Bonheur de vivre* what Stravinsky's *Le Sacre du printemps* is to the last quartets of Beethoven.

No one understood ... When Picasso showed the work to some friends from the Bateau Lavoir, they didn't know what to make of it. Braque got out of it with a pirouette: 'It's as if you wanted to make us eat dung and drink black oil!' Manolo, as usual, had something witty to say: 'If you went to pick up your parents at the train station and they arrived looking like that, you must admit you wouldn't be too happy about it.' Leo Stein was horrified. Others claimed that the work was unfinished. Derain was afraid they might come home to find Picasso hanging from his canvas.

But the worst was Apollinaire. He who was usually so prompt to defend the audacities and transgressions of modern art, especially when Picasso was the ringleader, kept quiet. He didn't write a word about the painting, or even mention its existence in his reviews and articles.

Only Gertrude Stein defended the painter. Without going so far as to buy the canvas, however ...

And the painting remained in the artist's successive studios for a long time. It was first exhibited in 1916, at the Salon d'Antin organized by André Salmon. It was he who suggested that for reasons of propriety, or perhaps of censorship, the name *Le Bordel d'Avignon* (the title Picasso had given it), or *Le Bordel philosophique* (the title given it by Apollinaire and Salmon) should be changed to *Les Demoiselles d'Avignon*. Picasso accepted reluctantly, and never really liked this name.

After the exhibition at the Salon d'Antin, the work was rolled up and shown very little. In 1923, André Breton convinced Jacques Doucet, the dress designer and patron of the arts, to acquire it. In 1937, a New York gallery bought it and later sold it to the Museum of Modern Art in New York.

Today, *Les Demoiselles* still excites controversy. Art historians debate among themselves the answer to two questions that have been asked since the painting first appeared: what is the role of Negro art in its composition, and can the work be considered as the starting point for cubism?

The answer originally given to the first question was that Iberic art was certainly an influence in the right part of the painting, the most 'revolutionary' part, with the borrowing being recognizable from the hatchings and the form of the ears and eyes of two of the demoiselles, one standing, the other crouching. It was said that this second figure was based on the portrait of a peasant that Picasso had done in Gosol – his sketchbooks prove this beyond reasonable doubt. And it was thought that the hollow eye of the demoiselle on the left reflected, on the other hand, the influence of Negro art. In support of this thesis, historians advance some dates which imply that when he began work on *Les Demoiselles*, Picasso already was familiar with Matisse's Vili statue and the Fang mask acquired by Derain – but did not know, or did not know well, the Ethnography Museum of the Trocadéro – and therefore that his sources of inspiration were limited.

It is true that it was only later that Picasso began to acquire the Negro objects which would soon encumber the studio of the Bateau Lavoir ('The Bird of Benin', the name chosen by Apollinaire to designate Picasso in *Le Poète assassiné*, refers to a piece from the painter's collection). It is also true that he owned fewer than did Matisse, who was champion in the field. Finally, it is no less true that from the late thirties on, Picasso himself declared that if, during the Bateau Lavoir period, everyone had seen the influence of Negro art in *Les Demoiselles*, it was only because everyone then was just discovering these cultural novelties – in reality, the most important influence on the painting was Iberic.

The importance of Negro art in the painter's work is also contested by Pierre Daix and by Pierre Reverdy. Reverdy, unlike Daix, argues clumsily, denying Cézanne's influence on cubism, Ingres' influence on the works of 1905 and the influence of Negro statuary on the period preceding cubism. The poet is wrong. But we can forgive him: he was writing in the twenties, and was thus too close to the story to see it objectively. In addition, he venerated his subject, thinking him as central to the history of art as Descartes was to the history of philosophy.

John Richardson recently tried to introduce a new nuance into this debate among specialists. Following the opinion of certain anthropologists and art historians, he affirms that the faces of the demoiselles are incontestably copies of African masks, and that Picasso repainted these faces after visiting the Trocadéro museum. Richardson reminds us, in addition, that at the time when Picasso was playing down the influence of Negro art on this work, the Spanish Civil War had just ended with Franco's victory: to underline the Iberic influence in *Le Bordel* was also to underline his Spanish roots. Between the conception of *Le Bordel* and the comments made by the painter in the late thirties, important events had happened: Guernica; the direction of the Prado museum being entrusted to Picasso by the Republicans; and finally, the massacres committed by the African troops engaged in the Franquist legions. The Spanish homeland thus needed to be defended all the more as it had been subjugated and beaten. This question was sufficiently important to Picasso to make him break with André Salmon without a moment's hesitation when the latter had to cover the war, on the side of the monarchists, for *Le Petit Parisien*. From that day on, he refused to shake his hand and turned away whenever their paths crossed.

The second question, that of cubism, remains unanswered. Salmon, like Jacob, always felt – and wrote – that *Les Demoiselles d'Avignon* was one of the first great original cubist paintings. Kahnweiler, who was soon to become Picasso's dealer, thought the same. And when one observes the right part of the painting, one clearly sees there the new forms which would be the mode of expression of this school. But Pierre Daix writes:

> Now, ever since the exhibition at the Museum of Modern Art of New York in 1989–90, it is considered that the birth of cubism implied, in addition to the reconstruction of natural forms, the in-depth exploration of the Cézannian expression of volumes, first perceptible in Braque's work in the course of the year 1908, and in Picasso's in the final version of *Les Trois femmes*.[5]

For Daix, the *Trois femmes* are a kind of final step in the development of the idea introduced by *Les Demoiselles d'Avignon*. If cubism there was, it was to be found there rather than elsewhere. Once again, the exegetes battled it out...

And what about Matisse, in all this? He saw *Le Bordel d'Avignon* in the studio of the Bateau Lavoir (where he was taken by the Steins) and understood perfectly against what and whom the violence of the younger man was directed. It was against what had been called modern art, until then – and therefore against himself. In the eyes of the foreigner, didn't *he* represent the newest tendencies in French painting? He was furious, of course, and declared that he would 'do in' Picasso.

The rivalry between the two men was strong. If Salmon is to be believed, it often took a surprisingly puerile form among Picasso's followers. When Matisse gave Picasso a portrait of his daughter Marguerite – a bad portrait, notes the writer to explain this gift – a group of Picasso's friends went one day to a bazaar on the rue des Abbesses, bought darts, and on their return to the Bateau Lavoir, aimed them as best they could at the little girl's face. Fortunately, the projectiles were of the Eureka brand, with rubber tips.

Matisse, for his part, wondered about the identity of the little smart alecs who painted slogans invoking him on the walls of Montmartre: 'Matisse will drive you mad!'[6]

His destiny, though, would soon lead him down the path of the prize juries and art academies. Another world...

In 1908, the relations between the two artists became even more strained when Braque was refused a place by the committee which decided on the works to be shown at the Salon d'Automne. Matisse, who three years earlier had caused a scandal at the very same Salon, was now a member of the committee. It was also said that he had criticized the emerging cubist movement. The claws of the wild beast had become a little less sharp.

The split, fortunately, did not last. By the eve of the First World War, Matisse and Picasso were going horse riding together in the Bois de Boulogne, meeting in their respective studios, exchanging works. In 1914, both escaped mobilization. In 1937, they were condemned by the Nazis, among other artists, as representatives of 'degenerate art'. When the Germans invaded Paris, Matisse was not there. Picasso protected his work in a strongbox at a nearby bank. For Matisse, in the words of Brassaï, Picasso was 'his friend and rival, his nemesis and his comrade in arms'.[7]

After the war, Picasso visited Matisse, who had taken refuge in Nice. All rivalry had by then disappeared between them. They spoke of their painting and of the painting of others. Matisse's attitude was almost paternal. He was soon going to die. He gave of himself, transmitted a message ... And Picasso listened. The rue de Fleurus was long forgotten. They didn't need Gertrude Stein any longer to keep them away from each other's throats. They knew now with certainty that they were the two great masters of modern art.

THE GOOD DOUANIER

A tiny bird, perched
On the shoulder of an angel
They're singing the praises
Of the good Rousseau

Guillaume Apollinaire

A strange painter, one whom no one would have expected to find in such a place, was also friendly with the Bateau Lavoir group. He was almost sixty-five years old, and seemed a very dignified elderly gentleman, with cane and soft hat, his back a little stooped, trotting up to the heights of the Butte Montmartre from Plaisance, where he lived. His face showed that he had a generous and kind character as well as a very emotional nature: he could blush violently at the slightest incident. Henri Rousseau was entering old age without ever having fully emerged from childhood. His painting reflected a naivety that Elie Fauré has compared to that of Utrillo, the two painters sharing, in his opinion, the same state of innocence.

He was known as the Douanier Rousseau, for he had been an employee of the municipal customs inspection bureau of Paris, responsible for examining the foodstuffs entering the capital. At the age of fifty, he had retired to devote himself exclusively to painting. He had never attended art school, but was totally self-taught. He knew nothing of perspective, or classical pictorial conventions. He painted instinctively, carefully. His story is a simple one, especially when it's not Apollinaire who's telling it!

You remember, Rousseau, the Aztec landscape,
Forests where mangoes and pineapple grow
Monkeys spilling all the blood of the watermelon
And the blond emperor shot to death there.

The scenes you paint, you saw them in Mexico,
A red sun decorated the façade of the banana trees
And you, worthy soldier, you exchanged your tunic
For the blue dolman of the good customs officers.

The poet let his imagination run away with him when he wrote that Henri Rousseau portrayed Mexican landscapes he had discovered during the war in Mexico, in which he had participated as a sergeant commanding a section of French soldiers. The truth was that the Douanier Rousseau had gone neither to Mexico nor to America, but only to Angers for his military service, and to the World Fair of 1889, where he had perhaps indeed seen reconstitutions of exotic landscapes which might have inspired him in later years. Apollinaire is thus wrong when, in a pithy phrase, he affirms that the works of Rousseau 'are the only thing that American exoticism contributed to the visual arts'.[1] And Blaise Cendrars was no more accurate when he in turn added to the legend:

Come to Mexico!
On the high plateaux the tulips bloom
Creeping ivys are the sun's flowing hair
As if created with a painter's palette and brushes
Colours as striking as gongs
Rousseau was there
His life forever dazzled.

But Rousseau was himself, and himself alone. He belonged to no school, and thus to no period: he was no closer to the impressionists, whose contemporary he was, than to the followers of Negro art. Perhaps there was an affinity with the Fauves, but only by accident: *Le Lion ayant faim* had indeed been hung alongside paintings by Matisse, Vlaminck and Derain at the famous Salon d'Automne of 1905. Louis Vauxcelles, who admired Rousseau, claimed that his case demonstrated 'that the most ignorant and untaught man can be a gifted artist'. It was said of him that he was a kind of deaf-mute of painting, alone and intuitive, going merrily along his way, a way that no one could share and whose rules he himself didn't know – if there were any rules.

The paradox of this artist who was absolutely one of a kind is that he shows a classicism which, though difficult to label, is still very far from the bold innovations of the Bateau Lavoir; ironically, though, fame came to him through them.

It was Alfred Jarry who introduced him to the two guiding spirits of the *Mercure de France*, Alfred Valette and his wife Rachilde, and then to Apollinaire. Jarry, also born in Laval, was the Douanier's great friend. One never knew – and he was not the only one of whom this was true – if he preferred the painter to the eccentric person, or the other way round. Whatever the case, it was he, the least conservative of authors, who got the kindly gentleman involved with the *Mercure de France*, which would help make his name. Then came the avant-garde painters, who had great respect for the childlike wonder with which Rousseau regarded nature.

Picasso was one of his greatest admirers. In 1908, he bought, for five francs, a canvas by Rousseau at the père Soulié's: *Le Portrait de Mme M.* (1895), a study of his first wife. Later, he would buy others. Picasso was obviously interested in the primitivism which so permeated the work of the Douanier. The man who was desperately seeking to distance himself from all forms of academic painting discovered in this work a manner which was unlike his, but which was definitely a manner of its own.

The Douanier Rousseau lived on the rue Perrel, near Montparnasse. He lived alone, having lost two wives and all his children except for one. A cardboard sign was tacked to the door: 'Drawing, painting, music. Private lessons, for a reasonable price.' He lived in poverty. Twice a week, he prepared a stew which he then kept under his bed and which was supposed to keep him nourished for the rest of the week. Unfortunately for him, all the poor people of the neighbourhood knew the day on which he cooked his big meal. The stew was no sooner ready than the neighbours began to arrive, and what was meant to nourish him for a week rarely lasted even two days.

He taught some students in his home and painted their portraits, which he sold to the shopkeepers and workers of the neighbourhood. (When the Museum of Modern Art in New York tried to track down his works, they discovered one at a plumber's, another at a farmer's ...) Until Vollard, Uhde, and Paul Rosenberg began to take an interest in him, only a few friends had bought his paintings: Delaunay, Serge Férat and his half-sister, Hélène d'OEttingen.

Still, poverty did not prevent the Douanier from inviting guests to his home. After saving money by fasting for eight days, he would send out invitations for a soirée, including a menu and a programme of dances. On 1 April 1909, the latter read:

Programme

Céciliette (polka)
The Little Bells (mazurka)
Eglantine (waltz)
The Babies' Polka
An Angel's Dream (mazurka)
Clémence (waltz)[2]

Among those invited to these little parties were the baker and the grocer who supplied Henri Rousseau with his everyday necessities, and practically the whole Bateau Lavoir group. The host invited his visitors to sit on chairs, all lined up in a row, and seated himself near the entrance in order to open the door to new arrivals. The guests ate and drank whatever was to be had – sometimes almost nothing. Each person recited a poem or a rhyme. Then the Douanier took up his violin and played a melody for the assembly. When fatigue overtook him, he would lie down, fully dressed, on the old couch in his studio, and not wake up until morning, happy as a baby and ready to paint.

But living alone began to weigh on him after a while and he decided to marry again and start a new family. He fell in love with a girl and courted her; when her parents appeared somewhat dubious about the idea of abandoning their sole heir to a penniless painter, he asked his friends for help. One fine day, he arrived at Vollard's, battling with a canvas that was much larger than him. He showed it to the dealer, who found it admirable.

'Good,' answered the painter. 'Do you think you could make me out a written testimony to the fact that I'm making progress?'

The dealer couldn't believe his ears. Rousseau explained that he wanted to get married and that a certificate of good behaviour would help convince his future parents-in-law to give him their daughter's hand.

'How old is your fiancée?' asked Vollard. 'Is she a minor? Does she have to have her parents' consent?'

'No,' answered Rousseau, with an ecstatic smile, 'she's fifty-four.'

He got the certificate, and another from Apollinaire. But the marriage never took place, and the good Douanier Rousseau remained a bachelor.

It had taken him several months to finish the portrait of Marie Laurencin and Guillaume Apollinaire. This was not due to any lack of inspiration or creativity. He was simply determined to have carnations at the bottom of the painting, and so had to wait for the season to offer him what he needed in the way of plant life . . .

Apollinaire also recounted that when the Douanier painted a canvas on a fantastical theme, the subject of the painting itself would sometimes frighten him and he would run to the window stricken with panic.

Another story about him that has been told by several people, including Georges Claretie, a journalist for the Figaro: after having been involved, without his knowledge, in a swindle, Rousseau was given a prison sentence. When he appealed, his lawyer, Maître Guilhermet, had barely finished pleading his case when the Douanier turned towards him and, in a voice audible to all, asked, 'Now that you're done, can I leave?' And when the judge finally granted him a pardon, the painter exclaimed, 'Thank you, Mr President! To show my gratitude, if you like, I'll paint your wife's portrait!'

Maître Guilhermet attributed two major achievements to Alfred Jarry:

writing *Ubu roi* and assuring the reputation of the Douanier Rousseau. But like many others, Guilhermet often wondered if the artist's frequent absurdities were due to a real simplemindedness or to an amazing comic talent. He first asked himself this one day when his client wanted to use the phone in his office to call someone in Laval. He shouted into the receiver. The lawyer suggested that he lower his voice. 'They can hear you, you know.'

'You can hear me. But not them.'

'Of course they can ... The telephone...'

'Foolishness!' interrupted Rousseau. He placed his hand over the receiver and added, 'I'm talking to people who live in Laval. It's not next door, Laval. How do you think they're going to hear me if I don't shout?'

His friends, painters or not, were amused by his naive reactions, reminiscent of a similar quality in his work. Picasso liked him, and the feeling was reciprocal. Rousseau once said to him, 'We are the two greatest artists of our times, you in the Egyptian, primitivist style, me in the modern style.'[3] The Spaniard didn't reply; he undoubtedly had his own thoughts on the subject...

In 1908, a few months before leaving the Bateau Lavoir, Picasso decided to organize a banquet in homage to the Douanier Rousseau. The purpose of the occasion was to honour the painting that he had bought from Père Soulié, along with its author. The evening had been planned for a long time, and the preparations carefully carried out. Fernande and Picasso had fastened branches of leaves to the beams of the room, and also covered the ceiling with them. Negro masks hung from the walls. In front of the glass wall, they had built a throne, using a chair placed on a crate. Behind this chair, on the walls, between the flags and lanterns, hung a banner which proclaimed, 'To Honour Rousseau!' The *Portrait de Mme M.* was set on an easel in the middle of the studio, surrounded by brightly coloured fabrics and garlands.

The table was set: it was a long plank of wood resting on trestles, on which had been placed plates and dishes lent by the Azon restaurant. As for the meal, ordered from a local Félix Potin grocery store, it had been paid for by all: the Bateau Lavoir had collected contributions for the occasion.

Everything was ready. The hosts were waiting for the food to arrive. At eight o'clock, the delivery still had not been made. The guests began to appear: Braque, Jacques Vaillant, Dalize, Gertrude Stein and Alice Toklas, wearing a brand new hat.

At eight-thirty, there was still no meal in sight. A few people ventured out to see what had happened – Félix Potin had got the date wrong. There was panic in the ranks, followed by a hasty war council. What was to be done? In a flash, all present trooped downstairs, and fanned out all over the neighbourhood – the rue Ravignan, the rue Lepic and the rue des Abbesses – to see what was to be had in the shops where they knew the shopkeepers. They then met up in the neighbourhood's bars to compare what they had managed to rustle up: mostly cakes and rice. The little band hurried back to the Trapper's House. They had to carry Marie Laurencin, too drunk by then to walk straight. Back in the studio, she flopped down onto the couch, not noticing the fruit tarts that someone had left in a corner of it. Jumping up again as fast as she had sat down, shaking her legs and waving her arms, screeching and sugar-coated, she fell into the other guests' arms. Soon all were sticky and gooey. Fernande began to insult the 'pretty ugly creature'; the two finally had to be separated.

Once calm had been restored, they sat down to eat. At this point, the door opened and Apollinaire, who had offered to go and fetch the Douanier Rousseau in a carriage, appeared with his charge. The painter, stunned and happy, stood motionless in the entrance hall, a little hat on his head, his cane in his left hand and his violin in the right. His friends pushed, pulled, and cheered him. Apollinaire recited a poem. So did Salmon. They all drank gallons of wine. Marie Laurencin, still pouting, sang songs from Normandy. Apollinaire scolded her quietly. Since this wasn't enough to quench her enthusiasm, he dragged her outside. When they returned to the room, she was quieter.

Rousseau sat down on the throne that had been prepared for him. Salmon danced on the table. When he started to get out of hand, Picasso pushed him out of the door. Leo Stein had decided to stand guard by the side of the evening's guest of honour to protect him from any unwanted familiarities from giddy revellers. But the painter had dozed off. Above him was a lantern with a candle in it, whose wax was falling drop by drop onto the top of his skull. When he woke up, he was amused at the charming hat which had slowly formed on his head. But when the lantern caught fire, several guests had to climb onto chairs and tables to put out the flames. Once things had calmed down, the Douanier took up his violin and, accompanying himself with the instrument, began to sing songs from his childhood: 'Aye! aye! aye! what a toothache I have!' Heartily applauded, he began on another rhyme:

Me, I don't like the big newspapers
That talk of nothing but politics
What do I care if the Eskimos
Have torn apart Africa?

Then, wearied by his efforts, he fell asleep again.
In the course of the evening, other guests arrived: Frédé and his donkey

Lolo, who immediately began to graze on the clothes and hats of all the guests; an American couple, she in an evening gown and he in a dark suit, astounded by the artistic pranks of these French jokers. They left again rather quickly.

At dawn, each of the guests contributed a little change so they could order a carriage for the Douanier Rousseau. They accompanied him to the vehicle, set him on the seat, and placed his cane and his violin on his lap. Giving him a hug, they sent him on his way.

This party, which was one of the last ones of the legendary period of the rue Ravignan, has been presented in varying lights in different accounts. According to Fernande Olivier, they were 'playing a joke on the Douanier'. In an article published in 1914 by Les Soirées de Paris, Maurice Raynal described the events as if everyone's game had indeed been to make fun of the artist. Gertrude Stein didn't take sides on the question. But Salmon disputed these unpleasant interpretations. He defended the painter:

> We didn't like Henri Rousseau for his clumsiness, his ignorance of the rudiments of drawing; we didn't cherish him for his immense candour ... We loved him, the man, for his purity, his courage in the face of an often cruel life, for a kind of angelic quality and, as an artist, for the surprising sense he had of the concept of grandeur, for his magnificent and ambitious desire to create vast compositions at a time when, with the exception of Picasso and, less fully, Matisse, so few artists really composed their paintings.[4]

It is probable that if Picasso took the trouble of organizing the party at his house, cleaning up the studio and the Trapper's House, covering up the Demoiselles d'Avignon, and putting away his painting materials, it was not at all to make fun of a bad painter, but quite certainly to honour an artist for whom he had affection and admiration.

Of course, Henri Rousseau made him laugh. He was amused by the naive ideas and the daydreams of this childlike old man. But they all enjoyed him, were amused by him. That doesn't mean that they thought, like Raynal and Derain – who would change his mind on the subject, in any case – that the Douanier Rousseau was a fool. (Derain is supposed to have said to Salmon, after the latter had published an article on the painter, 'What's this, the fool's triumph?') And even if Picasso was playing some kind of game, it is doubtful that he meant to mock the fellow; nor did Apollinaire. If Max Jacob is to be believed, Picasso would never have stood for it. Beatrice Hastings, Modigliani's future fiancée, learned this at her expense: Picasso refused to open his door to her after she had made some unkind remarks about the artist.

Whatever the case, Rousseau went his way without ever taking offence.
So what if people made fun of him? It was a sign that they were taking
an interest. And as far as painting went, he didn't have any lessons to
learn from anyone: he knew he had great talent.

It was he who had the idea of inaugurating a series of banquets in
which Braque and Apollinaire would later play the leading role, in another
time, and another place. It was also he who, as if in an apotheosis,
ushered out this legendary era in the life of the artists, who would soon
cross the Seine and in turn set Montparnasse on fire.

A month before his final departure from this world, he was in love
again. Alas, Eugénie-Léonie refused his hand. Henri Rousseau pleaded his
case:

> So man is meant to procreate, but at our age, we don't have anything
> to fear on that score. Yes, you are hurting me, for fortunately, I still have
> feelings. Let us unite our fates and you will see for yourself whether or
> not I am able to serve you.[5]

He never got a chance to prove his ardour. One day in September
1910, his friends received a death announcement: Henry Rousseau had
died at Necker Hospital, of gangrene. The funeral would be held at the
church of Saint Jean Baptiste de la Salle, on the rue Dutot.

Nobody came. The announcements had been sent out too late. By the
time they arrived, the funeral had already taken place.

THE THEFT OF THE *MONA LISA*

A Republican Guard accompanied him. Apollinaire – and this inadmissible severity of the penitentiary administration is regrettable – had handcuffs on his wrists.

Paris-Journal, 13 September 1911

The Picassos were moving house...

The movers transporting the little furniture they had from the Bateau Lavoir to the new apartment on the Boulevard de Clichy didn't understand it. These people must have just had a stroke of good fortune, or inherited a lot of money. What miracle had enabled them to leave the strange-looking, flimsy, wooden building for one of the most bourgeois houses imaginable, with a view of the Sacré Coeur on the studio side and a view of the trees along the Avenue Frochot on the other? The apartment had a living room, dining room, bedroom and pantry, and was quiet and comfortable.

A dream in square metres.

Everything changed, even the furniture. The bric-à-brac now became chic and snazzy: rustic mahogany, Italian woodwork, antique oak buffets, a Louis-Philippe couch, a piano ... The bedroom was a real bedroom, and the bed a real bed, with copper bars. Crystal and porcelain were displayed. Even better: when she arrived in her new home, Madame Picasso wrote to Gertrude Stein to see if she could ask Hélène, her cook, to find them a maid! She would be housed, fed, and receive forty francs a month.

When she found the rare creature, Madame Picasso gave her a room containing a round table, a large walnut-stained clothes chest, and the best of the furniture from the Bateau Lavoir.

But the young lady was not meant to share their bohemian lifestyle, of course: she was asked to wear a pretty white apron and to serve meals. She was to do the cleaning every day in all of the rooms except Monsieur's studio. There, the geometry of the arrangements was extremely complex. Canvases, brushes, tubes of paint, palettes, masks and Negro statues all over the room, musical instruments, furniture of all kinds. Not to mention the collections: one of little blue objects, another of cups, or of bottles, or fragments of frayed tapestries, boxes, old frames. And then there was the monkey, the dog and the three cats . . .

Monsieur requested that nothing be touched, especially the dust: when there was a layer of it everywhere it didn't do any harm, it was when it was shaken up by the duster that it became dangerous, settling on the paintings. To avoid problems, she was not allowed to enter: it was strictly forbidden territory. In this room, cleaning was done once every few months, no more. In the rest of the apartment, the day's activity would begin when Monsieur and Madame were awake, usually rather late in the morning. The girl took advantage of their schedule to get off to a slow start herself, which the lady of the house was not happy about: the maid was neglecting her duties.

Picasso became irritable in his new home, Fernande noted. He took refuge in his studio, a kind of reconstitution of the Bateau Lavoir. He called for well-balanced meals – fish, vegetables and fruit – which he felt were necessary for his health, which he thought was becoming delicate. He began a diet, and drank more water than wine. His mood darkened. He went out less, and with less enthusiasm. Was this perhaps because they were now invited to more elegant events than they had been to before? Frank Haviland, the porcelain manufacturer from Limoges, an admirer of Negro art and himself an occasional painter, entertained in style in his studio on the Avenue d'Orléans. And Paul Poiret, the well-known dress designer, received friends in great pomp. He had not yet achieved his place at the summit of the fashion world, but he was slowly ascending to it. Thanks to him and his dresses, women were already giving up corsets. He appreciated art and artists: when he came to Picasso's on the Boulevard de Clichy, he admired everything he saw, without delving into details. The canvases exhibited in the apartment were magnificent, extraordinary, marvellous, admirable, unique. The cushions were sublime, the view was splendid. Paul Poiret was a man of superlatives.

All this was undoubtedly gratifying to Picasso, who was not averse to allowing a bourgeois social life to intrude, on occasion, into his heroic artistic poverty. But too much of it could get on his nerves. His good humour would only return on Sundays, when he saw his friends: Salmon, Apollinaire and Max Jacob. Or when he was with his old friend Manolo, who had emigrated to Céret.

Céret at the time was a little Catalonian village located in the Western Pyrenees. Just as he had taken refuge in Gosol several years before, Picasso discovered the town for the first time in the summer of 1911. There, among the fruit trees, the country and the old houses, he found himself again.

To start with, he stayed in a hotel, then moved to a quiet house in the heart of the mountains. In the evening, he joined his friends. Braque came down from Paris, and Fernande followed soon afterwards. For a time, the couple's former harmony was restored. Picasso painted as he had in Gosol, and as with Gosol, when he returned to Paris, his painting had changed. And as at Gosol, again, their stay was interrupted by an unexpected development.

In 1906, it had been a typhoid epidemic. In 1911, it was a headline that appeared on the front page of *Paris-Journal*: the *Mona Lisa* had been stolen from the Louvre. When, on 29 August, a certain Géry-Piéret confessed in the columns of the same paper that he had taken three statuettes from the museum, Picasso and Fernande immediately packed their bags and left for Paris. The situation was critical.

Picasso knew this Géry-Piéret very well. All too well. He was a Belgian adventurer, a friend of Apollinaire, for whom he had also worked as a secretary from time to time. The poet had met him when he was working as a journalist for the *Guide des Rentiers*, and had introduced him to Picasso. In March 1907, Picasso had bought two Iberic stone heads from him for fifty francs. They came from the Louvre: at the time, the museum was like a sieve, in both directions. Francis Carco recounts that Roland Dorgelès had left a bust sculpted by one of his friends in the Antiques Gallery for several weeks, without anyone noticing the addition. Picasso himself had once facetiously asked Marie Laurencin, 'I'm going to the Louvre. Do you want me to bring you anything back?'

So Géry-Piéret knew his way around the museum. Things may not have been as easy as Blaise Cendrars made out; the poet, with his habitual exaggeration and his penchant for fanciful invention, describes the Belgian adventurer as a gay fellow who would bet a bottle of champagne that he could bring back a precious object from the Louvre hidden under his coat – after shaking hands with the guards. And Géry-Piéret, a very resourceful fellow, had indeed sold two heads from the Louvre to Picasso. The problem was that after the *Mona Lisa* disappeared, he sold a third head to *Paris-Journal* (for two hundred and fifty francs, far from the fifty thousand francs offered for the restitution of the *Mona Lisa*) and the newspaper gave itself some cheap publicity by exhibiting the statuette before restoring it to the museum. Of course, the poet's former secretary affirmed that it was also he who had spirited away the *Mona Lisa*. *Paris-Journal* then published an incendiary editorial criticizing the lack of security at the entrances and exits. Apollinaire himself published an article on the same theme in *L'Intransigeant* on 24 August. It began with the words, 'The *Mona Lisa* was so beautiful that her perfection had now become one of the commonplaces of art.' And continued, 'The Louvre is more poorly guarded even than a Spanish museum.'

This only went to show how naive he was, for the law could judge that he himself had been involved in the affair of the statuettes. He had served more or less as an intermediary between his two friends, the adventurer and the painter. In 1907, he had tried to persuade the latter to return the statuettes. Picasso had refused, saying that he had 'damaged them while trying to discover some of the secrets of composition of the antique and savage art they represented'.[1] The two Iberic heads constituted one of the sources of his research on primitivism, and they had their role in the creation of the *Demoiselles d'Avignon* (the round mouth of the woman on the right, the outsized ears of three of them, the general asymmetry).

This is why Picasso and Fernande returned from Céret in such haste: if Géry-Piéret had restored the third stolen head, the detectives of the Louvre, assisted by the men from the Préfecture de Police, might go looking for the other two.

As for Apollinaire, he understood the danger very well. He therefore came to fetch his friends at the station, and the three of them returned to the Boulevard de Clichy. One question had to be resolved: how to get rid of the stolen goods?

The poet was in a desperate mood. He accused himself of negligence, cursed the friend who had got them into trouble and predicted dishonour and the destruction of all they had achieved. Picasso wasn't in much better spirits. Fernande Olivier, a calm and somewhat cruel witness, noted that they were like 'contrite, frightened children'.[2]

In this critical situation, a fundamental fact, which both men had more or less forgotten, quickly resurfaced: they were foreigners. They could be thrown out of the country at any time.

They spent that evening on the Boulevard de Clichy, cooking up a thousand solutions, before adopting the one that seemed the least dangerous: throwing the statuettes into the Seine. Fernande recorded the scene. They had no sooner adopted this plan than they set out to execute it. Madame Picasso helped to find a large suitcase, slipped the works of art into it, and pushed them out of the door. They found themselves in the street. The always imaginative Blaise Cendrars would describe them hugging the walls, on the lookout for the police, struggling with their heavy burden. He mentioned an unexpected noise which sent them scuttling under an archway, their hearts thumping madly. Then he imagined them drawing close to the river, walking in single file, the man in front looking out for trouble coming their way, the man behind keeping constant watch to make sure they weren't being followed. But at some point, a movement in the shadows, more significant than anything so far, frightened them so much that they suddenly abandoned their murky route and hurried home, almost at a run, upset – terrified in fact.

When Fernande Olivier opened the door to find the two men standing before her at two in the morning, they were as white as chalk. And they still held the suitcase.

'Is it empty?'

'No, full,' muttered Picasso.

They entered the room, and began, once again, to mull over their choices. In the end, they adopted a solution that had already been tried by Géry-Piéret: they would give the Spanish heads to *Paris-Journal*. The only people who would be told would be the director, Chichet, and André Salmon, who worked for the paper. The publicity the newspaper would get should be worth, in exchange, a promise of confidentiality.

Apollinaire spent the rest of the night on the couch in the living room. In the morning, he took the suitcase and left to carry out the plan. According to Albert Gleizes, Picasso accompanied him. The two men first went to the Gare de l'Est, taking the outer boulevards, and put the suitcase into safekeeping there, while waiting for the newspaper to open.

The next day, through the intermediary of the paper, the statuettes were restored to the Louvre. A close escape!

Unfortunately, it wasn't. On the morning of 7 September, at the hour when the milkman usually did his rounds, the bell rang at Apollinaire's home.

But it wasn't the milkman. It was the police. They had come with a search warrant. Apollinaire was being arrested.

The poet was taken off to the Palais de Justice on the Quai des Orfèvres, and accused of sheltering criminals and of complicity in a theft. From there he was led directly to the Prison de la Santé. 'It seemed to me that, from that moment on, I was somewhere in another universe and I was going to be destroyed.' He had no rights. The clerk's office gave him a shirt, a towel, sheets and a cover. He was led down dim corridors to the eleventh division, the fifteenth cell. The door closed behind him. The bolts were drawn.

> Before entering my cell
> I had to strip
> And what sinister voice welled up
> To lament: 'Guillaume, what has become of you?'

He couldn't comprehend what was happening, he was groggy. On one of the posts supporting his narrow cot, a predecessor in this dark room had written: 'Dédé de Ménilmontant, for murder'.

He waited.

> How slowly the hours pass
> Like a funeral.

On the Boulevard de Clichy, Picasso lay low, quiet as a mouse. A day went by. He began to hope. But the next morning, at dawn, the doorbell rang. It was the court police. The man was dressed in civilian clothes, which didn't prevent him from showing his press card and requesting that Pablo Picasso accompany him to the Palais de Justice.

In the bedroom, the painter took off his pyjamas. 'Picasso, trembling, dressed hastily; he had to be helped; he was frightened out of his wits.'[3]

This was understandable. The painter was Spanish, and suspected by the French police of having anarchist leanings. He risked arrest, or even expulsion from the country.

Fernande watched him walk down the boulevard with his guard. They got into the bus that ran from Pigalle to the Halle-aux-Vins. Picasso swore that he had nothing to do with this affair, that he didn't even know what it was all about. But there was nothing the officer could do. The affair wasn't within his jurisdiction.

The men arrived at the judge's chambers. Picasso, who had been summoned as a witness, repeated that he didn't know what the whole thing was about. This did not impress the judge. The law had its sources.

'What sources?'

'There's a certain poet who claims to be a friend of yours.'

'I don't know any poet.'

He was stuttering. The judge read off the statement of the poet in question: he had mentioned the name of Picasso to Géry-Piéret, who was now known to be the thief of the art works; the aforementioned Géry-Piéret then went to see the painter and sold him two Iberic heads.

'I don't know what you're talking about,' repeated Picasso uncertainly.

'He also says that you didn't know where these two art works came from...'

No answer from Picasso.

'We have a witness.'

The witness had been waiting for four hours in a cell of the Palais de Justice, clutching at the bars of his prison. Then he had been taken from his hole and led, handcuffed, to a room next to the judge's office.

The judge opened the door. The witness entered. His face was marked; he was pale, haggard, with red eyes and two days' growth of beard. He had lost his tie, and his removable collar was hanging by a thread. He sat down on the chair he was shown. Picasso looked at him, then looked away. He stared at the opposite wall.

'Do you know this man?' asked the judge.

'No,' declared Pablo Picasso.

Guillaume Apollinaire started on his chair.

'No,' repeated Picasso, stubborn as a lost child. 'I've never seen him before in my life.'

That was all he said.

But soon he began to stammer, lose confidence, and contradict his initial declarations, while Apollinaire, incredulous, couldn't articulate a single word.

Seated at his desk, the judge, dumbfounded, observed these children, frightened by terrors more real than a nightmare, moaning and groaning as if the sky had fallen in. He sent one home, and the other back to prison. The same day, Géry-Piéret, using the borrowed name of the Baron Ignace d'Ormesan, which Apollinaire had invented in L'Hérésiarque & Cie, wrote to the Department of Justice to clear the name of the accused.

Meanwhile, in Paris, action was being taken. On the left, Apollinaire's friends, led by André Salmon, René Dalize, André Tudesq and André Billy, launched a petition demanding the poet's liberation (Frantz Jourdain, president of the Salon d'Automne, refused to sign it). On the right, the racist press, spurred on by Léon Daudet and Urbain Gohier, joined the fray:

> The secretary of the Jewish, or Polish, pornographer – one of the Louvre thieves – is a Belgian. When the identities of the entire band are ascertained, we will surely discover nothing but foreigners and aliens among them.[4]

Behind the bars, the alien was in despair:

> In a pit like a bear
> Every morning I walk, the same refrain
> Turning turning turning always
> The sky is blue like a chain
> In a pit like a bear
> Every morning I walk, the same refrain.

Fortunately, the situation would soon be resolved. On 12 September, Guillaume Apollinaire was let out of jail. But the affair wasn't over. Through the intermediary of Gleizes, the poet met the public prosecutor, Granié. This latter did not reassure him: Apollinaire had protected an individual who had stolen from the state and he had hidden goods taken from a National Museum.

'What are the dangers?' asked Apollinaire.

'Criminal court.'

'What else?'

'A conviction.'

The poet was alarmed.

'The best would be to present the case in the Court of Assizes...'

'What?'

'You can't deny the crime,' argued the lawyer. 'In the criminal court, the judges simply apply the law; there's no room for discussion. At the Assizes, one has a chance to explain...'

Apollinaire didn't really feel like explaining himself in a Court of Assizes. 'And there's no other solution?'

'For the case to be withdrawn.'

'Is there any chance of that happening?'

'We'll soon see...'

There was a chance. And Apollinaire was lucky. In January 1912, he was cleared of all suspicion. But this incident, which marked him deeply, left traces. In his heart, the heart of a friend, even if he never spoke of it, how could the Mal-Aimé not suffer from Picasso's lack of loyalty? Albert Gleizes was certain that he had:

> Hadn't one of his dearest friends denied their connection in a confrontation, so losing his head that he declared he didn't know him? He spoke to me of the incident with bitterness and unconcealed emotion.[5]

It should be mentioned in passing that this bitterness did not displease Gleizes. As he himself wished to be recognized as the inventor of cubism, he hated Picasso.

In any case, the painter was for a time treated very coldly by the poet's friends. This disgrace – nothing very serious – was accompanied by a generalized fear which obsessed him for some time: he refused to take the bus line from Pigalle to the Halle-aux-Vins, the one which had transported him to the police station; in the street, he was constantly turning around to see if he was being followed; every time the doorbell rang on the Boulevard de Clichy, he became fearful.

Fifty years later, in *Paris-Presse*, Picasso confessed to a journalist who was questioning him on the affair of the theft of the *Mona Lisa* that his own attitude had left him with a sense of shame which he still felt today.[6] This is understandable. For Apollinaire was so careful to protect the painter from the public's ire that his name was never once mentioned in the press, nor in the works that his contemporaries wrote on the relations between the two men. Better yet: in his preface to the poetic works of Guillaume Apollinaire,[7] André Billy, a witness of the time and an indirect actor in this unfortunate affair, doesn't even mention Picasso's identity; he speaks simply of a painter, a certain Monsieur X...

The *Mona Lisa* was recovered in 1913. It had been stolen by an Italian who worked at the Louvre and wanted to restore the work to his country. It would seem that the wheel had come full circle.

For everyone except, perhaps, Apollinaire.

One year later the First World War broke out. The poet immediately joined the armed forces. His friends all felt that this desire to defend a country not his own had a ring of revenge to it. It was as if Apollinaire wanted to cover over the shameful handcuffs with the three colours of the flag; it was his way of wiping out the memory of the devastating smile of the *Mona Lisa*.

SEPARATIONS

The F.O. affair: there are no two ways about it. I'm already in love,
in my imagination. I shall be very disappointed if nothing comes of
it. More than disappointed.

Paul Léautaud

The affair of the theft of the Mona Lisa was a turning point. A new era was
dawning, difficult for some, fortunate for others, fertile in forms and
colours. It was a time of new directions and breakups. In the book of the
arts, the page of Montmartre trembles. 'I will go to the Lapin Agile to
remember my lost youth,' Blaise Cendrars would soon write.

Marie Laurencin broke off with Guillaume Apollinaire. When one lives
in bourgeois Auteuil, a stay in jail is not treated lightly. Fernande Olivier
claims that Marie didn't even write to her lover while he was in the Santé
prison. This latest dishonour was the final straw, after the poet's numerous
infidelities and a chronic lack of domestic harmony. Marie had already
refused to marry him because he was too difficult to get along with. And
if Picasso is to be believed, the two were a bit bored with each other in
bed – when one thinks of the ardours recounted by Mony Vibescu in Les
Onze Mille Verges . . .

Deeply hurt, Apollinaire left Auteuil to go and live with Robert and
Sonia Delaunay, where he stayed for a few months. He was soon able to
take revenge on the Tristouse Ballerinette, in no uncertain terms:

> I was completely unknown, she thought, and now he [Croniamantal]
> has made me more famous than any woman alive ... I was thought ugly
> in general, too thin, with a large mouth, bad teeth, an asymmetrical
> face, a crooked nose. And now I am beautiful, all the men tell me so.
> People made fun of my jerky, manly way of walking, my pointy elbows
> which stuck out when I moved, like chickens' feet. Now I am thought
> so gracious that other women imitate me. What miracles the love of a
> poet can bring about!'

During the war, the poet in question would exchange letters that were a little more amiable with his former muse. But she did not miss her chance to get back at him, if Philippe Soupault is to be believed. Soupault, who admired Apollinaire enormously, could not accept the young woman's cruel and sordid mockery of the man who had shared several years of her life. And Marie Laurencin added to this two sins which were unpardonable in the eyes of the author of Le Nègre: she was pretentious and pleased with herself to a degree that nothing in her work could justify, and worse, she was very friendly with Marcel Jouhandeau.

Apollinaire was thus going through an extremely difficult period, both because his muse had left him and because he was plagued by doubts and uncertainties of all kinds: he hadn't yet managed to get the court case withdrawn, the attacks of the right-wing press had terrified him, and he feared not being granted his naturalization papers and so was always afraid that he might be ordered to leave the country.

To help him, his friends André Salmon, René Dalize, André Tudesq, André Billy and Serge Jastrebzoff put their funds together and took over a paper, Les Soirées de Paris, appointing him as director. In the space of a single issue, the number of subscribers went from forty to ... just one.[2] But requests for free press copies arrived from all over the world, which delighted Apollinaire. Once a month, in the company of Serge Jastrebzoff, he made the rounds of all the bookstores of Paris in a taxi, leaving them copies of the review.

Serge Jastrebzoff, better known by the name of Serge Férat, which he used as a painter, was the half-brother of the Baroness d'OEttingen. She was Russian, rich, very cultured, a socialite, and lived in an elegant home in the Faubourg Saint Germain. She had a polite interest in everything: particularly painting, literature and Apollinaire, whose mistress she was for a short time.

Meanwhile, on the Boulevard de Clichy, all was also not for the best in the best of all possible worlds, conjugally speaking. There too, the Mona Lisa episode had had repercussions. Was it because, as some have said, Fernande was very harsh on Apollinaire? Or because she expressed a certain irony about the situation, which would be clear in her later accounts of it and which was not appreciated by Picasso? Or because she was not entirely faithful? Or because their ever more fashionable social life was going to her head? Whatever the case, the couple was having problems.

The painter's irritability, during this period when he was working in tandem with Braque, has often been noted. Another factor mentioned as a possible source of discord is the beautiful Fernande's lack of understanding of the body of work which Picasso was steadily developing. Whatever the reasons, there were stormy scenes. She reproached him for paying too much attention to his little aches and pains; he accused her of buying too many clothes and too much perfume. She said he was 'as stupid as can be', that he didn't know how to do anything but paint, that he was a child genius, and nothing more. He criticized her constant complaining.

The scenes grew more frequent and more serious. One day, Fernande Olivier left. She went off for a few days, then returned. But the worm was in the fruit. It was going to grow, all by itself, until 1912. Years later, Picasso would admit that the first time that he and his Montmartre muse had separated, it was not just over arguments about eau de Cologne or overspending on clothes; it was because of Raymonde, the little girl who had been adopted and then returned.

The group of friends, for the moment, acted as if nothing was happening. They had abandoned the Lapin Agile for the Grelot, on the Place Blanche, or the Hermitage, on the Boulevard de Rochechouart: as ever, everyone followed Picasso. The painters found themselves together in a corner, regarded suspiciously by the habitués who drank their mugs of beer standing at the counter. Everyone had his place, and no one was supposed to move from it. When the young girls in the bar let themselves be seduced by the artists' banter, changing their allegiance just for an evening, fights could break out: Picasso was even seen knocking down one individual who had pushed him.

The regulars – Max Jacob, Apollinaire, Braque – counted points, assisted by newcomers, like Férat and his baroness sister, Metzinger, Marcoussis, the Italian futurists ... The latter could be spotted quickly: they liked to set themselves apart by all means available. They wore socks which matched their ties, but in different colours; they were painters and poets. Their leader, Filippo Tommaso Marinetti, had resolved the problem of the alexandrine and free verse, as an extract from his poem 'The Soldiers' Train' demonstrates:

tlactlac ii ii guuiii
trrrrrtrrrrr
tatatatôo-tatatatatôo
(WHEELS)
urrrrr
cuhrrr
gurrrrrrr
(LOCOMOTIVE)
fuufufufuufufu
fafafafafa
zazazazazaza
tzatzatza. tza[3]

Beyond the provocation caused by their attire and their declarations, and various other red flags waved in the face of the sensible climate of the time, the futurists must also be given credit for the role they played in the revolts to come: they lit the fuse, before Dada and the surrealists, for future explosions. But they clearly did it rather clumsily, especially when they boasted about being the precursors of tomorrow's art. They wanted at all costs to conform to the terms of the *Futurist Manifesto*, signed by Marinetti and published by *Le Figaro* on 20 February 1909:

> Article 4: We declare that the splendour of the world has become enriched with a new beauty: the beauty of speed. A racing car, its trunk overflowing with big tubes like snakes with explosive breath … a roaring automobile, which seems to be fuelled by shotgun ammunition, is more beautiful than the Winged Victory.
> Article 9: We want to glorify war – the only hygiene in the world, militarism, patriotism, the destructive gestures of the anarchists, great Ideas which kill, and scorn for women.
> Article 10: We want to demolish museums, libraries, to combat moralism, feminism and all opportunistic and utilitarian cowardice.

This gave rise to an exhibition at the Bernheim-Jeune gallery, and to a scathing article in the *Nouvelle Revue française*, in which Jacques Copeau spoke of 'a declamatory prose, incoherent and farcical'.[4] It also sowed the seeds for future political support of the Italian Duce, and reaped a poisoned arrow from Apollinaire:

> The futurists are young painters to whom one might accord one's confidence if the pretentiousness of their declarations and the insolence of their manifestos didn't wipe out any indulgence one might be tempted to have for them.[5]

And finally, they succeeded in definitively destabilizing the Picasso couple. Fernande ran off with Umbaldo Oppi, a futurist painter: when she came back down to earth, she understood that the present was now a thing of the past, for this time Picasso had gone off with somebody else, too.

She was Eva Gouel, and they were in Céret. Eva was Marcoussis' fiancée. They had spent a lot of time together at the Hermitage as a foursome; then it was just her and Picasso. Giving as a reason the small size of his studio on the Boulevard de Clichy, the painter rented another one in his old home, the Bateau Lavoir. Not the Trapper's House, but a room on the floor beneath it. This, most likely, was where he took on the role of clandestine lover, a role which he would play throughout the winter of 1911 and the spring of the following year.

It was not just a passing flirtation, and Marcoussis suffered. His friends urged him to forget, but it wasn't easy. They encouraged him to be magnanimous, and he tried. When anger got the better of him, they advised him to follow in Christ's footsteps.

'What did he do, Christ?'

'He forgave the adulterous wife.'

'Easy for him to do, it wasn't his wife who was adulterous!'

Picasso was madly in love with this young woman who was barely thirty, elegant, pretty, good-natured and even-tempered. He painted her and wrote, under the painting, 'My Pretty One'. To escape from Fernande, he went off with Eva to the Pyrenees, then fearing unexpected visits, left for Sorgues, where Braque joined him. Thus an eight-year passion ended in mediocrity. With Fernande gone from his life, he finally left the protective shadow of the Bateau Lavoir behind. She had been its queen, its only queen.

She was never to see Picasso again. After their breakup, she worked for Poiret, then for an antiques dealer, and finally in an art gallery. She recited poems at the Lapin Agile, became a cashier in a butcher's shop ... In the thirties, she was living in poverty, giving pronunciation lessons to the Americans who had begun flocking to Montparnasse. Max Jacob went to see Picasso and ask if he would help her. He didn't lift a finger. So she decided to publish her memoirs. She went to see a publisher, the Mercure de France. She was taken up to a dark office where she found a man with a pince-nez. He wore two jackets to protect him from the cold: the first was threadbare, stained, unravelled, the second was just dirty. It was shorter than the first, but in better shape, which must have been the reason its owner had chosen to wear it over its fellow.

Large sheets of newspaper were spread all over the floor. The headlines of the day were covered by crusts of bread drying at a safe remove from the piles of manuscripts that weighed down the shelves.

The man raised his glasses, greeted the visitor and introduced himself. His name was Paul Léautaud. He liked animals: in particular, cats. When he wasn't working at the Mercure, he took care of his little friends. He found them good homes or, more immediately, something to eat. The crusts were for them. If the young lady would like to take a seat...

Fernande Olivier had heard about Paul Léautaud shortly after her breakup with Picasso, perhaps through an anecdote told by Apollinaire. Léautaud was having dinner, accompanied by champagne, with a woman. As he raised his glass to his lips, his hostess stopped him, saying, 'Aren't you going to propose a toast?'

'Most certainly,' he said.

As he pronounced not a word, the woman finally cried, 'If you can't find anything better, we can drink to the health of beasts, at least!'

'Of course.' Léautaud clinked glasses with her, smiling, and murmured, 'To your health, my dear lady ...'

Fernande Olivier told her tale of woe to the author of *Petit Ami*. He was touched by her distress, in his own way, which never resembled anyone else's:

> Once Madame F.O. had left, I remarked to Madame de Graziansky (the subscriptions clerk) that if she's as poor as she claims, she is after all still a pretty woman and she can always take a lover.[6]

When he saw her again, he observed her carefully, and noted that she had 'a marvellous behind'. But also, alas, the 'pinkish skin of blondes'. Then he revised his opinion: she must be a redhead. He finally asked her, and discovered she had originally had reddish-brown hair. One day, he would find her beautiful, the next day rather unappealing: 'She has pink marks on her chest, above her cleavage.'

He gathered flowers for her in his garden, and brought them to her on the rue de la Grande-Chaumière, where she lived. Across from her was the Academy of Painting. Léautaud was a little jealous, thinking that if the young woman wanted someone to make love with, she wouldn't have far to look. He was angry with himself for being so old – sixty – and with her for being so young – forty, he thought. In fact, she was forty-six.

Léautaud was in love. All the more so when he understood she still had her 'monthlies', rather less when she told him about her artist's life, her bohemian existence, the Lapin Agile ... 'I much prefer a good bourgeois whore.'

But when she came to his house, usually in the daytime, he desired her. But he was shy. He didn't have the nerve. She was sitting on a deckchair in the garden. He discovered that her legs were 'enormous', that she had a roll of flesh around her waist, arms as wide as thighs, breasts which fell down to her stomach. It didn't matter: 'I was terribly aroused.' He had bought a bottle of champagne, which he ended up drinking alone after she had left.

Soon, she was telling him secrets. Marie Laurencin had never known sensual pleasure; Apollinaire could only make love if he was entirely clothed; Max Jacob preferred municipal sergeants and Republican Guards with moustaches; on the rue Ravignan, there was a street sweeper who had been in love with her and left coal in front of the Trapper's House without ever asking to be paid; she and Picasso got along very well on a 'sensual' level ...

She was still very attached to him, worrying when she learned he was ill, defending him constantly on any subject. When she talked about him, Léautaud could see emotion, maybe even regret, in her face.

One day, though, she burst out with a complaint: the problem with Picasso was that she was terribly bored when she was with him. He never talked, he was always so caught up in his work ... But then she would forget. She protested when Léautaud told her about the scene which Serge Férat had related to him, in confidence, about the dark day when the painter and Apollinaire had confronted each other in the trial judge's chambers and Picasso had claimed not to know him. Fernande protested, claiming this was just scandalous gossip, implying that jealousy was involved: Picasso having stolen Férat's mistress, this was his way of getting revenge.

At Georges Charenson's request, Léautaud wrote a preface for Fernande Olivier's memoirs (the Mercure published only a few excerpts from it, Valette having judged that the work would not sell). When Picasso learned that the book was about to be printed, he tried to intervene with the publishers, Stock, to stop its sale and distribution, proposing to pay all costs connected with the publication. He managed only to get its publication delayed, and the book finally came out in 1933.

Nearly twenty years later, once again finding herself in dire straits, Fernande Olivier wrote another book. When he heard about it from Braque's wife, Picasso sent his former lover a considerable sum of money – it isn't clear whether this was to stop its publication, or whether he was making a generous, disinterested gesture, as he would later do for Hans Hartung, helping him to flee to Spain during the Occupation.

For thirty years, the book remained in Fernande Olivier's drawer, unpublished.

CUBISM

Nature for us men is more in depth
than in surface.

Paul *Cézanne*

Marie Laurencin had left, as had Fernande. Max Jacob, after having savoured the charms of Cécile, and perhaps one other woman, almost fell in love with one of his cousins. In 1912, in Quimper, on Assumption Day, he was watching a procession pass by when he heard his name being called. He turned around to find one of his male cousins, with two female cousins, one of whom was named Eva. Max headed off with all these relations towards the bishopric. In the garden, they saw a mulberry tree. The cousins challenged Max to climb up the trunk. He performed this exploit, and Eva was seduced: an athletic poet!

This was apparently sufficient inducement for her to offer him a kiss, which Max was glad to accept. He was more than a little proud to have 'put Mademoiselle Eva in a good humour'.[1] But of the two exploits, he was in fact prouder of climbing the mulberry tree. And he soon abandoned his passing fancy for young ladies, and returned to his habitual tastes in lovers.

He was still a presence in Picasso's group of friends, but was beginning to lose some ground, for several reasons. He was inhaling too much ether. Picasso, who had taken no drugs since the death of Wiegels, disapproved of his friend's dependence on them. By now, he was taking almost anything. And, since this could sometimes spoil otherwise convivial evenings, Max Jacob was constantly inventing justifications for his need. He would pretend to be suffering from toothache, saying that the only way to soften the pain was with ether. His parents, when he visited them, were astonished to see the treatment for these dental pains plunging their son into near-delirium. They made him go to a dentist of their own choosing. Max Jacob, who hated dentists and in any case had no problems with his teeth, tried for a while to put a stop to his pharmaceutical habit. Perhaps he did so while he was in his native Brittany, but not in Montmartre.

This was his first offence. The second arose from his oversensitivity, which often led him to transform minor incidents into major battles. This occurred not only with Picasso but also with Apollinaire. The latter could sometimes be very cold to him. They were rivals for the painter's esteem, and Max complained that the poet only ever thought about joking and bantering with him, without really paying much attention to his literary production. And, while Picasso was beginning to make a good living, and Apollinaire was becoming better known (his *L'Hérésiarque & Cie* had won three votes in the contest for the Prix Goncourt, France's most prestigious literary award), Max seemed to remain confined to a smaller canvas. This situation only served to fuel his natural paranoia. In letters which are as childish as some of the Douanier Rousseau's remarks could be, Max accused Apollinaire of avoiding him, of coming to Montmartre without ever stopping by to say hello, of never inviting him to his dinners, of not showing up for various dates ... and all of this while swearing eternal and unfailing friendship.

This was a second reason. And finally, the poet himself could not forgive Picasso for a sin which to him was unpardonable: he had become rich. Ever since Vollard had started to buy his paintings, he had begun to forget his old friends and their unique complicity, born of shared suffering. It made Max want to weep. Unfortunately, he himself began to pull dangerously on the taut rope connecting the two men; shortly after the banquet for Rousseau at the Bateau Lavoir, he sold some Picasso drawings. He justified his gesture by invoking his (very real) poverty, which was no longer a problem for the others. Picasso hated to hear his former comrade in misfortune talk about, and thus remind him of, their period of dire poverty and the solidarity which had united them then.

Max's path was leading him away from his friends.

In 1911, he published, at his own expense, *La Côte*, 'a collection of ancient Celtic chants, never before published'. This work, as he would confess some years later to Tristan Tzara,[2] was designed to make fun of Paul Fort, Francis Jammes, and more generally, of popular literature, which he judged 'grotesque'. (This would seem to confirm the opinion of André Salmon, who thought that Max Jacob pretended to like this type of literature just to please Apollinaire.) He sold the book himself to make money. This way of making a living seemed to him almost like 'begging in disguise'. Picasso may have had the same thought.

When the others moved to larger and grander apartments, he remained in the poor neighbourhoods, on the rue Ravignan, the rue du Chevalier-de-la-Barre or the rue Gabrielle. Of course, he was sometimes invited to Céret by Picasso, but he couldn't afford the trip. The painter had to write to Kahnweiler to ask him to give his poet friend the few notes needed for the train fare, as well as some pocket money.

Fortunately, when Max Jacob was in the Pyrenees, harmony reigned. When in Montmartre, he lent Fernande a comforting shoulder to cry on, and in the mountains he became friendly with Eva. He liked her vivacity, her care in keeping an orderly house for Picasso, and her devotion to the master himself. The painter himself soon recovered his former first place in the poet's affections.

They went to Spain to attend a corrida. 'Spain is a square country, all angles,'[3] noted Max Jacob, thus expressing a rather silly idea that would soon be developed by Gertrude Stein, who was to consider Spain as the country of cubism.

In Céret, the poet drew geometrical landscapes; he didn't take long walks in the countryside, and nor did the others. They preferred the cafés (filled with etheromaniacs and 'pederasts', as Max wrote to Apollinaire) to the thyme and lavender of the mountains. Or simply staying at home, where they worked steadily. Max painted and wrote verse; Picasso, following Braque's example, was making paper collages.

It wasn't the first time that the two painters had worked together in Céret. During a previous stay, they had already found themselves together in an isolated house in the heart of the mountains. They had an old complicity, dating back to 1908, the year following the Salon des Indépendants where Braque had exposed his first landscapes of l'Estaque. Although different and carried out separately, their experiments with forms and volumes would inevitably lead them towards each other.

For Picasso, everything began with Negro and Iberic art. This double influence was to be found in his legendary painting, Les Demoiselles d'Avignon, which the painter kept covered or rolled up in his studio. Few visitors had the privilege of viewing the work. Nonetheless it was widely admired, even if it was considered shocking, and its reputation would only increase over the years.

For Braque, everything began with Cézanne. In his time, the master of Aix had been scorned and jeered, just like the Fauves and cubists, Berlioz and James Joyce – this is the fate of the avant-garde. Rejected by the official salons, laughed at by an ignorant public, Cézanne, who admired Delacroix and was praised by Gauguin, refused to exhibit his works for over twenty years. Camille Mauclair, an eminent commentator on the arts, congratulated him on this refusal: his painting, in the eyes of the critic, was 'the most memorable artistic joke of the last fifteen years'.

Ten years before his death, thanks to Vollard, Cézanne was finally recognized. Not only did he receive recognition at last for his early painting, born of his work with Pissarro and the impressionists of Auvers-sur-Oise, but he was also hailed for his experimentation with forms, volumes, the order of planes, fragmentation, and deformations. 'He raised the still life to the rank of an object which is still on the outside but full of

He wanted to discover the 'geological foundations' of the Sainte Victoire mountain, and tried hard to do so while respecting the human perception of space. He felt that nature was to be treated 'in terms of the sphere, the cylinder and the cone'. One can easily see why Apollinaire had decreed that Cézanne's final works were cubist in essence, and especially why Picasso was interested in him.

But Braque was even more interested. After Cézanne's death, accompanied by Othon Friesz, he went down to l'Estaque, near Marseille, and painted several works – structured, simplified and monochromatic – which he presented at the Salon des Indépendants in 1907. The following year, the Salon d'Automne accepted only two of his paintings, out of eight that he had presented. Braque refused to submit to this humiliation. Kahnweiler exhibited his work instead in his gallery on the rue Vignon, and asked Apollinaire to write a preface for the catalogue. The *Maisons à l'Estaque* was among the canvases shown. It was this painting to which the officials of the Salon d'Automne had objected, with its ochre-coloured cubes, its houses without doors or windows and its superimposed shapes. It was no longer an objective representation of nature, but an interpretation of it, reinvented outside the traditional canons, a simplification, an ordering and a deformation of volumes corresponding to an approach that was already known: that of Picasso. For Braque, this technique was almost becoming a vocation. If one is to believe Jean Paulhan, when he came to Paris, the painter from Le Havre went to the Louvre to copy works by Raphael. To begin with, they resembled the original. But the longer he painted, the more he deformed ...

Kahnweiler also exhibited Braque's *Grand Nu* (1908), which represented a kind of response to the violence of Picasso's *Demoiselles* and *Trois Femmes*, whose savagery and primitivism he had criticized as excessive. The *Grand Nu*, a close relative of Matisse's *Nu debout* (1907), was a work inspired by Cézanne, angular, devoid of the play of light and shadow, but less primitive and more 'accessible' than the Spaniard's fiery work. Braque's first large painting was an important landmark in the development of the new cubist movement.

Matisse didn't like it: he was one of the members of the jury of the Salon d'Automne which rejected Braque's work. He made fun of this painting made up of 'cubes', took no interest in it. After him, Louis Vauxcelles, in the issue of *Gil Blas* dated 14 November 1908, used the word 'cubes' again. At roughly the same time or soon after, the critic Charles Morice also used the word. The name of this movement (if it can be considered a movement) was thus probably invented by Matisse. Of course, he later denied it. But Apollinaire and Kahnweiler confirm that it first came from him. And the cubes in question were those in Braque's works, not Picasso's. In any case, Matisse would later affirm that the first cubist painting he had seen was a work by Braque that Picasso had shown him in his studio. A studio where he would soon be spending less and less time, angry with the Spanish painter for having won over Derain and Braque. And probably a little ashamed of himself for having rejected the latter at the Salon d'Automne...

Why was such a fuss made about the works of the two painters? For the simple reason that they were challenging tradition. Perspective no longer existed in their work, nor did the play of light and shadow, which they felt was a trick used to give a sense of depth, and nothing more. They moved away from a principle which dated back to the Renaissance, according to which the observer of a work looks at it from a single point of view. When they observed a landscape, they closed first their right eye, then their left, and realized they didn't see the same thing. Similarly, the object changed when the point of view changed. For them, these differences were essential, and they would take them into account in their work.

John Berger believes that cubism had a double origin: in Cézanne, because of the importance he gave to the relativity of the angle of vision, and in Courbet, who brought to classical pictorial tradition a materiality other than that of light and shadow.

> Before Cézanne, a painting was, to a certain degree, seen as though
> through a window. Courbet had tried to open the window to get
> outside. Cézanne simply broke the glass. The room became a part of
> the landscape, and the observer a part of the view.[5]

For one, dialectic. For the other, materialism. For both, if their ideas are combined – dialectical materialism. Cubism – no one has ever denied it – was a revolution.

Impressionism, in its time, had scandalized a public opinion that was not used to painters showing an interpreted reality, even if it was interpreted only through the prism of optical laws. The cubists went even further: they made free with light and shadow. Braque said, 'I was told: it's enough to put in shadows. No, it's not; what counts above all is the idea one has in mind.'[6]

They opposed an art of conception to an art of imitation. They didn't care about the respect for visual sensations advocated by the impressionists. What they wanted was to show the object in its essence – as it is conceived, not as it is seen. In this, they were close to Gauguin, who considered that impressionism had a tool, the eye, which the mind did not approach. Picasso said, 'When the cubist painter thought, "I'm going to paint a fruit bowl," he set to work, knowing that a fruit bowl in art and a fruit bowl in life had nothing in common.'[7]

The use of geometrical figures made it possible to present all the facets of an object, beyond its immediate appearance. There was no question of 'painting a likeness'. The artist had to go further. Colour itself did not have to adapt to passing phenomena like light, angle, and time, all elements which implied the intervention of the outside world; its role was to register the permanent essence of the object, inscribed in time. As Braque said, 'I don't need the sun any more, I carry my light with me.'

The impressionists drew their inspiration from their surroundings: for most of them, that meant the area around Paris, the banks of the river, moist landscapes with fluctuating light. The cubists lived in the city, and when they left it, it was to go to the villages of the south, where the countryside had sharper forms than the landscapes of the Seine or Auvers-sur-Oise. They were not the first to see the south in these terms. Baudelaire wrote, 'The South is brutal and positive' – this in opposition to the north, 'suffering and anxious'. He consoled himself 'with imagination'.[8] And Derain wrote to Vlaminck from Collioure, 'The light screams everywhere, in an enormous cry of victory. Not at all like the Northern mists, which have such compassion for one's sufferings.'[9] For the moderns, the idea of the South clearly carried a vital, if harsh significance.

The cubists integrated into their works elements of daily life which, they felt, played a role in the artistic perception of their fellow human beings: trees, houses, musical instruments, shop signs, advertising posters, newspapers, everyday objects. Collage made it possible to mix materials, textures, and colours, to assemble them in surprising juxtapositions which shed a new light on the most familiar objects – for example, Picasso's guitars and violins, notably *Le Violon* (1912), composed of papers pasted around a cardboard box.

The cubists used simple materials, sometimes even rough or vulgar ones, which were in opposition to a more precious vision of art. With them, there were no jewels, no fancy trimmings, but sand, paper, wood. They were presiding over the dawn of a century in which science would be increasingly important. It was the era of radioactivity, of Bakelite, of neon, of the emerging cinema and of Einstein's theory of relativity. The cubists were resolutely modern: they turned their back on romanticism.

The Fauves, for their part, had gone quite a long way in their experiments with colour. Coupling it with visible reality, they had made it conform to the vision imposed on it by their ideas. As Fernand Léger, who came to cubism quite late, would say, it was now necessary to ponder the question of composition and that of space. And Picasso observed, 'We were seeking an architectonic basis in composition, an austerity which would restore order.'

LEADERS OF THE PACK

> What is the modern conception of pure art? Creating a suggestive magic containing both the subject and the object, the world around the artist, and the artist himself.
>
> *Baudelaire*

After the first period, often described as pre-cubist or Cézannian and characterized by the deformation of bodies and objects, Braque and Picasso began to take a new direction, that of analytical cubism. They went straight to the heart of the matter: rather than using the play of shadow and light, a manipulation based on an illusion, they tried to express the third dimension – depth and volume – of the painted object by representing it from every angle, using superimposed planes. So that these objects could be easily identifiable, they chose subjects from ordinary daily life. This stage was characterized by monochromatic tones, greys and ochres, and by a certain austerity.

The two painters based their experiments on work with construction: they designed sculptures in paper, iron and cardboard. In this they were reacting very directly to Baudelaire, who saw in sculpture, other than that of the 'primitive period', an art of the second order, 'complementary'. It was as if they were taking the poet's viewpoint and rebutting it, showing the positive aspect of a negative point of view. What did Baudelaire find to criticize in sculpture? The fact that it did not afford a single point of view, that it obliged the observer to walk around it if he wanted to grasp its treasures (if it had any), that it showed 'too many faces at once'.[1]

But the things that were weaknesses to Baudelaire constituted so many treasures in the eyes of Braque and Picasso. So they started with their 'light' constructions, then tried to translate the results onto the canvas. They went from sculpture to painting, and from painting to sculpture, in a back-and-forth movement which would give birth, for instance, to the *Tête de Fernande* (1909), sculpted by Picasso from portraits of Fernande painted at Horta de Ebro, or around 1912, to the series of guitars, founded on a model in three-dimensional cardboard.

But the problem with these representations, which claim to be 'total art', is that the reference points have disappeared. The *Portrait de Daniel-Henry Kahnweiler* (1910), a masterpiece of analytical cubism, was done in two stages, after many hours of posing by the model. Its first manner didn't satisfy Picasso, because the painting was incomprehensible. So he added what he called 'attributes', signs, notations which helped the eye find its way: a shadow behind an ear, the bridge of the nose, a fragment of a tie, the hint of a hairstyle, crossed hands...

It was precisely in order to restore clarity to their works that the two painters would then inaugurate a new stage in their experimentation, arriving at synthetic cubism. This time, it was a matter of introducing into the canvas a detail, a sign, which made it possible to identify the object, thus giving back to the observer the hints that had previously been taken away. Examples are the nail that Braque painted in *trompe l'œil* in *Broc et cruche* (1910), or the printed letters, the glued papers and fragments of materials which would soon appear in the canvases of Gris and Picasso, shortly before the latter started to use Ripolin. Their experimentation also consisted in rendering the relief and volume of the objects chosen as models (such as guitars) in their painting, often using collages of papers on the canvas to achieve this effect.

The invention of cubism by Braque and Picasso was thus a joint enterprise, founded on similar preoccupations and on experimentation carried out in tandem. This exceptional complementarity has no parallel in the history of art.

One might wonder who did what? This question, though somewhat futile, is nonetheless worth asking, to ensure that credit is justly apportioned to all, and to achieve for Braque the recognition that Picasso's increasing fame would deny him.

The traces of Cézanne in the cubist style reflected Braque's influence, more deeply than that of Picasso. But the primitivism came from Picasso: if Picasso 'Cézanned' his primitivism, it was in total harmony with Braque.

The first of the two bodies of work actually to be labelled as 'cubist' was Braque's − but the work that was said to have opened the path towards cubism was Picasso's. The first cubist painting exhibited in an official Salon, the Salon des Indépendants of 1908, was Braque's. Fernande Olivier claimed that this work was inspired by a painting by Picasso (*Les Trois Femmes*, 1908) and that the Spaniard was furious with his friend. But Apollinaire never mentioned this, and Max Jacob affirmed the opposite: that Picasso, who never exhibited on official occasions (he was wary of the stupidity of the reviews and the controversies they fomented), encouraged Braque to go ahead.

In 1912, Braque entered a hardware store and bought a roll of wallpaper in imitation wood.[2] He stuck it on a canvas (*Compotier et verre*, 1912), thus inventing the principle of collage. Picasso would come to it in turn. It was he who would execute the first collage to use a piece of waxed canvas (*Nature morte à la chaise cannée*, 1912).

In 1911, in Céret, Braque had used *trompe l'œil* in *Le Portugais*, employing stencilled letters and figures to represent a musician seen through the window of a café. A year later, in *Le Violon*, Picasso inserted a musical score on which two words were written: 'Pretty Eva', in homage to his new lover. Before that, he had also painted on oval canvases, taking an idea from Braque.

In 1912, Braque employed ash and sand mixed in oil – Picasso would do so too, a few months later. In the autumn of 1912, Picasso executed a sculpture in cardboard, *La Guitare*, inspired by the cubist constructions in paper elaborated by Braque at the end of the previous year.

The verdict, then? One could almost agree with Pierre Cabanne when he described Picasso's art as a 'science of legitimate larceny'[3] – a judgement from which Picasso did not demur.

Nino Frank expressed a similar view in much harsher terms:

> Picasso is certainly one of the heroes of our times and its most admirable artist, having always indulged his sacred selfishness which lets him take advantage of everything and everyone, pilfering whatever he wants from any pocket, exploiting his friendships and his loves, and throwing everything and anything into his work. Some have even claimed that he is the 'pimp' of the era, and after all there is a bit of truth to it.[4]

Or one could heed Jean Cocteau's analysis – Cocteau who, during the war, managed to insinuate himself so thoroughly into the venerated Picasso's good graces that the painter let him accompany him to all the studios in Montparnasse. They were in fact welcomed with some reluctance; as soon as the artists learned that Picasso was coming, they were quick to hide their works before opening the door.

> He's going to take my manner of painting trees, one would say, and another would remark, He's going to take the siphon that I put in the painting. Everyone attached great importance to the slightest detail, and if his fellow artists feared Picasso's visit, it was because they knew that his eye would take in everything, swallow it, digest it, and reproduce it in his own work with a richness of which they were themselves incapable.[5]

And then there are Picasso's own words. Long after the cubist period, he explained that during all those years, he saw Braque every day (to the dismay of Max Jacob and Gertrude Stein, both jealous of this artistic bond that they could not share) – first in Montmartre, then in Céret, in Sorgues, and in Montparnasse. They judged and criticized each other's work: Braque spoke of a complicity comparable to that of two mountain climbers, attached together by a rope, blazing a trail up a mountain. True, one was more inspired by landscapes and still lifes while the other moved easily from objects to portraits. But they wanted to elaborate a collective, anonymous art, and their works almost belonged to both of them. This was true to such an extent that their paintings dating from this analytical period can scarcely be distinguished from each other. Most were not signed or, if they were, only at a later date. Kahnweiler, on this subject, sometimes confirms, sometimes contradicts the supposed authorship. He notes that between 1908 and 1914, the two painters signed on the back of their paintings, a practice in which he saw a desire, common to other artists, not to disturb the geometry of the canvas, while still indicating its origin.[6] But elsewhere,[7] he joins Picasso in recognizing, in both artists' attitudes, the desire for an 'impersonal execution'.

They did not intend to share this desire, which was clearly important to them both, with anyone else. They claimed it for themselves alone. Only Derain (vaguely) and Gris (especially) found favour in their eyes. But not Léger, who considered himself one of the pillars of cubism, a status which Kahnweiler too readily granted him.

Derain had been one of the first painters to take an interest in Negro art. He was also a great admirer of Cézanne. After a stay in l'Estaque, he had shown that, independently of colour, form and composition were extremely important in the representation of nature. His *Baigneuses*, exhibited at the Salon des Indépendants in 1907, affirmed the geometrization of lines, which probably inspired Picasso to eliminate the curved forms from the first version of the *Demoiselles d'Avignon*. Derain, an essential player in the birth of cubism, later adopted a low profile, letting the two pioneers of collage take the limelight.

Gris, more intellectual, more 'scientific' than Braque and Picasso, carried out his own experiments with collage and *trompe l'œil* at the same time as the other two. He liked to say, 'Cézanne starts with a bottle and ends up with a cylinder; me, I start with a cylinder and end up with a bottle.' At the Salon des Indépendants of 1912, he exhibited his *Hommage à Picasso* (1912), in deference to the man he considered to be the leader of the cubists. When war was declared, as the two founding fathers were no longer working together, he himself became the standard-bearer of orthodox cubism.

The war separated Braque and Picasso, as it separated many others. Years later, Picasso confided to Kahnweiler that the last time he had seen Braque and Derain was 2 August 1914, the day he took them to the station at Avignon. Of course, this was just an image, but it was significant. Afterwards, nothing would ever be the same again.

A second lieutenant at the front, Braque was wounded at Neuville-Saint-Vaast, and had to be trepanned. Picasso could never boast of anything but a rank jovially conferred on him by Apollinaire, and referred to again, more mockingly, by Derain: the general of cubism.

Braque and Picasso did see each other again, but only from time to time: the former mountain climbers were no longer symbiotically roped together. The pair were a little like the exploded forms that they had invented together and which, in their disarticulation, disruption, and splitting apart, so well anticipated the scenario of a war that would shatter the world.

With the passing years, Braque showed a bit of reserve towards his old companion. This distance enraged Picasso, who couldn't understand the reasons for his coldness. Unlike Max Jacob, Braque knew how to protect himself. He refused to be manipulated by the small but often hurtful manoeuvres that Picasso sometimes used on those close to him.

Picasso claimed that no one had cared for him as much as Braque, that he was a kind of Madame Picasso. His friend was ready to join in this game, but on one condition: that he would give as good as he got. He didn't mind Picasso's power plays, but only accepted them if he could respond in kind. In the fifties, he demonstrated his skill at handling Picasso, a subtle talent observed and appreciated on at least one occasion by Françoise Gilot.

Picasso had invited himself over to his old friend's home. Braque lived then near the Parc Montsouris, in an extraordinary house built by the architect Auguste Perret. Braque was rather cool, not going out of his way to be courteous to Françoise Gilot. Picasso was offended, all the more so as his friend hadn't even asked them to stay for lunch. When he came home to the Quai des Grands-Augustins, he removed from the wall of his studio a painting by Braque that had been there for a long time.

A few weeks later, he decided to stop by again with his companion. He meant to use the visit as a test of Braque's real feelings for him. They would arrive a few minutes before lunch, and if their host didn't invite them to stay this time, Picasso would know what was what and would break with him definitively.

A little before noon, Picasso and Françoise Gilot turned up at Braque's home. He let them in. There was a guest there who was already sniffing the delicious aroma of a leg of lamb that was almost ready to be eaten. Picasso expected Braque to add two plates. 'But', noted Françoise Gilot, 'Pablo knew his Braque by heart, but Braque knew his Picasso even better.'[8] He was well aware that if he invited Picasso to lunch, Picasso would feel that he had won the battle of wills and would make fun of his weakness.

He took him to his studio. For an hour, he showed him his latest works. The smell of the meat reached them on the first floor. Picasso was delighted at the idea of winning the match he had staged – but Braque even more so. He offered to show Picasso and Françoise Gilot some sculptures. They admired them. Picasso noted that the lamb must be cooked by now. Braque didn't answer, but suggested seeing the lithographs. Once again, the guests made admiring noises. It was nearly two o'clock. Picasso was getting nervous. He declared to Braque that Françoise wasn't familiar with his Fauve paintings.

'We can easily solve that problem,' answered Braque. He had understood Picasso's manoeuvre: the Fauve paintings were in the dining room.

They went downstairs. On the table were three plates. Nothing had been added.

Another half hour went by. Braque had still not said a word about lunch. Picasso became stubborn. To drag out the encounter, he asked their host to show him once again some paintings he had already seen. Calmly, Braque did as he was asked. They remained upstairs for another hour. Then spent yet another hour in the studio. At four-thirty, there was no longer any delicious smell coming from the leg of lamb, and it was teatime. Picasso finally took his leave. He was both angry and . . . impressed. After this appetite-building visit, he hung the Braque painting that he had previously removed on the wall of his studio again.

The two painters liked and respected each other, but they had become rivals. This rivalry was made worse by Picasso's almost congenital jealousy: Françoise Gilot testified to this, as Fernande Olivier had before her, though with greater irony and detachment. Gilot told of Picasso's anger when he discovered that after Reverdy had published a work illustrated by him, he had published a second book illustrated by Braque! And of his fury when he learned that this same Reverdy spent more time at Braque's home than at his. And of the day when, having stopped by Braque's, he found René Char there, René Char who had not been to see him on the Quai des Grands-Augustins for weeks!

When Braque died, Picasso executed a lithograph in his honour. On it, he engraved these words: 'Even today, I can still say I love you.' This surprised quite a few people, especially those who recalled some of his previous digs: 'Braque wanted to paint apples, like Cézanne, but he was never able to paint anything but potatoes.'* Or those who, like Sonia Delaunay, remembered the insufferable gossip and cutting comments that Picasso had sometimes indulged in at the expense of his former companion.

But it must be remembered that when Juan Gris had died, Picasso had also wept, which surprised more than a few people. Clearly, he was no stranger to crocodile tears . . .

* A pun in French, the word for apples being 'pommes', and for potatoes, 'pommes de terre'.

THE CUBISTERS

Some might be tempted to think I have something against cubism.
Not at all: I prefer the eccentricities of even a banal mind to the
boring, predictable work of a bourgeois imbecile.

Arthur Cravan

In 1912, the gallery La Boétie in Paris exhibited nearly two hundred
paintings that were described as cubist. Two years before, the painters
present, meeting in their studios, notably in Puteaux, at Jacques Villon's,
had founded the Section d'Or.* In 1911, at the Salon des Indépendants,
in Room 41, they had organized the first collective cubist exhibition.
Those represented were Delaunay, Gleizes, Léger, Metzinger, Jacques
Villon, Marcel Duchamp, Kupka, Picabia, Lhote, Segonzac, Archipenko,
Roger de la Fresnaye and Le Fauconnier.

Neither Braque nor Picasso was represented. They exhibited their work
only in Kahnweiler's gallery or at Uhde's. This stubborn refusal to mix
with those who aggressively claimed for themselves a title which was
rightfully only theirs showed the contempt they held for those whom
Braque called the 'cubisters'. Picasso was even more brutal, not hesitating
to proclaim, 'There is no such thing as cubism',[1] a pronouncement which
would prove to be as provocative as the sentence he was to pronounce
on Negro art in the twenties, 'Negro art? Never heard of it ...' This
attitude expressed both his wish to mark his difference and his contempt
for schools and theories.

In this, he was helped by the commentators. Reverdy, as we have seen,
denied Cézanne's influence, as well as that of Ingres and of Negro art, on
the master's work. During the war, he would go so far as to fight one of
the defenders of the 'other clan', to such an extent that Max Jacob
suggested creating two groups: one composed of Braque, Gris, Picasso

---

* The Section d'Or, or the Golden Section, was a faction of the surrealist movement which formed
around the Duchamp brothers and included such artists as Albert Gleizes, Fernand Léger, Robert
Delaunay and Francis Picabia. They wished to establish a more solid, theoretical basis for cubism,
and were preoccupied with the subject of the proportions issuing from the famous 'golden number'
and Leonardo da Vinci's theories of vision.

and Reverdy, and the other of Lhote, Metzinger and their friends.

Cocteau, another unconditional admirer of Picasso, was even more exclusive:

> When I speak of cubism, I ask that no one include Picasso in this category. A Picasso painting could not be cubist, any more than a Shakespeare drama could be Shakespearean.[2]

Robert Desnos was more critical of the cubisters, but subtler on the subject of Picasso:

> While so many other painters are imprisoned within the sterilizing formula of cubism, delighted to have finally found a means of concealing their impotence behind the incomprehensible, Picasso has never adhered to formulas. He paints what he feels.[3]

Braque and Picasso considered that even if the painters of the Golden Section had added geometrical forms to their works, this addition was not an inherent part of their creative process. They didn't agree with the popular wisdom which held that Bergson had had an influence on cubism (an assertion which the philosopher himself denied). Similarly, they discounted the thesis that cubism derived from mathematics. They made fun of simplistic interpretations which seemed to want to show that the cubists' experiments were based on the works of various scientists, notably Princet, a mathematician who worked for an insurance company and was friendly with the painters of the Bateau Lavoir.

If Princet liked to trace geometrical figures which aimed at demonstrating the relation of cause and effect between the compass and the brush, this may have concerned the painters of the Golden Section, but it didn't interest Braque or Picasso. For them, questions of the third, fourth, or fifth dimension were of little interest. They did not have recourse, and never had, to mathematical or geometrical laws which would have made them dependent on such a system. For them, there was no theory of cubism. Gleizes, Metzinger and Raynal, among others, were ploughing fields which were foreign to them.

Picasso, as always, distanced himself after having set the cat among the pigeons. Once the effects began to be felt, he was already elsewhere, far from the others. And Braque followed suit. Much later, he would confide to Jean Paulhan, 'I got out of there much earlier. I wasn't about to start producing customized Braques.'[4]

When the cubist tumult was at its height, the two founders of the new art let their allies slug it out. Max Jacob was one of them and, unlike some others, he liked to see himself as a refuge, a calm harbour from the insults, mud-slinging, sound and fury. To those who felt disoriented when faced with a cubist work, he gave four pieces of advice:

1 Come to the painting without any easy sarcasm or preconceived notions.
2 Consider the painting as you would consider a cut stone. Appreciate its facets, the originality of its design, its struggle with the light, the arrangement of lines and colours…
3 Home in on a detail which gives the key to the whole; observe it for a while and the model will emerge.
4 With this last comparison, let yourself be transported to the regions of powerful and exquisite Allusion.[5]

Max Jacob also saw himself as a cubist. A literary cubist, like Reverdy, with whom, on this point, he associated himself. In a work that was already heteroclite, complex, extraordinarily rich and unclassifiable, composed of prose poems, bits of overheard conversations, plays on words and the varied gymnastics of a very nimble mind, he added a cubist note:

Cubism in painting is the art of working on the painting for itself, outside what it represents, and of giving the central role to geometrical construction, proceeding only by allusion to real life. Literary cubism does the same in literature, using reality only as a means and not as an end.[6]

But the opinion-makers of the time did not understand Le Cornet à dés any more than they had understood l'Estaque, the bathers, guitars and other instruments of a music that was too atonal for their taste. For them, cubism was an attack on naturalism, and an attack from abroad. Italy was seen as one culprit, wanting to blow up the national art by sending its futurist submarines to torpedo it. Then there was Germany, which had delegated artillerymen in the persons of Wilhelm Uhde and Daniel-Henry Kahnweiler, the cubists' dealers. Not to mention Russia, which was dancing all over French traditions – Debussy, Ravel – thanks to the spying figures of Diaghilev and his ballets.

In 1912, a socialist deputy protested against the fact that this foreign painting was exhibited in national museums. There was talk of Kubism, of Kraut art. When the war came, the furore would only increase.

Even medicine got into the game. After having thought it over for a long time, a certain Doctor Artault of Vevey, called to the witness stand by Guillaume Apollinaire, explained cubism as the exploitation of a pathological phenomenon:

Picasso in the studio of
the Bateau Lavoir in 1908.

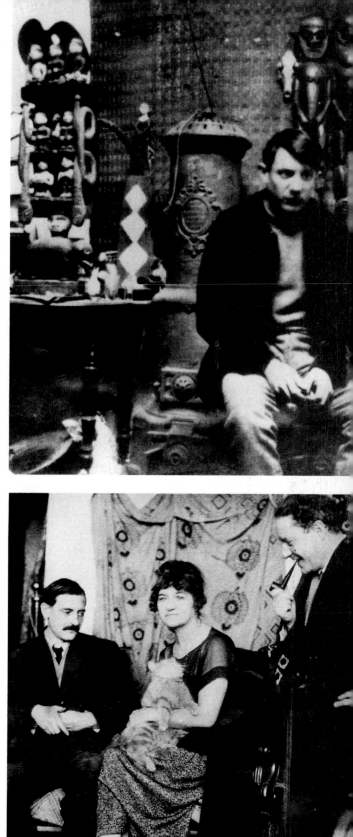

Max Jacob in 1915.

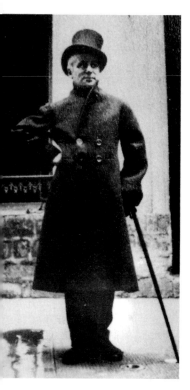

Utrillo, Suzanne Valadon
and André Utter.

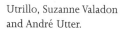

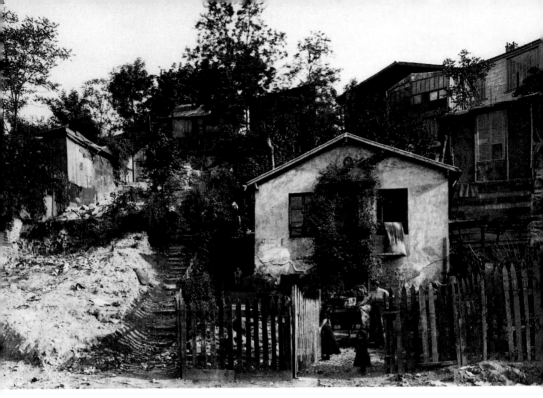

The Bateau Lavoir, to the right, dominating the Montmartre landscape.

The Lapin Agile cabaret in c.1905: a gathering of painters, including Poulbot and Dufy, listening to the père Frédé play the guitar.

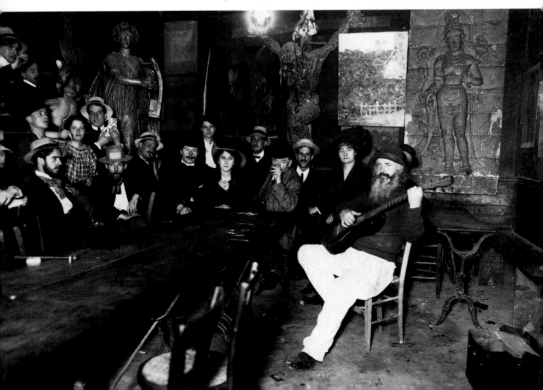

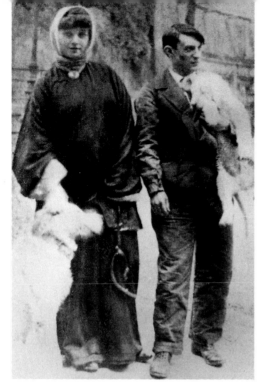

Picasso and Fernande Olivier in
Montmartre in 1906.

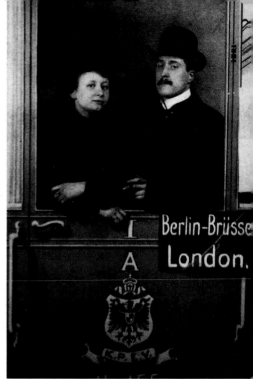

Guillaume Apollinaire and Annie Playden.

Lou

Guillaume Apollinaire and Marie Laurencin.

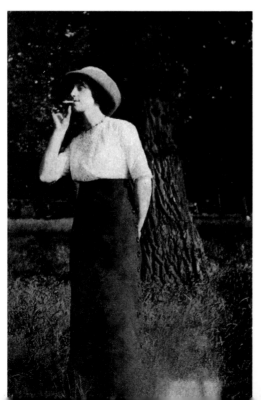

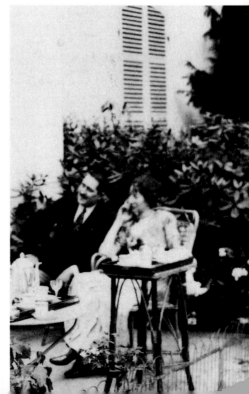

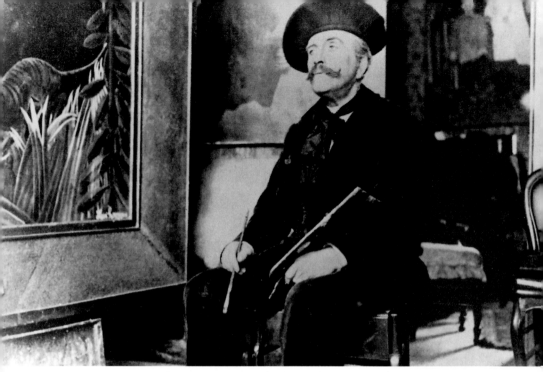

The Douanier Rousseau in his studio in 1904.

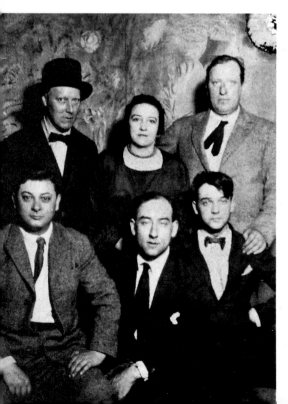

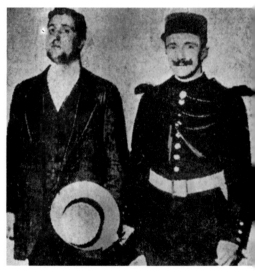

Guillaume Apollinaire with the examining magistrate in September 1911.

Top row: Derain, Madame Derain, Vlaminck.
Bottom row: Kisling, Florents Fels, Juan Gris.

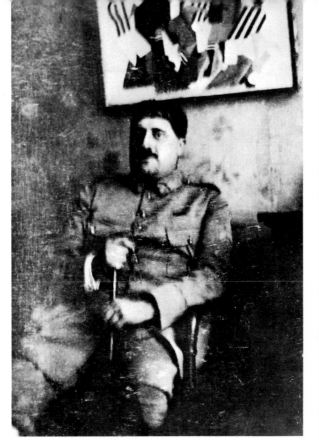

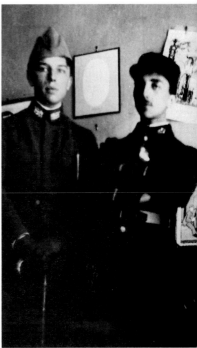

Guillaume Apollinaire

André Breton and Théodore Fraenkel in 1916–17.

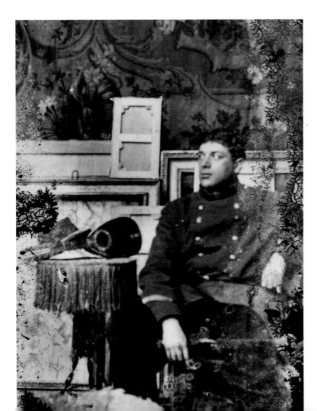

Braque in military uniform, photographed by Picasso in the studio of the Boulevard de Clichy in the spring of 1911.

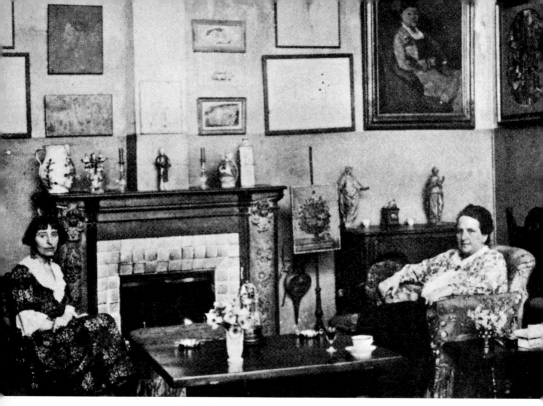

Alice Toklas and Gertrude Stein on the rue de Fleurus in 1923.

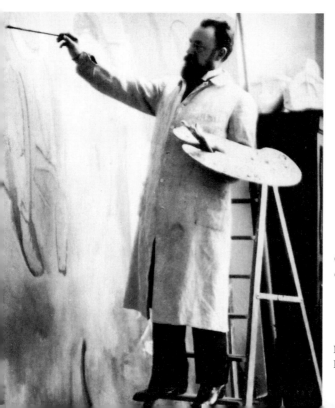

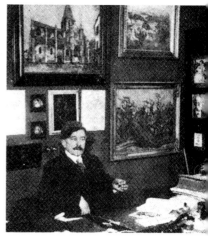

Commissioner Zamaron in his
office at the Prefecture of Police.

Matisse in his studio in
Issy-les-Moulineaux in May 1913.

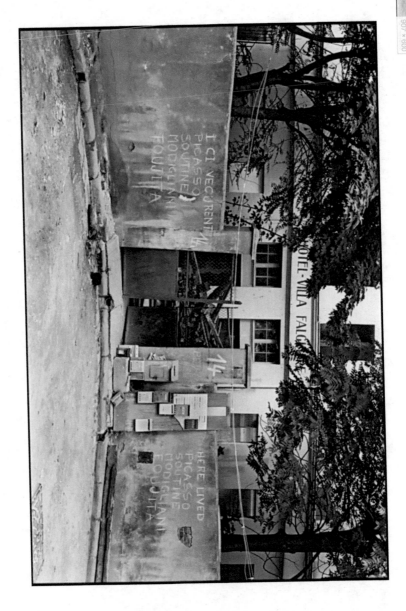

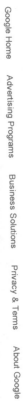

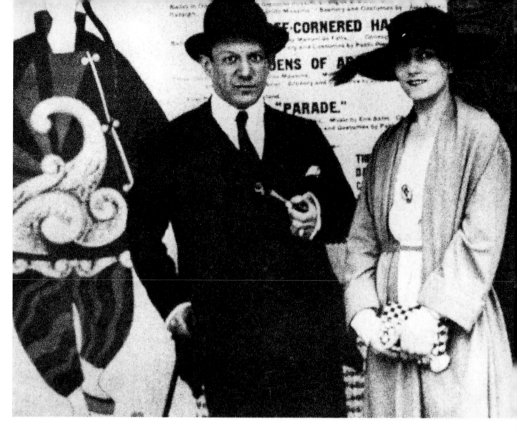

Picasso and Olga in London in 1919.

Modigliani, Picasso and André Salmon at the Rotonde.

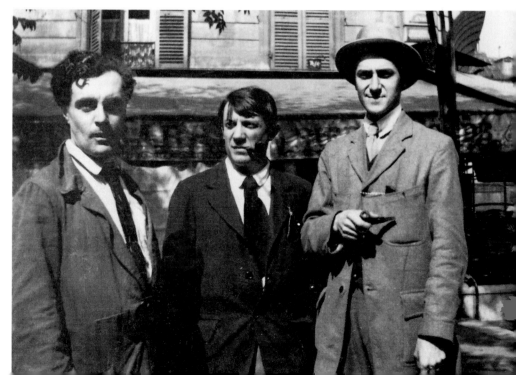

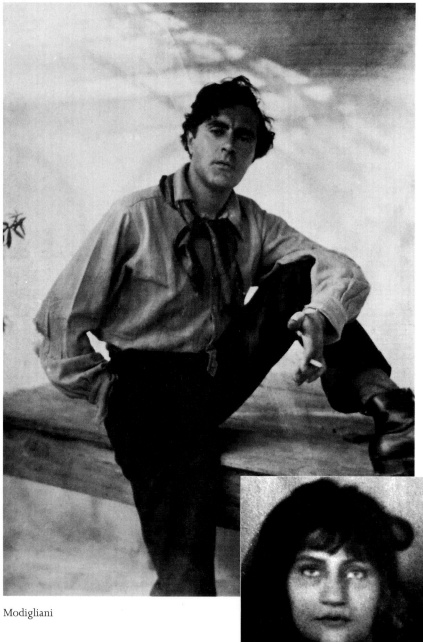

Modigliani

Jeanne Hébuterne at
the age of twenty.

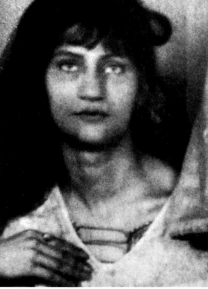

Indeed, it is enough to observe a cubist painting with half-closed eyes, to find there, in the mist of the zigzags and decreasing gleams of light, the deformations and the blurred forms of objects, characteristic of the monochromatic and vacillating irisations of the accident known as scintillating scotomar, the most common symptom of ophthalmic migraine.[7]

So for the medical profession, Braque, Picasso and their fellows were all suffering from migraines. A euphemistic way of putting the medical diagnosis, which was also that of popular opinion: they had all lost their minds.

Even Léon-Paul Fargue, who admired Lautréamont and liked Jarry, did not understand this painting which, in his eyes, suffered from a crisis of 'intellectuality'. He advocated a return to the great days of impressionism, and relegated the cubist painters to the dustbin of art:

> You are the painters of a public meeting, or a restaurant that serves no alcohol, or a vegetarian refectory ... You are half-educated, your heads are 'too weak for education'. So when you go to the country, you always take your half-baked ideas with you, your ideas from around the corner, from school, your sensible revolutionary ideas which don't even smell of oil, but only of an extinguished pipe, something sour, a wet tool, an old mustard pot, like rooms in which literary award banquets are held...[8]

Arrows were also flying from a camp that one might have thought more open-minded. Faithful to the image that he liked to project, Arthur Cravan let rip. His opinion of Metzinger: 'A failure who has jumped onto the cubist wagon.[9] His colour has a German accent about it. He disgusts me.' Of Marcoussis: 'Insincerity; still, one feels, as one does when faced with any of these cubist paintings, that there must be something there. But what?' Of Gleizes: 'No talent whatsoever.' Of De Segonzac: 'He doesn't do much but junky little things now.' Of Archipenko: 'A bit fake.'[10] And so on, down the line.

Montmartre also entered the fray. Dorgelès, then a contributor to *Paris-Journal*, could not tolerate this demolition of subjects, forms, and colours. He saw his best friends, Gleizes, Marcoussis, Delaunay, who had broken up the Eiffel Tower, and Maurice Raynal (whom he labelled an 'aesthematician') following a path which rejected tradition, the impressionists and the *pompier* painters. The steel bracket had replaced the paintbrush. The most important thing was to get noticed.

Supported by his friend André Warnod, Dorgelès decided to make news himself. There was no need to write devastating texts, to pronounce thundering excommunications, as others had done before him. Far better was the option of ridicule, playing a prank, a farce that would make headlines.

And so he launched his own movement: excessivism. And his own painter: Joachim-Raphaël Boronali, an Italian futurist born in Genoa. This artist, whom the press would indeed soon be talking about, was not at all like the others. He had a greyish face, quite long hair, walked on four legs, and didn't talk, but brayed. He was Frédé's donkey, Aliboron. The anagram of his name produced Boronali.

One morning, Dorgelès went to find a bailiff in the Faubourg Mont-martre. He told him about his plan and explained what he wanted of him. As a specialist in following straying husbands and gathering evidence in adultery cases, Monsieur Paul-Henri Brionne couldn't believe his ears or eyes. But the scheme made him laugh, and he was unable to resist going along with it.

The writer and his companion headed up the Butte Montmartre, where André Warnod awaited them. Dorgelès and he went and picked up Lolo at the Lapin Agile, and tied a brush dipped in ultramarine to his tail. They set a blank canvas on a stool, and placed it behind the animal. Then they began joking and playing with him, tempting him with carrots, and the contented beast started to wag his tail, thus making his first impression as an animal artist. The bailiff noted the event.

The two friends moved the frame to add to the vigour of the work in progress and, as monochromatics were not enough for the painter, they changed his palette, dipping the brush, which was still attached to the end of the rather unusual painting tool, into other pots of paint.

After ultramarine, they turned to red. Then cobalt, cadmium and indigo. When the quadruped showed signs of fatigue, Berthe gave him some tobacco to chew on, and the bailiff donated some cigarettes. Then Frédé sang 'Le Temps des cerises', and the donkey began to wag his tail in time to the tune. When he finally stopped, a masterpiece, *Et le soleil s'endormit sur l'Adriatique* ('The Sun Falling Asleep Over the Adriatic') was displayed before the admiring eyes of the art lovers. The bailiff noted the achievement.

Ten days later, the Salon des Indépendants was inaugurated. *Et le soleil s'endormit sur l'Adriatique* was prominently displayed. Dorgelès' friends, to whom he had confided his plans for the farce, expressed their enthusiasm for this important work by an Italian futurist, who was as yet unknown but who clearly would soon be scaling the heights of modern art. The name to remember was Joachim-Raphaël Boronali, one of the great masters of excessivism.

Everyone noted it. Some raved. Others criticized. The painting was found to be rather fauve on the side of the sky, a little vague in its forms, too imbued with the personality of the painter, enigmatic if not symbolic.

What did the red stains in the middle of the canvas represent – a nose, the moon, a divine Pierrot? *Le Matin, Comœdia, La Lanterne* ... all the papers were full of it. And even more so when Dorgelès arrived at the editorial desk of *Le Matin*, bringing with him the proof that the whole thing had been a practical joke. The revelation was met with stupefaction, then hesitation, which lasted only a few hours. The next day, in black ink splashed across the front page of the daily, the words appeared which defined cubism as it was thought of at the time: 'An Ass Leads an Artistic Movement.'

As the bailiff was there to attest.

GUILLAUME APOLLINAIRE GIVES A
LITTLE HELP TO HIS FRIENDS

Scholars are happy. If I were a scholar, I would know exactly how to paint one of my works all over again.

Georges Braque

On Monday 1 October 1912, at the inauguration of the Salon d'Automne, M. Frantz Jourdain, president of the event, welcomed the Minister of Public Instruction on the steps of the Grand Palais. After the usual congratulations, the distinguished assembly began to fan out into the galleries and the hallways.

A few days earlier, the artists, the richer among them coming in carriages and the poorer pushing wheelbarrows in which they had piled their works, had arrived from Montmartre and Montparnasse, shouting out greetings to each other, laughing and singing, to hang the paintings that had been accepted by the jury.

The officials visited the exhibition. They were enraptured by Renoir, Degas, Bonnard, Vuillard, Manet. They whispered together respectfully before the works of Fantin-Latour and Maillol. Their eyebrows rose slightly, but tactfully, as they passed in front of the former ugly ducklings who were now admitted to the fold, even given places of honour: Matisse, Van Dongen, Friesz. They marvelled at the *Portrait de Cézanne* by the worthy Pissarro.

Finally, they came to a darker room. Here, the view became quite obscene. They adjusted their pince-nez and removed their monocles. Frantz Jourdain and his vice-presidents had no choice but to accept a few of them, these dirty cubists, because as the official explained to the Minister of Public Instruction, the Salon d'Automne was supposed, after all, to represent modern art. One couldn't keep them out altogether. This was all the more true as two of them, Albert Gleizes and Jean Metzinger, had just published a book, *Du cubisme*, and the press was buzzing with reviews of it.

Among those present, opinions diverged. There was Paul Fort, the poet, Claude Debussy, the composer, Guillaume Apollinaire, a journalist. They looked at the paintings, murmuring comments to each other. Standing a little off to one side was Louis Vauxcelles, who was covering the event for *Gil Blas*, and who had copiously criticized Picabia ('the gilded cubist'), Léger (the 'tubist'), Picasso ('Ubu-Kub'), and many others, whom he merrily attacked on page after page.

This arbiter of artistic values offered his arm to his wife. He was about to come out with one of his skilfully aimed barbed arrows, when two of the painters he found so useless, but who were in excellent physical shape, jumped out at him from behind the geometries of Dunoyer de Segonzac and Roger de la Fresnaye, surrounded him, insulted him, and knocked him to the ground, while Marcoussis, Metzinger, Picabia, Lhote, Le Fauconnier, Gleizes, Léger, Duchamp and Villon watched, in gales of laughter.

There was talk of exchanging addresses and weapons, of sending witnesses. That evening, in *L'Intransigeant*, Guillaume Apollinaire recounted the event:

> A little incident occurred this morning. Some cubist painters approached one of our fellow critics, Monsieur Vauxcelles, and insulted him abundantly. But the altercation was limited to a lively exchange of words.[1]

Two days later, in the columns of the same newspaper, the criticized critic published a letter to the director:

> Please do me the honour of believing that it is not in my nature to let myself be insulted 'abundantly' without answering the offender.
>
> I did, indeed, tell the two young louts that the incident would find its natural solution on the duelling field. They withdrew immediately at this, the principles of cubist morality doubtless forbidding them to fight.
>
> I would be greatly obliged to you for publishing this letter, for I would not enjoy being cast in an unfavourable light in the eyes of your numerous readers.
>
> With all best wishes, your devoted servant,
>
> Louis Vauxcelles
>
> P.S. One last word: the two aforementioned young men might perhaps have had the delicacy of waiting until I was alone before 'approaching' me. As it happened, Madame Vauxcelles was leaning on my arm when the incident occurred. These questions should be settled among men alone.[2]

Clearly, cubism needed its advocates. The most energetic of these was Guillaume Apollinaire. For him, the defence of cubism, attacked on all sides, was something between a battle and a mission. In addition, the avant-garde movement in question was one in which, in the literary domain, Apollinaire himself participated as a poet. So it was in this arena that he first took up arms.

He knew all that he owed to symbolism, which had freed verse from its constraints and from the burdensome rules of prosody. But he wanted to be still more modern, to be the great advocate of free verse. Like the cubist painters, he wanted to combine poetry and the things of daily life, ordering this novel palette with his own personal touch, which lay in an amazing range of cultural interests and an immense inventiveness and imagination.

In 1913, he published *Alcools* with the *Mercure de France*. This collection contained texts written between 1898 and 1912. It was a mixed bouquet, containing both the flowers of his memory and greenery gathered in the outside world. There we find Guillaume in the prison of the Santé, suffering the thousand pangs of unhappy love, sleepless and anguished; but there are also the hangars of Port-Aviation, Pope Pius X, leaflets, posters, secretaries, aeroplanes, sirens' songs ... Punctuation has disappeared; the manner in which the verse is cut at the end of each line suffices to give the rhythm of the poem.

The following year, Apollinaire began to write his *Calligrammes*. The game of arranging letters to form figures was not originated by him. But how could one not see in these poem-images the visual application of what the words contained already in *Alcools*, further reinforced and accentuated now by the reproductions of newspaper headlines, typographical games, integrated drawings, and musical scales? Surely these were cubist collages in the form of poetry? Was this not the literary equivalent of the pictorial audacities of his painter friends? The product of the avant-garde? A generous and protean inventiveness, whose rhythms would find an echo fifteen years later in John Dos Passos' novel, *The 42nd Parallel*?

In defending the modernity of others, Apollinaire was defending his own as well. He was a participant in this revolution of modern art, not just its willing chronicler. He felt that he had to take up arms for the new language in the same way as in 1789 one fought for the revolution. He was a poet, his weapon was the pen – so he would fence with it.

Between 1910 and 1914, he officiated at *L'Intransigeant*. Salmon was at *Paris-Journal* (he signed with a pseudonym, 'La Palette', and would soon join *Gil Blas*, where he would assail the fortress defended by Vauxcelles). In the eyes of his comrades, Guillaume Apollinaire was an exceptional poet and a marvellous friend, but a mediocre art critic. Picasso didn't take him seriously. According to him, Apollinaire 'felt' more than he really knew or understood. For Braque, the poet didn't know the first thing about art; he confused Rubens with Rembrandt. Vlaminck spoke with irony of 'his incompetence and his whimsical verve'. Still others, like Juan Gris, were amused to discover in his articles opinions that they themselves had given in answer to a question he had asked.

But they needed him when the time came to do battle. Apollinaire adored everything new, and was always ready to oblige when a locked door had to be kicked in. He was the champion of the avant-garde. He was even ready to relegate to the shelf some 'antiquities' which could hardly be called that. Impressionism, for instance. In his preface to the catalogue of the Braque exhibition in 1908, after first invoking 'some magnificently talented masters', whom he did not name, he then sounded the battle cry: 'Ignorance and frenzy, these are the true characteristics of impressionism.' This movement had been 'nothing but a brief, poor and simply religious moment in the visual arts'; the impressionists had tried 'to express feverishly, hastily, and unreasonably, their wonder in the face of nature'.

The judgement was feverish, hasty, and unreasonable. As for Braque himself, who was after all the subject of the piece, since Kahnweiler was honouring him after the official salons had slammed their doors in his face, 'he expresses a beauty filled with tenderness, and the pearly tones of his paintings make our perception iridescent.' It was more poetry than criticism. Sentences which traversed painting without always discerning its novelties, its breaks with tradition, words scintillating like a palette in verse, images, an enormous amount of goodwill, but sometimes accompanied by a disconcerting lack of analysis.

In this preface to the works of Braque which had been refused at the Salon d'Automne, Apollinaire rejoiced in the success enjoyed by the paintings of Picasso, Matisse, Derain, and Vlaminck. And he deplored the fact that the Salon had not yet honoured Vallotton, Odilon Redon, Braque, and . . . Marie Laurencin.

If she was still his muse, then he was her troubadour: he sang her praises everywhere, in every register. In 1908, in *Les Peintres nouveaux*: 'Mademoiselle Laurencin has managed to express, in the magisterial art of painting, an entirely feminine sort of aesthetics.' That same year, in *L'Intransigeant*, for which Apollinaire wrote a regular column, 'La vie artistique', he wrote, 'I cannot find the words to properly define the very French grace of Mademoiselle Marie Laurencin.' In 1909, on the subject of the Salon des Indépendants: 'Mademoiselle Marie Laurencin brings to art a strong and clear grace which is very new.' At the Salon d'Automne of 1910, where Marie had been refused: 'Let us note that important artists, like Monsieur André Derain, Marie Laurencin, Puy, etc., did not exhibit their work.' In 1911: 'The high point of the Salon could have been the cubists' room, if they had all exhibited their work, if Delaunay and Marie Laurencin had been represented . . .'

A little later, the critic also expressed his regret at the absence of Picasso, Derain, Braque, and Dufy; no one apart from him would have thought of including Marie Laurencin – who painted on porcelain and whose works were pastel-coloured paintings full of soft curves – in the company of the other four! This is what is called stroking one's mistress in writing...

There were others, though, for whom Apollinaire didn't care. Perhaps because Picasso didn't either, or because these artists did not adhere to the new and controversial movements in art. Van Dongen, who preferred the round geometry of mother-of-pearl to the broken lines of cubist figures, took quite a drubbing in L'Intransigeant. 1910: 'The paintings of Monsieur Van Dongen are the expression of what a bourgeois suffering from gastric disturbance today calls "daring".' Several months later: 'Monsieur Van Dongen continues to progress along the path of banality.' In 1911, he was no longer anything but an 'old Fauve' exhibiting 'sorts of posters'. Two years later, his paintings appeared to the critic to be 'the most unnecessary in the world'.

In passing, Apollinaire shot a few arrows in Vlaminck's direction: 'He spoils his temperament by painting visiting cards.' He had a nasty word for Matisse in 1907, probably inspired, in the wings, by Picasso: 'Monsieur Henri Matisse is an innovator, but he renovates more than he innovates.' But soon Matisse's talent would become universally recognized, and Apollinaire would then help to consolidate the throne on which the master of the Convent of Des Oiseaux now sat, and which no one would think of demolishing.

As for Picasso, it was very simple: Apollinaire never said a word against him. When he didn't like something, if he didn't like something, he preferred not to write anything at all. Thus it was for Les Demoiselles d'Avignon: like Braque, Derain, and the handful of visitors who had seen the canvas at the Bateau Lavoir, he had probably not liked the work, or at best had been paralysed by its modernity. But from 1910 he began to beat the drum. He once again found the energy necessary to praise his friend and exalt him to the uppermost heights which, in Apollinaire's eyes, were his natural habitat.

In Poésie, a review published in the south-west of France, he gave an account of the Salon d'Automne, using the word 'cubism' for the first time and criticizing the 'visual metaphysics' that other journalists had detected in the exhibitors' works, such as those of Jean Metzinger. In his eyes, it was a question of a 'flat, lifeless imitation of other works, not on exhibit, painted by an artist gifted with a strong personality and who, in addition, has not breathed a word of his secrets to anyone. This great artist is named Pablo Picasso.' In another passage of the same article, he made his point even more clearly: 'The cubism on show at the Salon d'Automne resembles a bluejay parading in peacock's feathers.'

The peacock agreed, naturally, but nobody else did. In response to his articles in *L'Intransigeant*, the editors began to receive more and more complaints from painters panned in Apollinaire's reviews. They answered by publishing corrections, which wounded the critic's pride. He sent his witnesses to confront the painters who had complained. The directors of the paper finally placed the column in a less visible spot. Finally, Apollinaire left *L'Intransigeant* for *Paris-Journal*.

He was not Baudelaire, and Picasso was not his Delacroix. Sixty years after the Salons of his illustrious predecessor, it was clear that he was claiming as his own the mission of writing subjective, impassioned criticism – not analytical but playful, as advocated by the author of *Les Fleurs du mal*. But he couldn't penetrate the depths. Rarely does one read in his writings as incisive an analysis as 'La Madeleine dans le désert' or the 'Dernières paroles de Marc Aurèle',[3] not to mention the 'Eugène Delacroix',[4] signed by Baudelaire in 1845 and 1846.

Apollinaire had his opinions, of course – but he liked to share them a little too often. Not so much with his readers, which would have been perfectly reasonable, as with his friends, which was less so. He sometimes changed his mind in response to the tastes of his companions or, worse still, let himself be swayed by his friendships or animosities. In short, he did all he could to promote his friends, which would create new problems for him.

In 1911, when the works of the cubist painters were brought together for their first collective exhibition in Room 41 of the Salon des Indépendants, Apollinaire leapt to their defence, praising the 'cubisters'. Thus he contributed to creating a movement which in the minds of its two founding fathers – Braque and Picasso – did not exist. He recognized the preponderant role of one of them at least in the process of creation, and reiterated the point in many lines and many articles. However, he disregarded the feelings of the two themselves, who would soon be joined by Kahnweiler in this sentiment, by proclaiming that cubism *was* a school, one whose eminent members included Braque, Gris, Gleizes, and, of course, though only in some of her works, the omnipresent Marie Laurencin. Not to mention Metzinger, Lhote, Delaunay, Archipenko, Le Fauconnier, Dunoyer de Segonzac, Luc-Albert Moreau and Fernand Léger who, until the war, would all be praised by the poet with varying degrees of enthusiasm.

In fact, Apollinaire didn't really know exactly what to think. He loved too much, gave too much, discerned too little. He was stretched in too many directions, between his friendship for Picasso, his more recent ties with the Delaunays (who hated Picasso), his gratitude towards Picabia who, richer than all his other companions, financed an edition of Apollinaire's *Méditations esthétiques* ... And when, to please Picasso, Braque and Kahnweiler, he tried to go a little lighter on the theorizing, and to distance himself from what gradually appeared to him to be a system, it was too late. The deed was done, for better or for worse. Apollinaire had defended the young art so well that it had come to resemble a movement, a school – to such a degree that many, following the example of Vlaminck and Francis Carco, would soon wonder what would have become of cubism without Guillaume Apollinaire.

THE POET AND THE ART DEALER

Art is the child of its times.

Wassily Kandinsky

Cubism without Apollinaire? This wasn't something Daniel-Henry Kahnweiler gave a lot of thought to. Though the art dealer didn't write in the papers, he contributed as much as the poet did to the promotion of his painters. He was the dealer for the cubists, just as the Bernheims were for Matisse, Durand-Ruel was for the impressionists and Vollard was for Cézanne, Gauguin and the Nabis.

At the age of twenty-three, in an old workshop run by a Polish tailor on the rue Vignon, near the Opéra, Kahnweiler opened a gallery. It was barely sixteen square yards in size, but he was also starting out with twenty-five thousand francs in gold contributed by a family of German financiers. The challenge was great: they had given the young man a year to prove himself. If he failed in the art business, he would have to return home.

But he didn't fail. At the Salon des Indépendants, he bought paintings by Derain and Vlaminck. Then he turned to Van Dongen and Braque. In 1907, thanks to Wilhelm Uhde who had spoken to him of the *Demoiselles d'Avignon*, he went to the Bateau Lavoir and met Picasso. Unlike many others, he was fascinated by this painting. He immediately grasped the major break it represented in the history of art. He wanted to buy it but, claiming that it wasn't finished, Picasso refused. Kahnweiler had to content himself with some preparatory sketches. But he came back. When Vollard disappeared from the scene, he would replace him as the painter's dealer.

Fernande Olivier has described him as an audacious, determined man, extremely persistent, valiantly assailing whatever fortress it was he wished to take, and not giving up until he got what he wanted. We may suppose that this was his preferred method, since forty years later, he was still proceeding in exactly the same way. He would invite himself over to Picasso's and then just stay, settling in, making himself comfortable. The painter would try to provoke him with criticism or rough words, but the dealer would either calmly deny what he was accused of or agree good-naturedly. They would sometimes also get involved in philosophical discussions in which Kahnweiler was careful not to win the day, knowing full well that if he was the victor on the playing field of theory, he would be the loser in commerce. Picasso would never have accepted defeat twice. The hours passed, boredom overcame them, but still Kahnweiler wouldn't budge from his armchair. In the end Picasso would capitulate, and sell whatever it was Kahnweiler was after.

Françoise Gilot recounts that in 1944–5, when Kahnweiler did not have an exclusivity clause, Picasso played him off against another art dealer, Louis Carré. Carré's gallery, one of the most important of the time, was on the Avenue de Messine. The artist invited the two men to his home, on the Quai des Grands-Augustins, and left them together in a sitting room. First they waited there for an hour, just the two of them. Then the painter would ask one of the men to step into his studio. In general, it was Louis Carré. Respecting his own principle that 'he who loves well, punishes well', the artist made the dealer he preferred stew for a while.

In the studio, the men talked for longer than was really necessary. They talked for the time it would take the remaining visitor, in the sitting room, to become consumed with anxiety. When the painter and the dealer reappeared, Kahnweiler's face was grey. It was enough for Carré to look pleased, which implied that everything was settled (even if it wasn't), and poor Kahnweiler would turn green.

Picasso took him into the studio in turn, where it was now child's play to get him to raise his offer. 'This was one of my first glimpses of Picasso's technique, which consisted of using people as in a game of ninepins, aiming the ball at one person in order to make another fall,' concluded Françoise Gilot.[1]

In this cat-and-mouse strategy, it was always the cheese that won. How far away now seemed the days when Braque, Derain, Vlaminck and Picasso would arrive in their overalls at the little gallery on the rue Vignon, take off their caps and blurt out, 'Boss, we've come for our pay!'

Kahnweiler was the cubists' dealer, a title of which he was extremely proud. To which, ironically, Apollinaire could have answered by turning the question around: Very well, but which cubists?

If Kahnweiler considered Braque, Picasso, Gris and Léger to be the 'four great cubists',[2] then he was, indisputably, the cubists' dealer. But if they were excluded, the title was not truly his. Apollinaire knew this well, having been the victim of numerous poisoned arrows from this man who in one way or another, consciously or not, envied the complicity between the painter and the poet.

Both were friends of the arts. They both defended him passionately,

each with his own arms. Like Vollard before him, Kahnweiler published
works by poets, illustrated by his painters. These books were the joy of
bibliophiles, with limited editions of only one hundred copies.

He was Apollinaire's first publisher, and Apollinaire was his first author.
In 1909, they published *L'Enchanteur pourrissant* together, illustrated with
thirty-two wooden engravings by Derain (*Saint Matorel* by Max Jacob,
illustrated by Picasso, would follow in 1911). The printing was of one
hundred copies. Five years later, the records showed that only fifty had
been sold. A literary gem:

> The young lady touched him and felt that he had a very well-made
> body. She loved him immensely, fulfilled his desires and that, all that, to
> her mother and to others.

Kahnweiler appreciated and admired him as a poet, and respected the
erudite man of culture, but he scorned the art critic in Apollinaire, finding
him superficial and ignorant of art history. For him, the *Méditations esthétiques*
were nothing more than futile chatter. He couldn't tolerate the anecdotal
feel of the articles, and still less the poet's energetic defence of the cubist
painters collected in room 41 of the Salon des Indépendants in 1911. And
when Apollinaire repeated the performance the following year with the
artists of the Section d'Or, Kahnweiler became angry and protested. He
wanted the critic to make a clear and open distinction. Who was cubist
and who wasn't? And which side was he on?

The dealer asked Braque and Picasso to force their friend to clarify his
position. They refused to do so. They may have shared Kahnweiler's
opinion, but they were careful not to hurt the poet's feelings. Apollinaire,
who had just published *Alcools* with the *Mercure de France* (with his portrait
by Picasso as a frontispiece), learned of Kahnweiler's dubious game. He
picked up his pen and responded:

> I have heard that you find what I have to say about painting devoid of
> interest, which coming from you, seems quite surprising. Alone, I
> defended, as a writer, painters that you only came to admire after I
> spoke of them. And do you think it is a good thing to try to destroy
> someone who, in the end, is the only one who has managed to establish
> the bases for an emerging understanding of the arts?[3]

The art dealer answered, 'I received a very strange letter from you. As I
read it, I wondered if I should be angry. I preferred to be amused.'[4]

For Kahnweiler, things were clear: the painters he exhibited on the rue
Vignon, whose works he sold abroad, were the only cubist painters. The
others were just feeble imitators, to whom he paid no attention. In 1912,

he had established contracts binding him legally to his artists. The principle was simple. He bought their entire production at prices determined in advance. He demanded exclusivity. The prices varied, depending on the formats. Derain was better paid than Braque, who received three times less than Picasso. The latter had haggled over every clause of the contract, word for word. He had offered Kahnweiler exclusivity of three years for his entire work, excluding his older works and portraits that might be commissioned. He would keep five paintings and five drawings a year for himself. Kahnweiler would buy the other paintings, gouaches, and at least twenty drawings a year.

The dealer had signed. He was confident, and there was no lack of clients. These were no longer just Gertrude Stein and a handful of enlightened French art enthusiasts. For some time now, foreign collectors had been arriving in Paris to meet these cubists who weren't really cubists, but still were in a way...

The first of these collectors was Russian. He was called Sergei Shchukin, a textile industrialist who owned the Trubetskoy Palace in Moscow. He had bought works by Derain and Matisse: the latter had gone to Moscow to hang *La Danse* and *La Musique*. These works were exhibited on the walls of the palace, along with works by Van Gogh, Monet, Cézanne and Gauguin.

Shchukin had been interested in Picasso since 1908. He soon acquired the most important paintings of the blue, rose and cubist periods. (His collection would become the property of the state after the revolution of 1917, enriching the museums of Moscow and Leningrad.) Kahnweiler remained his privileged intermediary.

Kahnweiler was present on every front – except one, that of the national Salons. He advised his artists to follow Picasso's example, and forbade them to expose themselves to the sneers of the critics who toured the rooms of the Grand Palais with the dignitaries of the French Republic. To see the works of Braque, Derain, Gris and Picasso in France, one had to go to the homes of collectors with taste and understanding, or to the small gallery on the rue Vignon. Otherwise, one could go abroad. For paradoxically, while none of these artists exhibited any longer in the official Parisian Salons, their works were on view in Berlin, Cologne, Munich, Amsterdam, London and Moscow.

And this was only the beginning.

CUBISM ON THE AUCTION BLOCK

> We will all return to the rue
> Ravignan! Only there were
> we ever truly happy.
>
> Pablo Picasso

They were also on view in Paris on a certain Monday, 2 March 1914, in the Hôtel Drouot, rooms 6 and 7. Those attending ranged from the simply curious, journalists and dealers from Germany, to society figures and enlightened art lovers, like Marcel Sembat, a Parisian Socialist deputy.

In the crowd, it was easy to spot Picasso's rearguard: Max Jacob, Kahnweiler, Serge Férat and the Baronness d'OEttingen. In the first row, just in front of Maître Henri Beaudoin, the auctioneer, and his two experts, the founding members of the Peau de l'Ours (Bear's Skin), Druet and the Bernheim brothers, waited for the sale to begin. Ten years after creating their association, they were finally putting their works on sale. Since 1904, they had each added two hundred and fifty francs a year to the shared bank. They had divided the paintings among themselves as specified in the rules they had themselves devised, and were now about to part with them. They would recover their initial investment, augmented by minimal interest of three and a half per cent. André Level, the manager of the association, would receive twenty per cent of the sums remaining as payment for his services. The artists would share the rest. The operation had not been designed with any speculative purpose in mind, but to contribute to the promotion of modern art and help the painters live a little better. The preface to the catalogue set the tone:

> Some friends got together, ten years ago, to form a collection of paintings, and to decorate and enhance the walls of their homes. The fine works of the past were almost inaccessible, and so they readily let themselves, young as they were and with faith in the future, be persuaded to have confidence in artists who were also young, or recently discovered. It seemed to them honourable to take the risks implied by the new.

What had they bought in the space of ten years, these generous souls? One hundred and fifty works: Van Gogh, Gauguin, Odilon Redon, Vuillard, Maurice Denis, Bonnard, Vallotton, Signac, Sérusier, Maillol, but also Dufy, Van Dongen, Herbin, Dufrenoy, Flandrin, Roger de la Fresnaye, Othon Friesz, Marquet, Metzinger, Rouault, Dunoyer de Segonzac, Verhoeven, Vlaminck, Derain, Matisse, Willette and Picasso. Some painters who were almost traditional, some Fauves, and especially, the artists that everyone was expecting, the cubists. For even if they presented works that were less geometrical than those creating controversy elsewhere, it was still the first time that they were available on the national market. The Peau de l'Ours sale was clearly a decisive test for modern art.

Maître Henri Beaudoin sold the first work for seven hundred and twenty francs: it was Bonnard's L'Aquarium, described in the catalogue as a 'study of fish and shellfish'. Vlaminck didn't do quite so well with Ecluses à Bougival, sold for one hundred and seventy francs. Dufy's Boulevard maritime was offered at a hundred francs and sold for a hundred and sixty.

Metzinger, with a cubist landscape, did not get beyond a hundred francs, but Roger de la Fresnaye saw the cubes of his Nature morte aux anses rise to three hundred. Utrillo commanded the same price at best, and half that sum, at worst. Derain sold his Vase de grès for three hundred francs, and received two hundred and fifteen for Pêches dans une assiette, and two hundred and ten for La Chambre.

This was still not quite as good as the amount Marie Laurencin received: at four hundred and seventy-five francs, she finally justified the persistence of her former companion, who was still a critic. But Dunoyer de Segonzac fared even better, with La Mare which, offered at three hundred francs, was finally sold for eight hundred.

Gauguin's Le Violoncelliste sold for four thousand francs, as did Van Gogh's Fleurs dans un verre. With Etude de femme and La Mer en Corse, Matisse started off at nine hundred francs. Feuillages au bord de l'eau went for over two thousand francs, and Compotier de pommes et oranges doubled expectations, selling for five thousand, even better than Van Gogh.

The audience applauded, but Picasso had not yet said a single word; he remained above the fray. The canvases bought by André Level's friends were older than his more recent cubist works, but it didn't matter: it was the man – his innovative spirit, the movement he had initiated – that was being judged, not his blue or rose periods. After having worked in the shadows for many years, the Bateau Lavoir had finally emerged into the bright light of the auction room. And when he put up Picasso's first sketch, Femme et enfants, Maître Beaudoin, without realizing it, was burying Montmartre: the Montmartre of the old days, of splendid unknown artists awaiting their hour of glory.

For the hour had finally arrived. Femme et enfants was sold for one thousand one hundred francs – but it was only a sketch. *L'Homme à la houppelande* went for one thousand three hundred and fifty francs. *Les Trois Hollandaises* sold for five thousand two hundred francs.

All around the room, people were whispering to each other feverishly: this was more than for Matisse. Then a giant canvas was placed on the stage: the *Famille de saltimbanques* (1905). The starting price was eight thousand francs. (André Level had bought it for one thousand.) The bidding began. And continued. The prices rose, with some bidders enthusiastic, others furious. The spiteful critics were already sharpening the points of their pencils. The defenders of cubism were rubbing their hands in glee. And when the auctioneer's hammer fell, it was as though he was striking the death blow to the old world. Eleven thousand five hundred francs. It was the highest sum paid for a painting that day.

The assembly leapt to its feet, applauding wildly. Many began to head for the door. The more malicious gossips, and there was no lack of them, noted that the dealer who had bought *L'Homme à la houppelande* and *Famille de saltimbanques* was a German, Justin Tannhauser. Five months later, exactly five months, some might, retrospectively, detect a premonitory sign in this. But for the moment, the public simply scattered and began to disperse.

As they left, they bumped into another German, Daniel-Henry Kahnweiler, who was energetically pushing his way out of the room; he had to announce the news to Picasso. The sale had brought in one hundred and fifteen thousand francs, and Picasso alone was responsible for a quarter of what could only be called the 'volume of business'.

Kahnweiler, having finally fought his way free of the crowd, hailed a cab. He had to find Picasso. For Picasso wasn't there. He hadn't come. As usual, he was somewhere else.

And where was he, in this, his finest hour?

Not in Clichy, nor in Montmartre. Caesar, in his way, had braved the Rubicon: he had crossed the Seine. From now on, he would be mixing with a much wider world, whose electric lights would distance him for ever from the simple candles of Montmartre.

Picasso had left his artistic birthplace. He was no longer at the Bateau Lavoir.

He was on the left bank. In Montparnasse.

II
MONTPARNASSE
GOES TO WAR

THE RUCHE

Here is the Montparnasse which has become, for the painters and the
poets, what Montmartre was for them fifteen years ago: a haven of
fine, free simplicity.

Guillaume Apollinaire

On the other bank of the Seine, it was as if the Sacré Coeur didn't exist.
At the turn of the century the Mont Parnasse had been the kingdom of
stables and farms, with an occasional country fair brightening up a corner
of the boulevards, and flocks of sheep wandering in the streets.

The residents of the area were more men of letters than men of pictures:
many poets dressed in black, a few painters clad in blue overalls, sensible
and conventional, between the painting academies and the traditional
stone buildings with their imposing entrances. Montparnasse was perched
ambiguously on an unsteady base, as the bourgeoisie tiptoed its way
through horse manure. It had no symbolic monument in which to take
refuge.

Poetry set the tone of the place. Years before, students had come up
from the Latin Quarter to recite verses on the heights strewn with waste
from the nearby quarry yards. Later, they were replaced by farmboys,
produce growers, and the workers who were constructing the extension
of the Boulevard Raspail.

There were also some sculptors: the gardens and warehouses gave them
the space necessary for their work. They also took advantage of the way
the buildings of the neighbourhood were designed: the architects had
constructed bourgeois buildings for bourgeois people and, in the court-
yards, artists' studios for artists, with glass roofs and skylights which let
the light filter through in the best way, and high ceilings so that paintings
could be seen and judged from an elevated vantage point. A number of
studios had also replaced the farms, divided up and boasting large glass
roofs.

Montparnasse was thus becoming more and more receptive to the arts.
The area had a number of highly reputed painting academies: notably
Bourdelle's, whose teaching was more progressive than that of the official

masters. There were paint merchants and frame sellers, and even some markets for models, near the academy of the Grande Chaumière or on the corner of the street of the same name and the Boulevard du Montparnasse: boxers, typists, workers – many Italians, who were less inhibited than the others when it came to posing.

Montparnasse also had its Bateau Lavoirs. These were artists' residences where the tenants came, left, returned, depending on the state of their pocketbooks. There was one at the Impasse du Maine, where Bourdelle sculpted. There was the Cité Falguière, which was also called the Villa Rose because of its pinkish walls. Foujita lived there, and Modigliani, who was thrown out by the landlady, Madame Durchoux, for too often neglecting to pay the rent.

There was, above all, the Ruche, or 'hive', whose rotunda dominated the Impasse de Dantzig. It was one of the most important places in Montparnasse. All the artists stayed there at least once, and many remained. The Ruche was the Bateau Lavoir of the Jewish painters who had come from Eastern Europe.

The residence was the work of a patron of the arts, Alfred Boucher, a sculptor of the 'pompier' school. After the World Fair of 1900, he had bought up the remains of the pavilions constructed by Gustave Eiffel and had them assembled on a lot which he had previously acquired not far from the Vaugirard slaughterhouses. Numerous studios were located near the main building, the former Wine Pavilion, whose roof resembled a hive. On either side of the entrance, two caryatids had also made the trip from the Indonesian Pavilion; the outside gate came from the Women's Pavilion. The small buildings, including a three-hundred-seat theatre (where Louis Jouvet got his start) and exhibition rooms, were situated in the middle of the lawns and the alleyways – the Flower Drive, the Boulevard of Love, the Avenue of the Three Musketeers...

Boucher rented out the studios for a modest price to poor painters. They had a single room, which they called 'the coffin': a triangle with a platform above the door where the tenants slept on a thin mattress. There was no water, no gas, no electricity. The halls were dark, with rubbish heaped up in the corners, and leaky sewers. But once the numbered doors had been opened and the circular thresholds crossed, inside could be heard the songs of the Italians, the heated discussions of the Jews, and the shouts of the models posing for the Russians.

Before the war, Chagall, as he himself admitted, was an exile, working alone and late, receiving only rare visitors: first Cendrars, then Apollinaire. When they came home at night, in drunken, noisy groups, the artists of the Ruche threw pebbles at his windows to urge Chagall to come and join them. But the artist, the child of a poor family from Vitebsk, helped by a lawyer who was a deputy in the Russian Duma, was more serious

than the others. Alone, he cultivated an art that he defined as one of
moods, impressions, the spirit; painting his canvases in the nude, never
complaining, subsisting on a head of herring the first day of the week,
the tail of the same the next day, and breadcrusts the following days. His
studio had an inner balcony.

Except for a few, like Fernand Léger, who was from Normandy, most
of the residents of the Ruche were from central Europe. On Sundays, they
could indulge in some of the pleasures of their native lands. Fairground
performers would come, along with accordion players and minstrels. A
Jewish merchant with a long black beard came from the Saint Paul
neighbourhood and set up his handcart at the gates, selling herrings,
chopped liver, black bread – tastes and smells reminiscent of their
childhoods.

They were all immigrants who had arrived a few years before the war.
They didn't yet constitute the Paris School which was to become famous
throughout the world. Archipenko, a Russian sculptor who was a great
friend of Léger, had come in 1908. Lipchitz, a Lithuanian sculptor, had
arrived a year later. Kikoïne, also Lithuanian and the grandson of a Rabbi,
was a Socialist and a Bundist; he had studied at the school of fine arts of
Wilno with Krémègne and Soutine. Krémègne, who had crossed the border
clandestinely in 1912, was awkward in his manners and movements, and
rather sad and defeated-looking; he was a bit jealous of Soutine, whose
equal he considered himself to be. Mané-Katz had left Kiev for the Ruche
in 1913; Chana Orloff came the same year. The Polish Kisling, a brilliant
student from the Fine Arts School of Cracow, was livelier, more playful
than many of the others; he loved parties, wine, and painting. There was
Léon Bakst, a painter and decorator, who in 1909 designed the sets for
Cleopatra, the first of the Ballets Russes productions, which was a sensation
at the Châtelet theatre, with Pavlova and Nijinsky dancing. Soutine, the
most poverty-stricken of them all, sang in Yiddish as he painted. And
then there was Zadkine (who had come in 1909, at the age of nineteen),
Epstein, Gottlieb, Marevna, the sculptors Lipski, Joseph Csaky, Leon
Indenbaum...

When they first discovered France, these immigrants were only twenty
years old. They had left behind them family, friends, tradition. They had
no arms other than their pens and brushes. To a certain extent, they had
prepared for the battle before leaving home. But that preparation was
limited, both because there was not always a place for them in the
universities and because of the inflexibility of their spiritual traditions.
Hassidic law condemned idolatry and thus the reproduction of faces: 'You
will make no statues nor any images that are in the heavens above, nor
on the earth below, nor in the waters beneath the earth.'[1]

In the East, Jewish art was religious. There was no other tradition. The

Jews, tucked away in their ghettos, were impermeable to the outside world. The artists drew like children read: during the day, they worked on what they could show, and at night, on what they kept hidden. In the light of day, they carried on with normal life in the shtetl; and in the shadows, they unlocked forbidden images – first concealed and later expressed on the blank page, in the secrecy of locked rooms. The only way to find freedom was to leave.

Leaving was also the sole means of escaping anti-Semitism, official and ancestral. In many countries, the doors to universities were closed to Jews: they were notably forbidden from entering the Royal Academy of St Petersburg. When they arrived, these uprooted men knew only one word in the French language: Paris. They had chosen this city because others who had left before them had sent back a message. In Paris, one could live and paint as a free man. In Paris, Jewish artists worked alongside the others. They had the right to say anything, to show everything. Of course, they were very poor, but in most cases they had already known poverty before coming. They didn't know the language, but they would learn. The most important thing was to be able to paint openly at last – free, and far from schools and movements, whether impressionism or the newly invented cubism. Paris, as De Chirico would write soon afterwards, was a place where men, ideas, feelings, and creation all converged. Paris was, for everyone, the capital of the world.

UBU ROI

God is the shortest path from zero to
infinity. In which direction, one
might ask?

Alfred Jarry

Until the war, the painters of the Ruche did not cross paths or brushes with the artists of the Bateau Lavoir: a river separated the two worlds. When Picasso's group of friends crossed the Seine, it was usually to met men of letters, friends of Apollinaire. For Montparnasse rustled with the murmurs of the poets. Rhymers had always been kings in the neighbourhood, with scribblers following close behind. Montparnasse did not pace itself to the combined rhythm of the Dôme and Rotonde cafés, but to the versified cadence of the Closerie des Lilas.

The Closerie was the first of all the cafés to give an artistic reputation to the neighbourhood. Originally, it was a simple stop on the road to Fontainebleau. Its fame came from its proximity to the Bullier ballroom, which was located on the Avenue de l'Observatoire, across from the Luxembourg gardens. Until the war, one could dance amidst the lilacs there. Afterwards, one could have something to drink at this little bistro at the top end of the Boulevard Saint Michel, where it met Montparnasse, and where students mingled with artists. Many drank toasts there, in the shade of the statue of Marshal Ney, who had been shot to death on the Avenue de l'Observatoire after his return from the island of Elba. The statue had been brought back to be placed in the shade of the café when the Sceaux railroad was built.

The Closerie was a bastion of the Dreyfusards. It also became a second base of operations for habitués of the Flore, where Charles Maurras and his Camelots gathered.* Regular customers included Monet, Renoir, Verlaine, Gide and Gustave the Red, as well as a poet who would play a fundamental role in the intersection of the various arts in Montmartre and Montparnasse: Paul Fort.

---

* The 'Camelots du roi' were a group of right-wing nationalists.

Today, only very few remember him and sing his *French Ballads*: 'The little horse in bad weather, what courage he had!' But he was a prince, the prince of poets. He was elected to the post after Verlaine, Mallarmé, and Léon Dierx. Five newspapers, *La Phalange*, *Gil Blas*, *Comœdia*, *Les Nouvelles* and *Les Loups* organized a referendum in 1912 to name a successor to Dierx, who had just died. Three hundred and fifty writers voted for Paul Fort: he was judged the best person to inherit and carry on French literary traditions.

Paul Fort had no money. When he was asked how he managed to earn his living, he answered, with a smile on his lips, 'Why, with my pen, of course!' He copied his own works and sold them to collectors of rare manuscripts and autographs. Every Tuesday, he met his friends at the Closerie des Lilas, which was then run by the père Combes. All those assembled joyously toasted poetry, wine, festivity and song.

This master of hearts had the face and manners of a musketeer. Thin, with long hair and a pointed moustache, wearing a black tie beneath a jacket buttoned up to the collar, he laughed, drank toasts, told stories, lisped a little; he directed the show. Often, at midnight, in his shrill little voice, he would improvise wonderful poems. Sometimes, standing on a table, he would sing, accompanied by a piano and the voices of his friends, the cheers only dying out at dawn.

His friend Jean Papadiamantopoulos, whose pen name was Jean Moréas, listened, joked, and versified in the smoke and the haze of alcohol. This extremely erudite man, who led his readers on merry tours through the work of Chateaubriand, Vaugelas, Barrès or Madame de la Fayette, would sit at his regular table, drunk: his shiny silk top hat pulled down over his monocle, his monocle falling off constantly onto his dyed moustache, and the moustache presiding over sometimes quite disagreeable words emitted by a mouth with distinct rightist tendencies, which pronounced praise for Barrès and Maurras. This did not necessarily displease his evening's companion, the editorial secretary of the *Mercure de France*, Paul Léautaud, who went there once and swore never to return. But two other things did dismay him: Moréas' uncleanliness, legendary but confirmed, and the general level of alcohol. Moreover, on this particular occasion, Léautaud was depressed: he had just learned that in the space of five and a half years, only five hundred copies of his book, *Petit Ami*, had been sold.

It was with Moréas and Salmon that Paul Fort had founded a famous review in 1905: *Vers et Prose*. The three companions had borrowed two hundred francs, used them to buy stamps, and sent two thousand letters to the first future subscribers. *Vers et Prose* was a monument of French letters until the war, which destroyed it. In its pages it published eminent poets and writers such as Maeterlinck, Stuart Merrill, Barrès, Gide, Maurras, Jules Renard, Apollinaire ... Its offices were located in its founder's home, on the rue Boissonnade. Pierre Louÿs came up with the title. The stated purpose of *Vers et Prose* was to publish the 'heroic group of poets and prose writers who have modernized the substance and style of French letters, renewing the taste for great literature and lyricism which had long been abandoned.'

The troubadours of symbolism harnessed the power of the image, a mysterious force which was not easily analysed. It was a question of evoking the 'soul of things ... the secret affinities which our soul has with certain things.'[1] Their aim was to suggest, not describe.

The review brought together all the tendencies of the 'young literature'. Paul Fort nonetheless remained the key figure of a symbolism whose hour of glory had already come several years before. The great representatives of this school were Henri de Régnier, Saint-Pol Roux and, one day out of three, Jean Moréas, who changed schools more often than shirts. They were reacting against the realists (Zola), the romantics (Chateaubriand, Hugo, Lamartine), and the Parnassians (Banville, Leconte de Lisle, Baudelaire, Coppée). They reproached them for overvaluing analytical and critical qualities in their poems, and for having alienated the younger generation. They were unsparing in their criticism of these writers, but also of Flaubert and Catulle Mendès, who had judged Verlaine to be a very minor poet.

However, symbolism did not have a deep and lasting influence on the history of literature. It was a passing reaction which hardly lasted a dozen years. The great campaign of the symbolists, and later of the post-symbolists, concerned the question of rhythm. The conventional rules needed to be defied, the alexandrine liberated from its twelve chains, and free verse had to triumph. The columns of *Vers et Prose* were filled with debates and comments on this question; even Mallarmé joined in, *post mortem*, deploring in the alexandrine 'an abuse of the national cadence, whose use, like that of the flag, should remain an exception'.

From the first issue, the review had four hundred and fifty subscribers, and soon there were readers all over the world. The editorial team gave them free books, and welcomed advertising in its pages, from publishers, booksellers, bookshelf manufacturers, banks and financial firms.

In 1910, the publishing house Vers et Prose was founded. Enormous banquets were held, with nearly five hundred guests, for the most popular poets. On Tuesdays, at the Closerie, the merrymakers were fewer but just as noisy. They didn't come only from Montparnasse: many crossed the river, and some came on foot from Montmartre. When they entered the bistro to attend one of Paul Fort's Tuesdays, the painters of the Bateau Lavoir did not find themselves in unknown territory. Their riotous colours harmonized easily with the witty tastes of the poets of the Closerie des Lilas.

*

It was at the Closerie, around 1905, that the band of painters from the Place Ravignan got to know a friend of Apollinaire who sometimes came to the Fox – Alfred Jarry. It was Jarry who infected them with his passion for firearms. 'Jarry, he who revolver ...' was Breton's cryptic quip about this living monument whom the surrealists venerated, and with whom they shared two passions: poetry and gunslinging.

Guillaume Apollinaire was the first to take aim:

> Alfred Jarry ... seemed to me to be the personification of a river, a young beardless river, dressed in the damp clothes. of a person who's just escaped from drowning. He had a droopy little moustache, a morning coat with side panels swinging loose, a soft shirt and a cyclist's shoes. There was something formless and spongy about it all: the demigod was still wet; apparently he had emerged only a few hours earlier from the bed which was drenched by his wave.[2]

At the time, Jarry was the creator of pataphysics, whose praises Ubu and Faustroll would be the first to sing. Just what was pataphysics? 'A science that we have invented, the need for which was generally felt.'[3] This science proposed an observation of the world that began with its exceptions, its paradoxes, all that lay outside fixed habits of conventional thought. (René Daumal, and later Boris Vian and Raymond Queneau would continue to develop Jarry's experiments, with their 'College of Pataphysics'.)

When Apollinaire met Jarry, the latter had already published many articles in L'Art littéraire or Le Mercure de France. Several of his literary works had already appeared, such as César-Antéchrist, Les Jours et les nuits, Le Surmâle. He was best known as the author of a play which had created a sensation and revolted the well-mannered, respectable Paris audience, who were seated tranquilly at the Théâtre de l'Oeuvre, on 9 December 1896. At the first exchange – 'Merdre!'* – the audience was on its feet in protest.

Alfred Jarry lived on the rue Cassette, in an apartment just his size, if not proportional to his reputation. It was located between the third and fourth floors. Guillaume Apollinaire and Ambroise Vollard often came to visit. One knocked at a tiny door, encased in the stairway. The door opened towards the visitor, hitting him in the chest. A voice from inside asked the new arrival to bend down so that his face could be seen.

If it was a friend, Jarry invited him in. The visitor found himself in a room with a very low ceiling where he could only walk bent over: the owner of the building had divided his apartments in two, hoping to double his profits by renting them to short tenants. Vollard, who was tall,

---

* An invented word, the approximate equivalent of 'Shitly!'

relates that Jarry was just short enough to fit in. The dealer also recounts

that he lived there with an owl, the top of whose skull had been whitened
by plaster from the ceiling. The writer himself, who sometimes grazed it,
had some white hairs too. We don't know today if it was a flesh-and-
blood owl or only porcelain, although André Breton also complained
about the smell of the owl cage.

Jarry slept in a very low bed and wrote stretched out at full length. On
one wall hung a canvas (which later disappeared), a portrait of the writer
by his friend the Douanier Rousseau. It apparently showed Jarry in the
company of a parrot and a chameleon. But what one noticed most,
according to André Salmon, were the changes that the model had made
in the work: he had cut his own silhouette out of it, so that the canvas
contained a large gaping hole. Jarry couldn't stand seeing his painted
image – he couldn't bear to look at himself at all.

When he wanted some exercise, he would take his bicycle and pedal
to Plessis-Chenet, on the banks of the Seine. Near the estate belonging to
Valette, the director of the *Mercure de France*, and his wife, the novelist
Rachilde (her real name was Marguerite Eymery), he had bought a
minuscule lot where he had constructed a kind of house, called the
Tripode. It was made of wood and occupied nearly the entire surface of
his 'property': sixteen square yards. He stayed there in the summer,
devouring fish he had caught himself.

Jarry ate very little, except when he could make a joke out of it. Seated
one day at the table of a bistro on the rue de Seine with Salmon, he called
for the director.

'A brandy, please.'

'Is that all?'

'No, I'd like some coffee as well.'

'But ...'

'Coffee, a piece of cheese, and a fruit salad.'

'But you're ordering dessert!'

'To start with, yes. After that, please bring me half a chicken.'

'And then?'

'Then some macaroni.'

'Would you like a steak with it?'

'Rare, please.'

'All that at the same time?'

'No, in the order I asked for it.'

The bistro owner agreed, with a knowing look.

'After the meat, I'd like some radishes,' added Alfred Jarry. 'And soup.'

'Is that everything?'

'No, I'd like a glass of Pernod, too ... full strength.'

The owner put a hand on his customer's shoulder and sighed.

'Now stop it! You're going to make yourself sick!'

'Take your paws off me! And bring me some red ink in a little glass.'

'Very well, sir.'

The ink was brought. Jarry dipped a cube of sugar in the glass and drank all the ink. And that day he was dieting. Usually, he ate only cold meat and pickles.

This didn't keep him from drinking heavily, preferably 'herbe sainte',* the poetic name he gave to absinthe. According to Rachilde, his best friend, who remained faithful until his death, he consumed two litres of white wine and three Pernods between the time he got up and lunchtime. Then came liqueurs during the meal, coffee accompanied by brandy as an after-lunch drink, several apéritifs before dinner, and before going to bed, he would soothe his stomach with a dose of Pernod, a shot of vinegar and a drop of ink.

No one ever saw him drunk – only sick, when, to play a trick on him, Valette's daughter replaced the alcohol in his glass with water. It was too pure for him . . .

The first time he met Apollinaire, the two men stayed up all night walking around Paris. While they were on the Boulevard Saint Germain, a man came up to them to ask the way to Plaisance. Jarry whipped a revolver out of his pocket, aimed it at the stranger, ordered him to step back a few metres . . . and gave him the directions he'd asked for.

The six-shooter was our literary Ubu's great love. The stories of his exploits with it are innumerable. One evening when he was dining at Maurice Raynal's, Picasso's friend Manolo came up to him. He simply wanted to meet him, which didn't interest Jarry. He ordered the sculptor to leave him alone and to leave the room immediately. As the Spaniard made no effort to move, the writer pulled out his gun and fired into the curtains.

Another time, he was sitting in a café. A woman was seated at a nearby table. For some inexplicable reason, he conceived a sudden antipathy for a neighbouring customer. He rose, whipped out his revolver, and shot into a mirror. The mirror exploded, and the café went wild. Calmly, Jarry sat back down, turned towards the woman, and said: 'Now that the ice is broken, why don't we talk?'†

Once, shooting in the garden of a house he had rented in Corbeil (which he had named Le Phalanstère), he was practising uncorking bottles of champagne with his shots. The landlord suddenly appeared, frightened out of his wits, and pleaded, 'Stop, sir, stop! You're going to kill my child!'

* Literally, 'sainted grass', here a play on words with 'absinthe', with which it rhymes.
† In French, the word for 'mirror' and the word for 'ice' are the same: 'glace'.

'It doesn't matter,' answered Jarry, 'we'll make you another one.' He was boasting: Jarry didn't like women, and no one ever knew him to have a love affair.

He drew his gun on pedestrians who got in his way, he drew it to silence noisy children, he drew it when he couldn't get into an over-filled bus. Even when he didn't have his revolver on him, he never disarmed.

One evening, he attended a concert. He presented himself at the ticket office dressed in a paper shirt on which he had painted a tie, in Indian ink. This outfit did not please the direction, and he was sent to sit in the highest balcony. To begin with, he didn't say a word. But, when the theatre had quietened down and the conductor was about to launch into the score, he suddenly rose and shouted, 'It's a crime! How can they let the people sitting in the first three rows enter the theatre with those musical instruments? They're going to bother everybody!'

On 28 May 1906, after having received the last sacraments and drafted his will, he wrote to Rachilde:

> The père Ubu, who deserves his rest, is going to try to sleep. He believes that the brain, in decomposition, functions beyond death and that these dreams are Paradise. The père Ubu (this is conditional – he would so like to return to the Tripode) may be going to sleep for ever.

The next day, he added a postscript: 'I'm reopening my letter. The doctor has just come and thinks he may be able to save me.'[4]

He did indeed save him. Jarry survived for nearly another year and a half. Every day, armed with two revolvers and a lead-ended stick, he visited his doctor. The situation was dire. Debt-ridden and tubercular, he hid the truth from everyone. He dressed in friends' cast-off clothing. He was waiting for the end.

On 29 October 1907, Jarry didn't open the door when Valette knocked at the third floor mezzanine. Valette forced the lock. The writer was stretched out on his bed, unable to move. He was transported to the Hôpital de la Charité. For two days, ceaselessly, he exhaled, in a murmur, 'I'm looking, I'm looking, I'm looking . . .'

Dr Stephen-Chauvet, who examined him, noted that the sick man was exceptionally calm. He was very feeble. His liver was in shreds, his pulse weak. He didn't complain.

He died on 1 November, of tubercular meningitis. He was also suffering from chronic alcoholic intoxication, but this was in no sense the cause of his death.[5]

He had bequeathed the Tripode to his sister and, it was said (by Max Jacob, first of all), his revolver to Picasso. It is not known what became of his bicycle, a Clément Luxury 96 racetrack model, which had not been paid for at the time of its owner's death.

Dead at the age of thirty-four, Jarry never had time to play the role he deserved on the literary scene. His pranks and practical jokes were a language of their own, which his friends of the time knew how to interpret – Apollinaire more than anyone, who declared that 'Alfred Jarry was a man of letters of the sort one rarely finds. His slightest act, his games, every one of his gestures was literature.'[6] Breton concurred: 'Starting with Jarry, much more than Wilde, the distinction long deemed necessary between art and life was blurred, until it was finally abolished in its very principle.'[7]

What better homage can one render to Jarry, who so wanted to be Ubu and who played in life the role of this character whom he himself defined as the 'perfect anarchist'? But Jarry's intimate drama was that his reputation actually rested on an imposture: he was not really the father of Ubu, and never had been. This play which made him famous, so very famous, was not really his. He was indeed an author, and a great author; his books attest to that. But *Ubu roi* was a collective work to which Jarry barely contributed. The père Ubu was the hero of a long poem drafted by the students of the lycée in Rennes who wanted to make fun of their physics professor, the père Hébert, a man with no authority, whose pupils delighted in tormenting him. When Jarry was sixteen and at school, the play already existed. It was called *Les Polonais*, and the authors were the Morin brothers. Jarry came up with the title and the name of the main character. This name probably comes from a contraction of Hébert, who was called Hébée or Eb by the students – Hébée became Ubu.

It was probably also Jarry who added the anti-militaristic scenes when the play was first produced. But neither Chandelle Verte nor Cornegidouille are his creations. And still less the famous 'Merdre' with which the first scene opens. Charles Morin confided, 'We were still kids; our parents naturally didn't want us to use the word in its normal form, so we had the idea of putting in an "r", that's all there was to it.'[8]

But Ubu still owes to Jarry the fact of having travelled the world over, for it was he who first played the principal character on the stage: at the lycée in Rennes, to begin with, where the play was put on by the students, then in other places, sometimes with marionettes.

The reviews were superlative. Shakespeare was invoked, and Rabelais. *Vers et Prose* hailed this 'immortal burlesque tragedy, one of the masterpieces of French genius'. Long after Jarry's death, *L'Action française* was still applauding the caricature of Robespierre, of Lenin, of Bolshevism on the march ... All of which made the Morin brothers laugh, though they didn't react. Of course, they were still somewhat exasperated by the role that Jarry had ascribed to himself, making it seem as though he was the sole author of what was really a collective work. But they didn't give him away. Their explanation: the joke, which ridiculed the world of the time, and more particularly the pretensions of the literary milieu, amused them greatly. They had been friendly with Jarry during their school years, and knowing how much Ubu had helped him at the beginning of his career, they were delighted by the fame this farce had brought him. Finally, they had let him do what he wanted with Les Polonais, on two conditions: that he change the title and the names of the characters, so that no one would connect them to the père Hébert and the lycée de Rennes. For the rest, Ubu remained in the eyes of its two authors an amusement, a farce – better still, a 'ballbuster'.

Even if he undoubtedly was the author of Ubu enchaîné and Ubu cocu, even if the character of Ubu appears in his own works (notably in Les Minutes de sable mémorial and César-Antéchrist), the original Ubu roi was therefore not written by Jarry. His friend Ambroise Vollard knew this so well that during the First World War he accepted the task of writing a sequel to the saga: Les Réincarnations du père Ubu, with illustrations by Rouault.

This usurpation of the original work was to weigh heavily on Jarry's destiny, and also on his shoulders. We don't know of any confessions made by him on the subject of Les Polonais. Once though, he did confide:

I'm crushed by Ubu. It's only a student's farce and isn't even by me … I've done, and done well, many other things. But all they can talk about is Ubu, he's always there blocking the road. I have to speak him, mime him, live him. That's all they want![9]

Valette and Rachilde's daughter confirms that she never heard Jarry called anything other than Ubu: 'It was like a mask, that he sometimes left off when he was with us, his family. And occasionally we all began to talk like the père Ubu.'[10]

The role invaded Jarry's very being. But he played it and accepted all the curtain calls. He strode about on the stage of his life like a copy of this character, simultaneously displaying aspects of Macbeth, Falstaff, Garguantua, Tykho Moon and Polichinelle, who stands tall on the stage of existence, shouting 'Merdre'! He scandalized the habitués of fashionable drawing rooms with his provocation, his insolence and, again, with conduct which brandished the banner of libertarianism and anarchism, rejecting the plush chairs of official academies. In the end, Jarry's entire life was a tragicomedy in one act.

2 AUGUST 1914

On that day, lightning struck
the hearts of men.

Joseph Delteil

Ubu was not reasonable. But neither was the century. It had barely reached
the age of reason when it was already going off to war.

On 28 June 1914, the Archduke Franz Ferdinand was felled by the shot
of a Serb fanatic. On 28 July, Austria-Hungary declared war on Serbia.
On the 31st, Germany issued an ultimatum to France and Russia. The
same day, Jean Jaurès was assassinated. On 1 August, France mobilized
her troops. On the next day, which dawned bright and sunny, the soldiers
set off for the front, from the Ecole Militaire and the barracks of Paris.
With a flower on the end of their rifles and a helmet by their sides, in a
clattering of swords, sabres and bayonets, accompanied by waving flags
and music, the troops marched up the avenues and converged towards
the stations. Cavalrymen, dragoons, artillerymen, infantrymen and foot
soldiers of the marching army had one common cry: 'To Berlin!' They
estimated it would take a week to get there, and they would be back to
Paris just as quickly, bearing the scalp of the Kaiser on the end of their
guns.

In the cafés of Montparnasse, customers drank to the coming victories.
The Vavin corner had by now dethroned the Lapin Agile and the top end
of the Boulevard. On the eve of the First World War, following in Picasso's
footsteps, the artists crossed the Seine; they fled the tourists who were
beginning to arrive in Montmartre. The seeds had been sown on the right
bank, but the harvest would be reaped in Montparnasse.

The Closerie des Lilas was no longer the most popular place in the
neighbourhood – it had become too bourgeois. The price of *pastis* had
risen from six to eight sous: in retaliation, the painters and poets had
moved further on. They had ventured into two bistros set right across
from each other on either side of a wide crossroads, the Dôme and the
Rotonde. The former had opened fifteen years before the latter: it had three

rooms where Germans, Scandinavians, and Americans played billiards. The Rotonde offered two advantages: a slot machine and a sunny terrace. Soon it expanded, swallowing up its neighbours, the Parnasse and the Petit Napolitain. This is where the artists met to jeer the Kaiser.

On this 2 August, the Vavin crossroads was like any other place in Paris. Except that on the south side, a party was in full swing, while the north side rang hollow with defeat. The Rotonde was full of people – across the street, the Dôme was empty. The Germans had abandoned its green carpet: from now on, they would wear their pointed caps on the other side of the border. The painters, who until then had believed that art had no borders, sadly accompanied their German friends, summoned by Kaiser Wilhelm, to the train stations. They were leaving for Berlin or for Zurich, followed by angry boos from the crowds.

The air was rife with anti-German sentiment, in all areas, and art didn't buck the trend. The day after the Peau de l'Ours sale, *Paris-Midi* published an article which reflected a general feeling:

> Amazing prices were paid for the grotesque and formless works of undesirable foreigners ... Thus, the qualities of balance and order typical of our national art will gradually disappear, to the joy of M. Tannhauser and his countrymen who, one of these days, will no longer be content just to buy Picassos but will cart off the Louvre itself, free of charge, and, as the ineffectual snobs and intellectual anarchists will be incapable of defending it, they will thus become involuntary accomplices to the crime.[1]

Apollinaire himself set the tone. He condemned Romain Rolland and all the writers who only wanted peace. He proclaimed his 'anti-Kraut' feelings loud and strong. At the time of the publication of *Alcools*, he claimed that the Germans had translated 'Zone', the first poem in the collection, without ever giving him a mark's worth of royalties: 'When they are not setting fire to French cathedrals, they are cheating French poets.'[2]

Was it because he never went to the front that André Gide would be one of the rare writers to advocate Franco–German reconciliation – without which, he wrote, the consolidation of Europe could not take place? For many years, he was preaching in the desert. All French literature of the time, until the thirties, is filled with the narrow-minded patriotism that had already been denounced at the end of the preceding century by Rémy de Gourmont.

In 1917, people went so far as to rename eau de Cologne, calling it eau de Louvain; German shepherds became known as Alsatian shepherds; the rue de Berlin became the rue de Liège; and the rue Richard Wagner became the rue Albéric Magnard. 'I hope that when peace comes, they'll give the rue de la Victoire another name,' concluded Paul Léautaud, scandalized.[3]

The Rotonde escaped this treatment to a certain degree: nationalism there was less ferocious than elsewhere. As the armies marched by, the père Libion, owner and manager of the café, had been dispensing free drinks since morning, letting his artists partake of the varied pleasures his cellars had to offer. With one hand on his hip and the other smoothing down his moustache, dressed entirely in grey as was his wont, he watched the troops coming up the Boulevard. On the sidelines, women threw flowers at the young soldiers. The officers, in black tunics and red trousers, gave the military salute. The French national anthem, the 'Marseillaise', was on everyone's lips.

As they passed the Rotonde, though, the notes became shriller and the words died out. The troops and their followers began to boo the young men who were toasting the military marches but whose only uniforms were multicoloured shirts, worn over skin that was not made in France. And this Maurassian cry resounded, which, almost a century later, continues to scorch our ears: 'Half-breeds go home!'

They were not French, it is true, and this was visible to the eye. They were doubly foreign: they not only spoke with accents, but their clothes were different, as were their manners and occupations. Some came from far-away lands, others didn't. They still shared similar customs, incomprehensible to most French people. They stood there, on the borders, in the margins, on the pavements – apart from the thronging crowds who ran after the troops.

But on that day, there was a misunderstanding. Although they may have been foreigners, they were not cowards. Foreigners, certainly, different, yes, but if they all crowded into the café, taking refuge behind the père Libion's curtains, it was not through cowardice but to protect themselves from the storm of insults which were just as hideous at the time as they are today. What they didn't say, the foreigners, was that they had learned of the appeal made by two of their own, the Italian Ricciotto Canudo and the Swiss citizen Blaise Cendrars:

> Foreign friends of France, who, during their stay in France have learned to love it and cherish it like a second country, feel the imperious need to offer her their arms.
>
> Intellectuals, students, workers, healthy men of all sorts – born elsewhere, resident here – we who have found material nourishment in France, let us gather, in a solid group of good will, to offer our services for the good of the greatest France.

What they didn't say was that because 1 August fell that year on a Saturday, they were all waiting for the coming Monday to register in the recruitment centres. And on Monday, with the Poles leading the way, nearly a hundred thousand of them turned up on the rue Saint Dominique to join the legion. After which, map in hand, they descended upon the wholesale clothes market in the Temple neighbourhood to buy hoods, trousers, pea-jackets and képis that they would transform into military gear.

In a few weeks, the former residents of the Bateau Lavoir separated for ever, and Montparnasse lost its brothers from afar; they were all off to defend their adopted country in the entrails of the North. Apollinaire left for Nice, where he joined up. Picasso accompanied Braque and Derain to the Avignon train station, on their way to the war. Moïse Kisling returned from Holland to take up arms. Blaise Cendrars accompanied him, as did Per Krogh, Louis Marcoussis, Ossip Zadkine...

On 2 August in Paris, Frantz Jourdain, the enlightened president of the Salon d'Automne, cried, 'At last, cubism is doomed!' These were probably not the thoughts of Léger, Lhote, and Dunoyer de Segonzac, mobilized along with the others of their age. Nor those of Carco and Mac Orlan, who were also leaving. Still less those of Modigliani and the Italo-Chilean painter Ortiz de Zarate, who were turned away from the legion and elsewhere, because they were too weak and sickly to handle a rifle. Mané-Katz was too short, and Ehrenbourg was battling with tuberculosis. These men remained at home, in the company of Diego de Rivera, Brancusi, Gris and Picasso.

Foujita left for London; and from there would go to Spain, then return to Paris. Pascin would stop briefly in England before leaving for the United States, where Picabia and Duchamp had arrived before him. As for Delaunay, he was looking for an alibi. Some claim that he was turned away from the army for a heart murmur, or even bouts of madness. Cendrars would break with him, deeming, like many others, that he simply hid in Spain and Portugal with his wife Sonia.

In the days and weeks that followed, what remained of Montmartre? Of Montparnasse? Empty avenues, cafés forced to close before the curfew, the Bullier ballroom transformed into a munitions depot, and dire private poverty that had come to stay were the inevitable results of war. There was nothing to eat and nothing to drink. The mayor of the fourteenth arrondissement, Ferdinand Brunot, a grammarian and professor at the Sorbonne, resigned from his university post to concentrate on taking care of his district. He opened soup kitchens for the down-and-out. The socialist party opened what they called 'communist soup kitchens'. In their studios, those painters who remained suffered acutely from cold, hunger, and poverty.

The Ruche was requisitioned for refugees arriving from the Champagne region. The lawns became vegetable gardens. Trees lost their tops, which were chopped up for firewood. One winter morning, the concierge who, in the summer, sprayed his tenants with a hose containing ice water, climbed up to Chagall's studio. Chagall, who had left for Vitebsk on vacation on the eve of the war, had not been able to come back (he wouldn't return until 1923). The guardian of the temple took from the studio all the canvases he found there. After checking to make sure that the paint had made the canvas impermeable, he came back to the ground floor, satisfied. Paintings in hand, he returned to his lodgings. His roofing was faulty. He took it down and, with the beatific smile of a patron of the arts, replaced it with this protection come straight from the heavens: Chagall's paintings.

UNDER THE DIMMED STREET LAMPS

In Montparnasse we have artists' canteens, which let them indulge
their natural temperament and forget, at the expense of decency –
they even go so far as to dance – the national suffering, and all the
other suffering.

Max Jacob

Paris in wartime, Paris in poverty. The city was clothed in the dull colours
of deprivation and restriction. The lamp-posts and the headlights of cars
were dimmed. Shop windows were fitted out with anti-bomb tape. People
had to get used to new rules. Hunger weighed like a leaden sky over the
population. Everyone was learning the old law of the poverty-stricken:
life is nothing but a digestive tube. Only money lets one salivate: fifteen
sous for a pot-au-feu, thirteen sous for a helping of spinach, two sous for
a pound of pears, one sou for a hot chocolate...

The war cut off the revenues of all the foreign artists living in Paris:
the art dealers had left the city, the galleries were closed. The money that
some of them regularly received no longer crossed the border. They had
to wait long hours simply to obtain a few lumps of coal, sufficient to
warm the body for just long enough to remember what warmth was.
Rodin himself, though ill, was freezing over his marble slab, for no one
brought him the firewood he needed to keep warm.

But generally speaking, the artists demonstrated their solidarity. This
was nothing new. Caillebotte had supported his impressionist friends by
buying their paintings, organizing exhibitions, giving money to Monet,
Pissarro and Renoir. In the second decade of the century, the Russians of
Paris had organized charity balls to help out the poorest among them. In
1913, in Vers et Prose, Salmon, Billy and Warnod had announced the
creation of a literary mutual aid association that would collect funds for
writers without any sources of income. From 1914 on, Max Jacob wrote
to friends who had left for the front, sharing any news he received from
them with all the others. In 1915, the poet collected funds to send the
Italian painter Gino Severini, who was dying of hunger and tuberculosis,
to the south of France. Ortiz de Zarate, a great friend of Max Jacob (he
had also seen the Lord appear to him on a wall), followed Jacob's example

when he discovered Modigliani unconscious in his studio one day. He drummed up funds from all their friends to send the painter off to be cared for by his family in Italy.

Canteens were opened, and it was not only the city authorities who subsidized them. Marie Vassilieff opened one for the painters, in the Impasse du Maine where she lived. For the entire duration of the war, her canteen was filled with a mixture of artists: those who were long-time Montparnasse residents, those who had escaped the draft or left the Bateau Lavoir, and the great figures of the war and post-war years.

Marie Vassilieff came from Russia. After studying painting in Moscow, she spent some time in Italy and arrived in France in 1912. She studied with Matisse for a while and founded a painting academy in the Impasse du Maine. Youki Desnos recounts that only a few weeks after her arrival, when she was sitting on a bench somewhere in Paris, she was approached by a very polite, perfectly discreet elderly gentleman, who played the violin well and handled a paintbrush with aplomb. He asked for her hand in marriage. He was forty years older than the young girl and had worked in the customs house of Paris: his name was Henri Rousseau.

Marie Vassilieff had not given him her hand: she kept it for herself and used it to paint and sculpt, to read fortunes for her friends, and to provide them with a warmth and vivacity which, in these difficult times of war, helped them to cope with their sad past and worse present.

Rumour had it that before 1914, the Tsarina had sent her some roubles; and a contradictory rumour insinuated that she had been in Munich, distributing Communist tracts. At the end of the war, she would be suspected of working for the Bolsheviks.

Her canteen was well known throughout Montparnasse. As a private establishment, it was not subject to the curfew: the artists entered with the hope that the promises of the night might erase the betrayals of the day. On the walls were paintings by Chagall, Léger and Modigliani. On the floor were some fringed rugs. On the shelves sat the doll-portraits made in felt, which Marie Vassilieff designed and then sold to the dress designer Poiret, or to comfortable right bank customers who piled them up in their hideaways. Everywhere were mismatched chairs, cushions with the stuffing falling out, hundred of objects picked up at the flea market.

Behind the bar, washing dishes, as tall as a plum and more vivacious than an elf, this paragon of a hostess officiated. On one gas burner and one alcohol burner, Marie and a cook prepared the daily food. Each diner paid a few dozen centimes for a bowl of bouillon, vegetables, sometimes a dessert. The richest among them could also buy a glass of wine and three Caporal Bleu cigarettes.

They ate, sang, played the guitar. They recited poetry. They spoke in

Russian, exclaimed in Hungarian, laughed in every language. When the sirens sounded, they just sang a little louder to drown out fear and danger.

The next day, the painters would meet at the Dôme or the Rotonde during the day. They would sit for hours on end, as the cafés were heated, and one could sneak out bits of food: the owner of the Rotonde didn't care. Before the war, he had also turned a blind eye when his customers slipped into their bags or pockets the saucers and silverware which helped to furnish their lodgings with everyday necessities. He was only prickly on two points: ladies had to keep their hats on, and gentlemen had to go elsewhere to open their bottles of ether and their sachets of cocaine. Otherwise, he was exceptionally tolerant. He had instructed the waiters not to insist on drinks being regularly reordered, so that, in these times of poverty, one could remain inside with just one café-crème and keep warm for hours. Why a café-crème? Because it was a drink for the poor, not good enough to be drunk in one gulp, not bad enough to be left in the cup; in addition, it was hot and cheap. The café-crémistes of the Rotonde drank in tiny sips, washed themselves in the sinks of the toilets, and huddled next to the stove to keep warm. Libion even went out to stand in line and buy cigarettes for his artists, when they couldn't buy any themselves. He loved them, protected them. He was for Montparnasse what the père Frédé had been for Montmartre.

Most of the painters and poets of the Bateau Lavoir were at the front, but those who had stayed in Paris also met at père Libion's place. The former Montmartre residents came into contact there with the important figures of Montparnasse, some of whom they already knew. Braque, Derain, and Apollinaire were off fighting; Max Jacob, Vlaminck, Salmon and Picasso represented the much reduced contingent from the Place Ravignan. They crossed paths with the artists who would soon take over the Vavin crossroads and dress it in colours as lively and rich as those of the Butte Montmartre in times past: the Pole Kisling, the Italian Modigliani, the Japanese Foujita, the Swiss Cendrars, the Lithuanian Soutine ... For those who remained on the sidelines in Paris, for those home on leave, for those refused by the draft, for the convalescents: when they crossed the threshold of the Rotonde, the Marne seemed to be at the ends of the earth.

CHAÏM AND AMEDEO

My heart is tugging at me.

Chaïm Soutine

Chaïm Soutine came to the Rotonde to learn how to read. When the painter didn't have enough money to pay for the café-crèmes his teacher requested in exchange for her skills, Libion took care of it, thus contributing to the popularization of the French language. Soutine certainly needed the help.

He was one of the artists who had known the greatest suffering. Eaten up inside, gnawed at by anguish, devoured by the need always to do better, he was hated by many – Chagall first among them, who reproached him for his dark moods, his sullen manners, his roughness.

Soutine at the Rotonde was the equivalent of Quasimodo with a fever. Seated in the back of the café, he repeated after his tutor the words that she taught him. She was ugly; he didn't look at her. He protected himself from the cold in a grey coat which was falling apart. His wide shoulders were like a frame for his face. His chin receded into his neck, and his neck was hunched down into a woollen scarf. His shiny black hair was invisible beneath a hat with a turned-down rim, like a blockhouse which could barely contain his burning eyes. Soutine looked everywhere, at everything: to see who loved him, who didn't love him, who might hurt him, who would buy him a café-crème or offer him a cigarette. He was dying of cold and hunger; he would say, 'My heart is tugging at me.' Often, he foraged in the neighbourhood trash cans, to find some old clothes or a cracked boot that he might be able to exchange for a herring or an egg.

Buying Soutine a meal was the best present one could give him. At the table, he was an ogre. He didn't eat, he devoured: stuffed himself, chewed on bones, inhaled the sauce. His face, from forehead to chin, became a masticating palette. He got food all over himself, wiped his face with his hands, licked his fingers. He had absolutely no manners. He had never been taught the art of gracious living.

He liked beautiful houses, but was afraid of making a mess. One day he was invited to the private home of some rich people. After the meal, he excused himself, left the table and went out into the park. He was looking for a tree. He unzipped his pants and pissed against the trunk.

'Why did you do that?' he was asked.

In his horrible accent, he answered, 'It's so beautiful here, I don't want to get anything dirty...'

Another time, when one of his dealers offered to pay for a room for him in a luxurious hotel in Marseille, Soutine disappeared and took refuge near the port, in a sailors' bordello where he spent the night.

He liked boxing. When the audience howled and screamed because one of the fighters was down, his face all beefy and bloody from blows, Soutine would smile, ecstatic. He rose and applauded, at exactly the wrong moment. His painting was the same: tormented, violent, full of deformed shapes. He was untamed, like his work, intense.

He didn't paint on fresh canvases but covered over old and bad paintings that he had bought at the Clignancourt flea market. When he was unhappy with the result – that is, almost always – he would tear what he had just done to pieces with a knife. He did the same when someone to whom he had shown his work didn't express enough enthusiasm for it. The Montparnasse painters passed the word: nobody should criticize Soutine's paintings, because if they did, he would destroy them.

When he lacked materials for painting, he would retrieve his torn canvases, arm himself with needle and thread, sew the split fragments back together and begin once more to paint those deformed faces, those twisted limbs, those outrageous bodies that were the mark of his genius. He was more brutal even than Van Gogh; wilder, more 'fauve', than Vlaminck.

He didn't go to the Salons which exhibited contemporary painting, but spent his days at the Louvre, observing the Flemish masters, whom he venerated. And also the Courbets, Chardins, and Rembrandts; this last was, for him, the greatest of them all. He learned about light: he sought the opening that life was not bringing him. Turned in on himself, his eyes cast down, his hands shoved into the pockets of his coat, littered with a few cigarette butts, he cast around him for a bone to gnaw on, a glass to drink, a detail to paint, a reason to smile.

When the door of the Rotonde opened to let in Modigliani, his face would suddenly light up. He would lose interest in learning the French language, instead following the Italian's weaving path among the tables. Amedeo was the exact opposite of Chaïm. He went from one group to another, smiling, dressed in a jacket and velvet waistcoat which hid the fact that his shirt was cut from mattress material. A long scarf floated in his wake like a train. He was extremely handsome, affable, playful.

He would sit down opposite a stranger, push away the cups and saucers with his long nervous hands, take out a pad of paper and a pencil, begin to hum and sketch a portrait without even asking the man if he wanted one. He would finish it in a flash, taking only three minutes, sign it, tear off the sheet and hand it to his model with a flourish.

'It's yours, for a glass of vermouth.'

This is how he managed to drink, and eat.

But Soutine did not have this kind of ease with people. He made a living by carrying crates in train stations. He entirely agreed with Modigliani, who proclaimed loud and clear that artists should not work at anything besides their art, and who indeed would never earn his living except with his paintbrushes. But Soutine only managed to whisper this opinion, and only to himself.

Where the Italian would take Dante's *Divine Comedy* from his pocket – a book he carried around with him at all times – and read it aloud for all the diners in the restaurant to hear, the Lithuanian would wait until he was at home, in private, to read Baudelaire, and would attend the Colonne concerts on his own, where the music transported him into a seventh heaven.

Soutine gave away nothing, for he had nothing. Modigliani had only his drawings, but half of Montparnasse had one of these; when he didn't exchange them for a glass of something, he would give them away for free. He sold them as well, for a few sous each. His generosity was legendary. André Salmon recounts that the first time he met Picasso, in a café on the rue Godot-de-Mauroy, the Italian gave him the little money he had.

Modigliani wore clothes that were old and frayed, but he wore them like a prince. He was always freshly shaven. He washed regularly, even using freezing water if necessary. Soutine, on the other hand, was dirty. One day, a doctor actually discovered a nest of bugs in his right ear.

He didn't have much success with women. He was shy and didn't know how to approach them. In Vilna, a young, middle-class Jewish girl had fallen in love with him. She'd invited him home to her parents' house. His manners were terrible, as usual. He got tomato sauce on the walls and egg yolk all over the carpet. But much was forgiven him: artists have talents other than knowing how to behave in public.

The family waited for him to ask for the girl's hand. He sought the words, the gestures, but couldn't find them. He was clumsy and scared. He was given hints, but these escaped him. To help make him understand, the parents bought an apartment meant for the young couple. They took him to see it. Soutine exclaimed how nice it was. Maybe he pissed in the fireplace. But he didn't open his mouth. By the time they had left the building, the young girl had decided to find another husband.

Later, Soutine conquered his timidity. It was in a hotel room, with a maid. He dared to take her hand. He dared to caress her palm with his

thumb. Enchanted, his gaze fixed on her, he dared to utter a compliment:
'Your hands are as smooth as plates!'

In Paris, he went to a whorehouse. He sat down on the bench, which was upholstered in red velvet. When the manager's assistant clapped her hands, six women entered the room. They posed and postured. Soutine didn't even look at the most beautiful ones, the most desirable ones. He went off to a room with the ones who most resembled his painting: those with deformed features, their skin reddened by alcohol and a harsh life.

Modigliani was attractive to women: they were drawn by his energy, his good looks, his aristocratic air, which impressed everyone. He had a son (though he always denied it), born of a passing liaison with a young Canadian student, Simone Thiroux. She still loved him, and sent him extraordinarily touching letters:

> My tenderest thoughts are with you in this New Year which I wish could be the year of a reconciliation between us ... I swear on the head of my son, who is everything to me, that no bad idea has entered my mind. But I loved you too much and I suffer so greatly that I ask this of you in a final plea ... I beg of you, have a tender thought for me. Console me a little, I am too unhappy and ask only for a shred of affection, which would do me so much good.[1]

But Modigliani was in love with an English poetess, the Paris correspondent of a British paper, *The New Age*. Her name was Beatrice Hastings. She was beautiful and stylish; she often wore a black dress which her lover had decorated from top to bottom. She drank whisky. She had green eyes and sported incredible hats. She was lively, rich, well read. She played the piano. She was a friend of Katherine Mansfield and, for the times, a shameful radical: she championed abortion.

She took her lover off to Montmartre, where she lived. They made love and fought, insulting each other in public, playing a game of destructive, fatal passion – Modigliani had a jealous soul. At the Dôme, at Baty's or Rosalie's, or at the Rotonde, everyone counted the points in their match. The painter's attacks were loud and public, especially when the aniseed liqueur or the curaçao went to his head. Then he would become violent – or he might sing at the top of his lungs in the streets, harangue passers-by, pirouette in every direction on the pavements. He would sometimes fall asleep in a dustbin, where the rubbish collectors would find him and pick him out the next morning.

Soutine had to drink at least ten glasses of alcohol before he would begin to loosen up, agree to rise and do a few clumsy dance steps, accompanied by two couplets in Yiddish. Afterwards, he would sit down again, and cry.

Amedeo would sober up slowly: his laugh, a child's laugh, folded, broke, and became bitter until it finally disappeared into silence and memories.

A little later, if Amedeo asked Soutine to sing again, he would answer that he didn't know how.

'Well, say a few words in Yiddish then.'

'I don't speak it.'

'But yesterday...'

'You heard wrong.'

'And your name? Doesn't Chaïm mean "life"?'

'I've forgotten.'

He forgot everything. He swore that he didn't speak Yiddish. He also swore that his former life didn't interest him. He scorned his family and the shtetl of yesterday which, unlike Chagall and Mané Katz, he didn't paint, even if his fascination for the blood of animals may have had its roots in the rituals of his childhood.

Modigliani was from the south. The sun of Italy is less oppressive than the moon of Russia, and the Sepharads more at home with the beauties of the world. Amedeo was Jewish, and he wanted people to know it. On occasion he would even strike an anti-Semite. He was Italian, too, and he never forgot it. In Paris, he always missed his country, but once in Livorno, he would soon want to return to France. Invariably, he repeated that he found his strength in Italy, but that he could only paint when he was in torment. And torment was in Montparnasse.

The entire family had always supported Amedeo. When he had chosen to abandon his studies to devote himself to drawing, no one had tried to prevent him. In 1902, he registered at the Free School of the Nude in Florence; then, the following year, at the Beaux-Arts in Venice. In 1906, he came to Paris with his parents' approval and a little sum given him by his mother. He returned to Livorno many times. Modigliani never had to paint or sculpt in conflict with those close to him.

Soutine had lived in a ghetto of Smilovitchi, near Minsk. He was the tenth child of a very poor tailor who beat his son whenever he found him drawing. His elder brothers followed suit, mocking and condemning his desire to paint. His father's desire was for Chaïm to become a cobbler. At the age of sixteen, he transgressed the Law by painting a portrait of the village rabbi. The punishment was immediate: he was locked up by the butcher of Smilovitchi in the coldroom of the store, and violently beaten. To avoid a scandal, the merchant agreed to give a sum of twenty-five roubles to the family, in exchange for which Soutine left for Minsk, where he took drawing lessons while touching up photos in a laboratory. He then went to the Academy of Fine Arts of Vilna, where he met Kikoïne and Krémègne. Thanks to the generosity of the town's doctor, he was able to come to Paris. At the time, he had read practically nothing.

Modigliani, at the time of his arrival in France, was already familiar with Mallarmé and Lautréamont; and he had discovered Nietzsche, D'Annunzio, Bergson, Kropotkin and many other authors in the family library. He was the brother of a socialist militant who had spent some time in prison before being elected deputy. In the Soutine family, no one was involved in politics.

Until the advent of Barnes in his life in 1922, Soutine lived in a poverty which was close to distress. Thanks to the support of his family, Modigliani had more comfortable periods from time to time.

When he first came to Paris, in 1906, he moved into a respectable hotel near the Madeleine church. He took courses at the Colarossi academy, then rented a studio in Montmartre. He went from one hotel room to another, lived briefly at the Bateau Lavoir, then discovered a small, simple shed at the end of the rue Lepic. He finally ended up in Montparnasse in 1909, having dilapidated almost the entire sum of money that his mother had been sending him from Italy. He never regretted it: the important thing was to be free and to devote himself to his art.

Modigliani was courageous. When war was declared, he wanted to join the army. The military authorities refused him for health reasons. He was in despair over this rejection, which didn't prevent him from expressing in no uncertain terms his anti-militaristic sentiments: he was whipped for insulting Serbian soldiers passing through Montparnasse.

As for Soutine, he was afraid of everything, even of bureaucratic officials, who reminded him of the anti-Semitic functionaries in his own country. He could only go to an administrative office if he was accompanied by someone who would protect him from mishaps.

He had few friends. He was born in the same town as Kikoïne, and the two men studied painting in Minsk. They travelled together from Vilna to Paris, they had both lived in the same artists' residences – but they didn't speak to each other. Chaïm ignored his fellow countrymen, not only Kikoïne but also Krémègne, who boasted of being his great rival.

Modigliani was known to all. In 1907, a year after moving to Paris, he met the doctor Paul Alexandre, who was his first patron, as well as being one of his first suppliers of hashish. The doctor had rented a house on the rue du Delta, where he welcomed poor artists, including Gleizes, Le Fauconnier, the sculptor Drouard and Brancusi. Modigliani exhibited his paintings there. Paul Alexandre posed for him and bought a great number of his works. He persuaded him to exhibit at the Salon des Indépendants in 1908.

Apollinaire helped him sell his paintings. Paul Guillaume, who was his first dealer, was introduced to him by another friend, Max Jacob. With this latter, Modigliani talked religion and Judaism. He gave him his portrait dedicated as follows: 'To my brother, with great tenderness.'

He was also friendly with Frank Haviland, who offered to let him use his house to paint in. He showed Anna Akhmatova around Paris, and recited verses from Verlaine with her. He protected Utrillo, his great friend from the Butte Montmartre, to whom he felt closer than he did to Picasso.

He was also a friend of Soutine, who he took under his wing. It was he who taught him to chew with his mouth closed, to refrain from sticking his fork into his neighbour's dish, and to avoid snoring when he fell asleep in restaurants. For Chaïm, Amedeo was like a brother. He was infinitely grateful to him.

The two men were totally dissimilar, but shared strong bonds. Modigliani, like Soutine, destroyed things, particularly his canvases and his sculptures – and in Livorno, he threw several Carrara marbles into the town's canal.

Both of them shared the same desire for independence; they were not part of any clique. They weren't close either to the key figures of the Bateau Lavoir, nor to the Italian futurists, whom Modigliani refused to support. They were no more cubist than Fauve, they did not frequent Matisse's academy, and they rarely went to the Steins', on the rue de Fleurus. They wanted to be free, to remain independent of all schools.

Both had to struggle against a common enemy that ravaged them from the inside. Modigliani suffered from a pulmonary lesion that he had contracted in his childhood and which, with the help of alcohol and drugs, had become tuberculosis. Soutine had a tapeworm and stomach pains which quickly and predictably, given his chronic malnutrition, became an ulcer. The Italian was racked by horrible fits of coughing which left him exhausted; the Russian swallowed impressive quantities of bismuth which hardly eased the vice-like grip of his pain. In the end, both men kept their personal dramas to themselves.

Everyone knew Chaïm's, of course: it was his childhood. One had only to see him walking in the street, stooped, his hands dug deeply into the pockets of his threadbare coat, to understand how heavily his family history weighed on his shoulders.

Amedeo, by contrast, hid his problem under layers of exuberance; perhaps he drowned it in alcohol and drugs. But neither the quinquina, the stout nor the lemon mandarin, neither the hashish nor the cocaine could deceive Soutine. He knew what deep grief Amedeo was trying to overcome, what tears he stifled in the arms of women or at the counters of bistros.

He knew because they had lived together at the Cité Falguière, in the first decade of the century. This was the period when Modigliani was struggling with himself, fighting off bouts of illness to try to achieve the only true dream that mattered to him. In reality, it wasn't painting he cared about: it was sculpture. Only sculpture.

THE VILLA ROSE

Survage: 'Why did you paint a portrait of me with only one eye?'

Modigliani: 'Because you look at the world with one eye; with the other, you look into yourself.'

In the courtyard of the Cité Falguière, Foujita, Brancusi, Soutine and the sculptor Lipchitz watched Modigliani working in stone. Mallet and chisel in hand, the Italian hammered away at the rows of blocks that would become heads and caryatids. These were his 'columns of tenderness' that he meant to fashion into a 'temple of Beauty'. Around him, there was not a single bottle, not a glass in sight. Three years after his arrival in Paris, Amedeo drank little. He hadn't yet begun to see in hashish the virtues he would discover in it later, those of allowing him to imagine particular ensembles of colours. This was all the more true because at the time, painting was not his primary goal.

The Italian watched the sun. He tapped. A cloud of dust flew from the stone, entered his throat, descended to his lungs. He coughed. He tapped. He stopped, filled a watering can and dampened his work. He tapped. He coughed. He dropped his tools, bent over double, covered his mouth with his hand and stopped working.

Lacking the money necessary to buy the stone he needed, he got limestone from the Italian masons who were building the new Montparnasse. When they couldn't give him any, he would call on a few friends, wait until night, and drag his wheelbarrow over to the deserted construction sites where he would steal the necessary materials. Sometimes, the little group would go down into the Métro, then being constructed, and spirit away some struts or crosspieces which they carted off quickly to the courtyard of the Villa Rose.

In the evening, Modigliani and Brancusi talked about Rodin. They didn't approve of his excessive modelling, of all the mud he used. For them, cutting directly into the stone was more natural. And Rodin was too academic for them. They preferred the liberties and inventions of Negro art. Modigliani's work, and in particular his elongated and deformed faces, revealed this influence: one detects in them an inspiration similar to that of the pieces exhibited at the Ethnology Museum at the Trocadéro, which Matisse, Picasso, Vlaminck and Derain had already discovered.

Paul Guillaume, who would become the Italian's dealer in 1914, exhibited in his gallery on the rue de Miromesnil some primitive works with which the residents of the Cité Falguière were of course familiar. Georges Charensol recounts that one day, when he was in the boutique along with Francis Carco, he saw the dealer take a statuette from the Congo, lean down and rub it in dust from the ground. Carco asked Paul Guillaume what the purpose of the manoeuvre was.

'It's simple,' answered the dealer without batting an eyelid. 'I'm adding years to it.'

Between 1909 and 1914, Modigliani worked in stone, helped by Brancusi. The Romanian had arrived in Paris in 1904, having come on foot from Bucharest. He was the son of a poor peasant couple and had left home at the age of nine; he had learned to read and write by himself. He lent his tools and offered the use of his studio. For him, as for Foujita, Zadkine, or Lipchitz, Amedeo was only a sculptor. They knew of his innumerable drawings done in blue pen, but they didn't know that he also wielded a paintbrush. In 1914, in The New Age, Beatrice Hastings published a few articles devoted to her lover. She does not once mention his painting in them. For all of them, Modigliani was not a painter, but a sculptor. His daughter Jeanne would confirm this, writing that 'the first vocation of the young Dedo, when he had hardly emerged from childhood and was just being born to art ... was indeed sculpture.'[1]

This was the source of Modigliani's tragedy: shortly before the war, he had had to give up this vocation. Stone cost too much. Buyers were not exactly pounding at his door. He refused to accept the part-time menial jobs which would perhaps have enabled him to continue. But above all, the dust which issued from the process of direct carving in stone was making a painful path to his lungs. Modigliani would hit the stone, and cough. He was found once by friends, inanimate at the foot of his sculptures. Vacations in the sun, in Livorno or elsewhere, didn't help: his health would not allow him to become the sculptor he dreamed of being.

So he would be a painter. His wartime works and those which followed always revealed the traces of this unsatisfied desire. They were like sculptures on canvas. These pure forms, the elongated faces and busts, the long arms, long necks, long bodies: all are strangely reminiscent of the heads he sculpted between 1906 and 1913.

That year, Modigliani left the Cité Falguière for the Boulevard Raspail. He found a studio in a courtyard: a construction in glass where the cold, the wind, and the rain all entered through the cracks. He lived and painted there. He recited Dante. When he was paralysed by the cold, he would take refuge in the homes or apartments of richer artists, whose portraits he painted, thus taking advantage both of their roof and of materials that he lacked. In this way he painted Frank Haviland, Léon Indenbaum and Jacques Lipchitz, who posed with his wife. He executed this last painting in one sitting, as he always did. But Lipchitz asked him to continue: for him, the portrait was unfinished. Amedeo objected that if he continued, he would ruin everything. Lipchitz didn't give in. It wasn't to make Modigliani work longer, he simply wanted to be able to pay him a little more. In the end, Modigliani bowed to the will of his patron. The portrait of Lipchitz and his wife is one of the few by Modigliani not to have been painted in a single sitting.

When he left these work sessions, he drank. He took hashish, then cocaine. One day, when some friends had given him a few coins so he could buy a collective dose for them all, he came back 'hilarious and sniffing, having taken it all himself'.[2] He spent money heedlessly, paying whatever was needed to calm his fevers and his rages. But he was a generous soul. Vlaminck, usually quick to criticize, never had anything but praise for him:

> Yes, I knew Modigliani very well! I knew him when he was hungry. I saw him drunk. I saw him when he'd made a little money. In no case did I ever see him lacking in nobility or generosity. I never saw him show the slightest unworthy sentiment. I did see him irascible, irritated to note that the power of money, which he so scorned, could sometimes compromise his will and his pride.[3]

Rosalie was the first to feel the effects of the artist's excesses. This Italian woman was a former model in Montparnasse, who had opened a bistro on the rue Campagne-Première. It could hold about twenty-five people, standing shoulder to shoulder. Before the war, Rosalie served spaghetti to the establishment's customers: the masons who were developing the neighbourhood, the penniless painters, the rats who had come from the former stables nearby. The customers had remained faithful. If they didn't like the presence of the animal species, the price was the same, and if they didn't like the price, all they had to do was leave. There were some customers for whom Rosalie had a fondness, and she was a determined, stubborn woman. Alert at her oven, sharp in her speech, she kept a motherly and determined eye on these four tables of a former dairy store that she now called a restaurant. When someone knocked at the door, she opened it. If she didn't like the newcomer, she closed it again. She accepted people who couldn't pay, either offering them a free bowl of soup or granting them credit. She refused the cheapskates who came only because it wasn't expensive, and the snobs dressed in American-style clothing.

Among the customers, she had a particular fondness for a four-footed animal from Arcueil. She had met the dog at the same time as the master: he pulled the cart of the upholsterer who had restuffed the chairs of the place. His work had taken four days, and the animal had not wasted a minute of it. When they left, his belly was full. When it was empty again, he wanted to refill it. So the dog had an idea: to take the road from Arcueil to Paris again. He did it all alone, relying on pure instinct. Then he did it a second time. And on and on, for twelve years. He was without a doubt Rosalie's most faithful customer.

Along with Modigliani, that is. The bistro owner and the artist had a strange kind of friendship: they adored each other and fought with each other constantly. She scolded him for drinking too much; he asked for more wine. To the amusement of the other customers, they shouted insults at each other, sparing one another nothing, stopping just short of throwing plates. When he flew into a rage, the painter would take down one of his numerous drawings pinned to the walls, and destroy it. When he came back the next day, contrite, he would bring her a new one. Which he would soon destroy as well. It was almost a game between them. A game which went sour when Utrillo arrived: in this case, it would sometimes happen that the two drunkards' antics would land them in the police station at the rue Delambre. In these moments of crisis, the commissioner Zamaron had to be called in.

As the officer in charge of foreigners at the Prefecture of Police in Paris, Zamaron was the artists' friend. The walls of his office were covered with their works: Suzanne Valadon, Modigliani, Soutine, Kikoïne and especially Utrillo, one of his special favourites. Whenever a painter got into trouble, Zamaron came to the rescue. When he wasn't on duty, he would often come to the Dôme or the Rotonde to find his friends. He frequently defended them from Descaves, the other Paris policeman who was also an art lover. Descaves was nothing but a source of problems for the Vavin painters. He would offer his services in exchange for paintings. Sometimes he would buy one, pay a first instalment, and ask the artist to come and collect the remaining sum at the Prefecture. Of course, no one ever went.

When he left the police station, Modigliani would go to the home of one or another of his friends, or to the Dôme, the Rotonde, or Rosalie's. Sometimes he would walk along the wall of the Montparnasse cemetery, taking the Boulevard Raspail where it intersects the rue Edgar Quinet and then the rue Schoelcher, on the right. He would walk next to the high walls of the cemetery until he reached a little building, where he briskly climbed the steps. He would knock at the door. A young woman opened it: Eva Gouel. She concealed her pale complexion under a thick layer of make-up. She was ill. Tuberculosis was whispered of. She had tried to keep the truth from her lover, Picasso, frightened by the signs of illness. For a long time, she had remained silent, fearing that he would abandon her. But Picasso remained faithful. He accompanied her to the doctors and to the clinics which Eva had to visit regularly.

The couple spent the first months of the war in the south of France. In Paris he didn't stray far from the rue Schoelcher: in the cafés, Picasso was insulted too often by soldiers on leave who didn't understand why this man with the lovely companion was not at the front.

The studio's bay windows looked out over the tombs in the Montparnasse cemetery. The room, quite large, was cluttered with tubes, palettes, paintbrushes. Fearing he might lack materials, the painter had built up considerable reserves. Four or five hundred canvases were stacked against the walls. The floor was invisible under the paper that Picasso used for his collages.

He never stopped painting: not only canvases that were now closer to Ingres than to cubism, but also objects, chairs, walls ... He couldn't tolerate empty space.

He stood with his back to the window, in his undershorts. His features were drawn. He seemed preoccupied. It wasn't the war, which he didn't talk about except to ask for news of friends; it was Eva. He was consumed by anxiety.

When Modigliani arrived, Picasso was eyeing an envelope which the postman had just delivered. He gave his visitor that black look of his that struck fear into so many hearts. The Italian wasn't impressed by it. He recounted his adventures of the night before. Picasso listened distractedly. Eva had retreated to the other end of the apartment.

The two painters exchanged news. Kahnweiler was in Switzerland, the Rosenberg brothers were buying cubists, Gertrude Stein and Alice Toklas had come back from England and left again for Palma; Vlaminck was manufacturing shells in a weapons factory and writing mediocre novels in the evenings.

'Max Jacob wonders how one can be anti-militaristic and still give the sweat of one's brow to the military,' noted Picasso.

'He was ordered to do so,' objected Modigliani.

The conversation petered out. Amedeo didn't see that his exuberance was annoying the Spaniard. Picasso was now beginning to frequent more fashionable circles and putting the high jinks of the Bateau Lavoir period behind him. Amedeo would also never learn that several months later, Picasso, in the midst of a bombing, inspired and having no canvas to hand, would cover over a work by the Italian painter with a still life executed with a knife.

Scarcely ten minutes after the visitor's arrival, the two men had run out of things to say to each other. Modigliani turned on his heels, left the studio, took the stairs and disappeared into the grey mists of the rue Schoelcher.

Picasso turned his attention to the envelope he had opened just before the Italian arrived. It had already been used once before, which was typical of the stingy habits of his correspondent. But this friend was one of his most faithful companions. And Picasso couldn't keep from smiling as he thought of the poet, so refined, so subtle, so vain, so distinguished, as unctuous as a priest, as theatrical as the pope, naive like a child, now with his feet in the ice and his hands in the mud!

He reopened the envelope and plunged into a reading of the latest military and amorous adventures of Guillaume Apollinaire.

THE ARTILLERYMAN'S WOMEN

If I died there on the front in the army
You would cry one day O Lou my beloved.
Guillaume Apollinaire

Apollinaire had left for the army – a poet at war. He had a flower on his gun, a little straighter than the flower the others sported because to maintain his honour among men without a country, he had to eradicate the memory of a certain photograph: the one published in all the gazettes in the autumn of 1911, showing him with handcuffs on his wrists, being led off to the Santé prison. This was an extraordinary dishonour for a man whose greatest hope was to be definitively recognized and admired by the country which had adopted him.

He did not leave for the front as quickly as he had hoped. His goodwill met with administrative complications: when one is born in Rome of a Polish mother and a father too vague even to have acknowledged his child, the situation demands careful examination. And the Legion, over-whelmed by volunteers, was turning people away.

While the military authorities studied his case, Apollinaire joined some friends in Nice. Three weeks after his arrival, as he was lunching in a restaurant in the old city, he was called over to a nearby table where a young woman of about thirty was holding court. In a flash, the poet forgot all about Marie Laurencin, the muse who had betrayed him and who had just left for Spain with her husband of six weeks, Otto von Waetgen – 'a better engraver than painter', according to André Salmon.[1]

The woman who caught his eye was dark, pretty, and lively. She whirled among the guests and the crystal glasses, talking and gesturing. She was 'imprudent and daring, frivolous and wild'.[2] Her eyes were like craters filled with lava ready to erupt and she had so much energy that she didn't know what to do with it: she had grown up stifled by corsets and genuflexions, then married at the age of twenty-three and quickly divorced. Her noble name suggested an adventuress: Louise de Coligny-Châtillon. On the one hand, she played at being a volunteer nurse. On the other hand, she was a social butterfly, and an emancipated young woman. Apollinaire was enraptured.

The day after their first meeting, he declared his flame. Five days later, he had all his books sent to her. He promised to write one for her, for her alone. More concretely, he asked her to come out walking with him. Without chaperones, preferably. He was already declaring himself her 'servant for life'.[3]

They saw each other very soon in a house where opium was being smoked. Then in restaurants, at the seaside, on deserted beaches. Everywhere, except in a hotel. Whenever Guillaume tried to take things a little further, Louise would murmur that they were friends and should remain so. When she was stretched out with the pipe between her teeth, she would offer her hand and a few promises. The artilleryman clung to them: 'I wish we were alone in my little office near the terrace, lying on the bed where we smoked, so that you would love me.'[4]

When the drugtaking phase was over, they would go walking arm in arm; perhaps there was a little more between them but it was still not enough. Especially when the young woman told her smitten lover that her heart was already taken, by a certain 'Toutou', an artilleryman.

'What difference does that make?' asked Guillaume.

'Oh, none. I have other interests too . . .'

'So come with me . . .'

'No . . .'

After two months of this regime, Apollinaire was fed up. He accelerated the formalities of his army conscription and prepared for departure. Then it was that Louise finally gave in. Not just a little, nor even a lot – but totally, passionately. To the point where, for a few days, Guillaume almost regretted having joined up. When war was declared, friends had suggested fleeing to Switzerland. He had refused. This time, he was transferred to Nîmes, and almost wished he didn't have to go. But he went, his heart in tatters.

The next day, Louise was at the door of the barracks. She asked for Guillaume Kostrowitzky, second cannoneer-driver of the 38th regiment of artillery, 78th battery.

He joined her: they went to a hotel, and spent nine nights there. Then Apollinaire joined military life.

He discovered the joys of manoeuvres, of soup duty, of roll call. He learned to ride horseback, which made his rear end sore – he had diarrhoea. He was very short of money, a constant source of anxiety. He grew a moustache, which was obligatory. In his letters, he hid no detail of his life as a soldier from his beloved, all the while making passionate declarations of love. He reassured her that the war wouldn't last for more than a year at the most. Perhaps less, if Picabia was to be believed – five months before the mobilization, he had foreseen the conflict, and he predicted its end for the month of February. Apollinaire was confident and patriotic: 'French strength and valour will win the day. We are virile. The enemy doesn't amount to much.'[5]

When Lou didn't answer his letters quickly enough – three days was the maximum he could wait – the cannoneer despaired, whined, reminded her of their nights of lovemaking. This recollection brought to mind some of their other practices. He threatened her with the whip and a riding crop, depicted himself as the spearhead of national masculinity, ready to introduce himself ferociously into her personal trenches, to accomplish his duty as a hero.

In answer, she wrote that she 'used her hands' as she read his letters.

He used self-restraint. He sent her his portrait painted by Picasso.

On 1 January 1915, he obtained a two-day leave and went to meet Lou in Nice. They spent most of their time in bed. On the train back, between Nice and Marseille, Apollinaire found himself travelling in the company of a young stranger, a teacher of literature at a lycée for girls in Oran. Her name was Madeleine Pagès; they would meet again.

Five days after his return to Nîmes, to his great pride, Apollinaire entered the squadron of soldiers training to become officers. He rode more and more often on horseback. He took artillery classes. Why did he want to be an artilleryman? Because he was an artist, he explained.

His status as an apprentice soldier did not weigh on him in the slightest. He received packages from Sonia Delaunay, a sweater as a present from Archipenko's wife, a letter from Blaise Cendrars. But he was ashamed of his inactivity and felt guilty about not yet being at the front. At least this slow passage of time left him the leisure to pursue a decidedly erotic correspondence with his mistress. Unable to see her, he gave free rein to his imagination. He dreamed of her bottom. He thought of her fingers as she 'used her hands' and didn't always keep his own from roaming. He reminded her of their '69' position, and other geometrical figures. She was the woman of his dreams. Next to her, Annie Playden, Marie Laurencin, all his other mistresses, whom he described as being magnificent, inexhaustible in bed, were nothing, 'just sh–t'.

When she told him, in great detail, about her games with other men, he had trouble hiding his jealousy. Two, all right. Three, maybe. But any more than that was pure vice. Once, when she had been mentioning Italy frequently in her letters, he asked her, poetically: 'Would there be an Italian in a little flowerpot somewhere, at the moment?' He compared himself, the chaste artilleryman leading an ascetic life, to her, opening her heart and her bed to all as though they were brothels. Trading insult for injury, he advised her to watch out, for the inroads made by her sensuality were already beginning to fade her beauty.

When he was angry with her, he no longer addressed her as his adored Lou, his beloved Lou, his little darling, but as his 'dear friend,' his 'old colleague'. He no longer signed 'Gui', but 'Guillaume Apollinaire'. He played at being nonchalant, mimicked simple friendship, tried to make her jealous, which would have reassured him, by describing young girls who walked by and whom he might consider going off with to a hotel ... When it seemed to him that their love was unravelling, he began to play the part of a man of substance instead of a transfixed lover. He sent her money, and when she went to Paris, he lent her his apartment on the Boulevard Saint Germain. He described his work as a poet. She must save his letters and verses, he instructed her, for he meant to publish them after the war. He began to think ahead: from now on he would only write on one side of the page so they could be printed rapidly, and he wrote the more intimate passages on separate pieces of paper. He had already decided on the title of the work: *Ombre de mon amour*.

On Easter Day, Guillaume Apollinaire left for the front. It was one of the rare times in his life when he would remember that he was still not French, and that his country was Poland. He sympathized with his homeland for having suffered so much from the war. He saw his people as the noblest and unhappiest of all. If he was going to war, it was also to defend his countrymen.

On 9 April, he drafted a will in favour of Lou. He indicated to her that she must conclude an agreement with the *Mercure de France* concerning his book *Alcools*, which he thought would bring in some money. He drew up a resumé of his literary production, the contracts that were signed and those that were not, advances and percentages of royalties that she could claim in his name if something should happen to him and he couldn't do it himself. In the meantime, he asked her to behave herself in his apartment on the Boulevard Saint Germain. First of all, because a senator lived in the same building, and secondly because he wasn't paying any rent for the duration of the war and he needed this arrangement to be maintained. Finally, it seemed to him that there was something indecent about living it up in Paris while others were fighting for their lives and their country at Verdun.

When Lou complained about being anaemic, he answered sometimes like the virile husband he would have liked to be (get yourself vaccinated), and sometimes like the attentive lover that he no longer was (let the bathwater cool for twenty minutes), and sometimes like a madly jealous man who couldn't hide his bitterness (if you didn't kiss men who might be typhoid cases on the mouth, you wouldn't get sick ...)

With the exception of this last piece of advice, he addressed her in the same authoritarian tone that his own mother, La Kostrowitzka, still used with him when she wrote – demanding that he tell her where he was sleeping, wanting to know who this 'Comtesse' de Coligny is: young, old, a widow? She gave him advice which said a lot about how poorly acquainted she was with her son's situation; it would seem that she basically wasn't very interested, imperious egotist that she was, devoted first and foremost to herself. In the same tone as she had used ten years earlier, she reminded her son (now thirty-four!) to take care when he went riding in the woods not to run into shells which, apparently, made enormous holes — 'and it would be terrible if you fell into one with your horse! or even without your horse.'[6] The worst, according to La Kostrowitzka, was shells exploding in forests, because they made the trees fall. This fear led to a double helping of motherly advice: 'Get off your horse so as to not be crushed by a tree', and 'Pray to the Virgin Mary every day to protect you.'

On 11 April, the poet truly became a soldier. To his great pride, he was named a liaison agent. He rode horseback in the wilds, had fun with his friends, and wrote by the light of a lamp which burned animal fat. He was enjoying the war.

He pretended to be pals with Toutou, the other artilleryman who was Lou's lover. When she came to visit him, he told her to give him his best. Through her, he addressed his rival as a fellow soldier, telling him about his progress in shooting, asking if he wouldn't happen to have an extra sighting compass. When he hadn't heard from Lou in a while, he didn't hesitate to go a step further, and sent registered cards to Toutou, asking for news of their mutual beloved. And he reminded the young lady a little sharply that he had enlisted, after all, to defend her country . . .

Unfortunately, the lady in question seemed to be growing somewhat more distant. The flesh had been satisfied. The poet was still 'stiff as a cannon' but the opposing artillery was hardly responding. They still called each other 'mon Gui' or 'my darling Lou', however, and they had all kinds of little attentions for each other. Apollinaire sent her money without complaining. And on the rings that the soldiers made in the sockets of the shells, he engraved words of love. Climbing onto his high horse and assuming the tone of authority he sometimes affected, he reminded the lady that she belonged entirely to him, at least in one domain: 'Lou speaks only in bed.'

He suggested she look through his books and find Les Onze mille verges. He ordered her to speak of it to no one but to put it to good use herself. While she was at it, she might as well amuse herself with Le Nouveau Chatouiller des dames, included in one of the volumes of L'Enfer de la Bibliothèque nationale, which he had helped to inspire.

When she failed to answer his letters regularly, he rebuked her. And he got impatient when she sent him tea in tablets, for she should have known that these tablets melted only in boiling water, and that boiling water was not so easy to come by at the front ... These complaints, alternating with burning declarations of love, were the sign of the poet's suffering. Once again, he was the unloved hero of the story. Lou was drifting away, as Annie Playden and Marie Laurencin had drifted away. She was happy to be his friend, his correspondent, maybe his mistress, but this *maybe* was just what plunged the artillery soldier into despair: he wanted it all. The man should be the master, the woman submits; the couple is together for life, love is reciprocal. Otherwise, one could begin to look elsewhere.

Elsewhere might have meant, for instance, the arms of a friend of a friend's sister who, since April 1915, had been writing to the poet regularly. Her name was Jeanne Burgues-Brun. She had published a novel and some verses under the pseudonym of Yves Blanc. In the beginning, and also at the end, she was his wartime 'godmother'. The artilleryman had artfully tried to draw her closer to him, but the young woman had determinedly refused: no flirting between us. Not even a photo. Despite the soldier's insistence, she never sent him a picture of herself, and their relations remained strictly literary. They would only meet once, at the end of the war, in the Luxembourg gardens.

It was her loss, Apollinaire thought. In any case, he had someone else in mind. This was the girl he'd met on the train in January 1915. She was very young, just over twenty, and she had long eyelashes. Having just spent Christmas at her brother's, who lived in Nice, she was returning to Oran. He had been kissing Lou in the wagon's narrow passageway, until the train was ready to depart. Then he had sat down opposite the stranger. They had talked a little. About Nice, Villon, *Alcools*, which had been published two years earlier. In Marseille, he had helped her get off the train and had carried her suitcase. Then, he had asked for her address – why not?

Nothing ventured, nothing gained. In April, Apollinaire shrugged his shoulders over Lou, who hadn't written to him in three days, and sent a postcard to the stranger, bearing his respectful greetings and kissing her hand. He took care with what he wrote. Two weeks later, his speculative advance bore fruit, in the form of a box of cigars posted to him from Oran. It was more than he had hoped for. It deserved an answer. He put some thought into what he wrote. There were some general reflections on the war, a handful of verses, and a compliment – what a marvellous memory he had of that train journey! Respectful salutations, Guillaume Apollinaire.

Six days went by, then a card arrived. It promised enough to allow his correspondent, previously addressed as 'Mademoiselle', to become 'Little fairy' in his next greeting: more tender, less impersonal, a step forward. But Guillaume would have liked to progress even faster. He sounded her out, speaking of Goethe, Scott, Nerval and – an offhand reference – Laclos and his capital vices: ah, isn't it an interesting coincidence, wasn't Laclos also an artilleryman?

He moved on to her hands: Apollinaire proposed to make the young girl a ring. Could she send him the measurements of one of her fingers? Not the index finger, nor the middle finger. The ring finger, of course. And also a little photograph. He would put it next to his sabre and his revolver, which he carried on his left side, which also happened to be near his heart.

He was probably moving too quickly for her. Her answer was less spontaneous than her earlier missives. Kind, friendly, but lacking in warmth. Fortunately, this reserve would not last. The young girl sent him chocolates. The soldier answered with rose petals and a new ring: a stone in a copper setting, engraved with an 'M' for Madeleine.

He complained about her signing her letters with an icy M.P.; meanwhile, he moved from 'My charming little fairy', five weeks after the beginning of their correspondence, to 'My darling little fairy' a few days later. And on 10 July 1915, in an ecstatic sigh, the artilleryman began to stake his claim: 'I loved you from the moment I saw you.'[7]

The next day, he still wrote 'My darling Lou' to the young lady lodging in his apartment on the Boulevard Saint Germain. But if his heart was still hers, the tone was changing...

Apollinaire and Madeleine began to bombard each other with gifts. The artilleryman received a bottle of eau de Cologne, and in return sent a pen he had made himself from two German bullets. Madeleine answered with handkerchiefs, silk and lace, cigarettes, nougats and honeyed candies that had already been bitten into, as though she were kissing them. He replied with pencils, letter openers, inkstands carved out of cartridges, belts from the enemy with hearts carved in them, bullet clips, his soldier's kepi, butterfly wings, and books and poems which, with his usual foresight, he asked her to keep with a view to eventual publication.

Many of these poems had already been sent to Lou or to his 'godmother', but it didn't matter: it was the intention that counted, and the intention was not the same. With Lou, his feelings were passionate, dramatic, physical, violent. He couldn't go so quickly with Madeleine, who was shy, ignorant of men but knowing something of their ways. Apollinaire shed his carnal skin to take up his poet's gloves. Though he could not restrain himself from depositing a kiss on the young lady's breast, most of the time he was literary, wise, tender – both gentle and authoritative, as he recognized himself. He no longer spoke of whips, crops, or spankings, though he did allude to a portrait by Fragonard, La Correction conjugale – just in passing, to test the waters.

He was as sincere with Madeleine as he had been sophisticated with

Lou, for he no longer needed to parade around to the tune of erotic or amorous bagpipes. He laid bare his heart in a letter dating from July, 1915. He confessed that he had admired (and still admired) the talent of Marie Laurencin, who had inspired 'Le Pont Mirabeau' and 'Zone'. He had thought he loved Lou, but she proved in the end to be only a transitional figure, who helped him get over the pain of Marie's departure. He pitied her and saw her as a plaything for men; he had been attracted to her sensually, but his spirit had remained distant.

But Madeleine was different. To her he could express all his admiration for Gogol, and all his scorn for Henry Bordeaux.* Literature was one of the central themes of their correspondence. The rest concerned the war, not surprisingly, and their love. He said he wanted to have children with her; he wanted her to become engaged to him. On 10 August 1915, he asked her mother for her hand in marriage. After this, he behaved like a model son-in-law, declaring that he was very attached to his betrothed's mother, even though he had never even met her! He promised to come to meet her soon when he was on leave. He wrote to her. He kissed her as a son would . . .

The young couple now addressed each other in the familiar 'tu' form. Madeleine sent photos. He tried to discern her curves from the sepia lines, to make out her hips and breasts. Later, he would ask her to be less reserved. To please his olfactory sense, which he assured her was quite acute, he wanted her to rub the smell of her body hair on her letters. To thank her for her good will, he sent her a collection of poems, *Case d'armons* (the title referred to the name given to the casing of a large cannon); the collection was reproduced with the help of his fellow artillerymen, and its cover was decorated with military insignia and a dedication 'To the Armies of the Republic'. He also sent it to Lou, along with subscription forms for potential subscribers: 'Try to place them for me.'[8] The money she made from it would be hers to keep: 'If you sell even twenty, at twenty francs, that will pay for your dentist . . .'

On 25 August, Squadron Sergeant-Major Apollinaire, recently promoted, told his future in-laws about his advancement. He was very proud – and extremely pleased, a month later, to put on the new grey helmet, which no longer shone in the sun, and the regulation sky-blue uniform, which was a change from the bright reds he had been wearing, too easily seen from afar by enemy shooters. But aside from the security offered by the new uniform, what Apollinaire most liked about it was the silkiness and softness of the material, which comforted him and appealed to his taste for fine things.

---

* Henry Bordeaux, a writer from the Savoy region, wrote chiefly domestic dramas tinged with a kind of Catholic nationalism, in praise of family and religion.

He wouldn't be feeling comforted for long. In November, he volunteered for the infantry, and was named second lieutenant. His life on the sidelines was finished: he was now about to discover the trenches in all their squalor and the full horror of the footsoldier's life. The poet was finally becoming a fighter.

Until then, he had maintained an active correspondence first with some ladies, and then others, not to mention his Parisian friends. He had sent articles to the *Mercure de France* or elsewhere and had been able to monitor the details of their publication. The sound of the shells, miaowing like cats, had thrilled him. The drilling of the artillery fire had been like fireworks. He had slept in huts covered with canvas tenting, and observed with delight the snakes winding around his feet, the rats darting between his legs, the flies whose noses resembled those of bulldogs, and the charming spiders. The only thing he complained about was boredom. Though all his comrades in Montmartre and Montparnasse were worrying about how he would adapt to the rigours of the war around him, given his refined tastes and love of comfort, he himself wasn't suffering.

'How pretty war is!' This inscription, which he had engraved on his toothpaste kit in 1915 (and which echoes a line from his *Calligrammes*), would soon appear inappropriate to him, even if he initially found the sounds of the cannon 'splendid'.

The front was a different story. Suddenly, second lieutenant Kostrowitzky discovered signal boxes, machine guns, Marie-Louises, shit boxes, torpedoes falling out of the sky, and all the horror of life in the trenches. The German brute was only two metres away; the earth was torn up, ripped apart by explosions. He was in the front line, stretched out on the bloody ground, the cannon breathing down his neck. He slept in the mud, and sometimes didn't sleep. He shivered. He washed when he could, and fielded shells and shrapnel and gas attacks. The barbed wire ate into his skin, as did the vermin and the lice. He protected himself behind sacks of sand or piles of corpses. He learned to dig, to rebuild at night, like a troglodyte in the shadows. In a few months, his regiment had lost a million men; his comrades were falling one after another. From the front, Apollinaire sent a letter to Madeleine begging her to wait for him if he were taken prisoner. He made her the heir to all his worldly goods, replacing Lou, to whom he had bequeathed his fortune in March.

Of course, he thought about death. But he was not afraid. And he never complained, except about the military authorities who called war councils at the drop of a hat. When it was time to fight, he was the first to leap into battle, and he showed remarkable courage. His men loved him because he protected them and made sure that they had enough to eat; he shared his fire and his parcels, and lent his blankets when they were drier than theirs. But Kostrowitzky was too complicated a name to pronounce, so they called him 'Kostro the exquisite' or 'Cointreau-whisky'.

Submerged in the tumult of the war, 'Cointreau-whisky' fought. But whenever he had a moment, he wrote to Madeleine. The violence and rage which possessed him overpowered his customary reserve. In December, he wrote her a passionate letter, wildly erotic. It was the only one. In his mind, at the centre of his hopes, she was the key that might open the door to the leave he had been requesting for months.

She was going to come at Christmas. It would be his finest present. After leaving the front, the second lieutenant headed directly for Marseille, without even stopping in Paris to see his friends. After months of ardent epistolary exchanges, he was impatient to reach Laumur, in Algeria, and finally to get to know this twenty-two-year-old girl whose hand he had asked for in marriage, and with whom he had never spent more than a few hours: in a train, a year before – before the artilleryman had become a hussar . . .

THE WRITER WITH THE SEVERED HAND

The first virtue of a novelist is to be a liar.

Blaise Cendrars

'I'm sending you a note from a friend of mine who's one of the best poets writing today: Blaise Cendrars. He has an amputated arm!'[1]

On 6 November 1915, Guillaume Apollinaire told Madeleine about Frédéric Sauser's wound. Sauser, alias Blaise Cendrars, a Swiss citizen, was the co-author, with the Italian Ricciotto Canudo, of the appeal to foreigners to defend France.

Cendrars was a wanderer: at the age of thirty, he had been everywhere. He had run away from home when he was fifteen and had gone from country to country – Germany, England, Russia, India, China, America, Canada – before setting down his suitcases in Paris, first in 1907, and then again two years before war was declared.

He had worked at a thousand jobs, he had come into contact with people from all over the world and from every social class, he boldly defended libertarian and anarchistic ideas. He was also a poet: a travelling poet.

In New York, oppressed by poverty, he entered a Presbyterian church on Easter Day in 1912, to get warm and rest for a minute, and to listen to a few measures of Haydn's *Creation*. When he returned to his room, he sat down at his table and began to write a poem. He fell asleep. Waking up a few hours later, he continued his work, and so on, waking and sleeping, all through the night. In the morning, his head clear, he reread the work, and gave a title to this poem born of distress: 'Les Pâques à New York'.

Three months later, Cendrars was in Paris, living off odd jobs, luck and daring. With some anarchist friends, he founded a review, *Les Hommes nouveaux*. He financed the first issue by selling tickets to a show he had organized at the Palais Royal. He lodged with a poet in a hotel room on the rue Saint Etienne-du-Mont. He was still poverty-stricken: he hung out at the Dantzig, near the Ruche, and drank white wine at the Cinq Coins. He barely made a living, collaborating on reviews and selling original editions acquired several years earlier. At the Ruche, he met Modigliani, Chagall, and Fernand Léger. At an anarchist meeting, he met Victor Serge, who would translate his first novel, L'Or, into Russian.

But his dearest wish was to meet Guillaume Apollinaire. Why Apollinaire? Because he was a champion of the avant-garde. And because an individual suspected of having spirited away the Mona Lisa was necessarily an adventurer.

Back from America, Cendrars had sent his poem 'Les Pâques à New York' to Apollinaire, without receiving a response. One day in September 1912, the seasoned traveller was strolling by the bookstore owned by Editions Stock. He saw Apollinaire's L'Hérésiarque & Cie there, and began to read it. Discovering he didn't have enough money on him to buy it, he slipped the volume into his pocket and started to move away. Unfortunately, a passing policeman had seen him pocket the book. Blaise was arrested and thrown into prison. What did he do? He wrote to the author of the book, asking him if he could pay his debt to the Editions Stock and intervene to help have him freed. But he was released from prison before he even had time to send the letter.

A few months later, Cendrars met Apollinaire at the Café de Flore (this is the version told by Miriam Cendrars; others claim that Apollinaire wrote to Cendrars after having received 'Les Pâques à New York', inviting him to come and see him).

Apollinaire was seven years older than the author of 'Pâques'. He was close to Robert and Sonia Delaunay. If Salmon is to be believed, Delaunay made his reputation painting goldfish blue. He had no wit and never smiled. Apollinaire considered him to be the grand master of 'orphism' and praised the way he and his wife dressed. Sonia would wear a purple suit, the top part of which was composed of pieces of a sheet, taffeta, and rose, blue and scarlet tulle; Robert went about in a red coat with a blue collar, shoes of two colours, a green jacket, blue waistcoat and red tie. This was before the war. In August 1914, the Delaunays slipped off to Spain.

Cendrars became friendly first with Sonia Delaunay, with whom he spoke in Russian. She invited him to her studio on the rue des Grands-Augustins. There, in front of several guests (including, according to some, Guillaume Apollinaire), Cendrars read 'Les Pâques à New York':

Lord, today is your name day
I read in an old book the story of your sacrifice
And your anguish and your efforts and your noble words
Which weep in that book, in a gentle monotone.

The poem enchanted its audience. The verse was metrically entirely free, and the poem embodied a simple and direct approach to the modern world – its cities, its streets, its passers-by – in clear opposition to old-school symbolism.

Apollinaire was impressed (though if this reading really did take place, he should not have been surprised, since Cendrars had supposedly already sent him his poem). He was then working on a new collection of poems that the *Mercure de France* would publish in April: *Alcools*, whose title was then still *Eau de vie*. He assembled some of the works he had composed since 1898, arranged them in a particular but non-chronological order, then suddenly decided to eliminate all the punctuation: he considered that the rhythm of the verses was sufficient. Like Pierre Reverdy, he would play with the spaces between words and verses, a device which Jean Cocteau would use in turn in 'Le Cap de Bonne-Espérance'.

While correcting the proofs of the collection, he chose to open the book with a new poem, which he had probably composed during the summer and had certainly read in October in the Jura, at the home of Gabrielle Buffet and Picabia. This is where a title was found for the work, 'Zone',[2] published for the first time in December in *Les Soirées de Paris*.

> In the end you are weary of this old world
> Shepherdess of the Eiffel Tower the flock of bridges is bleating this
>   morning
> You've had enough of living in Greek and Roman antiquity
> Here even the automobiles seem ancient
> Only religion has remained completely new religion
> Has remained simple like the hangars of Port Aviation

There is the same modernity here as in Cendrars' work: unmetered verses (this was not new for Apollinaire), the city, the street, even religion...

When *Alcools* was published, Cendrars praised Apollinaire in public, but he was privately upset. 'Zone' was too much like 'Pâques'. When third parties told him that Guillaume was upset because Cendrars hadn't written anything on *Alcools*, he sent his elder a short letter in which he half-reproached him for not having dedicated 'Zone' to him. The question of which of the two works came first began seriously to threaten the relations between the two men. It clearly explains the coldness Cendrars showed towards Apollinaire, this latter trying in vain to obtain an explanation, which the Swiss poet refused to give.

But the quarrel didn't go any further than that. No one could prove anything, and no one did. Not even Tristan Tzara who, according to Jacques Roubaud, would sometimes show people a set of proofs of *Alcools* corrected in the light of the 'Prose du Transsibérien' and comment perfidiously: 'Everyone thinks that Apollinaire started it all! But Cendrars was there too!'[3]

This argument could have been valid, except for one thing: the poems in *Alcools* came before the 'Transsibérien', a work in which the author actually honours Apollinaire –

> 'Forgive me if I no longer know the old game of verse'
> As Guillaume Apollinaire says.[4]

While playing at this little game, one could also point out that certain of the *Sonnets dénaturés*, written in 1916, are reminiscent of *Calligrammes*. Or that the unpunctuated poems of Cendrars were composed after *Alcools* ... But Apollinaire was not Picasso any more than Cendrars was Braque. There was no rope joining them. They each had their own specific sources of inspiration, even if these sources intersected and were also nourished by others: cubism and futurism, for example, which had already expressed the modernity of this period in painting. Apollinaire clearly did not need Cendrars to write, and Cendrars did not wish to make an enemy of Apollinaire. In any case, Blaise would take a bit of revenge later, if this is what he was looking for; he would affirm that the choice of the title *Alcools* to replace the original *Eau de vie* was his idea.

Maybe, maybe not. Cendrars – this was another of his talents – was a great fabricator. According to Hemingway, he was 'a good companion, as long as he didn't drink too much, and at the time, it was more interesting to listen to him telling fibs than to listen to true stories told by someone else...'[5]

Did Cendrars really believe that, in addition to Apollinaire, he had also inspired Charlie Chaplin? According to him, the film maker had stolen his character Bikoff, whom Cendrars camouflaged as a tree trunk in *La Main coupé* and who appeared in similar guise in *Shoulder Arms*.[6]

Did he copy the *Romans de la Table ronde* for Apollinaire (who himself was acting for someone else) at the Bibliothèque Mazarine?

Probably.

Was he Apollinaire's ghost writer, as he claimed, composing erotic novels for him, and several chapters of historical romances of which René Dalize, Maurice Raynal and André Billy also wrote fragments?

Perhaps. Perhaps not.

Did he totally invent the version of Walt Whitman's funeral recounted by Apollinaire in an issue of the *Mercure de France* in 1913, which brought down upon the head of the author of *Alcools* the wrath of Stuart Merrill and numerous readers of this very serious review?

Almost certainly.

Walt Whitman was one of the greatest American poets of the nineteenth century. In France, his only translated collection of poems, *Leaves of Grass*, which was continually updated and expanded over the years, had noticeably influenced the poets of *Vers et Prose*. His life certainly fascinated the young Cendrars, who shared Whitman's taste for travel, for the most varied human company and for freedom. He told Apollinaire a story about the poet's funeral, which had taken place twenty years earlier. Using this information, which he seemed to think was authentic, Apollinaire let himself be carried away into the most unbridled lyricism. The article appeared on 1 April in the *Mercure*, and one almost might have thought it was an April Fool's joke. Perhaps it was. But only for Blaise Cendrars.

If the chronicler of the *Mercure de France* is to be believed, Whitman had organized his funeral himself. Its purpose would appear to have been less to deposit the coffin in the earth than to use the gathering as an occasion for riotous merrymaking. He had thus prepared musical fanfares, a banquet, barrels of beer and whisky ... The crowd was composed of joyous drunks mixed with journalists, politicians, farmers, oyster fishermen, handsome young men, many homosexuals ... All these people followed the coffin, kicking at it along the way, and the funeral had ended in a kind of gigantic orgy. The police, called to the rescue, had arrested fifty people.

Apollinaire went to town with the story. So did the readers of the review. It provoked a scandal: how could a serious publication like the *Mercure de France* publish articles that made Walt Whitman appear to be a depraved and alcoholic homosexual?

Eight months later, Apollinaire had to respond. He accepted full responsibility for his article. He reminded the readers that he had written it based on the account of an eyewitness. He refused to name the individual in question, indicating simply that the story had been told to him 'in the presence of a talented young poet, Monsieur Blaise Cendrars'.[7] He did not exactly give him away, then, but it was still a clear hint to Cendrars that he had better behave.

Finally, did Cendrars later totally invent the story of the death and burial of Apollinaire? It was certainly dreamlike, but also totally improbable from beginning to end.

It is certain that Cendrars did invent it, particularly as no one saw him at the poet's deathbed, where he claimed to have been. Apollinaire always admired Cendrars, and didn't hide it. Cendrars admired Apollinaire too, even if there was often a tone in his remarks which implied a touch of jealousy. Cendrars wrote in *Hamac*:[8]

Apollinaire
1900–1911
For 12 years the only poet in France

Why twelve years? Because after that Cendrars himself arrived on the scene.

After the war, the two men quickly cleared up the murky problems that had come between them. In 1918, the Editions de la Sirène, of which Blaise Cendrars would become editorial director, published Apollinaire's *Le Flâneur des deux rives*. Later, in his correspondence, Blaise would take up a most Apollinarian expression, which rang as a definitive homage to his comrade the poet. Preceding his signature, he would often use a phrase which all of Guillaume's friends knew well: 'With a friendly hand...'

On 3 August 1914, the day after Germany declared war on France, Blaise Cendrars joined the army. A month later, he got married. And a few days after that, he joined his regiment, the First Foreign Regiment in Paris.

Thus began a year of fighting for his adopted country. In the beginning, like Apollinaire and Cocteau, Cendrars discovered a world which fascinated his poet's imagination. But it didn't last. All the more so as he did not abandon his anarchism, which made him more insolent, more critical, and freer with respect to military matters. His attitude became mocking quite early on. In his writing, the spectacle he described could be surprising. For example, one day the troops were crossing Chantilly, where Joffre, his assistants and deputy assistants were studying maps at the headquarters. The great general didn't want to be disturbed by the noise of the infantry's boots striking the ground in rhythm. To preserve the silence necessary to a strategic union of his red, white and blue neurons, Joffre ordered tons of straw to be strewn over the streets of the city.

Cendrars had even more cause to mock when his regiment tried to reach the North Sea. They had to go quickly to block the enemy's passage. But since it was also necessary for the men to keep training so they would arrive in top form and ready to fight, the officers had a brilliant idea. Military brilliance and civilian brilliance are not the same thing. This time, it was decided that the troops would be escorted by the very trains that were meant to transport them. With their gear on their backs, the soldiers wore themselves out trudging along the rails, under the watchful gaze of the empty, well-rested and coal-covered locomotive chugging along slowly next to them. An ingenious scheme...

Blaise put up with everything: punishments, heavy work, the front, hand-to-hand combat. He hung on because by his side, always, there was a little fellow still in gestation who would later develop into a great character: Moravagine. He was Cendrars' closest companion during the war, and the most faithful. The others kept dying, one after another.

On 28 September 1915, in Champagne, a shell sliced through the writer's 'friendly hand', and Blaise Cendrars lost his right arm.

In May, in Carency, while they were fighting in the same regiment, Braque had been wounded in the head, and Kisling had been stabbed by a bayonet. Their wounds meant that all three of them had to leave the war zone. And they brought with them a considerable consolation prize; the war cross, with honours. More important still, they brought with them the promise of a reward which Kisling, Cendrars and all the foreign artists fighting in the trenches dreamed of: French nationality.

THE FRIVOLOUS PRINCE

Before he came, the cafés of the Boulevard Montparnasse had resounded only to the noise of quarrels or controversies over schools and tendencies; after him, people wandered about more elegantly in a maze of turns and detours as if he had, in a kind of game and without saying so, communicated to each of them his private art of 'complicating matters'.

André Salmon

Paris was disconcerting for those who were returning to it. After fifteen days of leave, spent in the arms of his official fiancée, Apollinaire stopped over in the capital for a few hours. The city was at war, but this was not the front, far from it. True, Zeppelins often attacked at night. Preceded by air raid sirens, they descended, grey and oblong, to a height of one hundred and fifty metres above ground level. The cannons wore themselves out trying to hit them. In the searchlights, the most curious Parisians could sometimes see the men who dropped the bombs, their arms raised above the cockpit, the murderous projectile in their hands. But the observers were not numerous. Most families scurried down to the cellars, waiting for the end of the raids.

It was also true that many people were still going hungry. The cold was very severe that winter. But there were many cowards, too. According to Jean Hugo, Léon-Paul Fargue used his influence with a non-commissioned officer from the Val-de-Grâce Hospital to get his friends turned away from the army. Apollinaire made a few barbed comments about some of his friends who had escaped combat by working in factories. Cendrars was no more indulgent about those who had run off to Spain or to the United States. In 1915, Derain had a brief falling out with Vlaminck, whom he accused in barely disguised words of having clung to the rear lines.

And what did the others do, those whom the war had not wanted to keep, those whom it had rejected after having mutilated them in the trenches?

They drank café-crèmes at the Rotonde. They waited for it all to end. Or they waited for it all to start – the Russian revolutionaries, in particular.

In Paris, there were several thousands of them, awaiting the great day. Having taken refuge far from their country, they studied the horizon for signs of the jolts and convulsions that might announce a possible revolution. They had chosen Montparnasse as their refuge.

Lenin lived on the rue Marie-Rose, near Alésia. Martov, Trotsky and Ilya Ehrenburg, who made a living from translating and guiding Russian tourists around the capital, were also in Paris. Trotsky had accepted an offer from a Kiev paper, the *Kievskaya Mysl*, which had asked him to be its correspondent in France.

Trotsky arrived in Montparnasse at the end of November 1914. First, he took a room in a hotel on the rue d'Odessa. Then, when his wife and children joined him, he moved to the rue de l'Amiral Mouchez, on the outskirts of Montsouris. Aside from his work for the *Kievskaya Mysl*, he helped to develop a daily news sheet which had recently been started by the Russian emigrants. He remained in France for two years before being expelled by the French authorities.

Trotsky often came to the Rotonde, and also to the Baty restaurant, on the corner of the Boulevard Raspail and the Boulevard du Montparnasse. Legend even has it that he left an unpaid bill at this restaurant, which was frequented by a chic, fairly well-to-do crowd and whose list of fine wines was appreciated by Apollinaire.

A few years later, the presence of the two Russian revolutionaries in Paris at that time would be hotly contested. But witnesses of the time remained firm.[1] They did sometimes go a bit overboard in their descriptions, which are caricatures, like Vlaminck's claim that when he met Trotsky one day at the Rotonde, he heard him say, 'I like your painting . . . But you should paint miners, excavators, workers. Exalt work, praise work!'[2] And they all acknowledged that even though Trotsky was already friendly with Diego Rivera, whom he would join much later in Mexico, he and his Bolshevik comrades didn't have much time to devote to artistic questions . . .

Some of the reported meetings are indeed difficult to imagine. Picturing Lenin, Trotsky, Martov and a collection of Mensheviks and Bolsheviks in the middle of the smoky dining room of the Rotonde, surrounded by the vapours of ether and cocaine, rather stretches the imagination. But it is enjoyable to think that the Russians might have encountered Modigliani howling antimilitarist slogans, Soutine grumbling, naked beneath his coat, and Derain, on leave that day, manufacturing little cardboard planes skilfully aimed to fall straight into these gentlemen's coffee cups.

Max Jacob's presence in the favourite meeting spots of these artists was a little more certain. One day in 1916, the poet walked into the Rotonde. He related his 'war experience' to the assembled company. He had served one month in Enghien as a civil ambulance driver, though the wounded were still rare at the time; he had spent his thirty days in a summery garden, surrounded by mothers and wives in tears, putting his poems and manuscripts in order, with a view to a posthumous publication of his works.

Then he spoke of Picasso, naturally. He cursed him. Not too harshly, because the painter was in mourning. Eva had finally succumbed to the tuberculosis which had been eating away at her for months. Several of them, including Juan Gris, had accompanied him to the cemetery. It was all so sad that Max ended up seeking some comfort. In wine, only wine. Thanks to which he began to tell some dubious stories. He had become a little too friendly with the coachman of the funeral carriage ... and had been scolded for his conduct.

Ever since, Picasso had been sulking. And Max was upset. After all he'd done for him! All he'd given him!

At the other end of the room, a young man was listening. When he heard Picasso's name, he raised his head. He was seated at the bar, across from the père Libion, swinging his legs, with their aviator boots laced up to the ankle. The red trousers hung impeccably straight, falling over little buckles in yellow leather. The black tunic was stylish, and better still was the helmet, painted mauve (mocking observers claimed that this was Paul Poiret's latest creation) which swung nonchalantly from the poet's lace-adorned wrist.

He was back from the war. He had first been sent to the Supply Corps, in Paris, then had obtained a transfer to an ambulance unit commanded by the Comte Etienne de Beaumont. He had found this magnificent. Beautiful. In the morning, there was nothing like the noise of the cannon to wake you up. And no landscape could be more splendid than the blue sky dotted with a volley of shrapnel cascading around the aeroplanes.

This very fashionable soldier moved with the rhythm of a lively and delicate thought, scattered effortlessly, like manna, on the little flowers all around him whom he tried – this was his weakness – to make love him. 'Admiration leaves me cold,' he murmured. 'My work demands love; I harvest it.'[3]

But a little love wasn't enough, and sometimes a lot wasn't either. He needed to be loved passionately. Often, he didn't harvest anything at all.

Vlaminck, who had just entered the Rotonde, walked by. He recognized the mobile, graceful wings of Cocteau the zephyr. He joined Salmon and Carco who, sitting side by side, were sneering at the gentleman soldier.

'He's the spiritual son of Picasso and Max Jacob,' groaned Vlaminck, 'but raised by Anna de Noailles.'[4]

Salmon lifted his glass. 'To the Ariel of the salons!'[5]

Carco toasted, 'To the darling of the old ladies.' He went on, 'To the tailor of the Arts.' He added, 'To the perfumed theoretician.'[6]

'To the frivolous prince,' concluded Vlaminck.

This was the title of a book that Cocteau had published in 1910, five years earlier. On the left bank, this work was scorned by the painters and poets, who detested everything that the right bank dandy represented. Though people smiled and simpered; though later many changed their tune; though Cocteau himself, after forcing an entrance into a circle that didn't really want him, in the end made a cosy little nest for himself there, becoming close friends with practically all of them, the truth of the early years remained: his manners were those of an outsider.

Francis Carco ascribed one virtue to him: 'Without Jean Cocteau who would ever have thought that cubism could enchant snobs?'[7] According to Philippe Soupault, Apollinaire didn't have much respect for him either: 'Beware of Cocteau ... He's a cheater and a chameleon.'[8] Reverdy considered him to be 'the anti-poet', as well as an 'exhibitionist, imitator, success-hunter, sneak, and master at creating complications'. This opinion would be echoed by André Salmon, who was as harsh on him as the others: 'He came from the right bank, which he used to return to as quickly as he could – Hey! Taxi! – until he left it one day for good; the poet would go off, having manipulated simple drinkers of café-crèmes into unexpected dialectical refinements.'[9]

Max Jacob was not the last to colour in the picture. And Cocteau replied to his criticisms with some very sharp observations of his own: the author of the *Cornet à dés* was an 'amateur Christian, the type who dabbles in everything, an unwashed sentimentalist',[10] and 'a Jean-Jacques Rousseau of the Water Closets, a vestry dancer'. All this did not keep the two men from becoming firm friends: Cocteau, as we have seen, would intervene, too late, to try to save Max Jacob when he was taken to Drancy.

He would also intervene for himself with the Vichy authorities in 1942, which would earn him the solid enmity of Philippe Soupault. The latter recalled that in 1983, at a public auction of letters and original manuscripts, during which the text of the *Champs magnétiques* was sold, he discovered two missives from Cocteau dating from 1942 and addressed to Pétain. After he and Jean Marais had been the victims of the wrath of the Milice and the collaborationist press, the author asked the Marshal to intervene so that his play, *Renaud et Armide*, which had just been banned, might yet be performed at the Comédie Française. Soupault quotes excerpts from the letters:

> I had decided, with the players of the house, to write for the Comédie Française a great lyric play exalting what your nobility teaches us ... My life is irreproachable, my work without a stain. I am a cousin of Admiral Darlan. But it is you, Monsieur le Maréchal to whom I address this missive, because I admire and venerate you.[11]

Well before this date, the surrealists had had nothing but contempt for

Jean Cocteau. In *Les Pas perdus*,[12] André Breton went so far as to excuse himself for having to write his name. He criticized him for the same traits that the poets and painters of Montmartre had already sensed in him before and during the First World War: his determination to get ahead at all costs, his superficiality, his tendency to play the social butterfly, his fawning attentions to the Princesse Bibesco, the Princesse de Polignac, the Empress Eugénie, Liane de Pougy, the wife of the Romanian prince Georges Ghika, and to the artists who shared his taste for gilded drawing rooms – the musician Reynaldo Hahn and the painter Jacques-Emile Blanche.

Jean Cocteau sparkled wherever he went. When he came to Montparnasse, his finest jewel, the one he most liked to show off, was the dazzling Ballets Russes. This triumph of artistry had developed from the *Mir Iskustva* group of artists, founded in St Petersburg in 1898. Under the direction of the choreographer Fokine, it brought together painters and musicians. In 1909, the ensemble found a French home at the Châtelet Theatre in Paris. Fokine and Sergei Diaghilev understood that if they wanted to break with classical ballet, they would have to add some of the leading proponents of the contemporary arts to their team. From this point of view, they were the founders of modern ballet. Turning their backs on conventional music, they commissioned works from resolutely modern composers: Auric, de Falla, Milhaud, Prokofiev, Satie, Stravinsky. And they did not neglect the need for modernity in the visual aspects of their work: after Bakst, the sets were designed by Derain, Braque and Picasso.

On stage, the dancing of Nijinsky and Karsavina created a sensation – or enraged the audience, as was the case for the *Prélude à l'apres-midi d'un faune* by Claude Debussy, and even more so, for *Le Sacre du printemps* by Igor Stravinsky, which opened in May 1913 at the Théâtre des Champs-Elysées. The latter set off a scandal reminiscent of the first night of *Hernani*.* The theatre was overflowing with pearls and furs, and all the finest flowers of the world of Parisian arts and letters were there: Debussy, Ravel, Gide, Proust, Claudel, Sarah Bernhardt, Réjane, Isadora Duncan . . . and of course, Jean Cocteau.

As soon as the curtain went up, a furore broke out. The audience was divided between those who defended Stravinsky's music and Nijinsky's choreography, and all the others. On one side, applause; on the other, boos. Insults rained; people hammered their walking sticks on the floor. No one could hear the music. On the stage, imperturbable, the dancers continued to dance. Moving among the rows of spectators, in top hat,

---

* When Victor Hugo's play *Hernani* was first produced in February 1830, the opening night was famously tumultuous, and the work sparked off a battle between the admirers of classicism and romanticism.

creamy white gloves, and ceremonial attire, Apollinaire kissed the hands
of the fashionable ladies – those who hadn't fainted, that is. The scandal
caused by the *Sacre* was similar to the one set off by the exhibition of
cubist painters at the Salon des Indépendants a few months before.

Like a busy bee, Jean Cocteau was gathering his honey. He had known
Diaghilev for some years, and met Stravinsky in 1911. One year later, he
wrote a ballet scenario that was set to music by Reynaldo Hahn: *Le Dieu
bleu* was performed in May 1912 by the Ballets Russes.

From then on, Cocteau's great idea was to bring together the avant-
garde of the different arts. He wanted to provide Diaghilev with what he
still lacked, the collaboration of the painters who, like the St Petersburg
troupe, most provoked the public. He wanted to become the orchestrator
of a new, total art.

After having mocked it at first, he later began to accept and move closer
to cubism. For this, he had had to meet Albert Gleizes, who took him to
see the artists of the Section d'Or. This was a beginning, but it wasn't
enough.

When he first came to Montparnasse, Cocteau understood right away –
as he wrote – that as most of his contemporaries had left for the front,
'Paris was there for the taking.'

Paris, in practice, meant Picasso. Very early on, Cocteau calculated that
if the painter had people as important as Max Jacob, Pierre Reverdy and
Guillaume Apollinaire at his side, then there was no reason why he, Jean
Cocteau, should not find a place in the painter's entourage. He determined
to do so. On every possible occasion, the young man (he was twenty-six
at the time) made little gifts to the painter he was trying to entice into
his golden net. He sent him tobacco. He wrote him tragically limpid
letters: 'My dear Picasso, you must paint my portrait quickly because I'm
going to die.'[13]

A few weeks before Eva's death, he managed without too much trouble
to make his way into the studio on the rue Schoelcher. Edgard Varèse was
the key. The poet was dazzled by what he saw there: 'I think I am one of
the few people capable of instantly entering your kingdom, and of
translating it into my language, in such a way that my syntax will obey
the same imperatives as yours.'[14]

In short, it was a revelation.

Ever since this first visit, Cocteau had dreamed of only one thing:
returning. Because, like Max Jacob, he had already understood that the
meeting with Picasso would be the most significant encounter of his life.
What did it matter if, to reach his goal, he had to spend time in the
Rotonde and become friendly with the cubists – whom he didn't really
understand, this group of shabbily dressed painters absorbed in futile
conversations, who found his chic tastes and fashion consciousness absurd.

He dreamed of seeing himself on a canvas signed by the Spanish painter.

In January 1915, Picasso executed a portrait in lead pencil of Max Jacob. Stylistically, it was strangely like the portrait he had done of Ambroise Vollard the same year. In the little world of Vavin, these two works had the effect of a bomb: was Picasso abandoning cubism for a more classical realism reminiscent of Ingres? Even Beatrice Hastings wrote of it in *The New Age*.

If he'll paint Max Jacob, why not me, Cocteau wondered. But how could he convince the painter to do him this enormous honour? There had to be a way ... To tell the truth, the method he found wasn't terribly original. When he saw the *Arlequin* painted by the artist during the last phase of Eva's illness, the idea began to take root in the poet's subtle mind. Léonce Rosenberg, who had bought the work, confirmed Picasso's interest in circus figures to him.

Cocteau deposited a coin on the counter, gave Libion a smile and slid graciously off his stool. He smoothed the folds of his red trousers, slipped the strap of his purple helmet over his right wrist and, nodding goodbye to all present, went off to carry out the plan that was beginning to hatch in his elegant brain.

THE COCK AND THE HARLEQUIN

I'm coming home. There are great storms here and in two days' time
I've lost the deep tan – a Negro's colour – that I had just spent two
months acquiring.

Jean Cocteau

He lived on the rue d'Anjou, at no. 10. He liked to entertain. This is
where Jean Hugo, the great-grandson of Victor Hugo, first met him:

> The poet, standing in the middle of a circle of male and female admirers,
> held a telephone receiver in his hand and marvelled, as he imagined
> the meandering path his words were taking as they flowed through the
> telephone line snaking along the carpet.[1]

It was also here that he read to a select group of visitors his poem 'Le
Cap de Bonne-Espérance', dedicated to the aviator Roland Garros, who
had introduced him to the joys of aerial navigation:

> so
> this angel whose thoughts were elsewhere
>
> that could
> appear
> to us
>
> The lovable giant slows down shrinks

The poet stood behind a desk decorated with painted flowers. He wore
a black dinner jacket and a white tie, and he had stuck a gardenia in his
buttonhole; he claimed he received one every day – not from Paris, which
would be too common, but from London.

When he had finished his reading, he moved about the group to take
the pulse of opinion. Misia Sert (the daughter of the Polish sculptor
Cyprien Godebski, and a great friend of Diaghilev) applauded, followed

by the actor Roland Bertin and the painter Valentine Grosz, the future wife of Jean Hugo, who had helped to bring the host into the Montparnasse group. André Breton, cramped in his military doctor's uniform, did not say a word. He disappeared at the end of the reading.

This was before the meeting with Picasso. Since then, some water had flowed under the bridge.

Cocteau opened his closet door, and this particular evening he chose the outfit which seemed most appropriate to him: a costume to be worn in a ballet he was preparing for Diaghilev. It was a clown's costume, composed of gaily coloured trousers and a shirt, in vivid diamond shapes.

He put it on. Just as he was leaving, he realized that walking about Paris in the middle of the war dressed in such a manner might be a little awkward. So he hid the disguise under a long coat. It still looked a little strange around the ankles, but if anyone asked him, he would just say that he was wearing camouflage gear . . .

Cocteau hailed a taxi and asked to be driven to the rue Schoelcher. He climbed the staircase with a pounding heart. How would Picasso welcome this guest in his unusual attire? Would his recent loss remove all desire to paint this gentle silhouette?

The poet rang the bell. The painter opened the door. The poet nonchalantly took off his coat and displayed his multicoloured finery. The painter didn't say a word. He didn't immediately stick a canvas on an easel to catch the light coming in from the bay window overlooking the Montparnasse cemetery; he didn't pick up his brush or palette. Cocteau was desperate. He consoled himself by rewriting the story: 'In 1916,' he was to claim, [Picasso] 'wanted to do my portrait in a Harlequin costume. This portrait ended up as a cubist canvas.'[2]

When Cocteau arrived at his home, Picasso was trying to get over the grief caused by Eva's death. He had begun to console himself with Gaby, a young girl from Montparnasse who would be succeeded by Irène Lagut, who left Serge Férat's arms for those of the Spaniard – who in turn would soon open his heart to Pâquerette, a model for Poiret, and then to Olga, his first wife.

Cocteau waited. Since Picasso was busy painting other things, for the moment, he posed for Modigliani and Kisling.

Like Cendrars, Moïse Kisling had been sent home from the front after the battle of Carency. He survived with the help of a Polish writer, Adolphe Basler (a great admirer of Manolo) who sold the artist's paintings in his apartment.

Kisling hung around Montparnasse, a merry partygoer wearing tattered overalls and sandals which had survived many battles with the pavements. The clothes he had come in from Cracow were no more than a memory: he had adopted the dress and habits of his new comrades. He was intrepid, and had already been so before the war. In 1914, he had fought a duel against another Polish painter, Leopold Gottlieb. No one ever knew the motive for this fratricidal combat, which took place in the Parc des Princes, near a cycling track. André Salmon was Kisling's witness, and Diego Rivera was Gottlieb's. The two men faced each other first with pistols, firing two shots each at a distance of twenty-five metres, then with sabres. Kisling had never used a sword before. The blades flew, the cyclists stopped their rounds to applaud, the onlookers were thrilled, the witnesses called for a pause to dress the wounds. The two Poles refused. They continued to battle ferociously for an hour, with a determination which earned them an impressive number of gashes. The end of the combat finally came after Gottlieb's sabre sliced off part of his countryman's nose. Kisling, his face bloody but smiling, turned towards the public and proclaimed: 'The fourth division of Poland!'

In fact, it was the fifth division. Six weeks later, Austria–Hungary declared war on Serbia.

While waiting for Picasso to accommodate him, Cocteau found himself one day on the rue Joseph Bara, in Kisling's studio. Modigliani was there too, and the two painters were to do a portrait of the poet. Cocteau had brought a bottle of gin and two lemons: he wanted to pose in front of a still life.

'Impossible!' Amedeo declared. He didn't like still lifes.

'But I love gin-fizz...' He picked up the gin bottle, squeezed the lemons, scrounged around to find a siphon of Seltzer water and served himself a drink. Then another. Then a third. Soon he had polished off the bottle.

Kisling was furious. Cocteau was still waiting.

A few weeks later, he could finally exult: Picasso had begun a portrait of him. Did the painter know then that under the impetus of the spirited young man, he was soon going to move into another universe altogether? That the Bateau Lavoir, which already seemed so far away, would disappear for good when, arm in arm, Cocteau and Picasso would venture out together into fashionable society.

He probably suspected as much, as did the others. Maurice Sachs' theory is that the former inhabitants of Montmartre – Max Jacob and Picasso first among them – let themselves be manipulated by Cocteau's subtle tricks because they needed a 'clever public relations agent'.[3] In exchange for his contacts, they offered him the novelty and the avant-garde approach that fascinated him. He himself was a marvellous 'presenter' and they used him for this. But between them, there was only really a 'friendship of façade, which hid beneath it deep rivalries and terrible contempt'.[4]

This is undoubtedly a somewhat exaggerated version of the facts, but there was some truth to it. *Parade* would come soon, and then a collaboration between Cocteau and Picasso on the Ballets Russes. But the painter would later move away from the poet. Gertrude Stein related a revealing story on this subject.[5] One day Picasso was in Barcelona, being interviewed by a Catalonian paper. The conversation turned to Jean Cocteau. Picasso declared that Cocteau was so famous in Paris that all the chic coiffeurs had copies of his poems on their tables.

The interview was published in the French press, and Cocteau read it. He tried to reach Picasso to demand an explanation, but Picasso avoided him. In order to put out the fire which threatened to scorch his reputation, Cocteau confided to a French paper that it wasn't his friend Picasso who had spoken of him in such terms, but ... Picabia. Unfortunately, Picabia denied it. Cocteau again assailed the Picasso fortress. He begged the painter to contradict Picabia's statement. Picasso still didn't answer.

A short time later, Picasso and a wife (probably Olga) were at the theatre one evening, where they ran into Cocteau's mother. She asked the painter to confirm that he was not the author of the calumny about her son that had filtered back from Spain. Picasso didn't react. It was his wife who, unhappy to see another mother suffering, answered that of course Picasso would never have spoken of Jean Cocteau in such terms.

So the poet was reassured; there was no murky misunderstanding between them.

But new storm clouds would soon build up. When, in the twenties, Picasso grew close to the surrealists, who detested 'the widower on the roof'* (their nickname for Cocteau) this was just a light drizzle. But it became a heavy rain when, during and after the Spanish Civil War, Picasso clearly leaned to the left on the political chessboard. The real storm came with the Second World War: Cocteau, who escaped somewhat miraculously from the after-war purge, had nonetheless leaned rather far to the right in his wartime political sympathies. He had even been heard publicly to praise Arno Breker ...†

Even if he forgave him much later, even if he would open his door to him again in the sixties, Picasso never forgot. And he wasn't alone. Françoise Gilot recounts that once when he was in Saint Tropez with Paul Eluard (whose real name was Eugène-Emile-Paul Grindel), a yacht came to moor in front of Senéquié's. Cocteau hopped off it. Eluard, who didn't like him, ignored him. But the other was so insistent that in the end Eluard had to shake his hand ... very coldly. It was better than nothing. It was enough, in any case, to enable Cocteau to write that Eluard was 'a great friend'.[6] Picasso was not much warmer on this occasion,

* 'Veuf sur le toit' in French, which rhymes with 'Boeuf sur le toit', the name of a fashionable restaurant of the time frequented by Cocteau.
† One of Hitler's architects.

though his attitude changed a little after Eluard's death in 1952.[7]

One question remains, which no one has ever been able to answer. In Montparnasse, during the years when Cocteau was at the height of his fame, there was another poet who was at least as important and talented, whose flame burned with a similarly varied and probably much longer-lasting light. He too had written poems, novels, and plays. His talent was protean and, although he too could kiss ladies' hands in salons, he had not made a concerted effort to enter the world of the avant-garde, or to insinuate himself with the geniuses of the time – for the simple reason that he was naturally one of them. This poet was Guillaume Apollinaire.

The two men had known each other since the end of 1916. To begin with, their relations were marked by doubts and mistrust. Writing to Picasso in the spring of 1917, Apollinaire confided that things between himself and Cocteau had improved a bit. Was this after he had received a letter dating from the month of March in which the younger of the two poets had practically gone down to him on bended knee?

> I swear to you that we will do things together and that I felt confident about our relations. Please forgive me if I overdid it a little, which made me look like 'the young man trying to make himself welcome'. I was acting bravely and seriously, for the common cause, and I was even glad of your mistrust, like a Freemason in disguise who tests another mason and runs up against his resistance.[8]

Or was it because Picasso, according to Cocteau, had urged the two poets to see each other and reach an understanding?

> I'm very happy about our meeting, which is so important and which Picasso desires with all his heart. 'If only you and Apollinaire like each other', he often says.[9]

They liked each other with some ups and as many downs. Cocteau complained that Apollinaire found something 'suspicious' about him. Apollinaire, according to Vauxcelles, was annoyed with Cocteau for trying to take the place in Picasso's life that he himself had stolen from Max Jacob. In any case, the gossip, the incidents, the rumours bandied about in salons, continued regularly to create shadow zones between them.

When, time having passed, Cocteau proclaimed that Paris during the war was a city to be taken, he was probably thinking less about the city than about his own place in it. A place, to be precise, that Guillaume Apollinaire had abandoned. This leads to a question that will remain unanswered for ever: what would have become of Cocteau if Apollinaire had lived?

THE POET'S WOUND

War is the legal return to a state of savagery.

Paul Léautaud

The date: 17 March 1916. In the 139th Division of the French Army, across from Berry-au-Bac, in the Buttes wood, Guillaume Apollinaire was setting up his corner of the trench. He stretched a canvas tent above the parapet: an illusory protection from the shrapnel falling all around. He donned his helmet and sat down in the mud. After his leave spent in Lamu with Madeleine and her mother, he had joined his unit in January. For two months, he had undergone intensive training, and had commanded his company. On 14 March, he left for the front. On the day of his departure, he wrote a letter to Madeleine in which he once again made her heir to all his possessions. Just one simple letter among others.

They wrote almost every day. He promised her eternal love and swore that as soon as he had time, he would take care of the formalities of their marriage. There was tenderness in his letters, but not passion. When the young woman seemed a little worried by this, he reassured her, explained in veiled language that because of the censor he could not make dramatic declarations of love. Sometimes, he seemed exasperated by her insistence. He begged her to be 'nice' and to write in a more literary, high-minded vein. He advised her to perfect her English, not to eat fish, to amuse herself more, and he was preoccupied by her aching feet: 'Massage them gently from the toe to the instep for two minutes each in the evening, and pass them through the philopode.'[1]

It was all very sensible. Their exchanges were a perfect reflection of the bourgeois nature of their entire romance: engagement, request for the daughter's hand from the mother, warm, reassuring gestures ... Was this really what Apollinaire wanted?

He no longer wrote to Lou. That page had been turned. His last missive dated from the month of January, in which he had asked her to send him a receipt from the pawnshop in Nice so he could retrieve a watch he had

left there. But he still corresponded from time to time with Marie
Laurencin, in an affectionate tone, and with friends from Paris – notably
Picasso, to whom he gave a ring he had made himself.

He wrote poems, and sent a few pages to the *Mercure de France*: his
Anecdotiques, which were about the war, futurism, Stendhal, Joan of Arc.
Whatever happened, he kept a book in his pocket, which he took out as
soon as he had a moment to himself on the front.

He still didn't complain, but he was depressed: he fell prey to a 'great
melancholy'. Less, it would seem, because of his separation from Madeleine
than because of the war itself. He had become accustomed to the rain,
the mud, barracks life, long marches and manoeuvres in the snow, the
asphyxiating gases. But he could not get used to the stupidity of headquarters. He had to make a report to explain why the men in his company
wore helmets while those in neighbouring companies had kepis. He was
probably also kept informed of the disciplinary measures inflicted on the
army as a whole. It was a time of war councils, in which voluntary
mutilation was punished by the death penalty. Any soldier who had
wounds on his hands and bore blackish traces around the wound risked
execution: these traces could be powder, which would prove that the
blow was received at such close proximity that it couldn't have been
inflicted by the enemy. Numerous soldiers were executed because of shells
which had exploded nearby and thus stained their hands.

Similarly, the refusal to obey was cruelly punished. In March 1915,
near Souain, the second company of the 336th infantry received orders
to attack enemy lines. The men refused to advance. They were exhausted
by the assaults and counter-assaults; moreover, they had to cross a zone
which was one hundred and fifty yards wide, covered with barbed wire
and constantly targeted by German machine guns: it was a suicide mission.

Faced with this characteristic lack of discipline, the general commanding
the division first had the idea of shelling the French trenches. When the
colonel in charge of the artillery objected, he changed tactics. He demanded
that six corporals and eighteen men be chosen from among the youngest.
The hostages would appear before the war council and immediately be
condemned to death.

In some such cases, the hostages were not chosen by their officers and
sub-officers, but had their names drawn in a lottery. They would then be
executed in place of those who had refused to charge into enemy fire or
to cross fields strewn with corpses, on top of which they would have had
to throw themselves, in order to dodge the German shells.

The sub-lieutenant Apollinaire was undoubtedly not insensible to the
case of another sub-lieutenant, Chapelant. He was twenty years old, an
officer in the machine-gun division of the 98th infantry. In October 1914,
he was attacked in the Loges woods. The Germans got around him, and

captured his two machine-guns and four servers. Then Chapelant was wounded near the German lines, and was caught between barbed wire for two days. When the stretcher-bearers picked him up, he was taken to see the colonel, who decreed that he must appear before the war council. Why? Because he had been found behind enemy lines!

Chapelant was lying on his stretcher when he heard his sentence: the death penalty. And not just any old death penalty. He was tied to his stretcher, the stretcher was raised to a vertical position, and he received twelve bullets in his chest.

These incidents disheartened the troops, and Apollinaire was as affected by them as anyone else. Derain, too, wrote of his distress to his mother:

> Millions of lives are being sacrificed in vain as if they were nothing, and for no well thought out or clear reason. Some people have given themselves all the power and use others like indefatigable and indestructible instruments, constantly demanding that they renew the most difficult of efforts. It's terrifying, the irresponsibility of the people giving orders.[2]

A few weeks before taking up his position across from Berry-au-Bac, Apollinaire went on leave for two days. He came back demoralized. How easy wartime was in Paris! Max Jacob had depressed him by foreseeing a thirty-year conflict. It was surely an exaggeration. But Guillaume didn't believe that an armistice would be signed before the end of 1917, maybe not even until the winter of 1918.

The only good news, the best in a long time, was contained in an official letter he had received a few days before. This letter, on official stationery from the department of Civil Affairs and of the National Seal within the Ministry of Justice, granted French nationality to Guillaume Kostrowitzky, known as Guillaume Apollinaire. At last...

The letter was in the poet's pocket, alongside an issue of the *Mercure de France*. Apollinaire's fingers brushed against the review, and he took it out and opened it. Around him, the bombing continued. But, aside from remaining vigilant, there was nothing he could do.

It was four o'clock on the afternoon of 17 March 1916. Apollinaire was reading the table of contents. He turned a few pages. Suddenly, there was an explosion about forty yards away from him, and at the same time he felt something strike his helmet. A slight hit, on the right temple. Apollinaire's hand flew to his head. There was a hole in the helmet. Something warm was coming down his cheek. Blood...

He called for help; he was evacuated and taken to the emergency station. The shard from a 150 mm bullet had entered his right temple. The chief doctor of the 246th regiment bound his wound. He was brought a jug of water and put to sleep. The next day, at two in the morning, an incision was made while he was in an ambulance transporting him to the hospital of Château-Thierry, and some fragments of the shell were removed. On 18 March, he wrote to Madeleine to keep her up to date on his health: the wound was only a slight one, he was only tired.

On the 22nd, he was given an X-ray. He was in pain, but this didn't prevent him from recording in his notebook the details of how he was wounded, or from writing to Madeleine, Yves Blanc and Max Jacob.

On the 25th, he was to be evacuated from Château-Thierry, but fever kept him in bed until the 28th. On the 29th, he arrived at the Val-de-Grâce Hospital in Paris. His friends came to see him: he was perfectly lucid. Apparently, the wound was healthy and the scar was healing.

But Apollinaire complained of headaches and dizziness. The doctors noted that he was tired. His left arm was getting heavy. On 9 April, Serge Férat, a nurse at the time at the hospital of the Italian Embassy, had him transferred to the Italian government hospital on the Quai d'Orsay. As the days went by, he developed a paralysis, accompanied by bouts of unconsciousness. On 9 May, at the Villa Molière (an annexe of the Val-de-Grâce Hospital, located on the Boulevard de Montmorency in Auteuil), Apollinaire was operated on for a cranial abscess. On the 11th, he sent a telegram to Madeleine to report that the operation had gone well.

In notes that were often short, he kept her informed of his transfers and the progress of his condition. In August, when she expressed the hope of coming to join him, he begged her not to. He asked her to write him cheerful letters, and not more than one a week. He also requested that she send him his artilleryman's notebook as well as a ring he had left with her. And a copy of *Case d'Armons*. And two watercolours by Marie Laurencin. He was starting to take back everything that he had given her of his, just as he had done with Lou.

Madeleine in turn would soon disappear from Guillaume Apollinaire's life. Was it because another woman, Jacqueline, who had come to see him at the Villa Molière, would begin to take her place? Or because, as he recognized himself in the last letter he sent to Algeria, he had become 'very irritable'? Whatever the cause, Guillaume Apollinaire was not the same when he returned to civilian life, wearing a magnificent uniform from which hung the cross of war, received in June, his head bandaged with a leather covering which replaced the turban of the first weeks. He was not just irritable. He showed a zealous patriotism which astonished his friends. He was preoccupied, less cheerful, disappointed by the selfishness he saw all around him and by Parisian life, so removed from the horrors of the front.

Yet he would still participate in it himself. He would sip drinks once again in the café de Flore and inhabit his apartment on the Boulevard Saint Germain; he would go to dinners and to parties. This period would last for as long as the war lasted: twenty-seven months.

Twenty-seven months: exactly the time he had left to live.

CAMOUFLAGE ART

War camouflage was the work of the
cubists: it was also, if you like, their
revenge.

Jean Paulhan

In February of 1916, Apollinaire had written to Madeleine to announce
some good news: he had a new uniform. He complained, however, that
the sky-blue colour recently adopted as replacements for the brightly-
coloured jackets and trousers, was not the same as the khaki reserved for
the army in the East. It would have been better if the colours had been
'harlequinized' so as to melt into nature and thus be invisible to the
enemy's eye. He had got this idea from Picasso. One year earlier, the
painter had written to his poet friend to give him the benefit of his
strategic insights: even painted grey, the cannons were easily picked out;
to hide them, one would have to play with forms, using bright colours
arranged like pieces of a harlequin's costume.

In *Le Poète assassiné*, Apollinaire writes that the Bird of Benin, who was
Picasso, camouflages pieces of heavy artillery. This Bird of Benin, if
Gertrude Stain is to be believed, exclaimed one day, as a military convoy
marched down the Boulevard Saint Germain, 'We did that!'

'We' meant the cubists. The experiment began on the eve of the war
in France near Toul. A decorator had the idea of concealing a cannon and
its servers under a canvas painted in earth tones. The military staff sent a
plane out above the camouflage cover; the aviator saw only the trees.

A few months later, at Pont-à-Mousson, a telephone operator was told
to transmit the order to fire the cannon. He did as he was told. No sooner
had the cannon fired its charge than an enemy shell blew it up. This made
the telephone operator wonder: couldn't one invent and develop an
effective system of protection enabling men and equipment to disappear
into the surrounding environment?

The telephone operator was a painter. He thought this objective could
be achieved by playing with forms and colours. He contacted military
headquarters, and in February 1915, the Ministry of War agreed to put

together a team to work under his direction. Thus it was that Lucien Guirand de Scevola (mentioned by Apollinaire before the war in his *Chroniques artistiques*)[1] founded the first camouflage unit in military history. To begin with there were thirty volunteers; three years later there were more than three thousand camouflagers and eight thousand manufacturers. And a symbol whose meaning was clear: a golden chameleon embroidered against a red background.

Whom did Scevola call in to help? People without the slightest competence in military affairs, equipment, strategy, or combat of any kind – the cubist painters. But as Jean Paulhan wrote, 'The only paintings that public opinion stubbornly condemned for looking like nothing were, in this time of danger, the only ones which could thus look like anything at all.'[2] The cubist painters knew better than most how to play with forms and planes, presenting, on the surface of their canvases, objects without volume but which were still shown from all angles. They reconstituted the object in its entirety and no longer only in terms of the point of view from which it is seen. They would do both that, and the opposite: they camouflaged objects by making their volume disappear. Others emerged, invented using a single plane which represented a totality. This was the principle of bait: the eye of the enemy aviator, flying over a false cannon painted on a flat plane and in *trompe-l'œil*, had to believe that the cannon was real, whatever angle he saw it from. And if cannons really were there, hidden by false branches, the eye of the enemy pilot had to believe that the branches were real, whatever angle he looked at them from. The aerial photographs themselves couldn't show anything that was supposed to be hidden. It was not only a question of hiding structures and arms. It was also essential to lead the enemy astray.

Under the command of Captain Guirand de Scevola, the cubists set to work. There was something stupefying about the whole thing: these painters who had been so insulted before the war, who had been seen as the great champions of 'Kraut art', painters whose dealers and buyers were Kahnweiler, Uhde, and others of Germanic extraction, were all working to defend the French nation! And not only painters, but also sculptors, theatrical designers, illustrators, and architects: Bouchard, Boussingault, Camoin, Dufresne, Dunoyer de Segonzac (who directed the camouflage workshop of Amiens), Forain, Roger de la Fresnaye, Marcoussis, André Mare, Luc-Albert Moreau, Jacques Villon ... Braque also joined in the effort, for a few months in 1916, but despite Scevola's repeated entreaties, Derain and Léger declined to participate.

Throughout the entire duration of the war, these artists drew, in watercolour, false trees which would be constructed behind the lines, in circuses or in schools of fine art, equipped with an inside ladder which allowed an observer to watch the enemy trenches (this is where Cendrars got the idea for Bikoff, who supposedly inspired Charlie Chaplin). They painted branches in natural colours on helmets and cannons, softened the angles of machines by covering them in brightly coloured shades or with raffia plants, and concealed shooting and observation posts behind false ruins, fake walls, mills made of cardboard, chimneys, bales of straw, corpses of men or animals painted with a brush. On giant canvases, they traced false forests sheltering real machine guns, railway lines, geographical markings. They concealed entire villages, trenches and bridges, and they painted heads of soldiers on poles, which the footsoldiers would wave from the depths of the trenches to attract enemy fire. In 1917, on the crest of Messina, several hundred footsoldiers would rise from the earth, drawn on canvases spread out to deceive the Germans.

Camouflage tactics would ultimately be adopted by all the world's armies: the French cubists would help the English and the Italians, and the Germans would start to use these strategies themselves from 1917. But when they came back from the war, many of these painters would be disgusted by an art whose sordid reality they had now witnessed at first hand: uprooted trees, villages turned inside out, monuments toppled over, corpses with the limbs wrenched off and scattered ... And some of them would then ask a very legitimate question: had not cubism, which so aptly illustrated the war, in large part anticipated it as well?

MEANWHILE, IN AMERICA...

Object-spear.

Marcel Duchamp

In 1914, Georges Braque had joined the 224th infantry regiment. Initially a sergeant, he had become a lieutenant and had fought in the front line of attack. In May 1915, he received a serious head wound at the battle of Carency; he was trepanned, then demobilized in 1916.

Léger fought at Argonne and Verdun: a victim of gas poisoning, he was sent home a few months before the end of the war.

In September 1915, Derain joined the 82nd artillery regiment. He fought in the battles – which became slaughters – of Verdun and the Chemin des Dames. He returned to civilian life when peace came.

Roger de la Fresnaye remained in the infantry until tuberculosis put him into a hospital bed in 1918.

Kisling was wounded during a one-on-one fight in Carency. Cendrars lost an arm in Champagne. Apollinaire came back to Paris after a bullet found its way to his head in the Buttes wood. All of these men criticized those of their friends from before the war who had continued to work, here and there, and to sell their creations. Not the ones who had been refused by the armies, like Modigliani or Ortiz de Zarate, but those who had fled, like Delaunay to Spain, or Picabia and Cravan to America.

America was part of a story that had begun before the war. But it would start again in Montparnasse a few months after the peace was signed. On 17 February 1913, in New York, the International Exhibition of Modern Art had opened, better known by the name of the Armory Show. It was the first American exhibition of contemporary international art and, according to Hélène Seckel, it represented 'the relaunching – if not actually the birth – of the art market'.[1] This exhibition would have considerable repercussions, for this is where European artists first met some of the collectors who would come to Paris in the twenties.

The works of the Armory Show were presented in a former hall of

arms (the Armory) near Greenwich Village. One of its promoters was the
American lawyer, John Quinn, who, after many battles, had managed to
ensure that avant-garde works would not be taxed when imported. With
the assistance of Henri-Pierre Roché, the future author of *Jules et Jim*, he
was to acquire a number of works in France. Walter Pach, Elie Faure's
translator into English, also furnished some paintings for the exhibition,
notably those of cubist painters of the Section d'Or.

The Armory Show exhibited nearly one thousand six hundred works
by European artists, including Cézanne (it was on this occasion that the
Metropolitan Museum of New York bought its first Cézanne painting),
Braque, Gauguin, Gleizes, Kandinsky, Léger, Marcoussis, Picasso, Duchamp
and Picabia. But in 1913, only Picabia was able to afford the transatlantic
voyage, and so was the sole French artist present at the Armory Show.
The American press devoted entire columns to this painter, the son of a
Cuban father and a French mother, who was the living incarnation of its
idea of the avant-garde.

Picabia had been an impressionist when young, a pointilliste later –
perhaps he was now somewhat Fauve, vaguely cubist, even orphist in
Apollinaire's eyes. America had given him a taste for the mechanical and
the technological. He discovered fast cars with electric starters, and all the
treasures of modernity. He inaugurated a new period, based on his taste
for machines. Picabia was fascinated by New York. For him, this American
city was the city of the future, and of cubism.

Back in France, this wealthy hedonist received his call to arms with
unconcealed disgust. Calling on his many relations, he found a way to
become the driver for an officer in Paris, which was at least better than
Verdun. But when he was summoned to go to Bordeaux, Picabia appealed
to his father for help. Through the Cuban Embassy in Paris, his father
managed to have him sent to Havana, on an official mission of a
commercial nature.

Havana wasn't America, and Picabia only went there when his wife,
Gabrielle Buffet, gave him a few kicks in the seat of his pants. He stayed
for two months, then came back to America. From there, he went to
Madrid, visited Switzerland, stopped in New York again, and then returned
to Spain.

During the summer of 1914, Delaunay, his wife and the boxer–poet
Arthur Cravan would arrive in Spain. Cendrars is not indulgent on the
subject of these three. They were friends. They had caroused together at
wild, alcohol-soaked parties. They had danced the tango in the Bullier
ballroom, decked out in richly coloured, strangely assorted, striking attire.
Cravan had made quite a hit with his trousers dipped in a painter's palette,
his shirts full of holes revealing tattoos and obscenities underneath.

They calmed down a little when war was declared. Yesterday's merrymakers all went to Lisbon, which they soon deserted when Portugal in turn declared war on Germany. They then turned up in Madrid. But the borders there weren't secure.

Cravan decided to go to America. To finance the journey, he had the idea of organizing a match in which he would challenge the title of the world heavyweight boxing champion, Jack Johnson. The two men had already met in training rooms in Berlin and in Paris. According to Cendrars, Johnson was a boxer full-time and a pimp half-time.

The two of them came to an agreement. The match took place in a hall in Madrid (though Cendrars claims it was Barcelona). It was announced in the press and on large posters and billboards all over the city: a veritable corrida. On the night before the tournament, Cravan had reserved a place on a transatlantic liner leaving for New York. Knowing that he could not compete with his adversary, he had asked him not to hit him too hard, and not to knock him to the ground at least for the first few rounds.

But things went much faster than that. The version told by Cendrars, who claimed to have got it from an eyewitness (as he had in the case of Whitman's funeral), portrays a terror-stricken Cravan, hunched over, immobile in the ring, sagging under the jeers of the crowd, faced with a Johnson who began by laughing, then gave him kicks in the rear to make him move a little, and finally delivered a monster punch which instantly laid Oscar Wilde's nephew out flat.

'One ... two ... three ...' intoned the referee. Cravan didn't waste time getting away. While the crowd and the organizers of the match were looking for him, together with Johnson, who swore he would destroy him, the fighter was already dressing his wounds in his ship's cabin.

He soon caused a scandal in New York. Duchamp and Picabia had learned that some high-society women had organized a lecture to hear more about modern art. They decided to send this snobbish, ignorant public their most exalted representative. Thus it was that Cravan was chosen to speak. He was taken to lunch before the talk, where he ate little but drank much. He arrived on time at the hall where hordes of stylish ladies, faint with admiration, awaited him. The speaker turned his back on them, removed his jacket, then his garters, then his shirt, and finally his trousers; turning around again, he began to insult the first rows of listeners, then the others. In the end he was carted away by the police. His friends paid his bail.

Cravan went next to Canada, which he soon fled disguised as a woman; he then found a job as a mechanic on a fishing boat on its way to Newfoundland. He later opened a boxing academy in Mexico City and disappeared off the Mexican coast after marrying the American writer Mina Loy.

As for Jack Johnson, he was never seen in a ring again.

Cendrars always recognized the 'immense' poetic talent of Arthur Cravan. But he never forgave him for leaving France on the eve of the war, neither Cravan nor his friends in New York, 'cowards of every stripe that the storm sweeping across Europe' had washed up there: a mixture of European deserters, internationalists, pacifists, and neutral observers.[2]

Among them was one essential figure in the history of modern art – perhaps neutral, certainly a pacifist, but in no way a deserter: Marcel Duchamp.

What was he doing in America? Creating a scandal, of course. He arrived in New York in 1915, preceded by a sulphurous reputation. Two years earlier, he had been the European star of the Armory Show. His *Nude Descending a Staircase* had provoked protest, enthusiasm, disgust and admiration. The press had lauded him, mocked him, damned him to hell and praised him to the skies.

It wasn't the first time. Already in 1912, at the very Parisian Salon des Indépendants, his cubist friends had asked him not to exhibit. Gleizes and Le Fauconnier had sent his two brothers, Jacques Villon and Raymond Duchamp-Villon, to ask the youngest brother not to show this *Nude Descending a Staircase*, too daring in its conception of movement to be accepted by the reviewers.

Duchamp had obeyed. Once, but not twice: the following year, his *Nude* was shown at the Salon de la Section d'Or. Then he had left for America.

At the Armory Show, Duchamp had sold all four of the works he had exhibited, thanks to which he had earned enough money to leave a Europe in flames and go to New York. He had been rejected from the army because of a weak heart. This didn't weigh on his conscience: he himself confessed to lacking the patriotism corresponding to the morality of the time. Once America entered the war, he decided that he should do something, and signed up at the French military mission as a secretary for a six-month stint.

When he arrived in New York, Duchamp recognized certain influences on his work: a little impressionism, a little fauvism, a little cubism, no particular admiration for Cézanne but a passion for Monet, a real respect for Matisse, and a shock on seeing Braque's work at Kahnweiler's during an exhibition of his paintings in 1910.

But the most important influence was not that of a painter, but rather of a writer, Raymond Roussel. Duchamp always admitted that he had begun his work *La Mariée mise à nu par ses célibataires, même*, after having seen a performance of *Impressions d'Afrique* at the Théâtre Antoine in 1912. Guillaume Apollinaire had been with him.

At this time, Raymond Roussel was the archetype of the wealthy young man to be found in the fashionable society of the Belle Epoque. He reminded Philippe Soupault of the Proust of Cabourg: the same elegance, the same taste for refinement, the same high standards in his literary tastes. After the failure of his first work, *La Doublure*, Roussel had succumbed to 'a frightful illness' which plagued him for a long time.[3] Later, he would on occasion roll around on the ground in rage and despair over his inability to reach the sublime heights he aspired to in his writing.

He drove about in a large caravan equipped with several rooms, a bathroom and a kitchen. Keeping all the shutters closed so that the spectacle of life outside didn't distract him from his work, Roussel wrote. At home, too, he paid a gardener to maintain flowers that he didn't even look at. He used his fortune to publish books that didn't sell, to produce plays which either found no audience or, quite the opposite, met with sound, fury and condemnation. Thus it was with *Impressions d'Afrique*.

He had the idea of adapting his book for the stage in order to reach a public which never asked for his books in bookshops. Only Edmond Rostand approved of the undertaking. As for the audience, it went on the rampage. The violence was directed against precisely that which fascinated Marcel Duchamp: the novelty of the language, the modernity of the show, the machines present on stage – notably the human machines, one of which represented a fencer. Roussel drew his inspiration from the sources that the avant-garde favoured – the technical revolution, movement, speed, the cinematograph.

Both the painter and the writer would abandon their art young. And both would then take up the game of chess, becoming the most brilliant players of their time. Roussel became famous for his invention of a new checkmate using the bishop and the knight, which would be praised by Tartakower.* Neither of them ever belonged to any artistic school.

Duchamp had an important reason for refusing to join a movement: the attack on his *Nude* by his peers in the Section d'Or had soured his faith in the joys of the collectivity for ever. In America, as in France, he remained alone: especially when the cubists Survage, Gleizes and Archipenko excluded the Dadaist painters and writers from the Section d'Or.

In New York, Duchamp, a good-natured young man, smoked his pipe and cigars amongst his admirers, going from one drawing room to the next, laughing to himself as he saw how he had become an object of cult worship or a source of scandal. He was the commander-in-chief of the entire avant-garde. He gave desultory French lessons to pretty young women, whom he taught the most indecent words in the language. He discovered jazz, played chess, smoked, drank, and danced in the company of Man Ray, the musician Edgard Varèse, Francis Picabia, Arthur Cravan

---

* Savielly Grigorievitsch Tartakower, one of the founders of the Hypermodern School of Chess, was a colourful international personality.

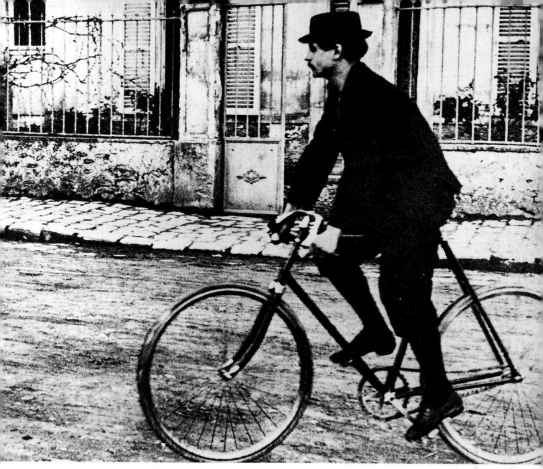

Alfred Jarry leaving his house in Corbeil to come to Paris, in 1898.

Paul Fort at the Closerie des Lilas, Boulevard du Montparnasse, in 1920.

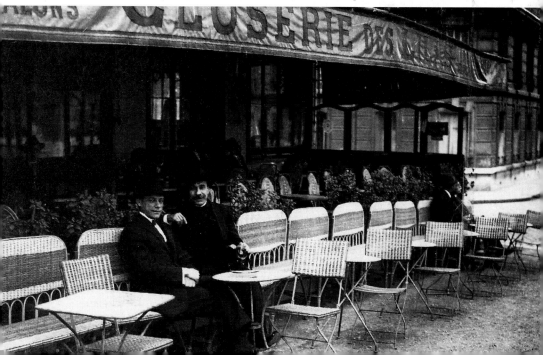

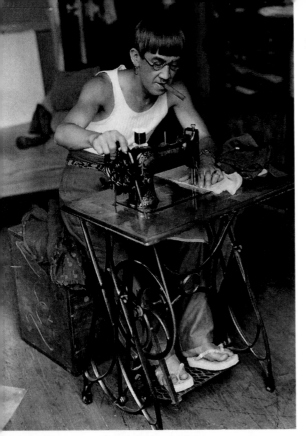

Foujita in 1928.

Arthur Cravan in c. 1902.

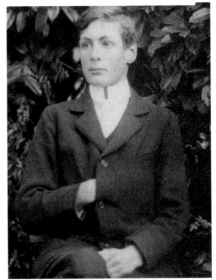

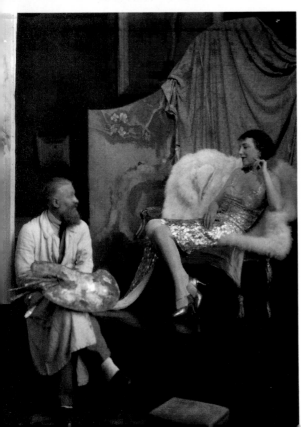

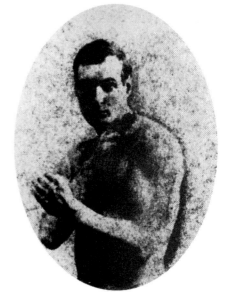

Arthur Cravan in 1916.

Session with a model at the painter Kees Van Dongen's studio in 1927.

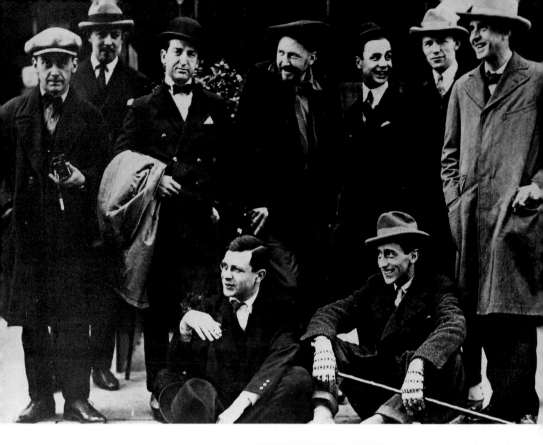

Opening of the Jockey Club. From left to right: Man Ray, Hilaire Hiler, Ezra Pound, the pianist Coleman, a waiter, Curtiss, Pöffer. Seated: Tristan Tzara and Jean Cocteau

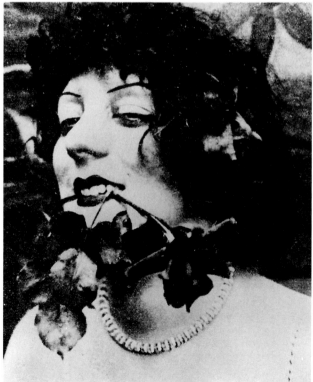

Kiki of Montparnasse.

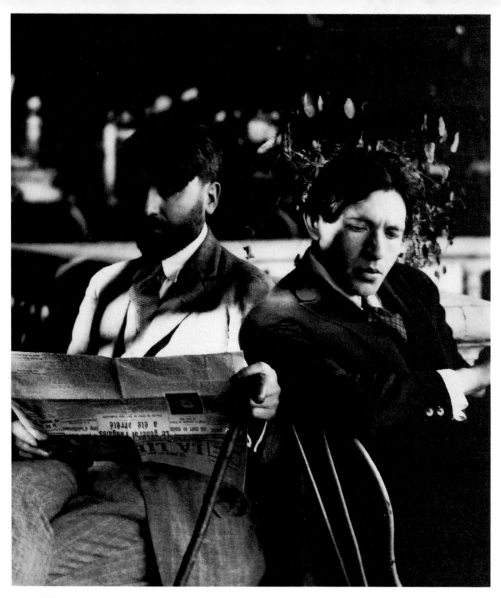

Zborowski and Soutine.

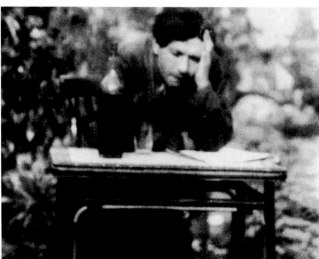

Soutine

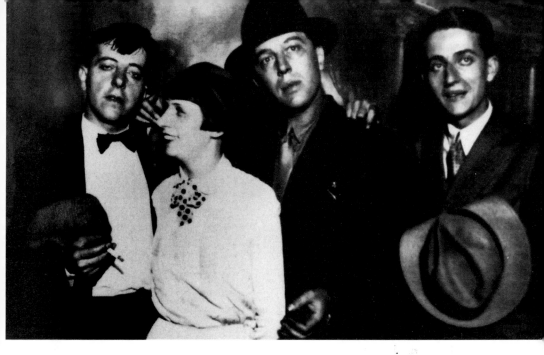

Jacques Prévert, Simone Prévert, André Breton, Pierre Prévert, in 1925.

André Breton at the Théâtre de
l'Oeuvre holding a work by Francis
Picabia on 27 March 1920.

Blaise Cendrars

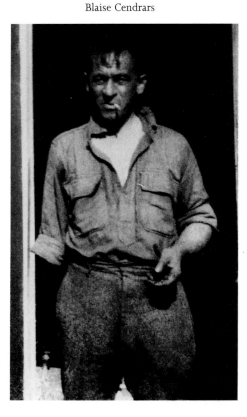

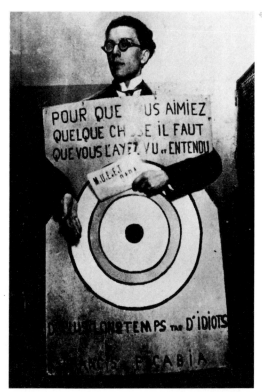

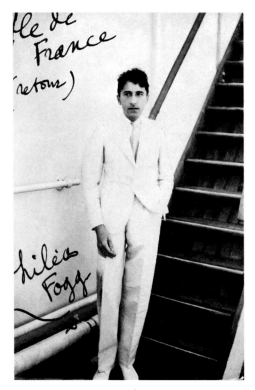

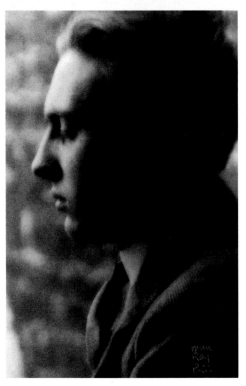

Jean Cocteau on the liner *Île-de-France* in 1925. Photo with commentary and signature of Jean Cocteau.

Raymond Radiguet in 1922.

A ball in Montparnasse in 1925. Foujita can be recognized by his bowler hat.

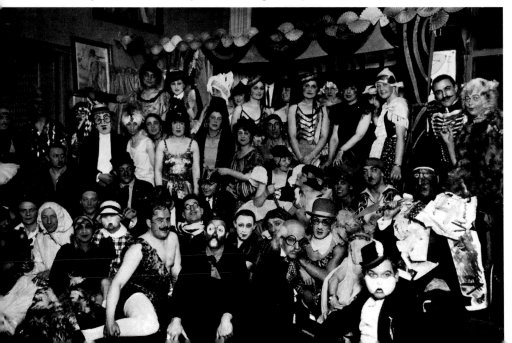

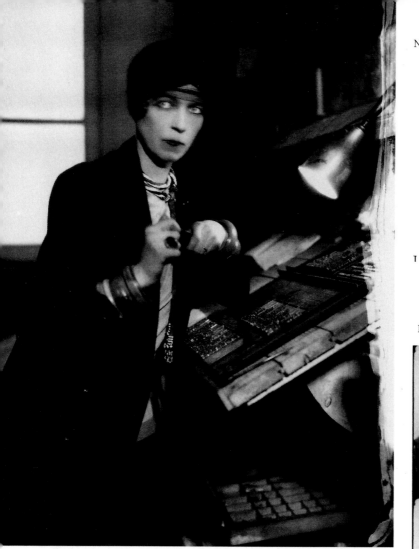

Nancy Cunard

Louis Aragon

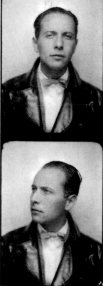

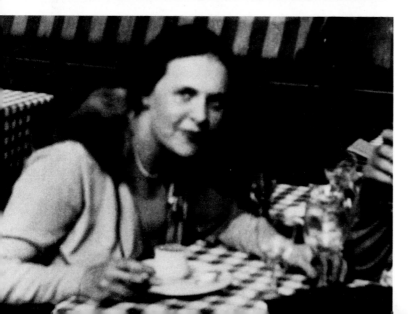

Elsa Triolet on the terrace of the Coupole in 1928 (detail). This was the first photograph that Elsa gave to Aragon.

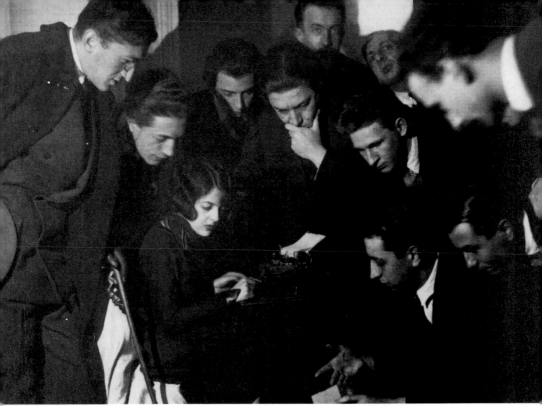

A session of hypnosis. From left to right: Max Morise, Roger Vitrac, Jacques Boiffard, André Breton, Paul Eluard, Pierre Naville, Giorgio De Chirico, Philippe Soupault. Bottom row: Simone Collinet-Breton, Robert Desnos, Jacques Baron, in 1924.

Russian ball at Bullier in 1929. From left to right: Iliazd, M. Guthier, Florent Fels, Ganzo, Michonze with Iliazd's wife, Pascin and Caridad de Laberdesque.

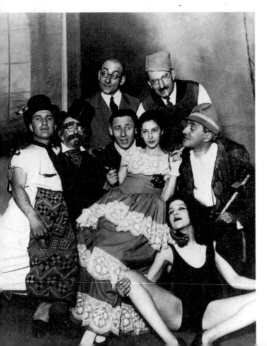

Pascin at the Coupole in the spring of 1930.

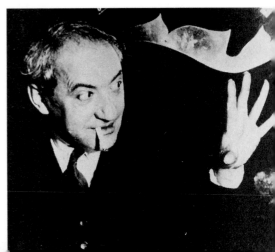

and Mina Loy. Women drifted through his life, disappearing and returning.

Money was not a problem, as he didn't need much. His father had always supported his three artist sons, and generous American patrons took over from there. Duchamp lived at the home of Louise and Walter Arensberg, who would soon pay him for the works they had acquired: not in banknotes but in months of free accommodation. Their walls were decorated with works by Cézanne, Matisse, Picasso and Braque; the Arensbergs were resolutely modern and ardent champions of the avant-garde.

With them and his friend Man Ray, Duchamp founded the Society of Independent Artists. The principle was similar to that of the Independents of Paris: anyone could exhibit, without censorship.

He played a game with his own Society, sending it a man's urinal, entitled *Fontaine*. He dated it and signed it with the name of a manufacturer of sanitary equipment, R. Mutt. Once again, scandal erupted. The urinal was not banned from the exhibition but it was hidden behind a curtain. Duchamp resigned.

Beyond the evident provocation implied by these works, what was Duchamp seeking? He wanted to invent new forms, to take an approach to art that would break the shackles of canvases, brushes, and palettes – all the traditional tools of painting. He also thought about the fourth dimension, invisible to the eye. His toilet reflected some of the pre-occupations inherent in his experimentation, which would pave the way for a great number of artistic vocations. As Pierre Cabanne has noted, 'the example of Duchamp brought about the greatest artistic mutation of the second half of the century, the neo-dada synthesis which would lead to pop art.'[4]

Fontaine was not the first 'ready-made' object displayed as art by Duchamp. The idea for these objects put to unexpected uses had come to him one day in Paris, in 1913. He had attached a bicycle wheel to a stool; he had also bought a draining board. These objects lay around for a while before he thought of giving them a specific use or value.

In New York, before the urinal, he had bought a snow-shovel in wood and iron, which he hung from the ceiling of his studio. The work was called *In Advance of the Broken Arm*. Soon to follow were *A Bruit secret*, a ball of string enclosed between two sheets of brass, *Pliant de voyage*, composed of the cover of an Underwood typewriter, and L.H.O.O.Q., a *Mona Lisa* with a goatee and moustache. Then Duchamp wrote to his sister, asking her to inscribe a short text (which has since been lost), and sign it, on the bottom of the draining board, henceforth transformed into a 'ready-made'.

From the twenties, these ready-mades would become more complicated. The artist would no longer be content with simply signing existing objects, but would also assemble them. Thus *Why Not Sneeze*, executed in 1920, was composed of cubes of marble, a thermometer, and a cuttlefish bone contained in a birdcage. *Fresh Window*, from 1920, was a small-scale French window, which he signed with a female pseudonym that he was to use often and which would turn up also in the poetry of Robert Desnos: Rrose Sélavy.

Duchamp explained how he chose this name. He wanted to change his identity and had at first thought of assuming a Jewish name. In the end, he preferred to play on the inversion of the sexes. The idea of Rrose Sélavy came to him when Picabia asked him to add his signature to those of his friends (Metzinger, Segonzac, Jean Hugo, Milhaud, Auric, Péret, Tzara, Dorgelès), whose signatures were inscribed around *L'Oeil cacodylate* (1921). Duchamp recalled, 'I think that I had put Pi Qu'habilla Rrose – "arrose" requires two Rs, so I was attracted by the second R, which I added – Pi Qu'habilla Rrose Sélavy.'* And he concluded, 'It was all plays on words.'[5]

Duchamp had a passion for words. On his ready-mades, he often added a short sentence, 'meant to lead the observer's mind towards other more verbal regions.'[6] The title of the piece he worked on from 1915 to 1923, *La Mariée mise à nu par ses célibataires, même (Le Grand Verre)*, in oil, lead wire on glass, contains the adverb, *même* (even) which seems to correspond to nothing, to make no sense. This nonsense is deliberate, however, and would be admired by people like Breton, who considered Duchamp the most intelligent man of the twentieth century.

Duchamp also owed his words to Raymond Roussel. Here again, there were similarities between the two men. They both had a flair for turning things inside out, for manipulations, word-games. The Rrose Sélavy of the painter is a distant relation of Roussel's 'Napoleon premier empereur' (Napoleon, First Emperor), whom he travesties in his 'Nappe ollé ombre miettes hampe air heure.'†

These words, these machines, this modernity were also present in the work of Francis Picabia, Duchamp's great friend in New York. For him, too, America represented a sort of laboratory of the future.

The two men walked the streets of American cities together. The one was as plump as the other was thin. Picabia looked like a chubby-cheeked baby of the family, and wore shoes with reinforced soles to make up for his short stature. Duchamp resembled a grand duke, in the style of Roger Vailland. They impatiently awaited the end of the war in Europe together. They often met at 291, Fifth Avenue, in the gallery of an American photographer of Austrian origin, Alfred Stieglitz, where the artistic avant-

---

* 'Pi Qu'habilla Rrose Sélavy' (or 'Pi, dressed by Rrose Sélavy') is pronounced the same way in French as 'Picabia Rrose, c'est la vie' (or 'Picabia Rrose, that's life'); 'arrose' means 'to water.'
† The approximate English equivalent is 'Na pole y on fur stem purr err'.

garde of both continents gathered. Stieglitz exhibited the works of other artists, and always gave them the entire sum earned from the sale of their works, keeping no percentage for himself. He made a good living from his photography; this was enough for him.

The gallery had a review, called the 291, which was the inspiration for Picabia when he created his 391 in Barcelona in January 1917 (the review would see its last days in Paris, in 1924). For the war had not put an end to travel, nor to meetings between friends. Picabia divided his time – the good times and the bad – between Barcelona, New York and Switzerland, and among Cravan, Gleizes, Roché, Varèse, Duchamp, Marie Laurencin and Isadora Duncan. He painted, wrote, visited his children in Gstaad, was treated by a neurologist in Lausanne, and in Zurich saw a little man with a monocle who would soon be talked about in a big way: Tristan Tzara.

For Cendrars, the Franco-Cuban artist was the 'flashy foreigner of art for art's sake'.[7] As for the Romanian, the 'grand mufti Tristan Tzara', he was just someone who spent his life in a bar surrounded by spies, aesthetes, and pacifists of various sorts who had all taken refuge in Switzerland.

Duchamp was almost the only one who escaped the imprecations of the man with the severed arm. And yet he was like the others, and the others were not, or not only cowards, shirkers, civilians frightened by the shock of shells exploding on the ground. The meeting point between the Cabaret Voltaire of Zurich (where the Dadaists gathered around Tristan Tzara), the New York drawing rooms frequented by Cravan, Duchamp and Picabia, and the surrealists, who revered these three men, was that all these artists boldly expressed an opinion which was anathema in that period: first and foremost, they were enemies of war.

DADA & COMPANY

I am against action, and for constant contradiction, for affirmation;
thus I am neither for nor against and I don't like to explain, because
I hate common sense.

Tristan Tzara

On the other side of the Atlantic, far from New York, hunkered down in
wartime Europe, two men played chess. One was forty-five years old. He
had a high forehead, with sparse hair, a moustache, and a goatee. The
other wore a monocle. He was barely twenty. A long lock of hair fell over
his forehead. He had a pasty complexion, and was short-sighted.

The older man was Russian, the younger, Romanian. They were in the
Cabaret Voltaire in Zurich, No. 1, Spiegelgasse. In the same city, at the
same time, Romain Rolland, James Joyce and Jorge Luis Borges were also
to be found.

The two men did not have much in common, beyond a taste for chess,
a solid mistrust of the war which had the continent in flames, and the
use of pseudonyms. One was known as Vladimir Ilyich Ulyanov, the other
as Samuel Rosenstock.

The revolutionary and the poet: Lenin and Tzara.

The former had recently been in Zimmerwald, where in September
1915, the socialist delegates gathered in this village near Bern had
published a manifesto in which they condemned the imperialistic war
that the Great Powers were waging – not that this was, by any means, a
declaration of pacifism.

The other was viscerally against war: not only this war, but all wars.
However, he had not organized or joined a group or party fighting for
peace, any more than Duchamp in New York or Breton and Aragon in
Paris had done such a thing. Politics was not Tristan Tzara's concern, and,
for the time being, it didn't interest the others either. At the time of the
Cabaret Voltaire, Tzara was a young man who liked Villon, Sade, Lautréamont and Max Jacob. He was perhaps undisciplined, but he had not
come to Zurich to change the world, simply to continue his studies.

Dada was born on 8 February 1916, at six o'clock in the evening. The word means nothing, which is why it was chosen. The movement owed its name to the chance falling of a letter opener slipped into a dictionary opened at random. This deliberate absence of the slightest meaning demonstrates the founders' desire to express the absurd and the grotesque. Hugo Ball, Christian Schad and Richard Huelsenbeck (German), the poet and sculptor Jean Arp (Alsatian-German), Marcel Janco and Tristan Tzara (Romanians), were in revolt not only against the war, but also against the civilization which had brought it about. They advocated the search for an absolute that was the total opposite of morality set in stone, based on the traditional foundations of work, family, country and religion.

The group met at the Cabaret Voltaire, founded by Hugo Ball. Poets, writers, painters and students all gathered there, most of them emigrants, anti-militarists, often revolutionaries: in addition to Lenin, Karl Radek and Willy Münzenberg also used to frequent the Cabaret. Hugo Ball put on shows there of a new kind, combining music, painting, poetry, dance, masks, and percussion instruments. Expression had to be spontaneous. Poetry was no longer simply expressed in writing. It was time to go even further than Baudelaire, Rimbaud, Jarry and Lautréamont. Words could be invented, exclaimed rather than declaimed. Artists accompanied each other, howling, hitting heavy boxes or crates with various utensils. They danced, they acted and they got the public to join in. To the poetry of sounds they added bodies of sentences, fragments of texts and of Negro chants. Tzara established a parallel with the pictorial experimentation of Picasso, Matisse and Derain, as well as with the collages of Arp, which were exhibited in the Dada Gallery.

June saw the birth of the review *Cabaret Voltaire*. Five hundred copies were printed, containing illustrations by Max Oppenheimer, Picasso, Modigliani, Arp, Janco, a poem by Apollinaire, another by the Italian futurist poet Marinetti, and the first scenic adaptation of a simultaneous poem written, sung, and recited in German, French, and English by Huelsenbeck, Janko and Tzara: *L'Amiral cherche une maison à louer*. And in his editorial, Hugo Ball announced the coming publication of an international review called *Dada*.

On 14 July, the first Dada evening took place. On the programme: Negro chants, a Dada concert and dances, simultaneous and 'movementist' poems, cubist dances.

A few days later, Tristan Tzara read, at the Cabaret Voltaire, *Le Manifeste de monsieur Antipyrine*, part of *La Première Aventure céleste de monsieur Antipyrine*, which would be performed again in Paris in 1920. The work was published in the Dada collection, with engraved woodcuts by Marcel Janco. Tzara sent a few copies to New York, thus introducing the Dada movement in the United States. Antipyrine was a medication which the author used frequently to calm his nerves, and the celestial adventure in question gave Tzara the opportunity to express his views in the first Dada manifesto:

> Dada is our intensity; it erects bayonets without consequence, the Sumatral head of the German baby; Dada is art without slippers or parallel ... we know in our wisdom that our heads will become soft cushions that our anti-dogmatism is as much an exclusivity as a civil servant that we are not free and are crying out for freedom Severe necessity without discipline or morality and let's spit on humanity. Dada remains in the European framework of weaknesses, after all it's still shit, but we now want to shit in many colours, to decorate the zoological garden of art with all the flags of the consulates do do bong hibo aho hiho aho.[1]

In July 1917, a year late, *Dada 1, A Literary and Artistic Collection* was published. Then came *Dada 2* and *Dada 3*. Soon, urged on by Picabia, whose energy more than replaced that of the founders of the Cabaret Voltaire, who had distanced themselves from the enterprise, Tristan Tzara published the *Dada Manifesto 1918* (the two men corresponded extensively before meeting in January, 1919).

This text was to have considerable repercussions in all of Europe, especially in France, where the future surrealists applauded the violence, audacity, and intelligence of this break with the past. Tzara condemned those who were seeking reasons, causes and explanations for everything – starting with the word 'Dada', which was an enigma for some, meant 'a nursemaid' to others, signified twice yes for the Russians and the Romanians, and 'tail of a holy cow' for the Krou Negros ... or whatever anyone wanted or imagined it to mean.

Tzara declared that the work of art was not synonymous with beauty, for if one were to define beauty 'by decree, objectively, for all' then it was dead. Criticism was thus useless, since all was a question of individual taste. Man was a chaos that nothing could put in order. To love one's fellow was hypocritical, to know oneself utopian. Psychoanalysis, 'a dangerous disease, put man's anti-reality penchants to sleep and systematized the bourgeoisie'. Dialectic led to opinions which were in any case those of others and which the individual would have discovered without it. Everyone spoke for himself, Tzara more than anyone, and he did not try to proselytize, nor encourage others to follow him: 'Thus DADA was born of a need for independence, a distrust of the community.'[2]

No more groups. No more theories. Down with the cubists and the futurists: they were nothing but 'laboratories of formalist ideas'. Cézanne looked at the cup to be painted from the bottom, the cubists from the top, the futurists saw the same cup in motion – but 'the new artist protests; he doesn't paint any more.' Brains have drawers that must be destroyed, just like those of social organizations. All that counts is the personal 'boom-boom'. Speculative science and harmony, which put things in order, are useless systems, like all systems. Morality atrophies the being: 'There is a great destructive, negative work to be accomplished. Sweeping, cleaning.'

Tzara's words had the impact of bullets, except that they didn't kill anyone. The *Dada Manifesto 1918* was a declaration of war on war. Or on the old world. A stunningly powerful text which preached a new humanity after the carnage, it would spearhead the Dada movement, crystallizing diverse sensibilities which the surrealists would soon grasp in their iron grip. And they wouldn't be the only ones. In New York, Marcel Duchamp would see in it numerous points of convergence with his own pre-occupations:

> Dada was the extreme point of protest against the physical aspect of painting. It was a metaphysical attitude. It was intimately and consciously connected to 'literature'. It was a kind of nihilism ... It was a way of leaving behind a certain state of mind – of keeping oneself from being influenced by the immediate surroundings, or by the past: distancing oneself from clichés – liberating oneself. The force of the vacuity of Dada was very healthy. Dada said: 'Don't forget that you're not as empty as you think!'[3]

This language was not shared by those with more conventional points of view, even literary ones – far from it. In September 1919, when the *Nouvelle Revue française* reappeared, the editorial direction, in an unsigned article, stigmatized this new form of expression from abroad:

> It is truly a shame that Paris seems to be welcoming silliness of this sort, which has come directly from Berlin. In the course of this last summer, the German press spoke several times about the Dada movement and recounted recitals during which the followers of the new school repeated endlessly the mystical syllables: 'Dada dada dada da.'[4]

A little later, André Gide would modify this opinion slightly, showing a more objective distance in respect to Dadaism. Opposing it to cubism, which was 'a school', he saw in it 'a demolition enterprise'. But he recognized that after the war, which caused so much physical ruin, it was natural 'that the mind should not lag behind matter; it also has a right to ruins. Dada will see to that.'[5]

Thus there was *Dada* in Switzerland, but also *391* in Europe and elsewhere (the first four issues were published in Spain, the following three in America, the eighth in Zurich, and the last eleven in Paris), and SIC and Nord–Sud in Paris. These reviews tried to make up for the absence of cultural material in the daily newspapers, whose few pages were devoted almost exclusively to war news. They also filled the hole left by the disappearance of the more conventional publications: the only one left was the Mercure de France, too traditional for the provocative advocates of the new art. In any case, the great dowagers of literature could only be offended by these hot-blooded younger poets. Unknown writers who first appeared in these pages were underestimated at the time, but after only a few years they became the Hugos, the Zolas, and the Flauberts of the twentieth century.

SIC (Sound, Ideas, Colours, Forms), took over from Ozenfant's review, L'Elan, which had been published in 1915 and 1916. It was the work of a single man, Pierre Albert-Birot. Before the war, he was a poet and a sculptor. Then he started a little business, making postcards that he printed at his own cost and sold to soldiers and their families to help facilitate their correspondence. Wanting to publish his own poems and those of his friends, Pierre Albert-Birot decided to found a review. He registered as unemployed, and was able to finance his project with the benefits received. SIC was eight pages long and five hundred copies were printed, priced at sixty centimes: it first appeared in January 1916. Its business office, at 37, rue de la Tombe-Issoire, was the home address of its director, who was also the author of all the articles and poems in the first issue. This issue opened with the words: 'Our will: to act. To take initiatives, not to wait for them to come to us from the other side of the Rhine.'

Pierre Albert-Birot was undeniably a man of action. When he founded his review, he didn't know a single poet. He was isolated and fairly ignorant of poetic matters. But he went ahead, and was soon to reap the fruits of his courage. He met Severini, who introduced him to Apollinaire, who agreed to give him a few poems. This was enough to launch SIC.

Nord–Sud was not as impassioned and unruly as its two rivals. Its title came from the name of the Métro line which went straight through the heart of Paris, from Montmartre to Montparnasse. When the first issue appeared in March 1917, Reverdy was known to few outside a fairly select circle. A literary editor by profession and Catholic by faith, he had joined the army but was sent home at the end of 1914. He didn't have any more money than Albert-Birot, but he had more contacts. A wealthy Chilean poet gave him the start he needed. Jacques Doucet also helped, as did Paul Guillaume (rejected from the army for medical reasons) whose regular advertisements for his gallery brought some revenues to the new monthly. Juan Gris contributed the cover page. The review's elegant appearance contrasted with the colours and the style of SIC, whose typographical effects could sometimes be aggressive.

If Nord–Sud was an instrument of the avant-garde, then this wasn't immediately apparent, but had to be discovered by delving into its pages. Pierre Reverdy, Max Jacob, the Baronness d'Œttingen (who used her two usual pseudonyms, Roch Grey and Léonard Pieux) and Guillaume Apollinaire exemplified this tendency for as long as the review survived; the last issue was published in May 1918. They persisted with it, despite a disagreement between Reverdy and Apollinaire (the former reproaching the latter for indulging in too much journalistic activity) and poor relations between Max Jacob and the same Reverdy (who would not accept the claim of the author of the Cornet à dés that he was the inventor of the prose poem, a form Reverdy also practised).

In June 1917, Cocteau made a brief appearance in the review as a guest contributor. His byline would not appear again; Reverdy mistrusted the author of Parade. He had similar feelings about the Italian futurists: these were systematically rejected at Nord–Sud (though welcome at SIC), with the exception of Marinetti – probably because in the second issue of the review, he admitted to having a few reservations about this movement which he had helped launch. (This would not prevent him, a few years later, from becoming friendly with the Duce.)

But new names, and not just any ones, also appeared in the review: André Breton in May 1917, Tristan Tzara the following month, Philippe Soupault in August, Louis Aragon in March 1918 (he published his first poem, 'Soifs de l'Ouest', in it), Jean Paulhan in May.

The same writers were collaborating with Tristan Tzara: Reverdy in Dada 3; Aragon, Breton, Soupault in Dada 4–5, which also contained a text by Georges Ribemont-Dessaignes. Finally, all these authors also published work in Pierre Albert-Birot's SIC, where they were joined by Raymond Radiguet and Pierre Drieu La Rochelle.

Through what coincidence did all these same signatures turn up in these three reviews, one published in Zurich and the other two in Paris, all tied to the avant-garde literary and artistic movements which were sweeping through wartime Europe?

It was all down to the efforts of a single person. The person who was celebrated by Nord–Sud, in the first editorial of its first issue, as the man who had 'traced new roads, opened new horizons'; a man to whom the review was fervently devoted, and for whom it had boundless admiration – Guillaume Apollinaire. That man again.

THE FRIENDS OF VAL-DE-GRÂCE

It was in the first meetings with Soupault and Aragon that the spark
was born which would give rise to the activity which, starting in
March 1919, would take its first exploratory steps in *Littérature*, soon
explode in *Dada*, and finally recharge itself completely to become
surrealism.

André Breton

He had been trepanned, but he was fine now. A little nervous, often tired,
but able to receive visits from his friends. In his hospital room, he was
dressed in his uniform, his forehead bandaged, his head shaved. He talked
readily and was generous with his time and energies.

Pierre Albert-Birot, who had discovered his work only recently, came
to ask if he would contribute to his review. From the front, Apollinaire
had already sent a poem that *SIC* had published in its fourth issue, entitled
'L'Avenir'. He promised Albert-Birot to give him something else soon,
and he kept his promise. For more than a year, he contributed texts
regularly. Together, the two men would soon publish *Les Mamelles de Tirésias*.
Apollinaire wrote a preface for the *Trente et un poèmes de poche* which Editions
SIC would publish. And when he left the Val-de-Grâce Hospital, the poet
would regularly come to the meetings held at the home of the journal's
director every Saturday, on the rue de la Tombe-Issoire. He brought
friends with him – Serge Férat, Pierre Reverdy, Max Jacob, Blaise Cendrars,
Roch Grey, and others. Thus the review continued to acquire new
contributors, which added to its prestige. Apollinaire remained a faithful
friend, in spite of some of the silly behaviour of Pierre Albert-Birot,
whom he didn't really take seriously. For instance, he didn't think much
of his theory of 'nunism', developed over many columns and pages by
the review's director. This was a kind of art of the moment which claimed
to extend to the entire world, preached universalism, and could supposedly
be applied to painting, poetry and theatre. This theory found few
supporters.

Relations with Tzara were more complicated. From Zurich, the father
of Dada had sent his publications everywhere. He had discovered *SIC* and
sent texts to Pierre Albert-Birot. He reported on the birth of *Nord–Sud*.
Using his energy to serve his cause, he contacted all the avant-garde artists

in wartime Europe to invite them to write in the columns of his own paper. Cendrars, Reverdy, and Max Jacob all received letters from him, and Apollinaire, naturally. But the poet, convalescing, took his time to answer. In June 1916, *Cabaret Voltaire* published a poem by him without asking his permission. He didn't take offence, but he did worry: was it advisable to publish his work in a newspaper printed in Switzerland, a country whose neutrality could be stained by the German spoken there?

He hesitated. Tzara persisted. Apollinaire finally answered him. In two letters, one dated December 1916, and the other January 1917, he reproached him for not defending France more vigorously in the face of German influence. He criticized 'the variety in nationalities' of *Cabaret Voltaire*'s editorial staff, 'some of whom have a very clear Germanophile tendency'. He concluded with these words: 'Long live French cubism! Long live France! Long live Romania!'[1]

As Tzara had published a portrait of the poet in *Dada* 2 in his honour, Apollinaire thanked him, but repeated his misgivings:

> I think it could be compromising for me, especially at the point we've reached in this multiform war, to collaborate with a review, however positive its spirit, which has Germans amongst its contributors, however much they're in favour of 'entente'.[2]

Apollinaire's stance may have been motivated not only by his ultra-patriotic sentiments, but also by his fears of the evils of censorship, which meant that mail to and from foreign countries could always be opened and read.

Whatever the case, this Germanophobia also became a source of conflict between him and Reverdy. The latter, very early on, solicited Tzara's participation in *Nord–Sud*. But a disagreeable rumour had begun to circulate about the Romanian poet: he was suspected of being registered on the 'black list' of German spies. This was somewhat ironic, given that Tzara was also interrogated by the Swiss police for having kept the company of dubious Germano-Bolshevik individuals...

Although he mistrusted Dada, it was nonetheless Apollinaire who, once again, would establish the link (albeit indirectly) between the *Cabaret Voltaire* group and the future surrealists. For it was at 202, Boulevard Saint Germain, the home of Guillaume Apollinaire, that André Breton saw the first two issues of the review.

The two men met for the first time on 10 May 1916, at the Val-de-Grâce Hospital, where Apollinaire had just been operated on. Apollinaire was thirty-six, Breton barely twenty. He was fairly handsome, with green eyes, a strong, solid face and good features. One year earlier, he had written to this 'great personage' whom he admired. He took advantage of a period of leave to come and visit him.

Breton had been mobilized in February 1915. After having spent three months in the seventeenth artillery regiment of Pontivy, his degree in medicine took him to Nantes where he had been transferred as a military nurse. He hadn't chosen medicine as a vocation, but had arrived at it by a process of elimination, and because it seemed to him that 'the medical profession was the one which best permitted the simultaneous exercise of other activities of the mind.'[3]

It was at the military hospital of Nantes that Breton met Jacques Vaché, a meteor-like figure who would have a considerable influence on him. Vaché, whom nobody ever knew very well, was to die of an overdose of opium in 1919, at the age of twenty-two. Breton was fascinated by his totally free behaviour in the middle of such terrible times, by the liberty of his acts and his words and his definitive insubordination. He never shook hands with anyone. He walked around the streets of Nantes dressed in the interchangeable uniforms either of a hussar or a pilot. When he ran into someone he knew, he would gesture in Breton's direction and say, 'Let me introduce you to André Salmon.' For Salmon was better known than Breton.

Vaché only had one thing in common with Apollinaire: his admiration for Jarry. Everything else separated them. Breton himself, who was very close to his comrade from Nantes, could not but be annoyed by the jingoist language of the poet–artilleryman. After having spent three weeks on the Meuse front, in the middle of generalized butchery, he considered the war the worst of monstrosities. Like Louis Aragon, Paul Eluard, Benjamin Péret and Philippe Soupault – the bright hopes of the coming surrealist movement – he had hated his days as a soldier. He had left the battlefields with a conviction that was shared by the other four: only a total revolution in every domain could cleanse civilization of this barbary. This was why Dada appeared to them one of the few viable paths to salvation. It was a path that was closer to Vaché than to Apollinaire, and Breton would later admit that he had transferred to Tristan Tzara the hopes he had originally placed in his friend from Nantes.[4]

But when he met Guillaume Apollinaire, their differences of opinion were dwarfed by the great poet's stature. These differences would only come to light in public in June 1917, during the performance of the *Mamelles de Tirésias*. The presence of Vaché in the theatre opened Breton's eyes: he could then measure in a more definitive way the deep divide separating the two figures close to him, and would choose his camp accordingly, moving away from Apollinaire.

For the moment, though, the latter remained the great poet of his time. Breton, a man of sometimes passing, sometimes long-lasting enthusiasms, had been dazzled by the Valéry of *Monsieur Teste*, by Rimbaud, Lautréamont and Mallarmé. But he was charmed by Apollinaire: the man fascinated him, with his vast culture, his presence, his prestige, and the new spirit which he still embodied, in Breton's eyes. To know him was a 'rare privilege'.[5]

> What ... impressed me about Apollinaire is that he would take his inspiration from the street, to which he managed to give dignity, whenever he decided to combine all the elements to create poems ... even if it was only bits of conversation.[6]

It was Apollinaire who introduced another of his admirers to Breton: Philippe Soupault, one of whose poems he had managed to get published in *SIC*. The two men soon found they had much in common. Soupault was the son of a doctor. He was bourgeois, fashionable, a bit of a dandy. Although mobilized, he hadn't fought in the trenches; he was used as a guinea pig like many others (who would die of it) and was vaccinated against typhus before his departure for the front. Poisoned as a result, he had to be hospitalized for several months.

He also had an immense hatred for this war that would not end. What weapon did he use to express this violence? His pen, of course: he wrote with rage. Inspiration came easily, suddenly. Sitting in a café, he would ask the waiter for a pen, close himself off from the outside world and compose a poem. He was the great initiator of automatic writing and co-author, with Breton, of the *Champs magnétiques*.

The third musketeer of surrealism was also a medical student. He had a thin moustache, was a year older than Breton and, like Soupault, studied at the Val-de-Grâce Hospital. His father, a man named Louis Andrieux, was a lawyer by profession; he became a deputy, then a prefect, an ambassador, and finally a senator. His son didn't have the same name: in fact, there was nothing to prove that he was his son, at least as far as the birth register was concerned. For when Louis Andrieux' mistress Marguerite Toucas-Massillon (who was thirty-three years younger than he was) gave birth to her child, the honourable prefect registered him as Louis Aragon, of unknown parentage – Aragon after a Spanish woman who was his father's former lover, it has been said.

The sin was so great that it had to be hidden not just once but twice: once for the state, and again for the neighbourhood. Thus the young Aragon was made to believe that his maternal grandmother was his mother and – three precautions being better than two – he was also told that she was only his adoptive mother. His real father was presented sometimes as his godfather, sometimes as a tutor, and the real mother became a sister. All these games apparently succeeded in preserving an appearance of morality, and the young Louis was able to attend a good school in the fashionable suburb of Neuilly and to register for medical studies. In 1917, the prefect insisted that the mother tell her son that she wasn't his sister, and that the godfather was the father: if the young man was going to die in the war, it was just as well that he be informed of his origins before his decease…

Aragon fought in the war without dying of it, and bravely enough to be given a medal. When he met André Breton, the two men were in comparable situations: they were each alternating periods of military service with terms of medical studies.

They shared a room at the Val-de-Grâce Hospital, and discovered many affinities and tastes in common. They talked about Picasso, Derain, Matisse, Max Jacob, Alfred Jarry, Mallarmé, Rimbaud, and Lautréamont – the greatest of them all – whom Aragon had discovered in the lending catalogue of a little bookshop which would become bigger, located at 7, rue de l'Odéon.

The medical student impressed Breton with his culture. He had read everything, and he dazzled with his conversation. His desire to please could be felt not only in the richness of his language but in that of his clothes: he was always dressed stylishly. This refinement was also evident in his manners, the way he spoke and the way he looked – sometimes ironically, sometimes with great warmth – at the person with whom he was conversing, when he wanted to charm them, which he invariably did.

When they weren't at the Val-de-Grâce, amongst former soldiers whom the war had driven round the bend, Aragon and Breton used to spend time in the bookshop on the rue de l'Odéon. One could buy books there, but also borrow them. One could listen to authors read from their works, and browse through the avant-garde reviews (SIC, Nord–Sud and Dada) which published the writers and poets of the coming generation. On the back of Nord–Sud were two addresses to write to if one wanted to become a subscriber. One was the home of Pierre Reverdy (12, rue Cortot) and the other was the bookshop on the rue de l'Odéon. This 'Maison des amis des livres', which had opened in 1915, was to play a considerable role in the development of cultural life in the twenty years to come. Its director, a short, plumpish woman with pink cheeks and blonde hair, was named Adrienne Monnier.

ADRIENNE MONNIER'S BOOKSHOP

A shop, a little store, a country house, a temple, an igloo, the backstage
of a theatre, a wax and dream museum, a reading room and sometimes
just a simple bookstore, with books to sell, or to borrow and return,
with customers there to browse, to buy, to take away books ... And
to read them.

Jacques Prévert

When they first opened the library one winter morning, Adrienne and
her young assistant set out a bookcase on the pavement, then came inside
and hid in the shop: frightened, moved, intimidated by the passers-by
who stopped one after another to browse through the boxes. There were
old volumes from family libraries, literary and artistic reviews, works on
modern literature. The bookshop couldn't afford to buy all the works it
wanted. Thus the speciality of the Maison des amis des livres derived from
a choice that was dictated first of all by financial circumstances. When the
shop first opened, customers found there all the books published by the
Mercure de France and the *Nouvelle Revue française*, whose backlist she had bought
up. Later, she acquired the entire collection of *Vers et Prose*. Paul Fort sold
her all that remained: 6,666 issues, to be paid for in several instalments.

These issues varied in popularity: some were never requested at all
while others remained barely a few hours on the shelves: Volume IV, for
instance. The first to buy it was André Breton, who intimidated the
shopkeeper:

> Breton didn't smile, but he laughed sometimes; he had a short sardonic
> laugh which interrupted his speech without altering his features, as with
> pregnant women who are being very careful to preserve their beauty
> ... The lower lip, almost abnormally developed, revealed, in accordance
> with classical theories of physiognomy, a strong sensuality ruled by the
> sexual element ... He really did have what Freud would call the libidinous
> power of the leader.[1]

He came back and bought another copy of Volume IV of *Vers et Prose*.
Then another, and another ...

Some time later, a very well-dressed young man appeared. He had a moustache, a hat, and pale gloves. In his right pocket was a volume of Verlaine, and in his left a collection by Laforgue. He approached the bookseller and, in the most pleasant voice imaginable, asked for Volume IV of *Vers et Prose*.

Adrienne Monnier rummaged around in the boxes which held Paul Fort's review and gave him a copy of Volume IV.

'What's so special about this volume?' she asked.

'Open it to page 69.'

The bookseller thus discovered the text that fascinated André Breton so much: 'La Soirée avec Monsieur Teste', by Paul Valéry.

She was to see Louis Aragon again often. He would come by the bookshop, begin chatting with someone or another, and stay for hours. Everyone was mesmerized by his art of conversation. Here he was able freely to express everything he wanted to say, none of which had found a natural outlet at the Val-de-Grâce, where the crudeness of his medical friends' conversation offended his natural delicacy.

Aragon, like Breton and Soupault, wrote in the reviews that Adrienne Monnier sold: *SIC* in particular, but also *Dada*. When one of her most faithful customers asked the bookseller one day whether she would agree to lend him the first two issues of the Zurich publication, he was told, 'All right, but on one condition: you mustn't cut the pages ... that way I can still send the horrible thing back to Switzerland later.'

The customer was Jean Paulhan.

Another time, the door opened to let in a big man with a pear-shaped head who had carefully studied the window display before entering. He looked for the bookseller. Finding her, he pointed an accusing finger at her and cried, 'It's really a bit much, not putting a single book by a soldier in your window!'

It was Guillaume Apollinaire.

The poet still had a great influence over Breton, who had spoken at length to Adrienne Monnier about Apollinaire before she first met him. He had a 'fanatical attachment' to him: he was, in a way, a disciple.

> I remember one or two truly unforgettable scenes: Apollinaire seated before me, chatting easily, and Breton standing, with his back to the wall, his eyes fixed and hysterical, seeing not the man who was there, but the invisible essence, the black god, from whom he was awaiting orders.[2]

Apollinaire was not the only living poet whom Breton admired. There was also Pierre Reverdy, the founder of *Nord–Sud*. Breton liked his incomparable 'verbal magic', and his marked taste for theory, but found him overly forceful in discussion, with too strong a tendency to defend 'a poetic expression related to cubism'.[3]

These reproaches were nothing compared to the storm of criticism that Breton unleashed on an unfortunate poet who, one day in 1917, wanted to organize a reading of his works in the presence of André Gide. The imprudent fellow went to see Adrienne Monnier and said to her, 'My dear Adrienne, M. Gide would very much like to hear my verses read in your shop. Would you be willing to lend me the place for an evening?'

Adrienne was perfectly agreeable to the idea, all the more so as she often organized events of this sort, to which she invited her friends: Léon-Paul Fargue, Paul Léautaud, Max Jacob, Erik Satie ... After the writers had read their works, the participants were invited to partake in a tea, where the sandwiches and sweets were accompanied by port.

Having obtained the bookshop's approval, the poet then went to see André Gide.

'Dear sir, Mlle Monnier has asked me to tell you that she would love for me to read "Le Cap" in her bookshop in your presence.'

'Agreed,' Gide answered.

'Le Cap' was 'Le Cap de Bonne-Espérance'. And the poet...

In May 1917, in the seventeenth issue of *SIC*, Jean Cocteau published a poem: 'Restaurant de nuit'. This text was much commented upon, less for its literary qualities than for the acrostic it contained. When the first letters of each verse were read in order, the result made up an insult to the review's director, reading: 'Poor Birots.' Cocteau immediately denied having written the poem, so Metzinger, Warnod, and a few others were then accused. The prankster eventually turned out to be Théodore Fraenkel, a great friend of André Breton.

Adrienne Monnier not only sold and lent books and organized reading sessions; she was also an occasional publisher. She published a few books, including one masterpiece, James Joyce's *Ulysses*. She agreed to produce the French version; the original English text was first published by Sylvia Beach, a friend of Adrienne.

Sylvia was American, the daughter of a pastor. She was in love with France and all things French. She discovered the bookshop thanks to a little notice for the review *Vers et Prose*, and went to the address on the rue de l'Odéon in order to buy a copy of the magazine. In 1919, advised and supported by Adrienne Monnier, Sylvia Beach opened her own bookshop, Shakespeare & Company, on the rue Dupuytren. Two years later, she would move to 12, rue de l'Odéon, just across from the Maison des amis des livres.

All the American writers who came to Paris after the war gathered in Sylvia Beach's establishment. Her shop was a meeting-point, a postal address, the first place that many literary people from abroad chose to visit in Paris. Among them was Hemingway, whom the young woman allowed to buy books on credit, all the while lending him works that he wanted to read. Another habitué was Ezra Pound, who persuaded James Joyce to come to Paris.

In 1918, in New York, *The Little Review* had begun to publish *Ulysses*. In 1920, after a complaint was lodged by the Society for the Suppression of Vice, the publication was interrupted. (American law would not authorize the work's publication until 1933, when it was published by Random House.) The following year, Joyce finished the work and Sylvia Beach offered to publish the English version in France. Joyce agreed: the work was published on 2 February 1922, his fortieth birthday.

Valery Larbaud had discovered *Ulysses* in *The Little Review*. The work fascinated this wealthy pharmacist's son, whose father owned and managed the Saint Yorre spring in Vichy and had made a fortune selling the bottled water. He wrote to Sylvia Beach to tell her he was 'absolutely mad about *Ulysses*' and that he would like to translate a few passages of it for the *Nouvelle Revue française*.[4]

In December 1921, he gave a talk on Joyce in Adrienne Monnier's bookshop. Adrienne Monnier and Joyce then asked him to translate the whole of *Ulysses*. After many discussions and changes of mind, the author of *Barnabooth* finally agreed to translate the end of the last part of the work, 'Penelope'. The rest of the book was translated by a young man, Auguste Morel, and by a British magistrate, Stuart Gilbert. Larbaud and Joyce had a hand in the final draft.

In February 1929, the French version of *Ulysses* was published by the Maison des amis des livres. Adrienne Monnier sent a copy to Paul Claudel, a regular visitor to her bookshop, who was the French ambassador to Washington at the time. Claudel sent the following reply:

> Please forgive me for sending you back the book which, I believe, has a certain commercial value but for me presents not the slightest interest. I once wasted a few hours reading the *Portrait of an Artist* by the same author, and that was more than enough for me.[5]

Two years later, Adrienne Monnier again wrote to Paul Claudel. She had learned in France that a pirated edition of *Ulysses*, copied letter for letter from Sylvia Beach's edition, was circulating in the United States. The bookshop was asking the ambassador to intervene, to contact the local authorities so they could take legal action against the publisher. Claudel refused, giving various reasons. His final argument was as follows:

> *Ulysses*, like the *Portrait*, is full of the most filthy blasphemy, in which one

can sense all the hatred of a renegade – who also happens to be afflicted with a truly diabolical lack of talent.[6]

Paul Claudel could not appreciate the modernist essence of *Ulysses*. He hated Joyce, and was himself hated in turn by the musketeers of surrealism – Breton, Aragon, Soupault, and Fraenkel, all friends of Adrienne Monnier – at a time when the defence of *Ulysses* was a literary cause célèbre.

Long before the work was published, *SIC*, *Nord–Sud* and *Dada* had disappeared from the scene. They had been replaced by the review *Littérature*, an instrument of André Breton and his friends, who didn't have any compunction about heaping anathema on Paul Claudel and the 'authors of infamous patriotic poems, of nauseating Catholic professions of faith'.[7] Adrienne Monnier, who had pardoned everything – and more besides – would never forgive André Breton for having attacked His Excellency the Ambassador in his review, and *Littérature* would no longer be sold in the bookshop on the rue de l'Odeon.

But this was after the war . . .

PARTY DAYS IN PARIS

My conscience is dirty linen, and tomorrow is washday.

Max Jacob

The front was sixty miles from Paris and the war was intensifying. It went through its fevers and rashes, which were eradicated by changing doctors (one day Marshal Joffre, the next Lyautey), or by administrating powerful – that is, fatal – remedies: napalm and chloride gas. There was talk about using aviation as an offensive tactic. It was said that the Americans were going to join forces with the Alliance. It was feared that the Russians, torn apart by internal troubles whose gravity was hard to judge, might defect. The corpses piled up in the trenches; the wounded poured back into the country.

In Montparnasse, all was well. The artists ate and drank as best they could – at the Rotonde, at Marie Vassilieff's, at the Samaritaine bakery shop, where croissants had reappeared. At night, cheating on the curfew, painters and artists crossed the city with covered lamps to take refuge in a comfortable apartment in Auteuil or Passy, where a jovial fellow in costume would be happy to provide drinks, just to have the pleasure of getting drunk with artists. Another evening, a studio would open its doors; all night long, although it was prohibited to walk in the streets after curfew, strangers would arrive, emptying their pockets of a few bits of bread or cheese which they passed around like so many offerings.

Cendrars' nightmares were surely haunted by his amputated arm, Kisling's by the rifle butt that had demolished his chest, Braque's and Apollinaire's by the blades, the saw and the hammers that had smashed into their skulls. But the wounds were soothed a bit by the joys and pleasures of peace; everyone had to put the war behind them.

In July 1916, in a gallery adjoining the showrooms belonging to the dress designer Paul Poiret, the Salon d'Antin was held. It wasn't the first artistic event since the beginning of the war (Germaine Bongard, Poiret's sister, had already organized several exhibitions) but it was indisputably the most important. It was organized by André Salmon, who wanted to mix French and foreign artists, to remind the public of the solidarity of the latter with France. Krémègne's work was next to that of Matisse, who was close to Severini, who was not far from Léger, De Chirico, Kisling, Van Dongen, Zarate ... Max Jacob was present too: French, but also, he had insisted, always a Breton.

Paul Poiret's residence was at 26, Avenue d'Antin (today the Avenue Franklin D. Roosevelt) at the end of a grandiose alley which cut across gardens reminiscent of Versailles. The exhibition took place in a fairly small gallery. An entire wall was taken up by a work that had been finished for a long time, but which the public had never yet seen, its author having refused until now to exhibit it: Picasso's *Les Demoiselles d'Avignon*.

Outside, the gardens were opened to the poets. Max Jacob read his 'Le Christ à Montparnasse'. Cendrars, with his amputated arm, and Guillaume Apollinaire, still wearing the bandage around his head from his operation, were applauded.

In the evening, there were concerts: music by Debussy, Stravinsky, Satie, performed by Georges Auric, Arthur Honegger, Darius Milhaud and a few others. It was there, among his musician friends, that Cocteau finally dreamed up a way to get his hands on Picasso.

A few days later, he invited him to collaborate on a realistic ballet he was writing with Erik Satie for Sergei Diaghilev and the Ballets Russes. The show would feature circus players performing their acts in order to draw passers-by into the tent.

It seems to have been the participation of Picasso which finally convinced Diaghilev to go ahead; he had taken no interest in *Parade* up until then. He met the painter, Satie, and Cocteau in the autumn and agreed to take on the project. The musician and the librettist set to work right away. Picasso was then leaving his studio on the rue Schoelcher for a house in Montrouge. He wouldn't stay there long.

At the end of 1916, other places opened their doors to artists' gatherings. The first of these was at 6, rue Huyghens, at the end of a courtyard. There, a Swiss painter, Emile Lejeune, had made his studio available to painters, poets and musicians who wanted to exhibit, read or perform their works.

Blaise Cendrars, Jean Cocteau and Ortiz de Zarate created the association 'Lyre et Palette', which would organize events attended by a widely varied public: the artist population of the Vavin neighbourhood, in sweaters and worn trousers, would mingle alongside chic society people dressed in the furs and jewels of the fashionable right bank, invited by Jean Cocteau. In a sometimes overheated, sometimes freezing room, these two worlds met.

Outside, the chrome-plated limousines left a little room for wheelbarrows to enter, transporting the works exhibited by the painters, or chairs lent for an evening by the attendant in the Luxembourg gardens.

On 19 November, the day of the opening of the first exhibition given by Lyre et Palette, Kisling, Matisse, Modigliani, Picasso and Ortiz de Zarate hung their works together. Paul Guillaume had lent some statuettes which were important examples of Negro art. In the evening, Erik Satie, who had come on foot from Arcueil on the outskirts of Paris, sat down at the piano to play some works with resolutely Dada-ish titles: *Melodies to Make you Run Away, Lopsided Dances, Secular and Sumptuous Verses, Truly Flaccid Preludes for a Dog*.

The next day and on the following days, a band known as the New Youth, who would become 'Les Six' – Arthur Honegger, Darius Milhaud, Francis Poulenc, Georges Auric, Louis Durey, Germaine Tailleferre – followed suit.

On 26 November, Cendrars, Max Jacob, Reverdy and Salmon read from their works. Cocteau recited a poem by Apollinaire, who was too weak to do so himself. He was present, however, standing off to one side, wearing a splendid officer's uniform bought the day before at the Belle Jardinière, and spotless tawny leather boots. He brushed off his sky-blue tunic, and proudly touched, from time to time, the black bandage tied around his forehead. A young woman was hanging on his arm. Her name was Jacqueline, though he had nicknamed her Ruby because of the colour of her hair. She didn't know many people there; he had met her again by chance after having run into her several times before, in the company of her fiancé, the poet Jules-Gérard Jordens, who had fallen in battle in the Buttes wood in 1916, where Apollinaire himself had been wounded.

On 31 December 1916, to celebrate the publication of *Le Poète assassiné*, a collection of stories and tales, Apollinaire's friends decided to organize an intimate lunch – two hundred people – in a discreet setting, the Palace of Orléans, on the Avenue du Maine. The menu had been cleverly put together by Max Jacob and Guillaume Apollinaire himself:

> Cubist, orphist, futurist (etc.) hors-d'œuvres
> Fish prepared by our friend Méritarte
> Zone of beef fillet à la Croniamantal
> Aretinus of capon hérésiarque
> Salad of aesthetic meditations
> Cheese in a cortège of Orpheus
> Fruit from Aesop's banquet
> The Masked Brigadier's biscuits
>
> The enchanter's white wine
> Red wine from the Case d'Armons

The artilleryman's Champagne
The coffee of Paris evenings
Liqueurs*

The occasion was a great success. The lunch was interrupted by a food fight with, on one side and at one table, Rachilde, Paul Fort, André Gide and a few other great literary figures, and on the other, some younger artists, who were noisier and extremely rude, to the general amusement of all.

Two weeks later, another party was held. This time it was at Marie Vassilieff's, in honour of Braque, who had also returned to civilian life after being trepanned. The organizing committee, which included Apollinaire, Gris, Max Jacob, Reverdy, Metzinger, Matisse, Picasso, and a few others, invited friends to join the festivities, for a six-franc contribution (André Salmon claims that Picasso had not written to Braque once during the entire war).

It was not a very happy evening. Marie Vassilieff had unfortunately invited Beatrice Hastings, who was separated from Modigliani. She came, but not alone: Alfredo Pina, a sculptor and her new lover, was with her. Amedeo, despite having been asked to spend the evening elsewhere, turned up. He paid his six-franc entrance fee, greeted his friends, and, reckoning that the admission charge entitled him to a show, went over to Beatrice and began to whisper verses by Dante and Rimbaud in her ear. When the sculptor approached, Amedeo tried to get rid of him. The other responded, to the stupefaction of all present, by pulling out a revolver. Chaos erupted. Max Jacob refereed the fight, Apollinaire kept score. Juan Gris contemplated, terror-stricken, these madmen with their shouts and insults who were leaping about like enraged cocks. Imperturbable behind his beard and glasses, Matisse tried to calm things down. In the end, Modigliani was ignominiously shoved out into the street.

Picasso, in a corner, was singing to Pâquerette, his favourite among Poiret's models. Their romance, however, would not last long.

A month later, the painter flew off on the gossamer wings of Cocteau the zephyr. He visited Naples and Pompeii, joined Diaghilev in Rome, fell into the arms of Olga, and came back on 18 May 1917 to the Châtelet Theatre in Paris. *Parade* was being staged there: a ballet in one act, written by Jean Cocteau, music by Erik Satie, costumes and sets by Pablo Picasso.

Once again, the evening was reminiscent of the opening night of *Hernani*, only in a modern setting. The bluebloods who had come that night to get a whiff of the troubling fragrance of cubist art championed by Cocteau in the programme received something of a shock. At the

* The menu contains many references to titles or characters from Apollinaire's works.

beginning, while the 'Marseillaise' was playing, all was well. They could take the tricoloured curtain with the harlequin, the horsewomen, and various circus actors. But the girl with the pointed hat, the Negro who served, the mare with wings, the cowboy wearing skyscrapers on his back – and the music! There weren't any notes, just noise...

Princesse Eugène Murat couldn't get over it. She was wearing a diadem. Exquisitely polite with her escort of the evening, she didn't hesitate for a second in hitting her neighbours with her fan if they didn't join her in the insults and whistles that they had practised that afternoon, in anticipation of the event. Fights broke out all over the theatre. The Comtesse de Chabrillan and the Marquise d'Ouesan cried, 'Foreigners! Shirkers! Reds!' It was thrilling. Society ladies sought out unwashed artists and attacked them with hatpins. Some, in evening gowns, were accompanied by gentlemen in smoking jackets or smart uniforms bearing the medals of the Legion of Honour and military decorations. Some, like the Princesse de Polignac, were dressed in nurses' uniforms, to remind Guillaume Apollinaire that he was not the only one who had served his country. For Guillaume was defending his friends in military dress, and the bandage that he wore around his head as evidence of his wound was impressive. Near him, Cocteau was jumping up and down to make sure that the theatre was filled with the people he had invited, those who would always be his crowd: high society and aristocrats. He bumped into a gentleman whom he heard telling his neighbour, 'If I had known this was going to be such a circus, I would have brought the children!'

The next day, the critics went wild. Parade was hailed as an exemplar of the best in German art. The reviewers attacked the typewriters, the dynamos, the mermaids. They pilloried Diaghilev who, a few weeks earlier, had unfortunately already created a stir by setting the Firebird ablaze in the folds of the Bolshevik Red Flag.

Erik Satie, the journalists' first target, would reply in the following terms to the chronicler of the Carnet de la semaine, who had accused him of offending French taste and of lacking talent, imagination, and mastery:

> Dear Sir and friend,
> You're nothing but an arsehole, and an unmusical arsehole at that.

The critic brought legal proceedings against him for insult and slander. Satie was given a suspended prison sentence. He was no less upset than Picasso had been, the day he was called before the examining judge for the theft of the Iberic statuettes. Suddenly he saw himself encumbered with a police record, ruined by the confiscation of his royalties and forbidden to travel (though in practice he never went any further than the round trip between Arcueil and Paris!). He did not have enough money to hire a lawyer to appeal against the verdict delivered. His friends – Gris, Cocteau and especially Max Jacob – contacted some of their prominent relations to help the musician.

Meanwhile, during this same month of May 1917, President Poincaré named Philippe Pétain as Commander-in-Chief of the armies. For, far up on the northern plains, the decimated battalions were emerging from the trenches to call for an end to the carnage.

Pétain had four hundred rebels executed to set an example. Four hundred more soldiers, to add to the forty thousand men who had already been butchered on the Chemin des Dames...

LOVE AT FIRST SIGHT

He was alone, with a thick dark fringe falling onto his forehead, horn-rimmed spectacles, a red-and-white checked cotton shirt, a little moustache in the form of an M, a suit made of very fine British cloth . . .

Youki Desnos

Sitting behind the bar of the Rotonde, his moustache quivering, Libion was keeping an eye on things. Blaise Cendrars had just entered, suitcase in hand. He spent his life going from hotel to hotel, and once again, he was on the move. He went up to Max Jacob, who was copying one of his manuscripts for Doucet, the dressmaker. Perhaps he was dressed in the attire described by Léautaud: worn out, flat, pointy shoes, thick woollen socks, washed out checked trousers that were too short, a tiny jacket that was too tight, a dusty hat.

Cendrars sat down. Max told him about the fight that Reverdy had got into with Diego Rivera on the subject of cubism: the painter and the poet had actually come to blows. It had all begun at the restaurant Lapérouse, at a dinner hosted by Léonce Rosenberg, and would end at Lhote, among the Louis-Philippe knick-knacks. Reverdy had defended the cubism of Braque, Gris, and Picasso, and did not hide his low opinion of the artists present. Offended, Rivera had slapped him. Reverdy had pulled his hair. They'd had to throw him out . . .

Libion didn't catch the bits of conversation coming from the café. He was watching the stratagems of half a dozen policemen on bicycles who were slowly surrounding the place, leaving their bikes and gathering again not far from the entrance to the café.

'Raid!' he shouted.

No one was impressed by the news. The customers were used to it now. Since the Russian revolutionaries and pacifists of all persuasions had chosen the Rotonde as their headquarters, the men from the prefecture made regular raids. All those who were against the war were considered defeatists. According to Marshal Joffre, this word was not in the French vocabulary. But it forced them to take certain precautions. So for a time, Libion plastered patriotic posters all over his walls. He hoped they would constitute sufficient proof of his good will. But they were not enough to rid the place of the tale-tellers, informers, and plain-clothes policemen who, since the beginning of the year, had been besieging establishments considered to be dubious. The Rotonde was one of the first among these, followed closely by the Dôme and the Closerie des Lilas. The Baty restaurant, across the street, was less often visited; its fine white tablecloths and its expensive menu pleaded in favour of the diners.

A squadron of rather stiff-looking individuals suddenly appeared at the entrance. They moved from table to table, checking the papers of the customers. No one could leave: the cyclists posted on the sidewalk would have immediately nabbed the offender. But this time, fortune smiled on those present: the identity check took place in the establishment and not at the police station.

The officers surrounded a little Japanese man dressed in a maroon robe. A chain sparkled around his neck, and his earrings gave him a strange appearance.

'Are you a woman?'

'A man,' replied the Japanese person.

'Prove it.'

'I was married once, and am soon to marry again,' answered the Japanese fellow with a delighted smile. He gestured towards a young girl sitting a little further on and speaking with her neighbour, paying no attention to the man looking at her.

'Love at first sight, gentlemen.'

'Let's have your papers.'

He handed them over. The policemen bent over to read: Fujita Tsuguharu, known as Foujita, born in 1885 in Tokyo, Japan.

'Father's profession?'

'General in the imperial army.'

'How long have you been in France?'

'Since 1913 ... But I went to London for a while.'

'To do what?'

Foujita glanced questioningly at the young lady who still hadn't noticed him. He returned his attention to the agents.

'I was working for a painter. We concocted paintings together. He signed them, sold them, and didn't pay me.'

'So why did you stay?'

'I had to earn a living.'

The police agents frowned.

'I was cheated, if that's what you want to know...'

'We want to know everything, and in detail.'

'This painter had an estate and a stable of horses,' Foujita explained carefully. 'The problem is that he knew how to paint everything except horses. I did them myself, and he did the rest, the grass, the rising or setting sun, the little country fences, the charming bucolic atmosphere. And of course the signature. One day, he went off to sell our joint work. I never saw him again.'

'And that's when you came to France?'

'After having been a designer in London, for Sir Gordon Selfridge. They're still selling blazers there that I cut.'

The agents stared at the maroon-coloured robe. 'Is that your work?'

'Hand sewn ... Would a little skirt in the same colour tempt one of you?'

The police agents headed towards the door – with a stop at the bar, where Libion was standing, hands on his hips. They warned him that if the rumours about his establishment persisted, it would be placed off limits for the troops.

Alone again, Foujita sought the eyes of the young girl sitting three tables further on. She was twenty-five, with laughing eyes, short hair, a turned-up nose, and slangy Parisian speech. She had turned towards him once and didn't seem surprised by the maroon robe. This did not astonish the little Japanese man. When he had arrived in France, he had gone about in the company of Isadora Duncan and her brother, who espoused a return to Greek ideals at that time. He wore a band around his forehead, a cape hanging from his shoulder, a necklace of large stones, a woman's bag, and sandals. This attire had not kept women from throwing themselves at him.

When he thought about it, Foujita recognized all he owed them. Marcelle had taught him how to drink his soup without making a noise and not to lick his spoon at dessert. Marguerite had taught him how to kiss. Renée had shown him how to enter a movie theatre without paying for his seat. Margot had given him a great repertoire of insults, of a rather bestial nature. Yvonne had taught him how to go to the pawnshop and pawn his watch, leaving it there while he bought himself a little cocaine. Gaby had shown him how to wear dresses or trousers that would remain in perfect shape now that he had learned to slide them under his mattress at night. But what could this girl teach him? And to begin with, what was her name?

Foujita rose and approached her. He bowed ceremoniously. They exchanged a few words. Then the Japanese man retreated.

The next day, he returned to the Rotonde. He came in all smiles, with a triumphant look on his face. On his arm was his latest conquest: the young girl whose name he had managed to learn – Fernande – as well as her address, the rue Delambre. She appeared to be madly in love with this diabolical Japanese fellow who had won her over with a simple shirt:

a blue blouse that she wore as proudly as if it had been the dress of a princess. Foujita, who could concoct a tunic in less than an hour, had spent the night sewing this gift. He had brought it to her in the morning, having obtained the previous night the address of the room near the Dôme where his future love lived. And as Fernande Barrey did not want to appear lacking in generosity herself, after he had offered her this handmade gift, and as he was complaining about how cold the little room was, she picked up a hatchet and hacked up the only chair she owned to provide him with some firewood.

Thirteen days later, they were married at the town hall of the fourteenth arrondissement. Foujita borrowed the six francs needed to publish the banns from a waiter at the Rotonde, whom he reimbursed by painting a portrait of his wife. They had brought a witness, but as they needed two, they recruited a professional witness who was standing around waiting outside the town hall.

A few weeks later, Madame Foujita left home with a portfolio of drawings under her arm. She walked to the right bank, where most of the art dealers operated. The story has it that, caught in an unexpected downpour, she went into Chéron's and offered him two watercolours in exchange for an umbrella, returning to Montparnasse without having sold a thing.

But at least she had won over Chéron. For after he had studied the watercolours attentively, the dealer crossed the Seine to the rue Delambre and, without even taking the time to notice the braided rugs on the floor, the lamps decorated with ideograms, the tables with sawn-off feet and – an incredible luxury – a real bathtub, he asked who the artist was and where he kept his works. He bought everything he saw, providing some welcome security for the young couple: seven francs fifty for each watercolour, as a minimum, made four hundred and fifty francs for a month's production.

To celebrate the good news, Foujita gave his wife a cage and a canary. But then he began to venture along a path down which no one could follow him, by mixing traditional Japanese art with that of the European avant-garde. Earlier, because of his lack of funds, he had painted animals and flowers in gouaches and pastels. Now he could afford the oil and the brushes he had lacked. Seated on the ground in the former stable which had become his workshop on the rue Delambre, with his paints all around him, Foujita serenely set out to paint the canvases that all of fashionable Paris would soon be buying up. After Van Dongen, and simultaneously with Picasso, he was about to discover the joys of luxury. Wealth was knocking at the door, and so was fame.

A PAINTER AND HIS DEALER

In the end it's great painters
who make great dealers.

Daniel-Henry Kahnweiler

The man who leaves his place open may well find it filled on his return.
As a German citizen who had taken refuge in Switzerland, Kahnweiler's
possessions (and therefore his collections) had been sequestered, and he
was finally running out of funds. He could no longer manage to support
his artists. From now on, his place was empty. It would not remain so
for long.

The quickest to pounce was Léonce Rosenberg, and it was he who won
the day. Advised by André Level and Max Jacob, he bought works by
Gris, Braque, Léger and Picasso. He became the official dealer of the
cubists despite knowing nothing about business, by his own confession.
And not only that: a few years after the end of the war he counselled
Miró to cut up his canvas *La Ferme* so that he could sell it to clients who
lived in an apartment with small walls. In the end, Hemingway fought
off other art lovers by winning the painting in a game of dice.

Léonce Rosenberg paid his painters rather badly – though sometimes
better than Kahnweiler. However, most of the artists didn't complain,
having no other door to knock on. Indeed, as Max Jacob noted, 'without
him, a number of painters would be drivers or factory workers.'[1]

Picasso was the only one who rebelled. He finally left Léonce for his
brother, Paul Rosenberg, who had more refined taste; he would become
Picasso's main dealer between the two wars.

Modigliani also changed horses in midstream. He was with Paul
Guillaume, but moved to Léopold Zborowski. The former was a great
defender of contemporary art, one of the first to publish the catalogues
of his exhibitions; the latter was a Polish poet who was in Paris studying
at the Sorbonne when the war broke out. Beneath his elegant clothes, he
concealed a poverty which was scarcely less pronounced than that of his
client. But he had a heart of gold, and a tongue of platinum: 'You're

worth two Picassos!' he said to Amedeo when he met him for the first time.

'Can you prove it?'

'Let's talk.'

This was during an exhibition mounted by the Lyre and Palette association, where they had been introduced to each other by Kisling. The artist and his future dealer walked towards the bar of the Petit Napolitain. Modigliani had just earned some money from a couple of modelling sessions. He left half of it on the boulevard, in the hat of Ortiz de Zarate, who had organized a travelling exhibition for the benefit of artists wounded in the war.

They sat down, and began by ordering, quite reasonably, two café-crèmes. They then ordered a third one for another poor artist with whom they identified. The man was wearing a torn overcoat, a shirt that was in even worse shape, and shoes that had seen better days, and he had a hacking cough. Modigliani slipped his hand into his pocket, brought out what remained of the money he had just earned, and discreetly dropped it on the ground. Then he leaned over, picked up the bill, and waved it over the table.

'Look what I just found on the ground! Ten francs!'

He put it down in front of the painter. 'It's for you ... It was under your chair.'

The man wanted to share it.

'Out of the question!' cried the Italian. 'I've just earned a lot of money.'

The proceeds of the second session's sitting vanished into thin air, to help the poor fellow. The painter bought them all a drink, then left.

The dealer, Zborowski, was a strange young man: stylish, with a well-cut jacket, an impeccably trimmed beard, an accent as pronounced as Soutine's and a strong desire to be associated with Amedeo. He offered to pay him fifteen francs a day, and to furnish him with a model and materials. For Picasso, this would have been peanuts; for Modigliani, it was a feast.

The Italian, stunned, stared at this man who was offering him manna from heaven on a regular basis, even though his market value was scarcely more than a small glass of brandy at the bar. The man was clearly as poor as he was: one had only to lift his tie to see the missing button, the darned shirt, the hollow chest, and to understand that he was as hungry as Modigliani himself. Fifteen francs a day!

'I have friends who are also very talented,' said the Italian.

He mentioned Chaïm Soutine. But, as he was about to launch into a catalogue of his friends in need, the dealer stopped him.

'I have to explain. To be very honest...'

He revealed his situation. He had nothing. The war had broken out while he was in Paris, studying French literature at the Sorbonne. He had become a dealer in works of art, books and engravings, because he spoke well and was gifted at negotiation. He hadn't enjoyed the work or been good at it. But he had discovered Modigliani through Lyre and Palette. He wanted to devote himself to his work and to promoting it.

Yes or no?

Amedeo had set his sketchbook down on the table, and was now observing an American girl, drinking alone nearby. He began to draw her face. Perhaps he was thinking about another meeting he had once had with a dealer, before Paul Guillaume had given him a contract. The fellow had negotiated with him for a bunch of drawings, making him go lower, lower, still lower. When Modigliani finally had the impression that sea level had been reached, he grabbed the drawings, stuck a hole in them, slipped a string in the hole, then went to the washroom where he hung his works from the toilet chain. Coming back to the dealer, he simply said, 'They're yours. Go wipe your ass with them.'

But now, Modigliani tore the sheet he had just filled from the pad.

'Yes or no?' asked Léopold Zborowski again.

Modi gave the American her portrait. She took the drawing, studied it first with suspicion, then with interest, kindness, joy, contentment, thrill, gratitude and happiness. When her ecstasy seemed exhausted, Amedeo said, 'That will be three stouts.'

These were immediately served to them.

'I want your signature!' cried the American.

'Saints are not always angels,' observed Zborowski.

Modigliani took back the drawing that the woman was holding. 'Why do you need a signature?'

'For the market value!' the good lady sighed. 'One day, you may be famous.'

In ten perfect blocks, in a diagonal line across the sheet, Modigliani covered over the portrait with the ten letters of his name. He gave it back to the American, who took it delightedly, looked at it with gratitude, then interest, then suspicion, and finally tore it up in a rage.

Modigliani turned towards Zborowski. He clinked the dealer's glass with his own and said, 'The answer is yes.'

Every day, the dealer went out to the galleries. Amedeo never asked for details of his activity, just for advances, to pay for the drinks, the meals, the bouquets of flowers ... And Zborowski gave him as much as he could. When he couldn't give him anything, he would take his wife's jewels to the pawnshop, play poker at the Rotonde, come to some arrangement with other art dealers or borrow money from shopkeepers. He could sometimes be seen seated at a table at the Rotonde, having eaten nothing for two days. His fate was no more enviable than that of Max Jacob, who went from table to table to sell his books, which he had published at his own expense; or that of the customers who washed themselves in the café's washrooms, having no access to a bathroom of their own. The dealer probably did the same as some of the other habitués, who filled their pockets with the crusts from the long loaves of bread sitting on the counter of the bar. When an art lover appeared, he sold Modigliani's paintings for whatever pittance he could get – works that would be worth a hundred times more, only five years later.

Zborowski was completely devoted to Amedeo. He made sacrifices for him, did without tobacco, coal, food, gave whatever he had to his client to alleviate his poverty a little. He did all this as much from affection as from admiration. He fought day in, day out to promote this painter in whom no one believed, aside from a few obscure Swiss collectors who had been intrigued one day by an article written in a Geneva paper by Francis Carco. They had acquired a few nudes for a tiny sum.

Zborowski sought potential clients everywhere, even among the shopkeepers of the Vavin neighbourhood. When he couldn't avoid it, Modigliani dealt with them directly. Francis Carco recounts that one day when his dealer was in the south of France, Amedeo ran into his wife, Hanka, whom he asked to pose for him; he was supposed to paint two canvases to sell to a hairdresser. She accepted, in exchange for a promise of a third work, which he was to give her. When the sitting was over, the last painting not yet having dried, Hanka Zborowska decided to come back the next day to get it. When she arrived at the studio, all three works had disappeared: two were at the hairdresser's, and the last had been sold to a buyer who had turned up unexpectedly.

Hanka posed often for Modigliani, as did Lunia, a friend of the couple. But whenever he had the five francs needed to pay them, Zborowski tried to find professional models for his client. He also tried to furnish all the materials the painter needed: brushes, paints, palettes, and canvases, not to mention the traditional bottle.

Amedeo used to paint at his hotel, then he would go to see his dealer on the rue Joseph Bara. He was now working in very different conditions from those imposed on him before the war by Chéron who, it was said, locked the artist up in the basement of his gallery on the rue La Boétie with a bottle of cognac, and only let him out once the painting was finished.

With the Zborowskis, Modi arrived in the afternoon. He needed to paint for several hours in order to finish a canvas. He never complained about his models. Once he had stopped working, he often shared a plate of beans with the couple, bought in the nearby grocery shop by Hanka. Then he would leave the dealer and his family, sometimes stopping by again at night to ask for an advance of a few francs; they would turn out the lights upstairs and pretend to be asleep.

Modi would often bring his friends to Zborowski's. Soutine was the first. Modigliani constantly urged the dealer to take him on, but the Pole was not that impressed by his work. Perhaps he was influenced by Hanka, who was terrified by Soutine's rough manners. She loved Modigliani, except when he was with his friend. For a long time she could not forgive him for having jumped up in the middle of a meal and, having stared at Soutine for a moment, crying, 'I'm going to paint you!' Which he proceeded to do immediately, straight on to the dining-room door.

Modigliani often came with the young girl who, from the spring of 1917, had succeeded Beatrice Hastings. She was nicknamed 'Coconut', because of the contrast between her dark hair with its auburn tints, and her very pale, translucent skin.

Jeanne Hébuterne had taken drawing lessons at the Colarossi studio. She was as gentle and shy as Beatrice Hastings had been hot-tempered and extravagant. She had lovely green eyes, pure as a mountain stream. She was beautiful and delicate: distant, inaccessible, with an infinite sadness in her deep, magnificent gaze. She resembled a frightened animal, seeking a little place for herself in the great wide world. Her parents, Eudoxie and Achille Casimir – practising Catholics, strict and stern – had not accepted their daughter's romance with a poor Jewish-Italian artist who was so much older than her. She was nineteen, and Modigliani thirty-five – but love had conquered all.

Zborowski found them a little artist's workshop on the rue de la Grande Chaumière, opposite the one that Paul Gauguin had once occupied. He continued to watch over his protégé, but in his own way, which was far removed from that of more wealthy, established art dealers.

Some people would criticize him later for his amateurism and unreliability, and the charge is not entirely unfounded. Daniel-Henry Kahnweiler, in particular, complained of his negligence in certain matters. These criticisms count for little in the end. All that matters is art, and it was between 1916 and 1920 – during the years, that is, when he was being looked after and encouraged by Zborowski – that Modigliani executed almost all of his painted work, notably his extraordinary series of nudes. Through extreme bad luck, or a sinister twist of fate, when the dealer died, twelve years after the Italian painter, he was a ruined man, as poor as Modigliani had been on the day that he died. That day, the morning after his death, Jeanne Hébuterne had returned to her parents' home at 8 bis, rue Amyot.

3, RUE JOSEPH BARA

Concierge? Yes, but concierge in a
building full of artists...

André Salmon

Young women were becoming emancipated. Passing romances were born
in the evening only to fade away in the morning. Cendrars claimed that
the war was emptying houses, with the men at the front and the women
out seeking replacements to occupy the vacant beds ... Passions flamed
like bonfires.

Kisling fell in love and became engaged to Renée-Jean, a twenty-year-
old blonde with her fringe cut short, just above her eyebrows. She was
lively and warm blooded, and she wore trousers with unmatched socks,
in the style of the Italian futurists.

Having inherited money from an American sculptor with whom he
had done much carousing before 1914, the bridegroom was able to
organize a grandiose wedding, the finest celebration in the neighbourhood
during these hard times of war. All of Montparnasse was invited. The
procession left from Kisling's house on the rue Joseph Bara. Drunk on
wine and joy, the little group set off towards the town hall, with a pause
at the Rotonde, then at the Dôme where old Cambron offered refreshments
to all. The group grew larger, from glass to glass, from café to bistro,
until Kisling and Renée-Jean finally exchanged their vows, fairly clearly,
before the mayor's deputy. The functionary had never before seen such a
sight as this band of noisy, unkempt artists, joined by a bunch of
uniformed soldiers on leave who clicked their heels together in the
marriage hall. The bride even called her new husband a 'stupid little
Polack', while the groom was in despair at marrying the daughter of a
commander of the Republican Guard: having expressed his anti-military
convictions in no uncertain terms, he was about to find himself with an
officer for a father-in-law. It was mortifying, a calamity.

After a lunch during which the wine flowed steadily, the company stopped
off in the whorehouses of the Boulevard Saint Germain, then came back to

Kisling's studio where Max Jacob was playing his finest role, imitating Jules Laforgue. Modigliani ran after him, begging him to let him recite Dante, Rimbaud, Baudelaire – anyone, provided he was allowed to play a part too. He went into the little room adjoining the studio, and returned covered in the young couple's sheets. He climbed onto a stool and pretended to be a ghost, reciting verses from *Macbeth*, then from *Hamlet*, oblivious to the boos of the bride, who was aghast at the idea that someone else was using her wedding sheets, even if it was to recite Shakespeare. There followed a chase in the stairwells, and a lot of shrieking, as the tenants responded in kind to Amedeo's bird calls and Mme Salomon's invectives.

Mme Salomon was the concierge, a stubborn Breton, tiny and dressed like a witch, but devoted and attentive to all the poor artists who made up her universe. She sang their praises to her fellow concierges all along the street. In the summer, she spent her nights stretched out in front of her door. In the winter, she came back into the apartment where, like the Douanier Rousseau, she slept fully dressed. There was no escaping her eagle eye. The moment she heard the slightest sound, she would bound from her niche. Night and day, she watched over her brood with a sometimes harsh, sometimes quizzical eye.

She had a particular affection for Kisling. When he came back from the war, wounded, she encouraged him to drink milk to relieve his ravaging cough. Each time he came in or went out, she leapt from her observation post, adjusted her pince-nez and asked, 'Have you drunk your milk?'

'Tomorrow, tomorrow . . .'

He kissed her unruly hair; he knew that she complained just for the sake of complaining.

She had welcomed Renée-Jean like a baby bird fallen from the nest, and she hoped that conjugal bliss would dampen Kisling's taste for night life. Before he had worn a uniform, Kisling often used to come home at dawn, dead drunk and rarely alone.

But she was soon disillusioned: his marital status had not changed her protégé's habits. The door of the studio was always open. In the morning, starting at nine o'clock, the models came by, one after another; in the afternoon, it was his friends. Evening was party time. And at all times, poor Mme Salomon was subjected to the horrible noise of the phonograph.

'It's scratching my ears! It's ruining my taste!' She hated Fréhel, and Argentinian tangos.

When it wasn't music, it was the sound of the platform on wheels on which the painter's models sat. He dragged it, pushed it, turned it around, moved it here and there to take advantage of the available sunlight, and when, finally, he had found the best angle, he began to whistle a little tune which came out like a roar, as he danced around the apartment, making a commotion.

And all this was just on the top floor. There were the others, too. For Kisling was not the only artist who rented a room at 3, rue Joseph Bara. André Salmon had also lived there before crossing the street to no. 6. Every evening, a passer-by walking his dogs would quite unintentionally give him the signal that it was time to go to bed. At eleven o'clock, almost like a ritual, this man pronounced a word, just one and always the same: 'Churl!' For the insects took advantage of the hour of the man's evening stroll to bite or bother another promenader, who would then insult the dogs' master, who in turn responded with his own somewhat literary insult, served up regularly at the same hour. The names of the animals remain unknown, but their owner, who lived near the rue Stanislas and worked at the *Mercure de France*, was Paul Léautaud.

Rembrandt Bugatti, a sculptor of animals and the brother of Ettore, the automobile manufacturer, had lived on the ground floor of no. 3. He had committed suicide there in 1915. And the previous year, Jules Pascin had left the last floor to return to Montmartre.

Their replacements were a great deal of trouble for Mme Salomon. Especially the last one: Léopold Zborowski, art dealer. He rented a two-room apartment on the first floor, which he shared with a number of people. First there was his wife, Hanka Zborowska, which was only natural; then a friend, Lunia Czechowska, the wife of a Polish man who had left for the front, which was a little more unusual; then there was Amedeo Modigliani, who lived elsewhere but who painted in the second room of the apartment. It was generous of the Polish couple to welcome their friends, but it made things rather noisy for the other occupants of the building.

Between the floors, there was a permanent to and fro. Modigliani would go to get his paints at Kisling's, who would later come down to retrieve them, running into Salmon on his way up the stairs. An onlooker in the building might often see Apollinaire opening a door, a model looking for the right floor, Renée-Jean waking up, Lunia asking someone or other if they thought her relationship with Amedeo was ambiguous, Hanka complaining because Soutine had just arrived, Soutine climbing up to the Zborowskis and Zborowski coming down, carrying Modigliani's latest drawings under his arm . . .

Madame Salomon followed and kept watch over the comings and goings of her tenants. When they were particularly rambunctious, she consoled herself by thinking about the grief she would have felt if by bad luck one of them hadn't returned from the war. Lying in her bed at night, after an exhausting day of work, she listened carefully, fearing other sounds that were more dangerous than the shouts and laughter of half a dozen painters and poets: the growl of the Zeppelins, and the explosions from the bomber planes.

LES MAMELLES DE TIRÉSIAS

I'm still very nervous, extremely irritable ... it appears it may take more than a year to get over the traumatic event which almost killed me.

Guillaume Apollinaire

Love had come to Kisling, Foujita, Modigliani and Apollinaire – Picasso would be next. Fernande was far away, Eva was buried, Gaby, Pâquerette and the others forgotten. On the canvas, tall, radiant, sovereign, Olga Khokhlova made her appearance. She was twenty-five, Russian, the daughter of a colonel in the Tsar's army, a dancer with the Ballets Russes. Picasso met her in Rome with Diaghilev. He followed her to Naples and Florence, then they met again in Paris, and went to Barcelona together with the dance troupe.

Picasso had changed. He now wore a suit, a tie, a handkerchief in his chest pocket, and a watch chain. His Spanish friends didn't recognize him. The fame and excitement of the Ballets Russes had brought him an aura that painting hadn't provided.

Ah, love ... In March 1917, Ruby announced to Apollinaire that she was pregnant. The child would not be born. Whether or not by coincidence, at this time Apollinaire was working on a play whose main theme was the repeopling of France: *Les Mamelles de Tirésias*. The work was performed on 24 June 1917, at the Théâtre Renée-Maubel in Montmartre. The cover of the programme was graced by one of Picasso's drawings. The play was to have considerable impact. Even more than *Parade*, it became 'the great avant-garde event of 1917'.[1]

The idea of producing *Les Mamelles de Tirésias* came from Pierre Albert-Birot. One evening in November 1916, in his study on the rue de la Tombe-Issoire, where his review had its offices, he was talking to Guillaume Apollinaire. Birot wanted *SIC* to publish not only contemporary poetry, but also modern theatre. Apollinaire suggested a text he had written in 1903: the story of Thérèse, who became Tirésias and, like the seer of Thebes, changed sex and took power from men. (The work is not without a certain resemblance to Aristophanes' *The Parliament of Women*.)

Birot agreed to publish it, and Apollinaire did some more work on the play, probably making some fairly important changes.

The most important of these was the addition of a prologue which didn't exist in the first version. This prologue expressed the author's true intentions: 'I bring you a play whose purpose is to change men's manners ...' He challenges the past: 'Dramatic art without greatness or virtue / Which whiled away the long evenings before the war.' He preaches a role for women comparable to that of men: 'I too want to be a deputy lawyer senator / Minister president of public affairs.' He shows himself to be resolutely anti-militaristic: 'They extinguish the stars with cannonballs.'

All this is enveloped in a debauch of travesties, sound games and outrageous effects that might have seemed to be purely provocative. Not only because pacifism (which was something fairly new to Apollinaire) is defeatism, but also because in these brutal times – although it was surely positive to encourage procreation in a healthy spirit of demographic concern – it was still not advisable to show a woman opening her blouse to unleash a cloud of balloons on a public stage.

Rehearsals began. The play was not directed so much as 'fought over', according to Pierre Albert-Birot's comment.[2] The actors were not professionals (Apollinaire even thought about playing a part), the sets, attributed to Serge Férat, were made at the last moment, and the musical score, which was supposed to be played by a full orchestra, was performed by a pianist who single-handedly replaced the instrumentalists who were so hard to find in wartime. The choruses were directed by Max Jacob, and the music was composed by Germaine Albert-Birot.

Apollinaire was never a great music lover. In 1917, at a concert performed at the Salle Gaveau, he spent the evening composing poetry while the orchestra played a work by César Franck, and he took advantage of the intermission to slip away discreetly. During the rehearsals for Les Mamelles, he heartily applauded the musician playing the work – less for the quality of her work than for her svelte figure. He liked Satie chiefly because he was a friend. But Mamelles was important to him because he was a resolute champion of the avant-garde.

When the programme was ready, Birot asked the poet what to put on the cover. Apollinaire said just the title, Les Mamelles de Tirésias, but Birot objected that this was not enough. They also had to describe the play.

'How about "drama"?' suggested Apollinaire.

'That's too short. And the public might think it's a cubist drama.'

Apollinaire thought for a second and said, 'Let's write "surnaturalistic drama".'

'That's impossible,' replied Birot. 'We're as far from naturalism as from surnaturalism.'

'Well, then, let's put Les Mamelles de Tirésias, surrealistic drama.'

The word had been pronounced. It would be taken up by André Breton and Philippe Soupault, in homage to Guillaume Apollinaire.

When *Mamelles* was performed, Breton was present. He was as disappointed by the work as by the actors' interpretation. At the end of the first act, he noticed a spectator making a scene in the audience. It was Jacques Vaché, dressed in the uniform of an English officer. He had pulled his revolver out of its holster and was threatening to use it. Breton managed to calm him down. The two men watched the show without enthusiasm. Vaché was as exasperated by 'the cheap lyric tone of the play as by the cubist repetition of the sets and costumes'.[3]

The evening was one of total chaos: it was the first of the long series of scandals which would line the path of surrealism. The press had a field day, and the public too. Despite the caution shown by Pierre Albert-Birot, the work was labelled cubist, Apollinaire roundly condemned, and Picasso, because of his drawing on the programme cover, crucified on the altar of 'national art'. Cubism, always considered as having been of German inspiration, was no more popular than in 1914.

But the painters who saw themselves as belonging to the cubist movement in its purest and most orthodox form loudly proclaimed their identification with this school. They even went so far as to write a protest to the papers, after the performance of *Les Mamelles de Tirésias*, specifying that there was no relationship between their works and 'certain literary and theatrical fantasies'. The allusion was clear. Aimed chiefly at Picasso, the accusation was signed by Gris, Hayden, Kisling, Lipchitz, Lhote, Metzinger, Rivera and Severini.[4] It upset Apollinaire, who felt that Blaise Cendrars had had a hand in the attack.

The day after the performance of *Les Mamelles de Tirésias* at the Théâtre Renée-Maubel, Apollinaire was appointed to work in the press office of the Ministry of War. This meant the bureau of censorship. At the time, he was writing in *Excelsior*, *L'Information*, *Nord–Sud*, Pierre Reverdy's review, and Pierre Albert-Birot's *SIC*. He had worked previously with André Billy at *Paris-Midi*. He hadn't lost the rebellious spirit which delighted his friends so much. In the *Paris-Midi*, for example, he published false news which supposedly came from London, Tokyo, or New York...

Carrying on the tradition of Paul Fort, he organized gatherings of his friends every Tuesday at the café de Flore, between five and seven in the evening. Max Jacob had called these meetings 'Paul Flore's Tuesdays' and Pierre Reverdy spoke of 'the fauna of the Flore'.

He saw Lou once, by chance, on the Place de l'Opéra. But their romance was over. Apollinaire was now living with Jacqueline, in his apartment on the Boulevard Saint Germain. The apartment was on the top floor; to reach it, one had to climb a succession of staircases. On the other side of the door, its inhabitant had made a minuscule opening which enabled him to see from inside the apartment who the visitor was. If it was a bailiff, he didn't open the door. On the ledge he had tacked a sign which read, 'No pestering the residents.'[5]

The apartment was criss-crossed by winding corridors filled with books, statuettes and a thousand fetish objects picked up here and there. It was a very strange place, a string of little rooms in which, thanks to the talent of a removal man with a magic touch, they had managed to fit in heavy, cumbersome furniture. Paintings hung on the walls; other canvases, sitting on the floor in corners, were waiting for a friendly hand to put them up. Apollinaire himself was clumsiness personified, incapable of hammering a nail without piercing three holes in his hand.

The room that the poet preferred was the dining room: dark, tiny, with lopsided chairs and a table set with chipped plates. In winter, there was a fire in the chimney. There was also a kitchen and an office in which a work table faced a narrow window. An inner staircase led to the bedroom. Through a glass door, one could walk out onto a tiny terrace with a view of the roofs of Paris.

This is where Apollinaire convalesced from his wound, and suffered from attacks of emphysema. The death in the war of his childhood friend René Dalize, to whom he had dedicated *Calligrammes*, had affected him deeply. Dalize was the companion of all his Paris evenings – with his ever-present umbrella under his arm, he used to stop in front of mirrors and sigh, staring at himself, 'A fine sabotage of an existence!'

Apollinaire at this time was at the height of his fame, recognized everywhere, constantly solicited, inspired by a thousand new projects. But he had left some of his *joie de vivre* at the front: he was worried about the future, and became more and more irascible. When his friends came to dinner at his house, they were careful not to touch anything, in order not to upset him. They glanced anxiously at the artilleryman's helmet, with the hole in it from the bullet to his forehead, crowning the table in the hallway.

In January 1918, a pulmonary congestion put the poet back in hospital, but he was released soon afterwards. By then, the nature of the war had begun to change.

PARIS–NICE

At dessert, champagne was uncorked 120 kilometres from Paris, or rather, above Paris, that evening. The entire company went down to continue their witty conversation in the wine cellar.

Max Jacob

In the spring of 1918, Paris was hungry and cold, but not sleepy. Everyone had an empty stomach, which did not prevent them from attending the theatre, cinema or concerts. Max Jacob wrote his poems on wrapping paper, but managed to find cigars for Picasso. In the evening, the night-birds got their hands on all the bottles they could find, then looked for places, either on foot or by taxi, where they could drink away all thoughts of their poverty. Cars would roll along at a snail's pace until one would finally pass the other, when one of its passengers had come up with an idea for somewhere to go. Everyone met up here and there: sometimes in the bakery on the rue de la Gaîté, sometimes in the back room of a department store on the right bank, where bottles and food were shared by all.

But in March, after two years of a chiefly defensive strategy, the Germans launched massive attacks on the French and English lines. The front was pushed back. Foch kept proclaiming that the country wouldn't lose an inch of ground, and Clemenceau exhorted the soldiers to hold out at any price, but the reality was that the war was now only fifty miles from Paris. At night, Big Bertha fired away. It was frightening: there were Krupp cannons thirty yards long, dragged along on railings, capable of projecting missiles twenty miles high and seventy miles in distance. The Germans called them the Pariser Kanonen. The cannonballs touched the rue de Grenelle, the rue de Vaugirard, the church of Saint Gervais and the Champ de Mars. One of them landed on the rue Liancourt. Another exploded at Port-Royal, in a Baudelocque maternity room, killing several children and their mothers. Half a million Parisians fled the capital for the south of France. Among them were Soutine, Foujita, Cendrars, Kisling, Modigliani, Jeanne, Zborowski and his wife.

The last group mentioned left not only to seek shelter from the bombing, but also because they hoped that the sun in Nice would help Amedeo's tuberculosis, which had got worse, and that it would be good for Jeanne, who was pregnant. When she learned of her daughter's state, Eudoxie Hébuterne decided to come along on the trip: there was no question of leaving her daughter alone in the hands of this badly-brought-up, useless, Jewish artist with no talent ... Once they all arrived in Nice, tempers flared, with the result that the future father had to go and stay at a hotel while Jeanne and her mother moved into an apartment on the rue Masséna.

Modigliani stayed in the south of France for almost two years. Besides the beneficial effects the sun was having on his condition, he couldn't come home any sooner as his identity papers had been stolen. He painted a lot, and drank a lot in the company of the many friends he found there: Survage, the sculptor Archipenko, Paul Guillaume and the painter Osterlind.

One day Osterlind took him to meet Renoir. Crippled by rheumatism, the painter could scarcely move from his wheelchair. He painted with brushes attached to his hands; thanks to a system of pulleys, he was able to raise and lower the canvas. He worked tirelessly in order to give as many paintings as possible to charity before dying. He also painted for the benefit of the poor children in families around him, but he stayed away from dealers. He still received visits from a few friends, like Monet, who made the journey to see him one last time. Paralysed in his wheelchair, smoking cigarettes which had to be placed between his lips, incapable of moving unless carried, he welcomed his eighty-year-old companion with these words: 'So, Monet, I hear you're losing your sight?'

Renoir also opened his door to young artists, which is why he received Modigliani. But the Italian wouldn't open his mouth.

'Go and take a look at my latest nudes,' Renoir suggested.

Amedeo and Osterlind went to the studio. The Italian looked at the canvases without commenting. Back at Renoir's side, he didn't say a word.

'So?'

So, nothing. Osterlind gave his opinion. For some unknown reason, Amedeo remained silent.

'Did you notice the colour of the skin?'

Silence.

'The curve of the breasts?'

Nothing.

'And those buttocks? When I paint buttocks, I feel like I'm touching them ...'

Modigliani suddenly straightened up, looked at the old painter and declared drily, 'I don't like buttocks.'

Then he left, leaving Renoir puzzled and Osterlind crimson with embarrassment.

He went to join Zborowski, who was spending his days going from door to door, trying to sell Modigliani's paintings in expensive hotels. When he saw that Modigliani was no more successful here than elsewhere, and that the idle rich of the South weren't buying much more than the Parisian dealers, he returned to the capital.

In Paris, Apollinaire had been released from hospital. He had left the bureau of censorship for the Ministry of the Colonies. On 2 May, he married Jacqueline Kolb. A religious ceremony took place at the church of St Thomas of Aquinas. The bride's witnesses were Ambroise Vollard and Gabrielle Buffet-Picabia; the groom's were the writer Lucien Descaves and Pablo Picasso.

Two months later, the Spaniard would be making his own appointment at the town hall. Gaby and Irène Lagut had turned him down, but Olga Khokhlova accepted. Diaghilev had warned Picasso: 'With a Russian woman, one must marry her.' More easily said than done, given the young woman's situation: her papers were not in order, and it was difficult to have them regularized because of the Russian revolution. Apollinaire intervened, calling on Lucien Descaves' brother, who worked at the prefecture. The marriage was set for 12 July 1918, at the town hall of the eighteenth arrondissement. When Max Jacob received the letter from Picasso announcing that he had chosen him as a witness, he thought he would faint with joy – all the more so as the wedding fell on his birthday. He ran to the Hôtel Lutétia, where the future bride had a suite. He didn't find her there. If he went to Montrouge, where Picasso still lived, he feared he might miss the future groom. He thus sent an ecstatic *pneumatique*:

> Dear godfather,
> Only death could keep me from being at the town hall of the 18th arrondissement on Friday at 11 o'clock; and in that case, even as I expired my last sentiment would be regret at having missed the wedding.

He was there. At eleven o'clock in the morning, Pablo Diego José Francisco de Paula Juan Nepomuceno Mariá de los Remedios Crispin Crispiniano Santísima Trinidad Ruiz y Picasso, born in Malaga, Spain on 25 October 1881, artist painter, married Olga Khokhlova, born in Niégine, Russia on 17 June 1891, no profession, in the presence of their witnesses: Guillaume Apollinaire, thirty-seven, man of letters, decorated by the war cross; Max Jacob, forty-two, man of letters; Valerien Irtchenko Svetloff, fifty-four, cavalry captain; Jean Cocteau, twenty-seven, man of letters. The religious service took place at the Russian church on the rue Daru, amidst incense and Orthodox chants.

A few weeks later, Picasso left his house in Montrouge to move in with Olga at the Hôtel Lutétia. He was there on the evening of 9 November 1918. The war was almost over. In the afternoon, he had been walking under the arcades of the rue de Rivoli when a war-widow crossed his path. A gust of wind blew the woman's crêpe over her face. Arriving back at the hotel, Picasso walked over to a mirror in his room and stared at his face for a long time. The chance encounter in the afternoon had upset him. He felt somehow that it did not augur well. He picked up a pencil and traced the face he saw in the mirror. Just then, the telephone rang. He left his drawing to answer it. After he hung up, he sat without moving for a long time. Then he returned to his self-portrait.

He had just been informed of the death of Guillaume Apollinaire.

THE END OF THE GAME

We won't go back to the woods again
The laurels have been felled
The lovers are going to die
and their mistresses only lie

Guillaume Apollinaire

On 3 November 1918, Guillaume left his house with Vlaminck and his wife, whom he was taking out to lunch. On the Boulevard Saint Germain, the two men talked about the poet's latest play, *Couleurs du temps*, which the Art et Liberté company was to perform two weeks later. Vlaminck was painting the sets. When they separated, Apollinaire headed off towards the *Excelsior*, a paper to which he regularly contributed.

That night, he had an attack of fever. He lay down in his room under the painting by Marie Laurencin, which showed him next to Max Jacob and Picasso. He felt ill, but in a different way from usual. He didn't want to go to the hospital again; he had been there far too often since he had received his head wound.

The fever rose. Guillaume was sweating. Jacqueline was alarmed, but didn't call the doctor yet. They waited.

The next day, Max Jacob came. Then Picasso. They soon came back. They went to see Jean Cocteau, on the rue d'Anjou, to ask him to alert Dr Capmas. Maybe it was a pulmonary congestion, maybe something else. They didn't know.

It was actually Spanish influenza. The disease was said to have been brought from Asia by Spanish sailors, but in reality, it came from the United States and had contaminated Europe through the arriving soldiers. It laid men out even faster than the war; in two years, there were twenty-five million dead. On the Chemin des Dames, generals arranged ceasefires simply in order to evacuate the victims. In Paris, the funeral processions followed each other to the cemeteries. One of them had taken away Edmond Rostand.

Guillaume Apollinaire felt death approaching. At the front, he had rubbed shoulders with it every day and had never been afraid. Here, panic overtook him. He begged Dr Capmas to save him. He didn't want to die this way; he couldn't fathom it. He had managed to survive a shell which had shattered his skull: how could he die just from a little germ?

His friends came, and returned. Jacqueline Apollinaire, Serge Férat, and Max Jacob didn't leave his bedside. There were flowers everywhere in the house. Outside, the sky hung grey and leaden over the roofs of Paris. Death came to 202, Boulevard Saint Germain, on 9 November 1918, at five o'clock in the evening.

How slowly the hours pass like a funeral procession.

Guillaume Apollinaire lay on the bed, dressed in his officer's uniform, his kepi by his side. The war was almost over. There were more than eight million dead and twenty million wounded. The poet was borne under a tricoloured canopy to the church of St Thomas of Aquinas, then to the Père Lachaise cemetery.

A section of the 237th territorial army performed the military honours. Mme de Kostrowitzky headed the funeral party. Picasso was next to her, followed by Max Jacob, André Salmon, Blaise Cendrars, Pierre Mac Orlan, Paul Fort, Jean Cocteau, Metzinger, Fernand Léger, Jacques Doucet, Paul Léautaud, Alfred Valette, Rachilde, Léon-Paul Fargue, Paul Guillaume, and many others. The armistice had been signed two days previously. In the streets, the crowd was celebrating the victory, shouting 'Death to Guillaume!'

They meant the Kaiser, not the poet.

> The shells miaow a love to die for
> Vanished loves are sweeter than others
> It's raining Shepherdess it's raining and the blood will stop
> The shells miaow Listen to our people sing
> Purple Love hailed by those about to perish.

On the evening of the funeral, Pablo Picasso left the Hôtel Lutétia and returned to his house in Montrouge. He collected his belongings. The next day he sent a letter to Gertrude Stein to tell her that he was moving to the rue La Boétie. Once again, he was crossing the Seine.

III
MONTPARNASSE, OPEN CITY

KIKI

Kiki? She deserved her reputation as the queen of Montparnasse.

André Salmon

A cold sun shone on peacetime Paris, where demobilization was in full swing. Tourists were arriving, the first of them the Americans from the expeditionary corps: they had discovered France in wartime and were eager to return, no longer in uniform but in civilian attire, to experience its pleasures. The bistros on the Boulevard du Montparnasse were full, both the older ones and the newer ones, such as the café du Parnasse, which thumbed its nose at the Rotonde.

Libion observed joylessly. It wasn't competition which worried him, but the authorities. He had already been fined or ordered to close his doors several times: firstly because deserters, or those suspected of being deserters, drank at the bar, then because Bolsheviks and their sympathizers sat at the counter, like Kikoïne, denounced for his relations with the Russian revolutionaries. Now it was because the smokers were smoking too much: Libion bought cigarettes on the black market, it was said, in order to be able to offer a few puffs to his poorer customers. He had been reprimanded for this, and had threatened to sell the establishment, which he would ultimately do. Everything seemed to be falling apart.

He noticed a curious individual, whom he knew he had already seen in Soutine's company, and whom he recognized, for she wore a man's hat, an old threadbare cape, and shoes that were much too big for her. She was a young girl, eighteen at the most, with a pale complexion, and short, very dark hair. She had a particular kind of beauty, a mixture of vulgarity, vivacity, and a verbal audacity that was echoed in her gestures, her bearing, her smiles. But this time, she didn't react when Kisling, turning towards Libion, asked in a loud voice, 'So who's the new whore?'

She just took a match out of her pocket, scratched it, blew out the flame, and delicately blackened her left eyebrow.

'So? Who's the whore?'

The young woman still didn't respond. She waited until Kisling repeated the question once more, then began to shower carefully considered insults upon him, to which the Polish artist responded by calling her a tart and accusing her of having the clap. After this, the painter hired the young girl to work as a model for him for a full three months, an unusual arrangement at the time.

These were the first steps of Alice Prin in Montparnasse. Nicknamed 'Kiki', then later 'Kiki of Montparnasse' – queen of the neighbourhood, a lucky charm for artists, a legendary figure, known the world over – she would pose for Kisling, Foujita, Man Ray, Per Krogh, Soutine, Derain, and many others. She would become the protégée of all the painters in the Vavin neighbourhood and the first important figure of this post-war Montparnasse, whose sulphurous reputation she would help to build – known as she was, as far afield as America, for her antics and high spirits.

Until then, Kiki had not had much luck in life: she had known more misery than happiness. A native of the Côte d'Or, she had emerged so quickly from her mother's womb that she was literally born in the street, before finding a more comfortable and appropriate place to stay. The father, a wood and coal merchant, had disappeared long before the birth.

Born out of wedlock: this was the first blot on Kiki's existence, and also, naturally, on her mother's. The moral rigidity of the provinces at the time soon convinced her to go off to Paris: she would stay in a Baudelocque maternity house, where the profession of obstetrics seemed to be trying hard to dissuade unwed mothers from ever becoming pregnant again, by disgusting them so much the first time.

Little Alice thus lived with her grandmother along with a band of cousins, all born out of wedlock like herself. Injustice and poverty reigned. The grandfather mended roads for one and a half francs a day, and the grandmother cleaned houses for the bourgeois inhabitants of the town. The mother sent what little money she could. The schoolmistress had no fondness for the poor, so that Kiki spent her mornings at the back of the class and her afternoons condemned to stand in the corner. In the evening, when there were no more beans to eat at home, she and her little cousin would go knocking on the door of the nuns. This experience would not make the young girl sympathetic to religion...

At the age of twelve, Kiki went off to Paris to join her mother, who had called for her. The little girl knew this woman, who had come to see her once a year, much less well than her grandmother, who had brought her up and whom she loved. In the train, she drowned her tears in her salami sandwich and red wine. Her neighbours in the compartment watched the spectacle with interest.

In Paris, little Alice discovered horse-drawn cabs, and grand avenues, all clean and straight. 'Tell me, mama, do they put wax on them to make them shine like that?'

This made her mother laugh, though she didn't have much of a sense of humour. She had left the Baudelocque establishment for a printing press where she became a linotypist. Wanting her daughter to follow in this profession, she sent her to the communal school on the rue de Vaugirard. Kiki stayed for just long enough to become permanently disgusted with formal schooling: 'I'm over thirteen. I've just left school for ever. I know how to read and to count, and that's all!'[1]

The young girl began working at the printing press as an apprentice binder. For fifty centimes a week, she bound the *Kama Sutra*. Then, in her own way, she participated in the war effort. She was hired in a shoe factory which recycled soldiers' shoes. When they arrived from the front, little Kiki disinfected them, softened them with oil and reshaped them with a hammer. From shoes, she moved on to soldering, then to dirigibles, aeroplanes, and grenades, though she still lived in the direst poverty. She chewed away at lumpy lentil dishes offered by the soup kitchens, and wore oversized men's shoes that she had found in a dustbin.

At fourteen and a half, she was fed, clothed, and lodged by a baker on the Place Saint Charles in the fifteenth arrondissement. Up at five o'clock to serve the workers leaving for work; off at seven o'clock to deliver bread to the floors where a few lazy souls were still asleep; at nine, housework, errands, cooking, and helping the baker's son. He was already a healthy adolescent; at the age of fifteen, he showed off his virility with all the arrogance of youth.

'Do you want to . . .'

'Not yet.'

But when, through her bedroom window, little Alice saw lovers kissing in the square, she was troubled. 'I felt all funny! I rolled around on my bed and it felt good . . . then I got frightened.'[2]

The frightened feeling would pass. The young girl decided to conquer her fear by taking the boy from over the road to the back of the shop. Their kisses and caresses were like paradise. But she was still afraid of going any further. It would be better to wait a little . . .

Kiki wore make-up; at her age, this wasn't done. Coming across her one day as she was painting her face, the bakerwoman cried out, 'Little tart!'

It was one remark too many. Her employer received a punch in the stomach, and the young pugilist took off.

She arrived next in the studio of a sculptor, for whom she posed – nude. The first session went well, but the second ended with a terrible scene. Having learned in the neighbourhood that her daughter was compromising herself with a man much older than herself, for the sake of an art she knew nothing about, Kiki's mother turned up, saw for herself, and shrieked, 'Whore! Miserable whore!'

This was the end of all relations between mother and daughter. The mother returned to the man she was later to marry, a linotypist younger than herself who had once been a soldier. The daughter ended up lodging with a singer from the Opéra-Comique.

She became a maid – but as she was quite talented at avoiding work, her musician friend soon sent her packing, and Kiki took refuge with her friend Eva, who lived in a tiny room at Plaisance. The bed was big, but not big enough for three – for from time to time, Eva received visits from a Corsican worker who was older than her. For two francs a day and a piece of sausage, he was welcome to the bed and to the bed's occupant.

'Watch,' Eva advised her friend, 'so you'll learn.'

Kiki sat down and followed the proceedings. She waited for the fever to pass: it didn't make much of an impression on her. She was pleased because, as she looked on, she could munch away to her heart's content on the sausage that the couple had forgotten.

But she began to wonder if she was normal.

'Why?' asked Eva.

'I'm still a virgin...'

'At the age of fifteen?'

'I've only done a little fooling around...'

'That's terrible. Come along with me, we'll solve the problem.'

The two girls went out walking on the Boulevard de Strasbourg. Eva promised that she would find an older man for her friend.

'Older guys are better the first time, they don't hurt you so much...'

Kiki supposed it was true: she knew a little about older men. Once or twice she had taken one with her behind the Montparnasse station, not far from the shack where she lodged. For two francs, she'd let him look at her breasts. For five francs, he could touch them. Never more, and never lower: Kiki was not a whore, she just wanted to have something to eat.

The first day, on the Boulevard de Strasbourg, Eva found an acceptable man of about fifty. She introduced him to Kiki: he smelled good, and he was willing. He bought them café-crèmes and croissants. The go-between slipped away, and Kiki followed the lucky man. He took her to where he lived, in Ménilmontant. He was a performer, a clown; he showed her costumes that were as fine as those of Fratellini. He fed her roast pork and served her good wine, after which he washed her, dressed her in a nightgown and put her to bed. Kiki was almost in love. She let herself be tucked in, listened to the lullabies that the clown played for her on his guitar, and fell asleep after some little intimate exchanges that were not at all unpleasant.

hadn't lost anything yet. Next, she met a painter called Robert. He bought
her a hot chocolate and took her home with him. He undressed first. His
socks almost ruined everything; they were cut off at the end. Kiki went
into fits of laughter and couldn't stop.

'I didn't know mittens for feet existed!'

He was annoyed. 'But they're all the rage at the moment...'

They tried, they almost managed – but not quite, not completely.
Robert had an idea. He came home one evening with two women he had
picked up at the Dôme.

'Watch how it's done, and learn.'

Kiki watched. Once, twice, three times. But if she was good at learning
lessons, she was bad at doing homework. Robert lost patience: he sent
her out to walk the street on the Boulevard Sébastopol. He wasn't far
from telling her that it was like going out to fight on the front, except
that there weren't any Germans there, but Yankees, Allies. Kiki didn't
want to. She preferred to endure the blows of her painter–pimp, who
fortunately disappeared one day and never came back.

She changed lodgings, lived in a dump on the rue de Vaugirard, a shed
behind Montparnasse. She discovered the Rotonde, with its painters and
sculptors. Like all of Libion's half-lodgers, she washed in the café's toilets
and slipped the few coins she possessed into the slot machine, hoping to
win a croissant in exchange.

But she found something better still: Soutine. Sometimes he would
house her at the Cité Falguière, burning half of the wood in the studio
to try to keep her warm. He introduced her to other artists, who initiated
the young girl into the pleasures of certain substances, which transported
her to delicious heights, but unfortunately left her still far from the
seventh heaven which she dearly wanted to experience.

In the end it was a Polish painter, Maurice Mendjizky, who turned out
to be the angel of grace, relieving her of what she no longer wanted and
giving her the nickname Kiki – a tender declination of Alice in Greek.[3]
Mendjizky was the first man in her life. She posed for him, and then for
those who would become her best friends, Kisling and Foujita.

The first time she went to the home of the Japanese artist, he was still
in his studio on the rue Delambre. When she entered, she was barefoot
in an overcoat and a red dress.

'Take off your clothes,' said the painter.

She removed her coat: there was nothing underneath. The illusion of
the red dress was made by a little square of cloth she had pinned to the
neckline of the coat. Foujita stared at his model, fascinated by her hairless
pubic area. He came up to her and examined the skin.

'You don't have any hair?'

'It grows while I pose.'

Kiki picked up a black pencil which was lying on the table and drew some makeshift pubic hair.

'How's that?'

'Amusing,' Foujita reassured her.

Kiki pushed him away from the easel and took his place. 'Don't move.'

The model picked up the coloured pencils and, sucking on them, biting them, tried to do a portrait of the artist who was supposed to paint her. When it was finished, she said, 'The fee for my modelling session, please.'

Stupefied by her audacity, Foujita paid. Kiki took the drawing and left. 'Goodbye, sir!'

She went to the Dôme, where an American collector bought her portrait of Foujita. The next day, the Japanese painter found her again at the Rotonde.

'You have to come back to my studio, and let me paint you!'

'All right,' said Kiki.

Foujita executed a very large canvas: *Reclining nude of Kiki*. He had never done anything so imposing. He sent it to the Salon d'Automne. It was talked about in all the press, and he was congratulated by ministers. The work was bought for eight thousand francs, an unheard-of sum. The painter invited his model to celebrate the event. At the end of the meal, he gave her a few banknotes. She left the table. When she reappeared in the studio of the rue Delambre, a few hours later, she was wearing a new hat, dress and coat, and shoes as shiny as glass.

'I want to paint you in that outfit,' cried Foujita.

'No,' said Kiki. 'I have to meet someone else.'

'A painter?'

'Kisling.'

At the time, Montparnasse had three Kikis: Kiki van Dongen, Kiki Kisling, and Kiki Kiki. What else could Foujita do but bow to the logic of the homonym?

DEATH COMES TO MONTPARNASSE

He was a child of the stars, and for him, reality didn't exist.

Léopold Zborowski

Kiki Kisling always waited for Kiki on the hour. When he said nine o'clock, it meant nine o'clock. For him – for her, it meant forty minutes later. This gave rise to some severe and noisy scenes, which Mme Salomon, with her delicate ears, complained about. The two Kikis' fights were carried out in insults, an art at which both were great masters.

But they also loved each other tenderly. When Madame Kiki was sad, Monsieur Kiki would try to get her to laugh. He sang and danced for her, urging her to imitate him. Each tried to see who could make the most noise. But they shut up when the neighbours arrived. Sometimes it would be Zborowski, other times just someone who was curious to see what was going on.

Sometimes it was Modigliani. He had come back from Nice in May 1919, followed three weeks later by Jeanne. In November of the previous year, a little girl had been born, whom they had also named Jeanne. They had had to find her a wet nurse as, according to the account given by Blaise Cendrars' first wife, neither the father, nor the mother, nor even the grandmother knew how to take care of her.

When she joined her daughter's father in Paris, Jeanne was pregnant again. On 7 July 1919, Modigliani promised in writing to marry her as soon as he had obtained the papers necessary for the administrative proceedings. This paper was countersigned by Jeanne herself, by Zborowski and by Lunia Czechowska. Many years later, Lunia admitted to Modigliani's daughter that she had often babysat for her in the Zborowskis' apartment on the rue Joseph Bara.

Modigliani would sometimes ring and ring at the door at night, dead drunk, to have news of his daughter. Lunia shouted out of the window at him not to make a noise, and he would quieten down, sit for a few minutes on the steps, and be off again.[1]

He still drank too much, and he never stopped coughing. He discovered Isidore Ducasse, alias the Comte de Lautréamont, whom he read sitting next to André Breton on a bench on the Avenue de l'Observatoire. The founder of the review *Littérature* published the *Poésies* in the second issue of the magazine, after copying them out at the Bibliothèque Nationale.

He received models in his studio on the rue de la Grande Chaumière, sketched a line, took a sip of rum, dragged his feet over a floor black with coal. When he went out, it was to sit in cafés. He would exchange a portrait for a drink, hand out some of the coins he had earned to those poorer than himself, swallow a sandwich, cough, drink, follow a group of friends, trip on the stones in front of the church of Alésia, fall down, and fall asleep in the rain.

He looked for Zborowski to borrow a little change from him, forgetting that Zborowski was in London for an exhibition of the work of his friend and client. He crossed the Seine and climbed up to Montmartre, where he greeted Utrillo and Suzanne Valadon, came back down towards the left bank and wrote a hasty note to his mother on the pre-stamped cards that she had sent him.

He was sick. No one ever heard him complain about the tuberculosis that was consuming him, not even the tremulously fragile Jeanne Hébuterne, whom he protected with his silence. For months, Zborowski had been trying to persuade him to go to the sanatorium in Switzerland for care. And each time, Amedeo answered with the same words: 'Stop preaching at me.'

But death was hovering, and he probably knew it. He drank to alleviate his suffering and pain, and the poverty and misery that had been his lot for so long. In the outside world, the war had been over for more than a year. Inside him, it had dug its trenches and cleared the ground for a final assault.

One January evening in 1920, Amedeo left the Rotonde with friends in the pouring rain. He headed off towards the Tombe-Issoire, waited for two hours in the cold, and left for Denfert, where he sat down under the Lion of Belfort. He coughed. But he didn't have the strength to drink any more. He came home, swaying as he walked, clutching onto walls for support, until he reached the rue de la Grande Chaumière. He climbed the narrow staircase leading to the studio, and fell onto the bed by Jeanne's side. He was spitting blood.

On 22 January, the painter Ortiz de Zarate, who lived in the same building, knocked at the door. He had just come back to Paris after a week's absence. He hadn't had any news of Modigliani. Nor had Zborowski, who was also sick and in bed, and nor had anyone else. Ortiz knocked, and knocked again. He couldn't hear any noise inside the apartment. The

Chilean waited a few more minutes, then gathering his strength, he kicked
in the door. Amedeo was on the bed, in Jeanne's arms. He moaned softly.
He called out to Italy: 'Cara Italia'. The heating was extinguished. An icy
veil covered the tins of sardines which lay on the floor along with the
empty bottles, in the lugubrious early morning silence.

Ortiz de Zarate ran down the steps four at a time to fetch a doctor. The
doctor ordered the sick man to be transferred immediately to the Hôpital
de la Charité on the rue Jacob.

Two days later, on 24 January 1920, tubercular meningitis finally won
the battle. It was quarter to nine in the evening. The news spread through
Montmartre and Montparnasse, and friends came from all over Paris. They
lined up in front of the hospital: painters, poets, dealers, models – everyone
was there, incredulous, horrified. Modigliani was dead. Modigliani, dead!

On the other side of the walls, in a room which was nothing but a
tomb, Kisling leaned over his friend's body. His hands were white with
plaster. Helped by the Swiss painter Conrad Moricand, he took the
impression for the death mask. The mask fell apart, taking with it pieces
of flesh. Lipchitz was called in to help collect the fragments; he would set
the mask in bronze.

Very early the next day, other friends came, accompanying a hieratic
shadow who broke through the crowd on the pavements. She was pale,
thin, tiny. Her hands on her stomach, she had the loping walk of pregnant
women. Jeanne Hébuterne had not slept at home on the rue de la Grande
Chaumière, but in a hotel. When she left, the cleaning woman had
discovered a stiletto under the pillow.

She was led from corridor to corridor until they reached the morgue,
where she asked to be left alone. She remained there for a long time. She
cut off a lock of her hair and placed it on the stomach of the father of
her two children. Then she left. No one could persuade her to go to a
clinic, where a room had been reserved for her. She went back to her
parents' home at 8 bis, rue Amyot. She spent the end of the day there,
and the beginning of the night. At three o'clock in the morning, she got
up, walked across the apartment, went into the salon, opened the window,
climbed over the railing, and threw herself into space.

She fell five flights.

The next day, a worker discovered the dismembered body. He gathered
it in his arms and brought it upstairs. No one knows whether it was her
father or brother who opened the door, nor why whoever it was asked
the man to take the corpse to 8, rue de la Grande Chaumière, where the
deceased had lived. One can only imagine the horror, the unspeakable
words, the fear of the two men facing each other.

The workman came back downstairs and laid the body on his wheelbarrow. Rue Lhomond. Rue Claude Bernard. Rue des Feuillantines. Rue

du Val-de-Grâce. Boulevard du Montparnasse. Rue de la Grande Chaumière. At no. 8, the concierge refused to let the man and his charge inside; she demanded to see a paper from the police. The man picked up his wheelbarrow again, with Jeanne lying in it. He went to the police station on the rue Delambre, or the one on the rue Campagne-Première. He obtained the paper requested, crossed the Boulevard du Montparnasse once again, and trudged back to the rue de la Grande Chaumière.

Friends were notified. Jeanne Léger laid the body out on a Russian sheet donated by Marie Vassilieff. Salmon came, then Kisling, then Carco; all of Montmartre, and all of Montparnasse. The next day, Jeanne remained alone as Modigliani was buried. Kisling paid for the funeral and notified the family. Emanuele, Amedeo's brother, a Socialist deputy, wrote, 'Bury him like a prince.'

And so he was, better than a prince in fact. All the painters, poets, and models pooled their resources to buy flowers. The artists collected some of their paintings to sell, to help support little Jeanne Modigliani, fatherless and motherless, who would be taken care of by Modigliani's family. Everyone was thinking of the child who wasn't there, as a large crowd, closely packed and silent, accompanied her father on a last journey.

At every corner, policemen saluted as the floats, flowers, and wreaths went by. The art dealers began to sniff the scent of good business. In this crowd brought together in such tragic circumstances, they sought out those who owned works by Modigliani. One of them approached Francis Carco, who was walking with the others, and offered to buy the paintings he owned by the dead painter. Fortune was finally knocking at the door, though it was the door of a tomb.

Modigliani was buried at Père Lachaise, and Jeanne Hébuterne would be buried at Bagneux. Her funeral was the next day, very early, just before eight o'clock, to avoid crowds and chaos. A pitiful funeral procession gathered in the rue de la Grande Chaumière. The coffin was narrow. The family accompanied it quickly, furtively, hoping that the news would not spread.

But it was already out. At the end of the rue de la Grande Chaumière two taxis were parked, alongside a private car. Salmon, Zborowski, Kisling and their wives were there, with white flowers.

Ten years later, the Modigliani family would finally persuade the Hébuterne family to let Jeanne be reunited with Amedeo at Père Lachaise – by then he was no longer just a poor, unlucky, and unknown Jewish artist.

Père Lachaise was, of course, also the place where another dead departed figure reposed: the artist of words who had so often used his pen to help the poets of forms and colours – Guillaume Apollinaire.

Montparnasse without the one, Montparnasse without the other ... It was not just the war that was ending, it was an entire generation. A moment in history, and a chapter of a story. Their story.

COMING TO BLOWS AT DROUOT

I wish I could live like a poor
man, but with a lot of money.

Pablo Picasso

There had been the Montmartre of the Chat Noir, Toulouse-Lautrec, Depaquit, Poulbot, Valadon and Utrillo; the Montmartre of the Bateau Lavoir, workers' overalls, pistols fired in the air, and parties at the Lapin Agile. Then the artists had crossed the Seine to shake hands with the poets: Alfred Jarry, Paul Fort and Blaise Cendrars. But the war had scattered the groups, leaving them dispersed like debris from an explosion. Montparnasse had known the hardships of lean times, clandestine celebrations, reunions of friends at peaceful exhibitions. But it was about to harvest what Montmartre had planted. Life was resuming a happier course. The armistice had been signed, and people were ready to forget the war. The death of Modigliani was the last tragedy of the age. He was part of the original fabric, and that fabric was undergoing a metamorphosis. Yesterday would soon be a memory. The surrealists were coming. Like many others, painters and poets were getting out of their horse-drawn carts to climb into spluttering automobiles, headed straight towards the future.

The artists of the Bateau Lavoir, the Fauves and cubists, had been pioneers of sorts. But Picasso had deserted. Max Jacob was preparing to retire to the banks of the Loire river. Van Dongen now wore felt jackets and immaculately tailored white shirts; he was busy playing the man of fashion on the boardwalks of Deauville, strolling about with countesses and marquesses on his arm, who later thronged to the artist's studio at Denfert-Rochereau to pose with all their jewels, or to give themselves the impression of slumming it at night at the outrageous parties that the Dutchman loved to give.

Derain was about to turn over a new leaf. He had a new hobby in his Bugatti collection, and plenty of new property with – in succession or simultaneously – a private home on the rue du Douanier Rousseau, an apartment on the rue d'Assas, another on the rue de Varennes, a studio on the rue Bonaparte and a house in Chambourcy. Until Ambassador Abetz had the unfortunate idea of inviting them both on the same sinister trip to Nazi Germany, the two great Fauve artists of Chatou hadn't seen each other in a long time.

At la Tourillière, between the Beauce and Perche regions, Vlaminck kept an eye out for his enemies (of whom he had many) with his buckshot gun in hand. Dressed in tweed, he watched over his estates, and inveighed against Picasso, Derain, Kisling and half of the earth. When his rage became too great, he climbed into his Chenard and calmed his nerves by careering around on country roads, striking terror into the hearts of chickens.

Juan Gris kept his distance from the others as he always had. He often went to the south, where the climate was helpful for his asthma, thought by the doctors to be linked to tuberculosis. It may well have been, but the latter in the end was less dangerous than the leukaemia which carried him off in 1927.

Braque, Derain's neighbour on the rue du Douanier Rousseau, had drifted away from Picasso, and from all the others as well.

Fifteen years had elapsed since the time of the Zut and the Austin Fox: once-empty wallets now bulged with money. Yet despite the houses, the estates and the magnificent cars, success would never totally transform these people. They may have become bourgeois, but never conventional. Daniel-Henry Kahnweiler, who knew them all at the beginning, and most of them for many years afterwards, often asserted:

> None of them, not even Derain and especially not Picasso, changed their style of life fundamentally ... What we know of the lives – not the private lives but the domestic lives of these painters – is that, all in all, they had very few needs. They didn't start to live like the bourgeoisie as far as daily life was concerned.[1]

But they didn't like each other very much any more and didn't seek out meetings. One event, though, would bring them together: the sale of Kahnweiler's collections of paintings. Kahnweiler had been the cubists' chief dealer before 1914.

His possessions, like those of Uhde and other residents of German extraction, had been sequestered during the five years of the war. The treaty of Versailles had now been signed and, as Germany baulked at paying the war reparations which had been forced upon her, there was talk of indemnifying creditors by selling possessions taken from the enemy. In the domain of painting, some were against it – Kahnweiler, obviously – and others for it, Léonce Rosenberg for one. The reasoning of the latter was simultaneously just and faulty. He thought he would preserve his position as prime advocate for the cubists by preventing the German dealer from retrieving the several hundred works which constituted his reserve. Moral considerations apart, this reasoning was probably sound. But he also thought that the market value of the cubist canvases would rocket, a judgement that turned out to be misguided, the market having been rapidly saturated by the sale of some eight hundred paintings.

Léonce Rosenberg was supported by all those who, fifteen years after the refusal to exhibit Braque at the Salon des Indépendants of 1908, hoped and believed that this last blow to cubism would get rid of it for good. Their self-interest conspired with their stupidity, and provided a prop for their obscurantism.

Kahnweiler returned to Paris in February 1920, one month after Modigliani's death. He went into business with a childhood friend, which enabled him to get around the problem of his nationality and to open the Simon gallery on the rue d'Astorg. Once this was done, he set out to achieve a double goal: to renew his ties with the painters whom he had lost because of the war, and to contain the threat represented by the sale of works that had been sequestered.

He had lost Picasso, and wouldn't retrieve him again so quickly. There was a double bone of contention between them. The Spaniard reproached the German for not having obtained French nationality, as he had advised him to do; this would have allowed him to avoid the impounding of his paintings, which had also damaged the artist. In addition, the dealer owed the painter twenty thousand francs, a sum which he was not able to reimburse just then.

The two men would not see each other again until after this debt was paid, around 1925. Even then, Picasso would not leave Paul Rosenberg, who had succeeded his brother Léonce.

But the other painters, Gris chief among them, remained faithful. Some of them would only be so for a few years; Vlaminck, Derain, Braque and Léger all ended by going over to the Rosenberg camp.

Neither Kahnweiler nor any of his friends could prevent the sale of works that had been confiscated by the French state. He simply managed to buy back in secret the paintings to which he was most attached – though none of these was signed by Picasso, their quarrel continuing. His nationality kept him from acting openly, so he created a syndicate with some friends and members of his family who worked to further his interests.

At Drouot, between 1921 and 1923, five sales were held of works in the collection acquired before the war by Daniel-Henry Kahnweiler: four sales of works from his gallery and one from his personal collection. They were a disaster, in every respect. Robert Desnos, who bought a charcoal drawing presented as a work by Braque when it was actually a Picasso, was scandalized on several counts:

> The paintings were piled up in no particular order, rolled up drawings were folded in boxes, others were carefully sealed so we couldn't look at them, yet others piled up in baskets or hidden behind the stage. All of this in an indescribably dirty and disorderly state, justifying the worst recriminations from the painters concerned: Messieurs Braque, Derain, Vlaminck, Gris, Léger, Manolo and Picasso. The way the paintings were hung, in particular, demonstrated an incompetence or a commercial servility which deserved whatever insults it received.[2]

At the first sale, on 13 June 1921, Braque opened fire first. If Gertrude Stein is to be believed, he had been more or less chosen by his peers as the one to lead the attack on Léonce Rosenberg, the supposed connoisseur. It couldn't be Gris or Picasso, who were Spanish, Marie Laurencin, German since her marriage, or the Russian sculptor Lipchitz. Vlaminck didn't have the necessary qualifications, having mostly fought in the back lines. They could have sent Derain or Léger. But Braque was the most suitable candidate: French, an officer, decorated with the war cross and the Legion of Honour and, moreover, seriously wounded at the front.

He bravely performed the task assigned to him, that of heaping insults on Léonce Rosenberg. He accused him of betraying the cubists, of being a bastard and a coward. The other answered by calling his aggressor a 'Norman pig', which managed to get him knocked down to the floor. The two adversaries were finally dragged to the police station by policemen called to put an end to the fight. Matisse, who had arrived in the mean time, took the side of the representative of the cubist painters once Gertrude Stein had explained to him what it was all about. 'Braque is right, that man has robbed France!' he declared.

Once the wounds were bandaged – though not yet healed – the auctioneer found himself once again facing the dealers: the young Bernheim, Durand-Ruel, Paul Guillaume, Leopold Zborowski, and numerous foreigners. There were also bankers, painters, patrons of the arts, and writers, not to mention the curators of French museums, who made so few bids that most of the works of the avant-garde slipped out of their hands. A sad spectacle.

The dealers bought little. Léonce Rosenberg couldn't because he didn't have any money left, his brother Paul didn't because he felt he had acquired enough Picassos since the war, and the foreigners hesitated because, except for Picasso and Derain, they didn't know the artists whose canvases were being sold for such meagre sums. At no point did the price of a painting ever really take off.

Kahnweiler's syndicate was able to buy most of Gris' and Braque's works. Derain was one of the front runners, closely followed by Vlaminck. As the days and sessions passed, Léonce Rosenberg's calculations turned out to be totally wrong. The prices were falling; the markets could not absorb all these works. Those who benefited were thus not the professionals of the art world, but private art collectors who often acted for a third party. Thus the Swiss painter Charles-Edouard Jeanneret, who wasn't yet known as Le Corbusier, bought a number of Picassos for an industrialist, Raoul La Roche; thus Louis Aragon bought Braque's *La Baigneuse* for two hundred and forty francs. Similar purchases were made by Tristan Tzara and Paul Eluard, and especially by André Breton, who acquired works by Léger, Picasso, Vlaminck, Braque and Van Dongen.

So the poets were present, but they weren't the same ones. The poets of pre-war times had died or disappeared, and others were taking their place. They would acquire the works of the artists of the Bateau Lavoir, and become the intermediaries between the old overall-clad painters and the new patrons of the arts. By occupying the space deserted by yesterday's writers, these poets would help change the face of Montparnasse for ever. At Drouot, in the early twenties, the surrealists were already there. It was their turn now.

SURREALIST SCENES

It was during this period that André Breton and I discovered this technique (at that time we saw it only as a technique) which we called, in memory of Guillaume Apollinaire, 'surrealisms'.

Philippe Soupault

In 1919, in the shabby little room in which he was living at the Hotel des Grands Hommes on the Place du Panthéon, André Breton had received a visit from his parents, who ordered him to stop engaging in his Dada activities with a bunch of dubious clowns. Unless he promised to return to his law studies, they threatened to cut him off without a penny.

And so they did. From the Val-de-Grâce Hospital, Breton had moved on to Editions Gallimard on the rue Sébastien Bottin, which employed him to do the tasks reserved for those of his age: sending the *Nouvelle Revue française* to subscribers, for example, or correcting the proofs of Marcel Proust's *The Guermantes Way*. But his great activity of the time was the writing of the *Champs magnétiques* with Philippe Soupault.

> In 1919, my attention was completely absorbed by those more or less fragmented sentences which, when one is completely alone, on the verge of falling asleep, appear in one's mind without it being possible to ascribe any previous deliberation to them. These sentences, remarkably vivid and constructed with perfect syntax, seemed to me to be poetic elements of the highest order.[1]

Every morning, for fifteen straight days, Breton and Soupault wrote together in the café La Source on the Boulevard Saint Michel and at the Hotel des Grands Hommes. Respecting the principle which rejects logic in favour of images and in consequence, eliminates self-censorship to promote a form of inspiration, the two men modified their rhythm of writing every day, not allowing themselves to erase or correct anything. Sometimes they worked alone, sometimes together, sometimes one after the other – following a method that would become known as the 'rule of exquisite corpses' – stopping at the end of the day and starting again the next. Thus they wrote this work, based on a revelation that had troubled Breton and which represented a key theme in the surrealist movement, with its interest in dreams, hypnotic sleep, mediums and automatic writing.

According to its authors, Les Champs magnétiques heralded the birth of surrealism, at a time when this tendency did not yet have a name. For up until then, all had been Dada – complete with its scandals.

Things had really begun to heat up in January 1920, just a few days after Tzara's arrival in Paris. The team of Littérature, headed by Breton and Aragon, had read poetry at the Palais des Fêtes, on the rue Saint Denis. The public, who had been expecting a speech by André Salmon entitled 'The Exchange Crisis', as announced on posters and in papers, had discovered a handful of strange-looking individuals reciting verses by Soupault, Tzara, Albert-Birot and a few others, who had no more to do with 'The Exchange Crisis' than did the works of Picabia, exhibited to an audience of curious onlookers, whose number steadily diminished as the minutes ticked by.

A few days later the future surrealists organized the second public Dada event, which was held at the Grand Palais on 5 February 1920.

They were faced with a simple question: how would they get people to come? And they soon found an answer, by sending out press releases announcing that Charlie Chaplin was in Paris, that he would come to the Grand Palais to see his Dadaist friends, accomplices even, since, like Gabriele D'Annunzio, Henri Bergson and the Prince of Monaco, Charlie had just joined the movement.

Charlie Chaplin didn't come, and nor did Bergson or D'Annunzio. But Tzara, Breton and Aragon read their manifestos to a full house. The debates with the audience were lively and highly charged.

On 27 March 1920, they once again set out to provoke the public, this time at the Maison de l'Oeuvre where, twenty years earlier, Ubi Roi had already stirred up controversy. Claiming they wanted to show up the absurdity of the rules of classical theatre, the 'actors' went wild. Ribemont-Dessaignes offered the audience an earful by playing Le Pas de la chicoree frisée, a piece for the piano composed of notes placed on the stave following no principle other than that of chance. André Breton, protected by a cardboard sheath decorated to represent a target, read Francis Picabia's Le Manifeste cannibale, which ended with these words:

> Dada itself feels nothing, it is nothing, nothing, nothing.
>> It is like your hopes: nothing.
>> Like your heavens: nothing.
>> Like your gods: nothing.
>> Like your politicians: nothing.

Like your heroes: nothing.
Like your artists: nothing.[2]

On 26 May 1920, the Dada Festival was held in the Salle Gaveau. The press and the sandwich-board men walking up and down the streets of the capital gave a clear indication of what was to take place: all the Dadaists would have their hair shaved in public. The show would not only be on the stage, thanks to MM. Aragon, Breton, Eluard, Fraenkel, Ribemont-Dessaignes, Soupault and Tzara, but also in the audience, which would, it was hoped, be large and quarrelsome.

Tzara opened the show by exhibiting Le Sexe de Dada, an enormous wooden phallus balanced on some balloons. Then the 'famous illusionist', Philippe Soupault appeared, made up to look like a black man, wearing a dressing gown and armed with a cutlass. He freed five balloons on which were written the identities of those who were flying high, balloons which had to be burst: a pope, Benoit XV; a man of war, Pétain; a statesman, Clemenceau; a woman of letters, Mme Rachilde; and Cocteau, the first to die, pierced by the blade of the surrealist poet.

In the audience, there was pandemonium. Though Gide, Dorgelès, Jules Romains, Brancusi, Léger, and Metzinger didn't move a muscle, everyone else went wild. Tomatoes, carrots, turnips, and oranges rained from the furthest reaches of the auditorium onto the stage where Ribemont-Dessaignes, disguised as a funnel, was the principal target. In one corner, the spectators began to sing 'La Madelon'. In another, strains of a vengeful 'Marseillaise' could be heard. Picabia was taken to task by a member of the public who challenged him to a duel. Elsewhere, a thickset young man leapt to his feet and shouted, 'Long live France and its fried potatoes!'

It was Benjamin Péret, who would soon leave the audience and climb onto the stage of surrealism himself.

Was it Dadaism or surrealism? For the moment, it was both, or one contained in the other without anyone realizing it yet. But Breton was becoming impatient. He was disappointed in Tzara, whom he respected as a poet, but less as an activist. What worked in Zurich would not necessarily work in Paris. Shouting was not enough; action was called for. Breton wanted less sterility, more results. Dada was a libertarian movement, as Breton acknowledged: 'Dada is a state of mind ... Dada is artistic free thinking.'[3] But where Tzara's heart was libertarian, Breton was attracted by Lenin. Indeed, on questions of method, he was already leaning towards a somewhat Stalinist approach.

On 13 May 1921, at eight-thirty in the evening in the Salle des Sociétés savantes on the rue Danton, the 'Barrès trial' began. It was a public spectacle, a public accusation, and a public judgement of the writer Maurice Barrès. Judgement by whom? Officially, the Dada group; in reality, André Breton. Why? Because Barrès represented what the *Littérature* team (as well as the left in general and a number of intellectuals of all persuasions) hated most: patriotism, nationalism, and conservatism.

Tristan Tzara opposed the holding of such a trial, feeling that Dada had no right to judge anyone. It was precisely this opinion to which Breton objected, and to fight against it he did everything in his power to ensure that the trial took place, making it into a judgement of Tzara as much as of Barrès. In this respect, the declaration of accusation expressed the double meaning given to the affair by Breton himself:

> Dada, feeling that it is time to put an executive power behind its negative spirit, and resolved, above all, to exercise this power against those who might oppose its dictatorship, is taking measures, starting today, to eliminate their resistance.

And to begin with, the resistance of Maurice Barrès, accused of 'crimes against the certainty of the spirit'.

The court was composed of a president, André Breton, and two assessors, Pierre Deval and Théodore Fraenkel. The prosecution was represented by Georges Ribemont-Dessaignes, and the defence comprised Louis Aragon and Philippe Soupault.

There were a great many witnesses, both Dadaists and well-known figures, some brought in for reasons which remain unclear: Benjamin Péret, Drieu La Rochelle, Tristan Tzara (against his will), Rachilde, the symbolist poet Louis de Gonzague-Frick...

The accused did not attend the proceedings. Summoned to appear before the court, he quickly left Paris. He was replaced by a cloth dummy who was enthroned beneath a banner which proclaimed that 'No one is supposed to be ignorant of Dada.' The court as a whole wore the caps and white coats of medical students.

Breton read the act of accusation, which he had drafted himself. The criticisms turned out to be fairly mild and praised Dada more than they condemned Barrès (Ribemont-Dessaignes was playing his role against his will). The prosecution hit harder on the points that the president was expecting. As for the witnesses, they simply bore witness.

The 'unknown soldier' was called to the stand. He wore a uniform and a gas mask and moved in a kind of goosewalk. His appearance provoked the usual whistles, the usual strains of the 'Marseillaise', and the usual departure of Picabia, who hated fights.

Benjamin Peret, who played his role well, retired behind the scenes and removed his gas mask. Tristan Tzara took his place. He was the most eagerly anticipated witness. He faced Breton. Between the two men, what was taking place was much more than just the parody of a trial: it was

Zurich against Paris, the past versus the future, Dada or surrealism. Tzara cast the dice:

> TZARA: I have no confidence in justice, even if this justice is determined by Dada. You must agree, Mr President, that we are nothing but a bunch of bastards, all of us, and in consequence the little differences, between greater or lesser bastards, are irrelevant…
>
> BRETON: Do you know why you have been asked to testify?
>
> TZARA: Of course. Because I am Tristan Tzara, though I'm not yet entirely sure of that.
>
> SOUPAULT: The defence, convinced that the witness envies the fate of the accused, asks if the witness dares to admit it.
>
> TZARA: The witness tells the defence to go to hell.
>
> BRETON: Besides Maurice Barrès, can you name some other great pigs?
>
> TZARA: Yes, André Breton, Theodore Fraenkel, Pierre Deval, Georges Ribemont-Dessaignes, Louis Aragon, Philippe Soupault, Jacques Rigaut, Pierre Drieu La Rochelle, Benjamin Péret, Serge Charchoune.
>
> BRETON: Does the witness mean to insinuate that he likes Maurice Barrès as much as all the pigs who are his friends and whom he has just listed? … Does the witness want to be seen as a total idiot, or does he wish to be carried off to an insane asylum?
>
> TZARA: Yes, I would like to be considered a total idiot, but I am not trying to escape from the asylum in which I already live my life.

André Breton probably hoped that Maurice Barrès would be condemned to death. The jury, composed of twelve observers, decided otherwise: the writer was sentenced to twenty years of hard labour. As soon as the verdict was announced, Breton started preparing a second round.

One year after the Barrès trial, when Picabia had begun to distance himself from the *Littérature* group as well as from Tzara's friends, he called an 'International Congress for the Determination of Counsel for and Promotion of the Modern Spirit'. This congress was to bring together the directors of the main reviews of the time and some independent artists: Paulhan, from the *Nouvelle Revue française*, Ozenfant, from *L'Esprit nouveau*, Vitrac, from *Aventure*, Breton, from *Littérature*, Auric, Delaunay, Léger.

Feeling that the form of such a congress did not correspond to the spirit of freedom dear to the Dadaists, Tzara refused, in the end, to participate. Breton then made an unfortunate move, as he himself would recognize later: judging that Tzara was systematically opposing the project, he published a press communiqué signed by the members of the congress's committee (only Paulhan's name was missing) in which Tzara was condemned as 'the promoter of a movement which had come from Zurich, which it was superfluous to designate by any other name, and

which no longer answers to any reality today'.[4] To ensure that no one
would fail to see the reality of the situation, the committee accused Tzara
of being a 'publicity-seeking impostor'.

It was a little much. Too much. In answer to Breton's xenophobic
attack, Tzara, aided by Eluard, Ribemont-Dessaignes and Erik Satie, called
a meeting of the entire movement at the Closerie de Lilas, as well as its
supporters and even the artists invited to the Paris Congress. Breton
showed up. Man Ray, Zadkine, Eluard, Metzinger, Roch Grey, Survage,
Zborowski, Charchoune, Brancusi, Férat and many others answered Tzara's
summons. By a majority, the attending artists condemned Breton for the
indelicacy of his approach: not only was he himself the sole instigator of
a communiqué that he had presented as a collective message, but he had
in addition insulted a public figure with the aim of harming him. The
artists withdrew the vote of confidence they had granted in his ability to
organize the Paris Congress, which then promptly fell apart.

Breton took revenge. A few days later, Comœdia published a text in
which he accused Tristan Tzara of giving himself credit for the invention
of the word 'dada', of having played a very small role in the drafting of
the Dada Manifesto of 1918, and of exercising little real influence in the
world of letters, since before him there had been Vaché, Duchamp and
Picabia.

Finally, in a less underhand move, Breton made an effort to strengthen
and unify the team of Littérature. The paper, founded in 1919, had welcomed
figures whom Breton considered to be the survivors of symbolism (Gide,
Valéry, Fargue), poets close to Apollinaire (Salmon, Jacob, Reverdy and
Cendrars), and other writers including Morand, Giraudoux, Drieu La
Rochelle. Then came Vaché, Eluard, and Tzara, who had eclipsed Valéry
and Gide. Reverdy, too Catholic to believe in surrealism, had also distanced
himself.

After the failure of the Paris Congress, the magazine became the
movement's war machine. Breton temporarily abandoned his skirmishes
with Dada. A more important struggle was about to begin, and Breton
needed to arrange his troops in battle formation: Aragon, Péret, Limbour,
Vitrac ... He also added a new recruit whom he placed in the front lines
of his little army right from the start. This man was Robert Desnos.

THE WAKEFUL SLEEPER

surrealism, n. Pure psychic automatism by which one aims at expressing, either orally or in writing or in any other manner, the true processes and functioning of the mind. Thought communicated directly, in the absence of any restraint exercised by reason, without regard for aesthetic or moral concerns.

André Breton

When Desnos had completed his military service, he was twenty-two years old and Breton twenty-six. Breton was struck by his young friend's 'great capacity for attack and resistance'.[1] In this respect, Desnos was indeed a phenomenon. He was small and dark, with a lock of hair falling over his forehead and deep circles under his eyes, which were the colour of a purplish oyster, and he dressed with no care for fashion. Passionate and excitable, he loved and hated with equal intensity; the happy medium was something unknown to him. Friendly with the anarchists of Bonnot's band, he was always spoiling for a fight. But, as he did not know quite how to set about it, one of his friends gave him some boxing lessons. This did not keep him from collecting plenty of black eyes: he did not suffer fools gladly and was always quick to leap to the attack.

He was as prodigal with his literary innovations as he was with his punches and uppercuts. Desnos was a dazzling practitioner of acrostics, anagrams, puns, and verbal inventions of all kinds. This cavalier defiance of logic and grammatical rules was not far from the preoccupations of the surrealists, a fact that Breton would be quick to recognize.

A journalist too, Desnos wrote on practically any subject, always with astonishing talent. He began by translating advertising brochures into languages of which he didn't speak a word, and moved on to articles on phylloxera, sailing, the growing of sweet potatoes, and run-over dogs: these purported 'news items' or features originated in reality entirely in his own head.

He was friendly with Eugène Merle, a man who, though a bit of a crook, had a heart of gold. Merle was the founder of *Paris-Soir* (which Jean Prouvost was to buy in 1930) and of *Le Merle blanc*, the paper which 'huffs and puffs every Saturday' and had been doing so ever since 1919. Eight hundred thousand copies of its jokes, gossip, and darkly satirical attacks, put together by the ebullient anarchists, were sold each week. It was Merle who, when he decided one day in 1927 to launch a new daily, *Paris-Matin*, called upon one of the *Merle blanc*'s most prolific writers, a young man of twenty-four who already had more than one literary string to his bow. This was Georges Simenon. Together, he and Merle, aided and abetted by Desnos, devised an elaborate practical joke. They signed a contract stipulating that the author would undertake to write a complete novel in three days and three nights, which *Paris-Matin* would publish in instalments as it was being written. To up the stakes, it was agreed that Simenon would base his story on a plot and characters that would be determined by the public. The readers would be present at the birth of the masterpiece. Far from hiding away in an ivory tower, the author would work in full view of the public. How? By writing in a glass cage set up in front of the Moulin Rouge.

The cage was constructed. It was announced that Simenon would receive an advance of twenty-five thousand francs, out of the hundred thousand eventually due to him. The exercise would go down in history, applauded with full honours by a thousand contemporaries, duped by those cleverer than they ...[2] Youki Desnos described the event, André Warnod presented his congratulations, Florent Fels expressed his admiration, Louis Martin-Chauffier fell over himself in praise ... and Merle had a hoot. For of course there never would be any glass cage, nor novel written in three days, nor fascinated public. Only Simenon was real. At the last minute, the operation had been cancelled.

Robert Desnos also liked to play games, though of a different type from those of his employer. Breton called him the 'wakeful sleeper' for, more than any other member of the group, he was tempted by the great surrealist experiments with sleep.

It was René Crevel who, in 1922, introduced the surrealists to the idea of hypnotic sleep. The previous year, a clairvoyant had congratulated him on his talents as a medium. Hypnotic sleep, like all phenomena having their roots in dreams or other kinds of unmonitored psychic activity, was in total harmony with surrealism, which 'wished nothing so much as to erase the boundaries between dream and reality, conscious and unconscious', and which 'constituted a kind of border area linking the unconscious, which provides, and the conscious, which receives and uses'.[3]

Soon they were all trying it. It was like a collective spell. Crevel was the first to succumb. Joining hands with Max Morise, Robert Desnos and André Breton, in a darkened, soundproofed room, he fell asleep and, as he slept, began to recite texts, to sing, to sigh, to tell wild stories ... And when he awoke, he remembered nothing.

Next it was Desnos' turn. Completely unconscious, he scratched at the table; this, according to Crevel, indicated a desire to write. So his companion set a sheet of paper in front of him and put a pencil in his hand. Miraculously, he began to write, as Crevel looked on. But the latter, whom Soupault admired for the speed with which he produced his books, driven by an extraordinary creative facility (he was probably rivalled in this only by Aragon), did not believe in automatic writing. To him, the phrase was a contradiction in terms. Unmoved, he sat and watched.

Despite their best efforts, Ernst, Eluard and Morise did not fall asleep. Aragon and Soupault were present, but did not take part in the experiment. As for Desnos, he slumbered on in the arms of Morpheus. He spoke, he wrote, he dreamed ... Soon he was falling asleep on every possible occasion, often at Breton's home. One night, the latter, unable to wake him, went off to fetch a doctor, who was greeted with shouts and insults when he arrived.

Another time, Desnos entered into telepathic communication with Marcel Duchamp in New York. Through Rrose Sélavy, who acted as a medium, Duchamp dictated sentences to Desnos in Paris. Desnos paid tribute to their intermediary in the line, 'Rrose Sélavy knows the salt merchant well.'[4]

He overdid it a little one day when Crevel, during a session of collective hypnosis, suggested to the group that they all go and hang themselves from the coatstand. Desnos chose instead to chase Eluard out into a nearby garden, with a kitchen knife in his hand. It took all Breton's efforts to prevent a murder from being committed. And it took all his persuasion to put an end to the experience as a whole:

> For years, Robert Desnos abandoned himself *Body and Soul* (the title of one of his books) to surrealist automatism. I tried as best I could to restrain him, from the moment I began to fear that it might do irreparable damage to his individual psychic structure. Yes, I still believe that if one takes this path too far, at a certain point one begins to run the risk of mental disintegration.[5]

This may well be true. But a crucial question remains: during these spiritualist sessions, organized by the enthusiasts of automatic speech and action, was Desnos really asleep, or only pretending to be?

Whatever the answer, one thing is certain: when he emerged from the trances, he was full of energy. Not only with words, but also, as we have seen, with his fists.

After inviting him to join *Littérature*, Breton soon turned Desnos into one of his most solid supporters, to be relied on in many combats still to come. He had not forgotten his first goal: to destroy Dada. But before moving on to the final attack, a general prepares his strategy. The Paris Congress had foundered in April 1922. Eight months later, new skirmishes broke out.

On 11 December, two plays were on the programme of the Théâtre Antoine: Raymond Roussel's *Locus Solus*, and a patriotic work, *La Guerre en pantoufles* ('The Stay-at-Home's War').

It was still in the name of Dada, and not surrealism, that Breton and his friends came to give a show of support for Roussel. Aragon, Desnos, Breton and a few others fanned out in the audience and, throughout the performance of *Locus Solus*, clapped, cheered, and congratulated the author effusively, each responding noisily to the comments of the others in order to drown out the insults of the public. But *La Guerre en pantoufles* sparked off angry retorts from all corners of the theatre.

'Long live Germany!' cried Aragon from one side.

'Down with France!' shouted Desnos from another.

'So what?' queried one of the actors, too absorbed in his role to notice what was happening in the theatre.

'So go to hell!' retorted Breton from the top of the balcony.

Total chaos ensued, to the delight of Raymond Roussel, who recalled that 'The incident caused a great stir and I became famous overnight. One thing at least was certain: the name of one of my works was now on everyone's lips.'[6]

It was talked about so much, in fact, that it even inspired two theatrical revues, produced the same year: *Cocus Solus* and *Blocus Solus, ou les bâtons dans les Ruhrs*.*

Eighteen months later, the surrealists leapt to the defence of *L'Etoile au front* ('A Star on his Brow'), also by Roussel. The pandemonium was so great this time that the curtain had to be brought down during the third act. To a member of the audience who shrieked at him, 'You're only the claque!' Robert Desnos answered, 'Yes, I'm the slap and you're the cheek!'† A loud and well-aimed slap . . .

The next blow was struck by André Breton at the Théâtre Michel, on the rue des Mathurins, on 6 July 1923. This time the target was Dada, and Dada alone.

On this occasion, Tzara had invited his friends to a seemingly harmless but strangely assorted production, *La Soirée du cœur à barbe* ('The Bearded Heart Evening') which presented not only several works by Stravinsky and others by Les Six, but also poems by Cocteau, Soupault, Eluard and Apollinaire, together with some dance numbers, a few previously unseen

---

* Loose English translations of these punning titles might be *Cuckolds Alone* and *Solo Blockade*, or *A Spanner in the Wurst*.

† The term *claque*, which literally means 'slap', also refers to a group of people hired to applaud at a performance.

films, and a three-act play by Tristan Tzara, *Le cœur à gaz* ('The Gas Heart').

Unfortunately, neither Soupault nor Eluard had been consulted, and they could not bear the thought of having their works read alongside Cocteau's. So of course they turned up at the theatre, accompanied by their usual accomplices.

To begin with, all went well. But, after the musical part of the evening, a young Dadaist, Pierre de Massot, climbed onto the stage and attempted to read a text condemning Gide, Picabia, Duchamp, and Picasso as having 'died on the field of honour'. Picasso happened to be present in the theatre. So did Breton, who rose to the painter's defence and leapt on stage, where he was soon joined by Desnos and Péret. They grabbed the speaker and Breton raised his cane, bringing it down on the young man's arm, which promptly fractured. The public booed the attackers and turned on Breton. Tzara, who was watching the scene from a distance, called the police. Breton, Desnos and Péret were thrown out, and calm was restored to the theatre. But not for long. Tzara's play had barely begun when a distinguished-looking young man, tall, fair, and dreamy-eyed, stood and addressed the author, demanding an explanation: why had he had Breton ejected from the theatre?

The forces of law and order had not all left the scene: they rushed at Paul Eluard, who was joined at once by his friends and allies. Poets and policemen were soon swinging away at each other. At this point, Tzara appeared on the stage. Swiftly changing targets, Eluard turned on Tzara and slapped him. He then slapped Crevel, who was coming up from behind. The fight descended into the theatre as audience and stagehands jumped into the fray. Soon the battle spread to the street. The next day, the theatre manager refused to allow another performance to be put on: art, yes, boxing, no.

Breton would not forgive Tzara until much later for having had him thrown out of the Théâtre Michel. He dedicated his *Pas perdus* ('The Lost Steps') to the father of Dadaism, with the following words: 'To Tristan Tzara, the novelist of 1924, crook of all trades, silly old chatterbox, police informer.' This book included a poem, 'Lâchez tout' ('Drop Everything') which resounded like a death knell for Dada:

> Drop everything.
> Drop Dada.
> Drop your wife, drop your mistress.
> Drop your hopes and your fears.
> Abandon your children in the corner of a wood.
> Drop the substance for the shadow.
> Drop, if need be, a comfortable life, what you have, for a better future.
> And set out on the open road.[7]

The two men were, in fact, to meet up again – but not until the publication of the *Second Surrealist Manifesto*.

The year 1924 was a milestone in the movement's history. Breton published not only *Les Pas perdus*, but also *The Surrealist Manifesto*. At the same time, Aragon published *Le Libertinage*, Péret *Immortelle maladie*, Eluard *Mourir de ne pas mourir* and Artaud (whom Breton met for the first time this same year) *L'Ombilic des limbes*.

In addition to the group's publications, which gave it a material reality in the world of letters, it also had an address. This was 15, rue de Grenelle, the headquarters of the 'Bureau of Surrealist Experiences', which was open every afternoon from half past four to half past six. The group soon opened a gallery, on the rue Jacques Callot, run by Roland Tual, an imaginative genius who unfortunately never became a writer himself. But he did launch *La Revolution surréaliste*, the first issue of which was published in December, directed and edited by Pierre Naville and Benjamin Péret.

Finally, 1924 saw an important change in André Breton's own life, which arose from the death of Anatole France and the scandal caused by the surrealists' reaction to the event.

Breton hated the writer:

> We were completely unmoved by the supposed limpidity of his style, and particularly repelled by his all too famous scepticism. On the personal level, we found his attitude contemptible and extremely shady: he had done everything to ingratiate himself with both the right and the left. He was rotten to the core from adulation, and riddled through with arrogance.[8]

At the time of the funeral, Aragon, Breton, Eluard, Delteil, Drieu and Soupault published a virulent diatribe against Anatole France, entitled 'Un Cadavre' ('A Corpse'). Breton in particular didn't mince words. Under the heading 'Refus d'inhumer' ('Burial certificate withheld'), he wrote, 'Loti, Barrès, France – let us mark with a bright white sign the year which eliminated these three sinister types: the fool, the traitor, and the policeman.'

'Have you ever slapped a dead man?' queried Aragon, blithely picking up where Breton had left off. Aragon continued:

> I consider any admirer of Anatole France to be a degraded human being … He was an execrable buffoon of the spirit who so totally reflected the ignominy of the French that the whole benighted nation rejoiced in having lent him its name … So go ahead, stutter out praises to your hearts' content for this decaying thing, this worm, soon to be

possessed by worms ... There were days when I dreamt of finding an eraser that would wipe out all the filth of humanity.

André Breton was to pay a high price for this collectively written pamphlet attacking Anatole France. The violence of its contents cost him the job he had held for several years, the position which had taken him to Drouot for the sale of the Kahnweiler collections. For he had been buying them not only for himself, but also for a man who employed him expressly for this purpose, a man who, for many years, had supported most of the artists in Montparnasse, painters and poets alike. This man was the fashion designer and patron of the arts, Jacques Doucet.

DRESS DESIGNER TO THE ARTS

*Thanks to Monsieur Doucet, until the end of the month I had nothing
to do but wander in the hills, lie in the grass, smoke, and dream.*

Blaise Cendrars

In 1924, Jacques Doucet was no longer very young, and haute couture
hardly interested him any longer. Moreover, he hated being introduced
as a figure from the world of fashion. Of course he was, and remains,
one of the great liberators of women during the early part of the twentieth
century: it was he who brought lightness to materials, laces, folds, see-
through styles, embroidery. He decided that women should not continue
to be weighed down by artificial corseted forms, but should appear as
they are, in fitted, open-necked, natural dresses.

He designed clothes for the greatest women of his time, and his shows
were true artistic occasions. On Sundays, at Longchamp, duchesses and
countesses liked to wear his soft, delicate pastel colours. He was friendly
with artists; Sarah Bernhardt and Réjane confided in him. But he had only
one wish, which was to sell his fashion house, for he was first and
foremost an art collector. There was something a little mad about him,
although it wasn't obvious. He was a rather handsome man, extremely
elegant, with silvery hair, and a soft, carefully trimmed beard. He wore
gaiters, and incredibly shiny shoes: rumour had it that he used a special
polish, and put his shoes in the oven every time he applied it.

He could be rather abrupt, and although he was subsidizing half of the
writers in Paris, he had few friends. Yet he was a sentimental man, a
lover, a solitary soul who had been unlucky in love. He had fallen in love
for the first time with a young girl who had refused her hand; on a
second occasion, the woman he loved had died before she could accept.
The lady in question was married, a certain Mme R., and he tried to
convince her to divorce her husband for him. Among his arguments was
a private home which he began to build for her on the rue Spontini, by
the edge of the Bois de Boulogne. When the object of his desire finally
succumbed to this extravagant enterprise, Jacques Doucet bought paintings

by La Tour, Fragonard and Boucher, and some porcelain and Chinese art objects, which he added to the Watteaus, Goyas and Chardins, the sculptures and hundreds of eighteenth-century works that he had already acquired. (In 1906, in a first sale at Drouot, the collector had already pruned and sorted out his collections.)

Alas, Mme R. was never to inhabit this dream palace: she died a few days before the separation from her first husband was finally declared.

Doucet never recovered from the blow. In 1912, he sold his collection. He obtained seven million francs in gold for it, which he decided to devote to building an art library.

As early as 1909, across from his magnificent home on the rue Spontini, he had rented a space in which to store various manuscripts and rare editions that he had bought. Then he had asked an art critic, René-Jean, to help him. He added on to the first location, which subsequently became one of the largest libraries in France. During and after the war, André Suarès, André Breton, and then Marie Dormoy would look after it. Jacques Doucet eventually bequeathed it to the University of Paris.

The collector could be superbly generous. One day when he was present at a fitting session at his boutique, one of his clients exclaimed, 'When I hear *Tristan*, I faint, I lose control of myself, I'd do anything in the world one asked of me at that moment!'

'Good ...' murmured the dress designer to himself.

The story doesn't say whether he himself was an admirer of Wagner. But he had enough respect for his client to do things elegantly. He rented an apartment, furnished it in style, and invited the melodramatic young lady to join him, which she did. Her host had scarcely closed the door of the drawing room when music began to filter through from the other side of the wall.

'Let's go and see what it is,' suggested Doucet.

And he led his soon-to-be sweetheart into a small room where musicians were playing excerpts from *Tristan*. It was a little paradise ...

Doucet showed the same generosity towards artists, whom he helped to keep alive during and after the war. And as was the case with his female conquests, he expected something from them in return: in their case, not their bodies, but their creations. For he did not only mean to acquire original editions and manuscripts, however rare these may have been (Baudelaire, Rimbaud, Chateaubriand, Verlaine, Mallarmé, Flaubert, then Claudel, Jammes, Gide ...); he also wanted the writers and poets that he helped to subsidize to write for him.

André Suarès, one of the first of those whom he contacted, was put in charge of a weekly newsletter on contemporary literature or a topical subject. In 1916, Pierre Reverdy received fifty francs for each bulletin he wrote on the artistic movements of the moment. Doucet also helped him when the review Nord–Sud was launched: not only financially, but also by giving him advice. Thus it was that he encouraged Reverdy to keep Jean Cocteau off the editorial board, which didn't prevent the latter from speaking of 'my old friend Doucet' when Raymond Radiguet in turn benefited from the generosity of the patron, receiving fifty francs for a weekly column.[1]

André Salmon was also asked to give his views on literature, as was Max Jacob. Through him, Jacques Doucet wanted to be kept up to date on the activities of the avant-garde. And so he was, but it was not the kind of news he necessarily wanted to hear. The poet brought him details of the fight between Reverdy and Diego Rivera at Lapérouse, the stormy first night of the Mamelles de Tirésias, and the problems Erik Satie was having with reviewers. He gave him the full benefit of his likes and dislikes in poetry and literature. But he categorically refused to give in to his patron's request to talk to him about Picasso:

> I haven't written anything on Picasso. He hates to have things written about him. He hates the lack of understanding and the invasiveness of it, and I have such respect and gratitude for him that I don't want to do anything to upset him … Some friends have lived off his name in their writings, their reviews, their imaginings … Anyway … maybe later … we'll see … but it will be much, much later and, in fact, probably never, I should think.[2]

He sold him a few manuscripts – Le Siège de Jérusalem, Le Cornet à dés, Le Christ à Montparnasse – some of them written for him, others copied for the occasion. He advised him to contact Apollinaire as well as other less well-known writers, and sometimes gave him the names of poor and still unknown painters. When he needed money, he didn't hesitate to ask him for advances, and thanked him for it by giving him gouaches.

Blaise Cendrars was also contacted. This was at a time when he was down and out. One day, the story went, he had gone to the Mercure de France to present a poem. Did he see Rachilde, Valette or Léautaud there? Whoever it was, when the person he spoke with had accepted his poem. Cendrars asked for an advance. The other man almost choked.

'An advance on what?'

'A sum in cash, please.'

The tension was rising, and the newspaperman's cheeks were getting red.

'You must know, my dear sir, that the Mercure never pays for poems in verse.'

'I don't care,' replied the writer, shrugging his shoulders. 'Put it into prose, and just let me have the six sous.'

He didn't get them. History doesn't record whether he left his prose at the *Mercure*...

Shortly afterwards, according to him, he received a visit from Jacques Doucet's valet, who brought him a proposal from his master: a monthly letter in exchange for a regular monthly sum of one hundred francs. The deal seemed risky to the poet: 'Monsieur Doucet wasn't a friend, there was no reason for me to write letters to him – what would I say, since I didn't have the honour of even being acquainted with him?'[3]

So his answer was negative, though because Cendrars declined the offer in writing, this meant a present of a free letter for the collector. But in this letter, Cendrars made a counter-proposal: he agreed to write for Doucet, on the condition that it was a book, a chapter of which he would write every month.

The messenger delivered the missive to Doucet's residence on the rue Spontini. When he returned, he deposited a hundred-franc note on Cendrars' table together with his master's letter of agreement. In response – this now made two free letters! – the poet specified the terms of the contract: it would be a little book written in twelve months, so many pages a month, so many lines a page, so many words a line, payable in advance on the first of each month, with publishing rights remaining with the author. This is how *L'Eubage* was written. But despite the couturier's munificence, Cendrars claimed that he never had the slightest dealings with Doucet on any other occasion.

André Breton, like so many others, was also to benefit from the patron's generosity. In December 1920, he was hired as a librarian. His role was to choose the works which he felt corresponded to the sensibility of the times, and he was also required to keep his employer up to date on modern art. He would encourage him to buy *Les Demoiselles d'Avignon* (for twenty-five thousand francs), *La Charmeuse de serpents* by the Douanier Rousseau, and works by Derain, De Chirico, Seurat, Duchamp, Picabia, Ernst, Masson and Miró.

In 1922, Breton got Aragon to help him set up a project to enlarge the library, which they proposed to Jacques Doucet. The idea was to acquire works that were ignored, neglected, or unrecognized by traditional literature. In addition to Lautréamont and Raymond Roussel, who were already represented, he suggested opening the door to Pascal, Kant, Hegel, Fichte, Bergson, Sade, Restif de la Bretonne, Sue, Jarry – and Dada. They also advised Doucet to buy manuscripts by Jean Paulhan, Tristan Tzara, Paul Eluard, Benjamin Péret, Robert Desnos, Jacques Baron and Georges Limbour, the finest of the surrealists.

Breton didn't conceal his ambitions: he wanted to help his friends. And so he did. Doucet was entranced with Aragon, whom he subsidized, like the others: he paid him, for example, to send him passages from the

Paysan de Paris and regular letters on literary subjects. Thus it was that the dress designer of the wealthy Neuilly and Passy neighbourhoods helped this young group of writers to survive, even as their outrageous pranks scandalized the rest of high society...

But the romance, as we have seen, would be over in 1924, with the death of Anatole France. Faced with the violence of their polemic, Jacques Doucet tore up his contracts with the surrealists. This was Breton's version, at any rate, but Marie Dormoy gives a slightly different account of the affair. She claims that Doucet had been informed of mocking and derogatory remarks that were being made about him by his young friends. He called the entire surrealist group into his office, and promised that he would pay them whatever he still owed them, but that the collaboration would end there – with all of them except Aragon.

In 1926, the writer fell in love with Nancy Cunard, heiress of the shipping company, whose mother had influence with the English royal family. The dress designer was pleased with this development. He doubled Aragon's monthly pension, asking him to keep him informed about the leisure pursuits of the fashionable young people of Paris. The poet did so until 1927. After he joined the Communist Party, though, he permanently broke his ties with Jacques Doucet, on political grounds.

Later, André Breton would also qualify his admiration for the patron, although he recognized the generosity and the talent of the collector who had helped him enormously at various points in his life. (When he married Simone Kahn, in 1921, Doucet, who had already given him presents and paid for his travel, doubled his salary to reassure the girl's family.) But he was sufficiently detached to remark that 'Since I don't feel it's a professional secret ... I might note that the pursestrings of this particular purse did not loosen up very easily to favour young painters.'[4]

Even worse: in the stories Breton tells, there is a little of the Clovis Sagot syndrome (Sagot was the dealer who advised Gertrude Stein to cut the feet off in a painting by Picasso). The writer claims that he convinced the dealer to acquire a painting by Max Ernst exhibited at the Salon des Indépendants. This work depicted five similar vases containing five similar bouquets. The price was five hundred francs.

'Ask the artist to paint us two vases for two hundred francs,' suggested Doucet.

It must be noted that Derain had paved the way for this attitude. Pierre Cabanne reports that one day, when Breton had taken the dress designer and art collector to his home to buy a still life, the artist had pulled a measuring tape out of his pocket, measured the painting that his visitor admired, and said, 'If we calculate the value based on the price of each square centimetre, that will cost you forty thousand francs.'

Another day, in front of a tiny Masson, Doucet had complained, 'There's something missing in this picture.' He scratched his beard as he studied the canvas, and finally exclaimed, struck by a brilliant thought, 'Let's ask the artist to add something . . . A bird! That's what we need. A bird would be perfect!'

As for Aragon, he did not present his former patron in a much more advantageous light. In *Aurélien*, he calls him Charles Roussel and portrays him along with a painter named Zamora, who was none other than Picabia. It is easy to recognize the faults of the latter: a socialite, he happily entertained 'famous jockeys, duchesses, scribblers, rich and idle men, pretty women of all kinds, chess players, people he had met on his travels, on ocean liners'.[5]

The patron is presented as a fashionable man, 'groomed as carefully as a poodle and dressed with such care it was almost in bad taste, in its effort to be distinguished.' He is probably exaggerating a bit, but he exaggerates less when he introduces a poet from Ménestrel's little band (Breton) who is knocked out during a tempestuous evening of surrealist shenanigans. The assailants, 'who couldn't stand Cocteau', had set out to create pandemonium during the performance of one of his plays. After a short fight, Ménestrel/Breton ends up with his nose smashed in and blood on his tie. Roussel/Doucet leads him to a café and asks, his eyes shining with greed, 'Couldn't you write me a little note, for my library, about this curious evening? I have the manuscript of the play, which I bought from Cocteau . . . I could publish it together with your note.'[6]

With their mockery and disparagement, neither Aragon nor Breton showed a great deal of gratitude to this man to whom in fact they owed a great deal. Enough in any case to encourage almost all the other artists, from Kisling and Cendrars to André Salmon, Max Jacob and Apollinaire, Radiguet, Cocteau and Desnos, to have passed the word around to take advantage of the generosity and gifts of a man to whom most of them wrote in a tone of humility, bordering sometimes on obsequiousness.

Cendrars was no better than the others. When he claims that Doucet contacted him through the intermediary of his valet, it is an empty boast. The truth is quite different. It was Cendrars himself who wrote to Doucet in 1917, to ask for five hundred francs which would enable him to finish his novel *La Fin du monde*. In exchange, he offered a manuscript which in the end would be that of 'Les Pâques à New York', written in 1912. After this, the two men struck a deal over *L'Eubage*. Thus, there was not only one exchange between them, as Cendrars claimed, but at least two. And it was certainly not the writer who dictated his conditions, just as he had not dictated the terms of the previous contract. He had asked for five hundred francs; Doucet had given him one hundred and fifty.[7] He could always call him an 'old dandy' in *Le Lotissement du ciel*; this didn't keep him from thanking him for his generosity in his letters, and bowing very low.

No one would agree with his description of Jacques Doucet's library: he
portrays himself accompanying the collector amidst a jumble of cases
containing boxes of letters and recopied manuscripts, but no major
works – except for *L'Eubage*. In his account, he listens to the old man
complaining about how much he receives, concluding in despair, 'Will
they never stop writing?'

This was clearly not Doucet talking, but Cendrars.

THE DRESS DESIGNER AND
THE PHOTOGRAPHER

Like many French artists, I was very impressed with the Ballets Russes
and wouldn't be surprised if they in fact had a certain influence on
me.

Paul Poiret

Doucet sold his fashion house in 1924. He had been dethroned by
younger designers, especially Paul Poiret, who had introduced more
vibrant colours into fashion, notably greens, reds and blues, which were
a change from the lilac and pink tones of his predecessors. He definitely
did away with the corseted woman, launched the brassière and developed
more narrowly cut dresses which hugged the contours of the female
figure.

Paul Poiret, who had learned the trade from Doucet, was also a patron
of the arts, but compared to the important work of the older man, his
activity in this domain was not much more than a footnote.

He first came to fame when he designed a coat in black tulle for Réjane.
He left Doucet after his fiancée had some of Poiret's designs made up by
a female dressmaker, for which Doucet never forgave him. Once free and
on his own, Poiret quickly made his mark, bought a magnificent private
house in the Faubourg Saint Honoré and began to dress women from
high, and very high society.

He was interested in the contemporary arts, though less in cubism than
in the Ballets Russes, whose influence on his own work he admitted. But
naturally boastful, Paul Poiret never forgot to add that his own reputation
dated from long before that of Monsieur Bakst.

In the heyday of Montmartre, he often went to the Bateau Lavoir. It
was he, as we have seen, who sent many of his fashionable clients to Max
Jacob's extremely humble lodgings, where these rich and glamorous ladies
could have their fortunes told. It was also he who invited some often very
shabby painters to the sumptuous parties where he would hold forth on
his aesthetic ideas: according to him, dress designing was an art like any
other. Apollinaire answered that if it was indeed an art, it was definitely
an inferior one.

But Paul Poiret did have a tender spot for Max Jacob. He consulted him on everything and nothing: the colour of his tie or of his socks, his daily schedule ... He asked him to put on his plays in Poiret's private home on the Avenue d'Antin, where Picasso had exhibited his *Demoiselles d'Avignon* during the war. He wove around him a web of worldly relations which enabled Max to find doors to knock on when he fell on hard times or was in despair.

Aside from his useful contacts, the poet did not hold the fashion designer in immense esteem. He reproached him for not liking his friends and for being very conservative in his artistic tastes. This is hardly disputable. Curiously, although he admired everything he saw at the Bateau Lavoir, Poiret never became a disciple of cubism: 'I wasn't indifferent to Picasso's experimentation and taste for novelty, but I always thought of them as workshop exercises or speculations of the mind, which wouldn't go beyond a small circle of artists and which the public should have ignored.'[1] His own great talent lay in his ability to mix different styles and disciplines: he was an eclectic rather than a purist.

He was very close to the dancer Isadora Duncan. After she had lost her two children, she spoke to Poiret about a plan she had hatched: she wanted a new heir who would have her superb physical attributes and the intellectual gifts of a poet of genius.

'Maeterlinck!' Poiret exclaimed. He had read one of his books the night before.

So Isadora went to see Maeterlinck to ask him if he would agree to give her a child. The writer refused. He was married, the situation would be too complicated ...

Poiret had also thought of Max Jacob. But he hadn't even dared to mention his name to the dancer ...

Fernande Olivier, who worked for the designer for a while after her break with Picasso, confided to Paul Léautaud that his shops were also a place where beautiful women could meet their lovers. She complained that while Poiret was always charming to people from the outside world, he was very hard on his staff. His only saving grace was his collection of avant-garde paintings, one of the finest in Paris.

This collection was also admired by a photographer who, one autumn day in 1921, appeared at the door of Poiret's home on the Avenue d'Antin. He was a young American, with a fairly traditional air about him, and he carried a large folder containing some of his work. He had been sent to see the dress designer by Gabrielle Buffet-Picabia.

He gave his name to the uniformed porter who was striding back and forth at the entrance to the gardens. He was led through the gardens, along paths which intersected lawns covered with crocuses in full bloom. Chairs and tables in bright colours were set here and there, amidst amazing expanses of grass, reminiscent of Versailles.

The visitor walked up the three steps of the threshold to the house, bordered by two bronze fauns brought back from Herculaneum, at the foot of Vesuvius. He walked through one of the ten doors leading to the inside, and across a magenta-coloured carpet, lit by crystal chandeliers, which stopped at the bottom of a massive staircase with a beautiful hand-worked railing.

A groom entered the elevator before him. On the first floor, the young man was led down a corridor punctuated by a multitude of fitting rooms. He came out into a large room where a number of distinguished ladies were milling about. They were all watching a model present a new dress. A statue by Brancusi dominated the centre of the room.

The visitor approached an orderly and asked where he could find M. Poiret, with whom he had an appointment.

'Follow me,' the servant told him.

From one room to another, through corridors and hallways, the American was led to an office, whose door sported the following notice:

BEWARE! DANGER!
Before knocking, ask yourself three times:
'Is it absolutely necessary to bother HIM?'

After being announced, the American was taken into a room where he found a man dressed in a canary-yellow jacket and striped trousers. He had a pointed beard and was going bald. The American photographer set his portfolio down on the desk. The designer opened it, looked through it attentively, and said, 'Very good ... and what can I do for you?'

'I don't know.'

'Have you ever done fashion photography?'

'No, but I'm willing to try ... Except that I don't have a studio.'

'Those who work with me work on my premises,' Poiret replied coldly.

With a wave of his hand, he took in his desk, the gardens and a second house that could be seen from the window.

'The photographers work here ... Do you have the necessary material?'

'I need a darkroom.'

'We'll lend you one.'

The photographer was authorized to take shots of the models outside working hours. He came back and did the job as asked. He developed the photographs in the tiny room where he was lodging, in a seedy hotel in Paris. He then came back to Poiret's to show them to him.

'They're splendid!' the designer exclaimed.

Taking advantage of the moment, the American photographer asked if he could be paid. Poiret answered with an astonished frown.

'I never pay photographers. The magazines take care of that part of it.'

'But I don't know anyone!' cried the photographer. 'I've just arrived in France.'

Poiret relented: he bought a few photos and paid two hundred francs for them.

His fortune was beginning to dwindle at the time. It would be consumed in just a few years, as the designer failed to adapt to the more sober and less extravagant lifestyle of the post-war years. By the middle of the twenties, nothing remained of Poiret's empire. The man himself, by his own account a victim of banks, tax collectors and 'socialist threats', left Paris for a little house in the Ile-de-France. He lived there like a hermit, cursing the entire world; he even considered presenting his case to the League of Human Rights, and finally gave up on the idea only out of fear that 'this organization might itself be stained with the masonic spirit and, in consequence, incapable of independent thought.'[2]

He still had one friend: the doctor who was taking care of him. One day, this man arrived on the American photographer's doorstep, to ask him to come with him to the country to see Paul Poiret. The former designer was writing a book of memoirs which would soon be published, and a photograph would be needed.

In memory of the two hundred francs Poiret had once given him in a time of need, the photographer agreed to make the trip. Poiret received him in style, with all the refinement he could now manage. They dined, drank, and went walking. But when they got back to the house, there was not enough light left to take the photo: they said a sad goodbye.

A few days later, the doctor who had served as an intermediary came back to see the American photographer. The American found he had a certain resemblance to Poiret in his days of glory, and amused himself by asking him to pose.

Twenty or so years later, when the former designer died, consumed by bitterness and paranoia, a weekly magazine asked the photographer if he had any shots of the deceased in his archives. The American sent them the portrait of the doctor, which they published. It accompanied an article on Paul Poiret, his life and his work. No one ever noticed the switch, except the doctor, of course. And the photographer, who had done it deliberately.

The name of the doctor is not known. The photographer, who had been living in Montparnasse since the summer of 1921, was named Man Ray.

AN AMERICAN IN PARIS

I made the acquaintance of an American who takes very good photos.
He said to me, 'Kiki! Don't look at me like that! I can't concentrate.'

Kiki of Montparnasse

When he returned to his hotel room, the day he had photographed Paul Poiret's models, Man Ray closed the curtains of the little room, lit a red lamp and began to develop the prints. He had very little equipment: just the necessary chemical products, two basins, paper, and a few accessories.

He soaked his sheets in the developing fluid. By mistake, he put one in that hadn't been used. After taking it out of the basin, he set a glass funnel down on it, and lit the lamp.

> Before my very eyes, an image was forming. It wasn't a simple silhouette of objects at all: these had been deformed and refracted by the glasses which had been more or less in contact with the paper, and the part that was directly exposed to the light showed through, as if in relief, against a black background.[1]

Man Ray set aside for a moment the photos he had taken at Poiret's. He picked up all the objects he could find around him, keys, handkerchief, pencil, string, and placed them on paper that wasn't even soaked in the developing fluid. Then he exposed it all to the light. He developed it, and dried it.

The next day, he hung the results of these experiments on the walls of his hotel room. In the evening, Tristan Tzara, who had arrived in Paris a year earlier, knocked on the door. Man Ray let him in and showed him his work. The young Romanian was enthusiastic. The two men spent a good part of the night setting out a thousand and one objects on the paper, developing it, and beginning again: rayography was born. This would make it possible to take photos without apparatus. One year later, Man Ray published his first album of rayographs, Les Champs délicieux, with a preface by Tristan Tzara.

Before becoming a photographer, Man Ray, the son of a Jewish tailor from Brooklyn, had been a painter. He had studied at the Ferrer School, given this name because it had been created by sympathizers of the anarchist cause, for which Francisco Ferrer (much admired by Picasso, we may recall) had given his life.* He had also spent time in the places frequented by the New York avant-garde at the time of the Armory Show, beginning with Alfred Stieglitz's gallery at 291, Fifth Avenue. This is where he had met Francis Picabia and, more significantly, Marcel Duchamp, with whom he was and remained very close.

Man Ray photographed his own work with his camera. As his career progressed, he discovered the richness of black and white reproductions and in the end 'destroyed the original and kept only the reproduction'.[2] He would soon come to look on painting as an 'outmoded form of expression', that would one day inevitably be dethroned by photography.[3] Later, he would change his mind on this subject.

In New York, he looked for models, not to paint but to photograph. Thanks to the portrait of the sculptress Berenice Abbot, whom he met in a bar in the Village – in Paris, she would become his assistant for three years – he won his first award for photography. In the space of a few months, he photographed Edgar Varèse, Marcel Duchamp, the writers Djuna Barnes and Mina Loy, Elsa Schiaparelli (who hadn't yet become a dressmaker), and others.

Duchamp was the first to leave for Paris. As soon as he managed to scrape together the money needed for the trip, Man Ray stuck his canvases and some Dadaist objects into a trunk, lugged it onto a transatlantic liner with him and set off to join his friend. The painter had reserved a room for him in a little hotel in Passy, where Tristan Tzara had also stayed. This is how Man Ray first met the Dadaists and surrealists of Paris, with whom he would become friendly: Breton, Aragon, Eluard, Fraenkel, Soupault, Desnos and the others.

Soupault was the one who had the idea of organizing an exhibition of the works that Man Ray had brought with him from New York. In the catalogue printed for the occasion, the Dadaists presented the artist as a coal merchant and at the same time a chewing-gum manufacturer, a millionaire who was also a talented painter. These credentials didn't help sell a single work. Man Ray retreated once again behind his camera's eye, photographing Picabia's canvases first of all. Then Cocteau, with his address book of useful contacts, crossed his path – Man Ray was launched.

In 1921, he had met a young woman who was going to become his first model, and soon the long-time muse of all Montparnasse. The

* The Francisco Ferrer Center and Modern School, founded in New York in honour of the martyred Spanish educator, advocated progressive education for children.

photographer was sitting with Marie Vassilieff in a café in the Vavin neighbourhood, near the Dôme and the Rotonde: the place was packed.

Everyone there was typical of the population of the neighbourhood since the armistice – painters who were a little less poor than before, American writers, Swedish dancers, an armada of models, a Redskin with all his feathers named Colbert, a Polish-Jewish painter disguised as a cowboy named Granowski, a poet from Laponia, Russians who were now white Russians, a mute Bulgarian who wore a shower-curtain ring in his nose, Cocteau with his young friend Radiguet, some people in costumes on their way to a party or a ball, barefoot men, a number of scantily clad women, the painter Jules Pascin who was just back from America, Antonin Artaud, a black musician trying out a saxophone softly, Adamov, still very young, barefoot in his Roman-style sandals, consumed by poverty and hunger...

At a distant table, two young girls were speaking loudly. They were made up like rainbows and adorned with jewels from ear to wrist. One of them was Kiki of Montparnasse, who gave a sharp answer to the waiter who refused to serve her on the grounds that she wasn't wearing a hat. He spoke firmly but softly, but she replied that a bistro wasn't a church: one could come as one liked.

'A Chambéry with strawberry liqueur, please,' requested Kiki, 'and another one for my friend.'

The waiter gave up and called the manager.

'Without a hat,' this gentleman explained, 'one might mistake you...'

'For an American?'

Americans were admitted anywhere, with or without a hat.

'That's not what I meant,' replied the stuttering manager.

'And what exactly did you mean?'

'Without a hat, one might think you were a...'

'A what?'

'A prostitute.'

Kiki leapt to her feet. Setting one bare foot on a chair, and the other on the table, in her inimitable Paris accent, speaking loudly, clearly, and very pointedly, she explained to the waiter and the manager that she didn't sell her favours. Which didn't keep her from having been born a true bastard in a true French province, Burgundy. Then she swore that she would never come back, neither she nor any of her friends, and jumping off the table, she revealed in a carefully calculated sweep of her skirt just what she had to show, and what she shouldn't be showing...

'No hat, no shoes, no knickers!'

Man Ray gestured to the waiter. Marie Vassilieff called out to the two young girls.

'Two drinks for the ladies,' said the American.

'Come and join us,' the Russian suggested.

Kiki sat down at their table.

'Are they with you?' asked the waiter.

'Yes,' answered Man Ray.

'Because I'm not allowed to serve women alone...'

'Unless they're wearing hats,' Kiki corrected.

They drank a toast. Then a second one. They left the café for another one, and then went on to a restaurant.

'Our American friend!' clamoured Marie and Kiki. They dined, and the wine flowed.

'Our rich American friend!'

They went to the movies, to see La Dame aux camélias.

'Very rich!'

The young girls were seated next to the chewing-gum millionaire. Kiki watched the screen, engrossed in the story like a child. Ray felt for her hand. He found it, pressed it. She didn't respond, but didn't take it away either.

When they left, he said that he would like to paint her but, overcome by emotion, didn't think he could. She answered that she knew all about that sort of thing. Painters were always in that state the first time she posed for them.

'Well, how about something else: let me photograph you.'

'Absolutely not!' cried Kiki.

But the next day, she turned up at Man Ray's hotel, went up to his room and took off her clothes; he wanted to photograph her nude.

He took a few shots. They went down to a café. He asked her to come back the next day for another session, and to see the first series of photos. She did. Together, they looked at the previous day's work. Then Kiki undressed, as Man Ray prepared his equipment. He was seated on the bed. She came over and sat down next to him, naked. He took her hand. She kissed him.

For the next six years, they would be inseparable.

A RADIATOR KNOB
SIGNED BY RODIN

And so he will come onto the stage, like a pretty, well-behaved child, self-possessed, with careful gestures, and eyes which seem to see without looking – he who scarcely ever drew anything but cats and women.

Roger Vailland

While Kiki and Man Ray were drifting off to sleep on the first page of their love story, a young girl of about twenty was pushing open the door of her apartment on the rue Cardinet. Her face was round and she was plump, with chestnut hair and dark, lively eyes. For the last three years, she had been an orphan. She didn't work; her parents had left her enough to live on.

Lucie Badoul set down the armful of books she had just bought. She went into the bathroom, carefully took off her make-up, picked up her books and went into her bedroom, where a little rust-coloured cat followed her. The young girl slipped between the sheets and chose one of the volumes to which she had treated herself for the simple reason that she liked the title: La Femme assise. She didn't know the author, Guillaume Apollinaire, any more than she knew Montparnasse, the neighbourhood he described. But when she had finished reading, the cafés seemed so extraordinary, the people who lived there so free, the atmosphere so different from that which Lucie Badoul knew, that she became almost feverish with curiosity.

She rose, got dressed again, put her make-up back on, tucked her cat under her arm and headed for the Métro, leaving the rue Cardinet behind.

She got out of the Métro at Montparnasse, and walked up the boulevard until she reached La Rotonde, the amazing bistro of which Apollinaire spoke. But it was packed with customers, both on the ground floor and the first floor. Disappointed, the young girl was about to leave when a group of Spaniards got up to go. She took their table. Seated, she looked around her. Never had she come across such a lively atmosphere, such a feeling of complicity amongst the regular customers who came in and out. Lucie was fascinated.

Late that night, she finally went home. The very next day she was back

more than mere silhouettes of people. Faces appeared and detached
themselves from the crowd.

That man, for instance, who was coming in the door. He was alone,
an Asian. His forehead was hidden by his fringe, and he wore horn-
rimmed glasses. Beneath his well-cut jacket, fastened at hip-level by a
cloth belt, was a red-and-white checked cotton shirt. Lucie watched him,
transfixed. She understood that she was helpless. She had just fallen madly
in love. But the man turned around and left. The young girl sat there,
motionless. She called to the waiter and asked for a liqueur. Then another.
And another ... Finally, after six glasses, she had summoned up the
courage to ask the question that was eating away at her. She got up, went
and stood in the middle of the café and asked if anyone knew the Japanese
man who had just left. A man stood up and said, 'Come with me.'

The man was a painter. He took the young lady to his home. In a
minute, he had traced a charcoal portrait of the Asian customer.

'Is that him?'

'Yes,' answered Lucie.

The painter rolled up his portrait and handed it to her.

'His name is Foujita.'

'Do you know him?'

'Of course!'

'Give him my address,' requested Lucie.

She wrote it on a piece of paper, and then went home. She hung the
portrait of Foujita on the wall. For eight days she didn't go out. She
waited. But the man of her dreams didn't try to reach her. Finally Lucie
returned to Montparnasse. The painter who had drawn the Japanese man
for her took her to 5, rue Delambre, where Foujita had his studio. Foujita
looked at the young girl, gave her a fan, and suggested meeting that night
at La Rotonde.

She was there, and they had dinner together. Afterwards, he took her
to a hotel, where they remained for three days without once leaving the
room. When they reappeared at the Rotonde, Lucie wasn't called Lucie
any more: Foujita had baptized her 'Youki', which was Japanese for 'Pink
rose'. She would keep the nickname he had given her even when, in
1931, she fell into Robert Desnos' arms.

What was life like with Foujita? Magical. Of course there was Fernande.
His wife didn't give up without a fight, even though she had fallen in
love with someone else long before. When Foujita exhibited his painting
Youki, Snow Goddess, at the Salon d'Automne, Fernande publicly insulted her
husband's mistress. But as soon as she was away, the party began.

In the twenties, life in Montparnasse resembled a son et lumière show,
filled with friends, social occasions, extravagant balls and parties. There

were often twenty guests at a dinner table, sometimes two or three times that number, or even more.

Everything depended on who the host was. When it was the Comte de Beaumont, entertaining in his home on the rue Duroc, the reception rooms, halls and even staircases were full to bursting. The ball was upstairs, downstairs, and in between, on the mezzanine. Most of the time, the guests were in costume, and Youki didn't always recognize everyone. Marcoussis came dressed as a peasant woman, Van Dongen as Neptune, Kisling as a prostitute from the south ... The women wore helmets and officers' uniforms, the men wore wigs. There were sailors, mutes and mimes, clowns with their faces painted white, toreadors. Foujita, the king of disguises, often came in a dress. One evening, he was seen completely naked, disguised as a porter with a cage on his back and a woman in the cage. Sometimes he wore earrings, a turban, or an opera hat. In every corner, people laughed and danced, couples formed or split up. The wine flowed freely ...

When the party wasn't on the rue Duroc, it was at the Watteau house on the rue Jules Chaplain, the Scandinavians' home ground. At least once a year, they held a sumptuous ball, attended by all of Montparnasse. And when it wasn't there, it was elsewhere: in studios specially fitted out for the occasion, with painters doing the decoration and sometimes even designing posters to be displayed in the streets. At the Bullier, the Union of Russian Artists sometimes gave its turn to the AAA (Amicable Assistance to Artists), which organized evenings for artists in need. There was also the Four Arts Ball, which began in the courtyard of the Beaux-Arts and ended, late at night or early in the morning, with the traditional bath in the fountains of the Place de la Concorde or in the Luxembourg gardens. On Saturdays or Sundays, or sometimes both, all the partymakers wound up at the Bal Nègre on the rue Blomet, near Vaugirard. There one danced the beguine (a dance from the West Indies), driven on by rum punch, drumrolls and vibrant clarinets. Crowds of people danced and had a riotous time, including many blacks but also mulattos, colonial soldiers and more and more artists.

Sometimes Youki and Foujita stopped at the Caméléon, at the corner of the Boulevard du Montparnasse and the rue Campagne-Première. Before, the place had been mostly empty in the daytime: one could get choucroute there which cost barely more than Rosalie's spaghetti, and hawkers sold mattresses or silk stockings to the occasional customer. But ever since Alexandre Mercereau, a sculptor by profession, had decided to take over this former bistro, the place had been full from morning until evening. Especially in the evening, when the Caméléon was transformed into the open university of Montparnasse. Musicians and poets from all over the world met there to read their poems, play their works and make speeches.

On Sundays, many of them came to see the satirical revues. Even the wealthy and the fashionable sometimes turned up: Cocteau had been known to attend, as had the Comtesse de Noailles.

The Comtesse was an admirer of Foujita's: less, perhaps, for the quality of his work than because he painted a milieu also favoured by Van Dongen, that of chic society. He had done portraits of the Comtesse de Clermont-Tonnerre, the Comtesse de Ganay, and the Comtesse de Monte-bello: why shouldn't he also paint the Comtesse de Noailles?

At the time, though they spent most of their days in Montparnasse, Youki and Foujita lived on the rue Massenet, near Passy. The Comtesse de Noailles was their neighbour. For the first sitting, it was she who came to them.

She was tiny but wore a gigantic string of pearls around her neck, which helped to keep her upright. She didn't have great esteem for the artists for whom she had sat before the Japanese painter, but then she didn't really have much esteem for anyone but herself. She was pleased with herself for many reasons, especially her poetry, which she practised assiduously. She saw herself as a great writer, an immensely gifted poet, and a beautiful woman, with magnificent eyes, a forehead revealing a subtle intelligence, the source of her infinite charm, and the body of a goddess. She sometimes had to protect these precious assets: 'You under-stand, my dear Foujita, why you must also come and paint me at my home, when I'm in bed, to give my flesh, my muscles, and my brain a chance to rest.'

So he went, the devoted Foujita. He took the servants' staircase because concierges didn't like to see a shabby little Japanese fellow like him coming to call on the wealthy inhabitants of their buildings. The Comtesse de Noailles was waiting for him, resting on the silken drapes of the canopy bed, wearing a dress designed by Poiret. She was in the shadows, and she constantly chattered and fidgeted. Foujita painted: the sittings were interminable. When he finally finished the portrait, the Comtesse de Noailles was furious: she didn't find in it all the beauty of her person, the splendour of her character, the divinity of her thought ... But that was just too bad; the painter signed and left. He hadn't even finished the work.

Life with Foujita was like a dream, because his career took off in such a spectacular way. Ever since Chéron had exhibited his gouaches in 1922, he had been much in demand everywhere. His works could be found all over Europe, and even in the United States, and his canvases sold for large sums of money. In the space of just a few months, he had become one of the kings of Montparnasse, and one of the most popular and wealthy artists. For his fiancée's twenty-first birthday (she was soon to become his wife), he decided that she should have a new driver. Until then, she had regularly taken a taxi, which always came to get her the minute she appeared at the door of a restaurant or a nightclub.

Foujita gave his beloved the present of which all formerly starving artists dream, a car. And not just any car: it was a yellow Ballot, with a body by Saoutchik and a radiator knob signed by Rodin. It was driven by José Raso, a Basque *pelote* champion who had just become a private chauffeur.

The mink coat which accompanied it hardly counted, and the stenographer–typist to whom Foujita henceforth dictated his mail was just another drop of water in the ocean of visible marks of success, which would only increase with time.

Foujita was in Saint Tropez.

Foujita was in Cannes, on the Croisette.

Foujita was bicycling along the promenade at Deauville. With whom? Maurice de Rothschild, Van Dongen, the Dolly Sisters or Suzy Solidor, who directed a dance troupe and liked to walk around in a bathing suit made of mother-of-pearl seashells, when she wasn't in a fishing net with a bikini bottom made of cork. Then there was Mistinguett, whom André Salmon encountered at the criminal court of Versailles, where 'the queen of feathers' was venting her rage and arrogance on a chambermaid who had stolen one of her one hundred and seventy-two fur coats. It was a strange world, pitiless, chic, diabolically worldly and superficial – even if, as all testify, Foujita himself wasn't fundamentally transformed by it.

Water had flowed under the bridge, and soon the bridges were of a different nature. Their studio on the rue Delambre faded from people's memories, as did their home on the right bank. From 1927 on, Youki and Foujita lived at 3, rue du Parc Montsouris, in a three-storey apartment with a terrace. Friends had contributed for the furniture, and a promising young writer had sold them a carpet, chairs, and a most original American bar. This writer signed his works by the name of Georges Sim, an abbreviation of his real name, Georges Simenon. He regularly attended the magnificent parties that the Foujitas gave in their home, which were as sumptuous as the Van Dongens' equally famous evenings. He also sat around in the Dôme and the Rotonde, stuffed his pipe with hashish, and waited his turn on the ground floor of whorehouses. He too left one bar for the next, went from one pleasure to another, to a second, a third, a fourth, until, very late in the night, the clouds of smoke and mists of alcohol drove him across the river to the right bank. For at 28, rue Boissy D'Anglas, Jean Cocteau, fulfilling the prophecy of Maurice Sachs, had become the most extraordinary of all Parisian hosts.

ONE COCKTAIL, TWO COCTEAUS…

Radiguet, with his monocle held to his eye, extremely distant, even pretentious: in short, Radiguet playing Radiguet…

Pierre Brasseur

Ever since 10 January 1922, Cocteau had been holding court at the Boeuf sur le Toit. He had invaded Louis Moysès' bar with his group of friends, who represented all that was most fashionable in Paris at the time, as well as the musicians of Les Six, Diaghilev, Coco Chanel, and a few others. There were enough of them to make this spot the right bank headquarters of the avant-garde.

Cocteau was the keeper of the flame; Wiener and Doucet were at the piano, and Williams was on the drums. But nobody really listened; people came to be seen. Or to drink. Or to admire Picabia's painting *L'œil cacodylate*, bought by Moysès after the Salon des Indépendants had refused it. It showed an eye that Picabia had drawn while suffering from an eye infection which was being treated with cacodylate (a medical allusion reminiscent of Tristan Tzara's *Antipyrine*). He had asked his friends to add their signatures and a few words to the painting. Some of the results were as follows: 'Isadora [Duncan] loves Picabia with all her soul'; 'I find him *Very*' (Tristan Tzara); 'I have nothing to say to you' (Georges Auric); 'My name has been Dada since 1892' (Darius Milhaud); 'I like salad' (Francis Poulenc); 'Crown of melancholy' (Jean Cocteau, with a photo).

Since his earliest ventures into Montparnasse society, Cocteau had made progress on the path he had cut out for himself. He had become a central figure in the artistic life of the times.

With a rare tactical sense, the young poet of the *Danse de Sophocle* (he was twenty-five in 1917) had won the admiration of fashionable society, whom he seemed to avoid after having understood and manipulated them with his strategic flair, and to whom he would return with his hands full – though always light – of presents which would leave them dumb with admiration.[1]

Salmon had found the words to express it, and even if it was said with cruelty, it was true: a dozen years after his first appearance in the artistic circles of Paris, Cocteau was firmly implanted. Everyone now knew all the frivolous details of his frenetic social life, but they were accepted. Even better: he was sought after. As for his poetry, it was viewed with indulgence. He so needed to be loved! He had such a gift for language!

Indeed, he was greatly admired by the youth of the time. When the young Pierre Brasseur was invited to meet him, he didn't hesitate for a second: 'In 1923, any young man would have jumped at the chance.'[2]

And so the future actor went to the rue d'Anjou to meet 'this high-wire artist whom we all admired'. The young man was fascinated, especially by the poet's hands: 'two hands which were worth four, which fluttered gracefully even to say hello, and which he used admirably, drawing pictures in the air, illustrating his conversation with them – like paintbrushes, like bolts of lightning, like feathers – in short, the finest hands I've ever seen!'

The master of the house let his visitor accompany him to the bathroom, where he shaved, talking all the while.

> His words were all topsy-turvy, the thoughts colliding with each other, resulting in a play of ideas like in a word game ... They took off like rockets, going up ceaselessly. All you had to do was give him a word or an idea for him to make a poetic joke out of it and set it aside, a handsome demonstration of his marvellous reflexes. He was never short of wit, the bastard.

The second time they met, Cocteau took Brasseur to see his bedroom, where the walls were covered with phone numbers. Another visitor, Georges Charensol, who was then a journalist for *Paris-Journal*, noted the ostentatious modesty of this room, compared to the bourgeois luxury of the entrance hall, which was dominated by a portrait of the master of the house, painted by Jacques-Emile Blanche. But Brasseur was still too young at the time to notice these details. All the more so as he had scarcely entered the room when a giant trundled out from under the bed. His face was crumpled and his tongue thick, probably the effect of the opium which the two men had doubtless been using and abusing in the course of the previous few hours.

Cocteau gestured towards the sleepy figure and said, 'That's a baby I gave birth to during the night.'[3]

It was Joseph Kessel.

All this, of course, could not fail to make quite an impression on a young man.

At the party for the opening of the Boeuf sur le Toit, Picasso chatted with Marie Laurencin, and Brancusi with a young man he had met several times in Cocteau's company. He wasn't particularly handsome: he had pale skin and light eyes; he was short, near-sighted, and his hair was badly cut. He rolled his own cigarettes, spreading tobacco everywhere. He wore broken glasses, which he took out of his pocket and held up to his eyes, like a monocle.

During the war, it had been André Salmon who had introduced this young man into Cocteau's circle. The poet was collaborating at that time with L'Intransigeant. In 1917, he had contacted one of his old friends, an illustrator, to commission some drawings to appear on the first page of the paper (Salmon had already helped Foujita out in this way). The man had accepted the proposal, which was for two drawings a week. As he lived in Saint-Maur (the Parc Saint-Maur at the time), he had given his son the job of delivering the finished work.

The son was just an adolescent, only fourteen and still wearing knee-length trousers: 'A nice boy with the lively eyes of a still innocent adult, but a good candidate for future cruelty; yes, he had a strange gaze, shadowed by rebellious hair falling into his face from beneath the rigid frame of the helmet.'[4]

His name was Raymond Radiguet. Twice a week, Raymond Radiguet delivered his father's drawings. After several weeks, he took André Salmon aside and said, 'You know, I draw too.'

Salmon said nothing.

'Do you want me to show you?'

As the journalist looked on in amazement, the young boy opened the portfolio containing his father's drawings and drew out some of his own.

'What do you think?'

André Salmon remained speechless.

'Maybe you could publish them...'

As the quality of the drawing wasn't bad, and as his illustrator friend needed money, Salmon agreed, but on one condition: that the boy use a different name from his father's.

'That's no problem,' said Raymond Radiguet. Before the editor's eyes, he picked up a pen and signed 'Rajki'.

One week later, when he returned, Raymond Radiguet delivered his father's illustration, added his own, and then said, 'I didn't tell you this, but I also write...'

And he took out a poem.

'Go see Max Jacob,' André Salmon suggested.

The next day, Raymond Radiguet phoned Max Jacob. Then he came back to L'Intransigeant to ask Salmon if he couldn't help him to get work as a journalist. Finally, he showed up at Léonce Rosenberg's, where a reading had been organized in memory of Guillaume Apollinaire. He read a poem, and Max Jacob introduced him to Cocteau. Impressed by the boy, the poet fell headlong into the arms of youth.

On the night of the inauguration of the Boeuf sur le Toit, realizing that he was out of place there, Brancusi invited the young man to return with him to simpler horizons. They left the party for Montparnasse. At dawn, the sculptor suggested taking the train.

'Fine, but where to...?'

'The South.'

They went to the station, got into the first wagon they saw and found themselves in Brittany. There they changed trains, and were in Marseille the next night. They were still wearing their party clothes: smoking jackets and patent leather shoes.

Marseille was depressing, so they left for Nice. Nice was deserted, so they went to Ajaccio. There were no women in Ajaccio, so they toured the island of Corsica. The island was not very large, and eleven days later they were back in Paris. 'Brancusi deposited Radiguet at the Boeuf and never turned up there again,' noted Jean Hugo without further comment.[5]

Like Pierre Brasseur, Paul Morand, who encountered the young man for the first time at a costume ball at Paul Poiret's home, found him taciturn, haughty and pretentious. Cocteau himself, fascinated, in love, transported, later wrote in terms that were both critical and self-critical: 'Undoubtedly he had a plan, that he was carrying out long-term. He would one day have orchestrated his work and even, I'm sure, taken all the necessary steps to make sure that notice would be taken of it.'[6]

But didn't he in fact do just that? And didn't Cocteau help him?

When Raymond Radiguet began to write the story of an affair between a young man and an older woman during the war, the poet had a hand in it. We don't know exactly how big a hand. Maybe, as he said himself, he simply locked his protégé in his room to force him to conquer his laziness. In any case, he was the one who brought the first pages of the work to Editions Grasset, to read to them.

Bernard Grasset immediately grasped what a goldmine he had in his hands: a very young author, a whiff of scandal, godfathers and protectors in every corner of Paris – both the Paris of the arts and letters, and elegant society.

Le Diable au corps was published in March 1923, accompanied by a well-oiled publicity strategy. Editions Grasset launched the book just as modern marketing executives launch a new product. Ads in the papers, extensive mailings of the book to journalists, friends writing reviews in their papers (notably Cocteau himself in the Nouvelle Revue française) – all this was very new at the time. The result was fifty thousand copies sold in the first two weeks. 'Baby', as Cocteau called him, could be pleased with himself.

And so he was. In the course of the year he had left to live, he drank to celebrate his triumph, smoked opium, and consumed everything he could, as fast as he could. He left behind him Marthe, the heroine of the *Diable au corps*, who searched for him in the editorial offices of all the papers; Beatrice Hastings, whom he had met at Brancusi's, and who was as violent and passionate with him as she had been with Modigliani; and Jean Cocteau, who still hadn't swallowed all these other lovers and couldn't accept the latest either. This was Bronia Perlmutter, a young model of Polish extraction, very popular in Montparnasse, who had been painted by Nils Dardel and by Kisling; she had come to the Boeuf dressed in a Poiret gown, and Radiguet had taken her off to a hotel.

The young couple claimed they wanted to marry. They hid out at the Hôtel Foyot on the rue de Tournon, trying to avoid him, whom the gossips would soon be calling 'le veuf sur le toit',* and on whose name the columnists punned: 'one cocktail, two cocteaus.'

Radiguet consumed his youth in a Montparnasse grown sluggish from all the singing and dancing, illuminated by garlands of moneyed pleasures, doped up with the cocaine that was easily to be had in cafés and restaurants, drowning in the drink consumed everywhere by artists, by stupefied tourists, by Americans toasting the joy of being in such a free and magnificent city. On both the right bank and the left, Paris was a cauldron, bubbling more dangerously than ever.

Only a few months after the publication of the *Diable au corps*, the lights were abruptly dimmed. On 12 December 1923, Raymond Radiguet succumbed to typhoid fever. When he was taken from his room at the Hôtel Foyot to a clinic in the sixteenth arrondissement, it was already too late. The senior doctor, sent by a desperate Cocteau, had not managed to diagnose the illness. Radiguet received absolution and died in excruciating pain.

Coco Chanel arranged the funeral. Everything was white: the coffin, the flowers, the horses, the harnesses. Cocteau, immobilized by grief, did not attend the ceremony. A few years later, he wrote these memorable words:

> Radiguet was too free. And it was he who had taught me to depend on nothing ... Since the little lucidity I had, I got from him, his death left me without instructions, incapable of leading my life coherently, of sustaining and nourishing my work, and providing for it.[7]

Raymond Radiguet was just twenty years old.

---

* 'The widower on the roof.'

A GENERATION LOST AND FOUND

You others, the young people who fought in the war, you're all a lost generation.

Gertrude Stein

In America, prohibition reigned. In Europe, one could drink in peace. Another advantage: life there was cheaper, and there were always friends willing to help.

Sylvia Beach, for instance, whose bookshop was a welcoming haven. Travellers could have mail sent to them there, and Shakespeare & Company was theirs for the asking. Sylvia organized literary evenings, helped people meet, encouraged encounters, events and exchanges.

For those who wanted to chat over a glass of wine when they left the bookshop, all they had to do was walk back up the rue de l'Odéon, cut through the Luxembourg gardens, take the rue Vavin, the rue Bréa, then the first street to the right after the corner, until they reached 10, rue Delambre. There was a bistro there that had just been bought by an American: the Dingo 'American bar and restaurant'. During the day, one could have lunch there, though it wasn't cheap, and in the evening drink flowed freely. Flossie Martin, a dancer who had left the other side of the Atlantic behind her, supervised her friends' ballets. They were hard drinkers and spoke with a Yankee accent. The Dingo was one of the centres of the American colony in Paris. Writers, of whom there must have been several hundred in Paris, also used to come there after dinner: Sherwood Anderson, Thornton Wilder, Eugène Jolas, who lived in Colombey-les-deux-Eglises, Sinclair Lewis, Archibald MacLeish, John Dos Passos, William Seabrook, Djuna Barnes, Mina Loy, and Robert MacAlmon, who would publish the works of his American friends. There was also George Gershwin, who wrote *An American in Paris* in hotel rooms; Ezra Pound – one of the first to arrive as the Paris correspondent for *The Little Review*, he would leave the country in 1924 to embrace Italy and, alas, the Duce; Natalie Clifford Barney and her companion Romaine Goddard Brooks, who welcomed their friends for open house dinners at their hotel on the rue Jacob. There was Henry Miller, who came through Paris for a short time in 1928 and who, two years later, would come back and stay for longer, perfecting, perhaps at the Dingo, an infallible method for finding as much as he wanted to eat every day. He would sit down at a table and write twelve notes that he sent to twelve diners in the room, asking each of them to invite him to dinner once in the week. In exchange for a bottle of champagne and a few free hours with one of the girls, Miller also drafted the publicity brochure for the biggest whorehouse on the left bank, the Sphynx, whose doors opened in 1931. He received a commission for every male client who came on his recommendation.

Then there was Sandy Calder, with his sculptures in metallic wire and all his rigmarole. There were, in particular, Scott Fitzgerald, Zelda, and even little Scotty. *The Great Gatsby* would soon be published, but even now, after the publication of *This Side of Paradise* in 1920, American reviews were frantic to buy up the writer's short stories, which gave him sufficient funds to enjoy the pleasures of Paris.

It was at the Dingo that he first met Hemingway. The latter had arrived in Paris in 1921, then went back to the United States for a year before returning with his wife Hadley and their child. Hemingway knew all the Anglo-Saxons in Paris, notably Joyce, with whom he went out drinking – when he was drunk, the Irishman used to sing operatic arias – and to whom he gave boxing lessons.

Hemingway and his family first lived in the fifth arrondissement, then moved to the rue Notre Dame des Champs. At the beginning of his stay, Hemingway made a living by writing sports articles for the *Toronto Star*. Ever since he had given up journalism, he had been trying to make enough to live on just by betting on horseraces and submitting his stories to American magazines, which systematically refused them.

He wrote at the Closerie des Lilas, which was quieter than the Dôme or the Select (the only poet to be found there was Blaise Cendrars). Sometimes he came with his son Bumby, who dozed while his father worked. When lunchtime approached, the trick was to go somewhere else where there would be no culinary temptations; in any case, there was no money with which to indulge whatever temptation might present itself.

Hemingway had worked out a route which was suited to his problems. First of all he would go to the Luxembourg gardens, where the plants and the trees gave off a fragrant smell totally unlike that of any tasty dishes. Between the Place de l'Observatoire and the rue de Vaugirard, famished walkers took no risks, as there were no restaurants in the area.

If the stroller wanted to change neighbourhoods and leave the garden, Hemingway advised taking the rue Férou to Saint Sulpice. Not a single tempting table was on the route. Then one could slip off towards the Seine, though one had to be warned that bakers, pastry chefs, grocers and other masticatory demons were legion here. The best option was to turn right on the rue de l'Odéon, avoiding the Place, where three restaurants beckoned, and to go up to no. 12. Sylvia Beach would always greet you pleasantly, and would even be so generous as to lend you books: Hemingway was able to read Turgenev, Gogol and Chekhov there.

In the evenings, he would often go to the Dingo. The first time he met Scott Fitzgerald there, the latter was downing champagne, one glass after another. At the end of the evening, he had to be packed into a taxi and sent home.

A few days later, the two men met again at the Closerie des Lilas. Fitzgerald told Hemingway how he managed to get his stories published in American papers. He would send one to the *Post*, then, after it was published, he would rework it, cut it, and revamp it a little before sending it elsewhere. When Hemingway became indignant and called him a 'whore', Fitzgerald exclaimed, 'I have to do it if I want to have enough money to write good books!'[1]

Then Fitzgerald asked a favour of his companion: could he come with him to Lyons to retrieve the Renault that Zelda and he had been forced to leave there when caught in a storm?

Hemingway agreed, and the two set out on an incredible trip. First Scott missed the train and Ernest had to leave alone. When they met up the next day, Scott had already made a good start on his daily dose of liquor. But he was only warming up. They bought supplies for the road before going to the garage where the Renault awaited them. It was a sedan without a roof. Surprised, Hem asked and Scott explained: the roof had been dented in Marseille, and Zelda had had it sawed off. Driving roofless in the rain was not much fun, so they had left the car in Lyons when it started to pour.

The two men got in, Scott at the wheel, Hem next to him. Soon another storm forced them to stop. They set off again, stopped again, set off, stopped ... On practically every stopover, they replenished their supply of wine. Scott was delighted: he had never before drunk straight from the bottle. But suddenly, between two gulps, he began to cough. Could this be the start of a congestion of the lungs?

'Of course not!' said Hemingway.

'It may well be ...' worried Fitzgerald.

That would be serious. He knew at least two people who had died from a congestion of the lungs and he didn't want the same thing to happen to him. But the situation seemed grave. At Chalon-sur-Saône, they stopped at a hotel. He was sick, and should be in bed.

In the hotel room, Scott put on his pyjamas and got into bed. Before closing his eyes, he asked Hemingway to promise to look after his wife and daughter if anything should happen to him. Hemingway promised with a light heart, since his friend's pulse was as normal as his complexion was healthy. But Fitzgerald wanted a thermometer. They called for the bellboy.

'If the crisis passes,' Fitzgerald declared, 'we'll take the train back and I'll go to the American hospital in Paris.'

The thermometer arrived. Scott slipped it under his arm. Five minutes later, he had the results, which were excellent: 37.6 degrees centigrade.

'Is that high?' asked the patient.

'It's normal.'

'What's your temperature?'

In a sign of friendship, Hem took his own temperature.

'Well?' asked Scott anxiously.

'37.6.'

'And you're not sick?'

'Not in the slightest.'

Fitzgerald jumped out of bed, took off his pyjamas and dressed hastily.

'I always make a speedy recovery...'

A few days later, in Paris, Scott invited Hem to lunch. He wanted to speak to him about an important, very personal problem. Zelda had told him that his penis was too small to satisfy women. What should he do?

'Let's see,' said Hemingway.

The two friends left the table and locked themselves in the washroom. The verdict was ... normal.

'No, you're wrong,' said Scott. 'It really is very short.'

'That's because you are looking at it from above ... From the side, it looks fine.'

'I have to be sure.'

'Let's go to the Louvre.'

'What for?'

'We'll compare you with the statues...'

Two Americans in Paris...

There was a third, whom Hemingway hadn't yet met, the patron of the arts who lived at 27, rue de Fleurus: Gertrude Stein.

When Hemingway went to her home for the first time, he was twenty-three. She found him handsome, and according to her account, he was also well-mannered and respectful. The lady was delighted. Not only might the newcomer be able to replace Ezra Pound, who had been kicked out since breaking a chair; he could actually be an improvement on him. For Hemingway sat down and listened. Even better, he sought advice. Hadn't he asked her if she might come and visit him to give her opinion on his manuscripts?

He showed her some poems which she found not too bad, and part of a novel, which she judged poor. To help guide him, she made him read her latest work, The Making of Americans. Hemingway was awestruck. Now this was a work. Gertrude Stein wrote that Hemingway told her 'that all that was left to him and his generation was to devote their lives to seeing that it was published'.[2]

And he did try to help. He copied the manuscript, corrected the proofs, and pushed for publication. This colossus of a man was kind and devoted to her. When Gertrude Stein advised him to give up journalism to devote himself to writing, Hemingway swore, his hand on the seam of his trousers, that that was what he would do. And he kept his promise. When he left for the United States, it was on the advice of the good Gertrude; he would work there so as not to have to return to Paris as a journalist.

A good pupil, by all accounts. That was what both Gertrude Stein and Sherwood Anderson said of him: 'Hemingway, such a good student!'

Why did they see this quality in him rather than some other trait? Because, wrote the great Gertrude, he had excellent masters in Anderson and herself. She felt that together they had educated the young man. She recognized, of course, that he had some aptitude, but he noted everything without necessarily understanding it. She compared him to Derain: modern, but still with a whiff of the museum about him.

Hemingway's version of all this is completely different, of course. First of all, when he went to Gertrude's, he was usually alone. His hostess did not have much taste for the wives of her friends: Alice Toklas was there to look after them.

He enjoyed these visits: he was offered as much eau-de-vie as he liked and could gaze at the magnificent paintings on the walls. The conversation was interesting, though Miss Stein had a tendency to spend more time discussing gossip and the private lives of writers than the works themselves. As for the sex education lessons she offered her visitor, they were hilarious. She tried to persuade him that male homosexuality was dirty and wicked, whereas female homosexuality was beautiful and noble. The young man's reaction, though he kept it to himself, was, 'It's not just a question of fucking, but of knowing how to settle your ass down.'

He admired her work, but with reservations. He found The Making of Americans interesting, but flawed: it was much too long, repetitive and difficult to digest. He tried to help get it published simply as a friendly gesture, and corrected the proofs for the same reason. Nothing more.

Their greatest preoccupation, though, was Gertrude Stein herself, as usual: her life, her work. Miss Stein wanted to be published in the Atlantic Monthly or the Saturday Evening Post, magazines in which, according to her,

Hemingway could not hope to have his work accepted; he was not a good enough writer.

The other American and English authors weren't worth much more in her eyes. They didn't count for a whole lot, she felt. Huxley? Useless. Lawrence? Sick. Joyce? 'Anyone who mentioned Joyce twice in her presence would be banished from the premises.'[3]

For Gertrude Stein, all the writers who had fought in the war thought of nothing now besides drinking, and had no respect for anything. They were, as she stated in a phrase that quickly became famous – because it was famously stupid – 'a lost generation'.

Having found so much to criticize in her acquaintances, Gertrude Stein would end by falling out with practically everyone who had ever come through the door of the rue de Fleurus, with the exception of Juan Gris, who was dead. Practically all the others, including her brother Leo, banded together against her when her memoirs were published in France in 1934. Braque, Picasso, Tzara, Matisse, and Salmon, notably, would each publish texts criticizing the lady's gossipy style, her pretension in giving herself a variety of titles and claims to fame, and her tendency to judge art through personal and biographical considerations rather than in terms of the painting itself.

Hemingway, more tolerant than some others, continued to see her. But he would never be as close to her again. Their old friendship only returned much later, in the sixties, when shortly before committing suicide, he looked back on his Parisian days to write the book that stands as a homage to the exhilarating freedom of the times: *A Moveable Feast*.

A WANDERING JEW

With his hat falling back on his neck, he looked like some turn-of-
the-century character from Broadway, rather than the charming painter
he really was, and later, when he had hung himself, I liked to
remember him as he was that night, at the Dôme.

Ernest Hemingway

Walking along the Boulevard du Montparnasse, coming back from Gertrude
Stein's or Sylvia Beach's bookshop, Hemingway passed the Dôme. A man
was sitting at a table, drawing. Two girls were with him: one had dark
hair, the other was very young and pretty. The man was well-dressed, in
a blue suit, a tie, a freshly ironed shirt and polished shoes. He wore a
long white silk scarf and a bowler hat pulled down towards the front of
his head. He had olive skin and dark, lively, penetrating eyes, which were
filled with melancholy at times. A cigarette hung from the corner of his
lips.

He gestured to Hemingway to come and join him.

'Have a drink with us!'

The writer asked for a beer. The other man answered that he had
money, and they could order whisky. He then introduced the two girls,
his models; he offered one of them to the American, along with his
studio, and they laughed.

When the waiter brought the drinks, the man with the hat asked for
some paper. He crumpled and tossed away the sheet he was drawing on,
took out a sulphur-treated match, lit it, extinguished it, dragged it over
the paper, diluted the line drawn with the coffee grounds and sketched
the portrait of one of the two young girls across from him, all without
interrupting the conversation for an instant. His voice was soft, and he
spoke with a central European accent. He smiled inwardly. He asked his
guest a thousand questions, all the while adding seltzer to his watercolours.
Little by little, the conversation progressed and a new drawing emerged,
which Jules Pascin stuffed under his seat. Then he called for another sheet
of paper and began again...

When Hemingway got up to go home, Pascin suggested to the two
young ladies that they had another drink at the Viking. From there they

went on to Alfredo's, on the rue des Martyrs. Pascin ate there often: the food was not very good, but it was expensive, which gave the painter the feeling that he was inviting his guests to one of the best restaurants in Paris.

At midnight, there were fifteen of them at the table: other models, other painters, a handful of strollers. Pascin paid for everyone. Then the night continued in a club in Montmartre or Montparnasse, on the ground floor of a whorehouse. Some of the guests went upstairs, others didn't. Pascin drew portraits of the girls: he was there and not there at the same time. Admired, toasted, surrounded by friends; sometimes laughing boisterously, sometimes alone with his feathers, his pens, his glasses of liqueur. He drank a lot, too much. His friends tried tricks as old as alcohol itself to try to reduce the doses; they rarely succeeded.

Pascin was the king of parties. Often, taking advantage of his friends' cars, he drove his little group of followers out to the country or the banks of the Marne. There were almost always more women than men. They ate cold meats and drank wine, half undressed because they'd been swimming. They came home late at night after having stopped for a last drink in a bar, or in several.

At least once a week, Pascin sent out invitations by mail or *pneumatique* to his friends. They were invited to come to his home at 36, Boulevard de Clichy, bringing whoever they wanted. The first guests would arrive to find their host in a bathrobe, shaving. He wandered down the hallway, with shaving cream on his chin, while his favourite models checked to make sure there was enough ham, chicken, lamb, wine, and liqueurs.

Aïcha, a young mulatto born in the Pas-de-Calais region, whom the painter had come across one day on the street, was the most faithful. She was very attached to Pascin, which didn't keep her from posing for Kisling, Van Dongen, Foujita and many others. She helped push back the chairs and cushions to make room in the studio. There would be drinking, dancing, maybe even a band. The party would be grand, but still simple: never sophisticated, not a stilted social occasion like at Van Dongen's. And maybe at the end of the evening, Pascin would suggest going to Saint Tropez. He actually did it once: at dawn, about fifty partygoers took the train for an improvised trip to the seashore, returning only after a few days of drinking and some inebriated nights.

Another time, in Marseille, the painter gave a banquet for his friends. Once they were all there, not a single seat remained. He himself went off to a nearby restaurant and ate alone at his table. Francis Carco is the one who tells the story, which may be a bit exaggerated. But it is still a faithful reflection of the temperament of Pascin, who loved parties and hated to be alone.

One of his favourite pastimes was ordering drinks for everyone ... You had to be there and see Pascin. He glowed with happiness, getting people to tell stories, listening to his friends and, as the level of alcohol increased, finishing the evening with a drunken dance in which everyone joined him. The more glasses that were emptied, the happier he was ... Nonetheless, at certain times, one could sense that he suffered from not being truly at home anywhere, even when he was in Montmartre, surrounded by his friends.[1]

At dawn, after having paid for the food and drink of all present, Pascin went home, his heart heavy, and not only from drinking.

In the morning other girls would come and he would dress them in his own black stockings, make them pose, give them something to eat, take them to bed with him ... They would buy him the tubes of paint he needed and help clean up the studio. There were dancers for whose lessons he paid, and others whose task was to cook or clean for him. These essentially theoretical jobs didn't keep them from wearing lace and light veils, and posing, often in suggestive positions, for their painter–employer, who was sometimes their lover and always their friend.

They were very young. Pascin didn't have the heart to send them home, particularly as they often had no home to speak of, or lodged in tiny rooms or cabins, the only sad shacks they could afford on the pittances they earned. So they would stay at his home, sleeping on couches or on the floor, wrapped in warm covers. Pascin liked the simplicity of these girls from modest backgrounds.

He was simultaneously an oriental prince and (as his friend Georges Papazoff, painter and fellow countryman, defined him) 'a Jew – the wandering Jew uprooted, pursued, persecuted.'[2] He was a man of great generosity, surrounded by a court upon whom he lavished food and drink, whom he could not do without, and who followed him around from bars to parties, like a shimmering shadow. 'At a restaurant table presided over by Pascin one could see all the shades of human skin,' noted one of his most frequent guests, his good friend Pierre Mac Orlan.[3]

As prodigal as Modigliani, Pascin gave away his drawings to whoever asked for them, his money to whoever needed it, his own possessions to friends who admired them, and the saucers on which waiters brought the bill to the poorest people sitting in the bistros. When a friend came to his home to buy a painting, Pascin let him choose it, and promised to send a bill, which of course never came. This was his way of giving.

In his studio, one drawer was always filled with money. When he received a friend in need, he would say to him, 'Open the drawer and take what you need.'

Sometimes his works were stolen, for the entire contents of his money drawer was not worth a single one of his drawings. These were so popular

that fakes were even made of them. Pascin didn't care: what he earned was more than enough for him. Though he appreciated the outward signs of wealth, he liked to live like Picasso or Derain, selling works for more than the latter and sometimes two times less than the former. But he didn't hoard: he spent everything, more on others than on himself. In addition to his friends, his models (whom he paid much more than the going rate), and the poor painters of Montmartre and Montparnasse, he was supporting two women. One was his wife, the other a woman he loved; he also loved all the nubile girls he painted. He was an alcoholic, a partygoer, an outrageous fornicator. But he was also uprooted, a man without a country, cosmopolitan. Finally, hidden behind the mirror of so much excess, was a shy, anxious man, consumed by the heartbreak of tormented love.

He was born in Bulgaria, on the banks of the Danube, the son of wealthy merchants. They were richer than the families of Soutine or Krémègne. His father was Turko-Spanish and his mother Serbo-Italian. They crossed the Romanian border at the beginning of the century in order to develop their business. There it was that Pascin first began to develop the voracious, scandalous aura of sexuality which would surround him all his life. He fell in love with a woman whose perfume was doubly dangerous. Firstly, because he was only fifteen years old and she was thirty. Secondly, because she directed a company whose profits earned her the contempt of every respectable citizen: she was the sole owner of the largest whorehouse in Bucharest. Just the kind of affair to intrigue the young Pascin – and undermine the family's authority.

His father sent the boy to Germany. Thanks to what he had learned from his mistress and her employees, all of whom he had sketched, the young man was already expert in drawing and caricature. After studying drawing in Munich, Vienna, and Berlin (where he got to know George Grosz), he was taken on by a satirical journal where Steinlen already worked, *Simplissimus*. This was the straw that broke the paternal camel's back. Not satisfied with turning away from the familial Judaism which had no meaning for him; incapable of taking over the family business, a prosperous grain company which would have guaranteed him a stable future; attaining personal and artistic manhood in an unspeakable whorehouse: now the boy was drawing for a newspaper that respected nothing and no one!

So that the family would suffer no further dishonour, the father ordered his son to change his name. And so Julius Mordecai Pincas became Jules Pascin. In the same way, Lautrec had become Tréclau for a few weeks, obeying a similar paternal decree. The difference was that the Frenchman soon gave up the anagram, while the Bulgarian kept his for life.

When he first arrived in Paris on 24 December 1905, at the age of twenty, Jules Pascin was a free man. He had broken with his family, turned his back on a stable future, chosen a name for himself and lastly, achieved a comfortable living from the monthly fees he was paid by *Simplissimus*. Exceptionally, for an immigrant from the East, he would be met at the station. The customers of the Dôme, mainly German, had crossed the Seine to welcome this artist whose work they knew so well. Bing, Uhde, Wiegels and a few others had come to greet him. They took the new arrival to Montparnasse, stopping on the way to book a room for him at the Hôtel des Ecoles, on the rue Delambre – and then the party began ...

It started on the Boulevard Sébastopol on Christmas Eve, with an unexpected present in his Christmas stocking: a girl.

It went on, filled with colours and images, at the Louvre, where Pascin, like so many others, went to copy the masters.

It continued in whorehouses, widely frequented at the time.

It ended each evening in Montmartre, in the hotels where Pascin was staying, as he hadn't yet moved into one of his studios. All his friends would soon gather, notably those who would later write about him: Paul Morand, Pierre Mac Orlan, André Warnod, Ernest Hemingway, André Salmon, Ilya Ehrenburg ...

And the party began again every morning at the Dôme, where Pascin met friends and business contacts alike.

Like Modigliani, he belonged to no school; and like him, he preferred to keep himself on the margins of established groups. In the heyday of the Bateau Lavoir, he would meet Picasso at the Médrano circus. It was he who led the funeral procession for the painter Wiegels, whom he had known in Germany and who had met him at the station the day he arrived in Paris. This artist had hung himself, and was followed to his final resting place, the cemetery of Saint Ouen, by the entire group of the Bateau Lavoir: Picasso and his friends dressed in overalls and Fauve attire, while Pascin was clothed entirely in black with his already legendary bowler hat.

Like Modigliani, Pascin liked women, parties and drink. His generosity was boundless. He had as many friends as the Italian, and everyone loved him just as much. They were of the same generation: their stories were based on exile, and they both suffered from an open wound. One was in mourning for his sculpture, the other for a woman. They were living symbols of their times, the first trying to subsist in pre-war poverty, the second celebrating post-war opulence. They shared a similar tragic destiny which would carry them off, sovereigns consumed by secret suffering, ten years apart.

Pascin, however, was not unlucky in his art. Starting in 1908, he exhibited at the Salon d'Automne, and also in Berlin, Budapest, and elsewhere. It was he who inaugurated Pierre Loeb's gallery in 1924. His works were sometimes found shocking, to such a degree that Berthe Weill had to hang them in a space well concealed from public view. This didn't keep him from welcoming a circle of private art collectors who came to his home.

In 1907, while he was still living at the Hôtel des Ecoles (which he would leave in 1908), he shared a studio on the rue Lauriston with Henry Bing, one of his friends from the Dôme. One evening, Bing told him they would be receiving a visitor the next day: a young girl who did engravings and painted miniatures on ivory. Pascin greeted her in his bathrobe, with a flower in his ear.

She was tall, dark-haired, and had one unstable eye, the result of an unhappy encounter with a corset stay when she was a child. In an hour's time, Pascin had won her over. He offered her enough cognac to get her to stretch out on a mattress, where he discovered that her undergarments had been sewn up. This archaic form of chastity belt was a precaution taken by her mother to ensure the daughter's virginity, even though she was already twenty-one.

Hermine David made her entrance into Jules Pascin's life that day. She was his first wife, and the only one he legally married: they tied the knot ten years later. For many years, they lived sometimes together, sometimes separately, in hotel rooms, or temporary studios, until the painter moved to the Boulevard de Clichy.

The second woman in his life, even more important than Hermine, was called Cécile Vidil – Lucy to the habitués of Montparnasse. She was an apprentice sausage-maker at the age of fourteen, an apprentice dress-maker the next year, then a model at the Matisse Academy. This is where she met the two men in her life, Jules Pascin and Per Krogh.

Pascin went to the Matisse Academy specifically to meet this woman, who was said to be one of the most beautiful in Paris. She was a brunette, with pale skin and luscious curves. Pascin invited her to pose for him – she accepted. He asked for something more – and again, she accepted. The encounter took place in a hotel on the Place d'Anvers. Afterwards, these lovers of a single night would not see each other again for ten years.

Per Krogh was the son of the painter Christian Krogh and the godson of Edvard Munch. He also met Lucy at the Matisse Academy. She came and posed for him; he took her to the Bullier ball; she fell into his arms. They both became tango dancers, performed in Norway, then came back to Paris where they married in 1915.

At this time, Pascin was far away. In June 1914, two months before war was declared, he had left his studio at 3, rue Joseph Bara, the same building in which Zborowski and Kisling lived. He had gone to Brussels, then to London. From there, he had gone to the United States, where he was not unknown: John Quinn had bought some of his works for the Armory Show.

He had spent the war years between New York, the Southern states and Cuba. He regularly sent postal orders to his painter friends fighting on the front, in the trenches. In 1920, he became an American citizen; his witness was Alfred Stieglitz. But in October 1921, he came back to France.

He went right away to the rue Joseph Bara, to get the trunk he had left in the basement before his departure. In the courtyard of the building, he ran into the person who had taken his place on the last floor. It was Lucy Vidil. She had become Lucy Krogh, and had a little boy who was three years old. This didn't stop them: they fell into each others' arms. The torture would last for ten years.

AT THE JOCKEY CLUB

Svelte, fashionable, Madame L. had small, piercing eyes and a singular expression. Her lips were curved in a permanent smile like a Madonna's. She doubtless represented a very distinct type of woman, a little mysterious perhaps but still sweet and charming. Dressed in the style of the time, she revealed the exact contours of her breasts, which were easy to see. It is undeniable that she answered in every way to the sentimental desires that a man might entertain. She also corresponded to the sexual sensibility of Pascin, a man who was constantly in love.

George Papazoff

He was madly in love with her. She returned his passion, but without excessive zeal. When Hermine David went off to live in Montparnasse, Pascin remained in Montmartre. He painted there, partied there and waited for Lucy there. Sometimes she came, often even, but she didn't stay. She claimed that she couldn't leave her husband and her son Guy. He begged her. She broke it off with him. He asked if they could see each other 'just as friends'. She didn't answer. He resorted to childish tricks, 'running into her' in cafés where he knew she would be, pretending not to notice her, ignoring her, waiting, hoping, all for nothing. Then he returned home, sending a note announcing that he was planning to come by the rue Joseph Bara to get his boxes out of storage: what day would suit her, he didn't want to be a bother?

He wasn't a bother, he was a whirlwind. He took away not his crates and boxes (which he realized might be more useful left where they were) but her. They spent a few hours together, maybe half the night, then she left again. And came back. He begged her not to abandon him. And she left. He returned to Montparnasse, or to the rue Joseph Bara. He rented a room in the hotel where they had met ten years earlier and sent her a letter to remind her of the anniversary. He gave her presents, promised her trips, meals fit for a king, a life of luxury. She agreed, then refused, she came, she went, she posed for him, took care of his studio, found him models, slipped between his sheets, made him happy. When she left, always too soon, he would paint. If she promised to come back and then didn't keep her word, he would become desperate again. He sent her tearful letters. He said that he couldn't work when he had to wait, when he knew she was going to come but wasn't there. He needed her, to paint, to live. When she spaced out her visits, he would negotiate minute by minute to squeeze some extra time out of her — then, to take his revenge, he would go out.

When he went out, he drank. When he drank, he would find a girl and bring her home. When it wasn't a girl, it was a young boy. Lucy would arrive in the morning and fly into a rage, which delighted Pascin. She said that when he drank, he did stupid things. He answered that he drank when she wasn't there; thus it was her fault if his health was becoming more fragile every day. She shrugged and punished him by turning away and walking out. He ran after her. She stopped, turned around, came back. He got her into bed. When she left, the eternal nightmare began again: when would she come back?

Pascin, a partygoer who always needed to have someone with him, was like a child. He was afraid of the dark, and when Lucy wasn't there, it was always dark. He wrung his hands and said that it was going to kill him. His wife Hermine tried to help him: she also posed for him, found him models and cleaned his studio. She often saw Lucy, with whom she was on amicable terms. Each of the women, in her own way, tried to save him. It was a lost cause, though neither of them realized it yet. Pascin always paid for everyone and invited the entire world to his parties. He was a little lonelier and a little sadder each time, but he still managed to put on a good show.

He went out with friends. There were Nils Dardel and his wife Thora, whom Modigliani painted a few months before she died; Abdul Wahab, a Tunisian painter who would welcome Hermine and Pascin to his country; Georges Eisenmann, a businessman and jazz lover; the Salmons, the Cremnitzes, Fatima, Morgan, Claudia, Simone, Aïcha, his most faithful models. There was also Hermine. And there were, above all, Lucy, Guy, and Per. For nothing was hidden from anyone. Everyone knew the situation and everyone closed their eyes. Scandal didn't exist here. In Pascin's entourage, all was freedom and excess, pure notes of passion and madness. Per knew all about Lucy's affair, as did Guy. Hermine didn't care. They would all go together in Lucy's little car to the country, to the banks of the river Marne, to the Jockey Club.

That was where Pascin's world met Kiki's: at the corner of the Boulevard de Montparnasse and the rue Campagne Première, in a club which had been opened in November 1923 by a former jockey, Miller, and an American painter, Hilaire Hiler. The Yanks immediately rejected the Caméléon at the other end of the street, and took over. A few months before the opening of the Select, which was coming, they launched the night life of the neighbourhood. From now on, Montparnasse would remain in full swing all night long. Merrymakers could sing, laugh, and dance under the sun and the stars. And the Jockey Club was the place to do it.

On the outside, cowboys and Indians painted by Hilaire Hiler himself stared down from the black walls; a crowd gathered at the entrance; limousines parked on the edge of the pavement. There was a miracle of modern technology, too: a brightly lit neon sign.

Inside, it was like the Wild West. There was just a bar, a few tables, and a dance floor, music and smoke. There were hundreds of posters on the walls, and a sign warning, in English: 'We only lost one customer ... he died!' Naked girls danced together without attracting any attention. When Hiler wasn't performing, a black musician played scales on the piano. Jazz was everywhere. People danced the foxtrot and the shimmy. Insults were exchanged in every language.

Pascin sat in his corner. Sometimes he was with Hermine, or Lucy, or Per. He was often alone with Per, on their way back from the Dôme, the Hamman, or elsewhere. Sometimes Pascin slept in the painter's new studio on the rue du Val-de-Grâce. Together, they spoke of Lucy − or of the young person who had just entered the Jockey Club and was weaving her way through the crowded room until she finally reached the dance floor, where she was applauded.

Kiki was the queen of the Jockey Club. Her Parisian accent was all the rage. She began her number after Marcelle, who did imitations of American stars, and Chiffon, nicknamed Chiffonnette, four feet ten in high heels, who sang sailor songs. There was also Floriane, tall and grotesque-looking, who tried to dance elegantly, and Barbette, a transvestite with a wig. When Ben, the black pianist, announced the star of the house with a trill on the saxophone, a symphony of applause greeted her. The room encouraged Kiki with its shouts of welcome.

She began fairly calmly with 'Nini peau de chien', then continued with 'Les Filles de Camaret':

> The girls from Camaret all call themselves virgins
> The girls from Camaret all call themselves virgins
> But when they're in my bed
> They prefer to hang on to my wick
> Than to candles, candles, candles…

Kiki only sang when she was drunk. Since she never remembered the words of her songs, the young girl who came and joined her on the dance floor whispered them to her. She was the one that Pascin was watching, and so was Per Krogh. She was about twenty, dark like Kiki, and with the same chubby face. She taught gymnastics. Her name was Thérèse Maure, but she preferred to be called by the nickname Robert Desnos, her former lover, had invented when she was giving him boxing lessons: Thérèse Treize (because, when he called her name in the street, the letters melted into each other and 'Thérèse' sounded like 'Treize'). With this pseudonym, her parents would never have to know anything about their daughter's adventures in free-wheeling Montparnasse.

Kiki and she adored each other. When they partied together, Kiki would forget herself; her companion served as her memory. Not only did she remind her of the words to her songs, but she organized her schedule. Thérèse was the one who told her, the day after a party, that she had made twenty different appointments for the same hour. Quietly, so that Man Ray wouldn't hear. It was she who danced with her friend when the men became a little too forward. And she who, at the end of the show, helped Kiki climb onto the tables and set her back on her feet when she had decided to walk on her hands – to the delight of the customers, who got an eyeful since Kiki never wore knickers.

Then the public, wild with enthusiasm, clapped madly enough to bring the house down. Thérèse Treize picked up a hat and offered it around the room.

'For the performers!' she cried.

The coins flew, and the compliments. Only one of these interested her, that of Per Krogh. For she had thanked Robert Desnos for a dance he had offered her with the handsome Scandinavian, whose long lock of hair falling over his forehead enchanted her.

When she was a few steps further on, Jules Pascin leaned over towards Lucy's husband and said quietly, 'That girl is sensational ... And she likes you, I can tell.'

Per smiled at the thought.

'*Mazel tov!*' said the Bulgarian, and gaily began to dance a little two-step.

PHOTOS, PHOTOS...

I was trying to do, in photography, what the painters did, with the difference that I used light and chemical products instead of colours, and even those without the help of a camera.

Man Ray

Kiki was not yet making love to Mosjoukine, the Russian comedian who would become her lover. She had not yet rejected the repeated solicitations of the Mexican minister who parked his Hispano-Suiza in front of the Jockey Club, eager to carry off the diva of Montparnasse to his suite at the Claridge Hotel, then abroad after that. She had returned from New York where, officially, she had followed a couple who suggested she try her talents in the movies, but where she had mostly played one of her finest roles, that of the husband's mistress.

Her love story with Man Ray was somewhat less than perfect: he was jealous and so was she. They would slap each other on the slightest pretext. She used to amuse herself by colouring over the telephone numbers of women in the photographer's notebooks. He sometimes sulked for days on end for no reason at all, or so she claimed. For instance, when he caught a venereal disease and accused her of being the origin of it, she had to furnish certificates of good health which were really certificates of good conduct. Another time, when he had given her two Schiaparelli dresses, she cut them up with scissors because she preferred her own efforts to those of haute couture...

They had always fought. And it didn't stop. They would throw water or ink at each others' faces. Sometimes Kiki would open the window of their hotel room and scream, 'He's going to kill me!'

The neighbours complained.

The couple moved.

Shortly after their meeting, Man Ray rented an extraordinary studio at 31 bis, rue Campagne Première. The building had been built by Arfvidsson in 1911. Inside were tall windowed façades, a staircase leading to a little loggia, and a bathroom that had been converted into a darkroom. When Man had clients over, Kiki hid in the loggia. Their life together wasn't easy, and they kept the studio but decided to rent an apartment as well. With a bathroom, where Kiki would stay in the bathtub for hours. Now that she had enough to eat every day, she was gaining weight. And, miracle of miracles, her pubic hair was growing back. She was happy. She was discovering the comforts of domestic life.

But there were scenes.

They moved again. First to a hotel on the rue Delambre, then to the Istria Hotel on the rue Campagne Première, near the studio. They went there a month after the Jockey Club opened, and had Tzara as their neighbour. He was Kiki's confidant; she complained to him about how cold Man Ray could be.

On the floor above them, Picabia, when he wasn't with his wife, used to come to be with his mistress, Germaine Everling. Satie, who stayed at the hotel briefly, composed the music for a ballet that Picabia would stage for Rolf de Maré's Ballets Suedois.

Marcel Duchamp, who had left 37, rue Froidevaux and his friends, the Matussières, played hide-and-seek with all the women who were looking for him. Sometimes they would go so far as to lie in wait for him at the door to the hotel's only bathroom on the ground floor. There was Mary Reynolds, a rich American with whom he had had a love affair and from whom he was now trying to escape; Fernande Barrey, with whom he had never had an affair but whom he was also trying to avoid; Elsa Triolet, who hadn't yet met Aragon and who would have liked at least a little kiss; Jeanne Léger, madly in love, ready to leave her painter husband and keep the room she had taken at the Istria Hotel just to be closer to this man, who didn't want to know anything about it. All he wanted was to be able to play chess, which his mistresses had trouble putting up with, and his wife of a few weeks even more so: she didn't see him in the evening because he was playing in a tournament at the Dôme, nor at night because he was sleeping in his own corner, nor in the morning because when she got up she would find him in the kitchen, busy resolving on the chessboard a problem which had given him nightmares all night. One day he found that he could no longer move the pieces on the chessboard − she had glued them to their squares.

Man Ray played with him sometimes, notably in René Clair's film, Entr'acte. The two men are seated on either side of a chessboard, on the roof of the Théâtre des Champs Elysées, until Picabia scatters all the chess pieces with a well-aimed spray of water.

Man Ray, who also worked for the cinema, was nonetheless chiefly interested in photography. He was well known everywhere by now. The rich and fashionable wanted to buy his photographs, as did former bohemians who had now become wealthy.

The Marquise de Casati opened the doors of the aristocratic world to him. He first came to her house in 1922, where she received the artist in her customary attire, that is, with three yards of live python wrapped around her waist. She spoke to him of her friend Gabriele D'Annunzio, then took him on a tour of the garden in which her famous parties were held: all the tree trunks were painted gold. After this, the Marquise returned to her house and asked the photographer to set to work. Man Ray plugged in his lights. This provoked a short circuit, as his lightbulbs made the electrical system explode.

What was to be done? The good lady decided to pose for him without light.

When he returned home, Man Ray developed his work. It looked unsatisfactory to him, but the Marquise thought otherwise. She loved the way her gaze had flickered and wavered, following an involuntary movement.

'Do you realize that you have photographed my soul?'

Satisfied, the lady bought the photos, then introduced the photographer to many of her blue-blooded friends. It was thanks to her that Man Ray was able to afford his studio on the rue Campagne Première.

After the Marquise de Casati came the Comte de Beaumont, a great friend of Cocteau, who invited the photographer to his home so he could immortalize the guests at his grandiose costume balls on film. Then it was the turn of the Comtesse Greffuhle, the Comte Pecci-Blunt, the Maharaja of Indora, and the Vicomte and the Vicomtesse de Noailles, who owned several Goyas and had installed a theatre in the garden, covered the gates of their estate with mirrors, and built a ballroom which could double as a projection room for films.

Man Ray also photographed Picasso dressed as a toreador, Tristan Tzara posing with his monocle in a hundred different ways, Ezra Pound, Sinclair Lewis drunk, Antonin Artaud, Philippe Soupault, Matisse, Braque, Duchamp disguised as Rrose Sélavy, Picabia at the wheel of his Delage ... He surprised Joyce as the writer was trying to cover his eyes, blinded by the lights. His portraits of Kiki of Montparnasse are the finest that exist. He took Meret Oppenheim, a friend of Giacometti's, to Brancusi's and immortalized her naked, her arms and hands stained by the ink of an etching press.

He also photographed Brancusi who, unlike the artists of Montparnasse, was rarely to be found in the cafés of Vavin. He lived in a large studio in the Impasse Ronsin. Everything there was white: the walls, the ceiling, the oven ... None of the furniture was bought from shops. Tree trunks served as benches. The table, where the guests ate lamb shanks grilled on the hearth, was composed of a stand sunk into the floor and covered by a gigantic flat plane of plaster.

When Man Ray came to his home for the first time, Brancusi asked him to teach him his art. He felt that no one besides himself would know how to photograph his work. They bought a camera, a tripod and the equipment needed for laboratory work. Brancusi built a darkroom, painted the outside white and, at a dinner at which he played the violin with Erik Sati, he showed Man Ray the results of his photographic work: blurred snapshots, pale, scratched. But the master was satisfied.

Man Ray photographed his era, and also the end of the preceding one. He even captured the face of Marcel Proust, though he had never met him. He never went to Cabourg at the time when Philippe Soupault used to run into the author of *A la recherche du temps perdu* in his seaside hotel. There, every evening, a wicker armchair was brought out onto the terrace and remained empty until nightfall when, once the sun had gone down, Proust came and sat in it. He would speak, first of time, 'like Englishwomen', he said, then of his illnesses, his 'dear companions'.[1] He dressed in a black overcoat and spoke in a slow, plaintive voice. His eyes were expressive and magnificent, and his skin had the white, almost waxy pallor of the very ill. But according to Jean Hugo, 'he would only speak to dukes.'[2]

Man Ray never went to a whorehouse with him and was never confided in by Paul Léautaud, who used to say, and write, that at one time, Proust would take a taxi to the door of a house of prostitution, ask for the directress, request that she send him some young people, have them get into the car across from him, then offer them milk and listen to them speak of love and death. (Was this the whorehouse of the rue Mayet where Léautaud once went to give away a cat? He was welcomed by the assistant directress who asked him to follow her, took him to a round room where six naked women were waiting, and said to him, 'Choose your cat, my dear sir.')

Man Ray was not in France in 1914 when, at the *Mercure de France*, Alfred Valette received a letter from Marcel Proust, half reproaching him for not having published a review of one of his previous works, and for letting Rachilde write an article in which she admitted to having given up trying to read *Du Côté de chez Swann*, which was putting her to sleep. He also suggested, as fair compensation, the publication of a favourable article by Jacques Blanche which had appeared in *L'Echo de Paris*.[3]

Man Ray definitely did not know Henri de Régnier, the permanent secretary of the Académie Française, to whom Proust wrote on 30 October 1919, asking what steps he could take to help be considered for the *grand prix* of the Académie, for *A l'ombre des jeunes filles en fleurs*.

Yet it was Man Ray on whom Cocteau called on 19 November 1922, to take a photograph of Marcel Proust, of which he was to make only two copies: one for the family and one for Cocteau. If he wished, Man

Ray could also make a copy for himself. The photographer agreed. Cocteau accompanied him to the writer's bedside. He was stretched out on his bed, fully clothed and motionless. Marcel Proust had died the day before.

DR ARGYROL AND MR BARNES

Dr Barnes has just left Paris. The golden clink of dollars preceded his arrival anywhere, desire and greed sprang forth in his presence like apparitions, followed him, teased him, pursued him like forest fires.

Paul Guillaume

One evening, Man Ray stopped his car, a Voisin, in front of the Jockey Club. He got out, went inside, and was engulfed by music, smoke, laughter . . . He tried to make his way to the dance floor, where Kiki would probably be. He exchanged a few words with Tristan Tzara, who was wearing a tie and a monocle and was soon to be married. He had met a young Swedish painter, Greta Knutson, whose family was so rich that they had promised to build a house for the young couple in the centre of Paris, designed by Adolf Loos, an Austrian architect.

That evening, Greta wasn't there. Tzara was with another heiress, a great friend of his and a great eccentric, dark, beautiful, slender, easily re-cognizable: it was Nancy Cunard, wearing a collection of ivory bracelets which clinked and clanked on her forearm. It was said that she had been Aldous Huxley's mistress. She was, in any case, going to become Aragon's, though on this particular evening he was not there either.

Aïcha, the young mulatto, Pascin's favourite model, came up to the Ameri-can. She asked him if she might pose for him some time. Man Ray said maybe, why not, and took the young girl's card. He read it: *Aïcha Goblot, artist.* He smiled and continued on his way. Where was Kiki?

Finally he saw her. A cowboy was asking her to dance. She refused. A little way away, the drums began to play. Pascin was the lead player; Man Ray recognized his bowler hat and white silk scarf. The painter liked music: sometimes he would play the drum or the heavy percussion. The American had often gone to his home, to his parties. He had also often witnessed fights there between the models. Once, after a meal with great quantities of wine to wash it down, fifteen of them had left for a whorehouse. Pascin and Man Ray both went upstairs with a girl, and both were too drunk to commit the slightest act of indecency.

As Man Ray finally reached the dance floor, the cowboy tried to take Kiki in his arms. She pushed him away. He hung on. Then Man Ray became angry. The man who was capable of going after his own mistress with a weapon leapt at the cowboy, grabbed at him from the side and knocked him to the ground. The two men rolled over and over on the floor. Kiki screamed. Everyone scrambled aside, to watch and applaud. Kiki shouted to Man Ray, 'Finish him off! Kill him!'

When the American got up, she kissed him proudly. Then she turned to the embarrassed cowboy and showered him with insults. That was Kiki. She didn't mince words. It wasn't rare to hear her answer, when asked if she had had a good night, 'Excellent. I screwed damn well . . .'

When she was asked why she didn't wear knickers, she would answer that the cafés didn't have any washrooms for women, and all she had to do was lift her skirts to do outside what men did downstairs, that is, in the basement toilets that were nothing more than holes in the ground.

She didn't like André Breton. She told him, 'You spend too much time talking about love to know how to make it!'

Ever since, the pope of surrealism had hated her. But Man Ray always defended her. When asked if she was intelligent, he replied that he had enough brains for the two of them – a remark which was more arrogant than kind.

He bailed her out when she ran into some problems in Villefranche, in the south of France. She had gone down there with her friend Treize. One evening, she went into a bistro and the owner wanted her to leave.

'No whores here!' he cried.

Kiki picked up a pile of saucers and hurled them in his face. There was a fight, and the owner filed a complaint. The next day a policeman showed up at her hotel.

'You're coming with me to the police station.'

Kiki refused.

The officer soon returned with the commissioner of Villefranche and a few of his men. The commissioner reiterated the order of his junior. Kiki answered that she was in no hurry. As her gestures reflected her words, the commissioner tried to get her moving. She responded with insults and blows, and was carted off to the prison of Nice. When Man Ray was told what had happened, he called all his friends. The painter Malkine put pressure on the lawyer assigned to her. Fraenkel, a friend of Breton's and a doctor, produced a certificate attesting that Kiki had a nervous disease. As she left the courtroom, Kiki confided, 'The hardest thing was when my lawyer told me, "You must say thank you to these gentlemen." '[1]

She said it, and was released. Man Ray, who had come down from Paris for the trial, took her back to the Jockey Club. From then on, Kiki had something new to brag about: she had spent more than ten days in prison.

She liked to recount this exploit to her friends. When she came back to the Jockey Club, and once Man had got rid of the enterprising cowboy, she went from table to table to boast of her latest adventures. She told the story to René Clair, to Foujita and to Kisling, who were sitting together a little way from the orchestra, not far from another group presided over by the builder André Citroën, sitting there with banknotes in hand. Nearby, Fernand Léger was keeping an eye on his wife to make sure she wasn't getting too close to Marcel Duchamp or Roland Tual. In any case, his watchfulness was useless; the painter knew of his wife Jeanne's little games, forgave them, and would even on occasion pick a fight with someone who gossiped about her. He had gone so far as to strike her lovers when they treated her badly; he had hit Thérèse Treize for the same reason.

As Kiki looked on, Thérèse Treize kissed Per Krogh on the mouth. Pascin, who had left his position at the drums, observed the scene. Alas, it didn't bring him any happiness. He now knew that this romance was not going to help him as he had hoped. Lucy, unfortunately, was jealous of Thérèse. She spied on the couple and went looking for them when they hid out in a hotel on the Boulevard Edgar Quinet.

The Bulgarian moved easily through the Jockey Club, less crowded now. He crossed paths with Soutine, who had just come in with his friend, the painter Michonze, but he didn't greet him. Kiki remembered that Youki Foujita had told her that she had introduced the two men recently, at the Select: the only other place in Montparnasse to remain open late at night, it was popular for its Welsh rarebit. Soutine had extended a hand to Pascin and said to him, 'I like your painting. Your little women really excite me!'

'I forbid you to excite yourself with my women!' exclaimed Pascin.

He was furious. Soutine, who had painted only a single nude in his entire œuvre, grabbed his hands and exclaimed, 'But I admire you so much, Monsieur Pascin! Very, very much!'

Kiki left Foujita and Kisling. She went up to Soutine, her poor friend who had become rich. Since the war years, when he used to lodge the young girl for the night in a freezing studio, Soutine had changed. He wasn't cold or hungry any more, and was no longer the virtual tramp he had once been. Now he smoked Lucky Strikes with a golden tip, and wore the suits he had long dreamed of and an overcoat that was as warm as his skin and smooth as a plate. It was a miracle: one that had a date – 1922 – and a name – Albert C. Barnes.

Barnes was an American industrialist, a little bit of a doctor, a little bit of a psychologist, altruistic but with a paranoid streak. He had built his fortune on the production and the commercialisation of an antiseptic he had invented, Argyrol.

He was born in Philadelphia, to a family of modest means, and had grown up not far from blacks; this had given him a taste for Negro art, which he would later collect quite judiciously. He also had a passion for contemporary painting, and felt that through art he would

be able to help his fellow men.

In his factory, he first exhibited American artists. Then he became interested in European painting. Before the war, he had sent an emissary to Paris, William James Glackens, an American painter whom he asked to visit the studios and galleries and to bring back works that seemed important. It was in this way that Cézanne, Van Gogh, Pissarro, Renoir and Picasso crossed the Atlantic.

In 1912, after having bought paintings by Renoir in New York, Dr Barnes made the trip himself. He met Ambroise Vollard and went to public auctions. Gauguin, Bonnard, Daumier, Matisse, more Cézanne (including *Les Baigneuses*) and more Renoir and Picasso entered his collection. He also bought some works by Matisse from Leo Stein. In 1914, before war was declared, Barnes had acquired fifty Renoirs, fifteen Cézannes and several Picassos. And this was just a start – a promising start.

In 1922, the collector bought a home in Merion, near Philadelphia. He built a museum there for his foundation. This was intended first of all to benefit the employees of the factory that produced Argyrol. They were meant to learn, and to develop their cultural life through contact with these works inspired by Negro art and by the most modern schools of painting. This pedagogical generosity was obviously most enriching for the workers of the Barnes Company and for everyone offered the exceptional privilege of entering the museum. But it was unbearable for the rest of the world. For in accordance with a principle which the collector had already articulated at the time of the Armory Show, when he refused to lend his works to be exhibited, the paintings, once acquired, would not be allowed to leave the foundation, and no one would have the right to reproduce them in any form. Thus art lovers and art historians would, for seventy years, be deprived of the slightest access to these paintings, including among others nearly two hundred Renoirs, some Cézannes, sixty Matisses and numerous Modiglianis...

In December 1922, Barnes returned to Paris. He settled in at the Hôtel Mirabeau on the rue de la Paix, and summoned the dealer he had chosen as an intermediary, Paul Guillaume. The dealer was a great specialist in Negro art, and had a number of works by Matisse, Vlaminck, Derain and Modigliani. For two weeks, every morning, he would come and pick up the American collector in his Hispano-Suiza. He made his way through the colleagues and dozens of poor artists waiting for the doctor on the pavement in front of the hotel, their portfolios of drawings under their arm. He took him to all the museums in Paris, to the antiques dealers, to the best restaurants. He patiently answered the industrialist's endless questions about the works and about contemporary artists. Finally, the ritual moment would come when, as night had fallen and the last liqueur had been swallowed, Barnes would stretch out in his armchair, hook his thumbs into his waistcoat and say, 'So, shall we go?'

'It's a little late...'

'Are you tired?'

'No...'

'Let's go then!'

And Barnes would get up, fresh as a daisy, climb into the Hispano-Suiza and, tirelessly, run down his questionnaire once more: why Negro art, why cubism, why Matisse, why Picasso, why Lipchitz?

He had gone to the sculptor's studio with his guide. He hadn't even noticed the artist's poverty; the man no longer had a dealer and was selling nothing. He had looked only at the work. He had enquired about this, that, the rest, and more. He had taken notes, and had bought eight sculptures. He had invited Lipchitz to lunch. The sculptor was speechless with joy. He tried to conceal the holes in his shirt so as not to present too great a contrast with the well-dressed Paul Guillaume, with his gold-framed pince-nez, cigar, felt gloves, and chequebook. Lipchitz thought he was in heaven. In fact, it was only purgatory.

'I'm building a museum,' Doctor Barnes explained. 'I need your help.'

This was over dessert. They had ordered cake.

'I want five bas-reliefs for the façade. Would you be able to do them for me?'

This was the icing on the cake.

And so it went on, for dozens of artists, hundreds of works.

The American's questions generally trailed off as they approached the rue La Boétie, where Paul Guillaume's gallery was. They would pick up again as soon as the lights were lit. Why the Fauves, why Vlaminck, why Kisling, why Marcoussis?

'I don't know,' muttered Paul Guillaume, exhausted.

'You don't know? Well, get them to come here, and I'll ask them myself.'

And so, at midnight, Paul Guillaume would call Vlaminck, Kisling and Marcoussis. Meanwhile, the doctor examined the paintings. One night, he paused over a canvas with bright colours and misshapen, twisted, elongated forms. He put it down, and stepped back to observe it more closely. It was a young man with a monstrous ear and a hat on his head, in a white smock coloured with yellow, green and blue reflections.

'What is it?' he asked.

'That's Soutine,' answered Paul Guillaume. 'Le Petit Patissier.'

'Do you know his dealer?'

'Zborowski.'

Barnes picked up his coat and moved towards the door.

'Let's go,' he said firmly.

'Where?'
'To the dealer Zborowski's!'
'Why? Why now?'
'Because I want to buy something! Everything. This Soutine is a genius!'

SOUTINE'S CROSS

I believe that he's one of the greatest painters of our times. Since
Goya, I really can't think of anyone as extraordinary as Soutine.

                                                            Chana Obloff

'He bought dozens of my paintings! For three thousand dollars!' Soutine
exclaimed.

'I draw too,' said Kiki. 'I'll have to show you some of my stuff.'

'After that,' the Lithuanian went on, 'my prices rose as fast as a Bugatti
on the racecourse. Today, a single painting of mine is worth ten thousand
dollars!'

She looked at him. Far off now was the time when he had had to fight
the bugs that invaded his studio and which, finding no warmer place,
had a tendency to take refuge in his ear. The time when he had nothing
to eat, when he had walked around naked under his coat. When, having
to invent his own fashion, he stuck his arms into the legs of a pair of
long johns, transformed the belt into a collar and the long johns into a
shirt.

This was a man who had suffered more than anyone. He still suffered.
The food he hadn't had the money to buy earlier he now could not eat.
He dreamed of the dishes of his native land, of spicy specialities, herrings,
sauces ... But he couldn't swallow anything, except bismuth.

Still, he had changed, so much so that he was almost unrecognizable.
The wary, unconfident immigrant, a little uncouth, who was teaching
himself French in the depths of the Rotonde, had been transformed. He
now wore shirts with polka dots and coloured ties, of which he had once
dreamed. No one had ever humiliated him as much as the Armenian
collector who had once asked him to accompany him to the Place
Vendôme, to an expensive shop which sold silk neckties. He wanted
Soutine to advise him on colours and tones. He had bought three dozen
ties without it even occurring to him to buy a single one for the painter,
who was looking on longingly, hunched up in his tattered overcoat.

Since then Soutine had had his revenge. Not only was he able to go to the Place Vendôme himself, but he could also have his hands manicured and wave them about nonchalantly (he knew he had nice hands). His nails were no longer caked in the paint which became encrusted when he dabbed on his colours with his palms and fingers, after throwing out his brushes in a rage. His jet-black hair shone with a new gleam; he had entrusted it to the care of a little sister of the poor who had darkened it for him with a special ointment. He even had the use of a car and a chauffeur, Daneyrolles. He explained to Kiki that all of this was not his but Zborowski's, who had become rich thanks to Barnes and himself. The American had come to the rue Joseph Bara to see Soutine's work. Every time the Polish dealer took one of his paintings out from under the bed, the other had exclaimed, 'Wonderful! Wonderful!'

Since then, Zborowski had opened a gallery on the rue de Seine, where he exhibited works by Utrillo, Derain, Vlaminck, Kisling, Dufy and Friesz. He had a house in the Indre where he invited his artists and collaborators to come and stay. Paulette Jourdain, who sometimes posed for Soutine and Kisling, occasionally went there, for example.

When he wanted to go to the Mediterranean, Soutine called Daneyrolles, lay down on the back seat of the American car, and woke up at the seaside the next day. He didn't like Paris, and was glad to escape from the scenes of his former misfortunes, avoiding both his companions of those times and the places where they gathered. He criticized Modigliani, although the Italian had been his only source of support during the war. He had fallen out with Elie Faure, who wrote the first book about him. He wouldn't say hello to Maurice Sachs, though the latter had published an article in praise of his work. When people recognized him in cafés, rose to greet him, approached him or called out to him, he would stare at them harshly and say, 'I don't know you.'

If the other persisted, he would answer, 'I've never seen you before.'

Then he would leave the table and the café.

His pride played tricks on him. It almost made him spoil his first meeting with the Castaings, patrons of the arts who would become as important to him as Barnes.

The Castaings lived in a castle near Chartres and were art enthusiasts. Marcellin edited the artistic sections of a review for which he was also the editorial secretary. He often came to Montparnasse to see artists.

One night, not long before Barnes first arrived in Paris, Castaing came to the Rotonde with his wife, Madeleine. Soutine stopped by. A painter suggested to the Castaings that they buy one of his paintings; the Russian didn't have a penny to his name and was almost starving. They called him over. Marcellin asked to see his work, so Soutine set up an appointment with them in the back room of a café on the rue Campagne Première. He arrived late, carrying two canvases. The Castaings looked them over quickly, in the shadows of the dark room, and suggested coming back the next day to get a better view, offering him a hundred-franc bill as an advance. Soutine took the bill and tore it up.

'I don't need handouts!' he said. 'And you didn't even look at my work!'

He was furious. The visitors left.

A few weeks later, Soutine exhibited *Le Coq mort aux tomates* in a gallery near the Madeleine. The Castaings wanted to buy it, so they sought out Zborowski. But he couldn't sell the painting because it belonged to Francis Carco. The merchant didn't say that he had in fact given the painting to the writer a few months before – given and not sold, for at the time a painting of Soutine's had been worth nothing.

As the clients wouldn't give up, Zborowski went and found Carco who, very graciously, gave back the painting and refused the money which the Polish dealer offered him. The Castaings bought it, then another, and yet another. When they came to the artist's studio, they remained there for ten straight hours.

Then it was Soutine's turn to go to the Château de Lèves. Soon he was staying for weeks at a time. His new protectors took good care of him, especially Madeleine, who posed for him. She was fascinated by this man who painted to save his soul, with unimaginable force and energy. Who looked for canvas from the seventeenth century, the only kind whose texture satisfied him since the brush could slide smoothly on it without slipping. Who begged, on bended knee, a washerwoman whose portrait he was painting, to recover a fleeting moment, find an expression she had lost. Who could remain concentrated for hours, for entire days, on one imperfect detail. Who, when he painted, needed silence and solitude so much that no one could talk to him or even approach him. Who awoke at dawn and asked for the car to be ready as early as possible to take him to the market, where he had to buy fish, and only fish, for he wanted to paint fish. Who, another morning, begged Madeleine and Marcellin to accompany him to some fields where he had seen an admirable horse. The horse turned out to be an old skinny mare, filthy with mud, pulling a wagonload of acrobats.

'I want to paint it!' exclaimed Soutine.

And he walked round and round the animal, almost in a trance. Marcellin Castaing talked with the circus members. They agreed to make a halt at the castle in exchange for food and drink. While they settled down on the lawn to enjoy the meal, Soutine went off with the horse. And painted a masterpiece.

He was very demanding of himself. He refused to participate in collective exhibitions for fear of being eclipsed by the other painters. He destroyed every canvas which didn't meet with approval or admiration from all those around him, including the Castaings and other close friends.

According to Man Ray, when Barnes bought his works, Soutine got drunk, then hailed a taxi and asked the taxi driver to take him directly to the south of France. He dreamed of seeing the sea; he visited Céret and Cagnes-sur-Mer.

Two years after his return, he was still systematically destroying canvases he had painted while in the South. When he found some at Zborowski's, he burned them. If he learned that a gallery had some, he tried to buy them back or exchange them for more recent paintings. He then took them home and cut them up carefully. They joined other fragments that he re-used sometimes, sewing them together before integrating them into new works. Most of the time, though, they ended up in the wastebin, where collectors – when it wasn't Daneyrolles acting for the Zborowskis – would retrieve them and take them to Monsieur Jacques, the owner of a bistro on the rue Mazarine, who sewed them back together with needle and thread, thus restoring a canvas which the collectors could sell to galleries.

The first works concerned were those dating from Céret, but the others didn't escape this treatment. The dealer René Gimple placed Soutine's canvases high on the wall, out of reach, whenever the painter came by. He never left him alone in a room with one of his own paintings.

Soutine destroyed everything including the fakes signed with his name. He set upon the works painted at the castle in Lèves or in the Zborowskis' house in the Creuse, the paintings done in Montparnasse, in the numerous places he had lived: the Boulevard Edgar Quinet, the Passage d'Enfer, the Avenue du Parc Montsouris, the rue de la Tombe Issoire and the Villa Seurat, where Dali, Chana Orloff, Lurçat and Henry Miller would all come.

In 1925, only his *Carcasse de bœuf* interested him. He worked on it in his studio on the rue Saint Gothard. He had already been at work for quite some time. He had often returned from Les Halles or from the farms around the Castaings' castle with turkeys, ducks, rabbits and chickens, all skinned or hung, which he represented on the canvas after hanging them from a meat hook. But an ox was something else. An ox was reminiscent of Rembrandt, whom he so admired. An ox evoked the butcher of Smilovitchi and the cold room in which as a child Soutine had been locked up after being whipped for painting iconoclastic images. Finally, an ox brought forth this extraordinary confession from the painter:

A long time ago, I saw the village butcher slice off the neck of a bird and empty it of its blood. I wanted to cry out, but he seemed so merry that the cry stuck in my throat ... That cry is still there. When as a child I drew a rough portrait of my professor, I was trying to coax that cry out once more, but in vain. When I painted the carcass of the ox, it was that cry again which I was seeking to liberate.[1]

Soutine went to La Villette, bought an entire ox and hung it from thick hooks in his studio. Days went by. The ox began to rot. Paulette Jourdain, as devoted to Zborowski as she was to Soutine, visited the slaughterhouses in order to get some blood, which she poured on the carcass to renew the colours. Soutine helped her: he splattered blood on the animal with his brush, painting the ox's flesh itself before painting the ox's image on the canvas.

Soon the flies got into the act. Soutine didn't even notice them, but the odour rapidly became unbearable. The neighbours complained, and one morning the sanitation services arrived. Frightened as usual by anything resembling a uniform, the painter hid. Paulette Jourdain had to explain the ox's presence. She convinced the municipal employees to disinfect the studio and obtained explanations as to how to keep the animal from decomposing and get rid of the odour: all they had to do was inject ammonia into the carcass.

After that, Soutine carried a trousseau of syringes with him everywhere. He simply stuck a needle into every recently dead animal he saw and felt like painting.

Kiki wanted to talk to him about his love life, but she didn't. She knew that he wasn't quite as lonely as he used to be. He had run into a woman from Vilno, a love of his youth, Deborah Melnik. Rumour had it that they had got married and had a child together. But Soutine quickly put an end to this affair, and when he was asked about his daughter, he claimed that he wasn't the father and changed the subject. He didn't want to know anything about it. Nonetheless, he wasn't as solitary as he had been. Women were now part of his life.

In 1937, he would fall in love with Gerda Groth, a German Jewish socialist refugee. He would nickname her 'Miss Watchman' because shortly after their first meeting, she stayed up an entire night looking after him when he was in bed, his stomach ravaged by an ulcer. They moved into the Villa Seurat together, then lived in Civry in the Yonne. During the war, they came back to Paris.

In 1940, Miss Watchman was taken off to the Vel' d'Hiv,* then to the camp of Gurs – miraculously, she would return to Paris in 1943. While she was in the camp, Soutine met a very beautiful young woman,

---

* The Vel' d'Hiv, or the Vélodrome d'Hiver, near Paris, was the scene of a grisly round-up by the French police, in the summer of 1942, of 13,000 Jews. Many, after first being detained there, were later deported to Auschwitz.

capricious and imaginative, who was introduced to him by the Castaings at an art opening. Her name was Marie-Berthe Aurenche. She had been Max Ernst's second wife, and she would become Soutine's last companion.

During the Occupation, the painter was sought by the Gestapo; he was Jewish and a foreigner. He used to walk around with his hat pulled down over his eyes, thinking that no one would recognize him this way. He didn't eat anything except boiled potatoes and soup; he was frighteningly thin, and he was losing his hair. To protect it, he would break an egg over his head and hide the omelette under a hat.

He took refuge on the rue des Plantes, with friends of Marie-Berthe Aurenche. He only went out at night. When the concierge betrayed him to the Occupation authorities, he fled to Champigny-sur-Veude in the Touraine. Marie-Berthe dragged him from hotel to hotel until they found an isolated house, where they settled down. Soutine's suffering grew constantly. In August 1942, his stomach lining burst. The painter was rushed to the hospital in Chinon, where he begged the doctors to operate immediately. Marie-Berthe refused; she wanted the operation to be done in Paris by a specialist. An ambulance was called. The ambulance returned to Champigny, where Marie-Berthe Aurenche wished to retrieve some of Soutine's paintings. Then she stopped elsewhere to pick up a few other works. And so on, for twenty-four hours. When, after this mortal journey, Soutine arrived in Paris, his stomach was in shreds. The operation took place on 7 August 1942. He died on the ninth, at six o'clock in the morning. Few artists accompanied him to his grave in the Montparnasse cemetery, where Pascin and his little women had been waiting for him for twelve years. There was only Picasso, and Max Jacob, with his star on his chest. He hadn't yet started down the tragic road to Drancy.

Chaïm Soutine's final resting place was in a plot belonging to the Aurenche family. He wasn't laid to rest under his six-pointed star, but under a cross. This was not the only paradox. A mistake was also made on his date of birth. And his name was wrongly spelt.

SCANDAL AT THE
CLOSERIE DES LILAS

The result was some rather bizarre behaviour which didn't really alarm his family until the day he went to some almost indecent extremes in public; then they understood that he was a poet.

Louis Aragon

For one morning at least, the men of letters had returned to the Closerie des Lilas. On a July day in 1925, *Les Nouvelles littéraires* organized a banquet in honour of the poet Saint-Pol Roux, a symbolist and a Catholic, who had retired to Camaret. The surrealists were invited, as they had contributed to a special issue of the *Nouvelles* dedicated to the poet. They forgave him his ideas on religion because they saw him as belonging to the same literary family as Mallarmé. André Breton dedicated *Clair de Terre* to him. Twenty years later, Aragon would again give homage to the 'great shadow' of the man he called 'the Magnificent One'.[1]

It was impossible for the surrealists not to respect a man who had written these lines:

> I admit to being legion like religions and heresies, and I willingly leave to the asses of the Sorbonne the stubborn signposts of their unchangeable opinions.

So Breton and his friends were present, and they were not alone. There was Lugné-Poe, who had been director of the Théâtre de l'Oeuvre when Jarry had created a scandal there with *Ubu Roi*. Breton accused him of having worked for the services of counter-espionage during the war. Mme Rachilde presided, seated at the table of honour. Breton noted, 'We were up in arms just at the words "*table of honour*".'[2] The atmosphere was tense. The presence of 'men of letters', letters which were nothing more than petty vowels as far as the surrealists were concerned, was not the only explanation for the rising anger. Under the plates of the noble assembly, the troublemakers had slipped an answer to the Ambassador to Japan, His Excellency Paul Claudel, who had just declared to the review *Comoedia* that surrealism and Dadaism were fundamentally 'pederastic', while reminding

all and sundry of his brilliant war service; he had bought lard in Latin
America to help feed the Allied armies. The answer was printed in blood
red, and its contents were no less bloody:

> All that remains is a moral rule, which is for instance that one cannot
> be both Ambassador of France and a poet. We take advantage of this
> opportunity to refuse our support to all that is French, in words and in
> acts. We declare that we find treason, and anything that can in any way
> harm the security of the State, much easier to reconcile with poetry
> than the sale of 'great quantities of lard' for the benefit of a nation of
> pigs and dogs ... Write, pray, foam at the mouth; we claim the dishonour
> of having called you once and for all a prig and a scum and a bastard.[3]

The room crackled with electricity. The slightest short circuit would
make the place explode. It was Mme Rachilde who set off the conflagration.
In the heyday of the Dada demonstrations, she had appealed to the
footsoldiers of the fight to attack the irresponsible strongholds and chastize
the insolent young. This time, she set things off by repeating some
Germanophobic remarks that she had pronounced a few days earlier in
an interview: 'A Frenchwoman should not marry a German!'

She didn't say it particularly loudly, but it was heard by all. This remark
touched on a point that was sensitive with the surrealists – Germany.
Firstly because a surrealist, as Aragon had said, always holds out a hand
to the enemy, especially when the enemy has been humiliated by the
treaty of Versailles, the reparations and the occupation of the Ruhr, and
even if the enemy did assassinate Rosa Luxemburg and Karl Liebknecht.
There was another reason which Breton, who had risen, expressed very
calmly: 'What you have just said, Madame, is extremely insulting to our
friend Max Ernst.'

Max Ernst nodded. Breton and he shared a good number of opinions.
The former was as little troubled by the defeat of Germany as the latter
was proud of France's victory. Breton's intervention was sufficient to break
the armed peace.

An apple flew through the air, then another. Breton, it was said, threw
a napkin in Rachilde's face, crying, 'Soldier's whore!'

'Pain in the arse!' another guest chimed in.

Saint-Pol Roux tried to restore calm.

'Please! One does not treat a lady like that. You must remain courteous!'

'Courtesy is another pain in the arse!'

The battle was on. On every side, food flew. The platter of fish in
cream sauce was a catapult, and everything served as ammunition: the
fresh vegetables, the silverware, the wine, the glasses, the plates ...

Philippe Soupault took a deep breath, grabbed on to the chandelier, hung there and swung from it, kicking out at everyone who passed. Rushing in from a neighbouring room, Louis de Gonzague Frick threw himself in turn on the surrealists. André Breton pushed open a window, shattering it. A crowd had gathered on the pavement. Max Ernst cupped his hands and shouted, 'Down with Germany!'

Michel Leiris answered, 'Down with France!'

'Long live China!' shouted someone.

'Long live the Africans!' cried someone else, in homage to the Berbers of Abd el-Krim who were fomenting an uprising in Morocco.

In the centre of the crowd on the pavement stood a young woman, whose gaze was fixed on the open window. She was Russian, not yet thirty years old. Inside, she had just seen a man dressed in a smoking jacket. He had left her speechless. Impeccably dressed, in the middle of all the shouts and blows, his gestures remained magnificently calm.

The stranger didn't see her. He stood there for a moment, looking down at the crowd. When he turned around to defend Max Ernst or Breton or another of his companions, grabbing a bunch of bananas and hurling them at the tables, Elsa Triolet asked one of her neighbours who he was. No one knew, of course. The young girl tried to find a spot which would give her a better view. On a corner of the Boulevard Saint Michel, she saw a bench and climbed onto it. Elsa searched, but the man had disappeared. The young girl kept looking for him. Finally she got down and moved off. Her heart was broken. She knew she had just seen the love of her life, the one she had been seeking for so long.

Inside the Closerie, in the middle of the maelstrom, Saint-Pol Roux was still trying in vain to calm things down. Michel Leiris went back to the window and shouted again, 'Long live Germany!'

The onlookers on the pavement demanded that he come out and explain himself. They almost lynched him. He was saved by the heroic arrival of the forces of order which took him off to the police station where, no less heroically, they beat him behind closed doors. (Youji Foujita claimed that he was freed thanks to the intervention of Robert Desnos, who appealed to Edouard Herriot for clemency.)

It was a great scandal. The next day, the whole of the press lashed out at the surrealists, accusing them of being 'the terrors of the Boulevard Montparnasse'. The Society of Men of Letters and the Writers' Association of Former Combatants, in conjunction with L'Action française, requested that the names of these men never be mentioned again, so as to cut them off from public view for good.

It wasn't the first time that the troublemakers had caused a stir. But never before had Montparnasse in general and the Closerie in particular seen poets, painters and writers assail each other for reasons which were so remote from art.

André Breton recognized the fact. 'What was significant about this episode – the banquet for Saint-Pol Roux – is that it marked surrealism's definitive break with all the conformist elements of the time.'[4]

But there was something else as well. On the morning of the banquet, Breton and his friends had joined in a protest condemning the war in Morocco and the dispatching of French troops to fight against Abd el-Krim. Seven years after the end of the 'war to end all wars', they were determined to participate in the fight for peace. Beyond the cries and confusion which shook the old walls of the Closerie des Lilas on this July day in 1925, a new reality was becoming apparent. Paul Fort and his comrades, whose verse had been composed amidst laughter and banter, now seemed very far away. Led by the surrealists, Montmartre and Montparnasse were once again preparing to change history. The poets were discovering a new prose.

It was called politics.

A LITTLE GEOGRAPHY
OF SURREALISM

Our father who is in heaven, please stay there.
Jacques Prévert

Surrealist theatre was played out on several stages. One was in the cafés, another was at Breton's home or on the rue du Château in the fifteenth arrondissement. These gentlemen – apart from Simone Breton, women were rarely present, and always remained silent – especially liked to meet in bistros. Not standing at the counter, but sitting in back rooms, where the seats were reserved. They went at regular hours, as though they were going to the office. They made appointments to meet people there, to read tarot cards, and to play charades and a question-and-answer game where one had to give answers to imaginary questions. It was there that the interrogations took place, which would include notably intimate questions about sexuality or character, which often ended in tension and fights. The press was pored over, events commented upon, revenge taken, and rarely discreetly. Friends were invited to drink an aperitif, at noon or at seven in the evening. Sometimes they were candidates for admission to the club, and were subjected to the ritual entrance exam.

Breton was always there and Aragon almost always. He was the only one to whom the father of the *Surrealist Manifesto* spoke with respect, even admiration. Breton was capable of flying into Homeric rages, but Aragon never lost his Olympian calm. This remarkable equanimity could be very helpful in some of their verbal skirmishes.

They drank grenadines because they liked the colour, or unusual drinks because they liked the names: pick me hup, kees me quick, omnium cocktail, Dada cocktail, pêle-mêle mixture, Amer Picon, porto flipp, pastis gascon, mandarin-curaçao. The Chambéry-fraisette (Chambéry with strawberry liqueur) had an additional virtue, which was that Apollinaire had touted its merits in L'Hérésiarque & Cie.

Each person paid for his own drinks; this was a fixed rule. Breton, who had become wealthy due to the many paintings bought during Kahnweiler's auctions and sold as needed, always kept other people's circumstances in mind. Paul Eluard also had some money, but he was practically the only other one. Thus they chose restaurants that all could afford.

Another rule was fidelity: this was almost obligatory. Aragon was regarded with suspicion if he preferred the jewelled arms of Nancy Cunard to Breton's welcome. And even if the others were happy to look at the photos of Gala nude which Eluard would show often and happily, his absences were remarked upon in no uncertain terms, justified or not. It was obvious that he loved his Gala, who loved him as much as she did Max Ernst, who loved her as much as he loved Eluard, who didn't mind forming a trio as long as he had what he wanted. But in any case, when Breton summoned his friends, no reason was accepted as an excuse for their absence, especially if it happened more than once. The 'pope' reigned over the gathering of the faithful, observing his little troop with a penetrating eye. Massively built, stiff in his dark, often bottle-green costumes, his hair waved back, he counted those present and those absent. If a woman came in, he rose and kissed her hand. So it was that kissing the hand became a surrealist ritual.

Where did they meet? During the Dada period, at the Source, on the Boulevard Saint Michel, which was close both to the Val-de-Grâce, where Aragon and Breton were, and to the Hôtel des Grands Hommes, where the latter lived. It was at the Source that Breton asked his best friend, Aragon, to read the two notebooks containing *Les Champs magnétiques*, the first three chapters of which were to be published by *Littérature*. And once again, the author of *Anicet* was sufficiently master of himself not to show the little pull at the heartstrings which he must have felt, he who, because he had been called to fight, had not participated in this founding experience.

He had his revenge shortly afterwards, when the group left the Source to frequent a Dada base of operations, which would soon become a surrealist one. This was the café Certà, at 11, Passage de l'Opéra, chosen precisely 'out of hatred for Montparnasse and Montmartre'.[1]

Breton, Tzara and Aragon interviewed potential new members there, and saw friends from the group, like Marcel Duchamp, Max Ernst, Jean Arp, or René Crevel, who was young, handsome and delicate-looking, always either enraged or ecstatic about something.

The café Certà helped Aragon fill his pockets a little, at a time when they were desperately empty; his friend Soupault commissioned a text from him on the Passage de l'Opéra for *La Revue européenne*, which he edited.

In the twenties, after Breton had moved to the rue Fontaine, near the Place Blanche, the movement held court at its founder's house, or at the

Cyrano, on the Boulevard de Clichy. They remained there until the arrival of Buñuel and Dali in 1929.

When they crossed the Seine, the surrealists went to the café de la Mairie, on the Place Saint Sulpice. From 1928, in the wake of Man Ray, Aragon and Desnos, they began going to the Coupole, where the painters also used to gather. Artaud and many others remained faithful to the Dôme and the Rotonde. But they all also met in two homes in Montparnasse which were the heart and soul of left bank surrealism.

The first was on the rue Blomet, in the Vaugirard neighbourhood. Three buildings stood together on a carpet of weeds. In 1922, André Masson and Joan Miró each moved into one. The two painters had met in Montmartre; both were friends of Max Jacob's. The Spaniard had crossed paths with Picabia, and therefore with a strand of French culture, in Barcelona. He came to Paris in 1919.

Masson had been wounded during the war. His war years had left some major damage, and he had spent time in a psychiatric hospital. When he was let out, he fell into abject poverty, as did Miró. He spent time as a deliveryman, an extra in films, and a corrector of proofs for the government's legislative publication, Le Journal officiel. In 1922, Max Jacob introduced him to Kahnweiler, who immediately offered to take him under contract. Thanks to this unexpected boon, Masson was able to move to the rue Blomet, with his wife and daughter, at the same time as Miró; according to the story, neither painter realized, although they were friends, that they were moving to the same spot.

In 1924, Robert Desnos took Breton to the rue Blomet, where he met Masson; the latter sent him over to Miró's. That same day, the man who hated Dada bought Terre labourée. He soon bought other paintings, and published reproductions of them in La Révolution surréaliste. For him, Miró was incontestably one of his own.

In November 1925, the names of most of the great figures of surrealism were on the invitation to the opening of an exhibition of the painter's work at the galerie Pierre on the rue Bonaparte. On the list were Breton, Aragon, Soupault, Naville, Eluard, Vitrac, Crevel (who, after having followed Dada for a while, had definitively come back to Breton), Leiris, Max Ernst ... The opening was to take place at midnight, as was often the case for group presentations at the galerie Pierre. Miró was there, of course: the Spaniard had nothing against the support of the surrealists, as long as they allowed him to keep his distance.

Masson was more enthusiastic. He regularly contributed drawings to Breton's review, and would remain faithful to him until 1928, when he began to back away from the authoritarianism of the 'chief'; as was the case with many others, this attitude would lead to his exclusion.

In the first years, all the surrealists, great and small, came to the rue

Blomet: Leiris, Artaud, Roland Tual, Bataille (who was close to the movement without ever being a part of it), Limbour, Aragon. They read, they drank, they took opium. And they were not the only ones. Those who, in 1926, replaced the first tenants – the sculptor André de la Rivière, the painter Georges Malkine, and the poet Robert Desnos – would sample the same pleasures, with the same nonchalance.

Desnos was no longer in love with Thérèse Treize, but had transferred his affections to Yvonne George, a Belgian actress who sang at times and demanded that her admirer, who was probably at her feet, furnish her with the necessary stimulants. Desnos did so, tasted the stuff in passing, and shared some with his friend Malkine, who was in love with Caridad de Laberdesque, a dancer.

When he wasn't sleeping, or pretending to sleep, Desnos went to the Bal Nègre: he was the one who helped to launch this successful and colourful nightspot. He would also often head up towards Gaîté, in the direction of the Montparnasse cemetery. He took the rue du Château, behind the station, which came out not far from Marie Vassilieff's old canteen, and stopped at no. 54. Pushing open a gate, he found himself standing in front of a house, on a floor which had formerly served as a sales room for rabbit skins. He climbed a few steps and arrived in a large room decorated with immense wall hangings by Lurçat, inspired by cubism. Scattered around on the floor were cushions and various objects picked up at the flea market or in neighbouring dustbins.

A strange piece of furniture was leaning against the back wall: it was tall and included a closet, a vivarium with sand and living snakes, a real record player with an electric motor and, sitting on the top, a cage containing white mice. On the other side, a loggia had been built. It was meant to house passing friends, which most often meant Benjamin Péret – or it had done before Louis Aragon arrived. Aragon at the time was going through a stormy love affair with Nancy Cunard – he was, that is, until the night of 6 November 1928, when in this very loggia, his life took a permanent turn for the better.

Concealed behind a door was the studio of one of the three occupants of the place, a tall man, with his hair slicked up on his head. This was the painter Yves Tanguy. On the largest wall of the neighbouring room, he had painted a bloody Christ, which he erased after having discovered De Chirico's art one day, with great surprise, from the platform of a bus. Ever since then, he had given up expressionism for much more iconoclastic works, some of which were published in La Révolution surréaliste.

The other two inhabitants of the house lived on the first floor. Marcel Duhamel hadn't yet begun his celebrated collection of crime novels, the Série noire; at this time, he was the manager of a hotel. Since he was the richest of the three, it was he who financed the construction and development of the house.

The last member of the little group already wore the cap which would become legendary, and walked around with a cigarette hanging from his bottom lip. He wrote film scripts which were refused (this wouldn't last) and songs in collaboration with Desnos – which they offered to Kiki, who didn't want them, believing that they were too 'clever' for her.

He played bit parts in his friends' films. He hadn't had much education; he was too busy playing hookey. When he was sixteen, he was already learning about life and cooking up trouble in the aisles of the Bon Marché department store, where he worked as a salesman. He had false bills delivered to real customers, or fixed the store's clocks so that they would all ring at the same time, preferably at the busiest moments. As he hadn't yet married Simone, he courted a young salesgirl who worked a little further on; her parents tried to keep him away from her and he found himself thrown out on the pavement in front of the Bon Marché, fleeing from two cops who were trying to nab him.

He did his military service in Meurthe-et-Moselle, and then in Constantinople, where he met his great friends Duhamel and Tanguy, who had tried in vain to get themselves sent home by swallowing live spiders.

The author of *Paroles* first met the author of *Corps et Biens* in a café in Montparnasse. The former was about to hit a man who was making too much noise, and the latter was getting ready to defend the threatened man with his fists. Florent Fels, who was present, introduced the two fighters to each other: they were Robert Desnos and Jacques Prévert.

They put their boxing gloves away and shook hands. Prévert dragged Desnos off to see Tanguy and Duhamel, and they became friends in turn. They soon discovered something they had in common: they were all born in 1900. At the time they met, then, they were not yet twenty-five.

Thus it was that the connection was established between the rue Blomet and the rue du Château; then between Montparnasse on the left bank, and the rue Fontaine on the right. The meeting would benefit a surrealism which was just coming into its own, and which would not be practised in quite the same way by its 'pope' and by its troublemakers...

THE BAD BOYS OF THE
RUE DU CHATEAU

We spent most of our time wandering around that ongoing carnival,
Montparnasse . . .

Marcel Duhamel

The first time that Prévert's group of friends went to Breton's, they had
just sniffed a good dose of cocaine to lift their spirits. Everyone ended up
feeling so good that they went back the next day, and the next. And, in
the other direction, people began to come every day to the rue du
Château – Aragon, Queneau, Max Morise, Michel Leiris . . . Leiris, the first
day, had sat down, his back very straight: he picked up a bottle of gin
and emptied it, sitting up straighter and straighter by the minute, and
becoming ever more inscrutable and silent.

It was a performance he would repeat.

When Benjamin Péret arrived, he picked up an accordion, took a deep
breath, and dramatically spread out his arms, so dramatically that the
instrument split into two equal halves.

This was not a performance he would repeat. But he would go one
better.

In the eighth issue of La Révolution surréaliste,[1] he had been immortalized
in the pursuit of his favourite sport: attacking the Church. Péret, in a
swimming costume, is shown calling out to a man of the Church passing
by in the street. The caption on the photo reads: 'Our collaborator
Benjamin Péret insulting a priest.' This took place at Plestin-les-Grèves,
near Lannion. Marcel Duhamel had taken the photograph. He had left
with the Préverts to find the Tanguys and take them all on vacation to the
Massons, who had rented a house in Sanary. They had zipped through
Pontoise at top speed, with the windows of the Torpédo down so that
Péret could annoy shopkeepers by shouting and shooting into the air with
a revolver, a weapon which he used and abused as much as Alfred Jarry
had done twenty years earlier.

Masson knew how outrageous Péret could be. When the painter had
lived on the Avenue de Ségur, before he moved to the rue Blomet, Péret

had come to see him every day. And every day for two weeks, the same scene occurred, without alteration. Péret would walk in front of the open window of a concierge on the ground floor, as he was sitting down with his wife and three children to a hot meal on the table. He would lean in at the window and ask this amiable question of the tranquilly lunching family: 'So how is that shit?'

He himself hadn't had anything to eat since the day before, or the day before that.

After two weeks of reflection, the brave defender of trampled family values finally got up the courage to react. Clearing his throat loudly, the next time the aggressor passed by, he leapt to the attack.

'Filthy German!' he muttered, and slammed the window shut as fast as he could, to avoid getting a punch in the face.

Péret admired Breton, who appreciated it. He never contradicted him and always defended him, except when Abbot Gegenbach was nearby. Then Péret would get up and slap him. The Abbot would leave. Breton reprimanded his most faithful surrealist friend, but to no effect; Péret would not listen. It made no difference to him that Gegenbach had joined the movement (which he would later denounce), that he was in love with an actress from the Odéon, that he danced in his cassock at the Jockey Club, that he drank at the Rotonde with a girl on each knee, that he spent time in whorehouses and went on retreats to Solesmes when he didn't have a penny. He was still a cleric. In its fifth issue, *La Révolution surréaliste* published a photo of the priest with his young ladyfriend. Péret couldn't stop the publication, but took his revenge elsewhere. Whenever the slightest shadow of a cassock crossed his path, he went crazy. Often Prévert was with him; he had no aversion to scandal either.

He was there with the group from the rue du Château one evening on the Boulevard de Clichy. They were standing in line at the cinema. The pavement was filled with people; it was raining, and they had umbrellas. Breton hated umbrellas, especially when they kept him from walking as fast as he wanted. Exasperated, he grabbed one from the hands of a passer-by, grasped it with both hands, and broke it in two. Prévert, amused by this game, did the same. Desnos, not wanting to be left out, destroyed a third umbrella. Tanguy, Péret and Duhamel took hold of other open umbrellas and followed suit ... The crowd began to get angry, Breton slapped someone who was in his way, then the police arrived on the scene. It soon became clear that they were not going to see a film that night ...

Another time, Prévert, Duhamel and Tanguy were on the beach in Brittany. Prévert walked around leering at all the women. When his pranks started to catch up with him, he hid in a restaurant where the dishes were excellent and the wines strong. At dessert, for a laugh, he threw the windows open and began to insult the peasants in the square. He just escaped being lynched. He was miraculously preserved from this fate again a few days later, when he punched a cyclist who had run into him by accident. In these cases, the best thing to do was to get home quietly and lie low.

The neighbours wondered if 54, rue du Château might be a whorehouse. How else could all the coming and going be explained?

During the day, the tenants didn't work, but instead wandered from bar to bar in Montparnasse, and went to the Ciné-Opéra. Desnos, it was said, went once a day, and Prévert almost as often. His brother Pierrot, who was a projectionist in a movie theatre on the right bank, let him and his friends in free. They saw the same films over and over again: The Golem, Nosferatu, The Brothers Karamazov . . . In the evening, when they came home, they read Georges Bataille's L'Histoire de l'œil, published clandestinely.

There were always lots of people there. Three of them rented the place, but at least fifteen slept there. Before going to bed, they would listen to American jazz records. They drank, smoked and played strange games. They would sit down at a table, with pieces of paper in front of them. They passed these around among themselves, wrote on them in secret, folded them, passed them, and began again. This 'game of scraps of paper', invented by Tzara, was cultivated by Prévert. It was he who invented the beginning of the famous sentence which gave the 'exquisite corpse' its name: 'The exquisite corpse will drink the new wine.' The painters played as well, forming teams in which poets would also pick up the paintbrush: Man Ray, Miró, Morise and Tanguy would take on Breton, Duhamel, Morise and Tanguy.

They also talked politics. They had become interested in the review Clarté: this magazine, founded in 1919 by Barbusse, had become more radical by 1924. George Grosz judged that in a France which was 'intellectually feeble, almost moribund', in which 'Romain Rolland, to whom people liked to point as the symbol of a better humanity, was as gentle a radical in the world of letters as Herriot was in politics,'[2] the Clarté group was the only true pole of radicalism around. Later the review would become the mouthpiece for leftist opposition to the Communist Party; for the moment, it was leading the struggle against the war in Morocco. Many intellectuals joined in this combat, including the surrealists. But Clarté raised the problem of communism. In 1926, Breton had published a long text in La Révolution surréaliste, entitled 'Légitime défense', in reaction to several attacks on intellectuals that had appeared in the newspaper L'Humanité, and in response to a question asked by Pierre Naville: were the surrealists ready for real revolution? Yes, answered Breton, but the revolution of the mind was as fundamental as political revolution; the members of the Communist Party were not the sole agents of revolution.

The great question in those years was whether the surrealists were going to get involved in communism. Prévert was dubious: 'They'll put me in a cell.'[3] He didn't need the Party in order to found the October Group in 1929 and perform with his theatre troupe in working-class suburbs.

Leiris and Tanguy were undecided. Artaud and Desnos refused. Breton, Aragon, Péret, Unik and Eluard took the big step in January 1927, though Breton, disappointed by the Party's cultural policy, would soon opt out again. They published a text, 'Au grand jour', in which they justified their decision. This elicited a sharp commentary from Paulhan, published in the *Nouvelle Revue française*, and a further response from Breton, labelling him a 'French-type arsehole'. Paulhan challenged him to a duel, and sent Marcel Arlan and Francis Crémieux to arrange it. But Breton was evasive. Paulhan responded with a note addressed to his two friends, published in the NRF:

> Dear Friends,
>   Thank you. I didn't bother you for nothing; now at least we have learned just how much cowardice lies beneath the violence and abjection of this character.[4]

Aragon had already answered this previously, defending Breton in a very surrealistic letter:

> Sir,
>   There are all kinds of bastards. I've always thought that the worst were the ones who conceal their names. You are a specialist of anonymity … But in the end you're too great a fool, and I can't just sit here and watch you say whatever you like. Go to hell, definitively.
>   P.S. You'd better send your witnesses fast; the day after tomorrow I'm running away.[5]

Crevel also joined the Party, and remained a member for longer: he wrote in communist papers and participated in militant actions. In 1935, during the International Congress of Writers for the Defence of Culture, he made a desperate effort to bring the communists and the surrealists together, but didn't manage to do so. He fell out with Breton and was in tears as he told the story to Salvador Dali.[6] A few days later, deep in despair, consumed by tuberculosis, he committed suicide.

As for Péret, he had been involved with communism since 1926. Moreover, he was head proofreader at *L'Humanité*, which earned him a little money. He left the Communist Party when the incompatibilities between communism and surrealism came to seem insurmountable. In 1936, in Spain, he supported the Trotskyists of the POUM.* As did Pierre Naville, also a Trotskyist, who joined the cell in1926, became editor of *Clarté* the same year, and was expelled from the Party in 1928 when he was director of the French section of the Fourth International.

On the right bank, surrealism was closer to Trotskyism than to communism. On the left bank, surrealism was closer to anarchism: it was fun-seeking, partygoing, libertarian – less rigid on principles, less worried about the party line, less inclined to excommunicate its members. On the rue du Château, the spirit of the old Montparnasse lived on a little. Of course, money, dazzle, and modernity had undermined it to a degree. But there was still something of Jarry and Apollinaire in Desnos and Prévert. Breton, by contrast, rather recalled Matisse. Even when he was in revolt, he was always in control: he kept his eyes fixed on the blue horizon of himself. The basic difference, at least until 1928 – the reason why Montparnasse remained Montparnasse and could never be confused with the rue Fontaine – was that in Prévert's crowd, the bad boys were kings. Whereas at the school on the rue Fontaine, the honours students took themselves very seriously indeed.

* The Workers' Party for Marxist Unification.

SETTLING SCORES

The conclusion to be drawn from my voluntary inspection is that
Morise spent all his time typing, and that Vitrac did absolutely nothing
at all.

André Breton

One day in 1928, Youki Foujita was having a drink at the Cigogne, on
the rue Bréa. At a nearby table, a man dressed in a smoking jacket was
laughing in a way which exasperated the young woman. A lock of hair
fell over his forehead. He was playing with straws. Because she seemed
to be observing his activity, he came over to her table and showed her
the latest surrealist game: he was putting together the wrappers of straws
until he had made a paper spider. Then he let a drop of water fall on the
insect, at which the animal waved its legs.

The man burst out laughing and introduced himself: his name was
Robert Desnos. Youki was unmoved.

The next day, she was having a drink with Breton, whom she knew a
little, having run into him several times in bars in Montparnasse. She told
him about the scene and admitted that she hadn't liked Desnos. Breton
immediately called over a waiter and had a sheet of paper brought
to him, on which he wrote a harsh note addressed to this surrealist companion who didn't know how to behave himself in cafés or with women.
Youki tried to restrain the hand of the chastizing disciplinarian, and keep
him from sending the letter. But she couldn't dissuade him: Breton was
furious.

A few days later, in another café, Youki saw Desnos again. She called
him over to her table, and apologized for having got him into trouble
with Breton. But Desnos didn't care a bit. He was free, he had just
returned from Cuba, he was happy . . .

Youki invited him to dinner that very evening at Foujita's home in
Montsouris. They became friends. Several years later, Youki Foujita would
become Youki Desnos. Breton would not be chosen as a witness . . .

The incendiary letter sent to the young joker after the meeting at the
Cigogne was typical of the severity of this pope of poets, 'as principled

and as rigid as St Andrew's cross', as Salvador Dali wrote.[1] Breton ruled his troops with an iron fist.

He played on various levels. For example, he felt that buying and selling paintings – which he himself did, like Eluard – was a noble activity. It was quite unlike journalism, a trade in which Desnos, who worked at *Paris-Soir*, was compromising himself, as were Crevel, editorial director of the *Nouvelles littéraires*, Soupault, and many others. In 1944, Soupault ran into Breton in New York, where he had taken up journalism for lack of any other means of making a living. Pierre Lazareff had hired him to read the news on the radio. The presenter had set himself an unchanging rule: that he would report on all events except those concerning the pope.

Music, one of the joys of Masson, Desnos and the guests at the rue du Château or at the Bal Nègre on the rue Blomet, was so little appreciated and little heard on the rue Fontaine that it was generally only listened to there in secret.

Idealized love was a virtue (as in *Najda*), and homosexuality a vice, an opinion to which Breton stuck fast. The eleventh issue of *La Révolution surréaliste*[2] included a report on a round table which brought together the faithful few to discuss a specific problem. That day the question was: 'What do you think of pederasty?' Prévert didn't condemn it, any more than Queneau, who deplored the prejudice against homosexuality common among the surrealists. Péret, Unik and Breton all spoke against it, especially Breton who felt that with the exception of Sade, homosexuals proposed 'to the tolerance of humanity a mental and moral deficit which they tended to systematize'.[3]

This mental rigidity undoubtedly explained in part the surrealists' contempt for Cocteau. It also justified the antagonism between Breton and Ilya Ehrenburg, a Soviet writer who lived in Paris and was a faithful follower of the Moscow line. The Frenchman reproached the Russian less for constantly changing his opinions to please the Party's directorate, than for having written some violent criticism of the surrealists, whom he accused of laziness, parasitism and, crime amongst crimes, ceaseless worrying about pederasty.

Shortly before the congress of the Association of Revolutionary Writers and Artists, Breton ran into Ehrenburg who was leaving his home in Montparnasse to go and buy some tobacco in a café. He followed him and slapped him methodically, without eliciting any reaction from the other.

Alternating slaps and insults, and often employing both together, the author of the *Surrealist Manifesto* was not sparing with either. Over time, it was hard to avoid finding oneself in the line of fire. His rages were often unpredictable. For instance, in 1929, when he and Simone Breton divorced, he considered it a crime of high treason for anyone so much as to speak to his ex-wife. Gossips even suggested that his break with Pierre Naville may have been partly motivated by the fact that Naville's lover (and future wife), Denise Lévy, was Simone's cousin.

With Breton, quarrels and fights were almost inevitable. They always occurred in a climate of hatred and insult, as violent as the passions that this man with his remarkable charisma would also inspire. The brutality with which first the Dadaists, then the surrealists, provoked the world around them was not only directed outwards; it came back at them like a boomerang whenever a member of the group had to be punished or excluded. Breton would later admit this: in 1946, in a notice advertising the reprinting of the *Second Surrealist Manifesto*, he regretted the 'unfortunate traces of nervousness' and 'occasionally hasty judgements' he had some-times expressed.

Soupault, although he was one of the crucial elements of the group and one of the two fathers of the *Champs magnétiques*, was expelled from it in circumstances that almost prefigured those of the expulsions from the great Stalinist brotherhood thirty years later. And just as a number of intellectuals felt like orphans after having been thrown out of the Party, Soupault had a nervous breakdown when he found himself alone, without the surrealist banner to hang onto.

He was summoned one evening in November 1926. As had been the case at the time of the Barrès trial, Breton directed the proceedings. Soupault recalled:

> I entered a fairly large, poorly lit room. I realized that, as usual, the numerous assistants present represented a court, presided over, of course, by André Breton, seconded by Louis Aragon and Max Morise. The accusation was pronounced in a hostile, even an insulting tone. I wasn't expecting a welcome of this nature from those I had always considered to be friends, whom I had tried to help when they had had problems of all kinds. I soon understood that this 'ceremony' which seemed silly and even slightly ridiculous to me had been prepared in advance to destroy me. The organizers had no intention of listening to my protests. Everything had already been decided.[4]

What were Philippe Soupault's crimes? Not having attended the group meetings at the Cyrano often enough. Contributing to 'bourgeois maga-zines' and having a 'disordered literary activity' by writing questionable books. Refusing to join the Communist Party. Smoking English cigarettes, considered more aristocratic than the black tobacco of the workers with their proletarian Caporals.

And what about Artaud, expelled at the same time? He was accused of acting ignobly, of being irrational, metaphysical, 'scum', 'vile'. Of having imbued the whole third issue of *La Révolution surréaliste* with a 'half-libertarian ... half-mystical tone which threatened to lead the movement in a direction foreign to its founder's wishes.'[5] Breton quickly regained control of the magazine, precisely in order to guard against such false directions.

Two years later, when Artaud produced *Le Songe* at the Théâtre Alfred Jarry, which Breton condemned as 'vaguely Strindbergian', he would be labelled an 'informer' motivated by 'money and prestige'.[6] The brilliant actor shrugged it off. For him, surrealism had signed its death warrant when it allied itself with communism.

Max Ernst and Joan Miró were also judged in 1926, in their case for having agreed to do the sets for a production deemed to be too conformist: *Romeo and Juliet*, staged by Sergei Diaghilev. This time, Breton, Aragon, and their troops assembled in the theatre. They couldn't accept the idea that the two artists would compromise themselves by making a pact with the forces of money and power. Hundreds of insulting tracts fluttered down from the balconies, and not far from the stage, Leiris unfurled a gigantic flag sporting the inscription 'Long live Lautréamont!' Aragon, impeccably dressed, insulted the crowd, and was seconded by the shouts of Péret and Desnos, which were soon drowned out by the whistles of arriving officers. The evening ended at the police station.

Soon it was De Chirico's turn. His early style had been much appreciated by the surrealists, but they hated his later work. In March 1928, against the painter's wishes and to counterbalance Léonce Rosenberg, who was exhibiting recent works by the painter, the surrealist gallery showed some of his older works. These had been bought by Breton in the painter's studio in Montparnasse, in the Passage d'Enfer, where he had lived until 1913. Raymond Queneau was in charge of the trial. According to him, there were indeed two periods in De Chirico's work: the early one, and the bad one.

On 11 March 1929, the rue du Château was the scene of another settling of scores. This time it didn't take place at the house, whose former tenants had handed the place over to even more orthodox newcomers, Georges Sadoul and André Thirion, but at the café across the street. Breton had summoned the rank and file of the surrealist movement to reflect on some major themes: revolution, Stalin's treatment of Trotsky, collective projects...

Members conspicuous by their absence included Naville, Artaud, Vitrac, Limbour, Masson, Tual, and Bataille, who had all chosen not to come. And two of the former tenants of the rue du Château, Duhamel and Prévert, had not been invited to the meeting, as the central surrealist committee had judged their 'occupations' or their 'characters' to be undesirable.[7] Man Ray and Tanguy came anyway, despite having also been 'forgotten'.

On the other hand, a number of recent recruits had come, and were quickly placed on the bench of the accused. The Grand Jeu group,* Roger Gilbert-Lecomte, René Daumal, and Roger Vailland, who worked together on the magazine of the same name, were accused of mysticism, and of preferring Landru to Sacco and Vanzetti† (as one provocative headline of the magazine Le Grand Jeu proclaimed). Finally, Roger Vailland published an article in Paris-Midi praising Chiappe, the prefect of police. The article was mocking and sarcastic, to say the least; it began by comparing Chiappe to 'a grandfather showering his grandchildren with presents' (the 'grandchildren' were clearly the Paris police) and ended with an arrow stuck straight in the heart of 'the purifier of our capital'.[8] But Breton didn't even see the mockery. Vailland was a journalist and for him, that was enough to nail him to the stake of surrealist fury.

The day after the Grand Jeu trial, Ribemont-Dessaignes sent a letter to the rue Fontaine, cutting all ties. He could no longer tolerate the judgemental zeal of God and his apostles.

But the worst was still to come. In 1930, Breton published the Second Surrealist Manifesto. It simultaneously represented a sorting out of the movement, a reminder of its founding principles, and an attack on 'the cowards, the simulators, the social climbers', all those who had betrayed the movement and compromised themselves.

It was already clear that Masson was jealous of Max Ernst and Picasso and that, like Artaud, he was guilty of 'social abstentionism'. Desnos' compromises and accommodations were now out in the open. It was supposed that Naville, to whom Breton had entrusted the direction of La Révolution surréaliste, as he had to Péret, because they appeared to be 'the most refractory to all concessions',[9] had joined the Communist Party – only to leave it again three months later, chiefly in order to garner some cheap publicity for himself (and perhaps also because of embarrassment at his father's wealth). Georges Bataille and Michel Leiris clearly deserved to be drawn and quartered: the former for having founded a rival review, Documents, which the latter edited. Both had committed the supreme act of betrayal by opening their columns to the renegades – Desnos, Prévert, Masson, Limbour...

* The Grand Jeu group, a faction of the surrealist movement which rejected both the materialistic world and the avenue of political engagement, was more drawn to the mystical, spiritual, and romantic tradition of Gurdjeff, Nerval and Rimbaud.
† Landru was a turn-of-the-century French criminal accused of seducing and strangling a dozen women whom he then burned in his stove. The tale of his exploits captivated and horrified the public imagination; he was guillotined in 1922. Sacco and Vanzetti were militant anarchists accused of murdering the treasurer and the guard of a factory in Braintree, Massachusetts. They were executed in 1927, despite numerous movements which sprang up around the world in their defence.

The *Second Manifesto* presented proof of all of this, and more. It revealed that Vitrac, who had the misfortune of writing for the theatre, was a 'true slattern of ideas', that Limbour's pen was dipped in 'literary coquetteries', and that Soupault was nothing but 'a rat running around the ratodrome,' the embodiment of 'total infamy'.[10]

A little bit of everything, and quite a lot of anything: it was too much for some. In answer to Breton's diatribes, Ribemont-Dessaignes, Vitrac, Limbour, Morise, Baron, Leiris, Queneau, Boiffard, Batailler, Desnos and Prévert published a pamphlet entitled *A Corpse*. It was a violent attack on André Breton, some presenting him as a false brother, others as a false pope and false bishop, many as a false friend, a collector of corpses and professional intellectual in the eyes of some, a cop and a priest in the eyes of all.

The icon-bashers used the title of the pamphlet brought out to dishonour Anatole France's death in 1924, and they repeated the same words with which Breton had concluded his own 'homage': 'This man, dead, must no longer raise dust.' This sentence was printed superimposed over Breton's face, his forehead adorned by a crown of thorns, a drop of blood dripping from a corner of one eye.

Breton, for his part, had mustered his troops, old and new. He had to unite those still at his side around a common cause. He found one, and prepared to mount a final assault on Montparnasse. The first attack had demolished the Closerie des Lilas. The last one, five years later, would devastate another establishment: a bar that was also a restaurant and dance hall, which had just opened on the Boulevard Edgar Quinet, not far from the rue du Départ and the Montparnasse railway station. This spot, devoted to nocturnal pleasures, had the misfortune to bear a name which the knights of Count Lautréamont couldn't bear to see flaunted on the awning of a watering spot: the Maldoror.

They weren't all there on 14 February 1930, the evening of the punitive night raid. The newcomers – Buñuel, Giacometti, Magritte, Dali, Sadoul, Thirion – were not all ready to fight in the front lines yet. There were several, though, who joined Aragon, Péret and Tanguy in the assault. Breton himself stormed the threshold of the Maldoror, proclaiming that he was a guest of the Count de Lautréamont. It was he who launched the first bombardment of glasses and plates which shattered the windows of the place.

'The surrealists are attacking!' cried a woman in a fur coat.

Thirion was bashed in the stomach. Tanguy was hit with a dish of snails cooked in champagne and fresh butter, and Eluard with a dried ham. In retaliation he struck out with his legs, then with his arms, and the fight spread. The women, in evening gowns, and the men, in smoking jackets, hid near the washrooms. René Char tugged on a tablecloth, and a soufflé cascaded creamily all over the brocaded carpets. A bucket lost its champagne, and the champagne its bubbles. The head barman hurled a piece of fruit which hit Aragon on the back of the head, setting off an offensive of vintage claret followed by some chairs and a table or two. All of this smashed against the door to the kitchens, which shattered. Three cooks came running out. Someone shouted, 'Call the police!'

Other bottles were thrown. Half a dozen roast beefs, accompanied by salted, peppered and spicy insults, were launched into the battle. Sirens sounded, and the poets huddled together. René Char was bleeding at the thigh, which had been pierced by a kitchen knife. Breton's shirt was in tatters.

The assailants slipped into the foyer, and stepped back to let the police through. In the general confusion, Breton deemed that Lautréamont's honour had been avenged: the battlefield of the Maldoror was covered with shards of glass and bottles, splintered tables, broken soup tureens, grease, gravy, and the remains of cheese sauces, cold, congealed, splattered all over the walls.

The surrealists disappeared. Char was taken away in a taxi. The others walked back along the cemetery wall. Breton's eyes shone with the enchanted flame which lit up his entire being after a fight. Péret rubbed his hands because a priest was approaching, not a hundred yards away, on the same pavement. Aragon's upper lip had been split open. Leaving the others, he turned into the rue Delambre, headed left when he reached Vavin, passed the Dôme and the Rotonde, and continued until he reached the crimson drapes of a restaurant which had opened two years earlier and where, ever since the night of its inauguration, Elsa had been waiting for him.

THE SOFT DRINK KING

For the last six months, the haste with which the artists are leaving Montparnasse has become accentuated. They are fleeing the expensive hotels, the studios which are no longer of use to anyone except rich American women, and a kind of picturesque image commercialized by the advertising of fifteen nightclubs and by a series of reviews and newspapers, each promoting its own interests.

Roger Vailland

The Coupole filled a space of 2,400 square metres, which was devoted to meals, dancing, flirtations, warmth, reunions and quarrels. On the ground floor, a chow room. In the basement, a pleasure room. And on the first floor, a games room.

In 1926, MM. Fraux and Lafon, brothers-in-law and restaurant owners from the Auvergne, bought the former wood and coal warehouse across from the Select. They had already bought the Dôme from old Chambon, but he then bought it back after three years of loyal service. Kept from seeing their dream come true, the brothers-in-law came up with a new dream: that of opening, in the middle of Montparnasse, the biggest restaurant in the neighbourhood, if not in the entire capital.

As soon as they thought of it, they set to work. Construction began in January 1927. Less than a year later, everything was finished. There were three floors for three different kinds of activities. On the ground floor, customers dined, observed by the very painters who had decorated the pillars of the columns. Those who came in through the revolving door on the Boulevard du Montparnasse found themselves in Bob the barman's domain; he officiated from behind his counter. Pushing open the door which joined the two rooms, one moved easily from the bar to the restaurant.

Those who wanted to play boule went to the first floor. The staircase was at the back of the room, to the right. It opened out onto a terrace where customers ate in the summer and played boule all year long. The painter Othon Friesz watched over the games room.

The nightbirds had to go downstairs. Two orchestras, one for blues, the other for tangos, enabled the dancers to get to know each other at different tempi.

In the afternoon, the embraces had a somewhat different flavour. The nightclub became a tearoom where heavily made-up, slightly older women came to seek out very young men who were a bit down on their luck. Certain skills were exchanged for money. And a young man could make quite a bit, apparently. Even into the nineteen seventies.

Why the Coupole? Because the Dôme and the Rotonde were already there, and this youngest establishment belonged to the same family as its elder siblings. MM. Fraux and Lafon even had a real cupola added after hitting upon the name for their masterpiece. It was five metres high, to allow the odours from the restaurant to rise and escape.

On the night of the restaurant's inauguration, 20 December 1927, two thousand people came to eat and drink. When supplies began to run out – the 1,200 bottles of champagne had been quickly consumed – taxis fanned out all over Paris to find more. On their return, there was such a crush around the buffet tables that some clever souls simply spirited away a bottle or two to the Select, the Dôme or the Rotonde, where they tranquilly asked for glasses, so they could drink in peace to the new Montparnasse.

At the Rotonde, in 1914, old Libion was helped by a trio which composed his entire personnel. At the Coupole, four hundred employees rushed to and fro. M. Fraux was nicknamed 'the soft drink king'. His kingdom? The Coupole. Four years before it opened, André Warnod had uttered the premonitory belief that 'The industrialist who opens the first late night restaurant in that neighbourhood will probably make a fortune, and the artists will leave for somewhere other than Montparnasse.'[1]

The industrialist opened the restaurant. He made a fortune. The artists were still there.

But not for much longer. And were they the same ones?

Derain now drove a Bugatti. Man Ray had bought a Voisin. Kisling, who lived as much if not more in Sanary as in Paris, zoomed about on his two American Willys Knights. Picabia had a six-cylinder Delage, and Cendrars an Alfa-Romeo. Zborowski didn't have a driver's licence, but he was rich. He would not remain so for long, though, and Foujita would also suffer a change in circumstances. He had exchanged Youki's Ballot for a Delage convertible with a top that the chauffeur refused to uncover, not wanting to let it get wrinkled. But changing the hood would not make much difference to the bill that the tax inspector had just presented for hundreds of thousands of francs, corresponding to various debts which had been accumulating since 1925. Foujita had to let some of his staff go. He organized a monumental exhibition in Japan which he hoped would rake in the profits. If not, he would have to sell the car. He was already preparing to leave his home in Montsouris.

The only one who never changed was Pascin. He was among the richest of them all, but he didn't flaunt it. When he arrived at the Rotonde with his models and faithful friends, he came on foot. He cut a path through the limousines parked outside, reached the bar, offered drinks to all and looked around for Lucy Krogh. For the moment, he was happy: he had just returned from a trip to the United States with Lucy. She was pregnant by him, and he did not yet know that a backroom abortionist had put a diabolical spell on her.

Pascin was as faithful to himself, to what he had always been, as he was to his love for Lucy Krogh. Elsewhere, though, all was mayhem and fickle hearts. Youki was about to leave Foujita for Robert Desnos, and Foujita would embark on a new romance with Mady Lequeux, a singer–model. Paul Eluard, who was returning from a solo tour around the world, had lost Gala and found Nusch, penniless in the street. Gala, who had hesitated for such a long time between Eluard and Ernst, now left the two friends to work it out between them and took advantage of a new opportunity in Dali. When she was with Eluard, she was called 'the pest'. For many, she would now become 'the cash register'.

Bronia had consoled herself after Radiguet's death and was going to marry René Clair, whom she had met during the filming of Entr'acte. Kiki was jealous and quarrelled constantly with her American photographer, who was about to wrap his arms around a young American model, beautiful and determined. She had come to France to learn photography, and had turned up on the rue Campagne Première to meet Man Ray. Since he wasn't there, she went off to wait for him in a café. He came in a little later. She walked up to him.

'Hello. My name is Lee Miller and I'm your student.'

'Excuse me?'

'Lee Miller ... From now on I'm your student.'

He looked at her, amazed.

'But I don't have any students!'

'Yes you do, you have me.'

Man Ray was leaving for Biarritz the next day, and told her so. She gave him a charming smile and asked one simple question: 'What time does our train leave?'

At the bar of the Coupole, Kiki threw plates at the insufferable seducer who was himself so jealous of any male who might approach Lee Miller that he now walked about with a revolver in his pocket, ready to execute anyone showing signs of wanting to take his place. Man Ray escaped from Kiki by slipping in between, and then under, the tables. The wheel was turning. Such was life.

But Kiki went too far. She married a journalist who also dabbled in illustration, Henri Broca. He launched new dailies in Paris, and launched his new fiancée in the wider world, thanks to exhibitions in which Kiki sold her (rather naive) works and to her now official status as queen of Montparnasse.

Derain settled his scores with as much zeal as Man Ray's former favourite model. He was about fifty, quarrelsome, and had a very rich mistress. Her name was Madeleine Anspach, and she was the wife of a Belgian banker. When he was in an alcoholic frenzy, she would watch him, roaring drunk, lift the glasses, the chairs, and the tables of the bar at the Coupole, and smash them all to bits. Then he would leap into his Bugatti and head off to Barbizon at a hundred and seventy-five kilometres an hour, come back the next day, excuse himself, pay for the damage and show off the motor of his little blue car, swearing that no work of art was more impressive. Madeleine Anspach would accept it all, and ask for two silver fox coats. She usually got them.

But the most passionate of all the Coupole's customers, the one whose romantic escapades were most eagerly followed, was Louis Aragon. The word 'escapade' didn't fit Denise Lévy, Breton's cousin and soon to be Naville's wife, with whom Aragon fell madly in love and whose portrait he drew in his novel *Aurélien*, as a result of failing to draw anything else out of her: Denise was the very chaste Bérénice of the tale.

Nancy Cunard was a different story altogether. Glamorous and beautiful, she preceded Elsa's arrival in the poet's life. Between 1926 and 1928, she offered him her arm, an arm graced by ivory bracelets which left traces on men's cheeks. She wore a hat, sometimes with a veil, and a cape to match her companion's. The latter sported one of the canes which he collected. He was as elegant as she was beautiful. They were both free: she because she respected above all her desires, made possible by her colossal fortune, which she spent with abandon from luxurious hotel to transatlantic liner; he because *Le Con d'Irène*, published clandestinely and illustrated by Masson, gave an even more sulphurous sheen to his reputation as a dandy who was interested in the life of the mind as well as that of the senses. He was a surrealist writer, she was a generous muse. She took him here and there with her: to the rue Le Regrattier, where she lived, like Bérénice in *Aurélien*; to one of her country houses; and into her bed, where she led him as soon as she had decided that he was the one she wanted out of all the regulars at the Cyrano.

He didn't need persuading. It happened on a winter's day in London at the beginning of 1926. Aragon discovered in her a woman who was not only free, but also independent. She had done what was necessary in order not to have any children, and she also did whatever was necessary to have the men she wanted. She saw them, laid claim to them, led them on. They drank, they played, then she got rid of them. Aragon stayed, but he was consumed with anxiety. He was at her feet. She could insult him with her English accent and French words; she would watch unmoved as he burned the fifteen hundred pages of the manuscript of *La Défense de l'Infini* in a Madrid hotel room; she reproached him for his jealousy, his

narrow-mindedness, his exclusiveness in sexual matters. But whatever
happened, he always had one knee to the ground, paralysed by his passion.

They went together to Spain, to Holland, to Germany. In July 1928, they were in Venice. Aragon was waiting to receive the money from *La Baigneuse*, the work by Braque which he had bought at Kahnweiler's sale in 1922. He had bought it for two hundred and forty francs; six years later, he sold it for a hundred times more. But the money hadn't arrived yet. He couldn't continue to live off Nancy. Still less so as his beloved was now strolling around St Mark's Square with another man. His name was Henry Crowder: he was an American jazz pianist, but the Cunard Line heiress had distracted him from the piano.

Aragon was alone in the hotel room. He wanted to die, and tried to. He would later say that he had thrown himself into the Grand Canal, or that he had taken sleeping pills – maybe both. Whatever the case, he was saved in time, so that when the money finally arrived, he was able to return to Paris.

He moved to the rue du Château. In 1928, two young men from the city of Nancy, communists and surrealists, had taken over the house that had previously been occupied by Prévert, Tanguy and Duhamel. Their names were André Thirion and Georges Sadoul, and they offered Aragon a room.

But Nancy returned from Venice, and it all began again. How long could it go on?

As it turned out, only until a Bugatti in every way like Derain's stopped one day in front of the Coupole. A young girl got out. She was dark-haired, lively, wore a hat on her head and carried a white mouse in her arms. She was a dancer, she came from Vienna and her name was Léna Amsel. Almost immediately, she was surrounded by men. But Aragon was the one she chose, and Aragon won out over all the others. His heart, though, was not completely hers: he would recall later that 'At the time, I told myself that I was in love with another woman, a German ... I pretended to no longer love another woman. An Englishwoman.'[2]

The romance with 'the German' would be short-lived. From a corner of the bar, a young woman was watching. She decided that her time had come. Leaning towards one of her friends, Roland Tual, who was sipping an ale, she said, 'I want you to introduce me to that man.'

'Aragon?' asked Tual.

'Aragon,' she answered.

'Why him?'

Elsa Triolet, with her deep dark eyes, looked straight at this surrealist artist who had never painted nor written, and answered simply, 'Because I've been waiting for this moment for the last three years.'

TAKEN IN PASSING

Love is a place which sums up an entire life – what am I saying? –
not just sums it up, but develops it.

Louis Aragon

On 4 November 1928, Mayakovsky was sitting at a table at the Coupole.
Mayakovsky was one of the greatest living Russian poets. He had arrived
in Paris a few days earlier, and was staying at the Hôtel Istria. It was Elsa
who had invited him to the café. She had known Mayakovsky since
childhood. She had been in love with him, but it was her sister, Lili, who
had won him in the end. She was known as Lili Brik, which was her
husband's name. Her husband was no more upset about the affair than
Eluard had been about Gala and Max Ernst. And Elsa had found consolation
in the arms of M. Triolet, a Frenchman who had been in Moscow in
1917. He had taken her to Tahiti, then to Paris, where he had deposited
her and left, almost as soon as he had married her.

Mayakovsky was surrounded by people from Ilya Ehrenburg's group of
friends. His height and build distinguished him from the others. He had
thick chestnut hair and enormous hands, but eyes that were infinitely gentle.

He was sitting next to a young girl of eighteen, Tatiana, with whom
he had been in love for a little while, without much hope of being able
to take her with him to the country of the Soviets. Not only was he
twenty years older than she, they weren't even on the same side: he was
a Red, she a White.

As Aragon was walking down the central aisle of the restaurant,
Mayakovsky asked for him to be called over. The two poets knew each
other by reputation. One didn't speak a word of French, the other not a
word of Russian. Fortunately, there were translators. Aragon invited
Mayakovsky to come to the rue du Château two days later, saying he
would organize a party in his honour.

On 5 November, when Aragon returned to the bar of the Coupole, one
of his friends called out to him. It was Roland Tual. Tual said to him, 'I'd
like to introduce you to a friend.'

The friend was sitting at a table, wearing a beige hat, a fur coat, and a
black dress. She was small, red-haired, pale-skinned, and serious-looking.

Aragon sat down. It was six o'clock in the evening. Before dark, Elsa
had already been invited to the party the next day for Mayakovsky.

'Yes, of course I'll come,' she said.

And so she did. She mingled with the other guests, but Aragon didn't
pay much attention to her. He was keeping an eye on Mayakovsky, and
also on his friend André Thirion who, moping about an unhappy love
affair, had taken refuge in the loggia.

Aragon went up to see how he was doing. From the lower level, Elsa
observed everything, understood everything, and saw her opportunity.
She climbed the staircase and joined the two men. She entered the loggia,
looked around and said, as if it were a joke: 'What's the point? Of making
love?'

Then she went up to Aragon and pressed her body against his. Thirion
could scarcely believe his eyes: 'She attacked right away, without the
slightest shyness, with a tenacious, patient desire for conquest that she
developed all her life.'[1]

A little embarrassed, the second man slipped away. He came downstairs
and remained at the foot of the steps, acting as a watchman. A quarter of
an hour later, the lovers came back to join the group. They were smiling.
They danced to music by Duke Ellington and Louis Armstrong, records
that had been left there by Marcel Duhamel.

This was Thirion's version. For Lilly Marcou, Elsa and Aragon did
indeed see each other again at the rue du Château, but they had already
spent a first night at the Istria Hotel, where Mayakovsky had passed them
on the staircase. In addition, on the day of the party, Elsa had arrived
with Vladimir Pozner, then asked him to disappear discreetly when the
time was right.[2]

The rest, however, was not so easy. The couple was just forming. They
hadn't had time yet to construct their legend: 'I didn't love you, I didn't
love you. I didn't tell you I loved you, because I didn't love you.'[3]

For the moment, Elsa's eyes did not have the brilliance that Aragon
would celebrate later. He preferred Lena Amsel's: the singer was livelier,
prettier, more fun to be with. But, like Nancy Cunard, she was too free:
she flirted with other men, notably with a sculptor.

When Elsa looked for her lover, she couldn't find him. As soon as
she ran across Thirion or Sadoul, she would ask them, 'Have you seen
Aragon?'

'No,' they would answer, evasively.

They had seen him, of course. But Aragon had asked them to keep
quiet. He hadn't chosen the Russian for her charms, he had just taken her
up in passing to get revenge on Lena and her sculptor. In any case, that's

what he told Thirion. He also told him that he was wary of Elsa. She was too clinging, too indiscreet. He even wondered if she were an informer, if she worked for the police. For the police were keeping an eye on members of the Communist Party. Might the cops try to pump the young woman for information garnered in pillow talk during long nights on the rue du Château?

Aragon was wrong, of course. Elsa was head over heels in love with him. But, even if she had won the first round, she had not yet won the second. She would have to wait several weeks for that. And then she would play her hand in an astonishingly adroit manner. Astonishing, and definitive.

One night, Aragon asked Thirion to go to the Jungle to tell Lena, whom he was supposed to meet at eleven o'clock, that he would be late. The Jungle had replaced the Jockey Club, which had been a victim of the battle being waged in the construction industry: Helena Rubinstein had bought up all the buildings on the corner of the rue Campagne Première and the Boulevard Montparnasse in order to construct a modern building there. The devotees of Montparnasse night life had only to cross the street to carry on the party. The same people were dancing to the same blues; it was just on another dance floor.

A few ice cubes short of eleven o'clock, Thirion entered and sat down at a table. The room was far from full; the night was young. The messenger from the rue du Château ordered a drink. He waited. At eleven o'clock and after a few drinks, a young woman sat down across from him. It wasn't Lena Amsel, it was Elsa. Suddenly it seemed quite hot in the restaurant. The discussion immediately hit on a subject which one of the two wanted to avoid but which was the only thing that interested the other: where was Aragon?

Uneasy, blushing, fearing the arrival of the legitimate mistress, Thirion ended up by confessing the truth: Aragon was with another woman.

'Who is she?'

'A dancer.'

'It's just a passing thing.'

'Not quite . . .'

He managed to get the second part out. 'He's in love with her. She's helped relieve the pain caused by Nancy Cunard.'

'He loves her, you said?'

'A bit . . .'

'No more than "a bit"?'

'Well, quite a bit . . .'

'Tell me more.'

Thirion gulped and sighed like a martyr.

'He really loves her. For good.'

It was a blow. Elsa didn't answer. She was crying.

Suddenly, on the other side of the dance floor, a couple appeared. It was Lena Amsel and Louis Aragon.

'Eek!' murmured Thirion.

'Ah!' cried Elsa.

Like a whirlwind, she leapt to her feet. When he saw her, Aragon turned and vanished. Elsa was watching Lena. She said to her, 'Why don't you come and have a drink with me?'

The two young women sat down at the table, where Thirion was cringing. Turning towards her, the Russian sent him away with the flick of a finger.

'Go find Aragon! What if something happened to him?'

Thirion didn't wait to hear it twice. At a few minutes to midnight, as if he were on springs, he catapulted out of the Jungle, gathered speed on the rue Campagne Première, accelerated at Raspail, sprouted wings behind the Montparnasse cemetery and braked on the rue du Château.

Aragon was there, methodically getting drunk in front of Nancy Cunard's portrait.

A few minutes later, a new crew entered the house: Lena Amsel and Elsa Triolet. The two women were wreathed in smiles. Elsa approached Aragon, stroked and petted him, and announced the result of the negotiations. Lena had understood that her love weighed nothing next to Elsa's own passion. So she was leaving.

Aragon didn't have time to say a word. Lena turned towards André Thirion and asked him, 'Could you take me to a taxi stand?'

When the communist–surrealist (who would one day be a Gaullist) came back, the lights were out on the rue du Château. In the loggia where Benjamin Péret used to sleep, the poet and his muse were now resting.

The curtain fell on the scene.

Marie-Laure de Noailles, who knew a thing or two about species of passion, compared Nancy Cunard to a rare type of night butterfly. Elsa, on the other hand, was like ivy: 'It's hard to fight ivy.'[4]

Madame Triolet hadn't been able to become Madame Mayakovsky; she would be Madame Aragon. Lili Brik was with the greatest Russian poet, and her sister would live with the greatest French poet.

In a twinkling, the man of letters was tied and trussed, taken away from the rue du Château and his friends, who were a bad influence – distanced from everyone who could have played the go-between for him with Nancy Cunard. Revenge is a dish which can be eaten cold, and since Elsa was still digesting the past, thirty-five years later, she prevented

Aragon from lifting a finger to help when Nancy appealed to him one day for assistance.

The heiress of the Cunard Line had by then run through her entire fortune. She had given generously to the surrealists, the Spanish Republicans, and black Americans. One night, she was in a taxi, drunk, ill, and frighteningly thin. The only thing that could be done for her was to keep her from having to end her life in a public ward in a hospital.

Aragon didn't do anything to prevent it.

In the case of Lena Amsel, revenge was more immediate. Circumstances lent a hand. On 3 November 1929, Derain invited the young dancer to go with him to Barbizon to have lunch. They would take Florence with them: Florence who had been waylaid the previous year by Max Ernst, and was ready to return to the rue du Château with André Thirion. They would take two cars, since there wasn't enough room in the Bugatti for three people.

So they drove in two cars. Florence came. They went to Barbizon. On the way home, Lena and Derain, each at the wheel of a vehicle, challenged each other to a race. The Bugatti was very fast and had only one defect: it was too light for its power. A weight in the back trunk had to be got rid of. Derain had thought of this, Lena hadn't. And it was the beetroot season. Her tyres didn't resist. The young dancer's Bugatti, which was following the painter's, slipped, veered off, overturned, once, twice, then burst into flames. Only two charred bodies would remain.

At the Coupole, on 14 February 1930, when Aragon came through the revolving door after the expedition to the Maldoror, he had become the man of just one woman. He was also a central figure of this new Montparnasse that the artists were abandoning daily.

Before, tourists and money had emptied Montmartre of its artistic population. Now, Montparnasse itself was starting to have trouble breathing. The shiny cars and the flash of gold and silver were still there, but the painters and poets were seeking out quieter spots. Some of them were already heading towards the plain of Saint-Germain-des-Prés which would one day succeed the hills of Montmartre and Montparnasse. Most of them were elsewhere. Many had turned their backs on a way of life and of being together that the First World War had swept away, and that the second would eliminate altogether.

Picasso had left a long time before. Max Jacob had fled to the banks of another river. Guillaume Apollinaire was dead. Vlaminck howled and raged on his own land. Van Dongen signed his contracts from the promenade at Deauville. André Salmon regularly wrote columns in the press, not always in the kindest terms. Braque hardly ever came near the place. Derain counted the fiscal horsepower of his cars. Juan Gris had

died. Modigliani had died. Kisling spent all his winters in Sanary. No one
ever heard from Zadkine. Soutine didn't come to the neighbourhood any
more. And Cendrars was off on his travels.

If there was only one artist left, it would be the one who always greeted
Bob the barman, with his bowler hat, his dark blue suits and his cigarette
hanging from the corner of his lips. He smiled a little smile at Aragon,
with whom he had at least one thing in common: he too was the man
of just one woman.

If only one man remained in Montparnasse, yes, it would be him. Jules
Pascin.

THE LAST OF THE BOHEMIANS

A free man, hero of dreams and desire
Pushing open the golden doors with bleeding hands
Bodily spirit, Pascin disdained choosing
And, master of life, he arranged his death.

André Salmon

The barque of love was broken by the current of life.

Mayakovsky

He was consumed by cirrhosis, by Lucy Krogh, by self-loathing. As he progressed in his work, he lost the early freedom he had enjoyed, to use his colours and his brushes as he wished. He liked the flowing line of the pen, the lightness of wash drawings. But he had to use oil; it sold better. Bernheim-Jeune had offered him an exceptional contract, which even Derain or Picasso would have envied. But he didn't want to become a 'pimp of painting'. He didn't sign it. Why should he?

Still, he needed to lodge Lucy Krogh, to clothe Hermine David, and to feed the dozens of models who came through his studio: flowers of the pavement, girls who were barely thirteen and who had been sent to him, whom he sometimes asked to pose without even painting them. He paid them, they smiled, spent a little time, and then left.

But they came back.

To escape his devils, Pascin moved from one hotel to another and sought out studios where no one could find him, where the bottles and the girls were few.

Lucy found him a little house, the villa Camélia, at the Porte de Vanves, on the far edge of Montparnasse. He went there, hoping she would join him, that they would live there together.

He returned to the Boulevard de Clichy. He painted. He wandered. He wrote heartbreaking letters to Lucy because she was late, because she was absent, because they had decided not to see each other any more, because he couldn't give her up. She reproached him for drinking too much, for not working enough, for coming home with blood on his face after his nightly rounds in bars. Each time, he would say to her, 'You're mean. You're too mean!'

Lucy, Lucyfer.

One night in the month of May, in 1930, she told him that it was all

over. He asked if he could come by to pick up his things and some
canvases which were in the house at the Porte de Vanves.

'All right, but before seven o'clock,' she answered.

'Seven in the evening?'

'In the morning.'

He called his friend Papazoff to ask him to help. They waited all night in front of the Montparnasse cemetery wall. Then they hailed two taxis, and asked to be driven to the Porte de Vanves.

Pascin returned to the Boulevard de Clichy.

And Lucy returned to the Boulevard de Clichy.

For a little while.

They didn't know how to live together. They didn't know how to separate. This had been going on for ten years.

On 1 June 1930, Pascin sat down at the table in the studio. He wrote a few lines in careful handwriting, then he chose a drawing from among his works. He dressed in the dark blue suit that all of Montmartre and Montparnasse knew well. Even if it was old now, like his shoes and his bowler hat, what reason did he have to change it?

He came downstairs and went to visit his regular physician, Dr Tzanck. Ever since he had been treating him, Dr Tzanck had refused to be paid. Pascin gave him the drawing.

He crossed the Seine, as he had done so often since 1905. He went back up towards Vavin, whose every doorway, every bench, every tree he knew by heart. He entered the revolving door of the Coupole. Bob was there behind his bar. Pascin ordered a brandy, and paid his old bills.

'Are you settling your debts, M. Pascin?'

'Yes, I am.'

That evening, that night, the painter went out walking, paying his respects to Paris. At dawn, on the Place Pigalle, he ran into Pierre Mac Orlan who was leaving a bar.

'Stay and have a last drink,' he suggested.

But the writer was tired, and continued on his way. Pascin had his last drink alone.

He went back home, and locked the door. A reddish dawn was breaking over the hills of Montmartre. Pascin closed the shutters so he would see nothing more.

He put two pillows on the floor, and two basins, on either side of them. On the back of an invitation for an exhibition in Berlin, he wrote a word of farewell to Lucy:

> Lucy, don't be angry with me for what I'm doing. Thanks for the packages. You're too kind, I have to leave so that you can be happy.
> FAREWELL! FAREWELL!

He went into the bathroom. He picked up his razor with its sharp blade. He slit his left wrist.

He came back into the studio and read again the will he had written that same morning. In it, he bequeathed the contents of his bank account and the totality of his works to Hermine David and Lucy Krogh.

He dipped his right index finger in the blood running from the left wrist, as though placing the point of a brush on the palette of his life.

On the door of the closet, he wrote, 'Farewell Lucy.'

He picked up the razor again and slit his right wrist. He lay down on the cushions and stuck his two forearms into the basins.

He waited. It was taking too long. An image came back to him from his childhood. The image of a hanging man.

He got up, and walked to the kitchen. He found a piece of rope in a drawer. He made a slipknot and tied it around his neck. He came back to the studio and looked around. He chose the doorknob, approached it, slipped the rope around it, kept the other end of it in his hand, and let himself fall to the ground.

When Lucy found him on 5 June, her shrieks combined with the cries of the young woman who was with her, and those of the locksmith who had forced open the door, and the tears of Hermine David, and the commissioner's report, and the hundreds of flowers brought by friends, and the lamentations in all of Paris when the terrible news was known, and the creaking of the gallery awnings, in mourning on the day of the funeral, and the tears, and the sighs, and the colours of the painters, and the verses of the poets … they all beat like a dying tide, washed up on the graves. Three little pebbles against the stone, three beats of a forgotten measure.

Guillaume Apollinaire.
Amedeo Modigliani.
Jules Pascin.

NOTES

PROLOGUE
1. *Vers et Prose*, no. 23, October 1910: L'Echoppe, Paris, 1993.

THE MAZE OF MONTMARTRE
1. Pierre Mac Orlan, *Le Quai des brumes*, Gallimard, Paris, 1927.

LITRILLO
1. Roland Dorgelès, *Bouquet de bohème*, Albin Michel, Paris, 1947.
2. Francis Carco, *La Légende et la vie d'Utrillo*, Bernard Grasset, Paris, 1928.

LIFE IN BLUE
1. Brassaï, *Conversations avec Picasso*, Gallimard, Paris, 1997.
2. Francis Carco, *Bohème d'artiste*, Editions du Milieu du monde, Geneva, 1942.

TWO AMERICANS IN PARIS
1. Ambroise Vollard, *Souvenirs d'un marchand de tableaux*, Albin Michel, Paris, 1937.
2. Georges Charensol, *D'une rive à l'autre*, Mercure de France, Paris, 1973.

CYPRIAN
1. Lecture at the Musée des Beaux Arts of Nantes.
2. Francis Carco, *Montmartre à vingt ans*, Editions du Milieu du monde, collection 'Mémoires d'une autre vie', Geneva, 1942.
3. Francis Carco, *Montmartre à vingt ans*, op. cit.
4. Max Jacob, *Correspondance*, Editions de Paris, 1953.
5. *Pour les cinquante ans de la mort de Max Jacob à Drancy*, Les Cahiers bleus, Paris, 1994.
6. Max Jacob, 'Le Christ à Montparnasse,' *Les Ecrits nouveaux*, April, 1919, Emile-Paul Frères.
7. André Warnod, *Les Berceaux de la jeune peinture*, Albin Michel, Paris, 1925.
8. Pierre Brasseur, *Ma vie en vrac*, Ramsay, Paris, 1985.
9. Max Jacob, 'Récit de ma conversion', *Correspondance*, Editions de Paris, 1953.
10. *Pour les cinquante ans de la mort de Max Jacob à Drancy*, op. cit.
11. Max Jacob, 'Le Christ à Montparnasse,' *Les Ecrits nouveaux*, op. cit.
12. *Pour les cinquante ans de la mort de Max Jacob à Drancy*, op. cit.
13. *Max Jacob et Picasso*, Réunion des Musées nationaux, Paris, 1994.
14. *Max Jacob et Picasso*, op. cit.
15. Paul Léautaud, *Journal littéraire*, Mercure de France, Paris, 1961.

GUILLAUME THE BELOVED
1. Guillaume Apollinaire, *Correspondance avec son frère et sa mère*, presented by Gilbert Boudar and Michel Décaudin, José Corti, Paris, 1987.
2. Marc Chagall, *Ma vie*, Stock, Paris, 1972.
3. Vladimir Divîs, *Apollinaire. Chronique d'une vie*, N.O.E.

THE LOVELY FERNANDE
1. Fernande Olivier, *Souvenirs intimes*, Calmann-Lévy, Paris, 1988.
2. Françoise Gilot, *Vivre avec Picasso*, Calmann-Lévy, Paris, 1991.

3. Guillaume Apollinaire, *La Femme assise*, Gallimard, Paris, 1948.

THE BATEAU LAVOIR

1. Guillaume Apollinaire, 'La serviette des poètes', *L'Hérésiarque & Cie*, Stock, Paris, 1984.

2. Guillaume Apollinaire, *La Femme assise*, op. cit.

3. Alfred Jarry, *Les Minutes de sable mémorial*, Fasquelle, Paris, 1932.

THE WILD BEASTS' CAGE

1. Henri Matisse, letter to Signac of July 14, 1905, André Derain, *Lettres à Vlaminck*, Flammarion, Paris, 1994, text edited and presented by Philippe Dagen.

2. Maurice Vlaminck, *Portraits avant décès*, Flammarion, Paris, 1943.

3. Maurice Vlaminck, *Portraits avant décès*, op. cit.

4. Georges Charensol, *D'une rive à l'autre*, op. cit.

5. Daniel-Henry Kahnweiler, *Juan Gris*, Gallimard, Paris, 1946.

WITH THE ACROBATS

1. Pierre Daix, *Picasso créateur*, Seuil, Paris, 1987.

2. André Salmon, *La Négresse du Sacré-Cœur*, Editions de la Nouvelle Revue française, Paris, 1920.

3. Hubert Fabureau, 'Max Jacob,' *La Nouvelle Revue critique*, Paris, 1935.

THE TIME OF DUELS

1. Arthur Cravan, *Maintenant*, July 1913, reprinted in Cravan, *Maintenant*, Seuil-L'Ecole des lettres, Paris, 1995.

2. Arthur Cravan, *Maintenant*, March, 1914.

3. Arthur Cravan, *Maintenant*, op. cit.

4. Arthur Cravan, *Maintenant*, op. cit.

5. André Salmon, *Souvenirs sans fin*, Gallimard, Paris, 1955.

6. Guillaume Apollinaire, *Le Poète assassiné*, Gallimard, Paris, 1947.

7. Francis Carco, *De Montmartre au quartier Latin*, Editions du Milieu du monde, Geneva, 1942.

8. *Vers et Prose*, no. 12, December 1907.

AN AFTERNOON ON THE RUE DE FLEURUS

1. André Salmon, *L'Air de la Butte*, Editions de la Nouvelle France, Paris, 1945.

THE BORDELLO OF AVIGNON

1. André Derain, March 7, 1906, in André Derain, *Lettres à Vlaminck*, op. cit.

2. Wassily Kandinsky, *Du spirituel dans l'art*, Denoël-Gonthier, Paris, 1969.

3. Daniel-Henry Kahnweiler, *Huit entretiens avec Picasso*, L'Echoppe, Paris, 1988.

4. Pierre Daix, *Picasso créateur*, op. cit.

5. Pierre Daix, *Dictionnaire Picasso*, Robert Laffont, Paris, 1995.

6. André Salmon, *Souvenirs sans fin*, op. cit.

7. Brassaï, *Conversations avec Picasso*, op. cit.

THE GOOD DOUANIER

1. Guillaume Apollinaire, *Anecdotiques*, Gallimard, Paris, 1955.

2. Article by Guillaume Apollinaire, *Les Soirées de Paris*, January 15, 1914.

3. Fernande Olivier, *Picasso et ses amis*, Stock, Paris, 1933.

4. André Salmon, *Souvenirs sans fin*, op. cit.

5. Lettre à madame Eugénie-Léonie V., August 19, 1910, quoted by Philippe Soupault, *Ecrits sur la peinture*, Editions Lachenal & Ritter, Paris, 1980.

THE THEFT OF THE MONA LISA

1. Guillaume Apollinaire, *Tendre comme le souvenir*, Gallimard, Paris, 1952.

2. Fernande Olivier, *Picasso et ses amis*, op. cit.

3. Fernande Olivier, *Picasso et ses amis*, op. cit.

4. *L'Oeuvre*, September, 1911.

5. Albert Gleizes, 'Apollinaire, la justice et moi,' *Rimes et Raison*, Editions de la Tête noire, 1946.

6. Peter Read, *Picasso et Apollinaire, les Métamorphoses de la mémoire*, Jean-Michel Place, Paris, 1995.

7. Gallimard, collection 'Bibliothèque de la Pléiade,' Paris, 1965.

SEPARATIONS

1. Guillaume Apollinaire, *Le Poète assassiné*, op. cit.

2. Roch Grey, 'Les soirées de Paris,'

Présence d'Apollinaire, Galerie Breteau, December 1943.

3. *Vers et Prose*, no. 34, p. 189.

4. *La Nouvelle Revue française*, Paris, August, 1909.

5. *L'Intransigeant* of February 7, 1912.

6. Paul Léautaud, *Journal littéraire*, vol. IX, Mercure de France, Paris, 1960.

CUBISM

1. Max Jacob, *Correspondance*, op. cit.

2. Max Jacob, letter to Tristan Tzara, February 26, 1916.

3. Max Jacob, letter to Guillaume Apollinaire, May 2, 1913.

4. Wassily Kandinsky, *Du spirituel dans l'art*, op. cit.

5. John Berger, *Réussite et échec de Picasso*, Denoël-Les Lettres nouvelles, Paris, 1968.

6. Jean Paulhan, *Braque le patron*, Gallimard, Paris, 1987.

7. Françoise Gilot, *Vivre avec Picasso*, op. cit.

8. Charles Baudelaire, 'Qu'est-ce que le romantisme?' *Salon de 1846*, Gallimard, collection 'Bibliothèque de la Pléiade,' Paris, 1976.

9. André Derain, *Lettres à Vlaminck*, op. cit., followed by the *Correspondance de guerre*, text edited and presented by Philippe Dagen, Flammarion, Paris, 1994.

LEADERS OF THE PACK

1. Charles Baudelaire, 'Pourquoi la sculpture est ennuyeuse,' *Salon de 1846*, Gallimard, collection 'Bibliothèque de la Pléiade,' Paris, 1976.

2. Pierre Cabanne, *Le Siècle de Picasso*, Gallimard, Paris, 1992.

3. Pierre Cabanne, *Le Siècle de Picasso*, op. cit.

4. Nino Frank, *Montmartre*, Calmann-Lévy, Paris, 1956.

5. Jean Cocteau, *Picasso*, L'Ecole des Lettres, Paris, 1996.

6. Daniel-Henry Kahnweiler, *Mes galeries et mes peintres, entretiens avec Francis Crémieux*, Gallimard, Paris, 1961.

7. Daniel-Henry Kahnweiler, *Juan Gris*, op. cit.

8. Françoise Gilot, *Vivre avec Picasso*, op. cit.

THE CUBISTERS

1. *Paris-Journal*, 1911.

2. Jean Cocteau, *Essai de critique indirecte*, Bernard Grasset, Paris, 1932.

3. Robert Desnos, *Escrits sur les peintres*, Flammarion, Paris, 1984.

4. Jean Paulhan, *Braque le patron*, op. cit.

5. Text published in *La Publicidad*, Barcelona, quoted in *Max Jacob and Picasso*, Réunion des Musées nationaux, op. cit.

6. Max Jacob, letter to his mother, 1927.

7. *Paris-Journal*, May 15, 1914.

8. *La Nouvelle Revue française*, Paris, January 1914.

9. Arthur Cravan, *Maintenant*, no. 4, 1914.

10. Arthur Cravan, *Maintenant*, op. cit.

GUILLAUME APOLLINAIRE GIVES A LITTLE HELP TO HIS FRIENDS

1. *L'Intransigeant*, October 1, 1912.

2. *L'Intransigeant*, October 3, 1912.

3. Charles Baudelaire, *Salon de 1845*, Gallimard, collection 'Bibliothèque de la Pléiade,' Paris, 1976.

4. Charles Baudelaire, *Salon de 1846*, op. cit.

THE POET AND THE ART DEALER

1. Françoise Gilot, *Vivre avec Picasso*, op. cit.

2. Daniel-Henry Kahnweiler, *Mes galeries et mes peintres, entretiens avec Francis Crémieux*, op. cit.

3. Pierre Assouline, *L'Homme de l'art*, Balland, Paris, 1988.

4. Pierre Assouline, *L'Homme de l'art*, op. cit.

THE RUCHE

1. *The Bible*, Exodus, 20.1.

UBU ROI

1. Robert de Souza, *Vers et Prose*, no. 2, 1905.

2. Guillaume Apollinaire, *Contemporains pittoresques*, Gallimard, Paris, 1975.

3. Alfred Jarry, *Les Minutes de sable mémorial*, op. cit.

4. Jacques-Henry Levesque, *Alfred Jarry*, Seghers, Paris, 1987.

5. Docteur Stephen-Chauvet, 'Les Derniers Jours d'Alfred Jarry,'

Mercure de France, no. 832, February 15, 1933.

6. Guillaume Apollinaire, Contemporains pittoresques, op. cit.

7. André Breton, Anthologie de l'humour noir, Jean-Jacques Pauvert, Paris, 1966.

8. Charles Chassé, D'Ubu roi au Douanier Rousseau, Editions de la Nouvelle Revue critique, Paris, 1947.

9. Charles Chassé, D'Ubu roi au Douanier Rousseau, op. cit.

10. Madame Fort-Vallette, as confided to Marcel Trillat and Nat Lilenstein, Magazine littéraire, no. 48, January 1971.

2 AUGUST 1914

1. Paris-Midi, March 3, 1914.

2. Guillaume Apollinaire, Tendre comme le souvenir, op. cit.

3. Paul Léautaud, Journal littéraire, vol. III, Mercure de France, Paris, 1956.

CHAÏM AND AMEDEO

1. Jeanne Modigliani, Modigliani sans légende, Jeanne Modigliani-Librairie Gründ, Paris, 1961.

THE VILLA ROSE

1. Jeanne Modigliani, Modigliani sans légende, op. cit.

2. Jean Arp, quoted by Billy Klüver and Julie Martin, Kiki et Montparnasse, Flammarion, Paris, 1989.

3. Maurice Vlaminck, Portraits avant décès, op. cit.

THE ARTILLERYMAN'S WOMEN

1. André Salmon, Souvenirs sans fin, op. cit.

2. André Rouveyre, Apollinaire, Gallimard, Paris, 1945.

3. Guillaume Apollinaire, Lettres à Lou, Gallimard, Paris, 1969.

4. Guillaume Apollinaire, Poèmes à Lou, Gallimard, collection 'Bibliothèque de la Pléiade', Paris, 1956.

5. Guillaume Apollinaire, Poèmes à Lou, op. cit.

6. Guillaume Apollinaire, Correspondance avec son frère et sa mère, op. cit.

7. Guillaume Apollinaire, Tendre comme le souvenir, op. cit.

8. Guillaume Apollinaire, Lettres à Lou, op. cit.

THE WRITER WITH THE SEVERED HAND

1. Guillaume Apollinaire, Tendre comme le souvenir, op. cit.

2. Guillaume Apollinaire, Oeuvres poétiques, Gallimard, collection 'Bibliothèque de la Pléiade,' Paris, 1956.

3. Jacques Roubaud, Cahiers de la bibliothèque littéraire Jacques-Doucet, no. 1, Doucet littérature, 1997.

4. Blaise Cendrars, 'Prose du Transsibérien et de la petite Jeanne de France,' Du monde entier, Gallimard, Paris, 1967.

5. Ernest Hemingway, Paris est une fête, Gallimard, Paris, 1964.

6. Blaise Cendrars, La Main coupé, Denoël, Paris, 1946.

7. Article published in the Mercure de France of December, 1913; Guillaume Apollinaire, Anecdotiques, op. cit.

8. Blaise Cendrars, 'Dix-neuf poèmes élastiques', Du monde entier, op. cit.

THE FRIVOLOUS PRINCE

1. Gustave Fuss-Amoré and Maurice des Ombiaux, Montparnasse, Albin Michel, Paris, 1925.

2. Maurice Vlaminck, Portraits avant décès, op. cit.

3. Jean Cocteau, Essai de critique indirecte, op. cit.

4. Maurice Vlaminck, Portraits avant décès, op. cit.

5. André Salmon, Montparnasse, André Bonne, Paris, 1950.

6. Francis Carco, Montmartre à vingt ans, op. cit.

7. Francis Carco, Montmartre à vingt ans, op. cit.

8. Philippe Soupault, Mémoires de l'oubli, Lachenal & Ritter, Paris, 1986.

9. André Salmon, Montparnasse, op. cit.

10. Jean Cocteau, letter to Albert Gleizes, 1916, quoted by Billy Klüver, Un jour avec Picasso, Hazan, Paris, 1994.

11. Philippe Soupault, Mémoires de l'oubli, op. cit., handwritten letter addressed to Marshall Pétain, signed and dated, February 1942, $3\frac{1}{2}$ pages in quarto.

12. André Breton, Les Pas perdus, Gallimard, Paris, 1969.

13. Letter of September 15, 1915. Quoted by Billy Klüver, *Un jour avec Picasso*, op. cit.
14. Jean Cocteau, *Picasso*, op. cit.

THE COCK AND THE HARLEQUIN
1. Jean Hugo, *Le Regard de la mémoire*, Actes Sud, Paris, 1994.
2. Jean Cocteau, *Picasso*, op. cit.
3. Maurice Sachs, *Le Sabbat*, Gallimard, Paris, 1960.
4. Maurice Sachs, *Le Sabbat*, op. cit.
5. Gertrude Stein, *Autobiographie d'Alice Toklas*, Gallimard, Paris, 1934.
6. Jean Cocteau, *Picasso*, op. cit.
7. Françoise Gilot, *Vivre avec Picasso*, op. cit.
8. Jean Cocteau et Guillaume Apollinaire, *Correspondance*, Jean-Michel Place, Paris, 1991.
9. Jean Cocteau and Guillaume Apollinaire, letter of April 13, 1917, *Correspondance*, op. cit.

THE POET'S WOUND
1. Guillaume Apollinaire, *Tendre comme le souvenir*, op. cit., letter to Madeleine of January 24, 1916.
2. André Derain, letter to Vlaminck, dated May 1, 1917.

CAMOUFLAGE ART
1. Guillaume Apollinaire, 'Chroniques et paroles sur l'art,' 1911, and 'La Vie artistique,' 1912, *Oeuvres en prose complètes*, Gallimard, collection 'Bibliothèque de la Pléiade,' 1991.
2. Jean Paulhan, *Braque le patron*, op. cit.

MEANWHILE, IN AMERICA...
1. *Paris-New York*, Editions du centre Georges-Pompidou-Gallimard, Paris, 1991.
2. Blaise Cendrars, *Le Lotissement du ciel*, Denoël, Paris, 1949.
3. Raymond Roussel, *Comment j'ai écrit certains de mes livres*, Jean-Jacques Pauvert, Paris, 1963.
4. Pierre Cabanne, *Duchamp et Cie*, Terrail, Paris, 1996. Marcel Duchamp, *Entretiens avec Pierre Cabanne*, 1995.
5. Marcel Duchamp, *Entretiens avec Pierre Cabanne*, op. cit.

6. Marcel Duchamp, *Duchamp du signe*, Flammarion, Paris, 1994.
7. Blaise Cendrars, *Le Lotissement du ciel*, op. cit.

DADA & COMPANY
1. Tristan Tzara, *Sept Manifestes Dada*, Jean-Jacques Pauvert, Paris, 1979.
2. Tristan Tzara, *Sept Manifestes Dada*, op. cit.
3. Marcel Duchamp, *Duchamp du signe*, op. cit.
4. *Nouvelle Revue française*, Paris, September 1, 1919.
5. *Nouvelle Revue française*, Paris, April, 1920.

THE FRIENDS OF VAL-DE-GRACE
1. Guillaume Apollinaire, letter to Tristan Tzara, January 14, 1917, quoted by Marc Dachy, *Tristan Tzara dompteur des acrobates*, L'Echoppe, Paris, 1992.
2. Guillaume Apollinaire, letter to Tristan Tzara, February 6, 1918, quoted by Michel Sanouillet, *Dada à Paris*, Flammarion, Paris, 1993.
3. André Breton, *Entretiens avec Madeleine Chapsal*, July, 1962, in Madeleine Chapsal, *Les Ecrivains en personne*, UGE, 1973.
4. André Breton, *Les Pas perdus*, op. cit.
5. André Breton, *Les Pas perdus*, op. cit.
6. André Breton, *Entretiens avec Madeleine Chapsal*, op. cit.

ADRIENNE MONNIER'S BOOKSHOP
1. Adrienne Monnier, 'Mémorial de la rue de l'Odéon,' *Rue de l'Odéon*, Albin Michel, Paris, 1989.
2. Adrienne Monnier, 'Mémorial de la rue de l'Odéon,' *Rue de l'Odéon*, op. cit.
3. André Breton, *Entretiens avec André Parinaud*, Gallimard, Paris, 1969.
4. Valery Larbaud, letter to Sylvia Beach of February 2, 1921. James Joyce, *Oeuvres complètes*, Gallimard, collection 'Bibliothèque de la Pléiade,' Paris, 1995.
5. Paul Claudel, letter to Adrienne Monnier of May 4, 1929. James Joyce, *Oeuvres complètes*, op. cit.
6. Paul Claudel, letter to Adrienne Monnier of December 28, 1931. James Joyces, *Oeuvres complètes*, op. cit.
7. André Breton, *Point du jour*, Gallimard, Paris, 1970.

A PAINTER AND HIS DEALER

1. Max Jacob, letter to Jacques Doucet, *Correspondance*, op. cit.

LES MAMELLES DE TIRÉSIAS

1. Michel Decaudin, Preface to Guillaume Apollinaire, *L'Enchanteur pourrissant*, Gallimard, Paris, 1972.

2. Pierre Albert-Birot, 'Guillaume Apollinaire,' special supplement to *Rimes et raisons*, Editions de la Tête noire, 1946.

3. André Breton, *Entretiens avec André Parinaud*, op. cit.

4. Pierre Cabanne, *Le Siècle de Picasso*, op. cit.

5. André Breton, *Perspective cavalière*, Gallimard, Paris, 1970.

KIKI

1. Kiki, *Souvenirs*, Henri Broca, 1929.

2. Kiki, *Souvenirs*, op. cit.

3. Lou Mollgaard, *Kiki reine de Montparnasse*, Robert Laffont, Paris, 1988.

DEATH COMES TO MONTPARNASSE

1. Jeanne Modigliani, *Modigliani sans légende*, op. cit.

COMING TO BLOWS AT DROUOT

1. Daniel-Henry Kahnweiler, *Mes galeries et mes peintres, entretiens avec Francis Crémieux*, op. cit.

2. Robert Desnos, *Ecrits sur les peintres*, op. cit.

SURREALIST SCENES

1. André Breton, *Les Pas perdus*, op. cit.

2. Michel Sanouillet, *Dada à Paris*, op. cit.

3. André Breton, *Les Pas perdus*, op. cit.

4. Michel Sanouillet, *Dada à Paris*, op. cit.

THE WAKEFUL SLEEPER

1. André Breton, *Perspective cavalière*, op. cit.

2. Pierre Assouline, *Simenon*, Julliard, Paris, 1992.

3. Gaëtan Picon, *Journal du surréalisme*, Skira, Geneva, 1976.

4. Robert Desnos, 'Rrose Sélavy,' in *Corps et biens*, Gallimard, Paris, 1953.

5. André Breton, *Perspective cavalière*, op. cit.

6. Raymond Roussel, *Comment j'ai écrit certains de mes livres*, op. cit.

7. André Breton, *Les Pas perdus*, op. cit.

8. André Breton, *Entretiens avec André Parinaud*, op. cit.

DRESS DESIGNER TO THE ARTS

1. François Chapon, *Jacques Doucet ou l'art du mécénat*, Perrin, Paris, 1996.

2. Max Jacob, *Correspondance*, op. cit.

3. Blaise Cendrars, *Le Lotissement du ciel*, op. cit.

4. André Breton, *Entretiens avec André Parinaud*, op. cit.

5. Louis Aragon, *Aurélien*, Gallimard, Paris, 1944.

6. Louis Aragon, *Aurélien*, op. cit.

7. François Chapon, *Jacques Doucet ou l'art du mécénat*, op. cit.

THE DRESS DESIGNER AND THE PHOTOGRAPHER

1. Paul Poiret, *En habillant l'époque*, 1930, Grasset, Paris, 1986.

2. Paul Poiret, *Art et phynance*, Lutétia, Paris, 1934.

AN AMERICAN IN PARIS

1. Man Ray, *Autoportrait*, Seghers, Paris, 1986.

2. Quoted in *Man Ray*, published by the Centre national de la photographie, 1988.

3. Man Ray, *Autoportrait*, op. cit.

ONE COCKTAIL, TWO COCTEAUS

1. André Salmon, *Montparnasse*, op. cit.

2. Pierre Brasseur, *Ma vie en vrac*, op. cit.

3. Pierre Brasseur, *Ma vie en vrac*, op. cit.

4. André Salmon, *Souvenirs sans fin*, op. cit.

5. Jean Hugo, *Le Regard de la mémoire*, op. cit.

6. Jean Cocteau, *La Difficulté d'être*, LGF, Paris, 1995.

7. Jean Cocteau, *La Difficulté d'être*, op. cit.

A GENERATION LOST AND FOUND

1. Ernest Hemingway, *Paris est une fête*, op. cit.

2. Gertrude Stein, *Autobiographie d'Alice Toklas*, op. cit.

3. Ernest Hemingway, *Paris est une fête*, op. cit.

A WANDERING JEW

1. Francis Carco, *Montmartre à vingt ans*, op. cit.

2. Georges Papazoff, *Pascin! ... Pascin! ... C'est moi! ...*, Editions Pierre Cailler, Geneva, 1959.

3. Pierre Mac Orlan 'Le Tombeau de Pascin,' *Pascin*, by Yves Kobry and Elisheva Cohen (eds), Hoëbeke, Paris, 1995.

PHOTOS, PHOTOS...

1. Philippe Soupault, *Mémoires de l'oubli*, Lachenal & Ritter, Paris, 1986, p. 71.

2. Jean Hugo, *Le Regard de la mémoire*, op. cit.

3. *Mecure de France. Anthologie 1890–1940*, Mercure de France, Paris, 1997.

DR ARGYROL AND MISTER BARNES

1. Kiki, *Souvenirs*, op. cit.

SOUTINE'S CROSS

1. Emile Szittya, *Soutine et son temps*, La Bibliothèque des Arts, Paris, 1955, in *Soutine, Catalogue raisonné*, Taschen, Paris, 1993.

SCANDAL AT THE CLOSERIE DES LILAS

1. Louis Aragon, *L'Homme communiste*, Gallimard, Paris, 1946.

2. André Breton, *Entretiens avec André Parinaud*, op. cit.

3. Jean-Jacques Brochier, *L'Aventure des surréalistes*, Stock, Paris, 1977.

4. André Breton, *Entretiens avec André Parinaud*, op. cit.

A LITTLE GEOGRAPHY OF SURREALISM

1. Louis Aragon, *Le Paysan de Paris*, Gallimard, Paris, 1953.

THE BAD BOYS OF THE RUE DU CHATEAU

1. *La Révolution surréaliste*, December 1, 1926.

2. George Grosz, article published in *Europa Almanach*, 1925. Quoted in the *Paris-Berlin* catalogue, Editions du centre Georges-Pompidou-Gallimard, Paris, 1992.

3. Marcel Duhamel, *Raconte pas ta vie*, Mercure de France, Paris, 1972.

4. *La Nouvelle Revue française*, November 1927.

5. Bernard Leuilliot, *Aragon, correspondance générale*, Gallimard, Paris, 1994.

6. Salvador Dali, Preface to René Crevel, *La Mort difficile*, Jean-Jacques Pauvert, Paris, 1974.

SETTLING SCORES

1. Salvador Dali, Preface to René Crevel, *La Mort difficile*, op. cit.

2. March, 1928.

3. André Breton, *La Révolution surréaliste*, no. 11.

4. Philippe Soupault, *Mémoires de l'oubli*, op. cit.

5. André Breton, *Entretiens avec André Parinaud*, op. cit.

6. André Breton, *Second Manifeste du surréalisme*, in *Manifestes du surréalisme*, Jean-Jacques Pauvert, Paris, 1979.

7. Maurice Nadeau, *Histoire du surréalisme*, Seuil, Paris, 1970.

8. Roger Vailland, 'L'Hymne "Chiappe-Martia"', *Paris-Midi*, September 15, 1928.

9. André Breton, *Entretiens avec André Parinaud*, op. cit.

10. André Breton, *Second Manifeste du surréalisme*, op. cit.

THE SOFT DRINK KING

1. André Warnod, *Les Berceaux de la jeune peinture*, op. cit.

2. Louis Aragon, *La Mise à mort*, Gallimard, Paris, 1965.

TAKEN IN PASSING

1. André Thirion, *Révolutionnaires sans révolution*, Le Pré aux Clercs, Paris, 1988.

2. Lilly Marcou, *Elsa Triolet, les yeux et la mémoire*, Plon, Paris, 1994.

3. Louis Aragon, *La Mise à mort*, op. cit.

4. Dominique Desanti, *Les Aragonautes*, Calmann-Lévy, Paris, 1997.

A SELECTIVE BIBLIOGRAPHY

AEGERTER, Emmanuel, LABRACHERIE, Pierre, *Au temps de Guillaume Apollinaire*, Julliard, Paris, 1945.

AKHMATOVA, Anna, *Poème sans héros et autres œuvres*, La Découverte, Paris, 1991.

ALLAIS, Alphonse, *Autour du chat noir*, Georges Bénard, 1955.

—, *Amedeo Modigliani*, Musée d'art moderne de la Ville de Paris, 1981.

APOLLINAIRE, Guillaume – PICASSO, Pablo, *Correspondance*, Gallimard-Réunion des Musées nationaux, Paris, 1992.

—, *Anecdotiques*, Gallimard, Paris, 1955.

—, Special supplement to *Rimes et raisons*, Editions de la Tête noire, 1946.

—, *Contemporains pittoresques*, Gallimard, Paris, 1975.

—, *Correspondance avec son frère et sa mère*, Librairie José Corti, Paris, 1987.

—, *L'Hérésiarque & Cie*, Stock, Paris, 1984.

—, *La Femme assise*, Gallimard, Paris, 1948.

—, *Le Flâneur des deux rives*, Gallimard, Paris, 1928.

—, *Le Poète assassiné*, Gallimard, Paris, 1947.

—, *Les Onze mille verges*, Jean-Jacques Pauvert, Paris, 1973.

—, *Lettres à Lou*, Gallimard, Paris, 1969.

—, *Lettres à sa marraine*, Gallimard, Paris, 1951.

—, 'Notes du mois', in *Le Festin d'Esope, Oeuvres en prose*, Gallimard, collection 'Bibliothèque de la Pléiade,' Paris, 1991.

—, *Oeuvres poétiques*, Gallimard, collection 'Bibliothèque de la Pléiade,' Paris, 1956.

—, *Tendre comme le souvenir*, Gallimard, Paris, 1952.

ARAGON, Louis, *Aurélien*, Gallimard, Paris, 1944.

—, *La Mise à mort*, Gallimard, Paris, 1965.

—, *L'Homme communiste*, Gallimard, Paris, 1946.

—, *La Défense de l'infini*, Gallimard, Paris, 1997.

—, *Le Paysan de Paris*, Gallimard, Paris, 1953.

ASSOULINE, Pierre, *L'Homme de l'art*, Balland, Paris, 1988.

—, *Simenon*, Julliard, Paris, 1992.

BAUDELAIRE, Charles, *Salon de 1846*, Gallimard, collection 'Bibliothèque de la Pléiade,' 1976.

BAY, André, *Adieu Lucy, le roman de Pascin*, Albin Michel, Paris, 1984.

BERGER, John, *Réussite et échec de Picasso*, Denoël-Les Lettres nouvelles, Paris, 1968.

BERNHEIM, Cathy, *Picabia*, Editions du Félin, Paris, 1995.

BRASSAÏ, *Conversations avec Picasso*, Gallimard, Paris, 1997.

BRASSEUR, Pierre, *Ma vie en vrac*, Ramsay, Paris, 1986.

BREDEL, Marc, *Erik Satie*, Mazarine, Paris, 1982.

BRETON, André, *Anthologie de l'humour noir*, Jean-Jacques Pauvert, Paris, 1966.

—, *Entretiens avec André Parinaud*, Gallimard, Paris, 1969.

—, *Les Pas perdus*, Gallimard, Paris, 1969.

—, *Perspective cavalière*, Gallimard, Paris, 1970.

—, *Manifestes du surréalisme*, Jean-Jacques Pauvert, Paris, 1979.

BROCA, Henri, *T'en fais pas, viens à Montparnasse*, SGIE, 1928.

BROCHIER, Jean-Jacques, *L'Aventure des surréalistes*, Stock, Paris, 1977.

BUISSON, Sylvie, PARISOT, Christian, *Paris-Montmartre*, Terrail, Paris, 1996.

Bureau de recherches surréalistes, *Cahier de permanence*, Gallimard, Paris, 1988.

CABANNE, Pierre, *André Derain*, Gallimard, Paris, 1990.

—, *Le Siècle de Picasso*, Gallimard, Paris, 1992.

—, *Duchamp et Cie*, Terrail, Paris, 1996.

CADOU, René-Guy, *Le Testament d'Apollinaire*, Rougerie, 1980.

CAIZERGUES, Pierre, SECKEL, Hélène, *Picasso–Apollinaire. Correspondance*, Gallimard, Paris, 1992.

CARCO, Francis, *Mémoires d'une autre vie*, Editions du Milieu du monde, Geneva, 1942.

—, *Bohème d'artistes*, Editions du Milieu du monde, Geneva, 1942.

—, *De Montmartre au quartier latin*, Editions du Milieu du monde, Geneva, 1942.

—, *La Légende et la vie d'Utrillo*, Bernard Grasset, Paris, 1928.

—, *Montmartre à vingt ans*, Editions du Milieu du monde, Geneva, 1942.

CARLUCCIO, L., LEYMARIE, J., NEGRI, R., RUSSOLI, F., BRUNHAMMER, Y., *Ecole de Paris*, Rive gauche productions, Paris, 1981.

CENDRARS, Blaise, *Oeuvres complètes*, Denoël, Paris, 1952.

CENDRARS, Miriam, *Blaise Cendrars*, Balland, Paris, 1984.

CHAGALL, Marc, *Ma vie*, Stock, Paris, 1972.

CHAMPION, Jeanne, *Suzanne Valadon*, Presses de la Renaissance, Paris, 1984.

CHAPIRO, Jacques, *La Ruche*, Flammarion, Paris, 1960.

CHAPON, François, *Jacques Doucet ou l'art du mécénat*, Perrin, Paris, 1996.

CHAPSAL, Madeleine, *Les Ecrivains en personne*, UGE, Paris, 1973.

CHARENSOL, Georges, *D'une rive à l'autre*, Mercure de France, Paris, 1973.

CHASSÉ, Charles, *D'Ubu roi au Douanier Rousseau*, Editions de la Nouvelle Revue critique, Paris, 1947.

CLEBERT, Jean-Paul, *Dictionnaire du surréalisme*, Seuil, Paris, 1996.

COCTEAU, Jean–APOLLINAIRE, Guillaume, *Correspondance*, Jean-Michel Place, Paris, 1991.

COCTEAU, Jean, *La Difficulté d'être*, LGF, Paris, 1995.

—, *Picasso*, L'Ecole des Lettres, Paris, 1996.

—, *Essai de critique indirecte*, Bernard Grasset, Paris, 1932.

—, *Romans, poésies, œuvres diverses*, Le livre de poche, collection 'La Pochotèque, 1995.

COGNIAT, Raymond, *Braque*, Flammarion, Paris, 1977.

CRESPELLE, Jean-Pierre, *Montparnasse vivant*, Hachette, Paris, 1962.

DACHY, Marc, *Tristan Tzara dompteur des acrobates*, L'Echoppe, Paris, 1992.

DAGEN, Philippe, *André Derain. Lettres à Vlaminck. Correspondance de guerre*, Flammarion, Paris, 1994.

—, *Le Silence des peintres*, Fayard, Paris, 1996.

DAIX, Pierre, *Dictionnaire Picasso*, Robert Laffont, Paris, 1995.

—, *La Vie et l'œuvre de Pablo Picasso*, Seuil, Paris, 1977.

—, *Picasso-Matisse*, Ides et calendes, 1996.

—, *Picasso créateur*, Seuil, Paris, 1987.

—, *La Vie quotidienne des surréalistes*, Hachette, Paris, 1993.

DALI, Salvador, preface to René Crevel, *La Mort difficile*, Jean-Jacques Pauvert, Paris, 1974.

DECAUDIN, Michel, *Apollinaire*, Séguier, Paris, 1986.

DESANTI, Dominique, *Les Aragonautes*, Calmann-Lévy, Paris, 1997.

DESNOS, Robert, *Ecrits sur les peintres*, Flammarion, Paris, 1984.

—, 'Rrose Sélavy,' in *Corps et biens*, Gallimard, Paris, 1953.

DESNOS, Youki, *Confidences*, Fayard, Paris, 1957.

DE VOORT, Claude, *Kisling*, preface by Henri Troyat, 1996.

DIEHL, Gaston, *Modigliani*, Flammarion, Paris, 1977.

DIVIS, Vladimir, *Apollinaire, chronique d'une vie*, N.O.E.

DORGELÈS, Roland, *Quand j'étais montmartrois*, Albin Michel, Paris, 1936.

—, *Bouquet de bohème*, Albin Michel, Paris, 1947.

DORMANN, Geneviève, *La Gourmandise de Guillaume Apollinaire*, Albin Michel, Paris, 1994.

DORMOY, Marie, *Souvenirs et portraits d'amis*, Mercure de France, Paris, 1963.

DROT, Jean-Marie, *Les Heures chaudes de Montparnasse*, Hazan, 1995.

DUCHAMP, Marcel, *Entretiens avec Pierre Cabanne*, Editions d'art, 1995.

—, *Duchamp du signe*, Flammarion, Paris, 1994.

DUHAMEL, Marcel, *Raconte pas ta vie*, Mercure de France, Paris, 1972.

DURIEU, Pierre, *Modigliani*, Hazan, Paris, 1995.

FABUREAU, Hubert, 'Max Jacob,' in *La Nouvelle Revue critique*, Paris, 1935.

FAURE, Elie, *Histoire de l'art, l'art moderne*, Denoël, Paris, 1987.

FRANK, Nino, *Montmartre*, Calmann-Lévy, Paris, 1956.

FUSS-AMORE, Gustave, and DES OMBIAUX, Maurice, *Montparnasse*, Albin Michel, Paris, 1925.

GAUZI, François, *Lautrec mon ami*, La Bibliothèque des Arts, Paris, 1992.

GILOT, Françoise, CARLTON, Lake, *Vivre avec Picasso*, Calmann-Lévy, Paris, 1991.

GIMPEL, René, *Journal d'un collectionneur*, Calmann-Lévy, Paris, 1963.

GINDERTAEL, R. V., *Modigliani et Montparnasse*, Gruppo Editoriale Fabbri, Milan, 1967.

GLANTON, Richard, BLIZOT, Irène, CACHIN, Françoise, DISTEL, Anne, 'Le Docteur Barnes est à Paris,' in *De Cézanne à Matisse, chefs-d'œuvre de la fondation Barnes*, Gallimard-Electra-Réunion des Musées nationaux, Paris, 1993.

GLEIZES, Albert, *Apollinaire, la justice et moi*, Rimes et Raison, Editions de la Tête noire, 1946.

GREY, Roch, *Présence d'Apollinaire*, Galerie Breteau, December 1943.

HEMINGWAY, Ernest, *Paris est une fête*, Gallimard, Paris, 1964.

HUGO, Jean, *Le Regard de la mémoire*, Actes Sud, Paris, 1994.

JACOB, Max, *Correspondance*, Editions de Paris, 1953.

—, *Les Ecrits nouveaux*, Emile-Paul frères, April 1919.

JARRY, Alfred, *Les Minutes de sable mémorial*, Fasquelle, Paris, 1932.

—, *Ubu*, Gallimard, Paris, 1978.

JOYCE, James, *Oeuvres complètes*, Gallimard, collection 'Bibliothèque de la Pléiade', Paris, 1995.

KAHNWEILER, Daniel-Henry, *Juan Gris*, Gallimard, Paris, 1946.

—, *Mes galeries et mes peintres, entretiens avec Francis Crémieux*, Gallimard, Paris, 1961.

—, *Huit entretiens avec Picasso*, L'Echoppe, Paris, 1988.

KANDINSKY, Wassily, *Du spirituel dans l'art*, Denoël-Gonthier, Paris, 1969.

KIKI (PRIN, Alice), *Souvenirs*, Henri Broca, 1929.

KLÜVER, Billy, MARTIN, Julie, *Kiki et Montparnasse*, Flammarion, Paris, 1989.

KLÜVER, Billy, *Un jour avec Picasso*, Hazan, Paris, 1994.

KOBRY, Yves, *Pascin*, Editions Hoëbeke-Musée de la Seita, Paris, 1995.

LACOTE, René, *Tristan Tzara*, Seghers, Paris, 1952.

LAMBRON, Marc, *L'Oeil du silence*, Flammarion, Paris, 1993.

LANNES, Roger, *Jean Cocteau*, Seghers, Paris, 1968.

LAROSE, René, *Guillaume Apollinaire l'Enchanteur*, Editions Autres Temps, 1993.

LÉAUTAUD, Paul, *Journal littéraire*, Mercure de France, Paris, 1961.

LEPAPRE, Pierre, *Gide le messager*, Seuil, Paris, 1997.

LEUILLIOT, Bernard, *Aragon, correspondance générale*, Gallimard, Paris, 1994.

LEVESQUE, Jacques-Henry, *Alfred Jarry*, Seghers, Paris, 1973.

LOUYS, Pierre, *Journal intime*, ed. Montaigne, Paris, 1929.

—, *Paroles de Verlaine*, L'Echoppe, Paris, 1993.

MAC ORLAN, Pierre, *Le Quai des brumes*, Gallimard, Paris, 1927.

—, 'Le Tombeau de Pascin', in *Pascin*, Yves KOBRY and Elisheva COHEN (eds),
    Editions Hoëbeke, Paris, 1995.

MAN RAY, *Autoportrait*, Seghers, Paris, 1986.

Man Ray, Centre national de la photographie, Paris, 1988.

MARCOU, Lilly, *Elsa Triolet, les yeux et la mémoire*, Plon, Paris, 1994.

MARE, André, *Carnets de guerre 1914–1918*, Herscher, Paris, 1996.

MAUBERT, Frank, *La Peinture moderne, du fauvisme à nos jours*, Fernand Nathan, Paris,
    1985.

Max Jacob et Picasso, Réunion des Musées nationaux, Paris, 1994.

MODIGLIANI, Jeanne, *Modigliani sans légende*, Jeanne Modigliani–Librairie Gründ, Paris,
    1961.

MOLLGAARD, Lou, *Kiki reine de Montparnasse*, Robert Laffont, Paris, 1988.

MONNIER, Adrienne, 'Mémorial de la rue de l'Odéon,' in *Rue de l'Odéon*, Albin
    Michel, Paris, 1989.

MORAND, Paul, *Lettres de Paris*, Salvy, Paris, 1996.

NADEAU, Maurice, *Histoire du surréalisme*, Seuil, Paris, 1964.

OLIVIER, Fernande, *Picasso et ses amis*, Stock, Paris, 1933.

—, *Souvenirs intimes*, Calmann-Lévy, Paris, 1988.

PAPAZOFF, Georges, *Pascin! . . . Pascin! . . . C'est moi!* . . . Pierre Cailler, Geneva, 1959.

PARINAUD, André, *Apollinaire*, Lattès, Paris, 1994.

Paris-Berlin, Editions du centre Georges-Pompidou-Gallimard, Paris, 1992.

Paris-New York, Editions du centre Georges-Pompidou-Gallimard, Paris, 1991.

PARISOT, Christian, *Modigliani*, Terrail, Paris, 1991.

PAULHAN, Jean, *Braque le patron*, Gallimard, Paris, 1952.

PENROSE, Roland, *Picasso*, Flammarion, Paris, 1982.

PIAT, Pascal, *Apollinaire*, Seuil, Paris, 1995.

—, *Picasso et Apollinaire, Les Métamorphoses de la mémoire*, Jean-Michel Place, Paris, 1995.

PICON, Gaëtan, *Journal du surréalisme*, Skira, Geneva, 1976.

PLANIOL, Françoise, *La Coupole*, Denoël, Paris, 1986.

POIRET, Paul, *Art et phynance*, Lutétia, 1934.

—, *En habillant l'époque*, 1930, Grasset, Paris, 1986.

Pour les cinquante ans de la mort de Max Jacob à Drancy, Les Cahiers bleus, Troyes, 1994.

PRAX, Valentine, *Avec Zadkine*, La Bibliothèque des arts, Paris, 1995.

READ, Peter, *Picasso et Apollinaire, les métamorphoses de la mémoire*, Jean-Michel Place, Paris,
    1995.

REVERDY, Pierre, *Pablo Picasso*, Gallimard, collection 'Les peintres français nouveaux,'
    Paris, 1924.

—, *Pablo Picasso*, Gallimard, Paris, 1924.

ROUBAUD, Jacques, *Cahiers de la bibliothèque littéraire Jacques-Doucet*, no. 1, Doucet
    littérature, 1997.

ROUSSEL, Raymond, *Comment j'ai écrit certains de mes livres*, Jean-Jacques Pauvert, Paris,
    1963.

ROUVEYRE, André, *Apollinaire*, Gallimard, Paris, 1945.

SABARTES, Jaime, *Picasso*, L'Ecole des lettres, 1996.

SACHS, Maurice, *Au temps du Bœuf sur le toit*, Grasset & Fasquelle, Paris, 1987.

—, *Le Sabbat*, Gallimard, Paris, 1960.

SALMON, André, *L'Air de la Butte*, Editions de la Nouvelle France, Paris, 1945.

—, *La Négresse du Sacré-Cœur*, Editions de la Nouvelle Revue française, Paris, 1920.

—, *La Vie passionnée de Modigliani*, Editions Gérard & Cie, 1957.

—, *Le Manuscrit trouvé dans un chapeau*, Fata Morgana, Saint-Clément-de-Rivière, 1983.

—, *Montparnasse*, André Bonne, Paris, 1950.

—, *Souvenirs sans fin*, Gallimard, Paris, 1955.

SANOUILLET, Michel, *Dada à Paris*, Flammarion, Paris, 1993.

SECKEL, Hélène, CARIOU, André, *Max Jacob et Picasso*, Réunion des Musées nationaux, Paris, 1994.

SOUPAULT, Philippe, *Ecrits sur la peinture*, Lachenal & Ritter, Paris, 1980.

—, *Mémoires de l'oubli*, Lachenal & Ritter, Paris, 1986.

STEIN, Gertrude, *Autobiographie d'Alice Toklas*, Gallimard, Paris, 1934.

STEPHEN-CHAUVET, Docteur, 'Les derniers jours d'Alfred Jarry,' in *Mercure de France*, no. 832, February 15, 1933.

SZITTYA, Emile, *Soutine et son temps*, La Bibliothèque des Arts, 1955, in *Soutine, Catalogue raisonné*, Taschen, Paris, 1993.

THIRION, André, *Révolutionnaires sans Révolution*, Le Pré aux Clercs, Paris, 1988.

TZARA, Tristan, *Dada est tatou. Tout est dada*, Flammarion, Paris, 1996.

—, *Sept manifestes Dada*, Jean-Jacques Pauvert, Paris, 1979.

VAILLAND, Roger, *Chronique des années folles à la Libération*, Messidor, Paris, 1984.

VLAMINCK, Maurice, *Portraits avant décès*, Flammarion, Paris, 1943.

—, *Tournant dangereux*, Stock, Paris, 1929.

VOLLARD, Ambroise, *Souvenirs d'un marchand de tableaux*, Albin Michel, Paris, 1937.

WARNOD, André, *Drôle d'époque*, Fayard, Paris, 1960.

—, *Les Berceaux de la jeune peinture*, Albin Michel, Paris, 1925.

WARNOD, Jeanine, *La Ruche & Montparnasse*, Weber, Paris, 1978.

MAGAZINES AND REVIEWS

Maintenant, reprinted in *CRAVAN*, Arthur, *Maintenant*, Seuil-L'Ecole des lettres, Paris, 1995.

Vers et Prose.

Archives du surréalisme, Gallimard, Paris, 1988.

Les Soirées de Paris, January 15, 1914.

La Nouvelle Revue française.

Paris-Journal.

Magazine littéraire, no. 48, January 1971.

Paris-Midi.

Mercure de France.

La Révolution surréaliste.

SIC, Jean-Michel Place, Paris, 1980.

Dada, Jean-Michel Place, Paris, 1911.

Nord-Sud, Jean-Michel Place, Paris, 1980.

Les Ecrits nouveaux.

Cahiers de la bibliothèque Jacques-Doucet.

INDEX

Action française, L' (periodical) 174
Akhmatova, Anna 190
Alain-Fournier, Henri 48
Albert-Birot, Germaine *see* Birot, Germaine Albert
Albert-Birot, Pierre *see* Birot, Pierre Albert
Alexandre, Paul 189
Allain, Marcel *see under* Souvestre, Pierre
Allais, Alphonse 4
Amicable Assistance to Artists 334
Amsel, Lena 401, 403-6
Anarchie, L' (periodical) 7
Anderson, Sherwood 342, 346
Andrieux, Louis 251
Anspach, Madeleine 400
Apollinaire, Guillaume (Wilhelm Apollinaris de Kostrowitzky): and Montmartre 6; attracted to Picasso 33, 64-5; Max Jacob and 34; nature of 44-55; and Fernande Olivier 57-8, 60-1; taking hashish 63; and Vlaminck's tie 72; nature of his dress 73; and the circus 74; influence of Picasso on 76-7; and duel 79; and Arthur Cravan 81-2; and Marie Laurencin 82-4, 121-2; and Gertrude Stein 90-1; on Fauvism 93; and Matisse's purchase of African statue 95-6; and *Les Demoiselles d'Avignon* 100; on Picasso 101, 138; and the Douanier Rousseau 104-5, 107, 109-11; Picasso's friendship with 113; and theft of Mona Lisa 114-20; in Le Grelot 123; and futurism 124; and Paul Léautaud 125; Fernande Olivier on 126; increasing reputation 129; Max Jacob writes to 130; on Cézanne 131; on cubism 142-3; as art critic 146-52; and Chagall 164; friends in Montparnasse 167; published in *Vers et Prose* 168; and Jarry 170, 172, 174; and anti-German sentiment 177; joins army 179; during World War I 183, 196-206, 214-15; and Modigliani 189; and Cendrars 208-12; and Cocteau 217, 219, 225; at *Sacre du printemps* 219; wounded 226-30, 234, 258; and Picabia 235; in *Cabaret Voltaire* 243;

and Severini 246; and *Nord-Sud* 247; and Dadaism 248-9; and Breton 249-51; and Adrienne Monnier 254; and Salon d'Antin 259; and 'Lyre et Palette' 260; and dinner for Braque 261; and first night of *Parade* 262; at rue Joseph Bara 275; and love 276; and production of *Mamelles de Tiresias* 277-8; living with Jacqueline 278-9; marries 282; death 283-5, 298, 406, 410; poets close to 309; Tzara and 313; Doucet and 319; reading in memory of 339; and surrealism 389; *Alcools* 34, 77, 84, 148, 177, 200, 209-10; (ed.) *Le Coffret du bibliophile* 46; *Les Maîtres de l'amour* 46; *Les Onze mille verges* 46, 201; *L'Enchanteur pourrissant* 48; *Mirely, ou le petit trou pas cher* 48; *L'Hérésiarque & Cie* 49, 53, 118, 129, 208; *Le Poète assassiné* 53, 82, 231; *Rhénanes* 53; *Calligrammes* 54, 63, 84, 148, 205, 279; *Le Chanson du Mal-Aimé* 54; *La Femme assise* 58, 60, 332; *Les Peintres nouveaux* 149; *Méditations ésthetiques* 151-2; *Ombre de mon amour* 200; *Case d'armons* 204, 228; 'Zone' 209; *Le Flâneur des deux rives* 212; *Chroniques artistiques* 232; *Les Mamelles de Tirésias* 248, 250, 276-9, 319
Apollinaire, Jacqueline (née Kolb) 48, 229, 260, 276, 278, 282, 284-5
Aragon, Louis: and Tzara 242, 247; as a soldier 250-2; and Adrienne Monnier 254; buys Braque 303; reads manifesto 305; and Dada Festival 306; Breton and 309; facility of 312; and Anatole France 315-16; and Doucet 320-2; and Man Ray 329; and Elsa Triolet 360, 403-5; and Saint-Pol Roux 376; magnanimity of 377; and surrealism 380-2; at café de la Mairie 382; and Masson 382; and Nancy Cunard 383; and Prévert 385; and communism 388; and Diaghilev's *Romeo and Juliet* 393; and Maldoror 395-6; and romantic escapades 400-1; and Mayakowsky 402-3; *Le Libertinage*

315; *Aurélien* 322, 400; *Anicet* 381
Archipenko (sculptor) 140, 143, 151, 165, 199, 238, 281
Arensberg, Louise 239
Arensberg, Walter 239
Arlan, Marcel 388
Armory Show (International Exhibition of Modern Art, 1913) 234-5, 237, 354
Arp, Jean 243, 381
Art littéraire, L' (periodical) 170
Artaud, Antonin 361, 382-3, 388, 392-4: *L'Ombilic des limbes* 315
Assiette au beurre (periodical) 20
Atlantic Monthly (periodical) 346
Aurenche, Marie-Berthe 375
Auric, Georges 218, 240, 259-60, 308, 337
Aventure (periodical) 308
Avril, Jane 4

Badoul, Lucie *see* Desnos, Youki
Bakst, Léon 165, 218, 324
Ball, Hugo 243
Ballets Russes, the, 5, 165, 218, 259, 276, 324
Banville, Théodore de 169
Barbusse, Henri 387
Barnes, Albert C. 366-9, 371, 373
Barnes, Djuna 329, 342
Barney, Natalie Clifford 342
Baron, Jacques 320, 395
Barrès, Maurice 168, 306-8, 392
Barrey, Fernande 360
Bataille Georges 383, 393-5; *L'Histoire de l'oeil* 387
Bateau Lavoir 3, 54-6, 60-5, 69-72, 76-7, 79-80, 84-6, 94, 98, 101, 104-5, 108, 112-13, 124, 129, 141, 158-9, 164, 167, 182-3, 299, 324-5
Baudelaire, Charles 33, 133-4, 151, 169, 243, 318
Baur, Harry 64
Beach, Sylvia 255-6, 342, 344, 348
Béarn, Pierre 35
Beaudoin, Henri 157-8
Beaumont, Comte Etienne de 216
Benda, Julien 47
Berger, John 132
Bergson, Henri 141, 305
Berlioz, Hector 130
Bernhardt, Sarah 218, 317
Bernheim brothers (dealers) 24-5, 157, 300

Bernheim-Jeune Gallery 124
Bertin, Roland 222
Billy, Andre 39, 118, 122, 181, 210, 278
Bing, Henry 352-3
Birot, Germaine Albert 277
Birot, Pierre Albert 276-8, 305
Blanc, Yves 229
Blanche, Jacques-Emile 218, 338, 362
Blum, Léon 47
Boissy (painter) 10
Bongard, Germaine 258
Bonnard, Pierre 8, 24, 65, 158, 367; L'Aquarium 158
Borges, Jorge Luis 242
'Boronali, Joachim-Raphael' 144
Bouchard (painter) 232
Boucher, Alfred 164
Bourdelle (sculptor) 163-4
Boussingault (painter) 232
Brancusi, Constantin 179, 189, 191, 306, 309, 341, 361-2
Braque, Georges: and Picasso 64; Vauxcelles on 67; appearance 69; Picasso envies; and Marcelle Dupré 77; at Académie Humbert 82; and Gertrude Stein 91, 347; Matisse jealous of 94; on Les Demoiselles d'Avignon 100; and the Douanier Rousseau 108, 111; working with Picasso 122; in Le Grelot 123; and Cézanne 130-1; and cubism 132-3, 140-3; and new directions in art 134-9; and Apollinaire 148-9, 151; Apollinaire on 150-1; during World War I 179, 183, 213, 234, 258; and Ballets Russes 218; in Armory Show 235; Duchamp and 237; Arensberg buys 239; dinner in honour of 261; and Léonce Rosenberg 268; work by Picasso sold under name of 300; works sold 303; and Man Ray 361; lifestyle 406; Grand Nu 131; Maisons à l'Estaque 131; Broc et cruche 135; Compotier et verre 135; Le Portugais 136; La Baigneuse 303, 401
Brassaï 103
Brasseur, Pierre 38, 338
Breker, Arno 224
Breton, André; and Picasso 33, 100; and Cocteau 222; and World War I 242; in Nord-Sud 247; and Apollinaire 249-51; and Adrienne Monnier 253-5; and surrealism 257, 380-2; and invention of term 'surrealism' 278; and Braque 303; disinherited 304; and Dada Festival 306; xenophobia of 309; and Desnos 310, 312; and Crevel 311; and Tzara 314; and Anatole France 315-16; and Doucet 318, 320-2; and Man Ray 329; Kiki and 365; and anti-German feeling 377; and fight at Closerie des Lilas 378-9; and Masson 382; and Prévert 385; Péret and 386; and communism 387-8; and Matisse 389; and Youki Foujita 390; morality of 391-3; and Second

Surrealist Manifesto 394; and Maldoror 396; and cousin 400; Les Pas perdus 218, 314; Clair de Terre 376; and Philippe Soupault: Les Champs magnétiques 304-5, 392, 381
Breton, Simone (née Kahn) 321, 381, 392
Brik, Lili 402
Brionne, Paul-Henri 144
Broca, Henri 399
Brooks, Goddard 342
Bruant, Aristide 4, 15
Buffet-Picabia, Gabrielle 209, 235, 282, 325-6
Bugatti, Ettore 275
Bugatti, Rembrandt 275
Buñuel, Luis 382, 395
Bureau of Surrealist Experiences 315
Burgues-Brun, Jeanne 202

Cabanne, Pierre 136, 321
Cabaret Voltaire (periodical) 243, 249
Cabaret Voltaire (Zurich café) 141, 242-3
Café de Flore 167, 278
Caillaux, Joseph 36
Caillebotte (painter) 181
Calder, Alexander 343
Caméleon, the (café) 334-5, 356
Camoin (painter) 66, 232
camouflage 231-2
Canudo, Ricciotto 178
Capmas, Dr 284
Carco, Francis: and Depaquit 5, 7; and Utrillo 10-12; in Montmartre 15; and Berthe Weill 22; and Apollinaire 51, 152; and Le Lapin Agile 63; manner of dress 72; on women 84; and Gertrude Stein 96; and Dorgelès 114; and World War I 179; and Cocteau 216-17; and Modigliani 271; and Modigliani's death 298; and Pascin 349-50; and Soutine 372
Carco, Hanka 271-2
Carnet de la Semaine (periodical) 262
Casa, Ramon 16
Casamegas (painter) 16-17
Casati, Marquise de 361
Casimir, Achille 272
Casimir, Eudoxie 272
Castaing, Madeleine 371-3
Castaing, Marcellin 371-3
Cendrars, Blaise (ps. of Frédéric Sauser): and Berthe Weill 23; and Max Jacob 33; and opium 62; and Gertrude Stein 96; and the Douanier Rousseau 105; and Picasso's stolen artworks 115; and Le Lapin Agile 121; and Chagall 164; victim of xenophobia 178-9; during World War I 183, 207-14, 234, 258, 273; writes to Apollinaire 199; and Cravan 236-7; on Picabia 241; and Apollinaire 248-9; and 'Lyre et Palette' 259-60; in La Rotonde 264; flees Paris 280; at Apollinaire's funeral 285; and Montmartre 299; Breton and 309; and Doucet 319-20, 322-3;

drives Alfa-Romeo 398; travelling 407; L'Or 208; Sonnets dénaturés 210; L'Eubage 320, 322-3; La Fin du monde 322; Le Lotissement du ciel 322-3;
Cendrars, Miriam 208
Cézanne, Paul 4, 16, 24, 28, 33, 67, 79, 101, 130-1, 135, 137, 140, 235, 237, 239, 367; Les Baigneuses 367
Chabrillan, Comtesse de 262
Chagall, Marc 24-5, 51, 164-5, 180, 182, 184, 188, 208
Chanel, Coco 337, 341
Chaplin, Charlie 210, 305
Char, René 33, 139, 395-6
Charensol, Georges 29, 68, 338
Charenson, Georges 127
Charivari (periodical) 20
Chat Noir, Le (periodical) 4
Chéron (dealer) 267, 335
Citroën, André 366
Clair, René 360, 366, 399
Claretie, Georges 107
Clarté (periodical) 387
Claudel, Paul 47, 218, 256-7, 318, 376
Clemenceau, Georges 280
Clermont-Tonnerre, Comtesse de 335
Closerie des Lilas (café) 3, 79, 167-70, 176, 265, 309, 343-4, 376-9, 395
Cocteau, Jean: and Picasso 33, 77, 136, 141; and Max Jacob 41, 43; and typography 209; and World War I 212; as 'the frivolous prince' 216-25; in Nord-Sud 247; in SIC 255; and 'Lyre et Palette' 259-60; and Satie 263; at Picasso's wedding 282; at Apollinaire's funeral 285; and Tzara 313-14; and Doucet 319; and Man Ray 329; at the Caméleon 335; as 'keeper of the flame' 337-41; and Comte de Beaumont 361; and Proust 362-3; surrealists' contempt for 391; Parade 261-2, 276
Coligny-Chatillon, Louise de 54, 63, 197-204, 226, 229, 278
collage 133, 135-7
communism 387-9; see also Communist Party
Communist Party 387, 392, 394, 404
Comoedia (periodical) 145, 168, 309
Congress of the Association of Revolutionary Writers and Artists 391
Copeau, Jacques 124
Coppée, François 169
Corbusier, Le see Jeanneret, Charles-Edouard
Corpse, A (pamphlet) 395
Coupole, La (café) 382, 397-8, 400, 406
Courbet, Gustave 66
Cravan, Arthur see Lloyd, Fabian Avenarius
Cremieux, Francis 388
Crevel, René 311-12, 314, 381-2, 404
Cri de Paris (periodical) 20

Crowder, Henry 401
Csaky, Joseph 165
cubism 67, 89, 128-33, 135, 140-5, 151-3, 157-9, 179, 238, 278, 299, 324-5, 368, 383
Cunard, Nancy 321, 381, 383, 400-1, 405-6
Czechowska, Lunia 275, 295

Dada Manifesto (1918) 309
Dada (periodical) 252, 254, 257
Dadaism 5, 124, 238, 241-9, 304-9, 313-14, 320, 329, 381-2, 392
Daix, Pierre 75, 99, 101-2
Dalì, Salvador 373, 382, 391, 395, 399
Dalize, René 108, 118, 122, 210, 279
D'Annunzio, Gabriele 305, 361
Dardel, Nils 356
Dardel, Thora 356
Daudet, Léon 118
Daumal, René 170, 394
Daumier, Honoré 367
David, Hermine see Pascin, Hermine
de Beaumont, Comte 334, 361
De Chirico, Giorgio 166, 259, 320, 383, 393
de Falla, Manuel 218
de Gonzague-Frick, Louis 307, 378
de Gourmont, Rémy 177
de la Fresnaye, Roger 140, 147, 158, 232, 234; Nature morte aux anses 158
de la Rivière, André 383
de Massot, Pierre 314
de Noailles, Anna, Comtesse de 335
de Polignac, Princesse 218
de Pougy, Liane 218
de Segonzac, Dunoyer 143, 147, 151, 158, 179, 232, 240; La Mare 158
Debussy, Claude 99, 142, 146, 218, 259; Prélude à l'aprés-midi d'un faune 218
Degas, Edgar 4, 10, 28, 31, 66, 74, 146
Delacroix, Eugène 31, 33, 130, 151
Delaunay, Robert 93, 106, 121, 140, 143, 151, 179, 208, 234-6, 308
Delaunay, Sonia 121, 139, 151, 179, 199, 208, 235-6
Delteil, Joseph 315
Denis, Maurice 31, 158
Depaquit, Jules 4-7, 51, 299; Jack in the Box 5
Derain, André: and Depaquit's Jack in the Box 5; and Berthe Weill 22; and Vollard 24, 26; and Apollinaire's mother 49; and Apollinaire 51, 54; as companion of Picasso 64; nature of his art 65-9; nature of his dress 72-3; Picasso envies 74; and Alice Princet 77; Picasso influenced by 88; Matisse jealous of 94; and African art 96-7, 101; and Gauguin 97; and Les Demoiselles d'Avignon 100; in Salon d'Automne exhibition 105; and

the Douanier Rousseau 110; and Picasso 132; on light 133; and new departures in art 137; Apollinaire on 149-50; at Peau de l'Ours sale 158; during World War I 179, 183, 214-15, 228; and Ballets Russes 218; and camouflage 232; Tzara and 243; Breton and 252; and Kiki 290; turns over a new leaf 299-300; Doucet buys 320; and Doucet 321; lifestyle of 351; and Paul Guillaume 367; and Zborowski 371; drives Bugatti 398; settling scores 400; and cars 406; and Léna Amsel 406; Vues de Collioure 67; Les Baigneuses 98, 137; La Chambre 158; Pêches dans une assiette 158; Vase de grès 158
Descartes, René 101
Descaves, Lucien 282
Desnos, Robert: and Rrose Sélavy 240; and surrealism 309-16; and Man Ray 329; and Youki 333, 390, 399; and Thérèse Maure 357-8; and Michel Leiris 378; and Doucet 320; at café de la Mairie 382; and Yvonne George 383; and Prévert 384; and cinema 387; and communism 388; Breton and 391, 394; at Diaghilev's Romeo and Juliet 393; and Breton 395
Desnos, Youki (formerly Fernande 'Youki' Foujita) 182, 266-7, 311, 332-6, 366, 378, 390, 398-9
Deval, Pierre 307
Diaghilev, Sergei Pavlovich 71, 142, 218-19, 221-2, 259, 261-2, 276, 337, 393
Dierx, Léon 168
Dome (café) 176-7, 183, 194, 265, 352, 360, 382, 396-8
Doneyrolles (chauffeur) 373
Dorgelès, Roland 5-6, 11, 15, 36, 63, 79, 93, 96, 143-5, 240, 306
Dormoy, André 318
Dormoy, Marie 321
Dos Passos, John 342; The 42nd Parallel 148
Doucet, Jacques 33, 100, 246, 285, 316-24, 337
Drieu La Rochelle, Pierre 247
Drouard (sculptor) 189
Drouot 157-9, 299-303
Ducasse, Isidore see Lautréamont, Comte de
Duchamp, Marcel: and the Section d'Or 140; and Vauxcelles 147; goes to America 179, 235-41; Breton and 309; and Dadaism 314; and Doucet 320; and Man Ray 329, 361; and relationships 360; and Kiki 366; and surrealism 381; La Mariée mise à nu par ses celibataires, même 237, 240; Nude Descending a Staircase 237-8; A Bruit secret 239; Fontaine 239; In Advance of the Broken Arm 239; L.H.O.O.Q. 239; Fresh Widow 240; Why Not Sneeze 240
Dufrenoy (painter) 158
Dufresne (painter) 232

Dufy, Raoul 7, 21-2, 150, 158, 371; Boulevard maritime 158
Duhamel, Georges 34
Duhamel, Marcel 383, 385-7, 393, 401, 403
Dullin, Charles 64
Dumarchey, Pierre see Mac Orlan, Pierre
Duncan, Isadora 3, 218, 241, 266, 325, 337
Dupré, Marcelle 77
Durand-Ruel, Paul 24-5, 300
Durey, Louis 260
Durrio, Paco 18, 54

Echo de Paris, L' (periodical) 362
Ehrenburg, Ilya 179, 215, 352, 391, 402
Eiffel, Gustave 164
Elan, L' (periodical) 246
Eluard, Gala 381, 399
Eluard, Paul (ps. of Eugène-Emile-Paul Grindel): and Picasso 33; and Cocteau 224-5; during World War I 250; buying art-works 303; and Dada Festival 306; and Littérature 309; and Crevel 312; and Tzara 313-14; and Anatole France 315; and Doucet 320; and Man Ray 329; wealth of 381; and Masson 382; and trading in paintings 391; and Maldoror 395; and Nusch 399; and Gala 402; Mourir de ne pas mourir 315
Elysee-Montmartre, the 4
Entr'acte (film) 360, 399
Epstein, Jacob 165
Ernst, Max: Doucet buys 320; and Marie-Berthe Aurenche 375; and anti-German feeling 377; and fight at Closerie des Lilas 378; and Eluard 381; and Masson 382, 394; Breton and 393; and Gala Eluard 402
Esprit nouveau, L' (periodical) 308
Eusenmann, Georges 354
Excelsior (periodical) 278

Fabureau, Hubert 76
Fantin-Latour, Ignace 146
Fargue, Léon-Paul 143, 255, 285, 309
Fauré, Elie 235, 371
Fauvism 66, 105, 130, 139, 299, 368
Fels, Florent 311, 384
Fenéon, Felix 8, 47
Férat, Serge (ps. of Serge Jastrebzoff): and the Douanier Rousseau 106; and Baronness d'OEttingen 2; and Le Lapin Agile 123; and Fernande Olivier 127; as Picasso's 'rearguard' 157; and Irène Lagut 222; and Apollinaire 248; and Apollinaire's death 285; and Dadaism 309
Ferrer, Francisco 17, 329
Festin d'Esope, Le (periodical) 48
Figaro, Le (newspaper) 67, 107, 124
First World War see World War I
Fitzgerald, Scott 343-5; The Great Gatsby 343; This Side of Paradise 343

Fitzgerald, Scotty 343
Fitzgerald, Zelda 343-5
Flandrin, Roger 158
Flaubert, Gustave 169, 318
Foch, Marshal Ferdinand 280
Fokine, Michel 218
Forain, Jean-Louis 232
Fort, Jean 48
Fort, Paul 129, 146, 167-9, 253, 261, 278, 285, 299, 379; *French Ballads* 168
Foujita, Youki *see* Desnos, Youki
Foujita (Fujita Tsuguharu): and Kiki 14, 290, 366; and World War I 179, 183, 280; and Modigliani 191; and Youki 265-7, 276, 280; and Lucie Badoul 333-6, 366; Salmon and 339; Aicha poses for 349; wealth of 398; and Mady Lequeux 399; *Youki, Snow Goddess* 333
Fraenkel, Théodore 255, 306-7, 329, 365
France, Anatole 315-16, 321, 395
Frank, Nino 5, 136
Fraux, M. 397-8
Frédé (café owner) 63-4, 183
Fresnaye, Roger de la *see* de la Fresnaye, Roger
Friesz, Othon 146, 158, 371, 397
Fujita, Fernande *see* Desnos, Youki
Fujita Tsuguharu *see* Foujita
futurism 123-4

Ganay, Comtesse de 335
Gauguin, Paul 16, 18, 24, 67, 88, 97-8, 130, 158, 235, 272, 367; *Le Violoncelliste* 158
George, Yvonne 383
Gérard, Frédéric 32
Géricault, Théodore 4
Gershwin, George 342; *An American in Paris* 342
Gery-Pieret, 114-18
Ghika, Georges 218
Giacometti, Alberto 361, 395
Gide, André xvii-xviii, 47, 67, 167, 177, 218, 245, 255, 261, 306, 309, 314, 318
Gil Blas (periodical) 147-8, 168
Gilbert, Stuart 256
Gilbert-Lecomte, Roger 394
Gill, Andre 63
Gilot, Françoise 138-9, 224
Gimpel, René 373
Glackens, William James 367
Gleizes, Albert 22, 116, 119, 140-1, 143, 147, 151, 189, 219, 235, 238, 241; and Jean Metzinger: *Du cubisme* 146
Godebski, Cyprien 221
Gohier, Urbain 118
Goldberg, Mecislas 47
Gottlieb, Leopold 165, 223
Gouel, Eva 124-5, 194-5, 216, 219-20, 222, 276
Goya, Francisco 15
Grand Jeu group 394
Grasset, Bernard 340
Grave, Jean 8
Greco, El (*properly* Domenico Theotocopuli) 17
Grey, Roch 248, 309
Grindel, Eugène-Emile-Paul *see*

Eluard, Paul
Gringoire, La (periodical) 93
Gris, Juan: jailed 7; sells sketches 20; and Max Jacob 34, 216; death 71-2, 407; married 84; and new departures in art 137; death 139; and cubism 140, 151; and Apollinaire 149; during World War I 179; and Eva Gouel's death 216; and Nord-Sud 246; and dinner for Braque 261; and Satie 263; and Leonce Rosenberg 268; attacks Picasso 278; and Rosenberg 300; works sold 303; *Hommage à Picasso* 137
Grosz, George 351, 387
Grosz, Valentin 222
Groth, Gerda 374
Guilhermet, Maître (lawyer) 107-8
Guillaume, Paul 22, 189, 246, 260, 268, 281, 285, 300, 367-9
Guitry, Sacha 41

Hahn, Reynaldo 218
Hartung, Hans 127
Hastings, Beatrice 110, 187, 220, 261, 272, 341
Haviland, Frank 190
Hayden (painter) 278
Hébuterne, Jeanne 272, 295-8
Hemingway, Ernest 210, 268, 343-8, 352; *A Moveable Feast* 347
Herbin (painter) 158
Herriot, Edouard 378
Hiler, Hilaire 356-7
Hommes nouveaux, Les (periodical) 207
Honegger, Arthur 259-60
Huelsenbeck, Richard 243
Hugo, Jean 214, 222, 362
Hugo, Victor 169; *Hernani* 218
Humanité, L' (newspaper) 387-8
Huxley, Aldous 347

impressionism 66
Indenbaum, Léon 165
Indora, Maharaja of 361
Information, L' (periodical) 278
Ingres, Jean Auguste Dominique 101; *Le Portrait de Monsieur Bertin* 87; *Le Bain turc* 88
International Congress for the Determination of Counsel for and Promotion of the Modern Spirit (1922) 308-9, 313
International Congress of Writers for the Defence of Culture 388
International Exhibition of Modern Art (1913) *see* Armory Show
Intransigeant, L' (periodical) 36, 114, 147-51, 339

Jacob, Max: in Montmartre 6; nature of 30-44, 138; and Apollinaire 46-9, 52, 54-5; and Fernande Olivier 60; entertaining friends 62; on artistic friendships 65; and Dolly Van Dongen 70; dress of 72; and Madeleine; and Raymonde 76; relationship with Picasso 77, 113, 219-20; and Apollinaire's projected duel 79; dining at Apollinaire's 83; and Picasso's early success 85-6; and Picasso's anger at his work

being varnished 91; and Picasso's interest in African art 95, 98-9; and Picasso's relationship with the Douanier Rousseau 110; in Le Grelot 123; and Eva Gouel 125; Fernande Olivier on 126; drug habit 128-9; and Fernande Olivier 130; and relationship between Braque and Picasso 135-6; and cubism 140-2; and Peau de l'Ours sale 157; and Jarry 173; during World War I 181, 183, 215-16, 228; and Modigliani 189-90; and Cocteau 217, 223, 225; Apollinaire writes to 229; Tzara and 242, 249; and Nord-Sud 247; and Albert-Birot 248; Breton and 252, 309; and Adrienne Monnier 255; and Salon d'Antin 259; and 'Lyre et Palette' 260; and dinner for Braque 261; and Satie 263; in La Rotonde 264; and Léonce Rosenberg 268; at Kisling's wedding 274; directs chorus of *Mamelles de Tirésias* 277; and café de Flore 278; at Picasso's wedding 282; and Apollinaire's death 285; preparing to leave Paris 299; and Doucet 319; Poiret and 324-5; and Radiguet 339-40; and Soutine 375; and Masson 382; leaves Paris 406; *Saint Matorel* 34-5, 37; *Le Cornet à dés* 35, 142; *Le Roi Kaboul ou le marmiton Gauvin* 35; *Le Siège de Jerusalem* 35; *Phanérogame* 35; *La Bande des habits noirs* 39; *La Côte* 129
Jammes, Francis 129, 318
Janco, Marcel 243
Jarry, Alfred: writing for *La Revue blanche* 47; and *Le Festin d'Aesope* 48; Apollinaire and 54; and opium 62; pistol-waving 79, 385; and the Douanier Rousseau 105; Guilhermet and 107-8; nature of 170-5; Dadaists and 243, 250; Aragon and 252; and Montmartre 299; and surrealism 389; *Les Minutes du sable memorial* 62; *Ubu roi* 108, 167-75, 305; *César-Antechrist* 170; *Le Surmâle* 170; *Les Jours et les nuits* 170
Jastrebzoff, Serge *see* Ferat, Serge
Jeanneret, Charles-Edouard (Le Corbusier) 303
Jockey Club 356-7, 359-60, 365-6, 386
Joffre, Marshal Joseph Jacques Césaire 212, 258, 264
Johnson, Jack 236
Jolas, Eugène 342
Jordens, Jules-Gerard 260
Jouhandeau, Marcel 122
Jourdain, Frantz 118, 146, 179
Jourdain, Paulette 374
Journal de Rouen (newspaper) 67
Journal official, Le (periodical) 382
Joyce, James 130, 242, 256, 343, 347, 361; *Ulysses* 255-7

Kahn, Simone *see* Breton, Simone
Kahnweiler, Daniel-Henry: Manolo and 19; Berthe Weill compared

to 22; and Max Jacob 38; and Braque 67, 131, 149, 237; Picasso and 71-2, 102, 129, 153-6; and Braque/Picasso collaboration 137; during World War I 142, 195, 268; and cubism 151; at Peau de l'Ours sale 157, 159, 401; and 'Kraut art' 232; and Zborowski 272; buying Gris and Braque 303; sale of collections 316; Breton and 380-1; and Masson 382

Kandinsky, Wassily 97, 99, 131, 235

Katz, Mane 165, 179, 188

Kessel, Joseph 338

Khoklova, Olga see Picasso, Olga

Kievskaya Mysl (newspaper) 215

Kiki (ps. of Alice Prin) 289-95, 330-2, 356-60, 364-6, 370-1, 374, 384, 399

Kikoïne (painter) 165, 188-9, 194, 289

Kisling, Moïse: and Kiki 14, 289-90, 295, 366; background 165; during World War I 179, 183, 213, 222-3, 234, 258-60; and Modigliani 269; and Renée-Jean 273-6; attacks Picasso 278; flees Paris 280; and Modigliani's death 297-8; in fancy dress 324; Aïcha poses for 349; living quarters 354; Barnes and 368; and Zborowski 371; and motor-bikes 398; leaves Paris 407

Kisling, Kiki 295

Kisling, Renée-Jean 273-4

Kolb, Jacqueline see Apollinaire, Jacqueline

Kostrowitzka, La see Kostrowitzky, Angelica de

Kostrowitzky, Albert 48-9

Kostrowitzky, Angelica de (La Kostrowitzka) 47-52, 200-1, 285

Kostrowitzky, Wilhelm Apollinaris de see Apollinaire, Guillaume

Kremègne (painter) 165, 188-9, 259, 351

Krogh, Guy 354-5

Krogh, Lucy (née Cecile Vidil) 353-8, 399, 408-10

Krogh, Per 179, 290, 353-8, 366; Kropotkin, Prince Peter, *Anarchy, Its Philosophy and Ideals* 8

Kupka (painter) 140

La Roche, Raoul 303

La Rochelle, Drieu 307, 315

Laberdesque, Caridad de 383

Lagut, Irène 222, 282

Lanterne, La (periodical) 145

Lapin Agile, Le (café) 63-4, 71, 79, 123, 125, 144, 176, 299

Larbaud, Valéry 35, 256

Laurencin, Marie: and Berthe Weill 22; Picasso introduces to Apollinaire 77; relationship with Apollinaire 81-4, 121-2, 128, 149-50, 197, 202, 204, 229, 284; and *Les Demoiselles d'Avignon* 99; the Douanier Rousseau and 107, 109, 121-2; Fernande Olivier on 126; and cubism 151;

at Peau de l'Ours sale 158; Picabia and 241; and attack on Rosenberg 300; at Boeuf sur le Toit 339

Lautréamont, Comte de (ps. of Isidore Ducasse) 243, 251-2, 296, 320

Lautrec, Henri Toulouse see Toulouse-Lautrec, Henri

Lazareff, Pierre 391

Le Fauconnier, Robert 140, 147, 151, 189

Léautaud, Paul 43, 48-50, 125-7, 168, 178, 255, 264, 275, 285, 319, 325, 362; *Petit Ami* 126, 168

Léger, Fernand: and Picasso 33; and Section d'Or 140; and Salon d'Automne (1912) 14; Apollinaire and 151; during World War I 179, 234; and Marie Vassilieff 182; Cendrars meets 208; declines to work on camouflage 232; in Armory Show 235; and Severini 259; and Rosenberg 268, 300; at Apollinaire's funeral 285; Breton buys 303; and Dada Festival 306; and Dadaism 308; wife ready to leave 360; and Kiki 366

Léger, Jeanne 298, 360

Leiris, Michel 378, 382-3, 385, 388, 393-5

Lejeune, Emile 259

Lenin, Vladimir Ilyich (ps. of Vladimir Ilyich Ulyanov) 215, 242-3, 306

Lequeux, Mady 399

Level, André 22, 86, 158-9, 268

Levy, Denise see Naville, Denise

Lewis, Sinclair 342, 361

Lhote (painter) 140-1, 147, 151, 179, 278

Libaude (dealer) 13, 20, 61

Libertaire (periodical) 7

Limbour, Georges 309, 320, 382, 393, 395

Lipchitz, Jacques 368

Lipchitz, Marc 165, 191, 278, 300

Lipski (sculptor) 165

Littérature (periodical) 257, 305, 307-9, 312

Little Review, The (periodical) 256, 342

Lloyd, Fabian Avenarius (aka Arthur Cravan) 80-1, 143, 235-6, 238, 241

Loeb, Pierre 353

Loups, Les (periodical) 168

Louÿs, Pierre xvii-xviii

Loy, Mina 236, 239, 329, 342

Lurçat, Jean 373, 383

Lyautey, General 258

Lyre et Palette 259-61, 269

Mac Orlan, Pierre (ps. of Pierre Dumarchey) 7, 15, 48, 63-4, 72, 179, 285, 352

MacAlmon, Robert 342

MacLeish, Archibald 342

Madeleine (Picasso model and companion) 57, 75

Maeterlinck, Maurice 168, 325

Magritte, René 395

Maillol, Aristide 24, 29, 146, 158

Maintenant (periodical) 81

Malkine, Georges 365, 383

Mallarmé, Stéphane 33, 47, 168, 251-2, 318, 376; *L'Après-midi d'un faune* 97

Manet, Edouard 4, 24, 66, 146

Manguin (painter) 66

Manolo see Martinez y Hugue, Manuel

Manyac (dealer) 16, 20, 22, 24, 31

Marais, Jean 217

Marcoussis, Louis 20, 123-5, 143, 147, 179, 232, 235, 324, 368

Mare, André 232

Marevna (painter) 165

Marinetti, Filippo Tommaso 123, 243, 247; *The Futurist Manifesto* 124

Marquet (painter) 66, 158

Martin-Chauffier, Louis 311

Martinez y Hugue, Manuel (Manolo) 18-19, 100, 113, 172

Masson, André 320-1, 382, 385, 391, 393-4

Matin, Le (newspaper) 48, 61, 145

Matisse, Henri: Berthe Weill and 22; and young artists 25; and Salon d'Automne 66-8, 105, 146; Picasso influenced by 88; and Gertrude Stein 92-3, 347; and Leo Stein 94; and Picasso 94-103; and Braque 131; and cubism 132; Apollinaire on 149; at Peau de l'Ours sale 158; and Marie Vassilieff 182; Duchamp and 237; Arensberg buys 239; Tzara and 243; Breton and 252, 389; and Salon d'Antin 259; and 'Lyre et Palette' 260; and dinner for Braque 261; and Rosenberg 300; and Man Ray 361; Barnes buys 367-8; *La Femme au chapeau* 67; *Le Bonheur de vivre* 97-8, 100; *Luxe, calme et volupté* 97; *Nu bleu: souvenir de Biskra* 98; *Nu debout* 131; *Compotier de pommes et oranges* 158; *Etude de Femme* 158; *Feuillages au bord de l'eau* 158

Mauclair, Camille 130

Maure, Thérèse (Thérèse Treize) 357-8, 366, 383

Maurras, Charles 84, 167-8

Mayakowsky, Vladimir 402-3

Melnik, Deborah 374

Mendes, Catulle 169

Mendjizky, Maurice 293

Mercereau, Alexandre 334

Mercure de France (periodical) 105, 168, 170, 210-11, 227-8, 275, 319, 362

Mercure de France (publisher) 125, 148, 200, 209, 253

Merle, Eugène 310-11

Merle blanc, Le (periodical) 310-11

Merrill, Stuart 168, 210

Metzinger, Jean: and Berthe Weill 22; and Apollinaire's cooking 83; in the Hermitage 123; and Section d'Or 140-1; Cravan on 143; and attack on Vauxcelles 147; Apollinaire on 150-1; and Peau de l'Ours 158; and Duchamp 240; and scabrous poem 255; and dinner in honour of Braque 261; and attack on Picasso 278; at Apollinaire's funeral 285; and Dada Festival 306; and Dadaism 309; *see also* under Gleizes, Albert

Milhaud, Darius 5, 218, 240, 259-60, 337

Milhaud, Gabrielle de 52; Vicomtesse de 52

Miller, Henry 343, 373

Miller, Lee 399

Mirbeau, Octave 47

Mirò, Joan 268, 320, 382, 387, 393

Modigliani, Amedeo: first exhibition 23; and Beatrice Hastings 110, 261, 341; in Montparnasse 164; during World War I 179, 183, 215; ill-health 182; and Soutine 184-90, 371; and 'Lyre et Palette' 260; sculpting 191-6; and Cendrars 208; and Cocteau 222-3; refused by the army 234; in Cabaret Voltaire 243; and dealers 268-72; and Zborowski 275; and love 276; flees Paris 280; in Nice 281-2; death 295-9, 410; prodigality of 350; nature of his art 350; portrait of Thora Dardel 356; Barnes buys 367

Modigliani, Emanuele 298

Modigliani, Jeanne 295

Molina da Silva, Linda 53

Monet, Claude 97, 167, 181, 237, 281

Monnier, Adrienne 252-7

Montebello, Comtesse de 335

Morand, Paul 352

Moréas, Jean 168-9

Moreau, Gustave 4, 167

Moreau, Luc-Albert 151, 232

Morel, Auguste 256

Morice, Charles 98, 131

Morin, Charles 174

Morin brothers: *Les Polonais* 174-5

Morise, Max 311, 385, 387, 395

Moyses, Louis 337

Munch, Edvard 353

Münzenburger, Willy 243

Murat, Princesse Eugène 262

Museum of Modern Art, New York 100, 106

Mussolini, Benito 124, 247, 342

Napoleon III, Emperor 66

Naville, Denise (née Levy) 392, 400

Naville, Pierre 315, 382, 387, 392-4, 400

New Age, The (periodical) 187, 220

Nijinsky, Vaslav 165, 218

Noailles, Marie-Laure de 405

Noailles, Vicomte de 361

Nonell, Isidre 16

Nord-Sud (periodical) 246-9, 252, 254, 257, 278, 319

Nouvelle Revue française (periodical and publisher) 124, 245, 253, 256, 304, 308, 340, 388

Nouvelles, Les (periodical) 168

Nouvelles littéraires, Les (periodical) 376, 391

OEttingen, Hélène d' 106, 122-3, 157, 247

Olivier, Fernande (*later* Fernande Picasso): and Max Jacob 34; early relationship with Picasso 56-62, 64; and Van Dongen 70; and Raymonde 75-6; as focus of Picasso's affections 77; and Marie Laurencin 82, 109, 121; as Picasso's inspiration 84; on holiday with Picasso 86; and Gertrude Stein 87-8; at Gertrude Stein's 91; in *Les Demoiselles d'Avignon* 99; and the Douanier Rousseau 110; moving house 112-13; and theft of Mona Lisa 115-17; relationship with Picasso 122-4, 126-7; and Eva Gouel 125; and Paul Léautaud 126; and Max Jacob 130; Picasso portrait of 134; on Braque 135; and Picasso's jealousy 139; break with Picasso 276; and Poiret 325

Oppenheim, Meret 361

Oppenheimer, Max 243

Oppi, Umbaldo 124

Orlan, Pierre Mac *see* Mac Orlan, Pierre

Orloff, Chana 165, 373

Osterlind (painter) 281

Ouesan, Marquise d' 262

Ozenfant, Edgar 136, 308

Pach, Walter 235

Pagès, Madeleine 199-206, 226-7, 229

Pallares, Manuel 16

Papadiamantopoulos, Jean 168

Papazoff, Georges 350

Paris-Journal (newspaper) 114, 116, 148, 151, 338

Paris-Matin (newspaper) 311

Paris-Midi (newspaper) 177, 278, 394

Paris-Presse (newspaper) 119

Paris-Soir (newspaper) 310, 391

Pascin, Jules 275, 348-58, 364, 366, 375, 398-9, 407-10

Pascin, Hermine (née David) 353, 355-7, 408, 410

Paulhan, Jean 131, 141, 232, 247, 254, 308, 388

Pavlova, Anna 165

Peau de l'Ours, La 86, 157-9, 177

Pecci-Blunt, Comte 361

Péret, Benjamin 240, 250, 307, 309, 314-15, 320, 383, 385-6, 388-9, 391, 393-5; *Immortelle maladie* 315

Petit Journal, Le (newspaper) 66

Petit Parisien, Le (newspaper) 102

Phalange, La (newspaper) 168

Picabia, Francis: and Berthe Weill 22; and Apollinaire 63, 151, 198, 209; and Section d'Or 140; and attack on Vauxcelles 147; in United States 179, 238; and Cocteau 224; and Armory Show 234-6; and Duchamp 240-1; and Dadaism 244, 314; and *Littérature* group 308; and Dada Manifesto 309; and Doucet 320; Aragon and 322; and Man Ray 329, 361; and Germaine

Everling 360; drives Delage 398; *L'Oeil cacodylate* 240, 337; *Le Manifeste cannibale* 305-6

Picasso, Fernande *see* Olivier, Fernande;

Picasso, Olga (née Khoklova) 276, 282

Picasso, Pablo: and Depaquit 5-6; and Sagot 13; early days in Montmartre 15-25; and Max Jacob 31-3, 35, 38-9, 41-4, 46, 48, 52; and Bateau Lavoir 54-5, 299; meets Fernande Olivier 56-65; and Van Dongen 70; and Gris 71-2; and the figure of the Harlequin 74-8; and fights 79-84; dining at Apollinaire's 83; early success 85-8; and Steins 87-8; and Gertrude Stein 91, 93-4, 347; and Matisse 95-103; and the Douanier Rousseau 106, 108, 110; moving house 112-13; in Céret 114; and theft of *Mona Lisa* 114-19; and Apollinaire's relationship with Marie Laurencin 121; relationship with Fernande Olivier 122-4, 126-7, 130; and Eva Gouel 124-5, 195; and drugs 128; relationship with Max Jacob 129; and cubism 132, 140-3; and new directions in art 134-9; Vauxcelles on 147; Apollinaire on 149-51; and Peau de l'Ours sale 157-9; and move to Montparnasse 167, 176; and Manolo 172; and Jarry 173; during World War I 179, 183; and Modigliani 186, 190; and Apollinaire during World War I 196; Max Jacob and 216; and Ballets Russes 218; and Cocteau 219-20, 222-5, 259; and camouflage 231; in Armory Show 235; Arensbergs buy 239; Tzara and 243; Breton and 252; and 'Lyre et Palette' 260; and dinner for Braque 261; and *Parade* 262; wealth of 267, 269; and Léonce Rosenberg 268, 300; and love 276; attacked by fellow painters 278; marries 282-3; witness at Apollinaire's wedding 282; at Apollinaire's funeral 285; Breton buys 303; and Dadaism 314; and Doucet 319; Sagot and 320; Poiret on 325; and Francisco Ferrer 329; at Boeuf sur le Toit 338-9; lifestyle of 351; and Man Ray 361; Barnes buys 367-8; and Soutine 375; Masson and 394; leaves Paris 406; *La Femme au casque de cheveux* 57; *La Femme à la chemise* 57; *Au Lapin Agile* 63; *La Femme à la corneille* 64; *Autoportrait en bleu* 72; *Famille d'acrobates avec un singe* 75; *Famille d'Arlequin* 75; *Maternité rose* 75; *Portrait de Raymonde* 75; *Les Demoiselles d'Avignon* 77, 88-9, 99-102, 110, 115, 130-1, 137, 150, 259, 320, 325; *Fernande à sa toilette* 88; *Grand Nu rose* 88; *Autoportrait* 98; *Autoportrait à la palette* 98; *Buste de femme à la grande*

oreille 98; *Portrait de Gertrude Stein* 98; *Trois Femmes* 131, 135; *Le Violon* 133, 136; *Tête de Fernande* 134; *Portrait de Daniel-Henry Kahnweiler* 135; *La Guitare* 136; *Nature morte à la chaise cannée* 136; *Femme et enfants* 158; *Famille de saltimbanques* 159; *Les Trois Hollandaises* 159; *L'Homme à la houpelande* 159
Pichot (painter) 16
Pina, Alfredo 261
Pissarro, Camille 24, 66, 97, 130, 181, 367
Playden, Annie 52-4, 202
Poche, Henri-Pierre 87
Poèsie (periodical) 150
Poincaré, Raymond 22, 263
Pointillism 66
Poiret, Paul 33, 37, 113, 182, 258-9, 261, 324-8, 335
Poulbot, Francisque 6, 63, 70, 299
Poulenc, Francis 260, 337
POUM (Workers' Party for Marxist Unification) 389
Pound, Ezra 256, 342, 361
Pozner, Vladimir 403
Prévert, Jacques 384-9, 388, 391, 393, 395, 401
Prin, Alice *see* Kiki; Alice 14
Princet, Alice 77
Princet (painter) 141
Prokofiev, Sergei 218
Proust, Marcel 47, 218, 238, 362-3; *The Guermantes Way* 304; *A la recherche du temps perdu* 362
Prouvost, Jean 310
Puvis de Chavannes, Pierre 10, 31

Quadrille Realiste, the 15
Queneau, Raymond 170, 385, 391, 393, 395
Quinn, John 235, 354

Rachilde *see* Valette, Rachilde
Radek, Karl 243
Radiguet, Raymond 247, 319, 330, 339-41, 399
Ravel, Jean 142, 218
Ray, Man 14, 238-9, 290, 309, 326-32, 358-66, 373, 382, 387, 394; 398, 399; *Les Champs délicieux* 328
Raymonde (Picasso's adopted child) 75-6, 123
Raynal, Maurice 110, 141, 143, 172, 210
ready-mades 239-40
Redon, Odilon 149, 158
Régnier, Henri de 169
Réjane 218, 317
Renard, Jules 47, 168
Renoir, Pierre Auguste 4, 10, 21, 24-5, 28, 31, 97, 146, 167, 181, 281, 367
Reverdy, Pierre: and Picasso 33-4, 101, 139, 141-2, 219; and typography 209; and Cocteau 217; nature of his work 246-7; and Tzara 248-9, and *Nord-Sud* 252, 254; reads works 260; and dinner for Braque 261; and Rivera 264, 319; and café de Flore 278; Breton and 309; and Doucet 318-19

Révolté, Le (periodical) 8
Révolution surréaliste, La (periodical) 315, 382-3, 385, 387, 391, 393-4
Revue blanche, La (periodical) 47
Revue d'art dramatique (periodical) 47
Revue européenne, La (periodical) 381
Revue immoraliste, La (periodical) 74
Reynolds, Mary 360
Ribemont-Dessaignes, Georges 247, 305-7, 309, 394-5
Richardson, John 101
Rimbaud, Arthur 33, 243, 251-2, 318; *Une Saison en enfer* 99-100
Rivera, Diego 179, 215, 223, 264, 278, 319
Roche, Henri-Pierre 235, 241; *Jules et Jim* 235
Rodin, Auguste 16, 24, 191
Rolland, Romain 177, 242
Romains, Jules 306
Ronsard, Pierre de 33
Rosenberg, Léonce 220, 268, 302-3, 339, 393
Rosenberg, Paul 106, 268, 302;
Rosenberg brothers (dealers) 22, 195
Rosenstock, Samuel *see* Tzara, Tristan
Rostand, Edmond 284
Rotonde, La (café) 158, 176-8, 183, 194, 214-15, 264-5, 332-3, 382, 386, 398
Rouault, Georges 25, 28, 158
Roubaud, Jacques 209
Rousseau, Henri (Le Douanier): 20, 22, 104-11, 129, 171, 182, 274; *Le Lion ayant faim* 105; *Le Portrait de Mme M.* 106, 108; *La Charmeuse de Serpent* 320
Roussel, Raymond 237-8, 240, 320; *Impressions d'Afrique* 237-8; *La Doublure* 238; *Locus Solus* 313
Roux, Saint-Pol 169, 376, 378-9
Rubens, Peter Paul 31
Rubinstein, Helena 404
Ruche, La 163-7, 180, 208

Sabartes, Jaime 16
Sachs, Maurice 223, 371
Sadoul, Georges 393, 395, 401, 403
Sagot, Clovis 13, 20-1, 61, 71, 82, 321
Saincere, Olivier 22
Salis, Rodolphe 4
Salmon, André: in Montmartre 6; and Utrillo 12; Manolo and 19; and Picasso 33, 61, 64-5; and Max Jacob 41; and Apollinaire 48; and Van Dongen 70; and Raymonde 75; relationship with Picasso 77; and Marie Laurencin 82; and Picasso's early success 85-6; on Matisse 93; and Matisse's purchase of African statue 95-6; and *Les Demoiselles d'Avignon* 100; Picasso breaks with 101-2; and the Douanier Rousseau 109-10; Picasso's friendship with 113; at *Paris-Journal* 116; and Apollinaire's arrest 118; and Apollinaire 122; on Max Jacob 29; as art critic 148; and Paul Fort 168; and

Jarry 171-2; creates literary fund 181; during World War I 183; and Modigliani 186; and Cocteau 216-17, 338-9; and duel 223; Breton and 250, 305, 309; and Salon d'Antin 259; and 'Lyre et Palette' 260; at rue Joseph Bara 275; at Apollinaire's funeral 285; and Modigliani's death 298; and Gertrude Stein 347; and Pascin 352; nature of his writing 406; *La Négresse au Sacré-Coeur* 76
Salon d'Antin (1916) 100, 258
Salon d'Automne (1912) 146
Salon d'Automne (1905) 66, 88, 105
Salon d'Automne (1906) 97
Salon d'Automne (1908) 131-2, 149, 353
Salon d'Automne (1910) 150
Salon des Indépendants 66, 69
Salon des Indépendants (1907) 130, 137
Salon des Indépendants (1908) 189
Salon des Indépendants (1909) 149
Salon des Indépendants (1911) 140, 151
Salon des Indépendants (1912) 137, 237
Salon des Indépendants (1913) 219
Salon des Refusés 66
Sarcey, Francisque 4
Satie, Erik 4-5, 10, 48, 218, 255, 259-62, 309, 319, 360, 362
Saturday Evening Post (periodical) 346
Scevola, Guirand de 231-2
Schad, Christian 243
Schiaparelli, Elsa 329
Seabrook, William 342
Seckel, Hélène 234
Second Surrealist Manifesto (1924) 315, 394-5
Second Surrealist Manifesto (reprint 1946) 392
Second World War *see* World War II
Section d'Or 140-1, 219, 235, 237-8
Segonzac, Maurice 140
Sembat, Marcel 22, 157
Serge, Victor 208
Sert, Misia 221
Sérusier (painter) 158
Seurat, Georges 66, 74, 97, 320
Severini, Gino 181, 246, 259, 278
SIC (periodical) 246-8, 251-2, 254-5, 257, 276, 278
Signac, Paul 8, 31, 66, 98, 158
Simenon, Georges 311
Simplissimus (periodical) 351
Society of Independent Artists, The 239
Soirées de Paris, Les (periodical) 110, 122, 209
Soulié (dealer) 21-2, 106
Soupault, Philippe: and Apollinaire 52; and Marie Laurencin 122; and Cocteau 217; and Roussel 238; collaborates with Tzara 247; during World War I 250-1; and Adrienne Monnier 254; and

'surrealism' 278; and Dada
Festival 306; and Barrès trial
307; and Crevel 312; and Tzara
313-14; and Anatole France 315;
and Man Ray 329, 361-2; and
fight at Closerie des Lilas 377-8;
and Aragon 381; and Masson
382; and Breton 391-3, 395; *see
also* under Breton, André
Souser, Frédéric *see* Cendrars, Blaise
Soutine, Chaim: background 165;
during World War I 183; and
Modigliani 184-91, 215, 269,
272, 275; and Zamaron 194;
flees Paris 280; and Kiki 289-90,
293; family 351; Pascin and
366; Barnes and 368-9; and success 370-5, 407; *Le Coq mort aux
tomates* 372; *Carcasse de boeuf* 373
Souvestre, Pierre, and Marcel Allain,
45-6; *Fantomas* 45n
Spanish Civil War 101, 224
Stein, Gertrude: and Vollard 26-7;
and Picasso 57, 64, 71-2, 87-94,
112, 136, 224, 231, 285; and
dinner for Rousseau 108; and
Rousseau 110; and Spain as
country of cubism 130; during
World War I 195; and Matisse's
purchase of African statue 95;
and African art 96; and *Les
Demoiselles d'Avignon* 100; and relationship between Matisse and
Picasso 103; and Braque's attack
on Rosenberg 300; Sagot and
321, and Gris 247; and
Hemingway 345-8; *The Making of
Americans* 346
Stein, Leo 26-7, 87, 90-4, 98, 100,
367
Stein, Michael 94
Steinlen, Théophile Alexandre 7,
351
Stieglitz, Alfred 240-1
Stravinsky, Igor 218, 259, 313; *Le
Sacre du printemps* 100, 218
Suares, André 318
surrealism 124, 140, 224, 241,
249-52, 277-8, 303-9, 313,
320-1, 329, 377, 379-84, 387-
9, 391, 393-6
Surrealist Manifesto 380
Survage (painter) 238, 281, 309
Svetloff, Valerien Irtchenko 282
symbolism 148, 169

Tabarin, Le (newspaper) 47
Tailleferre, Germaine 260
Tanguy, Yves 383, 385-8, 394-5,
401
Tannhauser, Justin 159
Tartakower, Savielly Grigoievitsch
238
Temps, Le (newspaper) 4, 47
Thiers, Louis Adolphe 3
Thirion, André 393, 395, 401,
403-5
Toklas, Alice 26-7, 92, 108, 195
Toronto Star (newspaper) 343

Toucas-Massillon, Marguerite 251
Toulouse-Lautrec, Henri 4, 10, 15,
17, 20-2, 31, 70, 74, 299, 351
Treize, Therese *see* Maure, Therese
Trenet, Charles 35
Triolet, Elsa 360, 378, 401-5
Trotsky, Leon 215
Trotskyism 389
Tual, Roland 315, 366, 383, 393,
401-2
Tudesq, André 118, 122
Tzara, Tristan (ps. of Samuel
Rosenstock): and Depaquit 5;
and Max Jacob 129; and
Apollinaire 209; and Dada 240-
50; and Braque 303; arrives in
Paris 305; and Barrès trial 306-
8; and Dada Festival 306; Picabia
and 308; Breton and 309, 313-
14; and Doucet 320; and Man
Ray 328, 360-1; and Gertrude
Stein 347; and surrealism 381;
and paper game 387; *La Première
aventure céleste de monsieur Antipyrine*
243; *Dada Manifesto* 244-5; *Le coeur
à gaz* 314; *Antipyrine* 337

Uhde, Wilhelm 106, 142, 232, 352
Ulyanov, Vladimir Ilyich *see* Lenin,
Vladimir Ilyich
Unik 391
Union of Russian Artists 324
Utrillo, Maurice 9-15, 20-2, 63,
70, 158, 190, 194, 299, 371
Utrillo Miguel 10, 16
Utter, Andre 10

Vaché, Jacques 250, 278, 309
Vailland, Roger 240, 394
Vaillant, Jacques 61, 108
Valadon, Suzanne 9-12, 15, 63, 84,
194, 299
Valéry, Paul 251, 254, 309
Valette, Alfred 105, 175, 285, 319,
362
Valette, Rachilde 105, 172-3, 175,
261, 285, 307, 319, 362, 377
Valloton, Félix 8, 149, 158
Van Dongen, Dolly 70-1
Van Dongen, Guus 70
Van Dongen, Kees: and Fénéon 8;
sells sketches 20; and Berthe
Weill 22; and Vollard 70-1; mar-
ried 84; at Salon d'Automne
(1912) 146; Apollinaire on 150;
and Severini 259; wealth of 267,
299; at Peau de l'Ours sale 158;
Breton buys 303; in fancy dress
334; Aïcha poses for 349; leaves
Paris 406
Van Gogh, Vincent 4, 24, 67, 158,
185, 367; *Fleurs dans un verre* 158
Varèse, Edgar 219, 238, 241, 329
Vassilieff, Marie 182, 258, 261,
298, 330-1, 383
Vauxcelles, Louis 67, 98, 105, 131,
147-8, 225
Verhoeven (painter) 158
Verlaine, Paul xvii-xviii, 33, 47,

167-9, 318
Vers et Prose (periodical) 65, 84,
168-9, 174, 181, 253, 255
Vian, Boris 170
Vidil, Cécile *see* Krogh, Lucy
Villon, Jacques 140, 147, 232
Vitrac, Roger 308-9, 382, 393, 395
Vlaminck, Maurice: and anarchism
8; and Vollard 24, 26, 28; and
Max Jacob 40; and Apollinaire's
cooking 47; and Apollinaire 49-
51, 54, 148-9, 284; drinking
habits 63; and Picasso 64; and
Salon d'Automne 66-9, 105;
nature of his dress 72; Derain
writes to 133; and Gertrude
Stein 92; and African art 96-7;
Apollinaire on 149-50; and
cubism 152; at Peau de l'Ours
sale 158; during World War I
183, 195, 214; nature of his
painting 185; and Trotsky 215;
and Cocteau 216-17; and
Rosenberg 300; Breton buys
303; and Paul Guillaume 367;
Barnes buys 368; and Zborowski
371; leaves Paris 406; *D'un Lit dans
l'autre* 69; *La Vie en culotte rouge* 69;
Ecluses à Bougival 158
Vollard, Ambroise 18, 22, 24-31,
70, 85-6, 106-7, 129-30, 170-
1, 220, 282, 367
von Waetgen, Otto 197
Vuillard, Edouard 146, 158

Wagner, Richard 318
Wahab, Abdul 354
Warnod, André 20, 72, 96, 143-4,
155, 181, 311, 352
Wasselet (painter) 63
Weill, Berthe 22-3, 28, 79, 86, 144
Whitman, Walt 210-11, 236; *Leaves
of Grass* 211
Wiegels (German painter) 63, 128,
352
Wiener (musician) 337
Wilde, Oscar 80-1
Wilder, Thornton 342
Willette (painter) 70, 158
World Fair (1889) 105
World Fair (1900) 16
World War I 120, 137-8, 176-80,
182-3, 214, 218, 258-63, 279-
83
World War II 224

Youki *see* Badoul, Lucie

Zadkine, Ossip 165, 179, 309, 407
Zamaron, Commissioner 194
Zarate, Ortiz de 179, 181-2, 234,
259-60, 269, 296-7
Zborowska, Hanka 275, 278
Zborowski, Leopold 268-73, 275,
278, 282, 295-6, 300, 309,
354, 368-9, 371-4, 398
Zola, Emile 33, 47, 169